DATE DUE

OCT 3 1 1997	
OCT 3 1 1997	
APR 1 7 1998	
APR 2 7 1998	
APR 6 1999	
OCT 1 3 2000	
APR - 7 2003	

BRODART   Cat. No. 23-221

LORD CHURCHILL'S COUP

LORD CHURCHILL'S COUP

The Anglo-American Empire and the
Glorious Revolution Reconsidered

STEPHEN SAUNDERS WEBB

Alfred A. Knopf   New York   1995

THIS IS A BORZOI BOOK
PUBLISHED BY ALFRED A. KNOPF, INC.

Copyright © 1995 by Stephen Saunders Webb
All rights reserved under International and Pan-American Copyright Conventions.
Published in the United States by Alfred A. Knopf, Inc., New York,
and simultaneously in Canada by Random House of Canada Limited, Toronto.
Distributed by Random House, Inc., New York.

Library of Congress Cataloging-in-Publication Data
Webb, Stephen Saunders.
Lord Churchill's coup : the Anglo-American empire
and the Glorious Revolution reconsidered /
by Stephen Saunders Webb.—1st ed.
p.   cm.
Includes bibliographical reference and index.
ISBN 0-394-54980-5
1. Marlborough, John Churchill, Duke of, 1650–1722.
2. Great Britain—Colonies—North America——History—17th century.
3. Great Britain—Politics and government—1660–1714.
4. Imperialism—Great Britain—History—17th century.
5. Great Britain—History, Military—17th century.
6. Great Britain—History—Revolution of 1688.
I.   Title.
DA462.M3W5   1995
941.06—dc20   95-22815
CIP

Manufactured in the United States of America

First Edition

For Jane N. Garrett

Editor, Priest, Friend

Contents

Illustrations follow pages 48, 112, and 240.

Preface

Armies were the agencies of modern European statehood. Navies transported them across the Atlantic (and around the world) to conquer colonies and command empires. *The Governors-General* depicted the military nationalization of England and the militant organization of its emerging empire, from the royal arquebusiers' defeat of the northern earls' tribesmen in 1569 down to the imperial compromise between the armed executive and the civilian legislatures in 1681. The central finding of *The Governors-General*—that Anglo-America was an empire and, like all modern empires, was administered by the army officer corps—has been called "the most provocatively revisionist interpretation of the British Empire to appear in this century, so sweeping that if it is finally accepted, even the history of the realm will have to be restructured to give greater weight to the army and much less to the county community." In *Lord Churchill's Coup*, that restructuring moves toward the eighteenth century to recast the so-called "Glorious Revolution" of 1688 (in England) and 1689 (in America) as a military coup and the beginning of a hundred years of war for American empire.[1]

In the age of European empire, war was the adjustor of competing colonial claims. In centuries of endemic imperial conflict, war drove the cycles of both economics and politics. In the new states mobilized for empire, war recruited, educated, and culled the new bureaucratic, meritocratic, militarized elite. War, therefore, ought to provide the narrative thread and the analytical impulse of overarching accounts of the Anglo-American empire. Yet only recently has *1676: The End of American Independence* been credited with "the rediscovery of war" as the driving force in the western world during the century prior to American independence. *Lord Churchill's Coup* finds war and warriors at the center of the public life of Anglo-America as our ancien régime begins.[2]

As this set of subjects suggests, much of what follows is a narrative of Anglo-American events (there were no distinct "English" or "American" histories until the American revolution eventuated in Jacksonian democracy). Only extended narrative can convey that depth of detail which authenticates historical rediscovery. The same reviewer of *1676* who applauded "the rediscovery of war" invoked the name of Francis Parkman, the master narrator of *England and France in North America*. Parkman has never had an equal as a history painter, but if the composition, the excitement, and the humanity of our past are to be recovered for the enlightenment and enjoyment of the present, he should have more emulators. What Parkman never forgot is that personality is the lifeblood of history.

Events, tendencies, and ideas were personified in *1676*. "17th century practitioners of Realpolitik," such as James, duke of York, were "unexpected." Others, like Garacontié of Onondaga, are "fascinating." New to the American story is the protagonist of *Lord Churchill's Coup*, John Churchill. These figures embody a conviction that individuals matter in history. As responsibility is personal, so change and consequence can be ascribed to persons, both as types and as actors. The unlikely alliance of the English absolutist, the Iroquoian aristocrat, and the Anglican officer to defend the American frontier against Louis XIV's aggression defined the boundaries of American empires until 1794. The alliance of the sovereign, the sachem, and the soldier, extended beyond the Restoration Empire by the greatest general of the age, also imposed centuries of anglican cultural hegemony on North America.[3]

Both the Iroquoian sphere and the Anglo-American empire were essentially religious regimes. These confessional cultures pursued the goal of perpetual peace by unending war. Such was the unity of transatlantic culture by the second half of the seventeenth century, that both the league of the Longhouse and the empire of the English were riven by the counter-reformation of European Catholicism. Religious rivalry motivated empire and incited war. In underdeveloped polities, then and now, religion and force prevail in public life, churches and armies are dominant institutions. Anglo-America was just such a primitive polity in 1688. Where priests and soldiers prevailed, "sugar and tobacco" could not be more important than "politics, war, and religion." Yet this is the mercantile mirage of the prevailing historical paradigm.[4]

In its place *Lord Churchill's Coup* places the hierarchies of the army and the church. These ordered institutions prevailed both in the politics of Stuart court and in the administration of the American colonies. The authoritarian alliance of the episcopacy and the officers with the Stuart monarchs was execrated by traditional elites—landed aristocrats and urban patriciates—in their parliaments and assemblies, as well as by religious dissenters and republican rebels. As the violent presages of lord Churchill's coup proved, however, the opponents of absolutism were helpless to resist a modern monarchy so long as the king could rely upon "the black coats and the red coats." But uniformed support for the king was conditional upon his preservation of the Anglican monopoly of office. When a bigoted Catholic sought absolute sovereignty in order to impose the counterreformation on an Anglican empire, the priests defected and the soldiers deserted. A religiously driven military coup, the Protestant putsch of 1688, felled James II.

Across the Atlantic, where extreme underdevelopment mandated even larger roles for religion and for force than they did in England, copycat coups toppled the various experiments in authoritarianism that had been imposed on American provinces in the wake of 1676. Yet, in America as in England, the advent of war with France limited the constitutional conclusions of lord Churchill's coup to a restoration of the imperial settlement of 1681. These post-exclusion constitutional compromises, in England and America, between authoritarian executive and elite parliaments, became the political parameters of the coming century, with one major militant modification. On both sides of the Atlantic, the forcible lessons of the coup, followed by the all-consuming war with France, rapidly institutionalized the military and its officers, regular and provincial, in the imperial polities. Instantly, military expenditure and army administration became the largest concerns of Anglo-American governance.

"The chief" of the politicized military officers was the premier of the putsch, John Churchill. As he continued his ascent from page to prince, he still personified the evolution of a militarized and meritocratic bureaucracy. Its leaders had emerged as the administrative "new class" of the Restoration Empire. Led by Churchill, as the duke of Marlborough and a prince of the empire, they became an oligarchy in the age of Anne. The most aspirant and accomplished officers of this new class, the men of Marlborough's staff, impressed English empire and Augustan culture on an anglicizing America, Marlborough's America.

Stephen Saunders Webb
Stella Point, Amherst Island
November 5, 1994

Acknowledgments

I am particularly grateful to Professors J. R. Jones of the University of East Anglia and W. A. Speck of Leeds University who read a late draft of this work and discussed it with me at length and in detail. Both of these readers have since published their own works on Marlborough: J. R. Jones, *Marlborough* (Cambridge, 1993), in *British Lives*, and W. A. Speck, *The Birth of Britain: A New Nation 1700–1710* (Oxford, 1994). Previously they had published the leading surveys of the period: J. R. Jones, *Country and Court England, 1658–1714* (London, and Cambridge, Mass., 1978), and W. A. Speck, *Stability and Strife England, 1714–1760* (London and Cambridge, Mass., 1977). Their readers will quickly discover how much I owe to these two learned authors. I have also to thank Dr. John Childs of Leeds University. To recognize that he is the leading historian of the later Stuart army does not begin to acknowledge the depth of context and the thoughtful commentary he brings to his four volumes on the subject. His advice, over Leeds ale, in his "1688" (*History*, 73 [1988]: 398–424), and in correspondence, have been continually helpful to the work presented here. Of course, none of these scholars bears any responsibility for the use I have made of their work or their advice.

Among English scholars, I must also thank Dr. Steven Smith, Secretary of the Institute for Historical Research, University of London, for innumerable courtesies and endless assistance over many years, first at the London Centre of Syracuse University and more recently at the Institute. In the Institute community, I have also to thank the members of the Imperial Seminar and the Eighteenth-Century Seminar for kind attention and helpful questions, as I do Professor Peter Marshall of King's College for the pleasures of his seminar.

At Syracuse University, I have again to acknowledge the unfailing assistance of colleagues and friends, in particular, Professors David H. Bennett and James Roger Sharp. The final revisions of this text could not have been completed without the devoted and intelligent research assistance of Ian McGiver, now of the University of Chicago. I am indebted to Matthew Rhoades for his help with the final round of citation verification. I also appreciate the secretarial services of Mrs. Judith Jablonski.

I have incurred many debts at research libraries, especially the British Public Record Office, the British Library, the Library of Congress, the Scottish National Archives, the National Library of Scotland, the Massey Library of the Royal Military College of Canada, and the University Libraries of Syracuse, Cornell, Harvard, Columbia, London, and Oxford. While the Blenheim Papers are now available, reorganized and catalogued in the British Library, I first made their acquaintance in several seasons at Blenheim Palace. I remain deeply grateful for the permission of the then duke of Marlborough to view and to quote his muniments and to the unstinting assistance of his grace's secretary, agent, and chief guide. I am very grateful to the present duke of Marlborough for renewing permission to reproduce and to refer to the manuscripts I viewed at Blenheim.

It is with particular pleasure that I thank Professor Bernard Bailyn, Adams University Professor in Harvard University, for his generous encouragement and valued advice over nearly thirty years. Perhaps his greatest gift was an introduction to his editor at Alfred A. Knopf, Inc., Jane N. Garrett. To her, this work is dedicated, with a depth of feeling for our dear friend and wise counselor equally shared with me by another contributor to this work, Margaret E. Webb.

LORD CHURCHILL'S COUP

Introduction

JOHN CHURCHILL rose through the disreputable Restoration court to become the greatest subject in Europe, the ablest general of the age, the first minister of Great Britain, and the arbiter of Augustan America. Churchill ascended from utter obscurity to princely power, wealth, and rank by the sword. In 1667, the favor of the duke of York made Churchill an ensign in the royal bodyguard. He was a colonel in eight years, a general in eleven. As the military favorite of James Stuart, duke of York and king of England, Churchill was an executor of absolutism. His identity with militant monarchy was enhanced because, from 1673 to 1675, Churchill received his advanced military training, found battlefield glory, and won rapid promotion in the mercenary service of Louis XIV, the would-be dictator of Europe and America. Churchill then became James Stuart's envoy to the French Hitler. He forwarded the secret diplomacy by which the two Catholic absolutists sought to secure James's succession to the imperial throne.

How much Colonel Churchill knew of the Catholic cousins' intent to have James restore the old religion in England as the ideological heart of absolutism is unknowable, but Churchill's growing alarm was closely linked to American developments. At the outset of Churchill's public life the only apparent alternative to authoritarian rule was anarchy. Such had been the lesson of the civil war and interregnum. As the Restoration wore on and the Atlantic world widened, however, political alternatives were tested in America and the imperial stakes there rose. After his return from France in 1675, Churchill was ever more involved in the military administration of English America. The American outcomes of the absolutist entente between Louis and James increasingly alarmed this soldier-diplomat. Churchill was ambitious for himself and for his nation. To both, America represented the future. Churchill grew increasingly unwilling to abandon the American future to France.

In 1685, James ascended the imperial throne and Churchill succeeded his master as the chief executive of the Hudson's Bay Company. During Churchill's governorship the Hudson's Bay Company became the most profitable and aggressive of English enterprises in America, and lord Churchill became the outspoken opponent of the 1686 Treaty of American

Neutrality between James II and Louis XIV. In Churchill's eyes "the Treaty of Whitehall" rewarded French aggression on every contested frontier in America. The treaty established interventionist principles that would endanger whichever of England's colonies the French king might covet. Already, King Louis publicly, violently, coveted all the contested frontiers between England and France from the sub-Arctic to the Lesser Antilles. In Hudson Bay, in Newfoundland and in Maine, in the Anglo-Iroquoian condominium of the Great Lakes basin (and its marchlands west and south to the Mississippi and the Gulf), and in the West Indies, lay England's makeweights against the otherwise overwhelming might of France. So lord Churchill resisted his master's willingness to concede the American future to France.

Resistance to France entailed resistance to Catholicism. Churchill's opposition to French imperialism was doubled when he realized that King James was sacrificing America to purchase King Louis's help in imposing Catholicism on England. That imposition had political as well as spiritual objectives. Counter-reformation, in the eyes of the two kings, was essential to complete monarchy's restoration. So it was as an Anglican and as a patriot, as a legalist and as an imperialist, that Churchill overcame gratitude and duty to challenge King James over America.

To all other appearances, during the twenty years from 1667 to 1687 in which John Churchill advanced from page to baron and from ensign to general in James Stuart's service, he was the sharp sword of his royal master's authoritarian intent. A year after being commissioned to carry the colors in the king's own company of the Guards, Churchill went out to soldier in Tangier, the particularly authoritarian outpost that James supervised. In 1672, Ensign Churchill fought against the Dutch aboard James's own flagship at Sole Bay and was promoted captain of a company of the royal duke's own marines. In 1673, Churchill took his company to France to fight for Louis XIV against the Dutch. He returned to England as a French colonel in 1675 and entered James's household. The subsequent interlude of pseudo-alliance and Protestant league with the Dutch introduced Colonel Churchill to William of Orange, the Protestant champion. The brief episode of the Triple Alliance only emphasized Protestant and parliamentary fear and hatred of Churchill's Catholic master, and of the monarchy and the military. The exclusion parliament drove King Charles to exile the duke of York. Colonel Churchill (accompanied by his new wife, Sarah Jenyns, maid of honor to the duchess) followed his master to Flanders. Two years later, in 1681, James was transferred to Scotland. "Church" (as the duke called his Anglican aide) followed him once more. He shared in the duke's harsh rule of the northern kingdom. After Churchill successfully negotiated James's recall to Charles's court, he saved the duke from the wreck of the *Gloucester*.

Back at his brother's court, James helped to inspire "the Stuart Revenge." The royal reaction against attempted exclusion and resurgent republicanism destroyed civic self-rule in old England and New. The Restoration Empire's assault on local autonomy was typical of those challenges to local self-government that marked the progress of absolutism in the Atlantic world. Churchill was a strong link in the military chain of command by which the absolutists tried to displace the traditional ruling classes. Churchill was the most talented of the English army officers who repressed rebels against militant monarchy. As the armed agent of an authoritarian executive, Colonel Churchill helped to dispatch the duke's marines to Virginia in 1676 and to convey Covenanters to Carolina after 1679, even before the crisis of his master's accession to the imperial throne.

Anticipating rebellion if not civil war on the accession of an avowedly Catholic king, in 1683 the crown recalled to England its most professional troops, the great garrison of Tangier. The Tangerines took control of the port cities of the south and east, and made possible the development of a field army in England. One of the elite units of that new army was the Royal Dragoons, whose cadres Churchill took from the Tangier Horse. His dragoon officers, ardent Anglicans and veteran soldiers, became the core of their colonel's own military "connection." That connection found its essential aegis, a royal patroness, when, in the same year, the duke of York's younger daughter, Princess Anne, married Prince George of Denmark. John and Sarah Churchill became the guiding spirits of the Denmark household. Its members came to constitute a countercourt, a military and political focus for succession politics.

Two years later, in 1685, Protestant and republican rebels rose to reject the Catholic James's accession to the imperial throne. Churchill and his dragoons crushed the rebels at Sedgemoor, eviscerated the survivors after the Bloody Assizes, and marched transportees in slave coffles for shipment to America. New England was excepted as already overinfected with puritan rebels. Instead the northern colonies were incorporated into a French-style dominion. The most notorious of the Tangerines, Colonel Piercy Kirke, lord Churchill's subordinate at Sedgemoor, was named to command the dominion of New England. Because he had sold pardons to rebels, however, Kirke was superseded by James's former governor of New York, the author of the Anglo-Iroquoian Covenant Chain, Churchill's old messmate and present colleague in the suppression of Monmouth's revolt, Sir Edmund Andros. England had had its dragonnade, New England its dominion. The parallel with France was all but complete. Authoritarianism needed only Catholicism to become absolutism.

King James rapidly embarked on a Catholicizing course. Lord Churchill was forced to choose between his conscience and his king. In the spring of 1687, at the apogee of his meteoric rise through James Stuart's service to a commanding position in the Restoration Empire, as a middle-aged general and a consummate courtier, lord Churchill made the most important decision of his life and age. He offered his services to William of Orange, the Protestant champion of Europe, if William would invade England to save it from King James's campaign to Catholicize the army and so to dragoon the empire of England.

England's leading soldier joined her most militant clerics to resist Catholicism. Lord Churchill openly facilitated the efforts of the American diocesan, Henry Compton, bishop of London, to protect Princess Anne from the crude Catholic canvass of her father the king and her stepmother, the devout Mary of Modena. Secretly, authorized by his confessor, Francis Turner, bishop of Ely, and under the aegis of Princess Anne, Churchill began to recruit the most Protestant and professional army officers for a putsch to protect their religion and the law (the law that preserved the Anglican monopoly of office, spiritual, military, and civil).

Disaffection on so large a scale could not be kept secret for long, but it was discounted by King James. He relied on the erastianism of the established church, the professional duty of the officer corps, and the gratitude of the "new class" of administrators whom he had raised from obscurity. James was a good general, a competent admiral, and (for a king) a splendid administrator, but he had never had much political sense and he had no liking for legalism. The English governing class was Anglican by law. To destroy that monopoly by fiat, as James attempted to do in 1687, might not be illegal, for his courts agreed that the king could dispense with the law, but it was unconstitutional, for the English state and the Church of England had been identical for a century and a half.

To preserve the church and the constitution, and to defy Catholicism and France, lord Churchill pledged that the military-political connection which Princess Anne emblemized would hamstring the defense of the realm against Prince William's invasion. William landed unopposed at Torbay on November 5, 1688, because the Channel Fleet had been paralyzed by the extension of the army conspiracy to the navy by Churchill's brother and by the kinsmen and brother officers of lord Churchill's co-conspirators. Then, between November 15 and 23, Churchill led hundreds of his Protestant, professional, patriotic officer comrades in a mass desertion from the field army of King James to that of Prince William. Abandoned by its professional officer elite and threatened by an invading army, King James's army collapsed. A series of garrison revolts seized the ports and citadels in England. In America, the king's governors-general and their red-coated bodyguards were overwhelmed by provincial armies.

The instant that its military instruments were dismantled, the monarchy of James II disintegrated. So did the monarch. "My daughter hath deserted me, my army also, and him that I raised from nothing, the same, on whom I heaped all favours; and if such betrays me, what can I expect from those I have done so little for," asked the king. Finding no answer, he fled to France. James II's assumption that loyalty was a function of favor missed the point of lord Churchill's coup. Neither profound personal debt nor royalist political principle, Churchill wrote to his king, could convince him to help James conquer his own subjects and deprive them of their religion by force, as King Louis had the Huguenots. Rather than do that, lord Churchill wrote, he had deserted to the invaders: "This, Sr. cou'd proceed from nothing but the inviolable dictates of my conscience, & a necessary concarn for my religion, (wich noe good man can oppose) & with which I am instructed nothing ought to come in competition." So John Churchill, personally, decisively, forcefully, and irrevocably, directed the course of Anglo-American history toward anglicanism.

Between January and July 1689, the distilled product of lord Churchill's coup and Prince William's invasion, a Protestant putsch, overspread America. In Maine and in Massachusetts, in New York and in Maryland, religious and military coups overthrew authoritarian or Catholic provincial or proprietary regimes. Each episode of the Protestant putsch enacted by American provincial armies reemphasized, even exaggerated, the religious and military themes of the decade-long debate between absolutism and exclusion. To leftover puritanism as to emergent whiggery, absolutism and Catholicism were one. So the same logic that had sent the earl of Danby to the Tower in the popish plot of 1679 chained Sir Edmund Andros to the walls of the Boston gaol in the Protestant putsch of 1689. Less logical appeals were made by demagogues to the demos. The pretended popish plot of 1679 provided a cast of fantastic characters for the Irish fright of 1688. The nightmare of Catholic conspiracy and Celtic native massacre that toppled the last loyalist authorities in England excited the hysterical reaction to a purported Jesuit and Indian invasion that propelled a Protestant putsch in the American provinces in the spring of 1689.

In each of England's American provinces, the Protestant putsch found its political resolution in the imperial constitution of 1681. Now revived and widened to include the growing number of royal provinces, this constitutionally conservative compromise extended while it defined executive authority, but it also recognized the rights of local elites to participation and representation. The balance that had been struck in 1681 between kingdom and colonies, monarchy and aristocracy, military and civilian, executive and elites, crown and parliament, became the English empire's "revolution settlement." This is something of a misnomer, wherever in the empire it is applied. Lord Churchill's coup in England and the Protestant putsch in America was a religious and military revolt in a politically underdeveloped polity. It was not a revolution, "glorious" or otherwise, unless by "revolution" is meant merely the turn of time. "Revolution," in England and

America, had put the constitutional clock back to 1681. The revolution of consequences, as imperial war impelled the construction of a modern state, took Churchill's whole life to accomplish.

In postputsch politics, lord Churchill at first took a second place to veteran imperial politicians of superior rank, the earl of Danby (now marquis of Carmarthen) and George Savile, the marquis of Halifax. Churchill had little experience of or faith in politics and parliaments but the lieutenant general would be driven toward both by the military fact that England was now commanded by a conquering prince and occupied by an alien army. Naïvely, the Protestant putschists had presumed that Prince William would lend them his might merely to force a wayward Catholic authoritarian away from the counterreformation and so away from France. Instead, Churchill and his co-conspirators found that William intended to be king himself. To seize the imperial crown, William displaced the English guards and replaced them with Dutch regiments in the metropolis. He commissioned his own generals to conquer the British kingdoms. He exiled the English army to fight against France in Flanders, Ireland, and America.

Bypassed and subordinated when he had thought to direct and command, Churchill had nonetheless to purge the English officer corps on the principles of the Protestant putsch. It was a wonderful opportunity to extend his military ascendancy, but Churchill had then to apply that ascendancy to distasteful ends. He had to neutralize the royal army while William made himself king. Churchill had to persuade his Anglican aegis, Princess Anne, to acquiesce in William's ascent to the imperial throne. He had to carry their "connection" with him in the convention parliament so that they did not vote against the accession of William and Mary. In the process Churchill began to create a political persona. In effect, he had begun to institutionalize the English army in domestic politics, as it had long been institutionalized in imperial administration, both in the other British kingdoms and in the royal provinces in America. Lord Churchill was rewarded at the coronation of William and Mary with the earldom of Marlborough, a title taken from his family's leading imperialist.

In the course of his transformation from English general to imperial politician, the new earl of Marlborough also had to assist William the Conqueror in Flanders against France in 1689. Marlborough commanded England's own defenses in 1690 while King William defeated King James at the Boyne. Marlborough then seized the Munster ports. Each of these military victories had immediate political effects. Marlborough's distinction in command of the English division at Walcourt, August 25, 1689, underlay his parliamentary assertion of Princess Anne's fiscal independence of William and Mary. Marlborough's defense of southern England during the summer of 1690 and his victories at Cork on September 25 and Kinsale on October 15 cemented his ascendancy over the English army and made him a menace to King William's armed and alien administration. The king disgraced Marlborough in January 1692. Queen Mary had him imprisoned in May. In the autumn, the house of lords refused to do business until Marlborough was released. The six subsequent years in unrelenting opposition were Marlborough's unpleasant but effective political and parliamentary education, in American affairs as well as English. Marlborough personified and directed the English army's resentment of the uncivil prince and his boorish generals. This bad blood bedeviled the conduct of both war and politics until it eventuated in the last of the standing army debates that had punctuated English politics for seventy years, and ever more frequently since the redcoats restored the Stuarts. All during the decade of the 1690s, Marlborough had advocated as that debate's essential outcome the removal of the Dutch army of occupation from England.

Once that was accomplished, the king was forced to return Marlborough to power as the favorite of the English army and the English princess. In June 1698, the king made Marlborough head of the new royal household established for Princess Anne's son. Then the king named Marlborough one of the lords justices. Finally, in July 1701, the king recommissioned Marlborough general of the English army and appointed him plenipotentiary to rebuild the grand alliance against France. As general, Marlborough would secure the succession of his princess as Queen Anne. As plenipotentiary, Marlborough would negotiate the terms under which England resumed the war against Louis XIV, a war for liberty in Europe and empire in America.

BOOK I

A SOLDIER'S SCHOOLS

Military men have seldom much knowledge of books,
their education does not allow it;
but what makes great amends for that want is,
that they generally know a great deal of the world;
they are thrown into it young;
they see variety of nations and characters;
and they find that to rise, which is the aim of them all,
they must first please;
these concurrent causes almost always give them manners
and politeness.
In consequence of which,
you see them always distinguished at Courts,
and favoured by women.

—Lord Chesterfield to his son, London, June 1752

CHAPTER ONE

The "Handsome Englishman": An Apprentice to Army and Empire: 1667–1679

O N AN AFTERNOON late in August 1667, beyond a screen of elm trees, sprawled the London suburb called Whitehall Palace. At a rickety back porch opening onto the palace park waited the king's coach and its six white horses. The king himself, a long-legged monarch, led a breathless band of courtiers down a shady park path at a furious pace. The royal rate, as his majesty often explained, exercised himself, entertained his spaniels, and silenced his courtiers. Oblivious to the royal passage, the palace dairy herd grazed alongside the path. So did sheep, kine, and a very handsome billy goat.

Across the background of this sylvan scene appeared a less bucolic, more royal reality. Mounted troopers of the household cavalry patrolled the park perimeter. Red-coated sentinels guarded the park gates. Cannon were "parked" on the premises, flanked by gunners. A company of the Coldstream Guards was on parade. Pikemen and musketeers, in black beaver hats and red uniforms, were aligned in rank and file by sergeants with their halberds. At the company's head stood a captain and a lieutenant carrying half-pikes. Their orders were echoed by young drummers. The focus of every eye in the company was its junior officer. The ensign bore aloft a silk standard, the red cross of St. George on a blue field, the symbol of English honor and royal identity, the company's own color, presented by the king, the commander-in-chief.[1]

The king's brother and heir, James Stuart, duke of York, drilled the company of his brother's Guards. The royal duke "placed his chief Delight in the Exercise of Arms." Formerly a lieutenant general in the French army and now a serving admiral in the English navy, the duke directed each of the sixteen steps by which the musketeers loaded and fired their matchlocks. He ordered the march and countermarch that moved the reloading firemen to shelter behind the hedge of sixteen-foot-long, steel-shod pikes borne by the biggest guardsmen. A step behind and beside the royal duke stood his beautiful page, the cynosure of the court, John Churchill. At seventeen, Churchill was already noted for "a most Genteel Air and obliging Deportment." His enchantment with the martial moment amused his master. "What," James Stuart asked his page, "should he do for him, as the first Step in his fortune." Churchill knelt before the duke and asked for "a Pair of Colours in the Guards." On September 14, 1667, "to Humour His forward Inclination to Martial Affairs," there was recorded in the royal army commission register John Churchill's ensigncy in the senior unit of the English infantry. Here, in the king's own company in the First Guards, began the career that would depose James Stuart from the imperial throne of England, deflate the dominions of France in both Europe and America, and transform Whitehall from a sylvan suburb of mercantile London into the military headquarters of the British empire.[2]

Empire began in England: "the King, being in authority at home, as he is at present, cannot fail of respect abroad." The restored monarchy's seven-year occupation of England, after twenty years of civil war and military dictatorship, was concluded in 1667. Under the relentless pressure of the duke of York, King Charles had regarrisoned the military strongholds of the former Cromwellian dictatorship. Now, 6,600 men in garrison companies provided a physical presence for the crown in every important port, provincial capital, and strategic town. No matter how shabby and ill-equipped they might be, the men of these infantry companies had no organized rivals. An equal number of regimented redcoats formed the royal bodyguard, garrisoned the Tower of London and the Thames Forts, held the administrative center, Westminster, and provided a mobile reserve with which to repress rebellion in the realm or, as in the cases of Barbados and Virginia, in overseas dominions of the imperial crown. During John Churchill's apprenticeship to army and empire, the Guards reinforced royal authority not just in England but in English outposts as far apart as the Channel Islands and the West Indies, North Africa and North America.[3]

"The sleeping lion" of executive power was now awakening in England. By 1667 it seemed that "the Guards and Garrisons," hitherto a mere gendarmerie, might move from peacekeeping to politics. "The design is, and the duke of York . . . is hot for it, to have a land army and to make the Government like that of France," but there were difficulties. "Our princes have not the brains or at least care and foresight enough," said one of their military bureaucrats, to use the army to make themselves absolute. In the words of Churchill's chaplain, in "the Unactive, Lazy Reign of Charles II . . . there was ever more business for the Cabinet than the Camp and greater Application to Luxury and Riot than either." King Charles was irresolute. Duke James was inflexible. Nonetheless, they now had soldiers enough to outfight their domestic opponents and officers enough to staff the royal governments overseas. Such new officers as Ensign Churchill, who, from his entry into the Guards displayed a "Natural Genius in Martial Affairs," became the willing instruments of the Stuarts' imperial authority.[4]

Imperial authority rested on the Cromwellian military model. Makers of that model were still present in the royal army when, in the autumn of 1667, John Churchill hired a veteran Cromwellian sergeant to teach him the drills of march, pike, and musket. The sergeant probably instructed Ensign Churchill in keeping the company orderly book and accounts, for the literacy and numeracy of Cromwellian noncommissioned officers was the foundation of the military bureaucracy that modernized English government. Then, as afterwards, senior sergeants ran the army, and the army ran the empire. Churchill learned this early. Subsequently, he sent sergeants by the score to organize and officer American companies of the imperial army.

So the ironic indispensability of the dictator's soldiers to the royal army extended from the routines of the drill field to the direction of the empire, and from noncommissioned officers, such as the sergeant who instructed Ensign Churchill, to the king's captain general himself, George Monck, the duke of Albemarle. He had formerly fought in Ireland, commanded Scotland, and reinforced Jamaica as a general of the Commonwealth and the Protectorate. Nonetheless, Monck had managed the royal restoration. What had been his own regiment in the dictator's army had become the king's Coldstream Guards on Valentine's Day 1660. Its title commemorated—and it still recalls—the then General Monck's headquarters and his regiment's river crossing from Scotland into England en route to the occupation of London and the restoration of King Charles. Monck, now duke of Albemarle, was still colonel of the Coldstream Guards and, as the king's captain general, Churchill's superior officer. So that most royalist of officers, Ensign John Churchill, was "Grounded in the Rudiments of War" by Cromwellian veterans.[5]

Churchill's commanders in the First (afterwards "Grenadier") Guards, however, were "king's men," veterans in the cause of the martyred King Charles I. They had followed his son, Charles II, into an impoverished exile, formed his first Guard in Flanders, and fought for their young king at the Battle of the Dunes. English patriots and Protestants, these senior Guards officers rejoiced in the royal restoration, and their own. Restored by one army and sustained by another, the king was bracketed between the Anglicanism of the Grenadiers and the puritanism of the Coldstream (to this day, when both of these regiments are on parade, they take opposite ends of the line). So the tolerant, even crypto-Catholic king reluctantly dismissed from his Guards all Roman Catholic officers. John Churchill stepped into one of their places. Indeed, for the next twenty years, every one of his promotions, from ensign to general, would be at the expense of a

Catholic officer. For Churchill, even more than for most officers in an army Protestant by law, the exclusion of Catholics from the service was the essence of his professional identity.[6]

Although Churchill's career depended upon the continued exclusion of Catholics from command, he rose by the favor of the Catholic duke. James's public status as a noncommunicant in the Church of England, from Easter of 1667, was not yet, nor, for many years to come, would be seen by the duke's Anglican followers as an irreversible commitment to Catholicism. In the factions of the First Guards, Ensign Churchill was marked not as a king's man or an Anglican but rather as one of "the duke's men," a servant and protégé of that martial monarchist, closet Catholic, and public francophile, James Stuart, duke of York. Churchill's elders among the duke's aides and servants had followed their exiled master to distinguished, rewarding careers in the army of France. Only after 1656, when Cromwellian diplomacy had forced the duke and many of his men from the French service to the Spanish, and so from pay to penury, did they encounter the hardship that had been the lot of the king's men for seven years already. The king's men, at the shabby Stuart court in Brussels, lived scantily on royalist loyalty, Anglican piety, and a decade of dashed hopes for their master's restoration (and their reward). When that long-awaited event occurred, however, both sets of royalists were received as poor relations by the Cromwellian garrison of Dunkirk (small wonder the royal military acquiesced so easily in King Charles's sale of the hated port to Louis XIV). Only after the restored monarch was forcibly challenged by republican, religious, and military irreconcilables, were both bands of exiles brought home and incorporated as the First Guards. The better fortunes and greater discipline of the duke's men still kept them loyal to their patron and long inclined them toward the absolutism he personified. The king's men, however, conditioned their loyalty to the crown on its alliance with the Church of England and on the king's adherence to legal forms in government.[7]

Ultimately, the Anglican allegiance of the royalists would wean John Churchill from the duke for, as the good child of a gentle family, Ensign Churchill aspired both to military honor and landed gentility, and he deplored deviation, religious or political, from the standards of an English officer and an Anglican gentleman. Religion and politics were one, as became clear when the Clarendon code and the Test Act combined to make English public life the exclusive preserve of communicants of the state church. These acts, like Churchill himself and his education, were the creations of cavaliers, royalists defeated in the civil wars, to whom their persecuted religion alone had remained during the Interregnum.

John was the eldest surviving son of Sir Winston Churchill, a royalist cavalry officer broken by physical wounds and military defeat, proscribed by puritans and fined by parliamentarians, living in the house (half-burnt by royalists) of his parliamentarian mother-in-law. Sir Winston spent his years of internal exile writing *Divi Britannici*, a tract justifying the divine right of kings from the moment of creation, and educating his children, with the assistance of the family chaplain, himself deprived of an Anglican benefice by a secular state. Together they educated young John in "the Church of England Principles" of religious royalism and Protestant patriotism.[8]

A defeated officer and a deprived clergyman bent their combined efforts to teach young John those "Sound Principles of Religion" that would compel him to help restore the authority of church and king and to rescue his family from the obscurity and penury imposed upon them by the republicans of the Commonwealth and the dictators of the Protectorate. It was the irredentism of such Anglican indoctrination that made the authorities of the Protectorate despair of making England one nation with the cavaliers who "have bred and educated their children by the sequestered and ejected clergy, and very much confined their marriages and alliances within their own party, as if they meant to entail their quarrel and prevent the means to reconcile posterity." The Church of England to which John Churchill was devoted from his youth was royalist and legalist. It was an institution concerned with governmental authority and national identity. It was as given to political rancor as it was to religious worship.[9]

Yet the Church of England was the avenue to divinity for Ensign John Churchill. The senior member of his family, from whom Churchill would take an aristocratic title, was the earl of Marlborough, James Ley. In John Churchill's youth Marlborough was famous as a soldier, a royalist, and an imperialist, an artilleryman who exercised his skill at Naseby, in Massachusetts, and in Bombay, but Marlborough was most marked as a fighting man whose faith became publicly eloquent on the eve of his fatal fleet action with the Dutch. As James Ley's successor in the title, John Churchill, earl and duke of Marlborough, ordered his chaplains to celebrate divine service at the head of his regiments and for his own staff in the last moments before battle. He rode into combat in a state of grace. He might literally be said to have "made a parade of his faith." For that faith, Churchill would subvert a Catholic king, just as his father had resisted puritan parliamentarians and the anti-Anglican protector. Both Sir Winston and his son were passionate defenders of Anglican moderation, the *via media* between popery and puritanism (and, as it would appear, of a parallel political moderation, a constitutional monarchy, midway between absolutism and republicanism).[10]

Ensign Churchill entered an army whose extensive, contentious, and decisive political history would offer him a variety of governmental commands as he rose rapidly through the commissioned ranks. His services to the state, to six sovereigns, and to the imperial army, during a professional career that covered fifty-five years, from 1667 to 1722 provide proof that the English military, for generations after the demise of the Cromwellian dictatorship, remained a decisive element in English politics. The army was as important to imperial politics as the crown or the parliament. Indeed, the army and the executive were one, and until 1689, parliament was only an occasional political participant. Before this date, and probably until 1697, the army was the key to an absolutism checked more effectively by the professional and Protestant self-interest of its own officers than by the parliamentary opposition to the Stuarts.

The army was the cadre of royal administration, increasing in governmental importance abroad as well as at home throughout Churchill's military career. In 1667, therefore, the flagrant factionalism of the Guards at home was even more apparent in the army's overseas administrations. The distinctions between royalists and absolutists, between religious ideologues and statist politiques, between the king's men, the duke's men, and the general's men, were clarified by the strictures of military service in the infant Englands overseas. Each colony's administration continued to be an English political experiment. Some were successful, in that the experience of garrison government formed the institutions and ideologies of successor states, a new nation, and an American empire. More immediately, what transpired in England's colonies offered options for England's own transformation from an association of late medieval counties and corporations into a modern, militarized nation-state.

One option was Cromwellian. In both Ireland and Jamaica, Albemarle's enormous influence as the maker of the Restoration and as captain general of the royal army helped preserve the Cromwellian regimental plantations. In them survived the Protestant, republican, legacy of the Commonwealth and the Protectorate, despite the arrival of newly ennobled royal governors, Charles II's "young lords." In Tangier, Cromwellian garrisons, commanders, and institutions coexisted uneasily with the Catholic protégés and absolutist programs of the duke of York. Virginia's royalist elite sought, as did Treasurer Southampton and Chancellor Clarendon at home, to turn the social and constitution clock back to 1641, an era before professional armies and secular bureaucracies and imperial income gave undue weight to the executive and challenged the sway of the church. Massachusetts still showed what could be wrong with such an autonomous model, from an Anglican, a royalist, or an imperialist viewpoint. The colonies, England's political laboratories, now, as always, exhibited more starkly, anticipated more clearly, the political issues masked and moderated in England by region and by class, by tradition and by time.[11]

In the ensuing conflicts of imperial authority with provincial elites, within England as well as overseas, the key players now became the faction-ridden royal regiments. Three of these regiments were cavalry formations, each composed of three to six troops, perhaps three hundred horsemen to the regiment. In 1667, the year of John Churchill's commission, the crown also employed eleven infantry regiments, each made up of between six and twenty-four companies, nominally of one hundred men per company. The fourteen royal regiments, three horse and eleven foot, were known collectively as "the Guards." The sixty-six independent companies were labeled "the Garrisons." In theory, the guards protected the king while the garrisons supported his governors, but increased centralization quickly eroded this distinction, and with it the autonomy of the provincial executives. When, in the fall of 1667, John Churchill joined the senior battalion of the first regiment of the household infantry, "the Guards" proper, many of its officers were on detached service in local governments. First Guards officers commanded the metropolitan garrison, housed in the Tower of London, the barracks of Westminster, the taverns of Southwark, and in three royal palaces. First Guards officers also served the crown as the governors of Guernsey, Portsmouth, old York, New York, and Barbados. Often these Guards officers and governors took their own companies with them to the provinces as their personal escorts and to stiffen local garrisons. Churchill's two seniors among the subalterns of the king's own company would command companies in the Guards battalion subsequently dispatched to Virginia. Four other First Guards contemporaries of Churchill joined the Virginia expedition, survived it, and returned to serve under Churchill's command. The imperial administrative service of the First Guards in the repression of Bacon's Revolution was one element in the Guards' developing "regimental connection." It created an institutional and personal link between the Old Dominion and the First Guards that grew throughout John Churchill's career until at last, now the colonel of the First Guards, he assigned his own staff officers to command the colony, which they transformed into an English province.[12]

On the first anniversary of his commission in the Guards, Ensign Churchill himself sailed for service in England's greatest overseas garrison, the embattled Mediterranean fortress port of Tangier. Tangier was the particular province of Churchill's patron, James, duke of York, the president of the Tangier commission. After the death of the captain general, Albemarle, in 1670 his institutional heir at court and in the empire, James Stuart, became the unchallenged director of the Tangier garrison and government. Its three British infantry battalions, plus cavalry and artillery, commanded by a governor-general, constituted the largest concentration of military force in the English empire, outside the garrison of the imperial metropolis itself.[13]

When, in the summer of 1668, Churchill prepared to join the relief fleet bound for Tangier, the colony was being spoken of as "the foundation of a new empire." If it could be made an all-weather, deepwater port by the

construction of the mole, certainly the greatest engineering project undertaken by Englishmen in the seventeenth century, Tangier would command
the straits of Gibraltar, "the great passage to the wealth of Africa and America." It was designedly a check on French imperial expansion and its garrison set itself to challenge the French monopoly of military reputation. At
the same time, in the ancient terms of European militarism and expansion,
Tangier was avowedly a Christian crusaders' bastion. It was besieged by
Moslem beys on land and beset by Algerian corsairs at sea. In ways both
ancient and modern, crusading and imperialistic, when John Churchill was
ordered there Tangier was intended to be the English crown's "Nursery of
its own for soldiers . . . without being altogether beholding to our Neighbours for their Education and breeding."[14]

There was fighting on other frontiers of the English empire in 1668. In
the Leeward Islands the Barbados Regiment was led by a former First
Guards ensign, Major Edmund Andros. In the spring of the year that
Churchill joined the regiment, Andros had been jumped up to major to
fight in the Antilles against the French, the Caribs, and the Dutch, and to
overawe the English republicans of Barbados. On the other side of the
world from Barbados, the first English commander of Bombay (beset by the
mutinies of unpaid troops symptomatic of England's imperial infancy,
mutinies that compelled the transfer of the colony's administration to the
East India Company, itself, especially in the 1690s, an employer and educa-
tor of soldier-administrators) was Churchill's exemplar, his cousin and
predecessor, James Ley, earl of Marlborough.[15]

More than either of these imperial outposts, however, Tangier was
the chief example of what each English colony was supposed to be, a self-
supporting "Magazine of Arms and a Military School or Seminary to breed
up Soldiers" without cost to the crown or reliance upon parliament. For
Churchill, an ambitious young soldier who wanted to learn "the rudiments
of Military Discipline" in the service of his own country, and so to lay "the
groundwork of that Reputation, which was the wonder of his Time," Tangier service was indispensable.[16]

Personal alliances as well as professional considerations presumably
promoted Churchill in the Guards and won him an assignment to Tangier.
His sister Arabella had fallen from her horse into the arms of the duke of
York. From January 1668, she received a ducal douceur of £1,000 a year.
For five years, Arabella Churchill was James's obsession, much to her as-
tonishment, for she was plain and James was incapable of appreciating her
wit. Still, she bore him four children (one of whom, James duke of Berwick,
became a marshal of France and, after his uncle John, was perhaps the
greatest general of the age). Although the duke of York married the beautiful and spirited Mary of Modena in 1673, he remained interested in Arabella, at least until her marriage to John Churchill's comrade, the army

officer Charles Godfrey. Doubtless the ducal involvement with his sister helped John Churchill's career, but the duke, as was the responsibility of royalty, "did not want Judgement to discern the early Promise [Churchill] made of being a Great Man, and therefore was not backward to Support him with his Favour." Obviously, it extended to the garrison of Tangier, which the duke directed and where Churchill could find combat experience, see imperial service, and observe a foreign culture—in short, where a young officer could find professional opportunity.[17]

In the summer of 1668, Churchill embarked in the royal fleet bound for the Mediterranean. The fleet made port first in Lisbon to pick up four hundred Cromwellian troopers, the survivors of a force sent out at the Restoration to relieve England of their politically dangerous presence and to protect Portugal, England's new imperial ally. To command the cavalry, Irish royalist officers had been commissioned, among them O'Briens and Dongans of the American gubernatorial families. English cavaliers also commanded in this fabled force of expatriates. One was Major Guy Molesworth, already a veteran of Bermuda and Virginia service. An amalgam of enemies, these British soldiers nonetheless had won a wide reputation under Schomberg's command, defending Portugal from Spanish imperialism. Now they reinforced the Tangier cavalry to help hold the African colony that England had acquired from Portugal. These troopers would become the veteran cadres of Churchill's first cavalry command, the Royal Dragoons, in 1683. His immediate assignment, however, was to the staff of "the Governor's Regiment" commanded by Tangier's lieutenant governor, Colonel Henry Norwood.[18]

An exiled officer of Charles I's army, Harry Norwood had spent the Interregnum in Virginia and he was still treasurer of that colony. Now Norwood alternated between military combat with the Moorish army and political encounters with the Tangier city corporation. Tangier's first mayor, John Bland, had his son Giles accuse Colonel Norwood of embezzling his soldiers' pay and provisions. Giles afterwards went out to Virginia and made equivalent accusations against Norwood's old comrade and commander, Governor Sir William Berkeley. Berkeley court-martialed and hanged Giles Bland but Norwood was merely amused at the Blands' badgering. "I am gotten out of the frying-pan into the fire," he wrote, "no sooner escaped the fury of the Turkes, but I am by the ears with the Mayor of Tangiers." Mayor Bland rejoined that the officers of the garrison were determined to "buy all, keep all, make slaves of all and get all, destroy all that will not doe as they doe, and make all fish that comes to their net."[19]

A winter on Norwood's staff introduced Churchill to the sordid squabbles of the military officers with the civilian authorities. These were envenomed by Tangier's constitutional place (like that of the American colonies) outside the realm of the common law and so subject to absolute, royal, martial authority. This extraconstitutional status would lead to parliamentary efforts to make Tangier (as well as Jamaica and Virginia) an English dominion by statute. The subjection of Tangier to martial law gave a political dimension to Governor Norwood's earnest efforts to quell the national quarrels of his garrison's English, Scots, and Irish regiments. In his resolution of both civil and military contests, Norwood attempted to preserve and express every Tangerine's especial respect for their royal commander, Ensign Churchill's patron, James, duke of York.[20]

In attitudes and in activities, Churchill became more martial daily. He wore the new tropical uniform that was being developed simultaneously by the English regiments in Tangier and Barbados. No doubt he shared his fellow officers' contempt for civilian concerns and behavior: "the effeminate designs and stupid procedures of the burghers." He helped supervise the perpetual digging that extended and reinforced Tangier's medieval walls with modern earthworks, places of arms, and artillery bastions. Tangier was notoriously a place of pleasure as well as danger. Garrisons always are. In Tangier, Churchill was subject to temptations that shocked even such a lubricious Londoner as Samuel Pepys. Certainly the Anglo-African colony had women enough to permit the officer polygamy by which 40 officers provided for 129 "wives" and 173 children.[21]

Perhaps some of these wives were other officers' widows rather than the mates or concubines of the officers in whose households they were listed. And serial remarriage of regimental widows to the men of the regiment was common at all ranks. The ever more extensive intermarriage of officers' families, and their marital alliances with families of provincial pooh-bahs in Port Royal, say, or New York, or Edinburgh, or Dublin was followed by the enlistment of their sons into what were, in every sense of the word, "parent" corps. These military generations quickly created imperial "interests" that were at once familial and professional. Then military service under the command of the regiment's actual commandants, its honorary colonels, general officers, and noble patrons, gave the children of the regiment English political and patrician contacts. These in turn facilitated military and imperial promotion, ideally capped by a triumphal return by the successful officer to his natal garrison government as governor-general. The Matthews of Antigua, the Lynch-Littletons of Jamaica, the Codringtons of Barbados and St. Kitts, the Parke-Evelyns and Elliot-Spotswoods of Virginia, the Carolinas and Edinburgh, the Mascarenes of Nova Scotia and Massachusetts, are but a few Anglo-American examples of the regimental families that Churchill found forming in the Tangier garrison. A Tangier regiment's garrison intermarriages produced two of Churchill's most distinguished future subordinates. Roger Elliot became a regimental commander under Churchill, who had him commissioned governor-general of Gibraltar. Elliot's younger half-brother, Alexander Spotswood, was the son of the garrison's surgeon during Churchill's service in Tangier. Spotswood was educated in the regimental school and commissioned an officer in the regiment's daughter unit in his teens. Spotswood rose to become Churchill's deputy quartermaster general (i.e., deputy chief of staff) and received the command of Virginia as the reward of his staff service.[22]

The commission to govern in Virginia that Churchill secured for the son of his Tangier surgeon completed another of the innumerable circles of army associations that connected Churchill—and so many other English officers—to Virginia. Information about the king's Old Dominion in America was wholesaled to Ensign Churchill when he dined at the table that Colonel Norwood kept for his officer "family." There the ensign inevitably heard the colonel's famous tale of his flight from republican usurpers in England to royalist refuge in Virginia. The governor told of a storm-racked voyage, of being marooned on the coast of Maryland, and of his rescue by the Accomacs. He described his venturesome voyage down the Chesapeake to Jamestown. He discussed the strange English province he had finally reached, beset by the natives, troubled by servant conspiracies, divided between west country Anglican royalist planters—Sir William Berkeley was their patriarch—and the scions of London merchant families like the Blands. Churchill himself would recruit the troops that finally settled the quarrel of Virginia's squires against its cosmopolites. Bacon's Revolution was Virginia's recapitulation of England's civil war and it anticipated the American revolution.[23]

The Virginia conflict was astutely analyzed by Norwood who, although he was Tangier's chief executive, remained a trader in tobacco with Sir William Berkeley of Virginia and Colonel Richard Nicolls of New York. Nicolls, formerly the duke of York's Catholic deputy governor at Portsmouth, had been transferred to America to conquer and govern the duke's new province, New York. Norwood not only facilitated New York's Iberian trade via Tangier (as he did that of Virginia), he also oversaw Tangier's entrepôt services for Newfoundland, Barbados, and Jamaica. Fleets of fishing ketches were convoyed by ships of the royal navy from Newfoundland banks to Tangier. Traders from American continental and Caribbean island ports also filled the Tangier roadstead during Churchill's term. Their captains came to dine at Governor Norwood's table to tell their tales of Englands overseas to his officers and to receive his licenses to trade and take convoy from Tangier.[24]

Besides offering Churchill an education in the economics, politics, and communications of the king's expanding empire, his service on Norwood's staff introduced the young officer to the ample authority of independent overseas command, that is, to garrison government. The king's commission promoting Norwood governor-general made him absolute. He was royal captain general, vice admiral, and chief governor of Tangier. As the king's governor-general, Churchill's commander could commission, discipline, and train the men of his garrison, subdue and slay rebels and traitors, legislate and judge and pardon, license or restrict commerce "as may best suite with your interests," restricted only occasionally by royal (that is, ducal) instructions.[25]

As viceroy, Norwood personified the absolutist union of army and empire. Ensign Churchill observed the governor-general exercise the sovereign's military authority not only to preserve and protect England's physical presence at this oceanic intersection but also to tie Tangier to the king's governments and colonial economies in North America and the West Indies. When, in later years, observers marveled at the imperial range of Churchill's strategic, imperial, and economic planning, they had forgotten his years of service in the Mediterranean outpost of the Restoration Empire.

The only missing element in Ensign Churchill's military curriculum was supplied at dawn on July 2, 1669. The forces of El Rasheed II, "the emperor of Morocco," attacked Tangier's James Fort. A red-coated sally beat them back. The Moors attacked again on July 18, only to be rebuffed by the entrenched garrison's gunfire. There followed two years of English patrol and native ambush, of the garrison's foraging forays, and its steady shrinkage from casualties and malnutrition, illness and neglect.[26]

On pain of summary court martial and, worse, loss of professional reputation, Ensign Churchill taught each of his men: "to defend his [company's] colors day and night"; to subordinate material gain to military community by awaiting pay patiently, eschewing freebooting, sharing plunder, provisions, and dangerous duty equally with his comrades; to be sober on watch and peaceable in garrison; to fight, march, drill, camp, quarter, and guard, never absenting himself from duty without leave; to maintain and to preserve his weapons; and in all times and circumstances to attend, respect, and obey his superiors.[27]

Two years of unending obedience to the commands of the king's officers in Tangier indoctrinated Churchill in a martial code of duty, first to God and to public worship, second to the king and to the duke, third to the army and his superior officers. To a garrison composed of civil war veterans and their sons, however, it was all too clear that these duties might conflict. Memories of civil war taught them the mathematics of military allegiance: the officer's first duty, to religion, if combined with his third duty, to profession, might outweigh his secondary loyalty, to the crown. And Tangier, as the decisive roles of its former garrison in 1688 would show, bred Protestant, patriotic, professional military values. From Tangier came the core of Churchill's own regiment. Tangier's military values shaped his fateful political decision. Tangier veterans executed his Protestant putsch itself, both on the land and on the sea.

The Tangier naval connection was nearly as portentous, professionally and politically, as was the Tangier garrison culture and its regimental connections. Churchill partook of both. On March 21, 1670, orders were issued in London for Ensign Churchill's naval equipment. He was assigned to the staff of Admiral Sir Thomas Allin. Churchill was the first of a succession of young officers from the Tangier garrison who, after they had fought "every fight on land . . . when their [sic] appeared no chance of [further] fighting, they went with the seamen after the Algerine Corsairs." Others were Charles Mordaunt (afterwards the famous fighting earl of Peterborough and a cat's-paw for Churchill's enemies in England, Iberia, and Jamaica) and William O'Brien (afterwards governor-general both of Tangier and of Jamaica), who lost an eye fighting the Algerines at sea.[28]

Admiral Allin and his Anglo-Dutch squadron were under the orders of the duke of York, as lord high admiral, to blockade Algiers and attack the corsairs. Presumably, Churchill was aboard the flagship when, on August 12, 1670, it met the Algerine fleet off Cape Spartel. Allin's command forced ashore or captured six Algerine warships and rescued 250 Christian captives. When Allin's battleships sailed home to England in the autumn of 1670, Churchill sailed with them, under the special orders of the duke of York to return to court.[29]

Disciplined, battle-tested, tanned, and hardened, the twenty-year-old officer of the Guards reentered Charles II's court "form'd with all the Advantages imaginable, both of Person and Address, to inspire Love," particularly in Churchill's cousin, Barbara Villiers, duchess of Cleveland. "Aging," at twenty-nine, and losing her preeminence in King Charles's affections, Cleveland shared her contemporaries' view that Churchill's "figure was beautiful, but his manner was irresistible." He offered romance and consideration to a sensual and spirited woman much put upon by royal machismo (if Charles was not the brute in bed that his brother was, still "there was nothing seraphic" in his lovemaking). Barbara was enraptured by "Jack" Churchill. Soon "it was visible to the whole Court," but it was some time before the jaded, unjudgmental, and otherwise occupied king was forced to acknowledge the affair between the duchess and the ensign.[30]

One afternoon, a year into the Cleveland-Churchill affair, King Charles unexpectedly entered Cleveland's bedroom. Her naked visitor dove through the window. It was three stories up, over a cobblestone courtyard. Such was the sanitary standard of the royal palace, however, that there was a huge dung heap handy to break the lover's fall (and intensify his humiliation). King Charles encountered Ensign Churchill on guard the next day. "Young man," said his sovereign, "I forgive you, for you do it for your bread." Whether or not Churchill had previously been paid by Cleveland for his sexual services, she now assuaged his (literal) embarrassment with £5,000.[31]

Barbara's bounty founded the Churchill family fortune. Such was his cold calculation, even at age twenty-one, in the midst of a spendthrift court, that Churchill invested the whole sum in an annuity (purchased from George Savile, earl of Halifax) that paid him £500 a year. (He also purchased for £800 an annuity of £100 from the most reliable of "the duke's men," Marshal Turenne's nephew, the earl of Feversham. (Forty years later, when Feversham, broken by his loyalty to James Stuart, begged Churchill, now the richest man in England, to let him buy back the bond, that monster of avarice refused, saying "he knew not where to put it for so good advantage.") Churchill was desperate to escape the poverty that had blighted his childhood, that had made his father dependent upon royal charity, and that had reduced Ensign Churchill to reliance on his cousin, "the royal whore."[32]

Like every aspirant officer in an aristocratic age, Churchill dreamt of acquiring a landed estate that would make him economically independent and that would free his children from the scrimping and humiliation he hated. Although Churchill had now set his foot on the military ladder he would climb to become "the greatest man, for a subject in Europe," it was as a subject to sovereign commanders, and as a landed aristocrat, as a member of the ruling elite, *primus inter pares*, that Churchill would break and make the kings and queens, the monarchs who constituted the horizon of his politics. His enemies would equate him with the tyrants of old, "King John," and with the recent dictator, "Oliver." Even his adulators could not help observing that, "had he fought for a Commonwealth so considerable as that of Rome, [he] had no doubt made himself the Head of it." Churchill himself was a monarchist. He never aimed at sovereignty. He sought simply first to join and then to dominate the aristocracy. He succeeded. His success transformed the ruling order of England. Churchill's ascent to aristocracy, with those of his contemporary "men of business" and of his military subordinates, transformed an ascriptive aristocracy into an oligarchy of achievement.[33]

The foundation of oligarchies is materialism. In acquisition and in saving, as in so many other aspects of his life, Churchill was a genius. As the Feversham anecdote indicates, Churchill's saving ways became an habitual miserliness and his penuriousness grew into an unbecoming avarice. When, in the heyday of his wealth and power, a Churchill despatch seemed especially indecipherable, it was remarked that he had probably left out the tittles of *i* and *j* "to save ink." But for the moment, Churchill was a young officer. An annuity sold to him seemed a safe investment. A soldier who, one way and another, lived as dangerously as Churchill did was hardly likely to survive long enough to recover his stake.[34]

Early in 1671, Cleveland was pregnant, probably by Churchill. The doubts about the paternity of the child led to duels with others of Cleveland's lovers. Churchill was wounded twice. Fortunately for his peace of mind, his health, and the progress of his military career, Churchill was ordered to take his company of the Guards onboard the flagship of Sir Robert Holmes, a creature of the duke of York and the agent of his antipathy to the Dutch. On March 13, 1672, Holmes's squadron attacked the Dutch Smyrna convoy as it sailed upchannel, the excuse being the Anglo-Dutch quarrel over the disposition of Surinam. The attack was a failure, if only because Holmes let Sir Edward Spragg pass homeward with his squadron rather than enlist Spragg's assistance and share in the anticipated profits. Holmes sent Ensign Churchill to report to the king and the duke the first shots of the Third Dutch War. To be the bearer of despatches was an honor, but to bring bad news was a dubious distinction. Still, Churchill's arrival at court produced his first, modest, mention in imperial despatches.[35]

In May, the duke took Churchill and his Guards company with him on board his flagship, the *Royal Prince*. Churchill's company was commanded by Captain Thomas Daniels and Lieutenant Edward Picts (both of whom, in a successful search for promotion, would go out to Virginia with the Guards battalion). These Guards now served as marines in the hard-fought battle of Solebay. There, on May 28, 1672, the English fleet, surprised by its Dutch enemies and deserted by its French allies, handicapped by contrary winds and a foul tide, faced odds of at least two to one.[36]

The *Royal Prince*, the duke's flagship, was the focus of the Dutch attack. Two hours' bombardment wrecked the ship and killed or wounded most of her crew. In extremis, the ship that was Churchill's battle station was rescued and towed out of the line of fire by Captain John Berry's *Resolution* (the captain had recently returned from distinguished service on the Jamaica station and his ship, on which Churchill had served, was just back from Tangier). One hundred and twenty of Berry's crew were killed during their rescue of the flagship. Aboard the *Royal Prince*, the most noted among two hundred casualties was Colonel Richard Nicolls. Recently retired from an historic term as the conqueror and governor of New York, Colonel Nicolls had volunteered for the duke's staff. He was cut in half by a cannonball as he stood at James's side.[37]

The duke's marine regiment, commanded aboard the *Royal Prince* by its colonel, the former governor-general of Jamaica, Sir Charles Littleton, had suffered severe losses at Solebay. Among them were four company captains. Into one of their places stepped Ensign John Churchill. This double jump in rank was the duke's recognition of Churchill's bravery in the most ferocious fight in the violent history of the Narrow Seas. It may also have been partly a petticoat promotion, for Cleveland allegedly paid 400 guineas for the commission (the payment, to the dead captain's widow, shows how the much-maligned purchase system served as an insurance policy). Churchill's elevation over the head of his immediate superior, Lieutenant Picts, inspired that Guards officer's bitter and vocal resentment and a remarkable range of comment elsewhere. It was not just Cleveland's favor but also Churchill's combination of ambition, charm, and merit that made the newly promoted captain an envied officer and a marked man. As "Caesar's Ghost" wandered the world (on the London stage),

It wonders what did Churchill recomend,
who never did to deeds of Arms pretend.
Love, all his active youth his business was,
Love that best suits his handsome shape & face.[38]

At the age of twenty-two, Churchill owned a company in a senior regiment in the corporate army of his day. He now controlled payrolls and muster rolls. He recruited men and discharged soldiers. He had a share in the nomination of his subalterns. If Captain Churchill was in any way like his officer colleagues (and, presumably, he was at least as avaricious), each of these functions provided him with cash. Payroll deductions, skewed musters, exemptions and dismissals from the service, gratuities for commissions—these were among the irregular profits that, far more than seldom-paid salaries, rewarded the European army officers of Churchill's age.[39]

Other, informal, recompense had larger imperial consequences. In his six years as a company commander in the duke of York's Maritime Regiment, Captain Churchill became part of a third regimental connection with the empire. In the Admiral's Regiment, as in the Guards and the Tangier Regiments, officers exchanged imperial information, influence, and commands. Besides his colonel, *"le sérieux"* Sir Charles Littleton, formerly lieutenant governor of Jamaica, now governor of Sheerness, Churchill's comrades in the Admiral's Regiment included Edward Nott, Charles Middleton, William Morrice, Francis Hobbyn, William Moryson, and John Jeffreys during the intervals of their American service. The regiment's officers connected not only England with its empire but both with the continent.[40]

Churchill's continental service with his company of the Admiral's Regiment was not entirely voluntary. King Charles was not best pleased with the new publicity given Cleveland's amour. He had permitted Churchill's jump to captain on the ground that the company was already in the Churchill family, but he refused to allow the duke of York to make Churchill a court intimate as one of the gentlemen of James's bedchamber (the duke promised he would give the post to no one else, an early and extraordinary instance of the duke's continued favor to his former page and current subaltern). Rather than let Churchill stay at court, in proximity to Cleveland, King Charles ordered him to country quarters at Yarmouth Camp (where Major Edmund Andros was organizing a force to invade the Netherlands). Deeply concerned at the "continuance of the king's displeasure towards his son," Sir Winston begged courtiers to get royal permission for Captain Churchill to travel on the continent "for a year or two to gaine some language & experience that may better fit him for his Majestys Service." Just in time, the Anglo-French entente offered Churchill a professional escape from the wrath of a cuckolded king. The duke of York personally acceded to Captain Churchill's request that his company be one of those that made up the nominal ten thousand troops sent from England to serve in the armies of Louis XIV.[41]

On December 27, 1672, Captain Churchill's company of the Admiral's Regiment landed in Calais and went into winter quarters. They were part of a composite English battalion, the vanguard of the 8,724 British soldiers who reinforced the armies of Louis XIV. The reinforcement's senior captain was Herbert Jeffreys of the First Guards, who, with a Guards battalion, shortly afterwards occupied, pacified, and governed Virginia. When, in 1672, troops from England, Scotland, and Ireland joined the French assault on the Netherlands, they were agents of the brothers Stuart's plan to weaken England's Dutch rivals for Atlantic empire, to make England itself more subject to the Stuart prerogative, and so to make possible Stuart restoration of the Church of Rome. The Anglo-French attack was intended to destroy not only Dutch seaborne commerce but also to eliminate the Netherlands as a sanctuary for civic liberties and the reformed religion. What was left of the Protestant provinces, after England took over the coastal enclaves and France absorbed the southern sections, would be made into an hereditary principality for the nephew of duke and king, William of Orange. Spurning this bait, the prince put himself at the head of the confederate resistance. William's determination "to die in the last ditch" in defense of the Netherlands helped inspire his countrymen to cut open the dikes, drown the land, and wash back the French attack. Meanwhile, the inability of the allies to destroy the Dutch navy prevented an English invasion by "Generalissimo" James and his eighteen thousand men, encamped on Blackheath and at Yarmouth.[42]

By the spring of 1673, one of the few Dutch fortresses still accessible to the French was Maestricht. Against it, in June, Louis XIV advanced in person. With him rode the English general, King Charles's brave and beautiful bastard, the duke of Monmouth. Among the volunteers in Monmouth's suite was Captain Churchill. All became enmired in a famous siege. Its orchestrator was the celebrated engineer Sébastien Le Prestre de Vauban, the masterbuilder of the new, geometric, earthwork fortress. On this occasion, Vauban invented what became the standard method of assaulting the new citadels. Angled communication trenches or "approaches" were dug from a fortified camp to the sites of battery revetments and assault lines. These "parallels" were excavated in positions at right angles to the enemy defenses. This process of crabwise advance toward the enemy fortifications was designed, first, to move up counterbatteries to suppress the defenders' artillery, then to dig in wall-breaching batteries on the very edge of the enemy defenses, and finally to bring up shock troops to storm the fortress over the breaches the batteries blew through the enemy walls. The successive parallels shielded the besiegers from cannonfire and musketry (though not from tunneled mines and mortar shells) but only at the price of plunging attacking armies, officers and men together, deep into the mud. As Monmouth wrote, the besiegers of Maestricht were "up to the knees in water" for their twenty-four-hour tours in the trenches, "which is not very comfortable."[43]

This was Churchill's introduction to the formal siege, the characteristic military action of his age. As one Anglo-Irish officer-governor wrote, "we make War more like Foxes, than Lyons; and you will have twenty Sieges, for one Battle; in which Sieges the scarcity of Victuals, the certainty of Blows, and the uncertainty of Plunder, . . . renders the usual parts of War full of Sufferings, and Dangers, and little or no Profit to the Soldiers." From his first moments at Maestricht, Churchill agreed that sieges were wasteful, indecisive even when successful. Churchill observed that even victory triply exhausted the besiegers. First they had to reduce the fortress by battering holes in its multilayered defenses big enough for an army to enter, at an enormous expenditure of men and munitions. Once the besiegers had stormed the defenses, or convinced the battered defenders to surrender rather than be massacred by the storming parties, the besiegers had to rebuild the breaches they had opened. Finally the victors had to garrison their conquest, weakening their field army and their offensive capacity. Sieges meant that sacrifices were rewarded by immobility. Even as a subaltern, and ever afterwards, Churchill sought to shorten sieges, if the orthodox generalship of present superiors or of subsequent allies made it impossible for him to avoid them entirely.[44]

At Maestricht, Churchill volunteered to head a direct assault against the Dutch defenses from Monmouth's sector of the French trenches. On the evening of June 24, 1673, Captain Churchill led picked troops "over the top." Two volunteers from the household cavalry, Piercy Kirke—afterwards commissioned governor-general of Tangier and New England—and Francis Watson—who concluded his army career as president of Jamaica—followed Churchill's lead. He personally planted the fleur-de-lis on the parapet of the Dutch bastion. His men drove out the defenders, dug out and defused a mine. The price of four hundred lives was paid for the bastion that covered Maestricht's main gate. Its capture was Captain Churchill's first European distinction.[45]

At first light on June 25, however, the Dutch exploded a second mine beneath the bastion Churchill's force had captured. Sixty of the soldiers who had relieved Churchill's assault force were killed instantly. At the moment of the explosion, the Dutch governor personally led a sortie to recover the work. The French and Swiss trench guards fled. Seeing this, Monmouth led his staff, Churchill among them, with a few bodyguards to counterattack. No more than a dozen all told, the English advanced "thro a Storm of Shot."[46]

Vastly outnumbered, Monmouth's little band nonetheless seized a sally port in the bastion. They held it until most of them were killed. Through this dearly bought entry, French reinforcements attacked the bastion. They lost 1,100 elite troops, among them the famous musketeer D'Artagnan, whom Louis XIV had ordered to direct and protect the inexperienced Monmouth. The duke himself was saved from certain death by Captain Churchill, who was wounded protecting his chief. The outwork was recaptured and the discouraged Dutch surrendered on honorable terms. Louis XIV himself was the delighted observer of the entire action. He paraded his entire army. At its head, the Sun King personally praised Captain Churchill as the rescuer of royalty. When Monmouth returned to court, he told his father, King Charles, and his uncle, the duke of York, of Captain Churchill's exploits. Monmouth added that "he owed his life to his bravery."[47]

It was not just by reckless bravery and royal rescues that Churchill became one of the most noted young officers of his generation. In the autumn of the year, he led his company to Westphalia to join the army of the greatest of Louis XIV's generals, the most innovative and daring tactician of his time, Henri de La Tour D'Auvergne, vicomte de Turenne and marshal of France. The master of movement and surprise, Turenne began to use the ferocious—and undisciplined—English as his shock troops. The marshal immediately recognized Captain Churchill as their leader and made him his protégé. "*Quel homme. Quel fortu homme,*" exclaimed the marshal of his intrepid captain. Under Turenne's tutelage, Churchill began his higher education in the art of war. His master's growing confidence in this apt pupil soon appeared in what became a famous anecdote about Turenne's "handsome Englishman."[48]

Under imperial attack, a French lieutenant colonel's command had abandoned a pass through the hills. Marshal Turenne turned to his staff and offered to "bet so many fat bucks and a Dozen flasks of Florence that his handsome English man should regain the Post with half the Number of men that were in it." The bet was taken. After a short sharp fight, Churchill and his company recaptured the pass, "won the Marshal his *Wager*, and gained for himself the Applause of the whole Army."[49]

In December 1673, after the campaign in Westphalia was over, Captain Churchill was given home leave. He arrived to find England convulsed by religious and political conflict. Its immediate excitements were the Dutch war and the French alliance. The duke of York's 18,000 men were ostensibly an invasion force bound for the Netherlands. When the expeditionary army did not sail, however, critics of the government began to fear the force's actual intent was to overawe London in the interest of the crown, Catholicism, and France. This fear was intensified by the recruitment and organization of eight new infantry regiments, some 4,000 men. At the same time, the imperial Barbados and Tangier regiments were brought up to strength and the former were converted into mounted military police and assigned to English patrols. Even more menacing to English critics of the crown was the arrival at the capital of Lockhart's Scots mercenaries, 1,200 strong. The duke's authority over this vastly expanded army, the political aggression of the new chief minister, lord Danby, and the Catholic and coercive premises of the assault on the Dutch, all antagonized the parliament that King Charles had assembled to finance the war. Instead parliament extorted—as the price of money for the Dutch war—the king's assent to a test act designed to oust all Catholics from public office, civil or military.[50]

The first and greatest casualty of the Test Act was the duke of York. He implicitly avowed his Catholicism by resigning from the admiralty and the privy council rather than take the test. The public revelation of the duke's Catholicism only made more menacing his continued influence over imperial policy, his hold on such outposts of empire as Tangier and New York (which he got back from its Dutch conquerors when peace was concluded on February 19, 1674), and his dominance of the British forces in France. The duke's Protestant and parliamentary critics were convinced that the army the duke championed would impose by force "popery and the french interest among us." The duke's "constant endeavor to have an army of both English and Irish always in France" was seen as evidence that he intended to enforce in England his axiom "that there was no way of governing the parliament but as Cromwell did govern them." The horrifying prospect of a Catholic Cromwell governing with French-trained troops persuaded Captain Churchill's father, Sir Winston, although he was, like his son, a member of the duke's household, to vote for the Test Act. The Churchills apparently preferred the Anglican confession and parliamentary politics to dynastic loyalty and monarchical absolutism. For them, the church and the constitution took precedence over the duke and the king.[51]

Fearful of the duke and the army, Catholicism and the crown, the parliament denounced the alliance with France and the war with the Dutch. As peace was achieved, parliament paid for the disbandment of the army's recent reinforcements. Instead of disbanding the forces, however, the crown moved them to posts just across the English Channel and the Irish Sea. The cadres of four infantry regiments, together with those of the Barbados Dragoons who did not accompany their major, Edmund Andros, to reoccupy

New York for the duke, reinforced the English army of occupation in Ireland. They were paid for by that dependent sovereignty's subservient parliament. Three oversized infantry regiments, plus drafts from other corps, new and old, totaling some five thousand soldiers, embarked for France and went on Louis XIV's payroll. If the English parliament would not pay for the enlarged Stuart army, the Irish, the Americans, and the French would. Such were the sources of Stuart strength.[52]

Besides Lockhart's Scots, the royal regiments diverted to France included two well-drilled new units. The earl of Peterborough's regiment introduced to military life such officers as lord Howard of Effingham and Virginia. Lord Vaughan, afterwards so much Churchill's friend, came over to France with his regiment in October 1673. He left it "in very good condition" on February 28, 1674. In the spring of 1675, lord Vaughan and a number of his regimental subordinates, constituting his staff and artillery officers, sailed for the West Indies, Vaughan having been commissioned governor-general of Jamaica.[53]

This shuffling of the English commands in France, Ireland, and America was Churchill's chance for another jump in rank. On March 3, 1674, King Charles gazetted "Captain Churchill, son of Sir Winston," colonel of an English battalion in France. A month later, at the opening of the campaign, Louis XIV issued a French colonel's commission to the twenty-four-year-old officer. Churchill immediately marched his battalion (which included elements of both Peterborough's and Vaughan's regiments) to join Turenne's army in Alsace.[54]

In the great marshal's most famous campaign Churchill won further distinction in no fewer than three pitched battles. Given the growing English sensibility about fighting the Dutch, Churchill's laurels were brighter because they were won against the Germans, not in France's other theatre, the Dutch frontier in Brabant. There six British regiments fought for the states general, even while their compatriots fought for France. The states' service made professional careers for officers such as Thomas Handasyde, afterwards Churchill's devoted subordinate in the command of Jamaica; Luke Lillingston, the West Indian expeditionary leader; and John Gibson (who may also have served with Churchill in France), afterwards commander of Newfoundland and Portsmouth. All told, ten or a dozen Anglo-American governors-general of Churchill's time served their apprenticeships to empire in the British battalions of the Dutch army.[55]

On June 16, 1674, Turenne ordered his inferior army across two rivers, in the face of the Imperialists. His infantry stormed the fortified village that anchored the Imperial line. Churchill's regiment, already renowned for its musketry, flanked and interlined the French cavalry. The combined arms charged uphill and routed the more numerous Imperial horse. Churchill recreated every feature of this battle thirty years later—albeit on a vastly larger scale, and with the fate of Western Europe and the Atlantic world waiting on its outcome—when he reentered Germany and fought the decisive battle of a century at Blenheim. What Churchill had learned from Turenne was more than tactical. The old marshal taught the young captain that psychological superiority over the enemy could be achieved by startling mobility and constant aggression; that advantages of position could be consolidated by carefully sited, skillfully served, fully supplied artillery; and that a clear eye for the ultimate opportunities in battle was preserved by coolness and calmness. Like his master the marshal, Churchill's sangfroid manifested leadership not only in quiet voice and precise orders but also by acts of personal courage. Commanding the marshal's assault troops, Churchill learned that an investment of life was required for battlefield victory, especially by an aggressive infantry, but a courtier's manner had its place in camp. All arms obeyed, all allies conciliated, the commander whose courtesy never failed him. This, too, the English captain learned from the French marshal. As Churchill's chaplain put it, "tho *England* made Him a General, 'twas *France* made him a Soldier."[56]

Turenne's victory at Sinzheim opened the Palatine to the terrible attentions of his army. Its British troops were among the worst of the looters who began to make refugees of that population which, a generation later, Churchill and his associates sent to New York. Fortunately for his fame, however, Colonel Churchill was noted for his personal clemency at the outset of this awful episode. Then he rode away from the sad scenes of the ruined countryside to a rare professional setback. Sent with some English troops to keep in contact with the Imperialist enemy on the Rhine, Churchill allowed them to advance to the west undetected. So Turenne was surprised. Rather than let the Imperialists "forage" upper Alsace, as his men had ravaged the Palatinate, Turenne marched his men through the mud for two nights and a day to attack the enemy at Entzheim, near Strasbourg, at daybreak on September 26, 1674.[57]

Despite their exhaustion, Turenne's British infantry cheered him as he formed them for the attack. As soon as the pouring rain let through enough light to see the battlefield it became apparent that its key was a treed copse on Turenne's right, ever afterwards notorious as "the Little Wood." At 8 a.m., Boufflers (who would be Churchill's formidable antagonist at Lille, twenty-eight years later) led his dragoons into the Little Wood to drive out the Imperialists already stationed there. As the fight for the woods ebbed and flowed, both sides pushed in reinforcements "so that there took place there one of the best and finest combats which ever was seen."[58]

Three British battalions were among the eight infantry units successively committed to this firefight. The first of these were Irish, commanded by their Catholic lieutenant colonel, Thomas Dongan. He succeeded his mortally wounded commander this day. So he acquired the rank that qualified him to command Tangier in 1678 and New York in 1683. In 1689, like his brother before him, Dongan would lead an army of exiles to the defense of Portugal, that Iberian adjunct of English empire. The second British battalion to enter the Little Wood was from Monmouth's Royal English Regiment. One of its companies was commanded by a lieutenant of the household cavalry, Piercy Kirke, who had served under Churchill's command at Maestricht. "Wounded in three places," Kirke was mentioned in the Entzheim despatches as being "certainly one of the bravest lads in the world and is much esteemed." Despite Irish sacrifice and English bravery, however, by midmorning the Imperialists had pushed the Franco-British force out of the Little Wood.[59]

Turenne now committed to the fight his penultimate reserve: a third English battalion. With Churchill at their head, "one and all performed miracles." They broke through the woods three times. Twice they were driven back before they fought forward once again to capture the Imperial artillery. Then Churchill's men drove the Germans from the deep ditch that covered their main front. The surviving English threw themselves into the wet shelter of this "very good ditch" (so a grateful Churchill described it) and began to count their casualties. Ten or eleven of Churchill's twenty-two officers were already killed or badly wounded. Their bitter colonel (so quickly was Churchill's tactical education advancing) criticized Turenne's dispositions: "half our foot was so posted that they did not fight at all." Unsupported by the French infantry, the English had been sacrificed. Yet Churchill himself, with the battle luck that never failed him, and which marked him as destiny's darling, was unscathed.[60]

Because Churchill's force was entrenched on Turenne's right, the Imperial counterattack fell on the marshal's exposed left flank. The Imperial cuirassiers attacked. They were checked on the verge of victory by the suicidal charge of three English squadrons. As Churchill lamented, all but three of their officers were killed (Sir Charles Littleton lost a brother) or wounded (as was Sir John Lanier, afterwards often mentioned with Churchill in proposed exchanges of imperial command and a co-conspirator of his in 1688).[61]

As night fell, the Imperialists retired. After claiming the rain-soaked battlefield on which his men had fought for ten hours, Turenne withdrew his sodden and exhausted army to the shelter of the village of Molsheim. Thence was sent the despatch to the duke of Monmouth at Whitehall which concluded that "no one could possibly have done better than Mr. Churchill had done" and that the "Mr. de Turenne is altogether pleased with him as with all our nation." Churchill's own assessment was much more modest: "I durst not brag much of our victory, but it is certain they left the field as soon as we."[62]

And indeed, it was time to leave the field. The campaigning season of

1674 was over. Cold, wet, sick soldiers, failing forage, impassable roads, all the inevitable outcomes of autumn sent seventeenth-century armies into winter quarters. Turenne retreated into Lorraine, assigned his troops their billets, and gave his officers leave. Most of the English officers reached Paris in November. At Christmas they wrote home that they daily expected Churchill to join them. But the colonel was with Turenne's secretly reassembled soldiers. Behind the mountainous Vosges, screened from Imperial scouts, Turenne's men slogged southward, from one previously prepared supply depot to another. They pitched a windswept winter camp in the Belfort Gap early in January. From it they swept down into Alsace, destroyed their enemies' scattered outposts, and smashed the Imperialists' hastily assembled main force at Turkheim. The makeweight of victory was the massed musketry of the British infantry, Colonel Churchill and his regiment prominent among them. Turenne's little army then retreated with 2,500 prisoners, 13 captured cavalry standards, and the colors of a famous Imperial infantry corps. When at last Turenne's men took shelter, Colonel Churchill rode on to Paris. There he received Monmouth's letter of congratulations and his confirmation of all Churchill's recommended promotions in the Anglo-French forces, "for you are the best judge of every ones deservings."[63]

CHAPTER TWO

In James Stuart's Service:

Regimental Connection and Shadow

Government:

1675–1683

A BYWORD FOR BRAVERY in combat and judgment in command, John Churchill was now perhaps the most highly regarded survivor of the Anglo-French officer corps. On January 5, 1675, he came home to be commissioned lieutenant colonel of the former Admiral's Regiment. The Test Act had compelled James Stuart to resign his cabinet-level command as lord high admiral but he had retained his personal regiment, now styled "the duke of York's maritime regiment." Churchill was now the regiment's executive officer. Although Churchill had won fame in France, and although the recommendation of Louis XIV to Charles II had weight, this double step in English rank, from company captain to regimental lieutenant colonel (without pausing at major's rank) was most unusual for a commoner. Observers saw it as extraordinary "for private captains to leap over old officers' heads to be lieutenant colonels; but the favour of great men goes far." More than to his own undoubted courage and obvious capacity, Churchill was beholden for his double promotion to the favor of the duke of York. So much was evident as, in good seventeenth-century fashion, Colonel Churchill parlayed that favor by promoting his own family in James Stuart's service.[1]

Churchill's brother George was commissioned as his ensign in the duke of York's regiment. George Churchill remained on leave from the regiment, serving at sea, building a career that would make him a royal naval captain before 1682, a key conspirator in the Channel Fleet in 1688, and the effective head of the English admiralty in his brother's heyday. Another brother, Charles Churchill, was promoted lieutenant in the duke of York's regiment in the autumn of 1675. Following his elder brother's example in the Tangier service and in the 1688 coup, Charles rose to become John Churchill's senior general of infantry.[2]

Churchill's immediate family and others of his officer colleagues in the duke's marines came to compose a regimental connection that reached from the court at Whitehall to the colonies in America. Edward Nott's commission (as Colonel Littleton's ensign in the duke of York's regiment) was the first step in a career that made Nott eminent in the garrison governments of Guernsey and Sheerness. Under John Churchill's aegis, Nott connected the border fortress of Berwick to Churchill's coup in 1688. After West Indian service, Churchill had Nott promoted to the command of Virginia. Three other marine officers took companies of the duke's regiment out to Virginia soon after Churchill became their lieutenant colonel. Marine officers also transferred to government service in New York and New England during Churchill's tenure as their executive officer.[3]

New York came to the fore early in Churchill's tenure with the duke's marines. The regiment ranked as the second of the line. Its colonel, Sir Charles Littleton, was an influential courtier and a veteran of both civil war and American government. He and his field officers therefore regularly sat as judges in the army's court martials. The most noted of these, held just as Churchill took up his command, was the trial of Colonel Francis Lovelace for his surrender of New York to the Dutch. The court martial found Lovelace guilty of neglect of duty (he had been on holiday in Connecticut when the Dutch fleet arrived off New York). It consigned Lovelace's property to the duke of York and condemned the colonel himself to imprisonment at the duke's pleasure in the Tower. There the disgraced officer became ill. He was released only to die in April 1675.[4]

The duke of York was a hard master. Colonel Churchill served him dutifully. The dislike that ducal service brought Churchill was multiplied by professional jealousy, which grew when the duke kept his promise to make Churchill one of his inner circle. The duke's household officers served as the comptrollers of James Stuart's personal estates and of his post office monopoly (which paid both salary and bounty to Colonel Churchill in excess of that received from the duke by any other commoner). Paid from the post office revenues, the duke's household officers were still a working administration in admiralty and colonial affairs (for the Test Act did not apply outside England) when Colonel Churchill joined their number.[5]

The duke not only named Churchill one of the gentlemen of his bedchamber, he also made him the master of his robes. The bedchamber post bespoke intimate influence. It afforded the adept courtier—one who knew that "sloth and too nice a modesty can be of no use"—with various "opportunities," sundry "discourses," and the "advantage" that lies in attending the informal conceptions of public policy. The mastership of the robes, with its control of the ducal clothing and livery contracts, was both extremely lucrative and bureaucratically central. The master of the robes in any royal household was a figure recognized in court circles across Europe as an official especially trusted by his royal employer. The retiring master of the ducal robes demanded 6,000 crowns as the price of his surrender of the office to Churchill. This huge sum the duchess of Cleveland was said to have acquired for Churchill by promising "a Gentleman of more Fortune than discretion, to bestow the last Favor on him . . . at the moderate Expence of 10,000£ for one Night." A last-minute substitution (arranged by Cleveland's procuress, Eleanor Waring, afterwards, as Lady Oglethorpe, Marlborough's Jacobite liaison and mother of the officer whom he set on the road to fame as the founder of Georgia) satisfied the silly swain, saved Cleveland some exertion, and bankrolled Churchill's first step into the councils of the English empire.[6]

Colonel Churchill's imperial opportunities in the duke's marines and in his shadow cabinet were the more welcome because the colonel's command in France had collapsed in the face of parliamentary hostility to the Anglo-French army. According to the fearful commons, King Charles's forces in France numbered ten thousand troops, being trained by Louis XIV to do the work of absolutism and Catholicism in England. In May 1675, parliament forced the king to forbid further English recruiting for the forces in France. They had been decimated by the campaign of 1674 and, absent recruits from England, had to be consolidated. Churchill's corps was absorbed in Monmouth's Royal English Regiment. Churchill's comrades in the Anglo-French force, Piercy Kirke and Charles Trelawney, took the field officers' commissions in the consolidated regiment and fought for Turenne in his last battle at Altenheim, but Churchill fulfilled his father's commitment to the commons. During the debate over the recall of the forces from France, Sir Winston had promised that he would "send for his son home, and engage he shall never go there again."[7]

Of course Colonel Churchill did go back to France. He arrived at Paris in August 1675, but his mission was fiscal and diplomatic, not military. He was assigned to get Louis XIV's subsidy to Charles II renewed. French funds enabled the English crown to govern without the parliamentary taxes that could only be obtained by weakening the royal prerogative, the royal army, and the Stuart alliance with Louis XIV. Still in France in October, Churchill arranged to get his campaign silver service shipped home, free of custom. This silver shipment was a sure signal that Churchill's French military career was canceled: he could not now keep a table at which to entertain his superiors and instruct his subordinates.[8]

Churchill soon followed his silver to Whitehall. There he attracted fresh attention by monopolizing the dance card of a fifteen-year-old "much favoured with the gifts of nature." Sarah Jenyns was also a member of the York household, a maid of honor to the duchess. Before long, Colonel

Churchill was taking "great delight in tying, and untying, M[istress] Jennings' garters." His liaison with Cleveland quickly collapsed. It had paid for Churchill's military promotions and his place in the Stuart household, the foundation of favor. Churchill's favor from the duke brought him to the notice of many ladies of quality. His father was busily arranging alliances with families of wealth and rank when John chose a penniless beauty. Sarah's dowry was her favor with the duke's younger daughter, Princess Anne, third in succession to the throne behind her father and her elder sister, Princess Mary. Jenyns's favor with Anne had been won by service every bit as attentive and devoted as Churchill's service to Anne's father. Alike ambitious to rise in the royal duke's favor, these household retainers allied their influence and found love. "Interest" became attraction and attraction bred passion because Colonel Churchill had found in his master's household a woman of a spirit, intelligence, and beauty to equal Barbara Villiers's. Their differences also were attractive. Young Sarah Jenyns's sexual reserve was refreshing, and tantalizing, to a jaundiced courtier colonel. And "little Jennings" was perfectly educated to be the consort of a courtier: "Books! prithee, don't talk to me about books. The only books I know are men and cards."[9]

Amid the usual recriminations, Barbara left for Paris. There she obviously had bad things to say about that "carpet knight," John Churchill, and his juvenile infatuation. In November 1676, both the rivals for command of the army (and so of the English throne), the dukes of Monmouth and York, recommended Churchill for the command of the Royal English Regiment in France. The French minister of war refused, alleging that "Mr. Churchill prefers to serve the very pretty sister [Sarah Jenyns] of Lady Hamilton than to be the lieutenant-colonel in Monmouth's regiment."[10]

Rather than being the lieutenant colonel in command of Monmouth's Royal English Regiment in battles along the Rhine, Churchill remained the lieutenant colonel who did the administrative work of "the duke of York's maritime regiment" in London. He helped draft officers and men from two companies of York's regiment to form the cadre of one of the four oversized companies that sailed, on November 18, 1676, with Sir John Berry to repress revolution in Virginia. The company flew the duke's standard, the emblem of his continued imperial influence and political power, despite the strictures of the Test Act. As an agent of the duke, Captain Charles Middleton, the most senior of the four company grade officers from the duke's marines who went out to Virginia, became an expert on the province. He was the particular champion of the duke of York's successful demand that all of Virginia's private proprietors surrender to the crown their pretenses to political power in the colony.[11]

As elimination of proprietary political power reduced aristocracy in the government of the crown's continental colony, so the ouster of the Berkeleyan oligarchy lowered gentility. To replace the two landed classes in political and military authority, the duke's military officers—themselves professionals "of no family"—nominated former Baconian revolutionaries, who were recent immigrants to Virginia and who had London commercial connections, to execute imperial orders. English-style absolutism, paramilitary and déclassé, began to impose state power upon the colony. The Old Dominion, a byword in England for rancor and hatred of the old civil war sorts, was civilized as well as pacified following Bacon's Revolution and Berkeley's Revenge, and became a province of Augustan Empire during the decisive administration of Churchill's quartermaster, Alexander Spotswood.

This was an unanticipated outcome in 1677. What was then clear was that, once again, England's political laboratories in America were testing governmental products. In its reaction to Bacon's Revolution, the crown essayed not continental absolutism but English authoritarianism, an alliance of the army and the aspirant in the service of the state. Forceful investigation of abuses in colonial government, restructuring of local charters, purging of local elites, their replacement with royal officers and new men, all took formal form in the quo warranto campaign against local governments everywhere in the empire, a campaign against entrenched local elites, not just, as is so often asserted, against legislatures.[12]

In this campaign the duke of York's officers royalized Virginia's government. Their collective tool was the punitive expedition of 1676, organized by such officers as Lieutenant Colonel Churchill. All the expeditionary commanders were the duke's men. Sir John Berry of the navy and Colonel Herbert Jeffreys of the Guards (who became governor-general of the province after its pacification) reported to the duke from Virginia by way of Churchill's distant cousin, ostensible friend, and chief rival in the duke's household, Colonel George Legge, the younger. Churchill himself presided over the court martial that cleared Lieutenant William Morrice for service in Virginia. It made Morrice a much consulted agent of the Old Dominion's new, royal, military, government. And Churchill's old superior in the Guards, Edward Picts, finally got a Guards company as a reward for his Virginia service.[13]

The Virginia expedition and the new government of the province also involved no fewer than seven of Churchill's former colleagues in the First Guards. An additional half-dozen Guards officers with whom Churchill afterwards served also held Virginia commands. Consider Edward Rouse. He had been six years an ensign in the Guards when he received a step to 2d lieutenant in the Virginia battalion. Its administration in the colony fell to Rouse because of Colonel Jeffreys's political preoccupations and his illness. When he came home, Rouse claimed his reward, the senior Guards captain-lieutenancy. Captain-lieutenant Rouse served in Churchill's Flanders battalion in 1678–79. He was wounded under Churchill's immediate command at Sedgemoor in 1685 and was promoted captain of Guards three weeks after the battle. Together with the other Guards captains, Rouse received the additional rank of lieutenant colonel from James II in 1687. Nonetheless, Rouse cooperated with Churchill in the conspiracy of 1688. In the ensuing war, Colonel Rouse served with the Guards in Flanders. At the peace of Rhyswick, in 1697, Rouse retired to the government of Upnor Castle. Here, in a minor key, were themes from that garrison-government of English empire in which Churchill was the leading player.[14]

Once Churchill and the other stay-at-home officers of the duke's regiment had helped get the Virginia expedition away from the piers, they were ordered to recruit replacements. Only parts of two companies had actually been drafted from the duke's marines for Virginia service. Yet the duke's regiment, like the First and Coldstream Guards and the Holland Regiment, claimed to have sent four companies, plus supernumeraries, to Virginia. Between them, these regiments immediately raised the better part of two battalions to replace the one they had sent to America. And the recruiting did not stop there. The pacification of Virginia was so popular with both the London merchant community and the parliamentary classes that few publicly objected when at least five thousand men were enlisted "for Virginia" between 1675 and 1677.[15]

"Virginia" enlistment violated the king's promise to parliament not to recruit the Anglo-French army, because most of the recruits actually were sent to serve with the English regiment in France. Even had parliamentarians wanted to, however, they could not protest, for the king prorogued the parliament during most of this period. Besides, Virginia recruiting was but one more episode in England's centuries-long supply of soldiers for European armies. Armed men were England's staple export and, in every emergency, reimport. The battalions that the English crown kept up at the expense of Louis XIV (and of the states general) were without cost to the English crown, so they were not subject to budgetary sanction by the English parliament. Worse, from a parliamentary point of view, the troops stationed across the Channel were equal in number to the regiments at home and they could, as they did, come home to support Stuart authority against domestic challenge. Yet only a few political critics cared or dared to denounce this particular siphoning of soldiers out of England and into the armed service of Louis XIV, "the Master of Absolute Dominion, the presumptive Monarch of Christendom, the declared Champion of Popery and the hereditary, natural, inveterate enemy of our King and Nation. . . ."[16]

Still, King Charles understood the unpopularity of his support for the national, religious, enemy. He finally felt compelled to offset his practical association with the Catholic tyrant, Louis XIV, by forging a symbolic link with the champion of Protestant liberties, William of Orange. Himself a

Stuart, the prince was potentially as good, or (as it turned out) a better prop of executive authority in England than was the Sun King. The British Brigades in the Netherlands embodied that fact. So the king of England ordered the duke of York to marry his elder daughter, Mary, to the Prince of Orange. As a gentleman of the duke's bedchamber, Lieutenant Colonel Churchill attended the nuptials of William and Mary on November 4, 1677. Obviously alarmed at this strengthening of the reversionary interest of his Protestant nephew to the imperial throne, James duke of York used the occasion to reassure his regiment's officers "that he never had any intentions to innovate Religion in the State, and . . . he never would." The duke then dutifully endorsed the king's recall of the Franco-British regiments. He added that the recall of eight hundred good soldiers from Virginia was also essential if England was to commit an expeditionary force to Flanders in support of Prince William against France. In a reversal of alliances the Stuart brothers now recruited troops to support the Nimwegen negotiation designed to put limits to French expansion. In fact, the king had no intention of impeding France but the popularity of such a pretense persuaded the parliament to finance an expanded royal army. This the duke intended to command in the interest of an enhanced royal authority (and the Netherlands now promised ten thousand troops to support royal authority in England, replacing the vague French commitment).[17]

Naturally, and correctly, the parliamentary opposition still feared that the crown's primary intention rather was "to set up an absolute monarchy than to make war with France." They told the newly assembled commons that "the King intended to raise an armie but never designed to goe on with the warr." The majority of the parliament, however, were convinced by King Charles's contention that he had exhausted his treasury in such popular projects as the repression of piracy in the Mediterranean, the suppression of rebellion in Virginia, and the Protestant marriage of his niece. The king claimed that he needed parliamentary help if he was to fulfill his military commitment against French aggression. The parliament financed no fewer than twenty-six new battalions of infantry and six mounted corps (four of cavalry, two of dragoons), and a navy of ninety ships, "for a war against France."[18]

English imperialists admitted that, in the first year of a war with France, the French would "ravage our plantations" in America and capture many transatlantic merchant ships. Thereafter, it was argued, English soldiers' "toughness of courage" and their voluntary obedience to their aggressive officers would recoup in Europe English imperial losses in America. For the control of Flanders was the essence of English empire. The imperialists observed that, if the Low Countries fell to France, the "dominion of the seas" would pass to Louis XIV. So the English strategists sent copies of the Nimwegen agreement to the governors-general in America because the treaty "has a relation to the present posture of Affairs in Europe and consequently those of America." This integrated view of empire, the idea that America must be won in Flanders, in alliance with the Netherlands and with Spain, and the recognition by English military administrators everywhere that "the greatness of France threatens all," came to the fore at the moment that Colonel Churchill was called up to help manage the war. They remained his imperial principles ever afterwards.[19]

On February 17, 1678, the duke of York summoned Churchill from his honeymoon (with the connivance of the duchess of York, Churchill had made "a final Resignation of his Heart" and secretly married Sarah Jenyns). Churchill was to command one of the new regiments but it seems never to have been raised. Instead, in March, Lieutenant Colonel Churchill sailed for Bruges to arrange Spanish and Dutch support for the expedition's vanguard. These four British battalions included the duke's. They were commanded by Churchill's own colonel, Sir Charles Littleton. To him Churchill wrote regularly of his anxiety to join the force, which reached the front early in May.[20]

The king and duke, however, had other plans for Churchill. In April 1678, they sent him to consult with their nephew, Prince William, about the organization of the allied army. The prince was enchanted with the envoy. He and the colonel were just of an age at twenty-eight. Both were hardened professional soldiers. Colonel Churchill instantly impressed Prince William "as the coolest head and the warmest heart" he had ever met. The prince was notoriously susceptible to male beauty and charm of manner, both of which he entirely lacked, but which Churchill had in superabundance. As a famous observer wrote, "of all the men that I ever knew in my life (and I knew him extremely well) [John Churchill] . . . possessed the Graces in the highest degree, not to say engrossed them. . . ." "Engaging" and "graceful," yet "cool" and "imperturbable," Churchill was gentle of manner but notably dignified. "The handsome Englishman" became the perfect diplomat.[21]

Churchill met William to ally the armies of the Netherlands and England against French absolutism and Catholicism. On that alliance rested the continued independence from France of the two northern, maritime, Protestant, constitutional powers. The meetings of the soldier with the prince marked the evolution of the Anglo-Dutch alliance. At the first, in 1678, Churchill was a very junior officer and England a very limited partner; at the second, in 1689, Churchill was a lord and a general and the captain of the coup that had brought William to the throne of England; and at the last, in 1701, Churchill was the earl of Marlborough, he was William's heir apparent as the allied commander in chief, and England had become an equal partner with the states general in Europe and was now infinitely her superior in America.

Despite his well-rewarded, military services to France, despite his recent diplomatic mission for Charles and James, and despite his subsequent negotiations with the French, both in London and Paris, Churchill's personal, Protestant, professional preference was for the union of England with the states general against the worldwide pretensions of France. So much he made clear in 1678 but, for a decade to come, Churchill was the servant of a Catholic, francophile prince. He was professionally dependent on James. He was personally grateful to the duke. As a monarchist and royalist, he was politically devoted to his royal highness. The interests of William, parallel though they were to Churchill's own religious, national, and imperial predilections, could only prosper in England if James were somehow set aside and William's positions as a princeling and a consort were somehow enhanced.

The key was William's marriage to James's elder daughter, Mary. This marriage, like so many aspects of England's nascent nationalism, was the work of the earl of Danby. William of Orange was now married to England, as well as allied with her. The alliance served to enhance his own dynastic interest in England's throne (William's mother was a Stuart princess) and it helped to cement his wife's royal inheritance. So Prince William pledged the services of the six British battalions in his army to crush any English insurrection. In addition, he promised that ten thousand Dutch troops would support Stuart rule in England if need be. These Anglo-Dutch forces influenced, determined, or secured the succession to the imperial throne at least three times over the next generation. In each instance, Churchill played the decisive role in applying Batavian force to British politics.[22]

Such were the dramatic outcomes of the Dutch prince's mundane consultations with the English colonel about bread rations and carriage contracts. Troop billets had to be assigned and marching orders mapped for the expeditionary army. The army was rapidly expanded in England during the spring of 1678. So Danby built up the military interest that was fundamental to his Protestant national and imperial objectives. This enlarged army was central to Danby's vision of a crown that could extend its empire abroad and increase its authority at home. That fifteen future governors in the British Isles and eighteen governors-general in America found their first commissions or major military promotion in the musters of 1678 attests to the ultimate success of Danby's Anglican imperialism, both at home and overseas. There is no measuring how much these officers, many of them Danby's personal clients and more of them devoted to his principles, resented his subsequent betrayal by Charles and James, their own loss of regimental investments and public prospects, and the abandonment of the Protestant patriotism Danby professed. Some regiments were obviously alienated—most dramatically the duke of Monmouth's cavalry corps. Apart from their colonel's notorious disaffection from 1679 on, and his outright rebellion in 1685, Monmouth's field officers, Sir John Lanier and Edmund Mayne, were among the leading army conspirators of 1688. Three captains whose troops of horse were transferred to Tangier when Monmouth's regiment was disbanded, Charles Nedby, John Coy, and Thomas Langston, came home to take commands in Churchill's dragoons. They were his key subordinates in 1688 and long afterward.²³

Actual recruits for the army of 1678 seem finally to have exceeded 14,000. The army totaled 26,500 men in 23 regiments (a paper strength of 35,709 was claimed by the crown, for purposes of parliamentary payment). Four thousand and fifty other men served the crown in 34 independent companies in English and American garrisons. Additional soldiers were recalled from service in France and Virginia. An army of this size required the royal army's first general staff. On May 1, Colonel Churchill became a brigadier general. Churchill's first qualification for command was his professional experience. It was unequaled amongst the officers of his age cohort, whose exemplar he was fast becoming. Churchill's extraordinary energy, the prestige he now acquired from his association with the Prince of Orange, and the religious liabilities of his Catholic senior, Thomas Dongan, all also helped him win promotion as the senior brigadier of the force in Flanders on September 3, 1678. His brigade, "the first," was "to consist of the two Battalions of Guards, one Battalion of the Holland Regiment, and the [new] Regiments of Her Royal Highness [the duchess of York] and [by his special request] Colonel Legg."²⁴

Among the Guards officers of imperial interest who served in Churchill's battalion were Captain Edward Sackville, Jr., afterwards commander of Tangier, and the subalterns just back from Virginia, Edward Rouse and his messmate Ralph Delavall. Another Virginia veteran, Captain William Meoles, brought his company home from the Old Dominion in March only to be immediately transshipped with them to Flanders. No fewer than three future commanders of the Leeward Islands served in the Holland Regiment under Churchill's orders. So did a newly commissioned ensign, Francis Nicholson, of whom Churchill would form a very favorable professional opinion. In all, seven future governors-general of England's American and West Indian provinces served under Churchill's immediate command in Flanders in 1678.²⁵

For most of them the Flanders expedition, as General Churchill had predicted, was mere spear carrying in the diplomatic drama that preceded the signing of the celebrated Treaty of Nimwegen on September 17. Although the English crown's share in this effort to put some limits to the northern and eastern expansion of France was no more than nominal, the officers of England's army now acquired an appreciation of the importance to Protestantism and civil liberty, and to English trade and empire, of checking the aggression of Louis XIV. Their expedition had elevated in

English opinion two potential captains in the cause, William of Orange and the duke of Monmouth, and it added to the prestige of that political spokesman of English religion, nationality, and empire, the earl of Danby.[26]

By February 1679, when the last units of the English expeditionary force sailed home, General Churchill was back in London. There he took stock of the anti-Catholicism and the francophobia that had been multiplied by England's expedition in support of the Nimwegen negotiations and which, by condemning General Thomas Dongan to a life of imperial exile, had mandated General Churchill's command in Flanders. About to lead the British expeditionary force, Dongan found he had no regiment. The Protestant civic authorities in Chester had arrested some of Dongan's recruiting officers. Catholic Irishmen bearing French commissions, these officers had English commissions as well, courtesy of the duke of York. The Chester magistracy deemed these officers' English commissions illegal under the Test Act and jailed their holders. The lord lieutenant of Ireland, the duke of Ormonde, disarmed the rest of Dongan's officers and interned their recruit companies, explaining that his English Protestant subordinates were sure that Dongan's Irish Catholic recruits could not really be intended to serve with English forces in Flanders. Instead, they must be meant either for the French service or an Irish rebellion. Rising fear of the Irish, of Catholics, and of France, drove General Dongan from London but also prevented his taking command as senior brigadier of the English in Flanders. That command fell to Churchill, a notable example of his professional ascent at the cost of Catholic officers.[27]

The duke of York had the king commission Dongan lieutenant governor of Tangier. When, late in 1679, Tangier's governor-general, the Protestant Irish officer William O'Brien, earl of Inchiquin, surrendered the crucial outworks on the hills commanding Tangier without fighting, Dongan reported his misconduct. Inchiquin asked for Dongan's recall. Instead, he was cashiered himself. Churchill, watching all this from his place in the duke's household, the Tangier command center, concluded that Inchiquin was "the worst possible officer" for a beleaguered imperial outpost. In an effort to make Tangier, that refuge for Yorkist Irishmen and Catholics, more palatable to English political opinion, Churchill's colleague on the Flanders general staff, Sir Palmes Fairburne, and Churchill's own subordinate, Edward Sackville, replaced both the Irish officers. General Dongan had to wait until 1682 for his master, the duke of York, to regain enough political power to secure him another imperial post. That was the government of the duke's own province, New York.[28]

The gap in General Dongan's army and imperial administrative career, from 1679 until 1682, reflected the eclipse and exile of the leading English militarist and imperialist, the duke of York. In the tumultuous years of the popish plot and the exclusion crisis, John Churchill became the beleaguered duke's political negotiator. In Flanders and in France, in Scotland and in England, in royalist politics and imperial administration, Churchill made himself indispensable to the duke, moved to the center of the Yorkist household, and committed himself to James's succession as king. Yet Churchill was ever more obsessed with the contradiction between his patron's deepening Catholicism and his own maturing Anglicanism.

The duke's decline began in 1679, after the Flanders campaign, with the dispersal of the royal army. By 1680, despite the recall of both battalions of the Royal Scots from France, the army in England numbered just 6,950, in Ireland but 6,428. Only in dire emergencies could the crown call home its 3,600 men from the Netherlands, 3,000 troops from Tangier, and 500 soldiers from the American garrisons. Without their immediate support, and deprived of the Flanders army, the crown was exposed to the religious fears and political jealousies of the parliamentary majority, empowered by the need for taxes to pay off the army. While not averse to crippling Danby's colonels (and so the minister's military arm) by disbanding their units before they could recover their recruiting costs, the legislators' greatest enmity was directed at the duke of York and to the possibility that this Catholic prince would become king.[29]

Paid by parliamentarians hostile to Catholicism and to James, informers concocted a "Popish Plot." Allegedly, it aimed at the life of King Charles. Allegedly, it would employ an army of Irish, Scots, and French Catholics to make the duke of York king of the English empire. Allegedly, James would legalize his title "by gift from the Pope." Allegedly, the Catholic king would erect "a tyrannical arbitrary government by an army, our common and statute law to be abolished and annihilated, and a mixture of military and civil law introduced, where counsel of war should supply the place of our courts of justice, and the racke for the jury."[30]

The military dictatorship supposedly intended for England and America was said by the professional witnesses to be but part of a larger popish plot to destroy Protestant churches and constitutional governments everywhere. On the ruins of the reformed religion and free institutions would rise Franco-Catholic armed absolutism. The duke of York, so the informers said, was both party to and beneficiary of this plot (certainly, many of his Protestant subjects in New York, and their neighbors from Jamestown to the Kennebec, believed in the plot and in the culpability of the greatest American proprietor). This testimony so inflamed parliamentary passions that, on the last day of February 1678/9, King Charles ordered the duke to defuse the clamor, either by conforming to the Church of England or by going into exile. The duke chose exile. On May 1, Colonel Churchill obtained permission to be absent for the whole session of the parliament "in order to the recovery of his health." He had been elected in March to a government borough, Newport, Isle of Wight, administered by his old

John Churchill, afterwards first duke of Marlborough, attributed to Sir Godfrey Kneller, in the Green Writing Room of Blenheim Palace, reproduced by the kind permission of His Grace the Duke of Marlborough.

Sir Winston Churchill, by Sir Peter Lely, in the Green Writing Room of Blenheim Palace, reproduced by the kind permission of His Grace the Duke of Marlborough.

Arabella Churchill.
Mrs. Godfrey Sister to John
Duke of Marlborough, *attributed
to the studio of Sir Peter Lely, at
Althorp, reproduced by permission
of Earl Spencer, with the assistance
of the National Portrait Gallery.*

Barbara Villiers. The Duchess
of Cleaveland, *P. Lely pinx.,
E. Lutterell fec., mezzotinto
engraving courtesy of the
British Museum.*

Sarah Jenyns. Mrs. Ienyns Wife to John Duke of Marlborough, *attributed to Simon Verelst, at Althorp, reproduced by permission of Earl Spencer, with the assistance of the National Portrait Gallery.*

The Lord Churchill's Two Daughters, *G. Kneller, pinx., I. Smith, fec., mezzotinto engraving from the author's collection.*

The first portrait is of John Churchill himself. Allegedly, this is the portrait at which the duke of Marlborough, in old age, looked up from his wheeled chair and said, with what speech remained to him after a series of strokes, "this was a man." Churchill here appears rather more stern of visage and more strongly featured than is usual in the early portraits of the man who was frequently described by contemporaries more as "beautiful" than "handsome." Churchill here wears antique parade armor, with visored bascinet at his side, of the style presented to him, with a commission as lieutenant general, by his patron, King James II, on the eve of their fateful march to Salisbury. Of course, lord Churchill wore such armor only on parade. No more did he actually carry the baton of command, which he here grasps in his long and slender hand.

In the same stateroom at Blenheim hangs Lely's portrait of Churchill's father, Sir Winston. Soldier of the martyred king, Charles I; royalist hagiographer; courtier, placeman, and parliamentary servant of Charles II: Sir Winston Churchill had spent his unwelcome and impoverished leisure during the Interregnum indelibly educating his eldest son in the old-fashioned virtues which here are emblemized by Sir Winston's own long hair, lace bands, slashed sleeves, and watered-silk waistcoat.

Two noble families descend from these two Churchills, so the family portraits are divided between two great houses. The portrait of Sir Winston's daughter, John's sister, Arabella Churchill, hangs at Althorp. Her fortunate fall from her horse, into the arms of her royal riding instructor, made Arabella the mistress of James duke of York and mother of James Fitzjames, duke of Berwick. Arabella opened James's household to her brother John and put him on the royal road to favor, fame, and fortune. Arabella subsequently married Colonel Charles Godfrey, a crucial Churchill confidante in the coup and his military liaison with the First Guards, in which Godfrey had been commissioned captain in 1670.

A cousin of Arabella and John's, Barbara Villiers, duchess of Cleveland, did not show to advantage in portraits. Nonetheless, even this rather late daub suggests something of her imperiousness, materialism, and carriage but it does not speak to the appetite, animation, and ambition that enabled her to dominate the jaded attention of King Charles long enough to promote her young lover, John Churchill. Of him it was said that he had "too indolent an air, and too delicate a shape, long to maintain himself in her favour; but all agreed that a man who was the favourite of the king's mistress, and brother to the duke's favourite, was in a fair way of preferment, and could not fail to make his fortune."

Indeed, Churchill did throw Cleveland over for the younger yet less demanding Sarah Jenyns, maid of honor to the duchess of York. Sarah appears here in her favorite picture, painted when she was fifteen, the year John Churchill fell in love with her. It hung in her dressing room at the Marlborough's modest home, Holywell House, the memento of an English rose (with thorns). Her husband called Sarah "the true born Whig." She agreed that "I was born with an inbred Love to my Country, I hated tyranny by nature before I had read a Line upon the Subject: I thought mankind was born free, and that Princes were ordained to make their people happy; . . . I also hated Popery, before I had ever looked into a booke of divinity; [I] thought alwaies, that the best way of Serving Princes, was to be true, & faithfull to them, and to Speake on all occasions to them without flattery, or dissimulation. . . ."

The oldest surviving children of the union of Sarah Jenyns and John Churchill were "The Lord Churchill's Two Daughters," Henrietta (b. 1681), afterwards countess of Godolphin and duchess of Marlborough, and Anne (b. 1684) namesake of her godmother the princess and afterwards countess of Sunderland. These sisters married the heirs of their father's and their mother's closest friends, respectively, Sidney earl of Godolphin and Anne, countess of Sunderland. So they confirmed in the Churchill connection England's leading financier, Godolphin, and its most devious politician, Robert Spencer, earl of Sunderland. Anne Churchill's husband, Spencer's heir, would become secretary of state in the Marlborough-Godolphin administration, responsible for America. In 1684, all that lay in the future of lord Churchill's two little daughters. They were his delight. "You cannot imagine," he wrote to their mother, in attendance on the princess, "how pleased I am with the children, for thay having noe body but their maid thay are so fond of me that when I am att home thay will be always with me, a kissing and huging me."

commander, Sir Robert Holmes, governor of the island, but there is no indication that Churchill sat, now or afterwards, in the commons. Instead, he and his wife followed the duke and duchess of York to Brussels, but Colonel Churchill was immediately sent back to London with the duke's advice to his brother to resist the republican tide by force.[31]

Through Churchill, the duke assured the king that they could still be sure of the navy's loyalty, the support of the English Guards, and the obedience of all the garrisons save that of Hull, which was commanded by partisans of the duke of Monmouth, Charles II's beautiful, brainless bastard, "the Protestant duke," the exclusionist candidate to displace the Catholic duke of York in the succession. Colonel Churchill told the king that the royal armies in Scotland and Ireland were also loyal to monarchy and hence to the legitimate succession, that of James, duke of York. Churchill echoed James's observation that the possession "of them two kingdoms will make men of estats consider well before they engage against the King" in a civil war to exclude the duke from the imperial throne. Colonel Churchill reminded King Charles that William of Orange was a firm supporter of the royal prerogative and of the dynastic succession that promised his wife, James's daughter, the throne of England and its empire. Political and military backing for James's succession by Prince William, the Protestant champion of Europe, Churchill was authorized to say, "can give no jealousy as to the Religion" of England.[32]

James insisted that any religious concession on his part was unnecessary as long as the crown retained military control of its dominions. Fundamentally, however, James's Catholicism was a matter of conscience, not of calculation. "As very a Papist as the Pope himself," had James possessed "the empire of the whole world, he would venture the loss of it, for his ambition is to shine in a red letter after he is dead." When Churchill returned from England with the pleas of moderate monarchists to James to save his nation from war and himself from disinheritance by eschewing the Mass, James replied, "never say any thing to me again of turning Protestant, do not expect it, or flatter your self that I shall ever be it, I never shall, and if occasion were I hope God would give me his grace to suffer death for the true Catholike religion, as well as Banishment." Here, from exile in Brussels, was the unyielding tone and unbending message of an heir facing civil war and the loss of an empire for his religion's sake.[33]

The duke sent Churchill home again with palliatives for Protestants. He was, said James through his messenger, no persecutor. He merely wanted the same toleration for his religion that he was willing to extend to others. Colonel Churchill himself could attest, James observed, that he and his wife worshiped daily in the Church of England chapel that James maintained for the Anglicans of his household (a chapel ministered to by Francis Turner, ever afterwards John Churchill's chief spiritual, and hence political, advisor; as the Church of England went, so Turner would direct Churchill to go). And James insisted that it was to his advantage to "preserve and protect" the privileges and rights of the Church of England. He had Churchill state this inescapable fact: the institutional support of the established church was indispensable to a divine-right monarchy. "I thank God," James wrote, that the English crown "yet has no dependency on Parliaments nor on nothing but God alone, nor ever can, and be a monarchy."[34]

Such assurances were welcome to Churchill and the Anglican monarchists who were now being labeled "tories." He had been bred by his father, that very religious royalist, to believe that "the Church of England & the Old Cavalier Principles" were inseparable. These were "the only Principles that are safe for the Government and comfortable to the Conscience." The child of a family broken politically and financially by a parliamentary revolution and by Protestant fanatics, Churchill loathed republican sectaries. He was horrified by religious persecution. He deeply respected property rights. It was on these reactions to the civil and religious wars that Churchill, like so many Englishmen, based his resistance to James Stuart's exclusion from the imperial throne. Churchill "thought it the Highest act of Injustice for anyone to be set aside from his Inheritance, upon bare Suppositions of intentional Evils, when Nothing that was Actual yet appeared to hinder him from the Exercise of his just Rights." Only as king would James provide Churchill with inescapable evidence of the "intentional Evils" that, in Churchill's eyes, would disqualify James for the command of England and its empire.[35]

In the meantime, Colonel Churchill was prepared to go a long way in support of his supposedly tolerant, certainly legitimate, master's succession. The colonel was at court when, at the end of August 1679, the king collapsed. With the succession at stake, Colonel Churchill consulted "the most considerable persons in the Fleet and Army." Then he carried to James a warning from Halifax. If the king should die, or even lose control of the government momentarily, the whig leader, the earl of Shaftesbury, was prepared to stage a coup to bring his puppet prince, the duke of Monmouth, captain general and colonel of the Life Guards, to the throne. James reacted with his customary speed and, as usual, relied on John Churchill to carry out his plans. In the first days of September, "dressed like a French officer in his scarf" and acting as "the best man of the party," Churchill led the disguised duke and two companions across the Channel and on a breakneck ride to the bedside of the ailing king. They found King Charles physically recovered and politically reinvigorated.[36]

The king decided to alter the odds in the succession crisis. James was compelled to return to Brussels, but the king himself resumed the captain generalcy of the royal army from Monmouth, transferred the command of the Life Guards from Monmouth to the young duke of Albemarle (a magnate much in favor with York, perhaps because the son and heir of the captain general exercised his military influence in the governments of Devon, Carolina, and Jamaica, rather than in the politics of the metropolis), and ordered Monmouth into exile in the Netherlands. Although such royal pieces in the succession contest as the governorships of Hull and Portsmouth were still in play, the duke of York's men took command of the relief expedition for Tangier. Imperial administrators in both England and America felt that James's influence over the Tangier forces was politically decisive. The duke himself, however, said that Monmouth had lost the throne when he lost the captain generalcy and the Life Guards.[37]

Even before James left Windsor for Brussels, he sent Colonel Churchill to Paris with news of Monmouth's disgrace. James wrote to both King Louis and his foreign minister that they should "give entire credit to everything" that his master of the robes should say. So licensed, Churchill first appealed for a renewal of the alliance between King Charles and King Louis and then asked for Louis XIV's backing for James's recall to Whitehall. The duke's brief return to court had not merely strengthened the crown in its struggle with the parliament about James's succession, Churchill added, it had also tipped the balance toward the crown in the larger contest of monarchical with legislative power. At this crucial moment, said the Stuart envoy, a French subsidy would confer a decisive advantage on the grateful royal brothers. French cash would permit the king to rule without parliament and it would enable the duke to succeed despite republican opposition.[38]

Now, the English succession, the Bourbon-Stuart entente, and so the likelihood of absolutism in the empire, apparently depended on which of the royal dukes, York or Monmouth, could get back to Britain first. On October 7, 1679, Colonel Churchill and the French ambassador persuaded King Charles to let the duke of York shift the seat of his exile from Brussels to Edinburgh. At first, neither military nor civil authority in Scotland was officially conferred on the duke, but his powerful personality, resident in the royal palace (still dignified by his reconstruction), could not fail to dominate the Scots army and government, multiply the duke's chances to survive the exclusion crisis, and help to insure him the imperial throne, should he outlive his brother.[39]

Churchill added a symbolic coup to this real shift in power. Landing from James's stormbound convoy, Colonel Churchill convinced the king that the duke could pass through the capital and thence overland to Scotland, without overexciting the exclusionists. The duke's men welcomed him to London at "the military feast" of the Honorable Artillery Company (of which Colonel George Legge, with Churchill the duke's favorite among Protestant professional officers, was a steward). As he watched the great

nobles and the city corporation assemble in his honor, the duke said to Sir
Charles Littleton that "this was pretty well for a poore banished man but so
little a while since." American administrators were told that the London
military feast reflected the royal force that had compelled Monmouth's disgrace, permitted York's movement to Edinburgh, emboldened King
Charles to dismiss the chief exclusionist, the earl of Shaftesbury, from the
presidency of the privy council and its plantations committee, and to pro-
rogue the parliament. With his chief political enemies in exile or disgrace
or limbo, and with Colonel Churchill as his ambassador at the courts of
England and France, with Colonel Legge controlling the artillery of the
metropolitan citadel, the Tower of London, and with Colonel Littleton in
command of his marines and the key Thames fort, the duke of York could
feel that whig politics were at a discount. His subordinates controlled the
martial keys to the kingdom. The odds were that the Yorkists could check
any exclusionists' attempt at the metropolitan coup that, as everyone re-
membered, was the military precondition of political revolution.[40]

In December 1679, Churchill joined the duke in Edinburgh to report
the latest military developments in the political struggle. Legge had extended his control of the artillery but that had brought into question his
simultaneous government of Portsmouth. Almost as crucial in the impending power struggle as Portsmouth was the government of Hull. Fortunately
the king had commissioned a Yorkist captain of the Guards, Lionel Copley
(afterwards the first governor-general of Maryland), as the professional
(lieutenant) governor. "I am glad that Captain Copley is at Hull," the duke
wrote, "for I look on him as an honest man and [one] that will be my
friend." The duke was also delighted to hear from Churchill that royal
troops had been quartered about the capital so as to prevent opposition
members of parliament from assembling in defiance of the king's proroga-
tion. Since the parliament was prorogued, James saw no reason why he
should not be allowed to return to England. To press his case, the duke
immediately sent Churchill back to the king.[41]

Through colonels Legge and Churchill, the duke argued at court that
only his own "bold and resolute councils," personally pressed, would encourage King Charles to prevent parliament's meeting, its pursuit of the
duke's exclusion, and its destruction of the monarchy. Instead of governing
with parliament, the duke said, the king must rule by his prerogative, exercised through key local governments controlled by units of the royal army.
Obviously, "the republic of London" was the first object of this forceful
policy. Its "republican" corporation must be replaced by a royalist one and
the capital's royal garrison must be doubled, so the duke had Colonel
Churchill insist. The "citizens" of the metropolitan estate, politically radi-
calized by the coincidence of the end of press licensing with the "discovery"
of the popish plot and the development of the exclusion crisis, had to be

physically cowed by the forces of monarchy. The capacity of "the City" to shelter the opposition, as it had in 1641, must be eliminated.[42]

In January 1680, the duke learned that Churchill had won his temporary recall to court. They reached court at the end of February. William Blathwayt, the colonial secretary, writing to Andros in New York, associated the return of the duke and his courtiers with the crown's first hearing of legal appeals from America and the reorganization of the plantations committees of the privy council. In May, as part of a plan to strengthen York's administrative hold on the empire and his military grip on the succession, James tried to promote Churchill. From London the lord lieutenant of Ireland was told that "here are some alterations in the military employments going on: Mr Churchill is to command the Duke's regiment of foot and the fort at Sheerness in the room of Sir Charles Littleton, who is to be Governor of Jersey; Sir John Lanier [the governor of Jersey] is to be lieutenant of the Duke's troop of Horse Guards in the room of Sir Richard Dutton, who is to go Governor of Barbados, and Sir Jonathan Atkins is to be recalled home" from the Barbados government (for which he had exchanged the captaincy of the king's own company in the First Guards). The duke's design was to dispatch the older, Anglican, cavalier colonels to provincial commands overseas and to replace them in the garrison of the metropolis with younger, French-trained, professional soldiers. The cavaliers could teach the colonists loyalty. The professionals would compel the Londoners' obedience. The Americans were warned that "the face of the court" had been transformed by York's return to full "credit and influence."[43]

Dutton did replace Atkins in command of Barbados and took with him instructions whose royalist rhetoric and prerogative prescripts anticipated in the empire a movement toward monarchism and militarism in England. The other exchanges fell through. Lanier said that command of the duke of York's troop in the Life Guards was both less rewarding materially and more exposed politically than was his independent command in Jersey. This he kept (in his lieutenant's hands) in return for taking command of the reinforcements bound for Tangier. Because Jersey's government was not open to Sir Charles Littleton, his lieutenant colonel, John Churchill, could not step up to command the marines. Sheerness, the vital Thames fort, the royal check on the economy of the capital, also remained in Littleton's loyal, but aging, hands.[44]

Littleton was the more anxious to retain the Sheerness command because its proximity to the capital permitted him to act as the agent of Jamaica and its governor-general and as a factor for Jamaican sugar planters. When the death of his Jamaica agent forced Littleton to sell the plantation holdings he had built up while in command of the colony he lamented the loss of the "faire prospect, as I thought of making a provision for my younger children from thence." Still dependent upon the "sweet negotiation of sugar," Littleton was doubly resentful that Churchill was willing to supersede him at Sheerness and in command of the marines. Jealous that his lieutenant colonel had replaced him in James's favor, Littleton labeled Churchill "ye only favourite of his Master," the duke of York.[45]

This was an exaggeration, but the entire episode spoke to the rise of a generation of young professional officers under the duke's aegis. Lord Halifax complained to James "that His Highness ought to consider thos that had escutions as well as thos that had none (three of the duke's chiefe favorits, viz; Legg, Churchill, and Hide, being scarce gentlemen.)" The officers of Churchill's ilk had been raised from social obscurity by royal favor and military merit. They were a "new class" of state functionaries. In return for their personal elevation, they would do the centralizing work of the crown, displacing the landed classes in both the British kingdoms and the overseas colonies. In the American colonies, both on the continent and in the West Indies, the process of armed administration would be carried on by provincial armies, officered by English cadres and by the upstart "middling sort" in each colony. Paramilitary politics would enforce a social accommodation to authoritarianism in the American dominions as in the British kingdoms. But authoritarianism in "Greater Britain" was conditional on the crown's satisfying the professional ambition and respecting the Protestant patriotism of the officer class. It was their institutional identification and national loyalty that made these military men constitutionalists and Anglicans. It was because they were "scarce gentlemen" that these officers had limits to their loyalty.[46]

In contrast to the usual view, consider that it was "gentlemen of long-tailed families," not Protestant professionals, who were apt to serve the sovereign unconditionally. As lord Halifax himself admitted, "Gentlemen in a general definition will bee supposedly more than other men, under the temptations of being made Instruments of Unlimited power, Their Relations, their way of living, their tast of the entertainments of the Court, inspire an ambition, that generally draw their inclinations towards it, besides the gratifying of their Interests." As the social composition of James's ultimate loyalists suggests, especially when contrasted with those who conducted the coup against him, family and dynasty were identified. Both were endangered by the rise of the professional officer. So, as the gentry drew closer to the crown, the professionals adhered to the nation. James was "hoist by his own petard." In militarizing and connecting English and American politics, James made the new class of military officers central to the operation of royal government both in England and in its empire overseas. So he made them the arbiters of sovereignty itself.[47]

Late in October 1680, the king, determined to meet the parliament, sent the duke back to Edinburgh. James left behind him, in England and the empire, a political position militarily reinforced. Lord Windsor, the former governor-general of Jamaica, had now enhanced the Yorkist presence at Hull. He took command of Copley, the garrison, citadel, and city. Colonel Legge was now effectively, if not officially, master general of the ordnance. It seemed that either Windsor or Albemarle (the past and future governors-general of Jamaica) would succeed Legge in the crucial command of Portsmouth. There the Guards officer John Mutlowe had returned from the duke's Virginia expedition to be commissioned deputy governor. And the regarrisoning of Chester pleased James. As he said to the officers of his household, despite antiquated fortifications, Chester "would still serve to keep that country in awe." Anticipating civil war, the duke saw a Chester garrison securing "a place for the loyal party to rendezvous in case of neede." And no royalist could forget that redcoated reinforcements from Ireland had debarked at Chester to crush Booth's rising in 1659 (and royal troops would land from Ireland at Chester to check Delamere's effort to support Monmouth in 1685).[48]

Across the Irish Sea from Chester, the power balance had shifted dramatically toward the duke with the arrival in Ireland from Tangier of that ultimate Jacobite, the earl of Dumbarton, and his highly professional Scots regiment. This reassignment reflected two other imperial command developments favorable to the duke of York: Monmouth's men had been sent overseas from the Scots border to reinforce Tangier, and the command of the colony itself had passed to the duke's escort, Colonel Piercy Kirke, Churchill's comrade in France. Kirke had also raised an English regiment that he took to Tangier to help control the colony and its growing garrison in the duke's interest.[49]

Colonel Churchill had impressed the military strength of James's imperial position on his friend (and banker) George Savile, the earl of Halifax. On November 15, 1680, lord Halifax spoke decisively in the house of lords against the exclusion of the duke from the throne. "How imprudent it would be to declare the Duke an enemy to the State," Halifax warned the peers, when James "was actually at the head of a powerful Nation [Scotland] where there was an Army too; that in Ireland his power was no less considerable . . . that he had a great interest in the Fleet, and credit with the English troops." Even exclusionists admitted that the duke was dominant in "The Plantations." Tangier, Virginia, Jamaica, Barbados, New York, even Pennsylvania, were at the duke's disposition. For all the drama of Halifax's lonesome eloquence—it was as if he alone had spoken for James, rising to meet every exclusionist argument of Shaftesbury's—the substance of Halifax's oratory was James's military hold on the empire, and so the inevitability of civil war if he were excluded from his imperial inheritance. The lords, profoundly sensitized by fears of 1641 and aware of the even greater role that the dominions would play in a recurrence of transatlantic civil war, acknowledged the obvious truth of Halifax's observation that the duke's influence in the armed forces and so over a militarized imperial government made it impossible to deny him the throne. They voted against exclusion.[50]

Despite Halifax's decisive declaration of the duke's power and right, James protested that "I could never understand his politics, and am sure they were never calculated for the meridian of a monarchy." Halifax, moderate and modern, considered monarchy to be bounded by constitutional law as well as empowered by military strength, and justified by good government as much as by royal right. James, blustering and bigoted, believed that monarchy was mandated by God, founded upon religious submission, and supported by military discipline. To James, kingly rule was as natural as patriarchy. So James was sure that his personal presence and forceful methods alone would save monarchical authority and preserve his inheritance. As James's envoy to King Charles from November 1680 to March 1681, Churchill argued that, if the king allowed his brother to return to England, James would neither take over the government nor provoke an insurrection against it. To James, Churchill said that the duke could only secure his return by recognizing the wisdom of Halifax's legal and pragmatic political prescriptions. Ever more anxious to return to court and command in England, James reassured the king, he bribed Charles's mistress with a colossal grant from the post office revenues, and he appeared to accept the counsels of moderation offered by his Protestant favorites, "scarce gentlemen," Churchill, Legge, and Laurence Hyde (the great chancellor's son, the duke's brother-in-law, a civilian, a churchman, and the first lord of the royal treasury).[51]

At the same time that he counseled moderation at home, Churchill was deeply implicated in the secret diplomacy of the Stuart alliance with Louis XIV, an alliance whose objectives were the antithesis of moderation. In January 1681, James once again sent Churchill from Edinburgh to Westminster. The colonel was ordered to tell King Charles that "the Monarchy must be either more absolute or quite abolished." Increased absolutism, James had his envoy say, required not only his own recall to England but also the elimination of parliament and a yet closer alliance with the object of parliamentary fears, Louis XIV. Cooperation with the Grand Monarch, James had Churchill say, would preserve European peace, make economical government possible in England, and so enable the crown to subsist on Louis XIV's subsidy. French cash, James ordered Churchill to say, would free the king from the trammels of parliamentary government and the indignities of popular politics.[52]

Admission of either of these political evils, the duke had his envoy warn both King Charles and the ambassador of King Louis, might give William of Orange an entry into English government. The French ambassador reported that Churchill said the duke believed "that it was designed that the Prince of Orange should come over with a view that he might become master of affairs, and be established now in a manner that could not be changed hereafter." William declined the offer to take his seat in the house of lords as duke of Cumberland, if only because he would sit in the lords as a subject, but the prince was heir apparent to his uncles, Charles and James. No one, Princess Mary least of all, expected that she, rather than her husband, would actually rule England if the imperial throne came to her from her uncle or father. The expectation of his ultimate sovereignty made William, Protestant, francophobe, and popular, the central fact of succession politics.[53]

In the summer of 1681, William did come over to England to test the political waters. Colonel Churchill, and the other leading moderates in James's household, openly discussed the prospect that Prince William would become the lord protector of England if James inherited the throne without first renouncing Catholicism. The moderates in James's service clearly approved of William's ultimate succession to their master, the royal duke, and seven years later they would propose a regency of William and Mary as a means of defanging James without deposing him. In 1681, however, they disapproved of William's obvious willingness to jump the queue and displace his father-in-law, their master, in line for the throne. Even the moderates still clung to the hope that, somehow, James might be persuaded to return to the Church of England and so preserve his succession and their careers.[54]

It was to preserve his patron's rights that Churchill had ridden down from Edinburgh. Louis XIV's ambassador wrote that "the principal cause of his journey was to press his Britannick Majesty to conclude a Treaty with your Majesty." It would so strengthen King Charles financially and diplomatically that he could face the fiscal and political cost of insuring James's succession. In the letter he sent with Churchill, the duke urged the French ambassador to negotiate the treaty immediately, "for if it is not begun at present, and while Churchill is in London, I fear some difficulty may yet occur." The duke said of the treaty to be completed by Churchill's agency that, "it will be an action altogether glorious for the King [of France] to re-establish the King of England . . . and to save the poor Catholics, who otherwise will be ruined without resource." Perhaps this was James's first public identification of his succession with the restoration of Roman Catholicism. Certainly, the association of English absolutism and Catholicism in an alliance with "the Most Christian King," just as Louis ordered his army to begin a pogrom of Protestants, were all awfully inimical to such Anglicans as Churchill. Yet he exercised himself in the cause of his king and his commander. The French ambassador put it a little unkindly. Colonel Churchill, he said, was one of those "docile personages who let themselves be led."[55]

Churchill's "soft and obliging deportment" concealed his determination to escape the religious dilemma posed by his master's succession. Churchill was repeatedly tipped for the Paris embassy. William of Orange asked that Churchill be appointed English ambassador at The Hague. Churchill himself sought to command the English brigade in the Dutch service. But on Colonel Churchill rested the duke of York's campaign to be reunited with King Charles. As the duke put it, "so long as I am from him, I would not willingly have Churchill from me." Churchill facilitated the secret treaty with Louis XIV on March 24, 1681. In return for a three-year subsidy, King Charles was to prevent parliament from legislating cooperation with William of Orange, or with Spain, in defense of Flanders against France. Churchill was allowed to tell James that King Charles was also pledged to veto any parliamentary act that excluded him from the throne of England or instituted an Orange regency.[56]

The king honored these understandings while Churchill was still at court. King Charles announced that he would summon the parliament to meet at Oxford, not Westminster. The empire awaited the outcome of this removal of the imperial legislature from the popular pressures of the capital. "We are under no ordinary impatience to hear of your proceedings at Oxford," wrote the Jamaican receiver general to his English principal, the secretary for the plantations. Oxford was garrisoned by the First Guards, purged for the occasion of all save the "true sons of the Church of England," officers devoted to passive obedience and divine-right monarchy. Still more reliable, the Coldstream Guards provided the king's immediate bodyguard. The earl of Oxford's "Blues" stationed its troops to protect the king's escape route from Oxford to his recently refurbished citadel at Windsor. All these precautions were necessary to prevent the armed households of the whig magnates from forcing the king to accept acts of parliament in violation of the French treaty. Four days after the treaty with France was signed, King Charles suddenly dissolved the parliament at Oxford. Surrounded by the Blues, he took his waiting coach to Windsor. The king and his Guards had foiled the whig scheme to seize the monarch and compel his acceptance of exclusion. Both sides were now prepared to abandon parliamentary politics and turn to physical force.[57]

In Scotland, the duke sought the king's authority to convene the legislature to authorize the use of force: "Mr. Churchill frankly owned that this Prince was not in a condition to maintain himself in Scotland, if the King his brother did not support him there." In June 1681, Churchill returned to Edinburgh with the king's commission. It authorized the duke to summon and direct the Scots parliament. That parliament's laws made the Scots army the duke's political tool and prescribed an officeholders' oath that forbade any challenge to Stuart rule.[58]

With this oath, the duke immediately disciplined the Scots aristocracy. He had the duke of Argyll condemned to death. Colonel Churchill privately did what he could to secure the king's pardon for Argyll but, before this was won, Argyll escaped from prison. Churchill publicly discounted that security lapse and he defended the duke of York's vindictiveness. Churchill promised that neither Argyll "nor his family shall not be able to signify anything." Churchill's public association with James's persecution of Argyll, and the private nature of his intercession on the duke's behalf, go far to explain the unending hostility of Argyll's heir to Churchill. Young Argyll grew to be a military and imperial figure whose interests reached from Minorca to Montserrat and from Argyllshire to the Carolinas. In every one of these provinces, and others in between them, Argyll would oppose John Churchill's influence.[59]

The duke of Argyll escaped from Edinburgh to London. The crown made little effort to apprehend him but Argyll delved deep into a plot to kill both duke and king. The Rye House plot was covered by the colonization of Carolina. The royal charter for Carolina permitted the proprietors to enlist provincial garrisons and to arm a provincial militia; to design, construct, and arm provincial fortresses; to collect capital funds and hire ships and mariners. So Carolina colonization, controlled by the earl of Shaftesbury, provided an ideal cover for conspiracy against the crown. It was the existence of this state within the state that enabled Argyll, even after he took up his exile in the Netherlands, to send to Shaftesbury the leaders of his ilk, Clan Campbell, and Scots Covenanters such as "Mr. William Veitch," Argyll's personal emissary and the founder of a family central to Scots colonization in America, from Darien to Nova Scotia. Argyll's emissaries met "the English Managers of the Plot in London, and Treat[ed] of a Joint Conspiracy with their Brethern there, under the disguise of planting *Carolina.*" A Cromwellian veteran, "a Stout and Able Officer," Lieutenant Colonel Walnut "was called out of Ireland" where he had been a leader of the "fanatic" interest, "under the colour of being the intended Governour of that Plantation." Walnut became Shaftesbury's chief military aide and, such was the magnetism of the whig earl, his devoted friend.[60]

As ostensible extenders of the Restoration Empire, the Carolina plotters played a double game. They "often attended at *Windsor* to make their Court, one day kissing the King's and the Duke's hands, the next consulting with the English Cabal, all in shew to sollicit the Interest of Carolina, whilst they really intended . . . 'To see what could be done for the delivery of the Nations.'" This British plot, under the cover of colonizing Carolina, to kill the Stuarts and restore the commonwealth, survived the death of Shaftesbury in exile and the execution of many of these conspirators. It is alleged to have ultimately involved twenty thousand plotters.

Actual Scots colonization in Carolina went forward under the same aegis. Indeed, plot and plantation were inseparable. Scots Covenanters were led across the Atlantic by Henry Erskine, lord Cardross, and his brother John. They returned from Carolina to the Netherlands just in time to take up commands in the Scots-Dutch brigade that spearheaded the invasion of England. Then they raised a regiment of Scots dragoons for the Protestant conquest of the northern kingdom. In the interim, in the Carolinas, Scots and English religious and political dissenters from the Stuart regime showed each other "the Word and Sign of the *Carolina*-Men" and hoped that "they might live, undisturbed, as Freemen and *Christians*," but they knew that their security was at risk from "the Stuart revenge."[61]

Whether they were refugees in Carolina, conspirators against the crown, or members of James's own household, "by the Duke's Government in *Scotland* . . . all men saw what was to be expected from him." Churchill was as alert as anyone to the likely results of transferring James's rough rule to England. He had exercised his blossoming favor with James to save several Scots from the duke's political use of the established church. In mediating the awkward alliance of the episcopal church and militant monarchy in Scotland, Churchill again relied upon the Anglican chaplain of York's household, Francis Turner. Turner's role in connecting James to the clerical establishment in England (which included legal redress for the duke's Anglican chaplain in New York) paralleled Churchill's work with the military and diplomatic corps. It was said in disparagement of both of them that they had "conversed more with men than with books." It was as Stuart courtiers, "zealous for the succession," and for the union of the army and the church, "the red coats and the black coats," in support of the monarchy, that both men rose to favor with their master and formed a friendship with each other. That friendship would determine the monarchy of their "best master," James.[62]

Both Turner and Churchill professed to believe that James's advocacy of episcopacy in Scotland was an earnest that, Catholic though he was, James would support the Church of England as the strongest prop of monarchy. So they were emboldened to take a further step toward reuniting the heir with the church. In September 1681, the moderates made their ultimate effort to reconcile the duke to English political reality: they sought to bring him back to the Church of England. If James would not return to the Church of England, Halifax wrote, sooner or later, "he must expect all men would desert his cause, as they would a town that could no longer be defended." Lawrence Hyde carried this prophetic counsel north to Edinburgh. There, despite the best efforts of the Anglicans, the duke rejected it.[63]

Disconsolate, Churchill rode south to the Scots border with Hyde. In the great fortress of Berwick, on September 12, 1681, Churchill forecast the Anglican moderates' bleak future under James. "Church" (as James had nicknamed his devout aide) told George Legge that "you will find that nothing is done in that which was so much desired, soe that sooner or laiter we must all be undone. . . . My hart is very foulle, soe that should I writt to you of the sade prospect I feare we have, I should tire your patience."[64]

Even as lord Hyde carried Churchill's letter south to Legge, Churchill shared the duke's table at Holyrood with John Lewin. Fresh from New York, the duke's auditor reported on both the province's finances and its politics during the imperial crisis of 1681. When Churchill himself came south, he found the governor-general of New York ensconced in the ducal household, having rebutted to the duke's officers Lewin's fiscal criticism and rebuffed in the king's court the charges of arbitrary action brought against him by a combination of religious and political dissenters. Quakers and republicans had combined against the duke of York's representative in New York's reflection of the exclusion crisis. Like his master, the duke, Sir Edmund Andros had been driven into a temporary exile by the exclusionists. Andros declined William Penn's offer to govern Pennsylvania, the province that James had just given Penn in return for "the Great Quaker's" abandonment of the republican cause and his willingness to tout James's purported religious toleration. Distrusting Penn, Andros accepted from the duke a watching brief as a gentleman of King Charles's bedchamber (another evidence of James's growing conviction that he would survive and succeed his brother). For the next four years, Andros and Churchill were colleagues in James's interest at Whitehall.[65]

Meanwhile, in the autumn of 1681, at James's court in Edinburgh, Churchill and the officers of the household had heard précis of the laws of Jamaica read at the duke's council. Immediately afterwards, James's enemy, that old Cromwellian, the earl of Carlisle, governor-general of Jamaica, returned to Whitehall. There the privy council arraigned Carlisle's failure to implement in Jamaica that central concern of Yorkist politics, the effective elimination of assemblies. In the debates about Jamaica's constitution in the privy council's plantations committee, lord Halifax capitalized on the credit his moderate politics had gained at court. Now was no time for the crown to seem hostile to legislatures, Halifax said. Whatever English statesmen decided about American government would be read as a declaration of political intent toward the entire empire. Halifax insisted that legislatures were an essential component of the imperial constitution, in both the colonies and in the British kingdoms. He won his case. By shaping the formative constitutions of 1681 for Jamaica and Virginia, Halifax helped underwrite the balance between executive and legislature, military and civil, direct and statute government that, by being preserved in the provinces, declared the moderates' intentions for England.[66]

To this balanced constitution, James remained essentially hostile. The moderates, by contrast, led by Halifax at King Charles's court and by Churchill in duke James's household, remained entirely committed to the imperial constitution of 1681. Halifax made his position clear in December

1684, when the settlement of 1681 was broken by the creation of a dominion of New England. The new dominion was to be governed absolutely by the king's governor-general (first the Tangerine Piercy Kirke, then the New York veteran, Sir Edmund Andros). Halifax protested to the privy council that "the same laws which are in force in England should also be established in a country inhabited by Englishmen . . . that an absolute government is neither so happy nor so safe, as that which is tempered by laws, and which sets boundaries to the authority of the prince." James declared Halifax's position to be subversive of monarchy. The duke supported the opposite contention, that the king "might, and ought to govern countries so distant from England in that manner which would seem fittest" to sustain English authority, power, and wealth. James then used Halifax's disquisition on "the inconveniencies of a sovereign power" in New England as reason for his removal from the royal counsels.[67]

As it happened, the crown's constitutional concessions of 1681 (and their application beyond Virginia and Jamaica to New York, Pennsylvania, and the Jerseys in the next two years) were the decade's last victory for moderation. Parliament was now dissolved. The last whigs were purged from the Guards. These elite regiments now occupied the Savoy barracks and Whitehall Palace to protect the king's court from the London mob and its radical agitators. The chief of these agitators, the earl of Shaftesbury, was arrested for treason. He offered to retire from politics, and even to go to Carolina. There, supposedly removed from plotting against the crown, he would expand the English empire and increase the king's customs, especially, the earl promised, if the king gave him £3,000 toward his equipage and assigned him a sympathetic naval captain and a warship as his convoy. The king declined either to make Shaftesbury a martyr by exiling him to the Carolina frontier or to enhance his authority there.[68]

John Locke had accepted Shaftesbury's bidding to write the aristocratic, slaveholding (insofar as the whigs were democrats, they were Athenian democrats), fundamental constitutions of Carolina in 1669. In 1681, Locke again expressed his master's views when, in two treatises of civil government, he justified the right of resistance to royal violations of the social contract. Locke's logic did not embolden even the most militarily professional and religiously devoted of Shaftesbury's associates. These republican rebels prepared to flee to the plantations they had purchased in West New Jersey. There that old Cromwellian-turned-Quaker, Major John Fenwick, together with Edward Byllinge, and their younger Friend, William Penn, had, in the Concessions of 1677, announced another American refuge for men of dissenting conscience and republican politics. The names of Waller and West, Norton and Trenchard—all famous in dissent in the latter half of the seventeenth century—joined Shaftesbury's men and the Penn partners in developing a commonwealth on the Delaware. On the lower reaches of that river, the proprietors of Pennsylvania and Maryland struggled to possess the carcass of the duke's dominions. Maryland itself had its own exclusion assembly and the defeated exclusionists prepared for another civil war. Here were other expressions of the ways in which, in the empire as in England, 1681 was as important as any way station on the road from revolution to revolution, from 1641 to 1776.[69]

With his enemies dispersing to America, King Charles concluded that it was safe to accede to Colonel Churchill's solicitation. At the end of February 1682, the king permitted the duke of York to leave Edinburgh and to join him at the Newmarket races. Once at his brother's side, the duke seemed so docile in behavior, so sensible in his reports of his reforms in the provincial government of Scotland, so well attended by military officers and imperial governors, and so modest in his demeanor ("ye Duke says he meddles in no business") that the king agreed to his permanent return to court. As the plantations secretary reassured the new governor-general of Jamaica, "all things go as well as we could wish at Court. The Quo Warranto [against the City of London's corporate charter] is in a fair way & the Whigs receive daily mortification. The Duke and Duchess & Lady Anne are expected here next week out of Scotland by Sea."[70]

To bring his household home from Edinburgh, the duke sailed from Margate Roads aboard HMS *Gloucester*, her captain Sir John Berry, on May 4, 1682. The duke was accompanied by two of his three favorites, John Churchill and George Legge (they stood just below "Lory" Hyde in that eminent servitude). Their ship first reached east and then beat northward in boisterous spring weather. Forty-eight hours out of Margate, twelve leagues from Yarmouth, just after daybreak, on an inshore tack, with the passengers still abed, the *Gloucester* struck the notorious "Lemon and Oar" shoal, three miles off the Norfolk coast.[71]

A strong sea was running. It drove the *Gloucester* onto the bar with "a terrible blow." When the rudder struck, the tiller smashed across the steerage, killing the helmsman. Out of control and pounding, the *Gloucester* opened up like a basket. "In a moment" there were nine feet of water in the hold. Clearly the ship could not be saved. But the duke refused to abandon her. Determined to appear courageous, humiliated by the charges that he had prematurely left the *Royal Prince* (and Churchill, who now again stood by his side in dreadful danger) to take refuge with Sir John Berry at Solebay, troubled by accusations that his imputations of cowardice had driven lord Sandwich to seek his death in that battle, his honor as lord high admiral involved in seeing the king's ship saved, James stood, apparently impassive, on the quarterdeck of the *Gloucester*.[72]

Only when the water surged in through the main deck gunports could "Mr. Churchill assisted by Sir John Berry" convince the duke, "always very difficult to be persuaded," that the ship was breaking up and could not be saved. George Legge brought the captain's barge under the great cabin's stern windows. Through them, out of sight of the sailors, he proposed to evacuate James. Still the duke dithered. He fussed over the safety of his strongbox, his priests, and his pugs. Churchill and Berry "had almost joined force to their Entreaties" before they could get James to move. Then, at last, discipline broke. The crew pressed aft into officers' country. They broke into the great cabin. They crowded up onto the afterdeck. They tried to jump down into the half-empty barge. They were held off at sword's point. In the bows of the boat, into which he was the last man invited by James, Churchill wielded the duke's own sword. Momentarily, the sailors shrank back. Churchill cut the painter and the lightly loaded barge was rowed out to the off-lying escort ships.[73]

Abandoned aboard the *Gloucester*, three hundred men struggled for life. As the ship was driven off the bar to sink in sixty feet of water, her boat was hoisted out and, overflowing with passengers still clad in their nightclothes, was fought free of the grasp of dozens of drowning men. The last man to leave the ship alive was her captain. Sir John Berry slid down a line into a boat bravely brought beneath the sinking *Gloucester*'s stern by the only captain in the fleet awake and on deck at dawn, John Wynbourne (Berry's colleague in a variety of American investigations and an influential enemy of New England independence). The *Gloucester* sank. Some of her complement escaped on bits of wreckage, for which they fought with the duke's mastiffs, but, by the duke's own count, 110 of the crew, uncounted servants, and 7 gentlemen, drowned. Lieutenant James Hyde was one. Not troubling to write himself, the duke ordered Colonel Churchill to inform Hyde's bereaved brother, the duke's favorite and kinsman, Laurence.[74]

A month later, in June 1682, at his court martial for the loss of the *Gloucester*, Sir John Berry insisted that the duke had behaved bravely throughout the disaster. On the crucial point, Berry testified that, when James finally abandoned the ship, he "took as many persons of quality with him in the boat as she could carry." The judges, who included Captain George Churchill, exonerated Captain Berry, although they imprisoned his pilot for life (the duke wanted him hanged) and cashiered a captain of one of the escorts. Despite widespread publicity of Berry's praise for the duke and although a medal was struck to celebrate his escape, James himself suffered a real loss of reputation. As Colonel Churchill privately told the Hydes— and we may safely assume that they, and Sir John Berry, did not forget it— James's "obstinacy" and his "false courage" were "the occasion of losing so many Lives."[75]

As James's protector, Colonel Churchill was ennobled. On December 21, 1682, King Charles created "the celebrated Colonel John Churchill" baron of Aymouth in the peerage of Scotland. In the same list "of distinguishing Favours, cheap and acceptable," were other clients of the duke's. Thomas lord Windsor, formerly governor of Jamaica and now of Hull, was created earl of Plymouth. Colonel George Legge, master general of the ordnance, took another step ahead of his intimate rival, lord Churchill, becoming baron Dartmouth in the peerage of England. Their close colleague, the royal (bastard) duke of Grafton, who had replaced the whig Russell as colonel of the First Guards, was now also commissioned admiral of England. The elevation of a generational cohort of the duke's clients proclaimed James's return to England and to imperial authority.

Churchill's contribution to the duke's restoration had been greater than his reward. Perhaps because of this, perhaps just because he was taking English composition classes, lord Churchill was soon touted as a secretary of state. "The King when he heard it," his business having suffered from the casual, if charming, earl of Conway, said he was resolved not "to have two idle secretaries." Instead, two of Churchill's closest friends, the earl of Sunderland and Sidney Godolphin, both converted from exclusion to support York's ascendancy, succeeded to the secretariat.[76]

William Blathwayt, the undersecretary of state and the head of the plantations office (who had done Conway's work for him and who, like Conway, took pains to forward Churchill's military career), was promoted to be secretary at war as well. Blathwayt hoped to become the English Louvois, and advance the development in England, as in France, of the administrative, rather than the political, state. In order to emulate Louis XIV's war minister, Blathwayt quickly collected copies of every available French order and drill book, town and fortress plan, hospital and logistical manual. These French war texts were to be Blathwayt's basis for modernizing and regularizing the English army, in cooperation with the duke's military staff, lord Churchill and lord Dartmouth chief among them. Here began a partnership in army and empire that, for Blathwayt and Churchill, lasted twenty-two years.[77]

During the spring and summer of 1683, the duke's household was preoccupied with the reorganization of his province of New York in accordance with the imperial settlement of 1681. The duke agreed that his permission for a New York legislature and his acceptance of a bill of civil liberties in that province would demonstrate his devotion to the imperial constitution of 1681 (James would withdraw both of these concessions as soon as he came to the imperial throne). Less to his advisors' taste, however, was James's determination to employ his coreligionists in imperial administration. The duke transferred the Catholic colonel Thomas Dongan from Tangier to succeed Sir Edmund Andros in command of New York. Dongan, as James's Catholic governors in the three British kingdoms would do, quickly restaffed the colony's crucial commands with Catholic officers.

New York's fanatically Protestant majority was as horrified as Anglicans in the British kingdoms would be when James as king followed the precedent he had set in New York as duke.[78]

Replying to Protestant protests, James insisted that toleration of all dissenters, not just Catholics, under a constitutionally revised regime, was his policy now and in the future. What he now did in New York, he intended to do in the entire empire later. To give religious toleration another imperial example, the Yorkists encouraged the development of Pennsylvania. William Penn's despatches were read to York's household council and they composed the duke's replies. The duke's household also saw the reorganization of the two New Jersey proprietaries as an opportunity to demonstrate, at a safe distance, the duke's purported political moderation and his vaunted religious tolerance.[79]

Real moderation, the prevalance of a pragmatic patriotism, lord Churchill's abiding interest, prevailed at last in the farcical episode of his brother George's Jamaica command. In the spring of 1683, Captain George Churchill was sent out in command of a fourth-rate man-of-war, the *Falcon* (42) and a sloop, ostensibly to reinforce the royal navy's Jamaica squadron. Actually, Churchill's orders were to convoy treasure hunters seeking the fabled wreck of the *Almiranta* of the Spanish treasure fleet (finally, dramatically, profitably, found the following year by William Phips of Boston, an episode with its own impact on the coming coup).[80]

George Churchill's orders had been written without the privity of either Secretary Blathwayt or his associate at the admiralty, Admiral Herbert, leaders of the military collectivity known as "the friends of the governors." When he heard of Churchill's sailing, Blathwayt warned Sir Thomas Lynch, the governor-general and vice admiral of Jamaica, that Captain Churchill was probably under orders to compromise Lynch as a whig. This was a congenial task for a tory, Captain Churchill, who sought to spoil the Spanish, because Lynch was a political moderate and the champion of the peace-oriented planter party. His conflict with the prerogative party of anti-Spanish privateers had come to hanging in the political crisis that accompanied the implementation of the imperial constitution of 1681 in Jamaica. Lynch had found that his moderation was at a discount in the island dominion and that Jamaica (second only to Ireland in imperial executive status and responsibility) was the focus of Anglo-American politics.[81]

If Lynch could be compromised or provoked, Blathwayt observed, there were several competitors for his place, chief among them the former governor-general of Jamaica, lord Vaughan, the new son-in-law of lord Halifax, himself the civilian champion of the new constitution. As it happened, Halifax ran afoul of Laurence Hyde, whose brother, lord Clarendon, was Lynch's patron. When Halifax lost face in this encounter, his son-in-law lost his chance to return to Jamaica. "Sir Charly" Littleton also

did good work at court on behalf of the Jamaica constitution and its im-
plementor.[82]

Neither of these was much approved of by Captain George Churchill,
especially as Lynch was one of the Cromwellian conquerors of the island, as
well as the head of the planter party. Captain Churchill naturally fell in with
the privateer party. Even their patron, Charles Howard, the earl of Carlisle,
admitted that the privateer party were "a company of drunken sots." They
did their drinking in a Port Royal tavern, "the Loyal Club." Their loyalty
became especially fervent in the summer of 1683 when they read of the Rye
House plot to assassinate the duke and king. The loyal club took to calling
their country critics "Whigs" and "Duke Killers." In Jamaica, as in English
counties, insults led to blows and to the abuse of power by tory partisans.
The chairman of the loyal club, Charles Morgan, acting as the town major
of Port Royal, arrested the leaders of the political opposition. He even persuaded Captain Churchill, already inflamed by rum and by the favor that
the governor-general showed religious dissenters, that the planter party
had tried to murder him.[83]

The proposal to try the local planter party leaders for attempted murder brought "the General," Sir Thomas Lynch, down to privateering Port
Royal from the planter capital of St. Iago. He cashiered Major Morgan,
suspended his brother, the famous privateer Sir Henry Morgan, from the
provincial council, and reofficered the entire Port Royal militia. Then, as
vice admiral, Lynch moved to discipline the navy. The commodore of the
squadron thereupon produced orders (presumably brought out by Captain
Churchill) exempting his officers from the governor-general's vice admiralty jurisdiction. Vice Admiral Lynch not only deplored this diminution of
his military authority, he feared that an autonomous naval command would
become the center of political opposition, perhaps even the basis of a provincial civil war between the army-planter and navy-privateer parties. Fortunately for Vice Admiral Lynch, his appeal to the authority of the lord
high admiral reached England just as the reaction against the Rye House
revelations propelled the duke back to power in the admiralty. Advised by
Blathwayt, and by Lynch's champions in his own household, James reaf-
firmed the governor-general's naval authority. Then the king-in-council
jettisoned the navy's complaints against Lynch.[84]

Vindicated, the viceroy set out to conciliate the crestfallen Captain
Churchill. The captain was ashamed to admit that the privateers had taken
advantage of his notorious intemperance, alcoholic and political, so he took
to drinking with the governor-general rather than with the privateers.
Nonetheless Churchill reported to the admiralty that Lynch took payoffs
from pirates. The vice admiral of Jamaica gave Captain Churchill profitable
patrols. Still, he told the colonial secretary that Churchill ruined his frigate's fighting capacity by crowding its decks with illegal cargoes. Alarmed at

the continued sniping between his viceregal client and lord Churchill's brother, Secretary Blathwayt met with Admiral Herbert, who promised to dismiss Captain Churchill's allegations. Then the secretary of war and plantations went to see "my lord Churchill himself." Once he had heard Blathwayt's account of the colonial contretemps, "his lordship," so the secretary reassured the viceroy, expressed himself as "well satisfied with your behavior towards his brother who he easily believes may have been indiscreet."[85]

George Churchill's political indiscretions were a growing embarrassment to his infinitely tactful and determinedly moderate brother. Lord Churchill, as a relieved Sir Thomas Lynch observed, was "to nyse a Courtyer to judg any thing can be don with or for such Foles" as the captain. Lord Churchill tried to get his brother to drop the issue when George returned to London in the winter of 1683–84. Undeterred, Captain Churchill connived with the earl of Craven, who was an old friend of the privateer chief, Sir Henry Morgan. Craven was further offended by Lynch's imputation that all the Carolina proprietors, even the loyal Craven, were implicated in Shaftesbury's plot to make "that Settlement a pretext to myne King & monarchy." Craven, colonel of the Coldstream Guards, and Captain George Churchill tried to convince "all the military men & seamen" that Jamaica was too valuable and too strategic a command to be left to an old Cromwellian, such as Sir Thomas Lynch. He boasted that he was "one of the conquerors" of the colony, and favored the puritan proprietors of the old army's regimental plantations. Besides, Captain Churchill said, "Port Royal was worse than Algiers" and required a firm, royalist commander. The port's heady mix of alcohol, sex, slave trading, piracy, and treasure hunting, all enhanced by Port Royal's centrality in a never-ending American war with Spain and France, made the government of Jamaica irresistible to military men of both services. When, a year after the Churchill episode, Sir Thomas Lynch died of an opium overdose, he was succeeded by two of Captain Churchill's drinking buddies, also overindulgers in rum and royalism, the duke of Albemarle and Sir Thomas Watson of the Life Guards.[86]

"The friends of the governors" deplored such appointments, for they agreed that "all His Maties Plantations as well Jamaica (as Jamaica indeed in an eminent degree) are worthy of his Maties care as They enlarge His Empire & Revenue very considerably and desperate adventures are now become necessary and important members of the main body, and deserve as good Governors. . . ." The "friends of the governors" favored plantation. In a policy statement that found its way into the standard instructions to governors-general, these imperialists supported close settlement and opposed engrossment of land. In particular, gubernatorial estates, "the Lands of ye E. of Carlisle and of Sr. T. Lynch ought to be made lyable to ye Quitrents or the forfeitures the rather as The Proprietors are not needy persons

& have therefore no excuse for not manuring their Lands." The "friends" were enemies of piracy and privateering. That privateering precluded planting was one reason to suppress it. To do that, so these imperialists argued, not only must the Jamaica executive be disciplined, but "the English Proprieties as the Bahama Islands, Carolina, Maryland, New England etc" must surrender the charters under which they "encouraged & supported privaters & Pirates." Freebooting had also to be put down because it both crippled trade with Spanish America and kept alive the Cromwellian vision of English conquest. True, it was "in His Maties Power to be Master of ye greatest and best parts of Their Dominion in America," but conquest was pointless because the Spanish were "already Subservient in ye Course of Trade to ye English Nation who reap the profit of their hazards & labour, without any expense to ye Crown." Aggression against the Spanish would also distract attention from England's real enemies in America, the French, who "may indeed do us and our Trade great prejudice by an Encrease of their Power there." Here were the major elements of the imperial program of settlement, plantation, trade, and resistance to France, which Blathwayt and his bureaucrats, Churchill and his soldiers propounded for a generation to come.[87]

Following this policy, the duke's household officials sought a better class of English executive, tried to resist French expansion, and appointed prerogative politicians. Cases in point were an island, St. Kitts, and an archipelago, the Leeward Islands, both split between the rival powers and dominated by a militant popular leader ("Colonel Codrington having distinguished himself by affecting popularity in ye assemblies"). So the Yorkists nominated Captain Thomas Hill to the Leeward Islands command. Hill had been lord Churchill's former comrade in France and Flanders and the lieutenant of the duke's own troop in the Life Guards. The duke's men praised Hill to the islanders, in much the same terms they used about Churchill himself, as a model of "courage undoubted" who was yet "free from pride," "affable," "courteous," "a trew & loyal Protestant, a stout soldier. . . ." The duke's household saw to it that Hill got munitions from the Tower, recruits from the Guards, and diplomatic assistance against the aggression of the French. In return, "Colonel" (his promotion came with the colonial command) Hill (like his senior colleague from the duke's troop, Sir Richard Dutton, the governor-general of Barbados) made sure that the household officers received a douceur from the colony for each item of help.[88]

Simultaneously, the duke's officers—with lord Churchill at their head as one of the duke's bedchamber, master of his robes, and lieutenant colonel of his regiment—daily refreshed and expanded James Stuart's imperial authority in the Tangier garrison, the African slave trade, the Newfoundland fisheries, and the fur trade of Hudson Bay. It was a comprehensive education in the administration, the politics, the personnel, and the economics of empire that the little circle of the duke's household acquired. For the next five years, as the leading figure in that household, lord Churchill's was an ever-growing part in James Stuart's imperial administration.[89]

Churchill's importance as a Stuart advisor and as a Yorkist executive was widely recognized. So much appeared when the king sent him out as the royal escort to bring back to England Prince George of Denmark, James's prospective son-in-law. At court, the gentlemen of the king's bedchamber, Sir Edmund Andros for example, protested this preferment of the duke's servant. In London, it was said on this occasion that lord Churchill "grows very great as they say on both sides, i.e., with ye King too." Writing to Paris, diplomats took particular note of the coincidence of Churchill's visit to the Danish royal court with the meeting of councils of war. Descriptions of the elite Danish troops (and their Scots officers) were combined with reports of the king of Denmark's personal attentions to lord Churchill. King Christian's presentation of a diamond-hilted sword honored Churchill not just as a Stuart envoy but also as a prominent military officer of a prospective, Protestant addition to the allied northern powers. Both the Danes and the English were presently in the French orbit, against their national interests, but lord Churchill's visit to the Danish court, and the impending marriage alliance that Churchill facilitated, were seen to underlie a potential diplomatic revolution against what American administrators were warned were "the french designes which at present threaten all Europe."[90]

Certainly, lord Churchill's own identification with moderate, Protestant, and legalist options was amplified on July 18, 1683, when he escorted Prince George to his marriage with James's younger daughter, Princess Anne. The princess's ideological attractiveness to Protestant patriots such as Churchill was celebrated by her marriage. Prince George had come to England to be a consort. He was not, like William, a foreigner who had taken home an English princess whom he politically controlled. In her marriage to George of Denmark, Anne was very much the senior partner, both by royal rank and force of personality. The marriage advertised as it enhanced Anne's distinct political identity as an English nationalist and an Anglican communicant. That identity was educated and protected by her tutor and chaplain, the militant Protestant and imperial metropolitan, Henry Compton, bishop of London and America. Compton was assisted by the princess's confessor (and lord Churchill's), Francis Turner, now bishop of Ely.[91]

As a married couple, the prince and princess of Denmark were entitled to form a household of their own. Given Anne's lack of education and George's amiable vacuity ("I've tried him drunk, and I've tried him sober, and there's nothing in him," was King Charles's dismissive summary), the courtiers of the Denmark household would be even more influential than was the Stuart wont. Lord Churchill's contemporaries saw him, "a very smooth man, made for a court," as privately and politically dominant in the Denmark ménage. Publicly, and personally, its leading spirit was lady Churchill's. The princess's preeminent friend since childhood, Sarah was Anne's preferred candidate to hold in her bedchamber the position that lord Churchill held in her father's. Anne wrote to Sarah that "the duke came in just as you were gone, and made no difficulty but has promised me that I shall have you, which I assure you is a great joy to me." The duke of York's compliance was lord Churchill's work.[92]

Other persons had blood claims to serve the royal newlyweds, foremost among them her mother's family, the Hydes and, in particular, the countess of Clarendon. The princess disliked the whole Hyde family (saving her mother, James's first wife, whose memory Anne revered: she was a commoner, and that degraded her daughters in Europe, but she was an Englishwoman, denizing her daughters in ways no other candidates to the throne, whether the Catholic Stuarts of Savoy or the Protestants of the Palatine and of Hanover, could claim). Still, Anne's aunt, the countess of Clarendon, was the titular head of the princess's household until, in 1686, she followed the earl to his command of Ireland, allowing Sarah to succeed as first lady of the bedchamber. The countess's son, Edward Hyde, lord Cornbury, became the prince's master of the horse. He neglected the post to fight in the defense of Vienna against the Turks. When he returned to England he served under lord Churchill's command against English rebels. Then Cornbury inaugurated lord Churchill's coup. Finally, Cornbury became governor-general of New York and the Jerseys. Another of Churchill's subsequent subordinates in imperial command, Edward Nott (afterwards governor-general of Virginia in Anne's reign and Churchill's ascendancy), acquired links to Princess Anne's new household through his sister Beatrice. But Sarah Churchill held Anne of Denmark's heart. So John Churchill, as much as any man could, controlled that willful princess's politics.[93]

Princess Anne's devotion to her vivacious elder, lady Churchill, was notorious and is famous. "There never was a more absolute favourite in a court" than Sarah in Anne's: "she is indeed become the mistress of her thoughts and affections, and does with her, both in court and in all her affairs, what she pleases." The princess's reliance on lord Churchill should be as well known. It was the more powerful by being one with her husband's. As a conduit for lord Churchill to Anne, the prince tempered her innate toryism and conveyed lord Churchill's moderate counsels. In this role, Prince George was as important as lady Churchill. No other royal death would ever so prostrate Churchill as Prince George's. None did him so much damage.[94]

Prince George's dependence on Churchill's younger brothers was of almost equivalent depth and duration. Charles Churchill, at age thirteen, had become page to the king of Denmark. At sixteen, he was promoted gentleman of the bedchamber to the king's brother, Prince George. Like his elder brother before him, Charles graduated from royal household to royal army. Commissioned ensign to his brother in the duke of York's regiment in 1674, Charles was promoted lieutenant in 1675 and captain of his own company in 1678 (when the Virginia companies of the regiment went to Flanders). Charles Churchill joined the Flanders expedition with the extra rank of captain-lieutenant to the earl of Feversham's dragoons. He went out with the last reinforcement to Tangier in 1682 as lieutenant colonel of a new garrison regiment. A year later, just as the popular, Protestant marriage of Prince George and Princess Anne was being celebrated, Charles Churchill's Tangerines (a renowned courier, Ensign Francis Nicholson, among them) came home to prop up the crown as "the duchess of York's regiment." Its lieutenant colonel, Charles Churchill, "the Danish Churchill," resumed his association with Prince George and became lord Churchill's right hand, forwarding the interests of the prince and princess of Denmark in the state and of the Churchills in the Denmark connection.[95]

A third Churchill brother, Captain George, had also been bred to arms. A naval favorite of the duke of York and an Anglo-Jamaican veteran, George Churchill returned from Tangier-based service of his own to become Prince George's naval aide, a place he held for twenty years. While serving the prince, George Churchill was distinguished in combat, rose to be an admiral of the blue and a commissioner of the navy. In the courts of Anne of England and George of Denmark, as well as in the fighting services, Admiral Churchill had reason for his boast that he was "frater non indignus" to his famous older brother.[96]

Lord Churchill's family dominated the new household of the prince and princess of Denmark. This wholesale enlistment seemed to be but a natural extension of the Churchills' courtly duties. To posts in the duke and duchess of York's households and military units they added more elevated positions in the service of the duke's daughter. Besides personal promotions, however, reversionary politics were apparent in the Churchill family's addition of posts in Anne's household to those they held in the service of her father the duke and her uncle the king. The Churchill family was taking out a dynastic insurance policy to preserve their position in case James Stuart died before King Charles or was subsequently deposed. It was to Princess Anne in the next royal generation (and perhaps in the subsequent one as well, for Princess Mary was barren but Princess Anne was still "hopeful") that the Churchills looked to continue their influence at the imperial court.

In part, the Churchills had to rely on Anne for their future because they could not establish themselves with James's heirs presumptive, the Princess and Prince of Orange. Lady Churchill was persona non grata to Mary of Orange. Mary disliked her sister's demeaning dependence on Sarah. Mary was further, and deeply, offended by Sarah's uncourtly candor, by her refusal to parade her piety, and by her obvious ambition for Anne (and so for herself, as Anne's "absolute favourite"). Young matrons together, Anne and Sarah were giving birth to the familial future denied to Mary. After five years of marriage, it was clear that William and Mary would never have an heir of their own. Anne was next in succession to her sister. Success in politics made Anne suspect to Mary and Anne's favorite, Sarah, was fair-haired, fecund, forceful, hated. As for lord Churchill, Princess Mary distrusted that accomplished courtier. Her husband admired the courtier and the commander both, but Churchill could not capitalize on this for the duke of York had repeatedly refused to let Churchill join Prince William's service.[97]

Ideological issues were also implicit in the Churchills' advance from service in James's household to dominance in that of his younger daughter. Lord Churchill's private unhappiness with the duke's religion, if not with James's authoritarianism, was ever more pronounced. Lady Churchill consciously cultivated Princess Anne's Protestantism and constitutionalism. Charles Churchill had imbibed militant Protestantism in Denmark, expressed francophobe feelings in Flanders, and advanced English imperialism in Tangier. Several of the Churchills were closely connected with that old trooper turned Anglican bishop, Henry Compton, who had insured the Anglicanism of his students, Mary and Anne, an Anglicanism that he exported to America as its metropolitan. All this suggests that the Churchill family saw the Denmark connection as an option in the imperial futures market, a "reversionary interest" in dynastic terms and an Anglican and constitutional one in imperial terms. The Denmark option could be exercised when need and opportunity combined to offer Princess Anne and her Churchill courtiers the leading roles in a Protestant, constitutional, anti-French future for England, and so for England's empire in America.[98]

BOOK II

LORD CHURCHILL'S INGRATITUDE

Since men are seldom suspected of sincerity, when they act contrary to their interests, tho my dutyful behaviour to your maiesty in the worst of times (for which I acknowlidg my poore servecas much overpay'd) may not be sufficient to incline you to a charitable interpretation of my actions, yet I hope the great advantages I injoy under your maiesty, which I can never expect in any other change of government, may reasonabley conveince your maiesty & the world that I am acted by a higher principle, when I offer that violence to my inclenation duty & intrest as to desert your maiesty at a time when your affaires seeme to challenge [the stricktest obedience from] all your subjects, much more [from] one who lyes under the greatest personable obligations imaginable, to your maiesty. This, Sr, cou'd proceed from nothing but the inviolable dictates of my consceince, & a necessary concarn for my religion, (which noe good man can oppose) & with which I am instructed nothing ought to com in competition, heanen knows with what partiallity my dutyfull opinion of your maiesty has hitherto represented those unhappy designes which inconsiderate & self interested men had framed against your maiestys true intrest to the protestant religion, but as I can noe longer joyn with such to give a pretence by conquest to bring them to effect soe I will allways with the hassard of my life & fortune (soe much your maiestys due) indeavour to preserve Your Royall person & lawfull rights with all the tender concern & dutyfull respect that becoms

Sr
Your maiesty's most dutyfull
& most oblidged subject &
Serunt

Lord Churchill to King James II, November 23, 1688

CHAPTER THREE

Rebellion and Empire:

1683–1687

THE STUART REVENGE STOOD on the shoulders of the Tangier garrison. James Stuart's favorite naval officers, lord Dartmouth as admiral and Sir John Berry as vice admiral, organized the great fleet that, in July 1683, sailed for the Mediterranean to evacuate Tangier, blow up its towers and walls, spoil its harbor, and bring back the veteran regiments of its garrison to "more immediate service at home." Learning from Dartmouth, the "Captain General and Commander in Chief of Tangier," of their transfer from Tangier to England, the regimental officers promised King Charles that "we shall never use unworthily those swords your Matie hath been pleased to put into our hands, but imploy them for the preservation and honour of yor Maties sacred person, and your Royal Service to the last drop of our blood."[1]

These officers were foreign service professionals, mercenary and militant, bred to regimental connections in the isolation of a distant garrison in alien territory. The Tangerines' physical violence and institutional loyalty shocked both the English patricians and the mobs of English cities they garrisoned. The Tangerine formations militarized the royal gendarmerie and palace guards. The Tangier officer corps intruded their professionalism into what had been an aristocratic patronage preserve. Dartmouth praised them, writing from Tangier that: "better officers can not be brought to the head of men, most having seen a great deal of service, & this place hath not been used so much for friends as being the proper refuge for those that are truly Souldiers, who have sought there bred, where finer gentlemen would not vouchsafe to come." Veterans, professionals, déclassé, the Tangerines also epitomized the crusading and patriotic characteristics of garrison government. They believed that their royal commanders personified these qualities. The Tangerines' disillusionment would end the Restoration.[2]

Besides the need to bring home the empire's greatest garrison to strengthen the English monarchy and to protect the royal brothers, there were an assortment of other rationales for abandoning Tangier. Perhaps the place was indefensible against resurgent Islam, whose jihad in this year reached the walls of Vienna. Certainly, the king himself was disappointed that his investments of men, munitions, and money—in excess of £330,000 since 1679—had not produced an equivalent increase in Tangier's commerce, colonization, and customs. Assuredly its large garrison of British, royal, professional troops—Irish and Scots as well as English; Catholics as well as Protestants—were offensive to the antimilitary, anti-Catholic, xenophobic majority of the English parliament. That majority had made the exclusion of the Catholic, militarist, British duke of York and Albany the condition of a subsidy to the crown for the support of Tangier. Neither exclusion nor subsidy had been forthcoming. Without that subsidy, the king could not finance Tangier, but to get it he would have to recall parliament and accept an act to incorporate Tangier into the realm and so subject it to parliamentary and common law. This concession the king had already rejected. Nonetheless, the opposition criticized the crown's decision to evacuate the colony as a diminution of English empire. They were horrified when they realized, all too late, that they had inspired the duke's household officers to convert the former Tangier garrison into the makeweight of crown control in England, to make Tangier officers into the instruments of direct royal rule in America, and so to secure the duke's succession to the imperial crown.[3]

On the eve of the Tangier evacuation, the rebellious, even murderous, temper of the whig extremists was revealed in the Rye House plot. The whigs' American affiliations appeared in the plot's Carolina cover. An American executive wrote scathingly of "the Carolina and Shaftesbury Cutt" in reply to Blathwayt's report of the attempted assassination. The whig plan to use "Carolina" arms and agents to kill the king and the duke and the threat of the whig magnates' household retainers at Oxford (Captain Charles Wilkinson, now governor-designate of Carolina, led Shaftesbury's troop) both triggered the Tangier evacuation and motivated a politically potent distribution of the returning Tangier troops. Those "great eyesores to the Whigs" landed in the crucial coastal garrisons. Colonel Piercy Kirke's first battalion was ordered to build a citadel at Pendennis that the colonel himself might govern, doubly displacing the local militia and magnate. Kirke's second battalion was to relieve the Guards companies from the Thames forts, tightening crown control of the capital's lifeline and increasing the size, specialization, and prestige of the household infantry. Brought back to London, "his Matys guards may be all at liberty to attend his Royal person only." The concentration of the Guards in barracks around the palace increased by a third the garrison of the capital.[4]

Colonel Kirke himself, however, was soon ordered to apply in an American command his African imperial experience. After he bypassed

Pendennis, it was rumored that Kirke would take command of Jamaica, a province whose elite now thought wise a loyal address deploring the Rye House plot. Then the royal courts' rescission of the New England colonies' corporate charters, just as the Tangier garrison was landing in England, opened a new American arena to absolutism. The impact of the Tangier garrison on Anglo-American politics was symbolized by Colonel Kirke's nomination as the first governor-general of the new dominion of New England. Lieutenant Francis Nicholson, the former Tangier subaltern (promoted captain and commissioned second in command of the royal garrison for New England), told the colonists that Kirke and company "had seen how . . . the Emperour of Morroco Governed the Moors and he would beat us into obedience. . . ."[5]

Secretary Blathwayt observed that the "Inspiration from England" of the opposition parties in the colonies "will cease for the king being in authority at home, as he is at present, cannot fail of respect abroad." Conversely, "the Resolution concerning New England must needs satisfy those who affect Popularity [in old England] that their game is at an end." Halifax's opposition to the elimination in New England of legislative, statute, and customary liberties and James's and Louis's support of absolutism in America demonstrated that the politics of the Restoration were decidedly transatlantic. The return of the Tangerines was intended to tip the balance of authority to the crown in old England as in New England.[6]

To impose authoritarian government in England, the second Tangier Regiment's first battalion were to land at Plymouth and garrison Charles II's new citadel there. Colonel Trelawney's family interest would assist recruiting. There too the regiment could reestablish its own family quarters and the school it kept for the education of such children of the corps as Alexander Spotswood. The second battalion of the regiment, commanded by Lieutenant Colonel Charles Churchill and Major "Tiffeny" (Zachariah Tiffin, afterwards a co-conspirator of lord Churchill and Colonel Trelawney, and Churchill's nominee to raise a regiment [the 27th] of foot), would take a battalion of the Tangerines to secure the great border fortress of Berwick. The Tangerines would also put some companies into Tynemouth. There they could command the loading docks for the coal supply of London, just as their comrades from the Tangier garrison now in the Thames forts commanded the colliers' access to the metropolis.[7]

Lord Dartmouth also proposed to ship some of Dumbarton's Scots to Portsmouth, the key to the Channel coast and the most direct link to London for forces from France (or other reinforcements for the capital's royal garrison). "I will not tell you," Dartmouth wrote, "how old a chore [corps], & how serviceable men & Officers these are, and therefore I chooze them for Portsmouth, where they are not to far out of his Majtys call, if ever he should have occasion in earnest for them." Dartmouth himself intended to lead the Tangier battalion of the Guards, "extraordinary men," up to London, together with the elite grenadier companies of all the Tangier battalions. After the triumphal entrance of the returned legate and his legions into the imperial capital, the Guards from Tangier would become the grenadier companies of the household battalions. The Tangier grenadiers would take over the Tower, under Dartmouth's own command as master general of the ordnance. Only Hull, of the great garrisons in England, was left unprovided for in lord Dartmouth's proposed distribution, but he had already ordered the construction of its new citadel. Commanded by the once and future American governors-general, Plymouth and Copley, the Hull citadel should overawe the town satisfactorily while it blocked the most obvious invasion route from the Netherlands.[8]

Only one of the Yorkist redistributions of the Tangier troops went off just as planned. It spawned a famous corps, the Royal Dragoons, potent politically as well as militarily. Even before the fleet returned from Tangier with the garrison, Sir Charles Littleton reported that the Tangier Horse would be "turned into a Regiment of Dragoons & My Ld Churchill Coll of them." At last, Churchill had his regiment. The command was a major promotion for lord Churchill, being not only a step up in rank but also from infantry to cavalry. It put iron in the jealous soul of Churchill's rival in James Stuart's household, lord Dartmouth. He said that the duke (and "Lory" Hyde, now earl of Rochester) favored Churchill only to degrade him. The jealous Dartmouth even alleged that "Churchill recommends himself by his lying with their wives, which is most certain as to my ladies Rochester and Sunderland."[9]

Other mounts were more assuredly involved in the raising of Churchill's Royal Dragoons. The battle-hardened Tangier Horse had been allowed to ship home their famous Andalusian steeds. Disembarked, the four Tangier troops rode up to London to become the cadres of Churchill's dragoons. Not since the Barbados Dragoons had been shipped to Ireland in 1674 and their commander, Edmund Andros, had sailed to New York to govern that province for the duke had there been such a regiment of military police in England. In the intervening years, Louis XIV's pogroms of Protestants in France had given "dragoon" a dreadful connotation. It was an ideologically loaded command that the duke gave lord Churchill. The First or Royal Dragoons, the heirs of the Tangier experience, were designed to be instruments of royal authority in England.[10]

Lord Churchill was commissioned colonel of the Royal Regiment of Dragoons on November 19, 1683. He quickly recruited and mounted the fifty privates of his own troop and quartered them in the neighborhood of his (wife's) estate at St. Albans. There their exactions, and their exemptions from civil arrest, outraged the local authorities. Lord Churchill's colleague in the household of the prince and princess of Denmark, the princess's

Hyde cousin, lord Cornbury, came home from Vienna and the Turkish war to be promoted lieutenant colonel of Churchill's dragoons. His rank and reputation quickly recruited his troop. Like his colonel, he quartered them near a family property, at Hereford. There they embodied their colonel's "interest" in the state and the state's authority in the community.[11]

By special favor, Churchill's and Cornbury's troops—each consisting of a captain (the colonel and his executive officer were also captains of their own troops), a lieutenant, cornet, quartermaster, two sergeants, three corporals, two drummers, two hautboys, and fifty troopers—were paid from the day each officer or trooper was commissioned or enlisted, rather than from the completion of the troop. These two troops were taken on the army establishment from January 1, 1684. On May 4, they were joined by the four Tangier troops. Their veteran officers, and particularly Thomas Langston and Charles Neatby, so distinguished in the battles of October 1680 outside of the beleaguered Tangier fortress, henceforward were among their colonel's closest military and political associates. Lord Churchill immediately sent them down to Hereford to drill lord Cornbury's recruits, both men and horses.[12]

Churchill's regimental staff also included the colonel's youngest brother, Theobald. He was commissioned as regimental chaplain, always a taxing post under Churchill's command. The colonel's Anglican devotion demanded daily prayers and weekly services, even on campaign. Lord Churchill also, invariably, used his chaplains as secretaries. His other nominations included the regiment's quartermasters (and provost marshals). These posts gave impoverished men a chance to enter the cavalry officer hierarchy, for quartermasters' commissions carried neither a purchase price nor its equivalent, the obligation to recruit troopers and their mounts. Lord Churchill's nomination of quartermasters for the Royal Dragoons began the tradition by which he promoted men recommended only by their military merit to positions on his staff from which they advanced to commands in the army and the empire as his clients and agents.[13]

The colonel also appointed the drum major, drummers, and hautboys, a regimental agent or banker, a surgeon, and a gunsmith as the remaining constituents of the "State Major, or Staff Officers of the Regiment of Dragoons." The colonel's staff, whose commissioned officers, save for Cornbury (who was just back from Austrian service against the Turks), were all veterans of either French or Tangier service, then distributed to the recruits the firearms and horse furniture supplied by the crown. They helped the colonel make up the muster rolls for each troop and then to write his first contracts for the regimental swords, clothing, saddlecloths, colors, banners, badges for the kettledrums, and the like. The nominal cost of each trooper's uniform and accoutrements was deducted from his weekly pay and credited to the regimental bank, controlled by the colonel through his agent. Colonel lord Churchill was left to make the best bargain he could with the manufacturers and tailors. Subsequent scandals suggest that Churchill profited from a goodly gap between what his men paid him for their uniforms and what he paid the suppliers. Churchill's share of the regiment's annual budget of £14,447/18/4 was his first substantial and regular perquisite after fourteen years in the army. This profit, and the regimental staff's planning, budgeting, and contracting that underlay it, were elements of the administrative experience that made military men the basis of the burgeoning bureaucratic state, both in the British Isles and in their American extensions.[14]

The imperial army was transformed by the Tangier garrison. The addition of four troops of cavalry and seven battalions of infantry doubled the size of the royal army in England. It more than doubled its toughness. The army could now provide a field force to meet the rebellion so long anticipated when James should come to the throne. The forces of the crown were no longer just the bodyguards and garrisons that the peacetime army in England had been since 1679. In October 1684, King Charles and his brother the duke concentrated more than four thousand troops on the outskirts of London and drilled them as a unit. The general staff was led by the earl of Craven, colonel of the Coldstream Guards. Lord Churchill was listed on the staff roster as the junior colonel of cavalry. No fewer than sixteen of the imperial governors-general, past or future, also appeared on the camp musters. Additionally, all "of the Governours, Lt. Governours, and Deputy Governours, throughout the Kingdom" were ranked in the "General and Compleat List Military" printed on this ominous occasion, the first peacetime army review in England.[15]

The "King's own Royal Regiment of Dragoons" followed their colonel's color, the royal cipher and crown, embroidered in gold on a field of crimson silk, from their quarters in Southwark out to Putney Heath. Churchill's troopers were coated and cloaked in red, lined and faced with blue. Their broad beaver hats, the products of the imperial alliance with the Iroquois, were bound in silver lace. Their colonel was determined that his regiment would rank as cavalry, not as mounted infantry, which dragoons were often considered. So the Royals, 388 strong, wore cloaks, jackboots, and gauntlets, and they completed the army's cavalry left wing, but their maneuvers, in the presence of the king and the duke, were cut short by "Wet & Showry" weather. On October 13, the Royal Dragoons were sent to winter quarters. Four of Churchill's troops were retained in the Thames Valley. The other two troops were ordered to ride north to repress religious dissenters, numerous and armed, at Oldbury, near Birmingham. There, Churchill's dragoons took their first police action in England. They insured that the local magistrates obeyed the royal orders to suppress dissenters' meetings, to arrest those who attended them, and to bring them to trial.[16]

On the night of February 6, 1685, all six troops of the Royal Dragoons were recalled to London. After a series of convulsions, mistreated, even tortured by his physicians, King Charles II had died that afternoon. For years, his heir, James, duke of York, had made military preparations for this crisis. He immediately ordered his elite regiments concentrated on the capital and alerted the garrisons and the navy. So "the King of England assures himself of all the sea-ports, the whole of the fleet, and the army." Even now, at the moment of his succession, James was aware of army opposition to his Catholicism and francophilia, and officer inclination to the Prince of Orange and to the existing constitution of the church and the state. Therefore, although he was in physical command of the imperial headquarters, James gave religious and political reassurance to his subjects that he would not abuse his power. In a message applauded across the English empire, he pledged "the word of a king, and a word never yet broken to preserve this government both in Church & State as it is now by law established." The principles of the Church of England and the laws of the English state, James declared, are "sufficient to make the King as great a monarch as I can wish."[17]

To power and pledges at home, King James added diplomatic action abroad. France was his first concern. As usual, James dispatched lord Churchill as his envoy to Paris. Churchill was ordered to make the official announcement of King Charles's death. Privately, he was to request both an extension and an expansion of Louis XIV's subsidy to the English crown. He "being already in the secret of a close alliance with Your Majesty. He is one of the Lords of the Bedchamber, and . . . this mission properly belongs to him." Churchill, so the French ambassador wrote to Louis XIV, "enjoys a great share of his majesties favours, and the choice he has made of him to send to Your Majesty is a mark of it." That being so, Churchill's candor should have been cautionary. Churchill was asked by Englishmen in Paris how seriously he took the new king's promise "to defend and support the Church of England." Lord Churchill is said to have replied instantly, clearly, and prophetically, that "if the king was ever prevail'd upon to alter our Religion, he would serve him no longer, but withdraw from him."[18]

In the meantime, lord Churchill carried back to King James King Louis's assurances of continued support. Secure, for the moment, on every front, James prepared for his coronation (at which bishop Turner was to preach the sermon) and rewarded those who had helped him to the imperial throne. Now a royal favorite, Churchill received the rewards, domestic and imperial, of a grateful sovereign to his loyal servant. The first of these was the stewardship of the reformed corporation of St. Albans. There, lord and lady Churchill now built their first home on land acquired from Sarah's family. There was probably raised and certainly quartered Churchill's troop of the Royals. Backed by the dragoons, lord Churchill's steward returned his brother George to parliament in 1685. George Churchill held the family seat for the next twenty-three years.[19]

Churchill's second reward reflected his master's changed position in the empire. As king, James had now to delegate to the officers of his former household many of the responsibilities that he had himself undertaken as his brother's chief imperial administrator. On April 2, 1685, lord Churchill succeeded James as governor of the Hudson's Bay Company. Churchill now began seven years of active service in the leadership of the corporation that carried the English flag to the top of North America. Churchill had acquired £300 of the company's closely held stock in March 1684. He added another £100 share immediately after his election. When he sold out, resigning the governorship of the Hudson's Bay Company after seven annual elections, he received nearly £5,000. Some of this enormous profit from Churchill's investment in America rewarded stock market manipulation, but dividends of 10 to 300 percent were paid in every year of Churchill's presidency. The fourfold rise in Hudson's Bay Company value during Churchill's governorship resulted in large measure from his corporate and imperial leadership.[20]

Far more than the princes, Rupert and James, who had preceded him as governor, Churchill was an active executive. It was a rare board meeting he did not attend after the summer of 1685 (which he spent on the battlefields of Monmouth's rebellion). Lord Churchill signed all commissions, correspondence, and orders. It was Churchill who continued to patronize Pierre Esprit Radisson, the effective founder of the Hudson's Bay enterprise. Churchill selected naval captains and military officers to command the ships of the company and the outposts that composed its colony, and he secured royal commissions for these officers. Churchill repeatedly moderated boardroom disputes, and always kept in close touch with a key corporate executive. Of course lord Churchill did the Hudson's Bay Company's public business with the king, the admiralty, the marines, and the diplomatic corps, both English and French.[21]

Diplomacy alone entailed a major investment of lord Churchill's time. The bitter rivalry between the English and the French for the lucrative fur trade of the Hudson Bay had already involved the duke of York, "both as governor of the company and as well wisher to our national interest there" in North America, in protests to Paris against French abuse and aggression. But this American manifestation of the growing Anglo-French imperial conflict, and the increasing doubt that King James, as a Catholic and a client of France, could effectively support the struggle, began to concern lord Churchill, as soon as the succession crisis was resolved.[22]

King James was anointed by the church and crowned on April 23, 1685. In a rare creation, the new monarch raised lord Churchill from the Scots peerage to the English nobility as baron Churchill of Sandridge in Hartfordshire and summoned him to take his seat in the house of lords. Parliament necessarily sat at the accession of a king, if only to grant the taxes that it had limited to the life of his predecessor. James had collected those taxes, illegally, since his brother's death. He had already shown how little respect he had for either the law or the parliament by his preparations to levy these taxes by military force, if parliament denied him its imprimatur. Some subjects had anticipated his autocracy. When, on May 22, King James repeated to the parliament his promise to protect the Church of England, Protestant rebels under Argyll's command were already in arms in Scotland to contest the claim of a Catholic to be king.[23]

From his exile in Holland, the duke of Monmouth denounced the king's Catholicism and claimed that James had poisoned King Charles. Having raised anew the abiding themes of the popish plot, the fuel of Anglo-American politics from 1588 to 1688, Monmouth prepared to invade England. On May 10, 1685, King James had ordered all his garrison governors to their commands, there to arrest without warrant every potential rebel leader and to keep them imprisoned without charge or hearing. The king himself had two hundred leaders of the opposition imprisoned in the capital. As London's sentiments were clearly for Monmouth, the king resolved not to leave the capital during the coming rebellion. Until he could call in troops from the Netherlands and Ireland, the king also retained the bulk of his field forces in the imperial metropolis, even though this left Monmouth free to land, to advance, and to recruit in the West Country. To check Monmouth's political partisans in the counties, however, the lords lieutenant were ordered to muster their select militias and send them to search the houses of the disaffected for weapons. The dungeons, gaols, and halls of every provincial town in England were quickly crowded with political prisoners. Monmouth's rebellion would be confined to whatever towns "the Protestant duke" could personally liberate.[24]

While Windsor and Copley secured the whigs of Hull in the new citadel, another Anglo-American executive, the duke of Albemarle, was sent down to Devon to raise his county's militia. The lords lieutenant were soon sent military advisors. Sir Edmund Andros and Sir William Stapleton (the latter freshly returned from commanding the Leeward Islands) were among the imperially experienced commanders who rode west to help hold down Monmouth's presumed partisans, the Protestant masses of the handicraft towns.[25]

Simultaneously, the royal army began a crash expansion. It originated on June 9, with the king's orders to lord Churchill to double the numbers of the Royal Dragoons. One of Churchill's new troops was given to the

Guards and Tangier veteran, Francis Russell, afterwards governor-general of Barbados. The Anglo-American political implications of royal army expansion and rebel repression were apparent to the French ambassador. On June 13, he told his master that Monmouth's rising would render King James "far more absolute in his kingdom than any of his predecessors were." The French ambassador added that "the levy of troops, which will soon be completed excites a belief that the king wishes to be in a condition to enforce obedience to his authority, and not to be constrained by any laws."[26]

Before dawn on that very morning, loyal burghers from Lyme had arrived at the London house of their member for parliament, Sir Winston Churchill. They reported that Monmouth had landed at Lyme and that the countryside had already begun to come in to him before the two loyalists escaped. Sir Winston took the burghers of Lyme to his son. Lord Churchill introduced them to the king at 4 a.m. The king commissioned Churchill brigadier general and ordered him to muster an elite mobile force, lead them west at speed, rendezvous with the duke of Albemarle, the lord lieutenant of Devon, and make contact with Monmouth's men.[27]

Lord Churchill left London the same day, at the head of four troops of the household cavalry (Oxford's "Blues," organized by their quartermaster, Walter Chetwynd, the future governor-general) and two troops of his own dragoons (one of which was lord Cornbury's, with his lordship in person at its head). In just four days of hard riding, this squadron covered 140 miles. Churchill met Albemarle at Bridport, did what he could to regroup the Devonshire militia ("half, if not the greatest part of them" lord Churchill wrote King James, "are gone to the rebels"), reached Aixminster, and found the rebel rendezvous near Taunton.[28]

On June 19, Churchill reached Chard and sent patrols toward Taunton. Three miles from the town, one royalist patrol encountered and beat up a rebel outguard, killing or wounding a dozen of them before being driven off by elements of Monmouth's main body. Harshly alerted to Churchill's presence, the rebel duke immediately called on his former subordinate to join the Protestant cause and to declare his personal allegiance. Churchill's response was vital to the rebellion. Unless the royal army was distracted by desertion and divided by disaffection, Monmouth knew he could not hope to succeed. His invasion had been premised on the results of a canvass of alienated officers. They had assured Monmouth's agents "that great Numbers of the King's standing forces, both Officers and Soldiers would desert and come to him." Instead, Churchill sent Monmouth's letter to King James and retired with his officers to church for a sermon enjoining obedience to monarchy. The text was Romans 13:2, "And them that shall resist shall receive to themselves damnation."[29]

If general lord Churchill's political and religious loyalty required military reinforcement, he received it two days later, on June 21, when Piercy Kirke, the governor-general designate of New England, newly commissioned an English brigadier general, joined Churchill's command with five companies of the Queen Dowager's Regiment and four of his own, the Queen's Royal Regiment. Kirke's ensign of grenadiers was Roger Elliot, the army brat from Tangier, he of the Carolina connections, and ultimately Churchill's choice for the government and defense of Gibraltar. Kirke's infantry had marched from London to Langport in less than a week. Here was a telling testimony to the toughness of the Tangerines and an early instance of the unmatched marching power of English infantry. On both, Churchill would ever afterwards rely. The cadres of the Queen's remaining companies were still in garrison at Plymouth. The governor, the earl of Bath, drew on them to form the regiment (afterwards famous as the 10th of the line) to be commanded by his nephew Sir Bevil Grenville (a regiment the command of which he exchanged for the government of Barbados). In Grenville's companies such Tangier evacuees as Ensign Elliot's half-brother, the young Alexander Spotswood, received their first commissions and began the imperial careers that culminated after a generation under Churchill's command.[30]

Of more immediate service than such new units as the 10th were the veterans whom King James called in from his reserves overseas to compensate for the failure of Albemarle's militia: the Irish Guards from Dublin; the Scots and English brigades from the Netherlands. Word of these pending reinforcements was immediately sent to lord Churchill (and by Blathwayt to Effingham, for the information of the Virginians, with assurances that "the Rebells in the west will be dispersed in a few days"). Churchill did not wait for help. Although his force was vastly outnumbered by the rebels, now numbering between three and five thousand men, eight hundred of whom were mounted, elements of Churchill's four hundred horsemen daily inflicted casualties on Monmouth's mob, retarded its recruitment, and harassed its transport. As Churchill forced the rebels to slow down and concentrate, he added to the strains on their feeble organization and scanty supplies. Determined, as he said, "to press the rebels as close as ever I can," Churchill proved impossible to shake off.[31]

"My Lord Churchill marches close upon the Rebells," the reports read. His troopers harassed the flanks and rear of Monmouth's thousands as they waded west toward Bristol through the slime of a typical English summer. Bristol was England's second city, the key to the Severn and to the campaign, and it lay just seventy miles from Taunton. There was no marching direct to the rebel goal, however, once Churchill's troopers got ahead of Monmouth's men. The dragoons stripped the countryside of supplies and terrorized potential rebels. "What we every day practice among these poor people," wrote one royal officer, "cannot be supported by any man of the least morality."[32]

And it was not just civilians whom Churchill's troopers terrorized. They beat Monmouth's mounted men in the Neroche Forest, ten miles southeast of Taunton. Forty royalist troopers broke double their numbers in a skirmish with the rebel rear guard near Langport and pursued them into Monmouth's camp. Anticipating Monmouth's line of march, Churchill rode cross country from Langport to Glastonbury and his troopers hit the rebel advance guard as they were about to encamp. Monmouth's essential calculation, that the royal army would not fight against their onetime commander and that, in particular, Churchill would not attack the royal son whose life he had saved at Maestricht, proved false. Monmouth had declared that the army's Protestantism would destroy its loyalty to a Catholic king. Indeed it would, but King James had just ascended the throne, he had promised to preserve the Church of England, and he had not yet had time to break that promise. So Monmouth's impatience doomed his rebellion.[33]

The rebels were hard pressed by Churchill's cavalry. They struck Monmouth's men again at Pensford after riding right around the rebels to obey King James's orders to get between Monmouth and Bristol. Monmouth's forces began to shrink, even before they saw the River Avon, the last barrier between them and England's second city. The rebel advance reached the bridge at Keynsham on June 24. They found the bridge broken and heard that Bristol had just been occupied by the leading elements of the royalists' main body. Nonetheless, Monmouth's advance guard repaired the bridge, crossed the Avon, and mustered in the meadows on the Gloucestershire side before heavy rain drove them back across the river to seek shelter in Keynsham. Churchill's tiny force had won just enough time for the royalists to relieve Bristol. From Bristol, patrols of the Life Guards rode toward Keynsham. Caught between elements of the royal army, Monmouth was without any clear line of advance. He proposed to march on Gloucester but his council of war, looking over their shoulders at Churchill's threat, objected "that there was a considerable body of horse and dragoons in our Rear who would continually be retarding our march till the foot came up and would necessitate us to fight before we could reach Gloucester." So Monmouth ordered his men to withdraw toward Wiltshire in hopes of acquiring some cavalry with whom to fight off Churchill's troopers. Instead, Monmouth's men began to melt away in the relentless rain. So far, Churchill had done more than any other commander to keep the kingdom from Monmouth's rebels. And as England went, so went the American empire.[34]

There were rebel sympathizers aplenty in Virginia and New England. They carried both Monmouth's and Argyll's campaign promises to every colony between Boston and Jamestown, and to the West Indies as well. Monmouth's pledge to restore "ancient Charters and Freedoms" spoke to provincial grievances everywhere in the increasingly centralized Restoration Empire where charters were falling to quo warranto proceedings. And Monmouth's pleas to Protestants struck chords in American consciences possessed by fears of the popish plot and a Catholic king. So American dissidents rejoiced at the news of Monmouth's invasion. They praised his Protestant and constitutional program.

"Ye Courage, or rather Impudence, yt some of them toke from ye Last Rebellion of Monmouth" led Virginia's country party to resist the prerogative program of the governor-general. Effingham declared that, had not the rebellion been defeated quickly, the colony would have been convulsed. The Virginians "let their Tongues run at large and demonstrated the wickedness of their hearts," vaunting the purported progress of the duke of Monmouth, the governor-general reported, "till I secured some and deterred others." In Nevis, faced with a "mutiny" by colonists who also took "Courage, or rather Impudence" from Monmouth's rebellion, the royal commander declared martial law and put his populace to building field fortifications "to secure that place from being attacked by the Rebells." In Bermuda, "when news reached us of a great army raised by the Duke of Monmouth and the defeat of the King's forces," the island's dissidents (Baptists, Cromwellians, and parliamentarians) "whispered about the country that now or never was the time, and that the Duke was rightful king and no papist, and that the Pope was the whore of Babylon and drunk with the blood of the saints. . . . Doubtless they intended to have seized the ports, great guns, and magazines had not the news arrived of the Duke of Monmouth's imprisonment." In Jamaica, an officer of "the old Army" declared that "James, Duke of York, was not rightful King of England, and that Monmouth, if God blessed him, would make work with him." The governor-general cashiered the officer and convicted him of treason, but recommended him for pardon on the grounds that the old soldier was as drunk as his sentiments were commonplace.[35]

From Boston, a royal customs official reported that "the generality of people" were "very full of Joy and Satisfaction at ye Whig News" that Argyll had conquered Scotland and Monmouth had beaten the royal army "or ye Popish Enemy as ye Trimmers & Whigg Brethren here basely term ye Loyalists." In the usual pattern of American resistance, "factious reports" were sent southward "every day" to every colony, "such damnable Reports from Boston & New England that I am sure the King Cannot Do himself better service in these partes yn Speedily to send a Governor to keep these people in order." Puritans rejoiced that London had supposedly surrendered to Monmouth; that the duke of York, "tearing his hair," had retired to Windsor; that the loyalist dukes of Beaufort, Albemarle, and Grafton had been slain. Reading this news with the eye of faith, the Bostonians declared that, "Everything now being Turn'd to its right Channel and the Crown sett upon the hopeful head of a protestant Prince, . . . that Popery was like to be extinguished and Liberty of Conscience Granted" (to Protestant dissenters only, of course). For all these blessings, the assembly of Massachusetts declared "a day of Thanksgiving."[36]

The lieutenant governor of New Hampshire condemned the tale-teller who reported, with some sense of British geopolitics, "that the Duke of Monmouth was proclaimed and crowned in Scotland and gone for Ireland where he had raised an army; and that the Duke of York was not yet crowned," and it was a question of whether he would be crowned. The Atlantic passage shuffled even the most urgent information. So imperial despatches, that reported as early as June 30 "the true particulars of the rebellion of the Earl of Argyle and the Duke of Monmouth," nonetheless trailed rumor and wishful thinking in the American colonies. High hopes for the success of Monmouth's rebellion only multiplied the American political disturbances that attended every imperial interregnum. These were not repressed until royal officers received the new king's commissions, often not until 1686.[37]

Whigs across the empire, who were prepared to attack King James's provincial governments the moment Monmouth actually won a battle (and who did so as soon as William seemed to have won, three years afterward) were disappointed. Churchill's obstruction of the rebel march to the Avon gave time enough for Louis Duras, the earl of Feversham (whom King James had commissioned to supersede Churchill in command of the west) and two hundred of the horse guards to reach Bristol at noon on June 23, 1685. The royalist troopers had ridden 115 miles in just eighty hours. They arrived to find the loyal duke of Beaufort, the governor-general Sir William Stapleton, and Beaufort's select militia about to lose their struggle to prevent the Bristol mob from declaring for Monmouth.[38]

Bristol secured, Feversham sent back the lieutenant colonel of his troop of the Life Guards, Theophilis Oglethorpe, to meet the rebels at Keynsham. Oglethorpe's troop charged through Monmouth's quarters on June 25, "A Successful but Desperate Attempt" that forcefully confirmed reports that King James's men were beforehand in Bristol (twenty years later, Churchill recalled their shared service in James Stuart's household and in the field when he opened a career in the Guards for Oglethorpe's son by Eleanor Waring, James Edward Oglethorpe, the founder of Georgia). A second squadron of royalists then roughed up the rebels. Finally, as some accounts have it, Churchill attacked Monmouth's men from flank and rear. The rebels now feared encirclement and Monmouth lacked the heart to fight on to Bristol, though that city held his only chance for success. The rebellion failed at Keynsham. Masses deserted Monmouth as he began to retreat after dark on June 26. To discourage new rebel recruitment, Churchill himself hung Monmouth's advance man, one "Jarvice a Feltmaker of Evell (a Notorious Fellow)." He died "obsinately and Impenitently."[39]

Churchill's troopers harassed Monmouth's men on their march from the bridge at Keynsham eastward to the gates of Bath. The city gates were held against the rebels by the governor, who was a royalist veteran, and his militia garrison. One of them shot Monmouth's messenger off his horse when he called for Bath's surrender. The rebels squelched off to the south and quartered in Philips Norton. The royal forces followed Churchill to Bath. There they concentrated. Elements of the Blues, the Life Guards, and the remaining two troops of Churchill's dragoons now formed Feversham's cavalry. Two small battalions of the First Guards (under Grafton's command and with companies commanded by the captains, afterwards Churchill's political associates and American governors-general, William Selwyn, John Seymour, and Francis Wheeler) arrived at Bath together with a battalion of the Coldstream Guards (whose officers included the future American commanders James Kendall and William Matthews). Five companies of Scots marched to the beat of "Dumbarton's Drums" (their officers numbered among them lord George Hamilton, subsequently Churchill's lieutenant general of infantry and so governor-general of Virginia, and Hamilton's lieutenant, John Johnson, who would be murdered while in command of the Leeward Islands). They escorted the artillery lord Dartmouth had dispatched from the Tower under the command of the Tangier gunner, Thomas Povey (his uncle, Blathwayt, would see to Povey's promotion to Massachusetts's government). All the while, that feckless son of a formidable father "the Duke of Albemarle continues in Devonshire."[40]

The royal army that assembled at Bath numbered about 2,500 men. It was commanded by Turenne's nephew, the politically reliable earl of Feversham. Perhaps the duke of Monmouth's letter to Churchill had reminded King James that "Church" might respond to a Protestant and constitutionalist appeal. Certainly, the king's commissions to Catholics to command in Ireland and Scotland were already exciting anguished apprehensions among Anglican officers. In any case Feversham, who had merely recorded Colonel Churchill's exploits at Entzheim, ended General Churchill's first independent command when their forces were united. Yet he depended utterly on Churchill in every crisis. Feversham was that figurehead commander limned by Sallust: "a man with a long pedigree and a houseful of family portraits, but without a single campaign to his credit, who, faced with a serious task which he does not know the first thing about, will find some commoner to instruct him in his duty. This is in fact what generally happens: the man you appoint to take command looks for another to command him." Churchill was bitter about his demotion, his subordination to a foreigner, and the thankless duty it entailed. "I see plainly," he wrote to Cornbury's father, the earl of Clarendon, now the lord lieutenant of Ireland, "that I am to have the trouble and that the honour will be another's." This was King James's intent. "Lord Churchill will be up with Lord Feversham within a day or two," the king had predicted, "and then there will be likelihood of some action." For this, Feversham, as the nominal commander, would be rewarded.[41]

That action came quickly but, to Churchill's dismay, it only embarrassed the royalists. The rebels had recoiled south from Bath to well-hedged high ground and the road junction in the stone-built village of Philips Norton. There, on June 27, Grafton's and Kirke's probe was ambushed in a lane between the rebel-held hedges. Although the rebel leader, a carpenter and dissenting preacher named John Coad, was shot through the wrist and body and, "falling to the ground, bleeding excessively, lay under foot during the fight," his comrades, just two companies at the outset, fought desperately and held the royalists in the lane, blocked at the village end by a barricade. Grafton's command was trapped. His subaltern, Matthews of the Coldstream, was wounded, left for dead, and taken prisoner. The royal infantry had to be extricated by Churchill and his dragoons, who then, with Kirke's Tangerines, covered the royalists' retreat until Povey's artillery came up. After two hours of intermittent artillery exchanges, "shooting at Hedges and Shot at, in desperate Rainy weather," Feversham decided to withdraw until his heavy guns arrived. He could not encamp on the field, for it was pouring rain and the royal army's tents had not yet arrived from London (Blathwayt was amazed when the Scots brigade landed from the Netherlands carrying full field equipment). Once again, the ill-equipped royalists took free quarter on the unfortunate villagers. Their "violence and wickedness" toward civilians made the king's troops "much their greater enemies than the rebels." Feversham's men made themselves comfortable in Bradford-on-Avon and took the next day, the Sabbath, "to clear our armes and recover the fatigue of the foregoing day." Churchill was furious that contact with the rebels, which he had sustained for weeks, was now lost. He complained to his stolid commander, who did not respond. Frustrated by the royal army's inexplicable inaction, Churchill wrote that Feversham "has the sole command here soe I know nothing but what it is his pleasure to tell me." Churchill himself did not dare insist on an advance "for feare that itt should not agree with what is the Kings intentions."[42]

The heavy artillery from London, escorted by Dumbarton's Scots and accompanied by the army's tents, reached Feversham at Westbury on the last day of June. The army encamped at Frome on July 1. There they were joined by more artillery, from Portsmouth, in the first days of July. Its escort was five companies of Trelawney's Tangier regiment (commanded by lord Churchill's brother, Lieutenant Colonel Charles Churchill, with the imperial officers, Captains Charles Fox, John Strode, Edward Saville, and Lieutenant Francis Nicholson, on Churchill's staff) and elements of the earl of Bath's new regiment (with the future viceroys Bevil Grenville and Andrew Hamilton among its officers). Now Feversham had ample artillery but he declared that the roads were too poor to advance. Besides, he did not know where the rebels had gone. Churchill stifled his fury: "we have had abundance of rain," he wrote to Sarah, "which has very much tired our soldiers, which I think is ill because it makes us not press the Duke of Monmouth as much as I think he should be. . . ."[43]

Monmouth had seen for himself the truth of reports that the regulars had arrived in numbers from London. At Philips Norton he heard "the unexpected news of Argyle's being defeated" in Scotland. (The duke's son, Neill Campbell, immediately took a well-laden ship to New York. There he was welcomed by Governor-General Dongan as a martial and articulate addition to the imperial administrative cadre Dongan was constructing. Campbell became deputy governor of New Jersey.) Monmouth was ever more depressed by his fatal miscalculation about the loyalty of the royal army, and of Churchill and Albemarle in particular. The duke decided to use the respite given him by Feversham's retreat to flee the country. Before he could act, the royalist advance resumed and, as Monmouth saw it, opened the loyalists to a fatal surprise.[44]

Feversham had finally resolved to leave behind the heavy guns (for which he had waited so long) and march with sixteen field pieces. The loyalists did not march far for, on July 4, a patrol of Churchill's dragoons found a rebel outpost within half a mile of Monmouth's quarters at Bridgewater, broke it, and drove the survivors into town. Having found the enemy, during the afternoon of July 5, the royal infantry, perhaps 1,500 strong, "march'd into the Levell . . . a Place copious and commodious for fighting," called Sedgemoor. The loyalists pitched their new tents behind "a Dry (but in some places Miry) Ditch" or drainage canal—"the Bussex Rhine"—on the edge of the Sedgemoor, only two miles from Bridgewater. Each of the regiments detailed a picket to cross the ditch and keep a lookout toward the rebels. Each regiment located its tents a uniform distance back from the ditch so as to have room to form up on an alarm. Dumbarton's veteran officers even laid tapes for the Scots to follow in the dark from their tents to the assembly points. The royal artillery lined the road to Bridgewater. The gun teams and their drivers took quarter in the nearby village of Weston-Zoyland (but Churchill stationed two troops of his dragoons to guard the guns). The cavalry detached patrols on either flank and Oglethorpe took a squadron out to watch the rebels in Bridgewater. After midnight, hearing nothing from Oglethorpe, Feversham retired to his field bed in the manor house of Weston Court. The cavalry had settled into the houses and outbuildings of Weston-Zoyland, which lay just to the rear of the infantry.

Although the troopers kept their mounts saddled, almost everyone seems to have indulged in the local cider and "we securely went to sleep."[45]

At 2 a.m. on July 6, 1685, "(Securely Sleeping) Our Camp was Rouz'd by the near approach of the Rebells, a dark night and thick Fogg covered the Moore, Supineness and preposterous confidence of our Selves, with an undervaluing of the Rebells . . . had put us into the worst circumstances of Surprise." Learning that the royalists had not entrenched, but ignorant of the Rhine, Monmouth had marched some 3,600 men right past Ogle-thorpe's patrol. The rebels' leading elements were within a few hundred yards of the royalist camp when one of the troopers posted in advance of the Langmoor crossing of the Rhine, to the right of the royal encampment, fired his pistol at the figures emerging from the ground fog. Then the trooper rode for the loyalist lines yelling "Beat your drums, the enemy is come. For the Lord's sake, beat your drums!" Monmouth immediately or-dered his mounted men to charge the nearest cattle crossing of the Bussex Rhine and smash into the sleeping royalist camp, but the right-hand patrol of 50 Life Guards and Royal Dragoons blunted the charge of hundreds of rebel horsemen. Although both the royalists's commanders, Sir Francis Compton (the bishop's brother) and his second, were badly wounded, their troopers made a fighting retreat and held the vital crossing.[46]

At the outbreak of the fighting only one senior officer was awake, armed, and on the spot. All the others "were doing the Duty of the Field in their Beds." Lord Churchill, despite his own prior judgment that Mon-mouth would abandon his infantry in Bridgewater and flee for the coast rather than fight the royal army, had taken seriously the last intelligence report: "that the Rebels had given out, they would fight in this place." As general of the day, Churchill sat up himself and he had ordered 150 of Dumbarton's Scots to the guard, fully armed, matchlocks loaded, matches lit. When the alarm sounded, he ordered them to fire into the dark mass of men and horses who had veered away from the crossing defended by Compton's patrol and who now suddenly appeared across the ditch from the loyalist camp. "Who are you for," shouted Douglas of the Royal Scots. "The King" came the reply out of the fog. "What King," demanded Doug-las. "Monmouth and God with us," was the rebel rallying cry. "Then take this with you!" The crash of the volley maddened the rebels' untrained horses. Most of Monmouth's cavalry fled.[47]

As the rebel cavalry broke, all along the lines of the royalist camp sen-tries fired their muskets and shouted for the drums. The drummers ran barefoot to their companies' assembly points and beat the alarm. Only half dressed but fully armed, the soldiers stumbled from their tents and moved forward to line up in the dark and fog. The Royal Scots, having been briefed before dark by their officers about a possible night attack, were first to join those of their comrades who were already ranked in the general's guard. Churchill's guard bought the rest of the loyalists time to rally, firing repeated volleys at the rebel infantry as its first three regiments, some two thousand men, deployed beyond the ditch that fronted the camp. Dumbarton's men kept up their fire even though their matchlocks, sparkling lines in the darkness, made perfect targets for the newly arrived rebel artillery. Three guns, trained by Dutch gunners, firing at pistol shot, killed or wounded every Scots officer of the guard and all but four of the battalion officers. Two-thirds of the Scots' picket fell. It is hard to know how Churchill himself escaped unscathed.[48]

The musketry of the Scots and the rebel fire defined the battle for Churchill. The rebels were in force before him and they outflanked the royal camp to its right. So lord Churchill held his own position but he ordered his brother Charles and Piercy Kirke to march their Tangerines behind the royalist lines from left to right, extending the royal infantry's front to match that of the rebels. He stationed two troops of his own dragoons behind the infantry to keep them to their duty. This proved to be unnecessary for the veteran Scots' discipline and lord Churchill's leadership had overcome the rebel surprise: "such was the extraordinary Cheerfullness of our Army, that they were allmost as readily drawn up to Receive them, as a Prainformed expedition could have posted them." Once his infantry was in line, Churchill organized his remaining dragoons and the Life Guards, who had now ridden up from the village, into two squadrons, one on each flank. The squadron commanded by Cornbury charged the rebel guns, killed their Dutch crews, and relieved the royalists from their murderous fire. Exposed, the raw rebel infantry, despite the leadership of such Anglo-Dutch regulars as John Foulkes, colonel of Monmouth's white regiment (who survived Sedgemoor to invade England once again in 1688 and then commanded in the English West Indies), began to falter. They had "stood near an hour and a half with great Shouting and Courage, briskly firing," but they would not cross the ditch and attack the camp, where, hand to hand, rebel scythes, spades, and numbers would have told against the rallying royalists.[49]

The rebel pikes shook and their musketry slowed when, "at last," the royalists acquired artillery of their own: "2 guns, which my lord Churchill ordered to be brought up on the right of our line, made them begin to run." Then the bishop of Winchester, the one-eyed, former Guards officer, Peter Mews, when the civilian teamsters could not be found, called out his own coachmen and horses to drag up six of Povey's fieldpieces. As these guns arrived, one at a time, Churchill placed three on the Scots' right flank and three between the Guards and the ditch. His line at last complete, horse, foot, and guns, lord Churchill ordered the Horse Guards to attack the rebel flank and rear, but Oglethorpe's troopers were beaten off by the inspired and desperate peasantry.[50]

It was now nearly 4 a.m. and day was breaking. Feversham, a sound sleeper and a slow dresser, at last arrived on the scene. He took command from Churchill. As soon as it was light enough to see the rebel confusion, Feversham ordered Churchill's dismounted dragoons and the grenadiers of the Scots and the Guards to lead the infantry charge across the ditch. Lord Churchill charged with his regiment but, with his usual sangfroid, paused to identify a colonel of Monmouth's who had been shot by some of Cornbury's under officers. Even as the rebels broke, they shot some of the leading loyalist officers, among them the Guards subaltern Edward Reresby. He survived and, like many others, found in his service at Sedgemoor the foundation of an imperial career in America. One hundred royalists fell before the rebels ran out of ammunition. After half an hour of hand to hand combat, Monmouth's men broke. The fugitives were run down by the royal grenadiers and ridden down by the Royal Dragoons. Two or three hundred rebel deaths on the banks of the Bussex Rhine were multiplied fivefold by sunset. Even then, a disgusted royalist observed, "our men are still killing them in ye corne and hedges and ditches whither they are crept." The royal pursuit, pushed by lord Churchill and Colonel Kirke, continued "until the Soldiers were weary of Killing."[51]

Churchill and Kirke did not halt the pursuit of the rebels at the edge of the moor. Rather ". . . there came down the Queens Guards (so they said) under the Lord *Churchill*," into the neighboring parishes, "and Terror march'd before them (for we could hear their Horses grind the Ground under their Feet, almost a Mile before they came)." Villagers (such as the Quaker John Whiting) were told that Churchill's troopers intended to burn six houses belonging to Monmouth supporters but they settled for one captain's farmstead, "cutting and tearing the Beds, Hangings, and Furniture to pieces, shaking out the Feathers and carrying away the Bed-stedes and what they could, letting out the Beer, Wine, and Sider, about the Celler." Then the Royals fired the barn. Only stone walls and a slate roof saved the house. Whiting hurried back to the safety of jail, but he heard that "many were hang'd in cold Blood by that cruel, inhuman, bloody Wrecht, Coll *Kirk*, the Shame of Mankind; and some were hung in Chains Naked to the Terror and Shame of the County."[52]

Having himself had four prisoners "hanged in Chains on the place where we fought," Feversham then had twenty-seven more prisoners barbarously executed for his amusement. He sent "presents to all the Whiggish towns of rouges to be hanged there." Then Feversham pushed on to Bridgewater. Thence he dispatched Oglethorpe to London to report the victory. The king knighted Oglethorpe and commissioned him colonel of the senior English line regiment. Five days after the battle, Feversham himself marched for London with the Guards. King James gave him the garter and the colonelcy of the first troop of the Life Guards. Lord Churchill was not recalled to London to share in the acclaim of court and capital, but his fellow directors of the Hudson's Bay Company sent him an address of congratulations and a lynx-skin comforter for his field bed. Churchill quickly took his place in the public eye and, more significantly, in the opinion of the army, as England's leading soldier. Meanwhile the London stage pilloried Feversham as "the General who had won a battle in bed."[53]

Churchill remained in the west, unrewarded by King James, who gave lord Feversham credit for the victory, just as Churchill had predicted. Churchill's was the horrid task of commanding Judge Jeffreys's escort to the "Bloody Assizes." Churchill's command provided the guards for as many as 324 torturous executions in fifty-two different towns and villages. Churchill's own dragoons, and the Tangerines commanded by his brother Charles, occupied Taunton itself during the butchery, "forcing poor Men to Hale about Men's Quarters, like Horse-flesh or Carrion to boil and hang them up as Monuments of their Cruelty and Inhumanity." Churchill's biographers uniformly put him in London during this infamous episode, but Judge Jeffreys himself, writing from Taunton on September 19, begged the king to "refer to my Lord Churchill for the particulars" of Jeffreys's judicial murders. On September 22, Judge Jeffreys again referred the king and the court to "my Lord Churchill's Relation, who was upon the place," for all "the Particulars of Taunton." These letters involve lord Churchill almost as fully in the awful aftermath of the rebellion as he had been both in the royalist victory at Sedgemoor and the terrible pursuit that had followed the fighting.[54]

Despite his thorough support for the vengeful king, lord Churchill only belatedly received hand-me-down promotions, and these were dependent on the departure of the discredited duke of Albemarle for America, save for the step to major general that Churchill and Feversham both received from the king after the battle. Albemarle thought that he should also have been promoted, just because he was a duke, but he had been disgraced by the flight and desertion of his militia. After that, Albemarle had not found any way to fight for the king (despite the great expectations held of one of his name and rank). Driven to tears by King James's public contempt, Albemarle exchanged his command of the First Troop of the Life Guards for the governor-generalship of Jamaica. Feversham took command of Albemarle's troop. Churchill succeeded to Feversham's former post, the colonelcy of the Third Troop, but he had to resign the command of the Royal Dragoons to lord Cornbury. Lord Churchill, as captain of the Life Guards, became the executive officer of the royal army's elite unit, but the disparity between Churchill's decisive accomplishment and his tardy promotion may have marked the king's growing distaste for Churchill's increasingly public Protestantism and his ever more moderate politics.[55]

Both of these qualities came increasingly to the fore after Churchill left the west country to take his seat in the lords, if only by contrast with the extended excesses of Churchill's former subordinates, "the Royals." Cornbury's Royal Regiment of Dragoons made "dragoon" an English verb. The Royals lived at free quarter (i.e., off the inhabitants) in one west country town after another, moving on monthly to punish a different place for its people's presumed rebel sympathies. Their "Violence . . . to ye Country in all kinds both to the persons as well as goods," Sir Charles Littleton wrote, "I have scarce known practised at any time in our former Civil Wars." The Royals, and the rest of the king's army of occupation, behaved "as in an enemy's country." The dragoons interrupted their looting just long enough to come up to town in August for King James's great review of his victorious army in Hyde Park. After being particularly inspected by the king in October, the Royals rode west once more, ostensibly to repress rebels turned highwaymen. In fact, the dragoons ransacked Devonshire for eight more months. After complaints of their robbery of a respectable royalist, one William Bird, reached London, the Royals' absentee colonel, lord Cornbury, was sent down to discipline his dragoons. He saw to it that his troops took to arresting supposed rebels as well as robbing them. Six months after the end of the rebellion, "they filled the prisons so full" that the prisoners "died as if the plague had been among them." Finally, the dragoons' outrages so angered even those fervid loyalists, the earl of Bath, Sir Bevil Grenville (whom King James had knighted at the head of the 10th in Hyde Park), and their kinsman and front man, the duke of Albemarle, that they together persuaded King James to recall the Royals.[56]

Worse than the dragoons' alternating indiscipline and oppression was the consistent cruelty of Colonel Kirke's Tangerines, "the Lambs." Belying the Pascal Lamb that adorned their crusaders' colors, Kirke and his men hung rebel fugitives as they found them—perhaps a hundred in the first week after Sedgemoor—and they looted every house in which they found a fugitive. In Taunton, Kirke and his officers drank a loyal toast as each rebel was executed. They turned out the regimental band to play mock accompaniments to the convulsive "dances" of the hanged men. One account has Colonel Kirke accepting an innkeeper's daughter's exchange of her favors for her father's life (but when she awoke, her father was dangling from his own inn sign). Another girl, who had killed one of Kirke's officers with his own sword when he attacked her mother, was supposedly pardoned by the capricious colonel. Desperate appeals to London finally persuaded Secretaries Sunderland and Blathwayt to tell Colonel Kirke that martial law had ceased in the west with the end of fighting. "Plundering and murder" by soldiers were now to be subject to the restraints of civil law. In King James's estimation, however, Kirke's crime was not looting and killing but veniality and mercy. Informed that the colonel had taken bribes to pardon persons the king would have condemned, James recalled Kirke to London, deprived him of the command of New England, and conferred it instead on Sir Edmund Andros (whose repressive work in the west had already won him a commission as lieutenant colonel of cavalry).[57]

Of course Colonel Kirke's alleged conduct as governor of Taunton was exaggerated (difficult although that was to do) in Massachusetts. There the general court was abuzz with reports that New England's governor-general designate "was Layd aside and quite out of his Matys favor for severall gross misdemeanors Committed while he was Governor of Taunton, where they report he invited 30 Gentlemen to dine with him, and after dinner hanged them up in his hall to satisfy his popish and blood thirsty Cruelty; and at an other Time, Not Long After, ye sd Col Hanged 12 men more upon the Sign post of a Tavern at wch ye [owner] seeming to be troubled, the col caused him to be hanged there also, & sending for a Justice of peace, whom came not so soon as his Honor the Governr expected upon his first approach pistolled him, whereupon his Majesty Turned him out of boath that and this Governmt" and substituted a presidency (to prepare for the arrival of a governor-general).[58]

The Massachusetts legislators "Rudely" remarked that "the King might have saved himself that trouble, for they, meaning the colony, had full power and a larger Jurisdiction for Election" even than in their prior period of overt independence. The arrival of the warship *Rose* with the royal commission to Joseph Dudley as president and to his council was a rude awakening for "the rageing furious, fanatic whiggs" of Massachusetts, those "stubborn Rebellious & unnatural haters & warrers agst the true mother church & spouse of Christ, Established," but it was nothing compared to the fate of the western towns of England.[59]

Their punishment now passed from Kirke and the "Lambs" to Trelawney's Tangerines, commanded by Lieutenant Colonel Charles Churchill. When they left Monmouth's capital city, Taunton, to spend eight months abusing the supposedly seditious inhabitants of Bristol, they were relieved by James Stuart's old regiment, the marines of Sir Charles Littleton and Edward Nott. They marched their command down the roads of the west. Every intersection was now sign-posted with some of the 1,200 heads and quarters of the rebels. Horrified, Littleton wrote that the west country was a "shambles," a human abattoir. Between 800 and 1,200 convicts escaped barbarous execution and revolting display only on condition of ten-year terms of servitude in "some of His Majesty's Southern Plantations in America, vizt. Jamaica, Barbados, or any of the Leeward Islands." A complacent King James wrote to his nephew the Prince of Orange that, "as for news there's little stirring, but that the Lord Chief Justice has almost done his campaign; he has already condemned several hundreds, some of which are already executed, more are to be, and the others sent to the plantations."[60]

The queen herself, and courtiers of every sort, strove to win shares in the slave trade in convicted rebels. The bulk of those who won contracts to purchase convicts for sale in America were those officers of the army, treasury, or court who already held West Indian properties. All were old servants of James Stuart. Several had or would command the very colonies to which they transported Monmouth's men. Sir Philip Howard of the Guards, governor-general designate of Jamaica, Sir William Stapleton, the Anglo-Irish soldier of fortune who was on leave from the command of the Leeward Islands, and Captain James Kendall of the Coldstream Guards, afterwards governor-general of Barbados, all secured consignments of rebel convicts. William Penn showed unusual moderation in support of the king's measures. He reported "about three hundred hanged in divers towns in the West, about one thousand to be transported. I begged twenty of the King." In Virginia, the governor-general, lord Howard of Effingham, promised the secretary of war and plantations that he would split with him the profits from the sale of one hundred rebels. He asked Blathwayt to send him the skilled artisans for which the west country was famous. "Ye more Tradesmen the better" the governor-general wrote. Effingham was disappointed to learn that his colony was judged too rebellious to receive many of Monmouth's followers. In the wake of Bacon's Revolution, Virginia could acquire only a few fresh rebels to add to the Cromwellians and Commonwealthsmen who still haunted its borders and continued to claim the silent allegiance of the tenants of the Northern Neck and the settlers of the South Side.[61]

From this infamous perquisite, "the buying and selling of free men into slavery . . . a necessary dependence on Arbitrary Power," as from most of the more honorable rewards of repression, lord Churchill was excluded. Indeed, he brought up to King James judge Jeffreys's protest that the king was rewarding courtiers rather than those "that served you in the soldiery." More creditably, Churchill presented petitions and petitioners for mercy to the king. Hannah Hewling had come to court seeking King James's pardon for one of her brothers, condemned like the others for rebellion but not yet executed. Lord Churchill agreed to exercise his privilege of royal access to introduce the petitioner. "I wish well to your suit with all my heart," Churchill told her, "but do not flatter yourself with hopes." Putting his hand on the mantelpiece, his lordship observed that "this marble is not harder than the king's heart." Hannah Hewling's last brother was hanged on September 30, 1685.[62]

Churchill's distaste for the cold-blooded royal revenge apparently counted not at all in the face of King James's increased power. The king had taken advantage of the rebellion to raise nine new regiments of horse (he had only two before 1685) and three new regiments of dragoons (previously he had but one, Churchill's old command). Nine new marching regiments more than doubled the numbers of the royal infantry. As the king told the Dutch ambassador, when thanking him for the dispatch of the British-Dutch brigades, Monmouth had performed an essential service in demonstrating to the English ruling class that the county militia were utterly unreliable. So Monmouth had given King James a reason to levy regulars and the parliament an excuse to vote taxes to maintain them. So, said James, he would soon be better able "to be of service to his friends & to be considered and loved by them." By the autumn of 1685, James had over sixteen thousand men under arms, most of them regimented and equipped for the field. By year's end, the royal soldiers numbered almost twenty thousand. Anglo-American officers innumerable would date their service (in their subsequent petitions to Churchill for promotions and posts in America) from 1685. Continuous military expansion (based in large part on taxes on American trade, another association of army and empire) enlisted twenty-two thousand soldiers by 1687. In the autumn of 1688, in the last moments of James's reign, Secretary Blathwayt estimated the authorized strength of the king's army at over forty thousand men.[63]

Mere numbers were not the most repressive part of absolutism's army. The disproportionate number of cavalry in these new formations indicated that King James's army was primarily intended to police England. This was remarked on across the empire. At the outset of militarization, a letter from London informed a Leeward Islands governor that "St. Christopher's may be a good retirement and a better abode than this in a short time, there being six [regiments of] new raised foot and, I think, no less horse to keep us quiet."[64]

Officers of heavy cavalry, however, seldom condescended to imperial service. One exception was Albemarle, who exchanged a troop of the Life Guards for the command of Jamaica. Another exception was Sir Edmund Andros, who traded the lieutenant colonelcy of a new cavalry regiment, Princess Anne's Horse (all of whose officers had household connections to the prince and princess of Denmark and to lord Churchill), for the command of the dominion of New England. The dragoons were more mobile, in every sense, than the heavies. Both the Royals and their new cohorts were full of Tangier veterans, famous for their willingness to fight and to command anywhere. The postrebellion Royals counted two future governors-general, Cornbury of New York and Russell of Barbados, amongst their officers. The newer dragoon regiments would be a ready source of imperial administrators in Churchill's heyday.[65]

Most imperial officers were infantrymen. They were promoted from the more senior marching regiments, as befit those formations' longer professional traditions and superior political connections. Only one of the nine new infantry regiments, the least aristocratic and most professional, bred future governors-general. Initially commanded, quite illegally, by a Catholic, Sir William Clifton's regiment, afterwards known as the 15th, counted among its original officers James Cotter, Thomas Fowke, William Dobbin, and Thomas Whetham, all of whom rose to imperial command.[66]

The first colonel of the 15th was ill, aged, and a mere figurehead for the king's determination to officer his army with Catholics. So the regiment was actually shaped by its officers' dual inheritance: the urban, politicized, garrison government tradition of Nottingham, home to several of the regiment's officers and many of its men; and the imperial, adventurous, and Anglican outlook of the Barbados Regiment and its field officers, Prince Rupert and Edmund Andros, whose captains became the field officers of the 15th. That is, the 15th, from its inception, was Protestant and professional, prepared to do the work of the imperial crown as readily abroad as at home, always providing that that work advanced the reformed religion as the prop and product of royal authority.

The 15th's service in Scotland and the West Indies, in Flanders and the Mediterranean, in Ireland and America, gave the regiment its own ties to each of the three British kingdoms and to every English dependency from Georgia to Minorca. The 15th would provide governors for most of these provinces before its first generation of officers, brought together in the summer of Sedgemoor and identified with lord Churchill and his princess, left the regiment's ranks. The history of the 15th shows in how many dimensions, and to what a high degree, regimental connections, traditions, and service were the cement of English empire.[67]

The lieutenant colonel of the 15th, James Cotter, was a veteran of the Barbados Regiment. He had been deputy governor of Montserrat and, after the 1673 campaign, had seen garrison government service in Ireland. The 15th's senior captain, Thomas Fowke, had also served in the Leeward Islands and in Ireland. As the regiment expanded in the next two years, it added to its field officers Rupert Billingsly, the godson of Prince Rupert and another veteran of the Barbados Regiment. These veterans had brought home with them from the West Indies a number of young planters who took commissions in the army, several in the 15th. Sundry of these American officers would return to the colonies, first as field officers and then as governors-general. James Kendall, Thomas Fowke, the senior William Matthews, all were English army officers and American planters who, through their connections with the 15th Foot, epitomized the legionary links between metropolis and dominion.[68]

The regimental connection exemplified by the 15th was self-consciously imperial, even Roman; its officers "Securing, Inlarging, and Peopling their Conquests . . . so that no Calling had so many Charms to allure at home, as the Profession of the Soldier had abroad." The legionary quality of the 15th Regiment was only one element in that Augustan ethos that grew and spread across the English empire, in large part because of the English army's American service. The Augustan ideal would be personified by lord Churchill in the age of Anne. But the legionary legacy was even longer lived. Regimental colonization had taken place in the wake of the civil war in Ireland and Jamaica. During the Restoration, regiments colonized Tangier, Barbados, and the Leeward Islands. In the reigns of William and of Anne, garrison units would develop the latter two colonies and Newfoundland and Nova Scotia as well. In the Georgian era, Georgia, New York, Florida, and Upper Canada joined the list of legionary settlements.[69]

The 15th legion was linked more closely to lord Churchill and to Princess Anne's household when Captain Edward Nott was promoted from Littleton's marines to become the new regiment's major. Nott's commission completed the alteration in the political and professional complexion of the regiment's field officers that followed the death of its Catholic colonel and that made the 15th an instrument of Churchillian policy. Sackville Tufton, Churchill's colleague in Tangier and in France, was commissioned colonel of the 15th when Rupert Billingsly became lieutenant colonel. The 15th was the most quickly raised and best drilled of the new units, but the moderate politics and Protestant connections of its new field officers boded ill for King James's plans to rule absolutely through a Catholicized army.[70]

The king's plans would be facilitated, and the façade of constitutional government would be preserved, if James could persuade parliament to vote sufficient revenue to support the standing army, to eviscerate the Test Act that forbade his employment of Catholic officers, and to authorize him to arrest and imprison political suspects without a warrant and to imprison them without a trial. The meeting of parliament had been interrupted by Monmouth's and Argyll's rebellions. The rebels' defeat, the execution of their leaders, and the expansion of his own army, all so emboldened King James that he dismissed Halifax from the presidency of the privy council on the eve of parliament's resumption for refusing to support repeal of the Test and Habeas Corpus Acts. These acts were "considered by the English as the bulwarks of the Protestant religion, and the privileges of the nation." Halifax's disgrace was designed as a declaration to the parliament that the Catholic king and his camarilla had rejected political moderation and religious temporizing.[71]

King James's opening speech, November 9, 1685, denounced the bad behavior of the militia during the rebellion. From this, the king concluded that "there is nothing but a good Force of well disciplined Troops in constant Pay that can defend us. . . ." He demanded doubled revenues to pay for the expanded army. In the same breath, James declared that he had commissioned no fewer than seventy-four Catholic officers in the English forces. The king added that he had pardoned each of these officers for their violation of the Test Act. James further asserted that he would keep the Catholic officers at the head of his troops, despite the law, if parliament did not alter it. Having now dispensed with parliamentary statute and armed his co-religionists, the Catholic king of England did not repeat his former promise to preserve the Church of England or to observe the law of the land.[72]

Sir Winston Churchill was the first commoner to support the king. He derided the militia. He mocked the opponents of a permanent, professional army. "The Colonel," as Sir Winston was always called, tended to sloganeering rather than to reason. It was, for him, but a step from his favorite aphorism, "no song, no supper," to saying that "Soldiers move not without Pay. *No Penny, no Pater Noster.*" Nothing could have been better calculated than this courtier's ill-considered contradiction of his previous constitutionalism to reinforce the country party's contentions that the army was to be Catholicized and that its commander, the king, was directed by his priests.[73]

Even those in parliament who had opposed James's exclusion from the throne on account of his religion now recalled that "the Arguments for it were, that we should, in case of a Popish Successor, have a Popish Army." They regretted that the Test Act, which supposedly guaranteed *"that No Papist can possibly creep into any Employment"* was now dispensed with by a Catholic king in favor of Catholic officers. Worse, they said, was the king's demand that parliament repeal the act itself. Some of "the military men" took the lead in opposing repeal for "they saw that, as soon as the king should get rid of the tests, they must either change their religion or lose their employments." Even more than the loss of their commissions, conscientious officers feared that a Catholicized army would restore the old religion by force. These Protestant officers observed that, within the month, Louis XIV had revoked the last edict that protected Protestants, their religion, their lives, their families, and their property. Then Louis had sent in his dragoons to force the Huguenots to convert to Catholicism. An American officer and agent in London learned of the dragonnades from an American governor-general visiting in France. He passed on to his colonial clients his fear that "such changes we may expect, and the consequences of them . . . the cruelties and inhumanities used by the dragoons, who are a new breed of missionary to make converts and settle religion."[74]

Imperial officers and issues also figured in the arguments against increased army expenditure and the commissioning of Catholics. Led by the coterie of the duke of Albemarle, governor-general-elect of Jamaica, headed by Albemarle's uncle, Sir Thomas Charges, the military members of parliament who carried on the imperial traditions of General Monck and the Protectorate now publicly regretted that, in its first flush of loyalty at the moment of King James's accession, the parliament had burdened American trade and naval resource with taxes on tobacco and sugar. Planters, merchants, and shipowners would be discouraged, but worse, so these officers declared, these new American revenues were sufficient to support the king's new army without any of the extra taxes the king now demanded.

Before they would consider additional taxes, the commons condemned James's employment of Catholic officers.[75]

The resolution was carried against the court, and an obviously angry monarch, by but a single vote. The vote was that of James Kendall, the colonist who was now a captain of General Monck's old regiment, the Coldstream Guards. Threatened with dismissal from the service for his vote, Captain Kendall replied that he could do without the king's shilling for "my brother died last night, and has left me £700 a year." Kendall's vote put King James on notice: the imperial ruling class, led by officers of the Anglo-American army, considered the king's employment of Catholic officers and his dispensing with the law to be alike unlawful, and they declared his burdens on imperial trade to be oppressive. The king contemptuously rejected the commons' address for he had discovered that the American revenues indeed sufficed to sustain, even to expand, his army without further recourse to parliament. Nonetheless, James Kendall had become a hero to those of the army officers who now saw that their professional, patriotic, and Protestant duty lay in resisting Catholicism, and France, and in supporting the English church and constitution. Captain Kendall continued to be a leader in the army's opposition to James. John Churchill saw to it that, once the religious threat to army and empire was forcibly eliminated, the former Guards officer was rewarded with the governor-generalship of Barbados.[76]

Churchill himself sat in the lords, a junior peer who had yet to make his maiden speech. The aristocratic opposition to royal dispensation with the law and to the king's commissioning of Catholic army officers was led by three Anglo-American figures. Lord Mordaunt was afterwards governor-general designate of Jamaica. The earl of Halifax had been dismissed from the presidency of the privy council not only because of his refusal to endorse repeal of the Test and Habeas Corpus Acts but also for his principled defense of legislatures and civil corporations, those of Massachusetts and Jamaica in particular. The king had ousted Bishop Compton, the metropolitan of Anglican America, from both the privy council and the chapel royal for arguing that Catholic army officers would create a Catholic kingdom. Speaking in the lords for all the bishops, "at which they all rose up," Compton reiterated his opposition and theirs to Catholic officers. But if the lords persisted in their opposition, they feared that the king might create enough new peers to control the house. When lord Churchill, at dinner with his friends, asked how the king could govern against the lords, that royal bear-warden, lord Sunderland, replied, "O Silly, why your troop of guards shall be called to the house of lords."[77]

When the angry monarch prorogued the parliament on November 20, 1685, contemporaries concluded that the king was now determined to rule "by open force." Even for military rule, however, the king required some aristocratic adjutants, the lords who commanded many of his regiments. In January 1686, no fewer than fifteen of these noble colonels were selected by Judge Jeffreys, acting as lord high steward, to be among the thirty-three peers commissioned as jurors in the treason trial of lord Delamere for complicity in Monmouth's rebellion. As captain of the Life Guards, lord Churchill was the senior officer among the thirty-three triers, but he was the most junior lord. So he had to vote first, in the presence of his commander-in-chief. King James had made it very clear that he expected a verdict of guilty. The verdict was demanded. "The Lord Churchill stood up uncovered," faced his sovereign, "and placing his hand upon his heart, answered Not Guilty, upon my honour. And so did the rest of the Peers." Lord Delamere was spared. King James was furious. Lord Churchill had led the military aristocracy to join the civil and religious lords in opposition to the excesses of King James's armed authority.[78]

King James was not the man to fear the falling barometer of political opinion. As he put it, "I have been used all my life to ruffe weather, and can ply to windward, and you know I do not love to beare up." Instead, he trimmed the military mainsheet of the ship of state. He began by cashiering sixteen officers of the new levies, all members of parliament, for voting for the commons' address against Catholic officers. First among the ousted officers was Captain John Coke of Princess Anne's Foot, a regiment that henceforth led the army's opposition to the king's commissioning of Catholic officers, and to his recruitment of Catholic soldiers. In the commons, Captain Coke had responded to the king's denunciation of the address against Catholic officers with the daring and prophetic words, "we are all Englishmen and we ought not to be frightened out of our duty by a few high words." The commons had sent the captain to the Tower for his disrespect to the king. As soon as the parliament was prorogued the king himself cashiered Coke. The Protestant officer corps's resentment at the royal disgrace of their parliamentary spokesmen (together, as some officers admitted, with the high cost and physical discomfort of the army's annual training camp) led to a rash of resignations. These only opened another dozen places to which the king commissioned Catholic officers, or divine-right Anglican royalists, when he assembled his field army on Hounslow Heath at the end of June 1686.[79]

In so large a force—"in all near 14,000 men" were encamped—the proportion of Catholic officers was small. It did not yet exceed 10 percent (although there are suggestions that a third of the rank and file were Catholics, mostly Scots and Irish). The Catholic officers, however, were disproportionately concentrated in command posts: the field-grade commissions of the royal regiments and the governorships of the key garrisons, both in the British kingdoms and in America. Dover in the Life Guards, Berwick at Portsmouth, Tyrconnel in Ireland and Queensberry in Scotland, Dongan in New York, were but a few of the Catholics who now commanded the strategic centers of army and empire. The most noted army commission to a Catholic was that to Sir Edward Hales as lieutenant of the Tower. It was not just the prominence of his post, the royal citadel in the heart of the metropolis, that brought Hales to the public eye and worried Protestant professionals. Rather it was the collusive challenge to his commission that led the royal judges to declare the legality of the king's power to dispense with the laws. *Gooden v. Hales* practically destroyed the test which had hitherto kept command of the English military the preserve of the established church. Catholic commanders reached the highest council of the empire when the king appointed Catholic privy councilors to replace the Protestant lords whom he had ousted for their opposition to Catholicizing the army. In this context, even the relatively small number of Catholics in the English officer corps seemed to anxious army officers the proverbial cloud, "no bigger than a man's hand," that foretold a monarchical and military storm of religious persecution, political oppression, and imperial subversion.[80]

Catholic courtiers multiplied Protestant anxiety about the English army by asserting that the soldiers were mere mercenaries, without ideals, patriotic, familial, or religious: "the King has not in vain his army at hand, on which he can place sure relyance if he keeps them in good pay, as soldiers & such sort of people do not mind ruining father & mother provided they get money by it, nor even to fight against the Mother Country." To fears of mercenaries, the Catholics added the spectre of the Irish and revived memories of native massacre and religious war by declaring that, in Ireland, King James "has upwards of 8000 well disciplined Soldiers, all of the Roman Catholic religion in readiness." The king could strike for Catholicism, "the more so because the other party are without a head and without arms."[81]

For the moment, Protestant commanders, clerics, and courtiers counseled caution and legality in opposing the king. As Churchill's chaplain explained, his lordship "declin'd acting too familiarly in the present Transactions, yet kept as near His Duty to the King as the Interest of his Country, and the Preservation of His Religion wou'd permit." So far, an American executive was told by his London agent, "we enjoy the free exercise of our religion, as by law established. And it is certainly the interest of every Protestant, as well as his duty, to be loyal and obedient both to God and the king." The Anglican clergy warned their flocks that the king's Catholic counselors hoped for another Protestant revolt to justify wrecking the reformed religion. To keep these obedient Protestants uninformed, the Catholic camarilla persuaded James to order London descriptions of the dragonnades to be burnt. But the court could not quiet the private testimonies of English diplomats, much less the tales told by forty thousand Huguenot refugees spread all across the English empire from London to the

Leeward Islands, from Carolina to New York. Each fugitive had a tale to tell of royal, Catholic religious persecution, property confiscation, and military oppression.[82]

Many of these refugees were soldiers. They invested their Protestant convictions, their financial capital, and their military skill in the growing army of England. King James had issued commissions for a fourth troop of the Life Guards. It was commanded by the Catholic privy councilor, lord Dover. It was supposed to be a military school for young Catholic gentlemen, hitherto barred by law from English military training. Instead, half of the commissions were bought from lord Dover by Huguenot officers, "for if a Turk had come, the fifty guineas had been acceptable to that Lord the Captain." Several of the Huguenot officers and gentleman troopers of the 4th Troop quickly became devoted subordinates of lord Churchill, now the executive officer of the Life Guards. Churchill himself continued in royal favor, despite his Anglican devotion, because the king considered him "a popular Man, and one that bore no small sway among the English nobility." Churchill, although he saw the crash coming, "by an Extraordinary vigalence, secur'd the King's good Graces, yet acted with that reserv'd caution as the present occasion requir'd."[83]

Leaving his Horse Guards in their Westminster barracks (some of them were meeting houses confiscated from Presbyterians, because they resisted the royal plans for religious indulgence, whereas the troops left Penn's Quakers undisturbed and they actively protected Catholic chapels), lord Churchill rode out to the camp on Hounslow Heath. There, in August 1686, he took up his command as a major general on the expanded general staff. The field army in England was now large enough to maneuver by wing or division instead of by squadron or regiment, and to march by brigade rather than by company. It exercised by the dicta of a uniform drill book. It was disciplined, in matters civil as well as military and, now, in peacetime as well as wartime, by court martials. In the first of these, at Hounslow, in June of 1686, the king declared "that in future the Soldiers should be placed under Martial Law." Critics instantly observed that martial law was "contrary to the Laws of the Country, which do not allow that in time of peace any other than the ordinary Civil Laws should be in force." The king's court martials were designed "to withdraw the soldiery from the civil power." James II sought to make the military a caste legally separate from (and superior to) civilian subjects.[84]

A law unto itself, the tent city of an entire army was now seen for the first time in England. At right angles to a front of a mile and a half ran the ruler-straight regimental streets, lined with the tents that sheltered more than ten thousand troops. At the foot of each street stood a triangle of officers' marquees, the colonel's at its apex. The opposite end of the regimental street was punctuated by a bell tent that protected the regiment's new snaphance muskets and its two brass field guns. Next door, the sergeants' orderly tent opened onto the vast parade ground, three miles long. The parade itself was bounded by the artillery park (its guards, lord Dartmouth's fusiliers, also held the Thames bridge) and by the general's camp. There the parsimonious lord Churchill was put to agonizing expense to entertain his royal commander-in-chief.[85]

There too stood the royal mass tent. When the weather permitted, the great tent's flies were furled so that all the soldiers could see their commander-in-chief worshiping at the daily Catholic celebrations. The officers who entered the mass tent, who knelt at the elevation of the Host (Captain Francis Nicholson among them, as Protestant soldiers in New York would angrily recall), made themselves marked men in the coming military struggle over the religion and the constitution of the empire. For, as the encampment continued, it became daily clearer that, despite the Catholic king's public example and the occasional officer's defection to his sovereign's religion, the army would remain Protestant and would therefore be essentially constitutional. The Protestant officers of the English army were militant members of the political nation. James II failed in his attempt to make them a separate caste, even as he put them on the road to becoming members of a military profession and to administering England's expanding empire as the preeminent representatives of a new class. The loyalist earl of Ailesbury wrote that he was not sure what use the king intended for the army encamped on Hounslow Heath, "but this I know, that instead of being a security to him, many chief officers so empoisoned the others, that in process of time, they were the instruments of all the King's misfortunes."[86]

The army intended to overawe London was instead confirmed in its Anglican faith by the imperial capital's defiantly Protestant clergy. "It was very plain," an Anglican observer wrote, "that such an army was not to be trusted in any quarrel in which religion was concerned." This was so because the camp educated the soldiers as much in mores as in marching. "In one tent is masses, in another common prayer," wrote a visitor to Hounslow, so "every sentinel will be able to dispute the point." "The point" the army debated was the religious and political future of the empire. It was the union of "arms and argument" that made the royal army the dominant force in imperial politics, "for what was before shared between the gownmen and the swords men will probably be found in one man." That man, the religiously informed, politically conscious, nationally patriotic soldier, and that soldier's exemplar, lord Churchill, would determine the future of the English church, monarchy, and empire. Even the king's Catholic confidants began to doubt the army's reliability in any constitutional crisis that was couched in religious terms: "God preserve the King when he realizes that his troops will not be faithful to him, for they are English."[87]

Even a king besotted with the idea that because he treated his soldiers well they would be loyal could see these problems. He applied brutal, but ineffective, remedies. The clergyman who distributed in the camp his "Address to the English Protestants in King James's Army" (asking them how they could save the reformed religion and the English nation if they obeyed Catholic and Irish officers) was pilloried, fined, and whipped at the cart's tail from Newgate to Tyburn. There his pamphlet was burned before him.[88]

The scourging of Samuel Johnson, the domestic chaplain of the Russells (whose master had been beheaded before his own doorway in Lincoln's Inn Fields, just as his lawyers had been executed at the gates of their Inns), infamous though it became, made little impression compared with the degradation of Henry Compton, the Life Guards officer turned bishop of London, the metropolitan of America, the tutor of Princess Anne, and an advisor of lord Churchill. On September 6, 1686, the king's new ecclesiastical commission silenced and suspended the bishop for reminding them that the commission itself was expressly forbidden by parliament; for his criticism in the lords of the king's speech on his Catholic officers; for implying that the royal dispensation of the test was unlawful; and for refusing to stop his clergy's preaching against Catholic "idolaters," a term, the ecclesiastical commission observed, that "causes an immediate and odious reflection upon our Sovereign." King James threatened bishop Compton with transportation to America if he was not silent and the bishop's American clergy were immediately informed of their metropolitan's suspension. Henceforward, they reported, reluctantly, to the episcopal commission that superseded Compton. King James complained that Compton spoke to him "more like a Colonel than a Bishop" about his suspension. Indeed, the bishop voiced many a colonel's sentiments when he replied that "H.M. did him honour in taking notice of his having formerly drawn his sword in defence of the constitution, and he should do the same thing again, if he lived to see it necessary."[89]

During the summer of 1686, the necessity of an armed defense of the constitution seemed more imminent to "the Protestant Bishop," to his army associates, and to the chaplains he had appointed to the garrisons, fleet, and colonies. They had begun to react against the Catholicizing work of lord Churchill's brother-in-law, a longtime member of James Stuart's household, "mad Dick" Talbot, earl of Tyrconnel. After a year's work in "reforming" the army in Ireland to King James's specifications, Tyrconnel was promoted the king's lieutenant general in Ireland in June 1686. To English officers it seemed that Tyrconnel had already transformed the Protestant English army of occupation into a Catholic national force, designed to undo the Cromwellian conquest and colonization of Ireland.

Having broken the English army's military grip on the greatest province of the empire, it seemed that Tyrconnel might even achieve the island's independence from England by defying the parliamentary acts of trade and navigation, by putting all royal offices in Irish Catholic hands, and by obtaining the protection of imperial France for an Irish client state. If King James did not entirely agree with Tyrconnel's objectives—for he shared the usual English prejudices against colonial elites as rebellious and against "natives" as heathen—the king nonetheless endorsed Tyrconnel's Catholic army—with its "Old English" officers and its Celtic recruits—as the instrument that would destroy the Protestant ascendancy in Ireland before being transported overseas to enforce Catholicism in England and America. The shorthand of these conclusions were the military appointments Blathwayt reported to his American correspondents: that (the Catholic purger of the Protestant army) Tyrconnel had replaced (the symbol of churchly legitimacy) Clarendon in command of Ireland, and that the king had cashiered the earl of Shrewsbury and lord Lumley (as colonels of English horse) and was giving their regiments to the likes of (the Catholic) lord Langdale.[90]

By August 1686, when Tyrconnel came to court to displace the Anglican lord lieutenant, the earl of Clarendon, he had made the Irish army officer corps more than one-third Catholic. By September, the muster master in Ireland estimated that two-thirds of the army had been recast in a Catholic mold. Thirty-six of Thomas Dongan's former subordinates from France got commissions in the remodeled Irish army, on the same Catholicizing principle that Dongan himself was applying to the garrison government of New York. Indeed, Tyrconnel personally ordered Dongan to come home from New York to take an Irish command. (Dongan declined.) In January 1687, Tyrconnel entered Dublin as lord deputy of Ireland. In the ensuing year he cashiered all but a few of the remaining Protestant officers. All of the ousted officers were long-service veterans of the English army in Ireland. Such officers as George Sloughter, cornet to the duke of Ormonde's cavalry in Dublin, Benjamin Fletcher, a garrison commander in Leitrim, and Richard Ingoldsby, who, after eight years of army service, had finally achieved company command, were ousted from their commands in Ireland. First they would fight to undo the Catholic counterrevolution in England and Ireland. Then they would supersede Dongan's Catholics in command of New York. Catholics or Protestants, James's officers or William's, all these officers embodied the forgotten, but essential, Irish military element in the transformation of New York from a Dutch and ducal colony into a British and imperial province.[91]

Sloughter, Fletcher, and Ingoldsby were military clients of the former, famous, loyal, and long-term lord lieutenant, the duke of Ormonde. Ormonde now began to withdraw his movables from Ireland, advised his officers to seek service overseas, and wrote that "I had rather live and die in Carolina than in Ireland." Driven from Ireland, Protestant professionals found commands in the expanding army in England. These refugee officers discovered in their new colleagues an attentive audience for their warnings of the Irish Catholic menace to Protestant English professionals. As more aristocratic and more whiggish officers evacuated Ireland, they told Churchill and others of their English peers that raw Catholic Celts—"the O's and the Macs"—would oust their Anglican betters in England as they had in Ireland, if James Stuart had his way. These warnings also spread from "the Plantations" in Ireland to the American plantations.[92]

The transatlantic transit of prejudice and politics was epitomized in the career of a fourth New York viceroy from Ireland, Richard Coote, afterwards earl of Bellomont. Despite his family's record of loyalism, even during the Interregnum, Coote was cashiered from his command as a captain of cavalry in the duke of Ormonde's own regiment in Ireland. He fled to London where, like other Anglo-Irish officers, he told his English associates that King James had "made his Will his Law" in Ireland and that Tyrconnel's military purge and the flight of the Protestant officer elite from Ireland were evidence of the king's intent to establish "*Popery* and *Arbitrary Power*" everywhere in the empire. Coote, and his fellow officer exiles, warned their English counterparts that Catholic commanders would not only impose a counterrevolution in religion and politics, but even in property. Not just in Ireland but in England, Protestants' estates—the lands of the pre-Reformation church—were in danger of confiscation. The creation of a Catholic military establishment, first in Ireland and next in England, was the first step toward a comprehensive counterreformation.[93]

Having warned English Protestant officers what Ireland portended, Coote, and many officers like him, crossed the Channel to commands in the British brigades being built up by William of Orange. As Coote put it when he informed King James of his transfer of allegiance, "now that his highness the Prince of Orange is pleas'd to give me the Command of a Company of Foot in the English troops that are in the Service of the States, I have thought it my duty to acquaint his Maty . . . that I accept his highness' favour, Intending to apply my Selfe to the study of arms the better to qualifie my self for the Service of my King and Country." That service, in Coote's case, involved the invasion of England, the deposition of King James, the reconquest of Ireland, and the reform of New York and Massachusetts.[94]

The two British brigades, three regiments each of Scots and of English, something over three thousand strong, in the service of the states general, were under the command of Prince William. On July 4, 1685, the soldiers of the Scots brigade had expressed their hostility to James II, his religion, and his francophilia when they paraded in London. They had been sent over to help repress Monmouth's rebellion but three Scots soldiers were condemned by court martial for drinking Monmouth's health as the Prot-

Henry Bishop of London, *I. Riley, pinx., I. Beckett, fec., mezzotinto engraving from the author's collection.*

The Seven Bishops prosecuted by order of James II for libel; acquitted June 30th, 1687, *I. Oliver, fec., mezzotinto engraving from the author's collection.*

The Right Reverend Father in God Gilbert Lord Bishop of Sarum, *Ino. Riley, pinx., I. Smith, fec., mezzotinto engraving from the author's collection.*

James, duke of Monmouth. G. Kneller, pinx., John Smith, fec., mezzotinto engraving courtesy of the British Museum.

The Right Honble. Lewis Earle of Feversham, *I. Riley, pinx., I. Smith, ex., I. Beckett, fec., mezzotinto engraving from the author's collection.*

The Portsmouth CAPTAINS, *R. White, fec., mezzotinto engraving courtesy of the British Museum.*

Frederick Duke
of Schomberg,
G. Kneller, pinx.,
I. Smith, fec.,
mezzotinto
engraving from
the author's
collection.

A Life Guardsman who turned cleric after the age of thirty, the scion of a great family in a church usually administered as an arm of the state by men elevated not by birth but by learning, sycophancy, and intrigue, Henry Compton, bishop of London, presided over the most political of English dioceses, one which included not just the metropolis but also America and the navy. Compton was responsible for the Anglican education of the Protestant princesses, Mary and Anne. He publicly defied the king their father's Catholicism. Although deprived of office by the furious James II, Compton carried out his threat to use force to defend the Anglican constitution by rescuing Anne and Sarah, Anne's favorite, from Whitehall at the crisis of lord Churchill's coup, escorting them to the head of the northern rising, and taking command himself of a rebel regiment.

Reduced to private status, Compton could not join the public resistance against the royal declaration of religious indulgence by the seven bishops who are here portrayed in a most popular print. Contemporary notes in the margin provide the surnames of, from top right, Francis Turner, bishop of Ely; Thomas Ken, bishop of Bath and Wells; Jonathan Trelawney, bishop of Bristol; Thomas White, bishop of Peterborough; John Lake, bishop of Chichester, William Lloyd, bishop of St. Asaph, and, in the center, the archbishop of Canterbury, William Sancroft. In their efforts to save their church, these bishops underwrote a Protestant putsch. Like bishop Turner, lord Churchill's confessor and counselor in the coup, the bishops all (save perhaps the militant and aristocratic Trelawney) wished to force King

James back onto an Anglican course. Like lord Churchill, they did not intend to depose the sacred monarch. Save for Lloyd and Trelawney, these bishops all refused to take the oaths of allegiance to King William and were deprived.

Their story—indeed, most of the stories of the age—are treated in Gilbert Burnet's *History of His Own Time*. It is at once its author's monument and his indictment, prolix, self-serving, and indispensable.

> *Prompt to assail, and careless of defence,*
> *Invulnerable in his impudence,*
> *He dares the world, and eager of a name,*
> *He thrusts about and justles into fame.*

Propagandist of the Protestant putsch, bishop Burnet became Marlborough's client when, in 1698, the earl nominated him to be governor to the duke of Gloucester. So Burnet acquired John Churchill's tory enemies to add to his own:

> *If such a soul to heaven stole,*
> *And passed the devil's clutches.*
> *I do presume there may be room*
> *For Marlboro' and his duchess.*

To the blackcoats of the clergy, contemporaries added the redcoats of the officers as the indispensable agents of the state and the essential opponents of King James. Rescued by John Churchill at Maestricht and subsequently captain general of England, James duke of Monmouth was Charles II's favorite child. In the words of Anthony Hamilton, the gossip of the Caroline court, the bastard duke was a man of "astonishing beauty"; however, "he was greatly deficient in mental accomplishments. He had no sentiments but such as others inspired him with." Thus this king's son became a republican tool. After being defeated by lord Churchill at Sedgemoor, Monmouth was beheaded by his uncle, James II.

Monmouth's nominal captor was Louis de Duras, earl of Feversham. Nephew of Turenne and brother of two French dukes, Duras became a Stuart courtier, was distinguished at Lowestoff, and made ambassador to France. He commanded the royal forces in the west in 1685 and King James's field army in 1688. Rewarded for his services of 1685 with the earldom of Feversham and successive command of the three troops of the Horse Guards, "he was an honest, brave, and good natured man, but weak to a degree not easy to be conceived."

The disaffection of the army Feversham commanded was epitomized by "The Portsmouth CAPTAINS." Led by Lieutenant Colonel John Beaumont, the executive officer of Princess Anne's Regiment, then in garrison at Portsmouth, these captains refused the king's three questions, rejected his attempt to recruit their companies with Irish Catholics, and printed their rebuff of the governor of Portsmouth, the duke of Berwick, King James's son by Arabella Churchill. The Portsmouth captains were court martialed and cashiered with all the publicity lord Churchill could arrange. So these officers served as the catalyst of Churchill's coup. He promoted most of them during his post-coup purge of the officer corps. Beaumont became colonel and Simon Pack lieutenant colonel of Princess Anne's Regiment (the 8th foot). Thomas Paston was promoted lieutenant colonel of marines and William Cook was commissioned lieutenant colonel of lord Lovelace's regiment. Thomas Orme and John Port are untraced. As the former was an elderly man of a loyalist family, he is apt to have retired.

Certainly an elderly officer, and another whose loyalty was determined by his religion, Frederick duke of Schomberg was a German Protestant, born in Heidelberg in 1615. An officer at age eighteen, Schomberg served in the Swedish, French, and Dutch armies. He joined the French general staff in 1652 and commanded the combined Franco-British force in Portugal 1661–1668, becoming a marshal of France in 1675. Schomberg left the French service on the revocation of the Edict of Nantes to command the forces of Brandenburg. Thence William of Orange recruited the most experienced Protestant general in Europe to second his invasion of England. Schomberg's reward was the ordnance office which Marlborough coveted. Sent to lead the reconquest of Ireland in 1689, Schomberg's refusal to advance destroyed the allied army in Dundalk camp and disgraced him with William. Even after Schomberg was killed leading the crossing of the Boyne, William denied him a distinguished burial. Schomberg's black page memorializes the two hundred Surinamese troops who were an impressive element of William's invasion force.

estant king. The French ambassador feared that these Protestant troops would act to advance Prince William's claim to the imperial throne. When they were brigaded under Hugh Mackay on Hounslow Heath in 1686, it was unclear whether the Scots were more affecting or affected by the anti-popery and francophobia of the English army. King James recognized the Scots' military and so political importance. He offered a major general's commission in the English army to the Scots' brigadier, and King James named Mackay a privy councilor in Scotland.[95]

When, early in 1687, lord Churchill once again sought leave from the army of King James to take command of the British brigades in the states' service, under Prince William's command, he made a political and religious statement as well as a military declaration. Churchill sought an honorable escape toward military advancement, away from the impending crisis of loyalty that, as the Irish counterrevolution had now made clear, faced every one of King James's Protestant English officers. Churchill's application to serve under Prince William's command may also have been the first public indication of his coming change of allegiance. Certainly Churchill now saw that every one of the king's steps away from the Anglican ruling class was a step toward France, Catholicism, and counterreformation. More than ever, William of Orange appeared to such officers as Churchill to be the last champion of the reformed religion, the ultimate enemy of France, "so warlike and daring a spirit that in history he may hereafter rival Lewis in the title of great."[96]

As he had since 1678, William wanted to command Churchill's military services. Once again, James refused to permit his Protestant heir presumptive to acquire his most able soldier. Instead, King James recommended an Irish peer, Francis Taafe, earl of Carlingford, whose qualifications for command were his Catholicism, his nationality, and his subservience to the king. When William refused to accept Taafe, James tried to disband both the English and the Scots brigades in the Netherlands. He ordered his subjects home. The king offered Catholics and Protestant loyalists from the British brigades posts in three new regiments, Irish, Scots, and English. They (as James hoped) were to be paid by Louis XIV. He apparently agreed with James that, by subsidizing the new corps, he would both weaken the Protestant Netherlands and strengthen his co-religionists in England. In these new regiments, King James told his French patron and exemplar, Catholics would be educated in arms and loyalty. King James hoped that these Catholic corps, when added to the re-officered English units and the new Irish Catholic army, would overawe the Protestant constitutionalists of the English army.[97]

If the army's Protestants revolted rather than accept service with the Catholics and the Irish, the king could "risk the chance with certainty." He would use the failed coup as an excuse to purge all the army's Protestant officers. Moderate Catholics, however, warned James that, by Catholicizing the army, he risked "his whole welfare, crown and life." For, they said, the English military opposition was rapidly organizing against this "threatening evil." The attempted recall of the British brigades from the Netherlands was seen, even by these Catholic observers, as a military act obviously designed to weaken the Dutch refuge of the king's opponents and to deflate the hopes of Protestant monarchists for the ultimate accession of William and Mary. The recall of the British brigades would force even politically moderate Protestants to plot with whigs and republicans to protect the reformed churches and the free, maritime states.[98]

The crisis was delayed because the plans of the Catholic kings of England and France to eviscerate the British brigades in the Netherlands were foiled. Fewer than half the British officers obeyed King James's command, and many of them were on a mission from Prince William. The privates were not allowed to leave the Netherlands on the grounds that no prince's commands could override the military law that bound the troops of the states to their posts on pain of death (even though there were Dutch officers who argued that it would be desirable to replace with Protestant refugees all the English: "those troublesome troops who always demand choice of quarters, the best garrisons, & higher pay"). The officer departures had two advantages. First, they enabled Prince William to infiltrate his uncle's new regiments and crucial garrisons with Protestant officers loyal to himself. Second, every officer who returned to England opened a command in the British brigades for one of the Anglo-Irish exiles or for one of the English officers who now declined to ask leave of King James (they saw how far that got Churchill) but quietly took commissions in the British-Dutch regiments they would lead back to England.[99]

For the same reasons that they objected to King James's Catholic, Celtic, absolutist, and francophile policies in Ireland, England, and the Netherlands, officers of Churchill's ilk—"Zealous Protestants" and "the anti-french party"—feared the imperial impact of King James's rapprochement with France in America. As governor of the Hudson's Bay Company, lord Churchill believed that the new Treaty of American Neutrality between England and France rewarded French aggression in America. Preliminary articles for "the Treaty of Whitehall" were signed in May 1686. It was the only public expression of the absolutist entente between the crowns of France and England. As such it was opposed in parliament. The final treaty, signed on November 6/16, 1686, did not satisfy imperialists any more than it did parliamentarians. It failed to counteract the large French trans-Appalachian claims raised by LaSalle's voyage; it did not settle the boundaries of Maine or New York; it did nothing to redress French aggression in Hudson Bay. Rather, because the treaty was concluded before the English learned of the French raids of 1686, it apparently endorsed both

French conquests in Hudson Bay and French attacks on the Seneca allies of New York. Most effectively, the treaty manifested the desire of the two Catholic kings "to establish more and more, day by day, mutual friendship between themselves and a sincere concord and correspondence between their kingdoms, dominions, and subjects" by concluding "a treaty of peace, good correspondence, and neutrality in America."[100]

Churchill had been the diplomatic agent of an Anglo-French entente as James Stuart's servant but he now made public his opposition to King James's imperial amity with France. Despite the peace between these two powers in Europe, in America Anglo-French hostilities extended from Hudson Bay to the Leeward Islands. In every theatre, lord Churchill thought the French at fault. In French estimation, Churchill's opposition to the treaty, officially on behalf of the Hudson's Bay Company, was its chief obstacle in England. Both at the time and after the coming coup, there were those who said that Churchill's opposition to the American expression of the entente of James and Louis was inspired, if not directed, by the Prince of Orange, to whom Churchill had already pledged his services in support of the Protestant religion and so (as he thought) of English interests, national and imperial.[101]

The American treaty that Churchill criticized had its origin in the local truce arranged between Sir William Stapleton, the Catholic governor-general of the Leeward Islands, and his French former comrades-in-arms who commanded the adjacent islands. In subsequent negotiations elsewhere in the West Indies, as well as in New York and about Hudson Bay, the French governors-general boasted the amity of Louis XIV and James II and projected an expansion of the Leeward Islands' truce into a general neutrality between all the provinces of the two powers in America. The French viceroys felt that a Franco-American peace, arranged by Catholic commanders, would benefit absolutism and Catholicism in England as well. Denonville wrote from New France to Dongan in New York that, as fellow soldiers and Catholics, "we should imitate our masters in the close alliance of friendship and union existing between them, for the re-establishment of Royal Authority in England and the restoration of the Gospel there in its ancient lustre."[102]

In Europe too, the Anglo-French Treaty of American Neutrality was seen as the alliance of the Catholic kings against the reformed religion and the decentralized, libertarian, and armed institutions (the Netherlands' states and the English counties and colonies) that protected religious and political dissent from Catholicism and absolutism. When the Dutch ambassador taxed King James with trying to neutralize imperial quarrels with France in America so that he could first disarm Anglicanism in England and then join King Louis in eliminating the states, reclaiming the refugees, and attacking Protestantism, James replied that "between him and France there existed nothing else but a treaty . . . respecting their differences in America, in which there was nothing suspicious &c." In fact, the Treaty of American Neutrality was James II's imperial offering to Louis XIV in return for his support for Catholicism and authoritarianism in England. The agreement about America was also the first earnest of England's support for French aggression in Europe. James's protestations about the isolation of American diplomacy from European concerns were not believed, either by the Dutch ambassador or by the English imperialists.[103]

Some colonists were more sanguine, seeking local advantage from both the proposed neutrality between England and France in America and the worsening religious and political climate in Europe. Colonial agents believed that they could recruit their tiny populations with Monmouth's rebels and disbanded Protestant soldiers, as well as with Protestant refugees from Scotland, Ireland, and France. The American agents expected that these religious, militant, anti-French settlers would be the successors of the puritans, expressing in a new generation the crusading character of American societies. Protestant English expansionists also hoped that this new generation of refugees from Catholicism and absolutism would increase staple crop production, expand the fur trade, and so widen the English imperial frontier until the French colonies were overwhelmed. Blathwayt, however, told American agents that he feared that if the French "tied our hands" by the proposed treaty, they would be able to eradicate the Dutch and Spanish presence in America. Then the French would also turn the English out of America. The colonial agents, the secretary of war and plantations added, made three erroneous assumptions in their negotiations with the French: that the French were blind to the menace of English expansion in America; that the French were foolish enough to keep to the terms of a treaty that permitted English expansion; that the French were prepared to abandon that militant expansion of their territory and their religion that had made them, as lord Churchill put it, "the ill Neighbours of all Mankind."[104]

On February 17, 1687, lord Churchill presented to King James the Hudson's Bay Company's protest—based in part on intelligence Churchill had just received from New York and Boston—that the French were continuing to attack English outposts and traders, ships and seafarers on the New York, Maine, and Hudson Bay frontiers. They had done so for the last five years. Instead of retaliating, Churchill complained, the king had completed the preliminary articles of the treaty in May 1686. Despite fresh French aggression, in November, the king had approved the Treaty of American Neutrality itself. He had then appointed commissioners to execute the amicable intent of the treaty. Unconfined by any specific terms, these commissioners were now negotiating a comprehensive settlement of all Anglo-French disputes, territorial, commercial, diplomatic, or military, in America. The ownership of the Leeward Islands and the "country of the Iroquois," the boundaries of Acadia, the seizure of New England fishermen on the Grand Banks, all were on the table, but to Churchill the chief dispute was control of the enormous territories of the Hudson Bay watershed. It was as governor of the Hudson's Bay Company that Churchill became the leading exponent of English imperial expansion.[105]

Lord Churchill protested to the king and the commissioners that, at the very moment that the French entered into the nonaggression pact of 1686, they had captured three English trading posts on the southern shores of Hudson Bay, together with the purpose-built frigate, the *Churchill* (another post was now named "Fort Churchill" and, with the Churchill River and its Cape, still memorializes the governor's abiding imperial influence). Then the French had turned the English traders out to starve in the wilderness. Lord Churchill reminded his sovereign that the company he represented had received "from your own Royall mouth, the assurance of Yor Maty protection and care to see them righted." Such was Churchill's own prestige, the influence of the imperial lobby (Churchill was backed by the earl of Craven, the Carolina proprietor and colonel of the Coldstream Guards, and, it was said, by the duke of Albemarle, and the governor-general of Jamaica's "interest"), and the king's own prior commitment to the Hudson's Bay Company, whose directors now stood before him, that King James replied, "Gentlemen, I understand your business, my honour, and your money are concerned, and I assure you I will take particular care to see you righted."[106]

The king had indeed instructed his commissioners to demand reparations and restoration, but the French had justified Canadian hostilities by vague references to Louis XIV's territorial claims and to Indian treaties. Despite Churchill's repeated interventions on behalf of the Hudson's Bay Company, and the facts presented by Churchill's chief contact on the board, William Young, the commissioners of the two crowns could come to no resolution. So, on May 17, 1687, lord Churchill widened the argument against France in America (having just agreed with William of Orange to join him against King James, and so against France, in Europe).

Churchill declared that "the wandering and variable dispositions" of the natives made concessions from them worthless, although, Churchill said, he could produce "Submissions and Capitulations of those people, wch do very much affect the ffrench Interests." If bogus French discoveries were added to vague native cessions, Churchill went on, "there would be no safety for his Majestys subjects in America" (or at least in those provinces of the Restoration empire acquired since the Treaty of Breda in 1667) "should the French think fit to seize them." Once the French had decided to attack an English possession, "it would not be difficult for them to allege imaginary Discoveries, or even to prove that 5 or 6 ffrench had passed that way before and made some contact with the Indians. It is more reasonable to reply [sic] upon actual Discoveries & upon possession taken in view of all the World. . . ." Such English possession the French could only offset by the violence with which they asserted the grandiose claims of Louis XIV. Mere monarchical claims to American territory, Churchill said to King James, were unsupported by "the Law of Nations & of Nature." Both these elements of international law provided that actual European exploration and permanent European settlement were the necessary preconditions of imperial possession. It was on these lawful foundations, lord Churchill stated, that the English empire in America rested.[107]

As instances, Churchill cited the Restoration provinces of Carolina and Pennsylvania, both founded since the last American adjustment with France, the Treaty of Breda. Both were colonies of which Churchill had acquired particular knowledge while an officer of James's household. Carolina was the quintessentially aristocratic colonial experiment, the laboratory of social and political ideas for several factions in the imperial privy council. Shaftesbury's (and his secretary, John Locke's) constitutions for Carolina are well known, but the Carolina basis for conspiracies against the crown, and the refuge that the colony offered to religious and political dissenters, were more widely remarked on in the latter 1680s. Even King James, however, had approved his Scottish Catholic councilors' suggestion that those who disliked their regime should migrate to Carolina. The loyalist military magnates, the earls of Bath and Craven, also held proprietary interests in Carolina, England's southern continental frontier. They passed them on to their military subordinates, Craven to Andros, Grenville to Elliot.[108]

Of course, Churchill also mentioned Pennsylvania to King James as a recent example of the actual colonization that authenticated English imperial claims. Published discoveries and lawful possession were the titles that Churchill was determined to establish in international law. Otherwise "His Majesties Plantations aforementioned and other Provinces and Countries in America would be laid open to the Pretentions and like Invasions of the ffrench" as Hudson Bay had been in 1682 and 1686. While Churchill was the then duke's agent in London, James had given Pennsylvania to William Penn in return for Penn's support against exclusion. Now "the Arch Quaker Penn" was "travelling through the Country in order to gain as many of his persuasion to the side and party of the king as possible." In fact, Penn was the leading man in King James's stagy effort to win the support of Protestant religious dissenters for the royal Declaration of Indulgence (that is, for the king's suspension of the laws that penalized dissenters from the Church of England). Indeed, Penn himself may have drafted the declaration for King James. Penn also favored packing parliament to repeal the Test and Penal Acts. Penn wished to import into England Pennsylvania's particular contribution to the imperial constitution: freedom for dissent from Anglicanism.[109]

The American provinces were the political laboratories of the English empire. The declaration, which argued for liberty of conscience as a public good, promoting trade, encouraging immigration, and stimulating artisan production and merchandise, reflected James's own policy in New York as well as Penn's in Pennsylvania. For both proprietors, however, it was hatred of the persecuting Church of England and devotion to their own dissenting beliefs that underlay their American policy and the Declaration of Indulgence. Both the prince and the proprietor expected their executive toleration to evoke personal loyalty from dissenting populations and to overthrow Anglican legalism. France must be conciliated and Anglican imperialism must be restrained if religious liberty was to be won in England, for a forward imperial policy required parliamentary financing and parliament was as yet the legal preserve of the Church of England. So it was that the Treaty of Whitehall was the American concomitant of the Declaration of Indulgence. Therefore, "Church," in his protest against the Treaty of American Neutrality, bespoke his faith as well as his geopolitics.[110]

In conclusion, lord Churchill moved from the English ownership of Pennsylvania to his main point: only force would check French aggression in America. The Hudson's Bay Company brief begged the king to "let loose Your Majestys Subjects in New England and your other Plantations upon the French in America." Churchill also asked for, and, more remarkably, he obtained, royal letters of marque and reprisal. These authorized the Hudson's Bay Company to outfit private men of war and to launch them against French shipping, presumably in American waters, to recover the company's losses. Secret though they were, these letters of marque were King James's concession to lord Churchill's determination to physically resist French imperial aggression. In public, however, the Anglo-French commissioners continued to seek an agreement about America between James and Louis that would manifest their entente in Europe. So Churchill learned from his most intimate friend, Sidney, lord Godolphin, one of the English commissioners under the Treaty of American Neutrality.[111]

Godolphin, and the English commissioners, were briefed on the English position in America by lord Churchill's colleague in the administration of the army and the empire, William Blathwayt, the secretary at war and auditor general of the plantations. Blathwayt began his brief by recapitulating lord Churchill's complaints of French aggression in Hudson Bay and Strait, and by repeating, almost verbatim, Churchill's arguments for English sovereignty in America and against the vast French claims to the American north and west. Turning east and south, Blathwayt demanded the restitution of English fishing vessels seized by the French off Acadia.

He insisted that New York's fishing and fur trading outpost at Pemaquid in Maine, a longtime concern of James's imperial household, was a possession of the imperial crown of England.[112]

Then Blathwayt discussed the western borderlands of the duke's old province and of those marcher lords, the Iroquois. Blathwayt argued that Churchill's old comrade, the governor-general of New York, Thomas Dongan, and the king's venturesome subjects in that province, were right to arm the Iroquois as New York's best protection against French aggression. The Iroquois, Blathwayt wrote, were English subjects. So the king was "obliged to protect and support those Indians in the like manner of his other subjects." Those of the Iroquois captured by the French (and, worse, enslaved in French galleys) must be reclaimed by the English negotiators. So too, said Blathwayt (repeating Dongan's despatches to Sunderland), others of his majesty's subjects, seized by the French during their pursuit of lawful trade, must be released. Besides the Hudson's Bay Company employees (whose case lord Churchill had argued), Blathwayt had in mind that venturesome Scottish imperialist, Major Patrick MacGregorie, and his men, both Iroquois and British, who had been seized by the French on the upper Great Lakes.[113]

The Scots and the Iroquois, both quintessential frontiersmen, acted on the orders and reflected the continental vision of that Irish aristocrat, Thomas Dongan, King James's governor-general of New York. The efforts of the French to have this aggressive and sharp-sighted enemy of Canada recalled were linked with Tyrconnel's effort to Catholicize the Irish military as the basis of an independent kingdom (to be declared on the advent of a Protestant successor in England). The Franco-Irish initiative was expressed in Tyrconnel's order to Dongan to return to Ireland to command the artillery, with rank second only to the lord deputy on the Irish general staff. Dongan resisted, writing to his royal commander-in-chief that he would accept no orders but the king's to leave the command of New York. Dongan's pecuniary reasons were obvious: the province owed him more than £6,000 for his advances to arm the provincial army against French aggression. Dongan's imperial interest was equally apparent: it was the Irish general who saw most clearly the dimensions of the contest for America between France and England. So Dongan recognized his own historic opportunity as the leader of the English and their Iroquoian allies. It was he who reported the French strikes against the Hudson Bay posts and the Iroquois towns; who explained them as assaults on the confines of Canada; who predicted the dangers to the future of every English province, from New York to the Carolinas, from French exploration and control of the Ohio and Mississippi rivers; and who took every opportunity to sabotage both the principles of the Treaty of American Neutrality and the specific orders for the cessation of hostilities produced by the Anglo-French commissioners to execute the treaty.[114]

In March 1687, Blathwayt sent Dongan copies of the treaty in English and in Latin but, Dongan replied, the crux was in the French version. "The French have been too crafty for us," Dongan wrote to Blathwayt. "In ye 3d article ye word Savage is used without adding Indians in ye french copy, but in the English its exprest wilde Indians, to distinguish them from those who submit themselves to Government," as the Iroquois had done, most recently in the 1684 brightening of the Covenant Chain. Given this loophole, the French had invaded Seneca country and burnt both the capital and the cornfields of the keepers of the western door of Anglo-Iroquoian empire.[115]

Dongan had responded with all the force at his command. He wrote his protest against the clever French in Albany, where he was spending the winter of 1687–88 with 450 men of the New York provincial army and 800 Iroquois warriors to counter French threats to ravage both Albany and the Iroquois towns. Alarmed by Dongan's despatches that Louis XIV had sent 3,000 additional troops to garrison Canada and attack the English and the Iroquois, King James ordered his viceroy in New York to protect the Five Nations of the Iroquois, as his subjects. Further French attacks were to be resisted by force of arms. Dongan might call up reinforcements from the armies of adjacent provinces. In January 1688, Governor-General Dongan accordingly asked Sir Edmund Andros, commander of the new dominion of New England (itself created to defend the Maine frontier from the French) to levy 400 foot and 100 horse from the dominion forces, to add to them one of Andros's two red-coated infantry companies, and to send them all to Albany to bolster the defense of the Anglo-Iroquoian frontier and so to enforce the cessation of hostilities.[116]

Dongan had already cited the cessation to win the release of Major MacGregorie and the provincials from Quebec. He had not gotten back the Iroquois prisoners, however, for the French, citing the treaty, refused to recognize them as King James's subjects. This distinction was repeated in negotiations about French forts on the Anglo-Iroquois frontiers. Newly returned to Canada, the viceroy, Count Frontenac, admitted that, as it was built during the negotiation of the treaty, the fort that bore his name (where the Cataraqui River brought the back channel from Quebec to Lake Ontario) would have to be demolished once the treaty was implemented. As for Fort Niagara, however, Frontenac declared that it had been built in Seneca country and that the Senecas were "rebells" against Louis XIV, not subjects of James II. Dongan's response was a plan that took four wars and three-quarters of a century to achieve. The governor-general proposed that the French Niagara be captured by the English; that an English Fort Oswego be built opposite the French Fort Frontenac on Ontario; that the Riche-lieu-Champlain-Hudson corridor be controlled by a fortress to be built at Crown Point. "If the French persist in such their Invasions, wee cannot be unconcerned Eastward," Dongan added, and so the English crown must also fortify Pemaquid and win an Acadian frontier. Reacting to the issues raised by the Treaty of American Neutrality, Governor-General Dongan had outlined the strategy of the coming century, a century whose history would be driven by the fact of an imperial struggle between France and England for northeastern America.[117]

Having used all of General Dongan's ammunition to attack French ag-gression against New York and the Five Nations, and with his confrère, lord Churchill, having apprehended Dongan's continental strategy of American empire, Secretary Blathwayt reviewed the hostilities of the French against the English in the West Indies. The secretary of war and plantations said that, even if the French could not now be forced to honor the American provisions of the Treaty of Breda (which Blathwayt inter-preted as recognizing English claims to Maine and the dominions of the Iroquois), Louis XIV must at least honor Breda's West Indian clauses. Therefore the French should evacuate St. Lucia and return the land and slaves captured by their French neighbors to the English colonists on St. Kitts.[118]

In all these cases, the negotiators at Westminster recognized that the greatest impediment to Anglo-French amity in America was the aggression of the governors-general and their provincial troops. So they wrote into the treaty a requirement that the viceroys respect their royal masters' entente by referring all American conflicts to the two kings. Then the commission-ers obtained from both monarchs orders to their viceroys not to attack each other during the coming year, that is until January 1/11, 1688/9, or until further royal orders were received. Lord Churchill was served with this order, as governor of the Hudson's Bay Company. Churchill, like every other governor and general, evaded obedience. When he forwarded the order to his deputies in the Bay, he added to it an injunction to meet force by force and gave orders to take every opportunity to recover company lands and goods from the treacherous French (he having won back Fort Nelson in the treaty negotiations). Because Churchill had expanded the company's territorial claims to include the vast drainage basin of Hudson Bay, Churchill's orders to his deputies were a prescription for expanded conflict with France in America. Just as Codrington in St. Kitts recovered lands and stockpiled munitions, just as Andros acted in Maine and sent his deputy, Nicholson, to scout Acadia, so Churchill's deputies in the Bay made the year of truce specified by the treaty one of preparation for war with France in America.[119]

In their opposition to the Anglo-French Treaty of American Neutrality, Blathwayt, Churchill, and Dongan had expressed the unanimous opinion of English imperialists, save for King James himself, that force alone could counter French aggression. True, King James chafed under his tutelage to Louis XIV. Certainly, James remained an English imperialist at heart, but the devout monarch had now subordinated all other considerations to those that would make his army, his realm, his empire, Catholic. That goal meant subservience to the Catholic champion, King Louis of France. Despite lord Churchill's further protestations in October of 1687, in December the commissioners for the Treaty of American Neutrality signed the agreement by which their masters would order the viceroys to preserve the status defined by the treaty. The Restoration Empire's military administrators agreed that these protocols devastated English imperial interests. Just sixteen months after the treaty was signed, lord Churchill and Secretary Blathwayt persuaded the new king whom they had brought to the imperial throne—a Protestant, francophobe monarch—to make French aggression in America, especially in Hudson Bay off Newfoundland, in New York, and on St. Kitts, the casus belli of an imperial war against France.[120]

CHAPTER FOUR

Lord Churchill's Coup:

1686–1688

I N NOVEMBER 1686, in the midst of the negotiations for the Treaty of American Neutrality, the king dispatched William Penn to The Hague. He ordered that "talking vain man" to badger Prince William for his public endorsement of the repeal of the Test and Penal Acts. If the prince supported the elimination of dissenters' disabilities, King James promised to honor his alliance with Prince William against France in Europe, even if that meant abandoning England's peace with France in America. James expected the Dutch to rise to this imperial bait. So they would defeat the intention of the Anglo-French treaty to weaken the commercial connection of England and its empire with the Dutch and their European correspondents. So they could conserve the capital capacities that underlay the two Protestant seapowers' military resistance to Roman Catholicism and French empire. If Prince William also pledged to maintain equal rights for Catholics in his own prospective English reign, King James promised to put known partisans of William's succession into English office.[1]

Despite King James's offers of European and American commercial and military advantage, Prince William refused to affront Anglican opinion by endorsing repeal of the tests. Instead, at the end of February 1687, the prince sent to England Everaard Van Weede, lord of Dykvelt. Dykvelt promised the opponents of King James's policies that "the prince would ever be firm to the Church of England and all our national interests." In return, Dykvelt asked "those who wished well to their religion and their country" to protect the prince's succession to the imperial throne. As heiress presumptive (in succession to her elder sister, Mary, William of Orange's wife), Princess Anne's cooperation in planning the succession was essential. In so vital a matter, her choice of agent was obvious. Princess Anne wrote to her sister that "I have desired Lord Churchill (who is one that I can trust and I am sure is a very honest man and a good Protestant) to speak to Mr. Dykvelt for me." Churchill passed on Anne's plea for William and Mary's help in securing King James's permission for her to join them at The Hague. Just as he had rejected lord Churchill's, so King James vetoed his daughter's effort (inspired by lady Churchill) to escape the crisis of loyalties that the king's Catholicism would soon compel.[2]

Even before he spoke for Princess Anne, Churchill's military reputation, long recognized by Prince William and recently reinforced by Churchill's victory at Sedgemoor, his captaincy of the Life Guards, and his resistance to France in America, made him Dykvelt's first English military contact. Churchill was the more responsive because Dykvelt's arrival coincided with the king's dismissal of the leading Anglican ministers, Rochester from the treasury and Clarendon from Ireland. This apparently prefaced a purge of Protestant officers from the English army and an overt alliance of the king with Catholic France. Therefore, on April 10, 1687, lord Churchill moved from mere consultations about securing the legitimate succession to actually planning a Protestant putsch.[3]

On April 4, James II had announced his Declaration of Indulgence. It was probably formulated by William Penn, duly grateful for the king's general gaol release of Quakers and for the king's protection of Penn's American proprietary from the quo warranto campaign of centralization. Penn was assisted in such matters by Robert Brent, the Catholic lawyer and royal election agent (his kinsman and namesake in Virginia would be accused of acting for the king and Catholicism). In the declaration that Penn and Brent likely composed for the king, James wished "that all the people of our dominions were members of the Catholic Church." Then he suspended the enforcement of all laws restricting religious profession and practice. Further, the king announced that he would dispense with the Test Act when he commissioned the officers of the crown. James's declaration "gave great offence to all true patriots as well as to the whole church party." To none more than to that Anglican imperialist and army officer, lord Churchill.[4]

Less than a month after King James's declaration of religious indulgence, on May 17, 1687, the very day that lord Churchill delivered his widest protest to the king against the Anglo-French Treaty of American Neutrality, Churchill wrote to the Prince of Orange that Princess Anne "was resolved, by the assistance of God, to suffer all extremities, even to death itself, rather than be brought to change her religion." As for himself, lord Churchill told the prince "that my places and the King's favor I set at nought, in the comparison of being true to my religion." It was not casually that Churchill considered the betrayal of his patron, or that this soldier of the crown contemplated treason. It was the king's assault on the Church of England, Churchill told William, that compelled him to consider action against the king: "in all things but this the King may command me, I call God to witness, that even with joy I should expose my life for his service, so sensible am I of his favours."[5]

In the coming crisis, lord Churchill assured Prince William, "the Princess of Denmark is safe in the trusting of me; I being resolved, although I cannot live the life of a saint, if there be occasion for it, to shew the resolution of a martyr." No one expected saintly behavior from Churchill, nor martyrdom for that matter. Rather, it was essential to Anglicanism that Churchill exercise his incomparable influence in the royal army to protect the established church and insure the succession of William and Mary. At the same moment, and despite King James's threat to transport him to America, Bishop Compton made the same pledge on behalf of the church. Admiral Herbert (whom James had just deprived of command in the fleet in favor of a Catholic, and from whom King James had taken the colonelcy of the 15th Foot to prefer a papist) and Captain Edward Russell (whose family had suffered a brutal execution on their very doorstep, as well as the loss of the First Guards command) together promised that the navy too would resist a Catholic counterrevolution and help to insure the Protestant succession.[6]

Such commitments as Churchill's might be no more than the usual succession politics. Princess Mary, as James II's elder daughter, was her father's heiress. Her husband, Prince William, was also James's nephew and he had long been acknowledged by the king as his likely successor. On the surface, therefore, all that Churchill and his military associates had pledged to William was that they would remain true to the legally established church and that the forces they led would insure the legitimate heirs' succession to the imperial throne. The formality of the pledge, and its religious premise, implied some division of the military's loyalty between the present sovereign and his presumed successors, but Churchill's promise to Prince William contemplated outright treason against King James only if the king, against all expectation, sired a male heir or launched an all-out attack on the Church of England.[7]

King James began his campaign against the church by trying to pack the house of commons. The king would rescind corporate charters, close borough electorates, and pledge likely members of parliament to vote to rescind the Penal Acts against religious dissent. In his electoral campaign the king's first targets were army officers. In the long run, religious toleration could only be sustained against the will of England's Anglican political nation by military force. In the short run, a compliant commons could only be obtained if garrison officers ran against local squires. If necessary (as was done at Queensborough, and, of course, in American provincial towns), the governors could use troops either to dragoon the electors or to replace them at the polls. So King James cashiered those officers who refused to promise to vote for repeal themselves, or who declined to use their electoral interest, or their troops, to support candidates pledged to repeal the penal laws. The most notable victims were the earl of Scarsdale and the duke of

St. Albans, two of the less dextrous members of the Denmark household. Contrast Piercy Kirke. Told by King James that he must become a Catholic if he was to retain his commission, the colonel pled a previous engagement: "Your Majesty knows that I was concerned at Tangier, and being often-times with the Emperour of Morroco about the late King's affairs, he oft desired the same thing of me, and I passed my word to him that if ever I changed my religion I would turn Mohometan."[8]

If the army was the weapon of the Anglican establishment, the clergy were its conscience. So King James moved from cashiering officers to as-saulting both the leading antipapists and the Protestant seminaries. Bishop Compton was silenced, removed from his American diocese, and forbidden to select chaplains for the navy and the garrisons overseas, as well as for colonial parishes. Not just the bishop but the entire church was subjected to an ecclesiastical commission, despite three prior declarations by the parlia-ment that such commissions were illegal. The commission's next act was to expel the clerical fellows of Magdalen College, Oxford, for refusing to admit a Catholic president. This was an inflammatory act. Magdalen's pres-ident was the duke of Ormonde's chaplain. The one fellow who defied King James to the end was Princess Anne's chaplain. The episode was widely seen as the precedent for the royal resumption of all the former property of the Catholic church from its Protestant possessors. William Penn played a prominent part in the process. Penn's ingenuousness is captured in his reas-surance that the king would stop confiscating colleges when he had added Magdalen to University and Christ Church because Magdalen's convenient location, and splendid walks, when added to the other colleges' fine build-ings, would give the king's Catholic fellows all anyone could desire.[9]

Penn was not alone in finding colleges for king and Catholics. Writing from Boston, Edward Randolph proposed not only that the Harvard presi-dent be dismissed and the college corporation replaced, but also that its resources, and those of the missionary New England Company, be con-verted to endow a Benedictine establishment (headed by Randolph's own brother-in-law). The puritan fugitive from the dominion of New England, Increase Mather, enlisted the aid of the Quaker William Penn and the Catholic George Brent to win King James's promise that Harvard College would be preserved. They convinced the king that he should demonstrate to the New England dissenters that they, too, would benefit from the Dec-laration of Indulgence. For themselves, they preserved Harvard as a bastion of opposition to Sir Edmund Andros's Anglican autocracy.[10]

Sir Edmund's legal counsel was Sir Robert Sawyer. As attorney general, Sawyer had led the quo warranto proceedings against the Massachusetts Bay Company charter. He was now dismissed by the king, however, be-cause he showed insufficient zeal purging sheriffs and justices who declined to cooperate in the king's campaign for repeal of the Test Act and penal laws (lords lieutenant and their deputies were also dismissed wholesale). Hostile as he remained to the puritan leadership of Massachusetts, Sawyer was reluctant to conduct a new round of quo warranto prosecutions against local government corporations, whether in England or America. After all, Sawyer was a lawyer, but, in place of the militia lieutenancies, the county courts, the civic corporations, and the collegiate foundations of the clergy—the constitutional structures of the ruling class—King James was "looking much to his formidable army by which he keeps everything in check." Yet the most vigorous and influential general of that army was alarmed by every one of his royal commander's attacks on the Anglican establishment in church, state, and military.[11]

During the summer of 1687, as the captain of the Life Guards, lord Churchill escorted King James in his royal progress across the kingdom. In this progress, James himself, as God's vice-regent, planned to touch and miraculously cure the scrofulous. He would do so in Anglican churches but with Catholic priests assisting. So the king expected heaven to manifest its mandate for his campaign first to elevate his co-religionists to political power and then to convert his Protestant subjects to Catholicism. Once again, and for the last time, Churchill warned his sovereign of the fatal consequences of his Catholic campaign. As they walked together in the garden of Winchester Cathedral, the king condescended to ask Churchill's opinion of his ceremonial. "What do my subjects say about this Method I have taken of performing the Ceremony of Touching in their Churches?" With uncharacteristic candor, lord Churchill replied, "why truly, they shew very little liking to it, and it is the general Voice of your People that Your Majesty is Paving the way for the Introduction of Popery." The king was outraged. Had he not given them "my Royal Word" that he would preserve the Church of England? After all their years together, after all their agonizing over the political problems posed by James's belief, Churchill must know that James intended only to establish toleration "for all Christian people." Of course the king expected "thos of my own Religion" to share in that toleration. Churchill again professed his loyalty and duty to the king but he boldly declared that they had a clear religious limit: "he had been bred a Protestant, and intended to live and die in that Communion; that above Nine Parts in Ten of the whole People were of the same Persuasion."[12]

In startlingly firm and frank terms, the captain of the Life Guards went on to tell his royal commander-in-chief that Protestants would not obey and that Anglican officers would not execute the king's orders to establish Catholicism. More, Churchill implied that James faced a religious revolt if he persisted in his assault on the Church of England. "The Genius of the *English Nation*" for rebellion, combined with "their natural Aversion to the Roman Catholick Worship," lord Churchill warned King James, will lead to "consequences which he dared not so much as to name." King James heard his favorite out, but his reply was uncompromising: "I tell you, *Churchill*, I will exercise my Religion in such a manner as I shall think fitting. I will shew Favor to my Catholic Subjects, and be a common Father to all my Protestants," but whatever their objections to his religious policy and to its political, corporate, diplomatic, and imperial consequences, "I am King, and to be obeyed by them." As for the consequences Churchill implied, the king declared that "I shall leave them to Providence and make use of the Power God has put in my hands" to repress any rebellion. Then the king went to dinner with the dean of the cathedral and directed all his royal remarks to that churchman on the religious duty of passive obedience. But even bishops had warned the king "that if he ever depended upon the doctrine of Non-resistance he would find himself deceived." The alleged author of the Declaration of Indulgence, "Quaker Penn attends the King very close and preaches at the Bath in the Tennis Court" on toleration and obedience, but "Church" had put King James on notice that he, otherwise the most obedient of subjects, would desert the king if he endangered Protestantism in England.[13]

Nevertheless, the king was determined to fulfill the first condition of a Protestant putsch, an attack on the national church. King James may also have spoken to the captain of his bodyguard with foreknowledge of the second precondition of a coup, a change in the succession. On November 14, 1687, it was revealed that the queen was pregnant. Catholic courtiers instantly, assuredly (in Protestant eyes, suspiciously), declared that the queen would give King James a healthy son, an heir to his throne and their religion, a prince to displace the Protestants Mary and Anne. For Prince William, the husband of the Princess Mary, and for lord Churchill, the champion of the Princess Anne, indeed, for European Protestantism and for the English empire, all expectations were instantly darkened.[14]

As lady Churchill said, now "every Body must be ruined, who would not become a Roman Catholic." Yet even now her lord refused "to do what the king required of him," that is to become a Catholic himself and promise to vote in the lords for repeal of the Test Act. Lord Churchill had made it clear at Winchester that, on the subject of religion, the clan Churchill had abandoned the courtier's chief characteristic: dissimulation. On December 29, 1687, Anne refuted those who had given her sister "so ill a character of Lady Churchill. I believe," Anne wrote, that "there is nobody in the world has better notions of religion than she has . . . she has a true sense of the doctrines of our Church, and abhors all the principles of the Church of Rome." In this, Anne insisted, lady Churchill "will never change. The same thing, I will venture . . . to say for her Lord; for though he is a very faithful servant to the King, and that the King is very kind to him, and, I believe, he will also always obey the King in all things that are consistent with religion;

yet rather than change that, I dare say, he will lose all his places, and all that he has."[15]

A few days later, at the outset of the new-style year 1688, convinced that the crisis of both their church and their careers was at hand, emboldened by the unanimous refusal of the Anglican ruling class to accept the king's measures, Churchill and other leaders pledged to the Protestant succession approached Prince William. The prince must reassure them, even publicly declare, that he would claim the throne and that, as king, he would preserve the Protestant ascendancy as protected by law. Otherwise they and other Anglican soldiers and statesmen could not remain in office without conforming to the king's religion and politics. If they either lost their commissions or became Catholics, the king could command the army to force the empire into Catholicism and absolutism. For the moment, the Protestant plotters declared that they could cling to the church and the constitution and that they could keep the army loyal to these loadstones. They warned William, however, that the king was attempting to force the army to rely entirely on himself. He allowed soldiers in garrison to commit the sort of abuses against civilians that the dragoons had inflicted on the west. The royal intention was to make the soldiers hateful to the people and dependent on royal protection from civil law.[16]

Admittedly, the soldiers were "bad Englishmen and worse Christians," Churchill and the other officers told Prince William, but as "yet the court found them too good protestants to trust much to them." The officers reiterated that this might not last, that the prince must act before the king could reconstitute the army as a caste above the law and employ them in a "dragooning system," copied from France, first to force civic corporations to surrender their charters (as Sir Bernard Howard was attempting to do at Winchester and as Berwick's regiment did at Huntington in the spring of 1688), and then to control parliamentary elections from the garrison towns (the border fortress town of Berwick was a test case in England, following the examples of New York and Port Royal). King James even proposed to reinstitute the free quartering of soldiers on civilians, although he knew that this had helped provoke the revolution against his father. Recognizing that all depended upon the army, King James determined to ask the same three questions of every officer and soldier that he was asking the courtiers in his "closet." Those who might be elected to parliament were asked if they would vote to repeal the penal laws and the Test Act. Those who could vote were asked if they would support candidates pledged to repeal. All were asked if they would live peaceably with those of another religion. The king began the questioning with lord Peterborough's regiment, in quarters at Bristol, on April 27, 1688. No ranker stepped forward. The officers declared that they "were determined rather to lose their places than to agree to it." English officers and governors warned their American correspondents that "the crises of our employments is at hand."[17]

Prince William replied to Churchill and the other conspirators that, given an invitation to "rescue the nation and the religion" of England, he would be ready to invade England "by the end of September," 1688. By May of that fateful year, the prince's immediate agent, Henry Sidney, had gone down the list of politicians publicly opposed to King James's program, looking for commitments to a coup. Halifax and Nottingham refused, the former out of conviction that James's excesses would fall of their own weight, the latter out of fear that they would not. Danby, Compton, and the duke of Devonshire promised their support to William. The prince's invasion plan "was next proposed to three of the chief officers of the army, Trelawney, Kirk, and the lord Churchill. Those all went into it."[18]

The two ex-Tangerines and Churchill, joined by Grafton of the foot guards and the young duke of Ormonde (representative of the Anglo-Irish officers and one of the first to reject King James's three questions), began to recruit officer candidates for the impending coup. Churchill's own troop of the Life Guards would follow him anywhere, and he counted on the backing of the Huguenot refugees in Dover's supposedly Catholic corps. As the Life Guards' executive officer, lord Churchill could at least confuse and subvert the rest of the royal bodyguard. At the head of the Denmark connection, Churchill spoke for lord Cornbury and the rest of Churchill's old regiment, the Royals. Churchill also represented another of his former subordinates, a fellow Tangier veteran, Thomas Langston, now the executive officer of Princess Anne's cavalry (succeeding Sir Edmund Andros). Of course, he could count on Charles Churchill, now colonel of the Buffs (succeeding Oglethorpe). Lord Churchill was also in daily touch with nets of Protestant professional officers in such new units as the 15th.[19]

Most important, Churchill could commit to the conspiracy the central figure of the Denmark connection, certain cynosure of any coup, Princess Anne. It was lord Churchill's crowning contribution to the growing conspiracy that he was able to promise "that Prince George and the Princess Anne would leave the court [of her father, the king], and come to the prince as soon as possible" after William invaded England. It was also important, if only because the princess loved her husband, that Churchill could assure the plotters of Prince George's services. The prince, had he any force of character, would have been the ideal supplanter of his father-in-law, at least in the Churchills' estimation. He would be at least as much influenced by them as the princess was. Reliance on the dangerous abilities, absolutist instincts, and professional army of Prince William could be reduced, if not avoided altogether, if only Prince George would fight to bring Princess Anne immediately to the throne.[20]

The conspirators canvassed the possibility of making the prince the putsch's premier, but they reluctantly dismissed him "as unequal to the crisis." Prince George's remaining use to lord Churchill and the rest of the plotters identified with Princess Anne's interest was as the authenticator of her involvement in the military conspiracy. So Prince George embodied the princess's claim to profit from a revolt against her father and he became the mediator between an essentially pacific princess and the military members of the Denmark connection. This unsung but essential role Prince George continued to play for the next twenty years, until his death destroyed the military association which dominated the English army and came to control the English empire after the military coup of 1688.

The young duke of Argyll recalled that each army officer recruited for the coup appeared before the prince of Denmark, the duke of Ormonde, and an officer of the princess's household (i.e., a Churchill connection). The recruit had to swear that he would desert the royal army and go over to the Prince of Orange "whenever he landed." Prince George was also the colonel-in-chief of Sir Charles Littleton's marines. Sir Charles's cavalier convictions, however, and the promotion of such Churchillian captains as Edward Nott from the marines to other (more easily corrupted) regiments, had made the old admiralty corps more than ever the servants of their founder, now their king. But the loyalty of Littleton and the marines to King James would be more than offset by the treason of his daughter and his general.[21]

Beyond the Denmark household were two other military connections with which Churchill had especially close professional contacts. The first of these was the Tangerines. Churchill's key subordinates in the western campaign and at Sedgemoor, Kirke and Trelawney, like Churchill himself and his brother Charles, all were veterans of the Tangier garrison. The professional regiments they had brought home from that garrison were the most feared units in England. The Tangerines also influenced many other units through their former subalterns and the children of the corps. Educated in the Tangier regiments, these young men were now among the most professional officers of the new formations. Elliot and Spotswood of the 10th, stationed in the vital garrison of Plymouth, were one in spirit with their numerous naval associates, the Tangerines at sea. There the Tangier connection extended upward from Lieutenant George Byng to Captain George Churchill and Admiral Arthur Herbert.[22]

The second of Churchill's conspiratorial constituencies, as important politically as the Tangerines were militarily, was the First Regiment of the Royal Foot Guards. The Guards' colonel, the duke of Grafton, was notoriously Churchill's creature. This was a connection of more than ordinary intensity, given Churchill's relation to Grafton's mother, Barbara, duchess of Cleveland. The connection had been cemented by Grafton's neglect by his uncle King James, even after Grafton's distinction with Churchill at Sedgemoor. The king had also deprived Grafton of rank in the navy, despite his successful command in the Mediterranean. Grafton had his own coterie among the naval captains and together Grafton and Churchill committed to the coup such Guards captains as William Selwyn, John Seymour, and William Matthew, the last of whom, a Leeward Islander, was embittered by his recent experience of the dragonnades in France. Perhaps the most crucial of these Guards captains, all of whom took imperial rewards for their part in the conspiracy, was Lionel Copley, the deputy-governor of the key eastern port and citadel of Hull. In an invasion, the plotters might also have to neutralize the officers of the Isle of Wight garrison. Fortunately, Grafton himself was the island's governor.[23]

In some ways, Churchill's old friend and comrade in France, afterwards his brother-in-law, Colonel Charles Godfrey, was his most active agent in the coup. Colonel Godfrey was Churchill's primary link to the most public club of conspirators, the whig officers who met at the Rose Tavern under the chairmanship of Richard Savage, viscount Colchester, a Life Guards colleague of lord Churchill's. Churchill's former subordinate, Lieutenant Colonel Langston, was also numbered among the Rose Tavern plotters. Many of them were old Monmouth men and most had strong Dutch military connections. Churchill's closest acquaintance among the Anglo-Dutch conspirators was his old comrade in France, Hugh Mackay. Having declined King James's offer to make him an English major-general if he would leave the Dutch service, Mackay had accepted a commission from the states as major-general commanding the British brigades. Now they constituted the Red Division, designated as the spearhead of Prince William's invasion.[24]

It was appropriate that a foreign invasion and a military coup premised on religious ideology, a Protestant putsch, should receive its greatest impetus from seven bishops. On April 27, 1688, James II's Declaration of Indulgence was republished. On May 4, the king ordered the Anglican clergy to read it in church. The king acted on the advice of "the well known Pen" who, driven by his hatred of the persecuting church, sought to disgrace the episcopacy by compelling them to disobey the king, the head of their church, and declare their opposition to toleration, uniting Protestant and Catholic dissenters from that church. After anguished, secret consultations at Ely House (it is not too much to say that Francis Turner, lord Churchill's spiritual advisor, sought the see of Ely simply to obtain its London palace) the episcopacy of the province of Canterbury resolved not to order their clergy to read the declaration. Despite William Penn's efforts, the bishops were supported in their refusal by the leading dissenting clergy. As they told Penn, the Protestant dissenters were all "for Liberty by Law" but they were "utterly against letting Papists into the Government."[25]

On May 17, seven bishops refused to obey the royal order themselves or to relay it to their diocesan clergy, on the ground that the king's declaration, by dispensing with acts of parliament, was unconstitutional. The bishops' disobedience, said the king, "was a Trumpet of rebellion." Summoned before King James, the bishops pled "Our Consciences and the law." They refused to obey their king's command. They declined to give bond for their future good behavior. King James ordered the bishops arrested and imprisoned to stand trial on a charge of seditious libel. On June 8, 1688, the fathers of the Church of England passed through the streets of the imperial metropolis on their way to prison. Amidst wrenching scenes of popular Protestant piety, led by the archbishop of Canterbury himself, they entered the Tower of London.[26]

That night, the garrison of the Tower drank the bishops' health. Told to stop by their colonel, the Catholic constable of the Tower, Sir Edward Hales, the men of the 14th Regiment replied that they would drink the bishops' health and no other, not their colonel's, not even the king's, as long as their fathers in God were imprisoned. This defiance in the kingdom's most crucial garrison ran up through the regiment to its senior captain, Richard Brewer (who was promoted lieutenant colonel in the coup and died in harness as lieutenant governor-general of Jamaica and colonel of a royal regiment in the provincial garrison). Revulsion at the bishops' arrest especially exercised Tangerines, for the brother of Jonathan Trelawney, bishop of Bristol, commanded the 2d (Tangier) Regiment. To this day, that regiment's slow march is the song written when Bishop Trelawney entered the Tower:

> And shall Trelawney die! And shall Trelawney die!
> Then thirty thousand Cornish boys will know the reason why.[27]

Escorted by sympathetic soldiers, the leading Protestant dissenters visited the bishops in the Tower during the week before their indictment. The ministers thus demonstrated that very religious solidarity, even with their erstwhile Anglican persecutors, that King James's conciliation of the dissenters had been designed to destroy. Nationwide, churches and sectarian meetings alike declared their support for the bishops and their antipathy to the prerogative and to the papists. This religious reaction deepened across the empire as the news spread of the birth of a Catholic prince of Wales on June 10.[28]

In the army, Roman Catholic officers were divided from their Protestant colleagues by the king's order that they give thanks separately for the royal birth. In the navy, Admiral Dartmouth and Secretary Pepys (what Churchill and Blathwayt were to the army) were told by the ecstatic king that they, and all other naval officers, must become Catholics. At court, it was widely reported that "the Archquaker Pen and his secretary have already declared themselves Roman Catholics." The Denmark connection had taken care "to be out of the way" when they were summoned to witness the royal birth. They soon began to cast doubt on it, asserting that a suppositious child had been introduced into the queen's bed. As the bishops were in the Tower, they could not witness the birth of a Catholic heir. Yet King James saw the birth of his son as heaven's instrument to execute his plans to "reconcile the Nation to the Mother Church." He began to plan for a Catholic regency to educate his son and govern a nation in which all ambition would be to be ever more Catholic.[29]

But the king, in challenging the Protestant succession as well as the Church of England, had completed the prerequisites for a putsch. The red coats and the black coats were uniting against him. The clergy of the capital refused to read the declaration in their churches. Other bishops joined opposition councils and "openly declare the acts of the king illegal." When the imprisoned bishops came to the bar, on a writ of habeas corpus, they were countenanced by twenty-one principal peers, headed by Halifax, Danby, Nottingham, and Carlisle, all of whom stood bail for the bishops. The populace of London lined the streets to cheer the bishops home. The king personally paraded three full battalions in Hyde Park to prevent a "general insurrection." He then called up the entire field force of England to camp on Hounslow Heath to overawe London during the bishops' coming trial. King James ordered that old viceroy, so long his supporter, Sir Charles Littleton, to lead the royal forces in Kent to the coast or put them onboard the fleet. Littleton was to meet the expected Dutch invasion. Royal frigates were ordered to scour the coasts of Holland. From Ireland King James called up Catholic regiments to replace English Protestant troops in crucial garrisons.[30]

As the bishops' trial came on, "even the army, that was then encamped on Hounslow-heath shewed such a disposition to mutiny" that the king hurried out to camp at the head of his Guards. He sprang a surprise drill on the entire army. Then he set them to dig. They built field fortifications and attacked them. The king was still in camp on the morning of June 30 when the seven bishops were declared innocent by a London jury. The royal presence "kept the army in some order" but the streets of London were quickly crowded with cheering citizens and the intersections were soon aflame with bonfires. So King James set off with his Guards toward his rioting capital. No sooner was he off the heath than the sound of a single great victory shout shook the royal party. The king asked his general, the earl of Feversham, what the army was cheering about. "It is nothing, sire, only the soldiers rejoicing at the acquittal of the bishops." "Nothing!" cried the king, "You call that nothing!"[31]

That night, seven civil conspirators sent Prince William an invitation to invade England. Their messenger was Admiral Herbert. His reward, as English officers were immediately informed, was a commission as vice admiral in Prince William's invasion fleet and a pension of 6,000 guilders. The message Admiral Herbert bore concerned the state of the English army. It was, wrote the conspirators, deeply divided, ". . . many of the officers being so discontented that they continue in their service only for a subsistence (besides that, some of their minds are known already) and very many of the common soldiers show such an aversion to the Popish religion, that there is the greatest probability imaginable of great numbers of deserters should there be such an occasion" as William's invasion. Besides being rent by religious disaffection, the plotters reported, the army was full of professional fear. It was widely rumored that the king had planned a military purge modeled on that in Ireland, "a great alteration which will probably be made both in the officers and soldiers of the army." If such a purge was effected, if the Test Act against Catholic officers were then repealed, and if the present changes in militia commands were completed, the conspirators told Prince William that they, and all the other opponents of the king's Catholicism and absolutism, would be helpless.[32]

The conspiracy's success therefore depended on William's ability to honor his promise to invade before winter. An immediate invasion would force a crisis on the army while it was religiously divided and while its Protestant officers still held their commands. Then too, the conspirators agreed that, without an invasion to distract the king's forces from domestic repression, "the people throughout the Kingdom who are desirous of a change" would be "destroyed before they could get in a posture to defend themselves." As one witness remarked, "England being a small Country, few strong towns in it, and those in the King's hands, the Nobility disarmed . . . and the Militia not to be raised but by the King's Command, there can be no force levied in any part of England, but must be destroyed in its Infancy by a few Regiments."[33]

Of course, this analysis assumed that the regular regiments would be loyal to the king. That assumption was soon put to the test. On July 22, King James ordered all officers below the rank of general, governors included, to go to their commands, to prepare to meet a Dutch invasion, and to repress the ensuing domestic insurrection. Many of the king's officers had agreed to join the conspiracy, supposing that William invaded and the coup came to fruition, but now some of them agonized over their conflicting loyalties: to king or to country; to professional duty or to religious conscience. All of these issues were touched upon by lord Churchill's letter to the prince, sent by the hand of William's English agent, on August 4, 1688. "Mr Sidney will lett you know how I intend to be have my selfe," Churchill wrote the prince. Of his intended treason he added, "I think itt is what I owe to god and my Country; my honor I take leave to put into your Royal hinesses hands, in which I think it safe; if you think ther is any thing else that I ought to doe, you have but to command me, and I shall pay an intier obedience to itt, being resolved to dye in that Relidgion that it has pleased god to give you both the will and power to protect. I am with all respect Sr, your Royalle hinesses obedient servant—Churchill."[34]

It was his religion that had taken lord Churchill from his duty to his king and put his military services at the disposal of an invader. Churchill had put his conflict of conscience to the bishop of Ely the moment the bishop was released from the Tower. That injured prelate had advised Churchill that not to assist the invaders "who come to the help of the Lord, to the help of the Lord against the mighty," the enslavers of the Israelites, was to become liable to the curse of Meroz (Judges, 5: 23). Turner, and Churchill too, took the prince's declaration at face value. They seem to have believed that William would invade England just to compel the king to call a freely elected parliament that would legislate to preserve Protestantism and the law.[35]

Churchill accepted Turner's counsel but, "qui nescit dissimulare, nescit vivere," or, as the manuals for the upwardly mobile of that day put it, "he that knows not how to dissemble, knows not how to live." In his tent, on June 27, 1688, at the opening of the Hounslow Heath encampment, lord Churchill had entertained his king at dinner. On August 4, he wrote to Prince William for orders. On September 6, six Protestant captains in the garrison of Portsmouth refused to accept the Irish Catholic recruits offered to their companies. Recruits were valuable commodities, but the Portsmouth captains saw in this tempting offer both the beginning of the threatened Celtic and Catholic infiltration of the English army and a menace to the security of England's most strategic port. The garrison regiment, Princess Anne's foot, first led to oppose the king's program by Captain Coke, were further encouraged in their resistance to Irish reinforcements by lord Churchill himself.[36]

The Portsmouth mutiny was merely the most dramatic element to date in the concerted opposition of both the militia and the garrison to the royal effort to put the strategic port in Catholic hands. Early in December 1687, the earl of Gainsborough, governor of Portsmouth and lord lieutenant of Hampshire, had resisted the royal "closeting." The king replaced him with his bastard son (by Arabella Churchill), that teenaged veteran of service against the Turks, the duke of Berwick. In February, Berwick put the three questions to his deputy lieutenants. Unanimously, they refused to support repeal of the Test Act and penal laws. Indeed, most of the militia officers declined even to appear before Berwick. Instead, they resigned their commissions to the king. Their example was followed by all the justices of the peace. The government of Hampshire had evaporated. Berwick then put the three questions to the regular army officers of Princess Anne's regiment in the Portsmouth garrison. Although Berwick threatened to have the officers cashiered if they gave the wrong answers, he was completely rebuffed. To make military administration possible, Berwick had to back down. He reconvened the officers for requestioning. Now the duke omitted the two questions regarding repeal of the Test Act and the penal laws. In response to the remaining question, the Portsmouth officers agreed that they would live peaceably with their neighbors, regardless of religion.[37]

When September brought reports of an imminent Dutch invasion, the security of Portsmouth could no longer be left to so vague an undertaking or to such disaffected soldiers. Berwick proposed to purge the regiment of its "old," "useless," and fictious men and fill the ranks with newly arrived Irish Catholics. Following the lead of the regiment's lieutenant colonel, John Beaumont, four-fifths of the officers told Berwick that recruiting was their business, not his, and that "they could find a sufficient number of Protestant and honorable people like themselves," who would be much more loyal to the English church and constitution than any Catholic Irishmen were apt to be. The duke cashiered six captains on the spot. They then published their reply to Berwick: "this spread a great disconent and jealousie throughout the army." All the subaltern officers at Portsmouth in their turn refused to accept the Irish Catholic recruits, resigned their commissions, and left the barracks, followed by most of their men. The regiment, "Princess Anne's Regiment," was true to the Protestant principles of its colonel in chief. The Dutch ambassador cheerfully reported that "the Court seems not a little disturbed" at the Portsmouth mutiny, "the more so as it is apprehended this will happen to the king in all the Regiments."[38]

The court was indeed enraged at the Portsmouth officers' rebuff to this attempt to repeat the military romanization so successful in Ireland, with the very Catholic sentinels whom Tyrconnel had recruited. An example had to be made of the Portsmouth officers. On September 10, the six captains who had refused to accept the Irish recruits were arrested for mutiny and sent to Windsor for court martial. Lord Churchill dominated the court. "Foreseeing that such a piece of severity would reflect upon the King and inflame the people," he supposedly called for the death penalty. Instead, the Portsmouth captains were censured and, again, dismissed from the service as a warning to other army officers that they must agree to "augment the numbers of Catholics in the Army." The Portsmouth captains won instant fame. Their portraits were published in mezzotinto together with a group portrait of the seven bishops who had defied the king, "in order together to be cannonized into the favour of the Nation." Here were the icons of a unified, uniformed, resistance to Rome.[39]

On September 22, seven of Berwick's subalterns were court-martialed for their refusal to accept Irish recruits and for discharging more than one hundred privates so they would not be contaminated by service with Catholics. Now the king demanded the death penalty but even his subservient privy council reminded the king that, in peacetime, the law of the land only permitted dismissal as punishment for officer offenses. "The faction and insolence among the military could hardly be bridled," and its impact was enormous. The drama of the court martials, reported by pamphlets, pictures, and songs, may have been even more subversive than the trial of the seven bishops. The two trials united the resistance of the army and the clergy to the king's Catholicizing campaign.[40]

Even in the Portsmouth garrison, resistance continued. The new officers of Princess Anne's Regiment, Anglo-Irish exiles such as Benjamin Fletcher (to be distinguished in the reconquest of Ireland and so promoted to the command of New York) among them, were as hostile to Celts and Catholics as the old officers had been. And there were soon more Irish Catholic soldiers to hate in Portsmouth. Unable to infiltrate Princess Anne's Regiment, the king ordered a full Irish corps into the garrison, backed by three troops of Irish dragoons and two of Irish cavalry. Patrick Sarsfield was sent to Ireland to bring back thousands of Catholic soldiers. The multiplying, subversive newssheets warned that the Catholic Irish would garrison the Tower of London and treat the inhabitants of the capital as they had the townspeople of Portsmouth, beating up the mayor, firing into the Church of England during divine service, fighting with the English troops (who then killed forty Irish), and driving the citizens beyond the walls. These fears began to be realized when the first of 2,460 new Irish arrivals were put into London. They were immediately accused of murdering citizens.[41]

The great fear, the Irish fright, the outcome of centuries of imperial conquest and religious hatred, was building toward an explosion. Before it could take place the Dutch would invade. John Beaumont, the cashiered lieutenant colonel of Princess Anne's Regiment, was now revealed to be a leading army conspirator. He wrote on September 25 that, "with the first North East Wind we expect the Dutch will land, but I hope the Business will soon be decided, and we may see Happy Days." On the same day, King James rescinded his entire program of authoritarianism and Catholicization. He announced that he would restore the bishop of London to his diocese, America included; that he would restore other bishops to the imperial privy council; that he would restore county government, recommissioning the purged and resigned deputy lieutenants of the militia and the justices of the peace; that he would restore the charter of the city of London and return its former magistrates to power; and that he would restore the Protestant president of Magdalen College and reinstate its fellows. But everyone knew that the king's "pretty promises arose only from fear" of the approaching Dutch armada, said to number hundreds of ships carrying more than twelve thousand troops.[42]

Resistance to invasion had demanded that the king conciliate the army. Even as Colonel Beaumont wrote of "Happy Days," King James ordered his generals to ride with him to Salisbury. General lord Churchill accepted a splendid gift from King James, the king's own armor, before he and the rest of the royal general staff began to concentrate 25,000 men around Salisbury. This field army was supposed to resist the invaders. The king retained 7,000 to 9,000 more men in garrisons or training regiments to hold down the localities. He ordered 3,000 recruits enlisted in his English regiments. He anticipated the arrival of some 6,000 to 8,000 additional Irish and 3,000 Scots regulars. His Majesty thought that more than 40,000 men were amply "sufficient to deal with the Prince of Orange." They "had really been so," the king reflected afterwards, but "the Duke of Grafton, my Lord Churchill, and others had already taken their measures with the Prince of Orange."[43]

To surround the suspect English generals with Scots and Irish officers the king planned to create a British general staff. Churchill staved off this plan on October 16. The next day he was the first of the officers who, "when they kissed their Majestys hands to go down to their respective commands . . . were the most profuse in their offers of shedding their blood for [his] Service . . . every one contributing therby to lull the King into an imaginary security, that when the Scene opened, he might be the more surprised and wors prepared. . . ." Not for nothing had John Churchill studied James Stuart for twenty-one years. "Those the king loved had no faults," and he loved lord Churchill. Even so, the army officers' "discontents were so visable and the conspirators were so hardy and indiscrete, thinking all sure," that Churchill, "he that was the great general afterwards, was seen to laugh and loll out his tongue" when the king reviewed his cavalry in Hyde Park. The arch-loyalists, Feversham and Ailesbury, fell on their knees before the king, "begging him to clap up seven or eight of the heads" of the conspiracy. Socially ranked, these were "the Prince of Denmark, the Dukes of Ormond and Grafton, Lord Churchill, Mr. Kirkk, Mr. Trelawney &c but . . . fatally, the King could not resolve. . . ."[44]

On October 23, however, lord Churchill barely escaped exposure. As William Penn informed lord Dartmouth, two of the conspirators' couriers were arrested for "dealing with the Kings officers of his army to revolt." One messenger disappeared before interrogation. The other bribed his guards and escaped from the very gates of the Tower. Such agents, many of them young officers, also broadcast Prince William's "Letter to the English Army," dated October 28, 1688. It again warned the rank and file about "Irish soldiers being brought over to be put in your places." It reminded King James's commanders "how many of your fellow officers have been used for their standing firm to the Protestant Religion and the Laws of England."[45]

The prince himself arrived right after his letter. The northeasterly storms of autumn, "the Protestant Wind," blew his armada of six hundred ships south and west, away from the aristocratic risings of Danby, Devonshire, and Delamere in the north and midlands, past the Channel Fleet, demoralized, divided, tidebound, fog-shrouded, windbound at the Gunfleet, to Torbay in Devon. There, on November 5, the fleet under Admiral Herbert put something between fourteen and twenty-one thousand men ashore.[46]

These dramatically disparate estimates of the prince's strength pose many questions. The first is the degree of the invader's dependence on potential deserters from King James's army, lord Churchill chief among them (and, therefore, the degree of pressure on the prince to make promises to the putschists about the future of the English empire). A rough figure of 14,000 men for William's invasion force (i.e., 12,000 effectives) finds support in the states general's contracts for 4,000 troopers and 10,600 infantry from the German states to replace the forces William took to England from the Netherlands. King James published his intelligence, which estimated the prince's army at 13,752: 3,060 horse and 10,692 foot. Certainly, William's force was numerically much inferior to James's. The king's nominal strength was over 40,000 and his effectives in the field numbered nearly 25,000. The odds against the Dutch were almost two to one. Even more crippling was the dreadful loss of cavalry mounts that William's force had suffered in the storm that drove back his first invasion attempt. If King James's army remained in Salisbury Plain to meet Prince William's advance, the prince's weakness in cavalry would be a distinct disadvantage. Therefore, the decisions of the English household cavalry and dragoons (so thoroughly infiltrated by the Churchill connection) would be vital militarily, as well as psychologically, to the outcome of the invasion.[47]

Of equal impact on the empire was the large number and diverse nationalities of the army officers in the Dutch service who landed at Torbay to begin careers in Anglo-American garrison government. The English and Anglo-Irish exiles already named—Foulkes, Coote, Gibson, Handasyde and lord Mordaunt—certainly came ashore at Torbay. Recent revisions suggest that several additional Scots-Dutch units landed, units led by Scots officers such as William Vetch, afterwards the conqueror and first governor of Nova Scotia, and Henry Erskine, lord Cardross, who had returned from colonizing Carolina to join William's forces in the Netherlands, and who would move from Torbay to serve William in Scotland. If the entire Anglo-Dutch brigade landed at Torbay, such future commanders in the West Indies as Luke Lillingston and Ventris Columbine must also be numbered among the invaders. Certainly, John Cutts, who had shuttled from London to Amsterdam with the messages of the military conspirators, now began the career in English commands that would make him the patron of such governors-general as Joseph Dudley. If all the Scots-Dutch came ashore, also among their officers was David Colyear, whom we shall meet again as lord Portmore, organizing the great West Indian expedition that counted him as governor-general of Jamaica and commander-in-chief in America.[48]

Observe that Prince William had already accomplished what King James intended, the creation of a British army, an army that anticipated and effected a British state and empire. The military unification of the British kingdoms was the necessary precondition of political union. First in the army's amalgamation, then by the conquest of Ireland and Scotland, and finally by the incorporation of American provinces in the new state, the Williamite regime transformed the English army and empire into a British union, "Greater Britain." The union with Scotland, the resubordination of Ireland, and the anglicanization of America depended upon and were realized by the British army that landed at Torbay, combined with the English force headed by lord Churchill.

For four days after the invaders landed at Torbay, led by Hugh Mackay and the British brigades, the prince's army, reduced to ten thousand effective men, struggled east and north. Among them were "200 Blacks brought from the Plantations of the Neitherlands in America" to exemplify interracial empire to the English. The invaders slogged twenty-three miles through mud and rain to shelter at Exeter. The occupation of Exeter was organized by John Gibson, a veteran of the Anglo-Dutch brigade and a key imperial commander in the coming reign. Gibson was but one of half a dozen officers who made the garrison government of newly occupied English towns a step toward imperial command in America.[49]

Across southern England, subalterns such as Richard Phillips, afterwards the military founder of Nova Scotia, distributed more copies of Prince William's "Letter to the English Army." The prince proclaimed that he had come to rescue England from the popery and slavery designed for them by the king's evil Catholic counselors who, "in contempt of" the law "have not only armed the Papists, but have likewise raised them up to the greatest military trusts, both by sea and land, and that strangers as well as natives, and Irish as well as English; that . . . they might be in a capacity to maintain and execute their wicked designs by the assistance of the Army, and thereby to enslave the nation." The prince asked English officers to abandon their military loyalty to a misguided king and instead "consider what you owe to Almighty God and Your Religion, to your Country & your Selves."[50]

On November 8, the day the Prince of Orange entered Exeter, the leading English officer, lord Churchill, received his last promotion from James Stuart. The king commissioned Churchill lieutenant general. Now Churchill faced the crisis of the coup. Prince William might not succeed without decisive help. He was outnumbered. He had landed in the midst of

Monmouth country. Thoroughly repressed, neither its people nor its gentry joined the prince. The first group of conspirators to try to reach William from London (badly led by lord Lovelace) had been defeated and captured by loyal militia at Gloucester. The incipient arrival at the royal camp of some five thousand Scots and Irish would weight the scales of war even further against the invaders.[51]

At this moment, the cavalry screen of the royal army—detachments from the Blues and the Royals, the Royal Dragoons, and Princess Anne's Horse—advanced toward the invaders. This detachment was commanded by lord Churchill's former subordinate and fellow Denmark household officer, lord Cornbury. It had taken the surprising absence of four senior officers to put Cornbury in command. The duke of Berwick recalled that "Mr. Blathwayt Secretary at War, to favour this design, had purposely delayed sending me the king's orders" for his transfer from Portsmouth to Salisbury to take command of the cavalry from Cornbury. Allegedly, Blathwayt then sent Langston, second in command of the cavalry at Salisbury, the false orders that launched Cornbury's escapade. It was further declared that these orders to his intimates were the work of the cavalry's executive officer, lord Churchill. Cornbury's orders allowed him, seconded by Langston, to lead the cavalry west. To do so was to lose the royal army's greatest advantage, by taking its dominant cavalry off Salisbury Plain and into hedge country, infantry territory. Questioned, Cornbury declared that he acted "by express orders . . . to attack a party of His Highness Cavalry." So Cornbury's command rode eighty-five miles in just thirty-six hours and entirely lost touch with the king's army.[52]

On November 13, 1688, the tired troopers rose early and rode another dozen miles closer to Prince William's advance guard. There, "the Troops of his Highness having previous information" of Cornbury's orders and intentions, had prepared a camp for three cavalry regiments and surrounded it with the prince's troopers. At the vital moment, a loyalist, Major Littleton, demanded to see Cornbury's orders. "Lord Cornbury had not the presence of mind that so critical a thing required." Their suspicions confirmed, the loyal officers tried to turn the regiments back. Seventy-five troopers, "who are papists," immediately obeyed. Lord Cornbury rode blindly on to meet the escort detached by the Prince of Orange. His lordship was followed by all the captains and sixty dragoons of the Royals, and some forty of the Guards. A much more successful treason was that of Lieutenant Colonel Langston. A stern disciplinarian like the rest of the Tangier professionals, and in command of a regiment closely connected to lord Churchill and Princess Anne's household, Langston carried the whole of his command over to Prince William.[53]

Princess Anne was pleased by the treason of her partisans, the first of many desertions that she expected the Denmark connection to engineer.

She explained to her uncle, Cornbury's father, "that people were so apprehensive of Popery, that she believed many more of the army would do the same." Prince William was disappointed. He had expected Cornbury's desertion both to increase his desperately weak cavalry by a third and to inspire thousands of royalists to follow their example. Instead, William welcomed little more than a single regiment. Even some of these troopers soon found their way back to the royal ranks (demonstrating, as King James bitterly remarked, "a greater honour and fidelity in the common men than in the generality of the officers, who usually value themselves so much for these qualifications"). The effect of Cornbury's defection was more moral than material. As one of the invaders wrote, they were heartened "that we had not been deceived in what was told us of the inclinations of the king's army." That news was immediately reinforced by the arrival in the invader's camp of Colonel Godfrey, the Churchill connection's coordinator, and Lieutenant Colonel Beaumont, instigator of the Portsmouth mutiny. They brought further news of the disaffection of the royal army at Salisbury. Where the army led, the gentry of the west would follow. As King James put it, "not one man of consideration in the Western Countys went in [to the Prince] till my Lord Cornbury's treachery began the general defection."[54]

Cornbury's desertion not only moved the gentry, it devastated the royal army and demoralized its commander. The first reports that reached the king were "that 3 entire regiments are gone over to ye Pr. of Orange." Worse, the king's advisors expected what the prince hoped for, that "ye foot, when they are advanced far enough to have an opportunity, will follow the example" of the horse. And indeed, (false) reports soon arrived that the royal vanguard, "the whole brigade commanded by Kirke & Trelawney" had deserted. "This news has putt ye King into greater disorder," but it set the chief military conspirator dancing. Churchill, his friend Godolphin, and the enigmatic Sunderland, are said to have been seen at Whitehall skipping "hand in hand along the Gallery in the greatest transports of joy imaginable." Well might the plotters prance. Even loyal officers concluded that the impact of Cornbury's and Langston's desertion "was exceedingly great for . . . it broke the Kings measures, disheartened the other troops and created such a jealousie, that each man suspected his Neighbour and in effect rendered the army useless."[55]

Cornbury's desertion was a dramatic demonstration of the army's disaffection. As the king's amanuensis wrote, it "seem'd to pull up all his hopes and expectations by the roots, when his chief and only support began to fail him." King James made one last effort "to animate the officers of the Army, and to examine whether they will stand by him or not." He called together "all the General Officers and Collonells that remained in town." The king told them that he would meet all their demands. In particular, James prom ised to call a free parliament to legislate protections for English "Liberties, Priviledges, and Religion," as soon as the invader had been driven from the kingdom. If his promise did not satisfy them, however, the royal commander said that he wished to spare his officers the dishonor of desertion. He would take back their commissions. He would free them to serve the prince. But "he looked on them as men of too much honour, to follow my Lord Cornbury's example." Apparently moved by the royal generosity, perhaps intimidated by the king's threat to "divide the estates of as many as should be found abettors to the invasion amongst such of the soldiery as should signalize themselves in the action," and certainly unwilling to give up the military commands that constituted political currency, as well as physical power, in the cresting coup, the officers assembled before their king "vow'd they would serve him to the last drop of their blood. The Duke of Grafton and My Lord Churchill were the first who made this attestation." The commanders of the royal bodyguard, monarchy's ultimate recourse, had again misled their master.[56]

Accepting their apparent fealty, the king ordered his generals to join their commands. Late as usual, lord Feversham did not reach the army he supposedly commanded until November 15, four days after Cornbury's cavalry had left the royalist camp. The king himself, having left five thousand troops to hold down London, was escorted by lord Churchill, in the king's own armor ("which was very beautiful to behold"), at the head of his and Dover's troops of the Horse Guards, and by the duke of Grafton, in command of three battalions of the Foot Guards, but they did not leave London until November 17. That was Queen Elizabeth's ascension day, notorious for its antipapist riots, so the king had batteries of cannon emplaced at Whitehall and saw the day out. But his danger was in his own family and his own Guards, not in the London mob. On November 18, Princess Anne wrote to the Prince of Orange that her husband, Prince George, would join him the moment he was told to do so by the conspirators. The king arrived at Salisbury on November 19 to find his army divided by distrust, riven with recrimination, blinded by the loss of some of its cavalry and the dubious loyalty of the rest.[57]

Even with the king's army in the field, "Churchill and Grafton and Kirke made no secret of their dissaffection." Feversham now advised King James to send Churchill, as the most dangerous of the conspirators, to Portsmouth, and to execute him, together with Kirke and Grafton, the other leading professional captains of the coup, as soon as court martials could sit. If even Feversham was so well informed, the conspiracy was indeed transparent, but the king allowed Churchill and all the rest to swear once again that they would be loyal to him. He readmitted them to the council of war. He even listened to Churchill's advice that the royal army should advance. As in the previous western campaign against invaders, in

1685, Churchill's aggression was opposed by Feversham's conventionality and caution, but it could also be said that Churchill's plan would destroy the royal army's tactical advantage by entangling its cavalry in cropland. Certainly Churchill's purported plan might facilitate further desertion for, on November 21, the Prince of Orange had at last advanced from Exeter, advised by Churchill's intimates, Godfrey and Langston, that their chief would himself desert the king if all else failed. King James, ever more cautious, even paralyzed, rejected any movement to meet the advancing invaders.[58]

The king afterwards recalled that Churchill, undaunted in his effrontery, proposed that the king should at least hearten his army, and threaten the enemy, by visiting the advance post at Warminster, on the western edge of Salisbury Plain. As gold stick in waiting, the Horse Guards officer attending the king, Churchill himself would ride in the royal coach. The escort would be composed of Life Guards under Churchill's command. The post at Warminster was held by the ex-Tangerines under Kirke, Trelawney, and Charles Churchill. Suddenly, even as he listened to lord Churchill propose that he put himself in the hands of the Tangerines, King James collapsed, his nose bleeding profusely. "This bleeding . . . happen'd very providentially," the king's amanuensis wrote, "for it was generally believed afterwards, that My Lord Churchill, Kerke, and Trelawney, with some others in that quarter, had laid a design to Seize the King either in his going hither or his coming back, and so to have carry'd him to the Prince of Orange."[59]

It was midnight when the king's collapse dissolved the council of war. Before dawn on November 23, 1688, lord Churchill, escorted by the horse grenadiers of his troop of the Life Guards, followed by Grafton of the Guards and four hundred other officers and troopers (Churchill's immediate party may have included three future governors-general, Goddard, Kendall, and Brewer), rode west to William of Orange. This mass desertion by his elite officers was fatal to King James. Its leadership shattered, the loyal rank and file of the royal army could not fight, or at least so the king believed. "I have Nothing to do in this mischevious Conjuncture," said the king to Feversham, "but to trust myself to the Care of Providence, since there is no Reliance upon Troops who must needs have taken Infection from their faithless Commanders." The army was James's last hope. Although he had attacked their religion and threatened their careers, the king had continued to believe that personal loyalty, professional duty, and fear of chaos would keep his Protestant officers loyal to him, as it had Churchill for so many years. Disabused of that notion, the king collapsed. His remaining generals panicked. "I can never forget the confusion the Court was in," the advocate general recalled, "the Lord Churchill had gone over to the Prince of Orange from Salisbury the night before, and the Duke of Grafton that morning; the king knew not whom to trust, and the fright was so great," the army's apprehension of Churchill's dash and daring was so deep, that the king's staff believed an impossible account of an advance by Prince William and his new recruits. King James's generals ordered the entire royal army to flee for the Thames.[60]

This was the decisive moment of lord Churchill's coup. The desertion of the leading royal officers had disintegrated the royal army and demoralized the king. James II's army was in full retreat toward the Thames. Crippled physically and psychologically, the king was powerless to resist the combined forces of the invaders and his own officers. Lord Churchill had precisely fulfilled his promise to Prince William, made four months earlier. He would, Churchill had promised, "when the prince should come over, [to] go in to him; but to betray no post, nor do anything more than the withdrawing himself, with such officers as he could trust with such a secret." The number of officers in Churchill's confidence, and under his influence, had proved to be large: one-half of the officers of the most professional royal regiments and most of the king's general staff either deserted to William with Churchill or followed him by prearrangement. On November 25, Churchill's closest associates—the prince of Denmark, Colonel Trelawney, Lieutenant Colonel Churchill, and the duke of Ormonde—together with their staffs, rode away from the retreating army. Their desertion masked by military disorder, they rode west to join lord Churchill, captain of the king's Life Guards, the coordinator of this officers' coup; the duke of Grafton, colonel of the king's First Foot Guards; and lord Cornbury, the king's cousin, in the camp of the invader.[61]

True, lord Churchill's master stroke had missed its mark. He had arranged with Kirke, Trelawney, and Churchill to bring off in a body to Prince William the Tangerine-dominated brigade from Warminster. The plan had been rumored for days. So the moment word reached the king of Churchill's desertion, James (or more likely his son, Churchill's martial nephew, Berwick) had Kirke arrested and withdrew the Tangier battalions to Salisbury. Unaware of this development, when lord Churchill reached William, he reported his intentions. William ordered twelve hundred cavalry to support Churchill. They reached Warminster only to find the troops withdrawn and the royalists in retreat. Still the Tangier officers came over in a body to join lord Churchill in Prince William's camp. Within a week the officer-deserters had been followed by between three and five thousand men. The duke of Grafton's successor in command of the Guards remarked "with a sigh: Poor man (meaning the King) they will leave him so fast they will not give him time to make terms."[62]

Of all these military desertions, contemporaries agreed, Churchill's was the most devastating to King James. It was "the last and most confounding stroke." The Protestant principles Churchill professed had erased the personal gratitude and offset the military duty of the king's longtime favorite and most professional officer. When Churchill deserted him, James "did not know upon whom he could depend." What was he to expect from equally Anglican but far less favored army officers? Lord Churchill proclaimed the religious foundation of this Protestant putsch in the letter he left behind. "I am acted by a higher principle," lord Churchill wrote King James, "when I . . . desert your Majesty at a time when your affaires seeme to challenge the stricktest obedience from all your subjects. . . . This, Sr, could proceed from nothing but the inviolable dictates of my conscience, & a necessary concarn for my religion. . . ." Lord Churchill explained that he had deserted the royal army rather than help the king win "a pretence by conquest" to support "those unhappy designes" which James's evil advisors had "framed against your Maiesty's true interest and the protestant religion."[63]

The king immediately ordered the seizure of lord Churchill's property, the arrest of George Churchill, "and (as I take it) my Lady Churchill herself." After midnight, the guard around the Cockpit, Princess Anne's residence, was doubled. Rumor had it that not only lady Churchill but also the princess herself were to be arrested. Possessed by Sarah's speculations, Anne feared for her life at the hands of the queen. The arresting officer only sought lady Churchill. Princess Anne asked for half an hour's delay. When the time was up, both the princess and her friend had disappeared. The arrangements had been in place for months. A new flight of stairs, supposedly for the convenience of the maids, had been built from the back of the princess's apartments to the street below. The bishop of London had offered his services to his former pupil, Princess Anne, in any emergency. Called up by a message from Sarah Churchill, delivered by lady Berkeley (wife of the cavalry officer who had just joined lord Churchill), Compton's coach stood ready in the street. At first light on November 26, the heavily cloaked ladies stepped into the bishop's coach. The fugitives arrived at the Comptons' town house to find Princess Anne's religious advisor wearing a cloak of episcopal purple over the jackboots and armor of his old regiment, with pistols at his saddlebow, at the head of a mounted guard. This force had been organized by Lieutenant Colonel William Selwyn of the Guards, the senior officer in town, the governor of the Thames forts, and, in due course, the governor-general of Jamaica. The princess's escort also introduced into the imperial service such young recruits as the Scot, Robert Hunter, subsequently Churchill's aide and governor-general of New York, New Jersey, and Jamaica. At daybreak, the escort surrounded the bishop's coach and the princess and her lady rolled north to lend royalty to the regional revolt being organized by the duke of Devonshire at Nottingham.[64]

The objectives of the northern rising were stated in the "Declaration of the Nobility, Gentry and Commonality," dated at Nottingham November

22, but not issued until the princess arrived with such emblems of the church and army as "the Protestant bishop" and the general's wife. It was the king's attack on the church, his expansion of the army, and his reliance upon "Jesuitical Councils" for an "Arbitrary and Tyrannical Government" that, the northerners declared, had moved them to call for a free parliament and to support the Prince of Orange's invasion. This document began the anglicization of Prince William's declarations and, sent via the West Indies, gave a little English color to the pending puritan putsch in New England.[65]

The Nottingham demonstration, like the town takeovers led by the Anglican officers Lumley at York and Lanier at Chester (three of Lanier's cavalry troops had already gone over to William of Orange), as well as Devonshire's personal declaration for the prince, each was premised on the king's rejection of addresses for a free parliament, but, as the Dutch ambassador observed, while these acts were ostensibly in favor of the Prince of Orange and his promise to procure a parliament they were really fueled by fear and hatred of Roman Catholicism. The northern risings survived only because the desertion of the three key officers, Grafton, Churchill, and Trelawney, followed as they were by Denmark, Ormonde, and Berkeley, was providentially timed to check the planned dispatch of regular troops to attack the rebel rendezvous at Nottingham and then move on to York. All anticipated that the regulars would have quickly dispersed the "whish-tail militia" of the northern lords and officers, the more quickly because Nottingham was now an open town. The civil war had been fought in its streets. Garrison government had been personified by the town's parliamentary governor, a famous Independent colonel, John Hutchinson. So the restored monarchy had leveled the walls of Nottingham, as it did those of all the most notoriously puritan and parliamentary inland towns.[66]

The crown built new forts, batteries, blockhouses and citadels, but these were designed to defend and discipline the major seaports. The professional commanders of the seaport garrisons had been the objects of James Stuart's political concern since his brother's restoration. John Churchill had been James's agent for these garrison governments for almost a decade and the first concern of the king's Catholic advisors had been to replace Churchill's confrères with Catholic loyalists. Berwick had succeeded Gainsborough and cashiered Beaumont at Portsmouth. Langdale superseded Copley in Hull. Lord Widdrington took command of Rupert Billingsly and the 15th Regiment at Berwick. Sir Edward Hales displaced Richard Brewer in control of the Tower itself. These seaports and citadels, not such county towns as Nottingham, easily seized but indefensible, were the keys to the coup of 1688.[67]

In the outport garrisons, most of the superseded commanders still served as subordinates to the newly commissioned Catholics. Every one of these Protestant professionals joined the conspiracy organized by lord

Churchill and his associates. Some Protestant officers were supposedly of such superlative loyalty that they had been allowed to retain their commands: Selwyn of the Thames forts; Sir John Reresby at York; Sir Peter Shackerly at Chester; and, in the new citadel of Plymouth, key of the west, that famous royalist, John Grenville, earl of Bath. Such an aristocratic executive, of such wide territorial influence, and with such a cavalier past and so active a court connection, could not be removed from his command of Plymouth—citadel and militia, town and port—without announcing a royal aversion to all Protestant officers whatsoever. Because he was a Protestant constitutionalist, however, and because his deputy lieutenants, county justices, and corporate officers in Cornwall and Devon were early and unanimous in rejecting the king's three questions, Bath's loyalty was suspect at court. In the fall of 1688, he was ordered to accept a Catholic lieutenant governor, the earl of Huntington, and to take his regiment (the 13th) into the Plymouth garrison.[68]

The regiments at Plymouth were the only regular royal units near the invasion beaches at Torbay. When William's army got ashore, unopposed and in force, Bath sent his own company's lieutenant in the 10th to promise the prince that he would join him. No one believed that Bath would actually do so until William's victory was clear. Bath assured both the king and the prince "that he was managing the garrison" in their interest, "whereas he was staying till he saw how the matter was like to be decided." Bath promised the prince that he would turn over the fortress by November 15 or 16. He felt forced to keep his pledge in part because lord Cornbury's desertion brought over to the invaders Sir Edward Seymour, Bath's great rival for territorial influence in the west. William trusted him as little as he did the other grandees, and he assigned Colonel Gibson to shadow Seymour, even after he made Seymour governor of Exeter. Nonetheless, Sir Edward's presence in the prince's camp put weight behind William's letter to Bath. It called on the earl not just to preserve the Protestant religion and parliamentary government but also to protect Bath's own political influence by bringing Plymouth over to the constitutionalist cause.[69]

In reply, on November 18, 1688, Bath promised "perfect obedience" to the prince's commands. There followed a model for the garrison government coups of 1688. On Saturday afternoon, November 24, the day after Churchill had led the desertion from the Salisbury camps, Bath and the Protestant officers of his staff met and agreed to join the prince in his "generous great design of defending the Protestant religion the country and its liberties or the ancient constitution of England." The Protestant officers immediately burst into the city quarters of lord Huntington, found him in the company of his six Catholic subordinates, and arrested them all as agents of a purported popish plot to poison the governor (by sprinkling arsenic on his roast lamb in lieu of salt) and seize the citadel.[70]

By a most fortunate coincidence, the royal frigate *Newcastle*, commanded by Captain George Churchill, was anchored in Plymouth harbor. Despite the king's anger at Captain Churchill's subversion and sabotage in the Channel Fleet, and James II's protests to lord Churchill about his naval brother's backwardness to act against the invaders, the captain had stayed in London almost until the moment when lord Churchill left for the Salisbury camp. Only then did Captain Churchill get the *Newcastle* to sea. Immediately on joining lord Dartmouth's fleet, however, the *Newcastle* was blown westward. Helpless before the storm, the ship's pumps overwhelmed by "a great leak," so her captain wrote, the *Newcastle* had been carried right past the invader's fleet and into Plymouth. Captain Churchill hurried to tell the earl of Bath (the vice admiral for the region, as governors-general usually were) that his entire ship's company was pledged to the anti-Catholic cause. Presumably, Churchill also relayed word of his brother's impending disruption of the king's army, with a predictable effect on Bath's resolution to turn over Plymouth to the prince. That resolution Churchill independently reported to his brother at the prince's headquarters. Captain Churchill added that the *Newcastle* and its crew would control Plymouth harbor in the interest of lord Churchill's coup. So they did.[71]

That afternoon, the soldiers and sailors ratified their officers' political acts. The governor paraded the purged companies of his garrison. He read the prince's declarations in favor of Protestantism and parliament and "the Officers and Soldiers (as one Man) with great and repeated acclimations of Joy assented thereto; declaring They would live and die with the Prince and his Lordship, in defence of the said Declarations." The disarmed Catholic rank and file were turned out of the city gates. Simultaneously, Churchill's crew pledged their loyalty to the prince, the Protestant religion, and the parliament. So did the town fathers of Plymouth in a meeting at the guildhall.[72]

There followed the consequences of a coup, fiscal, military, and political. The governor seized the royal revenue in bank at Plymouth and issued full arrears of pay (a revolutionary event in itself) to his soldiers and Churchill's sailors. After consulting the prince, Bath remodeled the garrison regiments. Protestant professionals and Cornish clients rejoiced in promotions. Bath also took three hundred men from Prince William's army into the garrison, ostensibly to replace the Catholics ousted from Huntington's regiment, actually as a guarantee of his newfound loyalty to the prince. Bath sought to reassert his own influence by calling up the formidable Cornish miners to garrison the citadel. Prince William's supremacy was made militarily manifest, however, when the Dutch battle fleet, and much of the rest of the invaders' armada, in all some 250 ships, anchored in the shelter of Plymouth harbor and the adjacent Tamar estuary. Although the prince would recommission Bath governor of Plymouth and colonel of

his elite (the 10th) regiment, he was never trusted again. The imperial influence that Bath had wielded, in Carolina for example, passed to the officers
of his regiment. Sir Bevil Grenville, Roger Elliot, and Alexander Spotswood became governors-general, the first by John Churchill's arrange-
ment, the latter two as his aides. Churchill's brother Charles ultimately
took command of the citadel and city of Plymouth.[73]

With the port physically secured and the Dutch fleet protected from
autumn's gales by Plymouth's splendid harbors, "all behind him was safe."
Prince William could follow King James's retreating army toward the
Thames. Both armies marched faster when they learned that the great citadel of Hull, the original invasion target, had also fallen to the Protestant
plotters. In 1681, James had been delighted at the king's commission to
Guards captain Lionel Copley as deputy governor of the port and town.
This command included a new citadel designed, like the Restoration refor-
tifications of Plymouth and Portsmouth, to put a bit in the mouth of popular government. Then the king "reformed" the charter of the Hull
corporation. He commissioned that old cavalier and former Jamaican viceroy, Thomas Windsor, earl of Plymouth, as governor of Hull and colonel
of a new infantry regiment (afterwards the 11th of the line). Added to the
citadel, the royal charter, governor, and regiment completed the system of
crown control—garrison government—in the key royal arsenal and port of
eastern England.[74]

The effective quashing of Monmouth's sympathizers in Hull during
the summer of 1685 proved the effectiveness of the new order, but then
Windsor's death weakened the Hull government. On November 4, 1687,
King James commissioned a local Catholic notable, Marmaduke, lord
Langdale, as governor. Langdale also was commissioned captain of the
grenadier company in the 11th Foot. The regiment itself passed to a some-
what more experienced Catholic officer, William Herbert, viscount Montgomery. Montgomery was one of the covey of Catholics educated in arms
in Hungary with Churchill's nephew, the duke of Berwick (who would
become one of the great tacticians of his time, a marshal of France, and who
took care never to lose touch with his Uncle John).[75]

To Hull, besides militant Catholics, the king sent modern cannon, for
the port was generally considered to be the most likely target of a Dutch
invasion. Hull was indeed William's first objective, but the mid-October
storm that drove back the initial Dutch attempt to cross the Channel spared
Hull from invasion. Sailing again on November 1, William's fleet once
more set a course for Hull but, on receipt of last-minute intelligence from
the conspirators at London, William altered course south and west to Torbay. After waiting two weeks for some word of encouragement from the
prince, and for the officers and arms William had promised to send if he
could not come north himself (and he would not, since the issue would be

settled in the populous, prosperous south and west, not the underdeveloped north and east, and by professional officers, not by feudal magnates), the northern conspirators finally rose rather than lose their claim to share in the spoils of lord Churchill's coup. Danby (with the professional assistance of a colonel from the Anglo-Dutch brigade, Sir Henry Belasyse, who asked for Jamaica's government as his reward) seized York. Devonshire rallied the dissidents of Nottinghamshire. Delamere had early on raised Protestant irregulars in Cheshire and Lancashire. Nonetheless, it was left to the Protestant and professional officers of Hull's garrison to attack the Catholic military and to inflict the most material injury on the king's cause in the northeast.[76]

At nine o'clock on the night of December 3, 1688, Captain Lionel Copley, as lieutenant governor and officer of the watch, was about to review the newly posted sentries. Suddenly, lord Langdale appeared and told Copley that he had ordered lord Montgomery and his major, both Catholics, to do the rounds instead. As a Guards officer, Protestant and professional, Copley was insulted and alarmed. Like Bath before him at Plymouth, Copley said that he feared that at Hull "the Popish officers (who were in number more than the Protestant) had an intention of Rising that night." The army conspirators had long since organized the Protestant officers to resist a new popish plot. Outnumbered by the Catholics, the Protestant officers had also involved many of the leading townspeople, much of the seafaring population of the port ("they having had a long Jealousie of the Governour &c"), and several of the Protestant nobility of the region, headed by Danby, in planning for a putsch.[77]

Dismissed from duty by lord Langdale, Captain Copley rallied the other Protestant officers. They went quietly through the darkened streets of Hull and collected the men of their companies from their billets in taverns, stables, and even private homes. Within an hour, Copley and his comrades had enough men in hand to overpower Langdale's sentries, man the city gates, and arrest the Catholic governor and colonel "in their beds." Then the military conspirators captured the remaining Catholic officers. Hull's Catholic command had collapsed. Popular antipopery was unleashed: "the Mobile forthwith fell upon the Mass-house, and all the Houses of the Papists in Town, which they ransack't and demolished by 3 o'clock." An hour later, at first light, Copley and Sir John Hanmer, the senior Protestant officer of the garrison, sent their men across the bridge from the town to seize the old castle. They also stormed the two blockhouses. Finally, the new citadel itself, and the great royal magazine of munitions it housed, were surrendered to the Protestant professionals. Not a shot was fired, for the citadel had been entrusted to the unprofessional care of one of the governor's Catholic confidants, a Cheapside linen salesman lately turned soldier.[78]

At dawn, orange flags flew from every Hull turret and spire. Copley and Hanmer paraded their troops and dedicated "that Strong Garrison for the Service of the Protestant Religion and a Free Parliament." Before nightfall, Copley, using his troops to protect the Catholic nobility and gentry of Hull from "the Mobilee" who were looting their town houses and chapels, escorted the Catholics out of town. Meanwhile, Copley had called in the militia of the east riding to help him hold Hull. Copley's coup made it easy for Churchill and Danby to obtain Prince William's order for Copley to retain the command of Hull. Copley subsequently received a brevet to command as colonel (the military rank of governors on both sides of the Atlantic). On June 4, 1689, Copley was commissioned lieutenant governor to the earl of Danby, who "had gott the government of Hull as a place of retreat, and whereby to make his terms, should there be any change of times." In 1691, Colonel Copley was promoted to the command of Maryland. Copley was the colony's first royal governor-general. He replaced the Catholic proprietor, lord Baltimore (a royal captain of cavalry who had been arrested by lord Churchill's troopers). So was effected, alike on an eastern English estuary and on the Eastern Shore of the Chesapeake, lord Churchill's coup.[79]

The great border fortress of Berwick was garrisoned by the 15th Regiment. King James had cashiered the regiment's colonel, Admiral Herbert, just before Herbert left for Holland with the invitation to Prince William. Effective command was in the hands of Lieutenant Colonel Rupert Billingsly. He had "served from his youth in [the] Army," but, having been ousted as major of the Irish Guards by Tyrconnel, Billingsly had just succeeded his former lieutenant in the Barbados Regiment, James Cotter, as the executive officer of the 15th. In December 1688, the serving officers of the regiment included half a dozen future governors-general. The most notable was the 15th's link with the Denmark-Churchill connection, the regimental major, Edward Nott. At the regiment's church parade, following divine service on the morning of December 16, Colonel Billingsly told his officers that "I was resolved immediately before I dismissed the Regiment to declare for preservation of the King's person and Protestant religion and a free Parliament, and to assist the Prince of Orange in these affayres, to which the Officers all concurred." Billingsly ordered the mayor, still present in the church, to assemble the corporation, and have them endorse the regiment's determination to join the military coup. That done, Billingsly ordered the Catholic governor, lord Widdrington, to leave the fortress, "soe that nowe I have the sole government of this place, at the Prince's service." The lieutenant colonel immediately reported the coup at Berwick to Danby's London agent. On February 20, 1689, Billingsly was duly commissioned lieutenant governor of Berwick and, in recognition of his signal service to the Protestant putsch, knighted by the new sovereign.[80]

Displaced from Berwick by Anglo-Dutch veterans, cadres of the 15th

Regiment, led by Major Nott, and including Lieutenant Colonel Cotter, captains Thomas Fowke, William Dobbyns, and Ensign Thomas Whetham, all previous or subsequent colonial commanders, formed a regiment under the patronage of the duke of Bolton. "Bolton's Second Regiment" took over the governments of the Leeward Islands in the fall of the year, a crucial stage in imperial careers that would reach from Antigua to Scotland and from Guadeloupe to Virginia. The regiment's American service, although a natural outcome of its officers' longstanding and extensive ties to the Leeward Islands, was not entirely a matter of choice. The victorious Prince of Orange found service outside of England for the surviving units of King James's army. The prince did not intend that the army could undo its choice of sovereigns in 1689 as it had in 1660. Once again, the political menace of the old army meant that the American dominions received an influx of military manpower and leadership just in time to fight another imperial war and to impose another round of political centralization.[81]

Like the army in which it occurred, the coup had had two elements, "the guards" (i.e., regiments, mostly in the field) and "the garrisons" (often independent companies, stationed in the ports and provinces). In the guards, lord Churchill's influence had been paramount. His organization, his action, and his example had been decisive for the most professional of the Protestant regimental officers and general staff of the English army. When general lord Churchill left King James II, the royal field army lost its head. So much King James himself said to his privy council on his return to the capital November 26, "in particular inveighing very much against lord Churchill who he had made great and who he considered the only cause of all the desertions, and of the retreat of her Royal Highness," Princess Anne. The army coup was a conspiracy centered on the lieutenant general, lord Churchill. In the English garrisons, although most were linked to the Churchill connection, the varying relations of the long-service Protestant governors with their troops, and of both governors and garrisons with the local and regional patricians and populace, gave a distinctive cast to each urban uprising. In these local contexts, the politics of each garrison unit, the tensions between the troops and the townsmen, and the uneasy interaction of town and hinterland (as burghers and professionals competed for local influence with the regional aristocracies, Protestant or Catholic) produced half a dozen distinct mini-coups. What they had in common was that the seaport and citadel strategy of the Stuarts failed King James in the face of professional and Protestant outrage at the king's imposition of new Catholic commanders, an outrage emboldened by lord Churchill's coup and Prince William's invasion.[82]

The weekend after the Hull coup came the test of King James's reorganized field army. At last, James had implemented his Catholic and Celtic plan for the military. After Piercy Kirke was arrested for conspiring to take the Tangerines over to Prince William, the front line of the royal army was reconstituted. Kirke's brigade, mostly ex-Tangerines, was superseded as the advance guard of the English infantry by some of the twelve thousand Scots and Irish soldiers who had now reached England (one Scots regiment had occupied the Churchills' own St. Albans). In the cavalry, the English regiments disorganized by Cornbury's desertion were supplanted by Scottish and Irish horsemen, all officered by Catholics. The king also hurried Catholic officers to the fore of those units whose officers had followed lord Churchill to the invaders' camp, especially the Guards. King James had at last created a British army, under royalist, reactionary, and, increasingly, Catholic command. It remained to be seen if it was too late for the king to use this army to hold out until French aid arrived. Then, with the promised troops of Louis XIV, James II could impose Catholicism and absolutism on Greater Britain or, as lord Churchill had put it, give "a pretence by conquest" to destroy the Church of England and the imperial constitution.[83]

On Sunday morning, December 9, 1688, most of the British forces King James had left to hold the Twyford Bridge over the Thames fled from the approach of Prince William's vanguard. Of those who fought, sixty Irish "Royalists" were killed. Their compatriots were disarmed. Claverhouse's Scots cavalry withdrew over the bridge, still firing their pistols, but six entire companies of the Scots Guards, who had warned the king "that they will not fight against Protestants," went over to Prince William in a body, "officers and all, in full uniform." King James's almost inexhaustible capacity for surprise that his soldiers were men of religious conscience (or, as Grafton had said when the king twitted him, "It is true, Sir, I don't pretend to much conscience, but I belong to a party that have a great deal") was exercised once again. For James had been convinced that his Edinburgh reign had won the undying loyalty of all Scots soldiers, religion regardless.[84]

Even some of the Irish proved unreliable. Arthur, lord Forbes, Churchill's colleague under Turenne, had managed to keep a quarter of his Irish regiment Protestant, including half of the commissioned and most of the noncommissioned officers. When the regiment (afterwards famous as the 18th Foot, "the Royal Irish") reached England, Forbes refused successive solicitations by Churchill, Grafton, and Ormonde, to subscribe to the coup. Once it was under way, however, the regiment disarmed and discharged its Catholics and Celts. Forbes recalled to the colors a dozen of the regiment's former officers, who just happened to be in the vicinity of Forbes's headquarters (they included one of the regiment's three future governors-general, Lieutenant Richard Blakeney). Then the reformed regiment faced down an anti-Irish mob with an impressive display of Anglican piety. The regiment's refusal to fight for King James demonstrated both the passive disobedience that so amplified the effect of the Churchills' active conspiracy and the regiment's self-starting religious and professional reorganiza-

tion, the institutional initiative of a veteran corps. Protestant religious belief, anglican ethnic identity, and regimental self-consciousness, all elements of a conservative constitutionalism, combined as the constituents of
the military coup that so rapidly undid King James's Catholic and Celtic
intent. As one of the 18th's officers recalled, "it is to be observed to the
honour of the Army, that it was they in a great measure, who saved the
Nation at this juncture. They seeing their Religion, Laws, and Liberties at
Stake, refused to fight for their King, because he had overturned the Constitution; and declared for the Prince who came over to restore it."[85]

The king's last line of defense against the invaders was broken when the
invaders crossed the Thames. Those of his British soldiers who had not
deserted him were overmatched. He had been abandoned, first by his best
English general and that general's followers, and then by his younger
daughter. Her loss courtiers equated with that of an army. The king's elder
daughter was married to the invader, who conquered in her name and interest, and she was anxious and active to depose her own father. Most of the
outlying English garrisons had taken the king's citadels, ousted his Catholic
and loyalist governors, and declared for the Protestant putsch. Lord
Churchill's coup aimed to compel the king to convene a free parliament,
which would legislate to protect the Anglican ascendancy and legitimate the
interim administration of the Prince of Orange.

The defeated king agreed to summon parliament to meet on January
15, 1689. He sent Halifax, Nottingham, and Godolphin to the Prince of
Orange to arrange an immediate truce and to negotiate the military context
of the parliament's meeting. William called in Churchill and a few other of
the military lords to concert a reply. It embodied an analysis of English
security policy and, if implemented, would conclude the coup. To control
London, the Tower and Tilbury Fort were to be surrendered to the Orang-
ists. To secure communications between London and the Netherlands, the
Thames ports below the bridges were all to be garrisoned by elements of
the invading army. To prevent French troops from landing, Portsmouth
was to be neutralized. The king and the prince were to have equal numbers
of guards in London when the parliament met. Otherwise, the metropolis
was to be demilitarized and the main armies were to withdraw to points
thirty miles (two days' march) from the capital. Finally, the prince's army
was to be paid from the king's own revenues until the free parliament made
other provisions.[86]

To accept these conditions was to concede the kingdom to the coup.
On December 10, 1688, King James II read the prince's demands. He
found them unacceptable, but he rejected loyalist plans for a cavalry break-
out and an assault on the northern lords and their "broomstick and whish-
tail militia, and some raw bubbles . . . who will all run away." Instead,
deserted, demoralized, and diseased, James II decided to flee. First, how-

ever, he gave orders for the evacuation of his infant son, the prince of Wales, with his mother, the queen, to France via Portsmouth, the only major garrison still in his hands. But the port was now controlled by naval conspirators. So, to play for time, the king maintained the façade not just of imperial government, but of its reform. He met with the privy council plantations committee during the day on December 10. In committee, the king announced his intent to recommission Colonel Molesworth to the command of Jamaica, to order him to undo the excesses of Albemarle's saturnalia there, and to restore the 1681 constitution. Given Jamaica's role as the colonies' bellwether, this was as profound a political concession for America as those he had promised his officers that he would make in England. James had as little intention of keeping this promise as that.[87]

That evening, the king retired at his usual hour, leaving his faithful guards commanders—Craven of the Coldstream Guards and Northumberland of the Horse Guards—asleep in the antechamber. At 4 a.m., when the top of the Thames tide touched the private steps behind Whitehall, the king boarded his barge. One account has it that the king took with him the symbols and the agents of his failed regime, Father Petre and Judge Jeffreys. All three, ironically enough, given Churchill's coup, were "disguised in Soldiers Habits." In this account, the royal barge rowed down the Thames, shot London Bridge at slack water, and tided downriver on the ebb, its uniformed passengers bound for France. In fact, Petre had fled days before and Jeffreys was taken at Wapping, disguised as a sailor, his trademark eyebrows shaved. An alternative account had it that the king crossed the Thames almost unaccompanied, save for Sir Edward Hales, and rode for the coast of Kent. All accounts agree that, before he fled from Whitehall, determined to disrupt the kingdom he could no longer command, and to prevent any legal usurpation of his prerogative, the king burned the writs summoning members to the parliament and, as he escaped, dropped the Great Seal into the Thames.[88]

As he waited for daylight and a rising tide, James Stuart wrote to explain himself to his old intimate, lord Dartmouth. The king declared that, "having been basely deserted by many officers and Souldiers of my troops, . . . and [realizing] that the same poyson is gott amongst the fleet . . . I could no longer resolve to expose myself to no purpose to what I might expect from the ambitious Prince of Orange and the associated rebellious Lords, and therefore have resolved to withdraw till this Violent storme is over." In the face of the military coup, the king had lost his nerve. Repeatedly, the king denounced the ingratitude of his armed forces. He had, as he reminded his admiral, enlarged, equipped, and favored those forces. He had relied on them to impose his religious and constitutional counterrevolution. Devoted to the established order in church and state, however, the English navy had failed the king and the army had betrayed him. "Neuer any Prince took more care of his sea and land men as I have done, & been so very ill repayd by them," James wrote to his admiral. Still blind to the Protestant and parliamentary principles of the resistance, the king personalized both his decision and Churchill's coup. "If I should go," he asked the loyal earl of Ailesbury on the evening of his flight, "who can wonder after the treatment I have found? My daughter hath deserted me, my army also, and him that I raised from nothing, the same, on whom I heaped all favours; and if such betrays me, what can I expect from those I have done so little for. I know not who to speak to or who to trust."[89]

Army loyalists there still were, however, and they awoke at Whitehall on the morning of December 11, 1688, to find that their commander had effectively abdicated. Then Craven and Northumberland learned that Feversham had taken a broad hint from the migrating monarch not to "expose yourself by resisting a foreign Army and a poisoned Nation." That loyal general had thereupon disbanded four thousand royal troops. By turning them loose into the countryside, armed and undisciplined, Feversham infuriated Prince William. He wanted the men for himself. In large measure, it was to seize control of the English armed forces and commit them to the war with France that William had invaded England. And Feversham's military disbandment terrified both the capital and the countryside. Rumors ran rampant that the Irish soldiery were out to plunder and murder. English Protestants expressed their atavistic fears of the Catholics and Celtics in the mass hysteria of the "Irish fright."[90]

"I am now Allarum'd with ye Reportt of a Body of 8 or 9000 Bloody Irish coming this way from London," the governor of Chester wrote to Secretary Blathwayt. The governor of the gateway to Ireland reported that he had disarmed King James's Catholic garrison with the help of the local militia. Now Sir Peter Shackerley asked that "the victorious Prince of Orange" order his troops to protect Chester against the king's disbanded Irish army. The governor had been warned that the Irish "Burn all Places they come at, and kill Man, Woman, and Child." To resist the Irish, he had armed the Chester citizens from the citadel's magazine and he had mounted cannon at the city gates. The Irish fright had completed the coup at Chester but the governor feared that even an armed citizenry could not resist the Irish "Enemies of our Honest Protestant Religion and Country."[91]

The morphology of the Irish fright was straightforward and, as also appeared in England's American provinces, it was designed to be widely replicated and to terrify the populace to complete the work of the Protestant putsch. Instructed by mail from conspirators in London, persons posing as yokels, "Country Fellows," arrived in town after town, in the dead of night. They roused the sleeping inhabitants with drumbeat and gunfire and the cry "Rise, arm, Arm! The Irish are cutting throats." When the trained bands turned out, they were told to follow the directions in the "Third Declaration of the Prince of Orange." This was a production not of the prince's household, but rather of practiced antipapist plotters. In the prince's name, it ordered Protestants and patriots to disarm all Catholics and arrest every partisan of King James's government. The next town was then informed, often by an anonymous letter in the post, that the Irish had attacked their neighbors. No eyewitness ever appeared. No local person ever admitted to receiving the message. So the rumormongers have never been identified, but their invention, the Irish fright, and its American version, the Indian plot, was admirably contrived to involve every Protestant with access to arms in the work of the putsch.[92]

As the London mob rose, even the most loyal soldiers resisted the results of King James's plans for chaos. Craven and Northumberland paraded the Coldstream and the Horse Guards, accepted the resignations of every Catholic officer, and disarmed and discharged the Catholics from the ranks. With this purged police force, the guards commanders took control of Whitehall and Westminster. Then Craven and Northumberland consulted the thirty-three Protestant peers who remained at court. Organized by the earl of Rochester and the bishop of Ely, the peers constituted themselves as a provisional government. These lords met first at the Guildhall to consult with the City magistrates and then at Whitehall to emphasize that they were the government. They included two former governors-general, Vaughan of Jamaica and Culpepper of Virginia. Their enmity to James or, in American terms, their support for the imperial constitution established in 1681, focused the irreconcilables and so prevented the majority of the peers, who were loyal to James, from declaring in favor of his return.[93]

VAUGHAN, A "COUNTRY" PEER, had been active in that interest's oligarchical and representative colonial policy during his tenure in command of Jamaica. The royal reaction to the Vaughan regime was the attempt to impose Poynings's Law—the constitution of Ireland—on Jamaica (prefatory to imposing it on all England's provinces in America). On Vaughan's return from Jamaica, he became a member of the reforming admiralty commissions of 1679 and 1682 and married Halifax's daughter. Doubtless Vaughan supplied his father-in-law with some of the Jamaican materials with which he defended the legislative privileges of the American provinces, and Vaughan became Halifax's candidate to institute the constitution of 1681 in Jamaica. In 1688, Vaughan (so known from his English barony; he also held the Irish earldom of Carberry) was the only peer to participate in every act of the provisional government. He was marked by his rapid response to the Irish fright, his initiative in the incarceration of Jeffreys in the Tower, and his participation in the council of eleven peers at

Windsor that advocated the prince's seizure of the king. Churchill joined Vaughan in that discussion, and they remained the closest of confidants in the new regime, to William's extreme displeasure.[94]

The second irreconcilable Anglo-American enemy of King James was Thomas, lord Culpepper, who was bitter over his recall from Virginia and his political disgrace, which he blamed on James Stuart. Culpepper had led the formulation of the 1681 compromises between executive and legislative, military and civil, imperial and provincial government, which ended the effort to subject the American provinces to Poynings's Law. Now Culpepper made it clear that he was a champion of constitutional government at home as well as in the empire. In the crisis of the coup against King James, lord Culpepper allied himself with the radical whigs. Culpepper did as much as any peer in the provisional government to make sure that King James's flight was considered an abdication and that William was made monarch in James's place. He led "the violent party" in the maneuvers that deleted from the Guildhall declaration the assertion that the provisional government intended to bring "the King home againe with honor and safety." Indeed, Culpepper objected to every phrase supportive of James's authority or dignity. Culpepper was one of the lords who carried the Guildhall declaration to Prince William.[95]

So he linked the provisional government with the prince's emerging ambition to ascend the imperial throne. Culpepper brought back to the peers William's announcement that, at the invitation of the City, not theirs, he intended to march on London. Culpepper then led the movement for a convention parliament. He helped draft the peers' invitation to William to take over the administration of government until the convention could meet. William's possession of the administration effectively dictated the convention's choice of the prince as king. Lord Culpepper had avenged his Virginia disgrace. The constitutional settlement that Culpepper had championed in the Old Dominion would be the model for England's imperial order under the new king. For Culpepper, as for another enemy of tyranny, "nothing in his life became him like the leaving it." He died on January 27, 1689.[96]

THE GUARDS AND THE PEERS began their provisional government by recognizing that the city's first fear was bombardment from the Tower of London. The peers replaced King James's governor with a well-known Protestant soldier, lord Lucas. He dismissed all Catholics from the Tower garrison and dismounted the mortars that threatened London. The city was safe from the citadel but not from its own inhabitants. The mob rose on the night of December 11. Covered by the longest night of the year, assuming that the flight of the king had ended government, and believing that the threat of the Irish licensed action, the mobs pulled down the Catholic chapels and assaulted the embassies of Catholic kings. Then criminals took over the mob and began to direct the sack of the royal palaces. The capital of the English empire had to be preserved from its own people. The general responsibility was lord Craven's as colonel of the Coldstream Guards and lord lieutenant of Middlesex, but the tactical response was in the hands of Lieutenant Colonel Selwyn and the battalion of the First Guards left behind in London when King James took the field.[97]

After purging his Catholic officers and men, and promising the Protestant Guardsmen their regular pay ("on which they unanimously declared themselves for His Highness," the Prince of Orange), Selwyn had four hundred of the First Guards in hand. Colonel Richard Baggott mustered four hundred of Prince George's men, their colonel, the loyalist Sir Charles Littleton, being elsewhere. The Guards and the marines reached St. James's just behind the mob. They pulled iconoclasts off the organ and statuary of the chapel royal and they ran down the looters of the royal apartments. The next morning, December 12, "whereas the rabble are grown to an ungovernable height," the peers authorized Selwyn "to use force, and fire upon them with bullet." That night, the peers ordered the regulars paraded in St. James's Park. Cannon were "planted in the Park, Charing Cross, at the entrance into Picadilly from Hyde Park side, and other proper places." The earl of Craven, as lord lieutenant of Middlesex, summoned the militia of the suburbs into the capital. Dartmouth's fusiliers were called up to protect the peers themselves "from the rage of the rabble." So the peers kept their promise to the Prince of Orange (by the hands of lord Culpepper and bishop Turner) that they would keep the peace of the imperial capital until he arrived.[98]

The next morning, December 13, the Prince of Orange summoned the secretary at war, William Blathwayt, to Windsor "to the end I may know the exact number of troops now on foot in this Kingdom." Blathwayt was a realist and an imperialist, formerly a diplomat in the Netherlands, now deeply implicated in the conspiracy. He had anticipated the prince's command and came to Windsor with the information that would enable William to take over the English army. Having begun the process of collecting the king's army, the prince ordered the chief military conspirators in his camp to complete their coup by taking control of the capital, and so, as it happened, of the empire. On December 14, lord Churchill, commissioned lieutenant general of the prince's army (the rank he had held in the king's), rode into Whitehall at the head of his troop of the Life Guards. There he completed the purge of that corps' Catholics. In Whitehall Palace, one of Churchill's troopers seized King James's religious advisor, the Pennsylvania proprietor, "Father Penn," asking "what does this Jesuiticall fellow here?" Penn represented the Anglican bugaboo, the union of the papist and the puritan in a regime of dissenting religion and absolutist politics in England and America.[99]

The Life Guards officer on duty then arrived. He compelled Penn to come before the peers. "Mr Pen (the great Quaker, who had joined with the papists in all their late councils at Court)" explained to his captors "that the King was always his Friend, & his Father's Friend, and was a Friend to those of his Persuasion, and in gratitude he was the King's . . ." friend. He was savagely attacked before the peers by Sir Robert Sawyer, the former attorney general and enemy of colonial corporations, Pennsylvania in particular. In reply, Penn himself was not above a little prevarication, declaring that his support for liberty of conscience had been aimed only at preventing its subversion by papists. The lords had to appear to act against so notorious a supporter of the king's religious policies. They required the Pennsylvania proprietor to give bail for a subsequent court appearance. He very reluctantly complied, the more so as the amount was huge, £6,000. The Catholic proprietor of Maryland, lord Baltimore, was also arrested at this time, whether in Whitehall or Wapping is unclear. Lord Baltimore made no speeches but he surrendered to lord Churchill both his person and his troop of cavalry. Baltimore's American government as well soon passed to an officer distinguished in lord Churchill's coup.[100]

The duke of Grafton came to town with lord Churchill, they being the two most senior of the English deserters and of all the coup commanders the two closest to the prince. Grafton, as colonel of the First Guards, took command of Lieutenant Colonel Selwyn's reformed battalion and led them down the Strand en route to the barges from which they would land at the Thames forts to oust their Irish garrisons. In the midst of the Strand, a drunken Irish trooper rode up to Grafton, fired his pistol at the duke, missed, and was shot dead by a Guardsman.[101]

Seen as an Irish Catholic attempt to assassinate one of the Protestant English leaders of the coup against King James, this incident took on added meaning when, on Sunday, December 16, to everyone's surprise, not least his own, King James was welcomed back to London by cheering crowds. Disguised as a servant of Sir Edward Hales's, the king had been captured on the coast by fishermen who took him to be an escaped priest. The fishermen abused the king, robbed him, and locked him up in "The Arms of England" pub. The king was rescued by a party of the Horse Guards, brought back to London, and escorted to Whitehall by lord Craven and the Coldstream Guards in a triumphal parade. The peers sent Van Citters, the Dutch ambassador, to warn Prince William that his safety, his entrance into the capital, and the conclusion of the coup, all were suddenly cast in doubt, first by the assault on Grafton, then by the king's return.[102]

Welcomed by his fickle subjects' loud huzzahs, the king stood in the way of the awakened ambition of the prince. On December 17, bishop

Turner pressed on King James the program of the prince's declarations, as they were understood by the authors of lord Churchill's coup. After that meeting, Turner declared "that he now believed his Majesty was willing to do all that could be required of him, and even to be reduced to the state of a Duke of Venice." But the Prince of Orange had moved beyond his declared intention of forcing King James to accept the will of a parliament, protect the Protestant religion, and secure his own ultimate succession. The prince now intended to capitalize on lord Churchill's coup and his own invasion of England to seize the crown immediately.[103]

On the evening of December 17, 1688, the firelock matches of three battalions of Prince William's Blue Guards suddenly glowed in ranks across Hyde Park. Then, drums beating, the prince's bodyguard marched up the slope toward St. James's. There the king was and there the earl of Craven had drawn up the Coldstream Guards. The Dutch general, Count Solms, ever afterwards the nemesis of English soldiers, rode up and ordered lord Craven to withdraw his men. The little earl replied that "he would rather be cut in pieces." Instead, he went in to his king. On his knees, the colonel of the Coldstream Guards begged King James's permission to resist, to fulfill his promise to his loyal troops "to at least have one blow for it," and so to redeem the English army's lost honor. James refused. Instead he ordered the Coldstream Guards, the last loyalists, to give up their posts to the Dutch. The king of England was the prisoner of the invaders.[104]

The next day, having taken the advice of lord Churchill and others of the peers with him at Windsor, Prince William ordered his royal prisoner to leave London. Three hours after the king took barge for Rochester, surrounded by boats full of the prince's Blue Guards, Prince William rode into London, now garrisoned by 6,800 of his own troops, posted by lord Churchill. The prince was personally protected by four regiments of the English and Scots brigades in the states' service, commanded by Major General Hugh Mackay. "The Shouts, the Huzza's, the Oranges on Swords, Pikes &c., and the numbers of the People were incredible," but not all Englishmen were pleased. "A forraign enemy in an hostile manner march through the metropolis of the Kingdom," grumbled one observer. His view was echoed by many English soldiers: "the army seem generally out of humour and uneasy at what they have done." William's first order on arriving in the capital of the English empire was that Churchill disperse all the English Guards to country quarters, away from the capital and away from the possibility of reversing the outcome of the coup. Grafton and the First Guards were sent to take over Portsmouth from Berwick and the Irish. Lord Churchill's own troop of the Life Guards were ordered to ride all the way out to his estate at St. Albans, twenty miles from Whitehall, and displace the Scots whom King James had quartered there. The English Guards, "which both in their persons and gallantry were an ornament to the town," were displaced by twenty-six companies of Prince William's Blue Guards, "ill-lookeing and ill-habited Dutch" in the eyes of English soldiers. The invaders took over the guard posts in Whitehall and Westminster. Even the spearheads of the invasion, the three thousand men of the Anglo-Dutch and Scots-Dutch brigades, were quartered across the Thames in Southwark as soon as they had led Prince William's parade into London.[105]

As this momentous changing of the palace guard proves, the events of 1688 were no revolution. They were not even a revolt, whether by peers, parliament, or people. Instead, King James and the counterreformation of the seventeenth century were overthrown by lord Churchill's coup and Prince William's invasion. The coup d'état of 1688 was the first stage of the military transformation of British government, moving it from an underdeveloped early modern monarchy towards nationalism and statehood. The ensuing decade of world war with France propelled England out of underdevelopment and into modernity. England became a centralized, bureaucratized, armed state. This statist outcome was the consequence of the coup organized by young, ambitious, professional, political, and Protestant officers, led by their exemplar John Churchill. He and they saw their church and their careers, their constitution and their empire, all in danger from a bigoted and absolutist, francophile and Catholic king. Churchill and his co-conspirators had volunteered their support to the Prince of Orange, commander-in-chief apparent of England, the Protestant champion of Europe, the greatest enemy of France, if he would invade England and so help them save its Protestant church, its parliamentary laws, its national independence, and its imperial future.

In return for Prince William's leadership, his invasion force of twelve thousand troops, his armada of hundreds of ships, the officers of England's armed forces, lord Churchill in particular, promised the prince that they would divide, disrupt, and desert the army of James II. If their plot succeeded in defanging the royal army, the military instrument of Stuart policy, Churchill and his colleagues could expect, from their experience of Prince William over the preceding fifteen years, an English future more militantly Protestant, national, and imperial than the Catholic clientage to France that King James had intended them to impose on his kingdoms and his colonies. They did not expect William to convert their coup into his kingship. Naïvely, they believed William's declaration that he "had no intention of removing the King from the Throne or to make himself Master of England, but only to take care that by the convocation of a free Parliament summoned according to the Laws of England, and composed of legally qualified persons," that the reformed religion "might be placed in Security," that the English political nation could be assured of its liberties and privileges, and so, by bringing king and people into harmony, England might be made more useful to its allies, especially the states of the Netherlands in their war with France and their defense of the reformed religion.[106]

To these ends, the officers of Churchill's cohort, officers of like age, professionalism, and ideology organized a classic military coup. The military were necessarily predominant in an underdeveloped polity. Indeed, it is appropriate to think of England and its dependencies in 1688 as analogous to a "third world" state in which the army and the church are the only bureaucratically advanced institutions and so constitute the national administrative structure. To be sure, English aristocrats' cooperation was important to the coup in remote regions. Certainly the army command was essentially aristocratic in ethos, if seldom by blood. The very vitality of aristocracy was the mark of a primitive polity. The overwhelming administrative importance of the army in so primitive, so personalized, and so parochial a government had meant that Churchill's disintegration of the military command structure, with the blessing of the Protestant priesthood, had stripped the king of authority in England.

So too in America. Since 1681, in order to seize his royal inheritance in England, James had withdrawn from the provinces of the empire the regular military forces that were everywhere the makeweight of royal government, yet he had made imperial administration even more identical with the chain of command. Therefore lord Churchill's coup in England eviscerated American provincial governments and left them exposed to a series of coups by the provincial armies. Each American coup reflected, in the exaggerated way characteristic of colonies, aspects of the coup d'état in England.

Lord Churchill's coup was so successful on both sides of the Atlantic that, a year after the fact, it was doubly misnamed the "Glorious Revolution." The "revolution" of 1689–1702 followed the coup of 1688 and was its consequence. The unconstitutional convention that "offered" the crown to the conqueror merely ratified the military verdict of lord Churchill's coup and Prince William's invasion. The political struggles of the next generation were essentially about the degree to which the monarch could be made to share the direction of the army (and so of policy, domestic, foreign, and imperial) with the "men of business," the oligarchy that emerged from the coup and from the ensuing wars with France. The triumph of this new class, in which John Churchill's part was to rescue the English army from Dutch command and to put an English princess at the head of the army and so of the empire, was indeed revolutionary. It was "glorious" too, in a parochial way, for the bloodshed that made England a major power in just a dozen years was externalized to Scotland and Ireland and Europe and America. This was the "Glorious Revolution" of 1689–1702. It was altogether consequent upon lord Churchill's coup in 1688.

The coup d'état and the invasion together determined the dynastic question as to whether the Catholic or the Protestant branch of the ruling family would sit on the imperial throne of England. In a monarchical government, the military factions were necessarily devoted to one or another royal commander-in-chief. In every succession crisis in John Churchill's lifetime, the choice of monarchs lay in the hands of the dominant army commanders. It had done so in 1649, 1659, 1660, 1685, and 1688/9. It would do so again in 1702 and 1714/5. The centrality of the army to "empire," in both the sense of monarchical rule and of widespread dominion, was clearest in 1688/9. It was to win control of the fighting forces and financial resources of the English empire for his war with Louis XIV that Prince William had connived with the Churchillian conspirators and the dissident aristocrats. The flight of King James and the replacement of his guards by those of Prince William made manifest a military coup far more extensive than Churchill and his colleagues had intended. Because lord Churchill had deserted him, King James effectively abdicated. What remained of his army was either committed to the conqueror or defanged by lord Churchill's post-coup purge. Suddenly the extent of William's ambition, and the firmness of its foundations in force, appeared to the military conspirators, to the dissident aristocrats, to the population of the imperial metropolis, and so to the entire empire. A second "William the Conqueror" seized the imperial throne. He thrust the empire into war with France. To serve that war, he transformed English society and government, reinvolved the island empire with Europe, and made all America a theatre of combat.

"That all power flows from the barrel of a gun" was made manifest in 1688, and for a decade afterwards, by the military occupation of the imperial metropolis by foreign troops. London was garrisoned by William's Blue Guards from 1688 until 1698. This was the unintended military consequence of lord Churchill's coup. It brought home to Churchill and his fellow officers the transforming reality of their act in deposing King James and ending the Restoration Empire. "The posting of the Dutch guards where the English guards had been, gave a general disgust to the whole English army." That army found itself first rusticated, then purged. The loyalists of the Coldstream Guards left London with particular unwillingness. Their new lieutenant colonel, William Selwyn, promoted for his part in the putsch, had to use all of his persuasive powers to get most of the Coldstreamers to obey lord Churchill's commands. Only four companies of the Coldstream Guards left London willingly. Privileged to attend their king, these Guards arrived at Rochester, only to find that James II had disappointed their loyalty one last time.[107]

The king had been terrified by the suggestion, allegedly lord Churchill's, that he be incarcerated in the Tower of London. King James said to the counselors who begged him to stay in England that, "if I do not retire I shall certainly be sent to the Tower, and no king ever went out of that place but to his grave." In the small hours of December 22, 1688, King James sailed for France. He landed at Cherbourg on Christmas morning "still talking bitterly of Churchill's ingratitude." That, King James concluded, was the key to "the greatest conspiracy ever formed," one that, "by so general a defection in my army," had encompassed three ancient kingdoms and one new empire.[108]

BOOK III

ARMY AND REVOLUTION

Kirk has Fire, *Lanier* Thought, *Mackay* Skill,
and *Colchester* Bravery;
but there is something in the Earl of *Marlborough*
that is inexpressible.
All those Virtues seem to be united
in his single Person
And I have lost my wonted knowledge of Physiognomy,
if any Subject you have
can ever attain such a Height of Military Glory,
as this Combination of sublime Perfections
must one Day or other advance him to.

—Charles Henri de Lorraine, the prince of Vaudemont,
to King William III, 1691

CHAPTER FIVE

The Coup in the Colonies:

1689–1690

Changing the Guard

O N T H E D A Y after King James left London to the Prince of Orange, the newly freed press reported that "the Lord Churchill and Colonel Kirke are in great favor with his Highness, and that he has left it at their discretion to cashier what officers of the army they dislike and put in new ones." Churchill (for it was he who took control of the English army when Kirke was diverted to Ireland) purged two English officers in three for refusing to join the coup d'état. Churchill's officer corps were now outnumbered by the British, Dutch, Danish, and Huguenot followers of Prince William. The successful conspirators held but a tenuous command of a rank and file still largely loyal to the exiled king. The creators of the coup could neither restore the domestic authority that the army had exercised under King James nor themselves seize the governmental power they thought that they deserved as the authors of the coup against the Catholic king.[1]

Churchill and his co-conspirators had hoped to use the prince to coerce the king. Instead they were used by the prince to oust the king. They had intended to use the prince to force reform of James's regime. Instead, they had made possible William's conquest of England. The army of England was reduced to being a sword—two-edged to be sure—of a second "William the Conqueror." Or rather, as contemporaries observed, the army were the agents of another Cromwell. There was, wrote Archbishop Sancroft, "no difference" between these military dictators, "but that the one's name was Oliver and the other's William." As another Cromwell, William would equal his prescient predecessor in modernizing the army and, with it, ruling the British kingdoms and the American dominions, but the army of the Restoration Empire would not serve the prince's English political purposes. An army was the sine qua non of William's sovereignty. As the speaker of the commons put it, "if the Prince was King he must maintain it by an army," but the army which had been James II's "was not to be trusted against their natural prince, for as the late English army would not fight for poperie, soe neither would they fight against their King, as was apparent by their [the men's] daily deserting and [the officers'] quitting their commands." So William the Conqueror took control of the metropolis and the ports of England with the units of his own invasion force. Churchill and company were reduced to the task of making the British forces the professional instrument of King William's European purposes. As anglican imperialists, however, they redirected what military resources they could divert from the European continent to English America. As in Cromwell's time, redcoats once again became the shock troops of empire.[2]

Lord Churchill's immediate task was to combine his personal military commands, which had been the center of the coup, with those units of the English and Scots armies which had remained loyal to King James, and then to lead this politically divided and militarily demoralized force overseas to join the allied army in Flanders. Colonel Kirke took most of the other English and Scottish regiments across the Irish Sea to relieve Londonderry, the last Protestant stronghold in Ireland. From that base, Kirke's troops could begin the reconquest of England's greatest colony. The remaining English and Scottish regiments, the survivors of lord Churchill's coup and purge, were to be divided between the policing of Scotland and the protection of the West Indies.

England itself was largely stripped of English troops. They were displaced in the imperial capital by Prince William's own praetorians, the Blue Guards, and in the citadels and seaports of the south and west by the Anglo-Dutch brigade. William's troops had won him the imperial throne because the most professional parts of the English officer corps and crucial units in both the guards and garrisons had betrayed King James. Prince William would give them no chance to recall King James or to oppose the prince's own ambition to become king in James's place. For almost a decade to come, William's men held London and the Channel ports. That is, the Dutch controlled England while the British served overseas.

So, the Prince of Orange parsed the declaration he had published on the eve of his invasion of England. The prince had pledged that "as soon as the state of the kingdom will admit of it, we promise that we will send back all those foreign forces that we have brought along with us," but William never thought that state had arrived. So William denied domestic influence to the English army and its best general, although their coup had put him on the throne, effected England's alliance with the Netherlands, and launched the English army toward services in Flanders, Ireland, and America unequaled since Cromwell's redcoats had conquered and consolidated the first English empire. So Churchill and the English army were balked of the political power that the coup d'état had promised them by a prince who was himself a master manipulator of armed authority. William's Blue Guards at Whitehall were the emblems and the instruments of an alien prince's command of the English empire.[3]

In this, the second episode of praetorian politics that London had experienced in a generation, lord Churchill was William's chief subordinate. His name grew "very formidable, both in the Court and in the Camp." Lord Churchill executed Prince William's orders to move the English household troops more than a day's march from London but he himself remained in the capital to reform the English army under William's aegis. The whig aristocrats were outraged by Churchill's elevation. They told the prince that Churchill was a mere mercenary, a professional soldier and social climber. He had led his military connection to desert because "their ambition was not answered" by King James, and because their commands were in danger: "they were like to be laid aside" when the king Catholicized his army. These officers' only interest was their own careers, the prince was warned, and "nothing can make them faithful to you." What the whigs failed to anticipate was that, while the Denmark connection indeed expanded their authority in the English army by purging their elders and their enemies in the prince's name, Churchill and his colleagues then were bound to execute William's orders. These were to ship the reformed English army overseas. With their own power base abroad and the prince's troops on guard at Whitehall, the officers of the Denmark connection could not preserve the succession (subsequent to the childless Mary) of their candidate for the imperial throne, Princess Anne. Even so, Anne became the figurehead of army-tory politics and English xenophobia.[4]

The princess lost her place in the succession when the prince made it plain that he would rule in his own right, the right of conquest, not as a regent for his father-in-law nor as the consort of his wife, "being unwilling to possess any thing by apron strings." William's claim by conquest to sole sovereignty was but slightly masked by Mary's hereditary title and by the convention's resolution. His overbearing ambition found no obstacle in his wife's submission and incapacity, and his military control of the capital meant that the irregularly elected and assembled legislature, a "convention" not a parliament, ratified a physical fact: the prince possessed the kingdom. Arguments about social contract and parliamentary power, about providence and the people, faded before the forcible fact of the Protestant putsch as the foundation for a change of regal command. That militant fact was the more menacing because it implied the continued rule of force, the absolutism of the armed state. The conqueror and his troops, "the present Possessors [of the property called "England"] may turn them out of their Freeholds, and sell them to the West Indies without any legal Injustice. For where a People are Conquered their Lives and Fortunes lye at the Mercy of the Conqueror."[5]

To the authority of a foreign prince and his army, lord Churchill emerged as an armed obstacle. The anglican patriotism and military professionalism, the religious faith and personal devotion to Princess Anne that had moved Churchill to destroy James's popish and francophile regime now led him to subvert the rule of the Dutch prince and his army. To begin with, as Princess Anne's champion, lord Churchill threatened to thwart the prince's passion to be a king and to exercise sole sovereignty. Likewise, lady Churchill stood between Anne and Mary's determination to subordinate her younger sister. Lord and lady Churchill's influence over Princess Anne reminded the would-be king and queen of John Churchill's notorious indispensability to King James. Churchill intended to become equally important to the prince and princess whom he had put within reach of the imperial throne, but William "said that Ld. Churchill could not govern him nor my Lady the Princess his wife, as they did the Prince and Princess of Denmark." Thwarted, Churchill became the center of the opposition to the prince's supremacy and the champion both of Princess Anne's immediate influence and her ultimate succession.[6]

Anne was now heard to say that she should never have deserted "her father to come in to the Prince, who was now endeavouring to take away *her right, and to get the priority of Succession before her.*" As Anne's representative, out of residual loyalty to his old master, King James, and from a belief in the hereditary principle, Churchill supported a regency in the convention debates about the succession (he always retained minutes of those debates in his papers). A regency was compatible with the Churchills' original hopes for the outcome of the conspiracy (that the presence of the prince and his army would enable the conspirators to force reforms on King James that would protect the Church of England and the Anglican monopoly of public life). A regency was in accord with the views of the Church of England, as formulated by Churchill's spiritual advisor, Bishop Turner. A regency had been inherent in Churchill's relationship with William since 1678. As regent, Prince William would preside over a government premised on King James's incapacity and absence, but that did not dethrone the king. Instead the regency would be sanctioned by a collectivity of Mary's inheritance and Anne's reversion. Ruling in James's name and by Mary's right, William's position would be too weak to resist accommodations with Anne's partisans, headed by the Churchills.[7]

The Denmark interest (lord Churchill had just been named groom of the stole to the prince of Denmark), however, could not deny that military realities—the Dutch guards at Whitehall Palace, the Dutch fleet in Portsmouth harbor, the Dutch command of the allied army in the coming war with France—made William monarch. Swallowing their semiarticulate but heartfelt hopes of personal elevation from their coup, lord and lady Churchill acknowledged "that in reality there was nothing to be done but to yeild with a good grace." It thus became lord Churchill's distasteful duty to persuade the princess (whose chief counselor he was, and whose military supporters he headed) that she should put off "the sunshine day" of her succession to the throne of England and its empire. Anne, Churchill said, would have to wait for the throne not only until the demise of her elder sister, Mary, but also until the death of Mary's husband, Prince William. Lord Churchill sabotaged the Clarendon connection's efforts to establish Mary's sole sovereignty and Anne's right to succeed her sister as queen. The Churchill party's absence from the lords provided much of the margin by which William became king, not regent.[8]

Churchill's political recognition of military reality was rewarded, modest though those rewards appeared to the ambitious general who had managed the coup. A week after William and Mary were elevated to the imperial throne of England, King William recommissioned lord Churchill to the offices he had held under King James: lieutenant general of the English army; colonel of the Third Troop of the Life Guards; gentleman of the king's bedchamber (a new, whig, presence occasionally intruded there in the form of lord Mordaunt, although he had spent the crisis of empire in Jamaica, hunting treasure; afterwards, as the earl of Peterborough, he was Jamaica's soi-disant governor-general). Churchill was also elevated to the new king's privy council. Churchill's importance outraged the courtiers of the new regime. They cooled their heels in the antechamber for hours on end while the general and the king reformed the administration of the army, and so of the empire. On March 8, 1688/9, Churchill began to organize ten English battalions for the allied army then assembling in Holland. Such was his success that, as part of his own coronation as king, William raised Churchill a step in the English peerage, creating him earl of Marlborough.[9]

THE TITLE CHURCHILL TOOK on April 9, 1689, had been made famous by a combative cousin killed at Lowestoft on the eve of Churchill's own enlistment. The military career of James Ley, earl of Marlborough, had marked out, on opposite sides of the world, the frontiers of the English empire that his successor would dominate. James, earl of Marlborough, had inspected Massachusetts in 1637 as the herald of the imperial order that was implemented by Sir Edmund Andros fifty years afterward. Marlborough came home from Massachusetts to fight for King Charles, as so many Massachusetts men did to fight against him. By 1643, Marlborough commanded the royal artillery. His command and the king's cause were destroyed together at Naseby in the summer of 1645. The earl took the path of English exile and imperial expansion chosen by so many other cavaliers. Marlborough led out the English expedition that reconquered the colony of Santa Cruz from the Spanish. Then he forwarded the royalist cause in Barbados.

Immediately after the royal restoration, King Charles II commissioned Marlborough admiral and governor in command of the force that occupied Bombay and so founded the English empire in India. He was "employed to the American plantations in anno 1662." In 1664, Marlborough was named viceroy of Jamaica. Before he could return to America the Dutch war broke out. The earl immediately volunteered for service. On June 3, 1665, in command of the *Old James*, Marlborough was cut in half by a cannonball just as his ship recaptured the *Montague* from the Dutch. He was forty-six years old.

The great earl of Clarendon wrote that James, earl of Marlborough, had been a "man of wonderful parts in all kinds of learning, which he took more delight in than his title." He was famous among his contemporaries for that religious faith which is so often found in battle. Marlborough anticipated his death in a valediction written six weeks before the fatal fight off Lowestoft: "let us be more generous than to believe that we die as the beasts that perish; but with a Christian, manly, brave resolution, look to what is eternal." Marlborough was borne to his tomb by the lords of the privy council, his imperial achievements were proclaimed by the royal heralds, and he was laid to rest in Westminster Abbey. There, fifty years later, he was joined for a time by the kinsman and namesake who had succeeded him in the profession of war, the title of Marlborough, and the administration of the empire.[10]

THE ACHIEVEMENTS of John Churchill, the new earl of Marlborough, in army reform and imperial administration surpassed those of the old earl. They were also more controversial. In the first years after the coup, Marlborough's activities disappointed revolutionary idealism. They were marred by military mutinies. They were imperiled (in the American provinces of the empire as they were in its British kingdoms) by the political conflicts consequent on lord Churchill's coup.

Idealism was Marlborough's first victim. The newspapers had played up a planted story about the disbandment of the regiments commanded by King James's household officers. The story promised that "none but Sober and Discreet Persons shall be put in Comand, that no places, either Civil or Military shall be bought or sold; and that singular Merit, Parts and Valour, shall be the only means to recomend Persons." Yet it was precisely his refusal to make "the mean applications I found wd. be required of me from ye noble Peer my Ld. Marlboro to keep myself in" command, Sir Charles Littleton wrote, that cost him the government of Sheerness and eliminated his regiment of marines. There was more to this episode than Marlborough's avarice or Littleton's pride. The royal marines, formed as James Stuart's own regiment, were at the center of the mutinies that swept the army of England as Marlborough tried to transform it from a political police force into an expeditionary corps. The marines rejected lord Churchill's command to march to Harwich for embarkation to Holland. "Their pretence is, and what we can't bring them off," Colonel Sir Charles Littleton wrote to William Blathwayt (now King William's secretary at war and of plantations as he had been King James's), "is that they are to have Dutch officers put over them when they come beyond the sea, that they are to have Dutch pay, and are to be banished England, that they see no reason why they should be so used, while the Dutch troops stay here and eat up the fat of the land."[11]

The English army had lost its kingdom to a Dutch invader. That humiliation underlay military unrest throughout William's reign. Churchill himself would come to conduct the army chorus of resentment but, with the outcome of the coup still in the balance, military discipline required that an example be made of the mutinous marines and of a tory colonel who had refused to bow to his former subordinate. Other regiments struck for and won concessions—promises of English pay, of rotation home, even an alteration of field officers—but Churchill eliminated the royal marines, his own former corps, and the only senior regiment to be entirely disbanded in the Marlborough purge. First he refused to authorize Littleton's officers to recruit. Then he told King William that they had connived at their men's mutiny and desertion. Finally Marlborough had the king cashier the marine regiment's officer corps. Churchill took their men for his own regiment, the Royal Fusiliers (formerly Dartmouth's command). Littleton protested: "I have plainly told my Ld. Church, who's now Ld. Marlborough, we think we deserve better usage as being the Regiment who's officers have stuck best together in ye Service of any in the army." Indeed, the marine officers had been united, but in the service of King James. So they were broken at the instance of their old executive officer, the commander of the coup against their king. Then Littleton lost Sheerness (he handed over his commission as governor to Queen Mary, rather than give it to her hated husband). His public excuse was that, at his age, he could not stand wartime attendance at his command. His political declaration was a refusal to "sign and address renouncing my later master." His real resentment was having to submit to Marlborough.[12]

So in 1689 ended the imperial career of an officer whose first independent command had been that of Jamaica in 1661. Littleton's resignation from the government of Sheerness was an epitaph for the Restoration Empire, and another indication of Marlborough's imperial ascendancy. Marlborough replaced Littleton by promoting Colonel William Selwyn to garrison government. Selwyn's services to the coup in London had already won him a double step to the lieutenant colonelcy of the Coldstream

Guards. Now it was alleged that two payments to Marlborough, each of 1,000 gold guineas, secured Selwyn the government of the Thames garrisons. This command was Selwyn's first step in a garrison government career that concluded with his governor-generalship of Jamaica (again achieved under Marlborough's aegis).[13]

When the governor of Chester applied to Secretary Blathwayt for the renewal of his commission, Blathwayt replied, "write to my Lord Churchill about it." The governor not only wrote to Churchill, he sent his banker. So much for promotions "according to Meritt, not Price." One of his intimates asserted that "the harvest My Lord Churchill made by this was vast, for all is sold." Purported profits of £70,000 supposedly came Churchill's way as he "reformed" the army command system in royal regiments and garrison governments. To the redoubtable Sarah, now the countess of Marlborough, this enormous sum seemed little enough to purchase a landed estate suitable to their new title, much less to provide their daughters with dowries suitable to their newly exalted station.[14]

It seemed likely to go on raining gold into the Churchill cashbox. Marshal Schomberg, William's general, the military head of the Huguenots, remarked that "My Lord Churchill proposes all, I am sent for to say the general consents and Monsieur Bentick is the secretary to write all." William Blathwayt, the secretary at war, and the earl of Marlborough did what they could to put garrison government, in America as in England, into the hands of army officers who combined coup connections with conservative politics. In the Jamaica case, Blathwayt and Marlborough were previously committed to the succession of the provincial lieutenant governor, Colonel Hender Molesworth, as the protégé of Sir Thomas Lynch, the governor-general who had created the planter party and promoted the imperial constitution of 1681. Molesworth's commission was duly confirmed by William but, before it could pass the seals, a prominent officer from among the English conspirators and another from the Anglo-Dutch brigades both claimed the Jamaica command as a reward for their recent military-political service. As were the officers now commissioned to New York, Virginia, and the Leeward Islands, the competitors for the Jamaica command were ideologically as well as professionally qualified for American government.[15]

Richard Savage, viscount Colchester, had been lord Churchill's own lieutenant in the Third Troop of the Life Guards. A violent whig and a rakehell, Colchester had left Churchill's command to become one of the least likely recruits of lord Dover's Catholic school for military gentlemen, the Fourth Troop of the Life Guards. Colchester had become its lieutenant colonel, represented the Protestant officers of the Life Guards in the "Treason Club," and was one of the first of King James's officers to desert to William of Orange. The prince commissioned Colchester colonel of a cavalry regiment. When the unit was posted to the cold and unrewarding wilderness of Scotland, however, Colchester sought the warmer, richer, viceregency of Jamaica. His competitor was Sir Henry Belasyse, a Tangerine in Churchill's time and, since 1674, an officer of the Anglo-Dutch brigade. In 1678, William of Orange had promoted Belasyse a colonel in the brigade. It was Belasyse, so the loyal governor of York reported, who "had lurked long here in Yorkshire" before the putsch, and who, with his troop of horse, conducted the coup in the northern capital. King William duly promoted Belasyse brigadier general in April 1689, just as he sought independent command in Jamaica, presumably as Danby's nominee.[16]

Yet neither of these well-qualified and well-connected candidates for imperial command ousted Molesworth from the Jamaica succession. Colchester and Belasyse were victims of the rule that every one of James II's American viceroys—linked, as each of them was, with the "friends of the governors," Admiral Herbert, Secretary Blathwayt, and the general, Marlborough—who offered to serve King William was recommissioned. Molesworth's strengths were those of a capitalist and constitutionalist entrenched with the imperial establishment. After Marlborough sailed to Flanders, however, Molesworth suddenly died. He was succeeded by "the worst man in the world" for an imperial government, in Marlborough's view, the earl of Inchiquin. This former governor-general of Tangier was rewarded for his part in the Irish episodes of the imperial coup. Inchiquin's appointment was the first American product of Queen Mary's connection with Irish exile officers. That connection would promote a succession of Anglo-Irish officers to the command of New York.[17]

Contests for no fewer than nine American governments continued between the constituents of the coup. To settle them, King William increasingly relied on the recommendations of Marlborough, Blathwayt, and the other tory imperialists because the king quickly came to suspect the whigs of republicanism and to appreciate that the tories were ideologically committed to monarchical authority. The anglican imperialists won military and administrative power for themselves (Blathwayt even displaced Constantine Huygens, William's Dutch secretary at war). They kept their old correspondents and comrades in American commands. They adjusted their American policies to the new Anglo-Dutch condominium in ways which largely forestalled a Dutch resurgence in America and that also prevented provincial opponents of English empire from retaining the local authority they had won by their shares in the American coups. The reappointed administrators of the army and the empire, all of whom had served King James, continued under King William to resist four perils to the English imperial prerogative: the French enemy; the Dutch allies; the "republicans" (in both old England and New England); and the private provincial proprietors.[18]

As for the French enemy, even before his coronation, William had heard Churchill (and Blathwayt) complain about the French attacks on the Hudson Bay outposts. He listened to them predict French assaults on the Leeward Islands and Newfoundland. On April 25, 1689, the newly created earl of Marlborough petitioned the new king to honor their imperial bargain. The English imperialist had organized military resources for the champion of European Protestantism to fight Catholic France in Europe. He expected to have William's approval for his plans to forward empire in America. Marlborough now offered to King William the argument for northern development and against French designs on English America that he had vainly pressed on King James. Marlborough claimed colonial status for "Rupertsland" as part of "the Imperial Crowne of this Kingdom." He repeated that "the French Nation at Canada (the ill Neighbours of all mankind)," under cover of the negotiations for the Treaty of American Neutrality, had captured the ships, destroyed the factories, stolen the goods, burnt the houses, and murdered the Englishmen of Hudson Bay. For losses of £100,000 no recompense had been given by the French because, Marlborough said, the Company of Canada was the fiefdom of the Jesuits. But the danger was much more extensive than that, Marlborough warned William. The French had insolently announced their intent not only "utterly to extirpate" Hudson Bay but also declared "that in a short time they intended to have New York & New England too, their Priests acting in all their Councils with their Indians against Your Matys Subjects." Marlborough again annexed the latest letter he had received from Boston as evidence of Franco-Catholic-Indian aggression against "your Territories and Plantations in America." He called on King William to protect the American empire and authorize retaliation against the French.[19]

To resist French aggression in America, Dutch aid would be useful. Marlborough and Blathwayt, however, shied at paying an American imperial price for Dutch military aid (in addition to the £600,000 the parliament had voted to reimburse the Dutch for their invasion costs). English imperial exclusiveness meant that the war in America during the 1690s would be wholly English and, whenever it moved beyond defense, a failure, yet the Dutch had neither the political will nor the physical capacity to invest heavily in the American theatre. Certainly King William willingly left America to his English ministers and he acknowledged English naval preponderance in the Atlantic, just as he accepted for the states the greatest burden in Europe. He thereby determined that he and his compatriots would control the continental outcomes of the war while the English would harvest whatever the war won in America. That was to be no more than the *status quo antebellum* on the islands and in the established American provinces. Hudson Bay was not recovered by the English until 1718. All provincial frontiers were still exposed to French and Indian raiders. All Anglo-American commerce was decimated by French corsairs. English xenophobia and

Dutch weakness combined to deprive the American provinces of the military benefits Churchill proposed for them from his coup against King James.[20]

In the spring of 1689, in "the Business which your Lopp has now in Charge, namely how to regulate a Conjunction of our Forces with Holland," the English imperialist was advised to accept as little Dutch aid at sea, and so in America, as possible, "for this is the Soul of Power in those Parts." Sea power, especially on the Atlantic routes to America, should be essentially English, the imperial negotiator was advised, but the allied army should be as much Dutch as possible. So the Dutch, eviscerated by the land war with France fought on the Netherlands' own frontiers, would have neither resources nor attention to spare for an America presumably cordoned off from European rivals by the English navy.[21]

Marshal Schomberg's presence at the head of King William's general staff repeatedly reminded the English imperialists of two facts. Louis XIV had given a great gift to the enemies of his intolerance: the Huguenot refugees who now manned the allied armies. These militant Protestant exiles also provided the Dutch with a perquisite of empire increasingly precious in an age of falling European populations: skilled, soldierly settlers. The xenophobic English imperialists feared that these Huguenots might man Dutch conquests in America. Although these conquests would come at the expense of Spain's empire, "the great Carcasse upon which all the rest do prey," the English imperialists feared that any recrudescence of Dutch empire in America would disrupt the monopolistic Anglo-American exchanges "that furnish a full third part of the whole Trade and Navigation of England."[22]

England's American objectives in the world war with France ought to be to protect the existing provinces, not to conquer new ones, the imperialists of 1689 argued. It seemed to them that "wee have already but too much Territory abroad, and to get more, were but to drain England of People." Instead, what was required in America, besides sea power, was a restoration and reinforcement of garrison government. Otherwise the French would successfully attack England's provincial frontiers, Indian allies, trade, fisheries, and populations in America. Refreshed garrison government seemed to English imperial planners essential politically as well as militarily. The private provincial proprietors were poised to resume the authority taken from them in the previous reign. The cause of imperial defense and direct government, so the imperialists asserted, was even more endangered by "the Republicans," especially in New England. They would seek to emulate lord Churchill's coup in order to oust Sir Edmund Andros's autocracy, undo the dominion of New England, and revert to "a Commonwealth, to coine Money, to destroy Our Act of Navigation, and to shake off all Dependence but what they think fitt."[23]

The Protestant Putsch in the Dominion of New England

Less than a month after the imperialist manifesto of March 23, 1689, "the Republicans of New England" began to fulfill its predictions. Conjoined, lord Churchill's coup and Prince William's invasion promised a Protestant putsch. Intimations of invasion and insurrection had crossed the Atlantic with King James's warning dated September 28, 1688. The king denounced the "Design of Our Enemies, who expect to find Our People Divided, and by publishing perhaps some plausible Reasons of their coming hither, as the Specious, though false Pretences of maintaining the *Protestant* Religion, or Asserting the Liberties and Properties of Our People, do hope thereby to Conquer this Great and Renouned Kingdom." The king commanded all his military executives "to defend their country." He prohibited all his subjects from aiding the enemy, although the king admitted that this design of foreign conquest "is promoted (as We understand, although it may seem almost Incredible) by some of Our Subjects." Such subjects, wrote James II, had no memory of the horrors of civil war nor any value for the present peace.[24]

Forwarded to the governor-general of New England on October 16, 1688, the royal rescript reached the hands of Sir Edmund Andros on January 1, 1688/9. After a further nine-day delay, having also been warned from New York that the Prince of Orange was preparing to invade England, the governor-general decided he had no choice but to replicate his master's mistake and announce the coming coup. Adapting the royal text, on January 10, 1689, Andros also denounced the "false pretences" of the Protestant putsch "relating to Liberty, Property, and Religion." His proclamation prohibited all "Attempts" against the dominion. No more effective advertisement for the coup could have been conceived.[25]

Andros's New Year's Day denunciation of a potential putsch was dated from "*Fort Charles* at *Pemaquid*," the Maine headquarters of Sir Edmund's expedition against the Abenaki. A war against French-backed, Jesuit-inspired Indians should have authenticated Andros's patriotic and Protestant credentials, even to puritans. Indeed, the military purpose of the dominion, as lord Churchill himself had observed, was to meet New Englanders' pleas for protection against the French, their priests, and their Indian allies. Yet Sir Edmund Andros became the personification of Protestant and provincial fears. These fears were most marked among the men of the Massachusetts provincial army in Maine, especially as they were not serving under their traditional commanders. Provincial generals in Massachusetts preferred to leave hard duty to professional officers and conscript soldiers. In the long run, the unserviceability of the county militias opened commissioned careers to aspiring provincial officers and military service to landless sons and to the survivors of indentured servitude. So provincial regiments strengthened the military hand of the governors-general for nearly ninety years, the period of provincialization between two episodes of Protestant putsch. In those two episodes, however, the provincial armies proved lethal to imperial authority. Always the American provincial armies had annually to be recruited and retrained, at a high cost to morale and discipline. Now Sir Edmund Andros was about to experience the ineffi- ciency and the insubordination of local levies.[26]

After the provincial generals had declined to serve, the governor- general had himself led nine Massachusetts companies, leavened by two and a half companies of regulars, to the Maine frontier. The local leaders had been humiliated by the governor-general's contempt for their habitually ham-handed provocations of the Indians. They resented "the Release and setting at liberty sundry Indians," whom they had arbitrarily incarcerated while the governor-general was away in New York. The provincial pooh- bahs were also alienated by Andros's rejection of their military dispositions in Casco Bay. They were appalled by his negotiations with the Iroquois and the French, none of which he condescended to discuss with the dominion's councilors and provincial generals. They fitfully recognized that their own failure (and Andros's success) in King Philip's War had morally justified the crown's revocation of their corporate autonomy. They clearly understood that a successful war with the French and the Abenaki would fulfill the pre- rogative purposes of the dominion. "So serviceable another Indian war might have been to the Designs which we saw waiting for us" that some provincial leaders concluded that the governor-general had planned the war to exalt imperial authority. At a more personal level, the hardships of a winter campaign, far from home, in a war provoked by their own col- leagues, against an Indian enemy well supplied with arms and ammunition by Boston's own merchants, was neither to General Waitstill Winthrop's taste nor Colonel Samuel Shrimpton's.[27]

It was even less to the liking of the 709 Massachusetts recruits, who were mixed with local levies and redcoats in Maine. At Pemaquid, and in a string of riverine and coastal forts, the men of the provincial army fell under the brutal professional discipline of Andros's regular officers. Lieutenant James Weems cheerfully predicted to the provincials that "Hell is like to be youre winter quarters and the Devill your Lan[d]lord," calling them "damed sons of whores and often beating them." Lieutenant John Jordan introduced conscripts from Maine to the tortures of the stake and the picket. Officers' fists pummeled every hesitant trainee, officers' whips pun- ished disobedient soldiers, and officers' pig ropes bound the recalcitrant recruits' necks to their heels.[28]

The men of Massachusetts and Maine were disciplined and drilled both by the officers of fortune whom Andros had brought with him to Maine from New York and by noncommissioned officers promoted to the command of provincial units from the two and a half companies of red-coated regulars—the bulk of his garrison command—that the governor-general had brought with him to Maine. These centurions were supervised by such seasoned professional officers as Major Patrick MacGregorie and Captain Anthony Brockholes. These officers were all Scots or English. Some of them were Roman Catholics. They all declared their contempt for "the country" and the politics of Massachusetts. They all exalted the person and the prerogative of the king, and of Sir Edmund Andros as James II's viceroy. So the regular officers provided the ethnic and religious, the professional and personal bases for the provincial recruits' resentments of martial discipline.[29]

That discipline—the social stigmata of the modern state—was essential for, according to the British officers, the Massachusetts troops refused to help the people of the Maine communities they had been marched north to protect. Rather than undertake patrols, even in the best of weather, the provincials cowered in the forts they filled with filth. They habitually filched precious provisions and sold stolen supplies. The professional officers observed that such sociopathic provincials bitterly resented even basic discipline, much less forced marches through the Maine winter in pursuit of an elusive enemy. Naturally, their subsequent "Charges Against Sir Edmund Andros, Governor" featured complaints of "the Cruelty of Sir Edmund's Officers Eastward."[30]

In a characteristic effort to improve his men's morale in Maine, Andros left punitive measures to his subordinates while he played the patriarch. Sir Edmund was "a tender father in his family" of soldiers. He "took care that they had what was necessary for them in their Sickness." He visited every bivouac, tent, and barrack where his soldiers slept "and if he found them uncovered would cover them." He even unbent enough to loosen the knee-strings of sleeping soldiers' breeches lest their circulation suffer. Andros's personal attentions might mitigate his men's physical discomfort but they did not erase the provincials' resentment at the "frequent partyes, marches and pursuits after the enemy, sometimes above one hundred miles into the desart further than any Christian settlement."[31]

On March 16, 1689, the governor-general received word that the Congregational clergy of the dominion capital, Boston, were circulating the Prince of Orange's declaration. Like their Anglican counterparts in the imperial metropolis, London, so in Congregational Massachusetts, the "black regiment" was embittered by the royal effort to break their monopoly of religion, to reduce their congregants' political predominance, and to increase the status of Protestant dissenters and Roman Catholics. To counter the clergy's campaign, Sir Edmund took ship for Boston, "leaving the garrisons and souldiers in the Eastward parts in good condition, and sufficiently furnished with provisions and all stores and implyments of warr and vessells for defence of the coast and fishery."[32]

Mere materiel would not satisfy the men of Massachusetts. Absent Andros's commanding presence, then informed that King James, deserted and defeated, had fled for France, and finally assured that the victorious Prince of Orange, supported by "almost the whole bodie of the Kingdom," was enforcing his several declarations, the Massachusetts provincials mutinied. They declared that military discipline, even the entire campaign against the Abenaki, were parts of the ongoing popish plot. This phase of the plot was designed to destroy them. Wasting the Protestant provincial army in winter war, so the soldiers said, would make way for a French-Catholic-Indian invasion, led by King James's viceroy, Sir Edmund Andros himself. "There were several things happened, which made the Armies Suspicious that Sir Edmund had conducted 7 or 800 men into the Eastern Wilderness in the Depth of Winter on purpose to Sacrifice them there": the soldiers saw Sir Edmund actually talking to Indians; they saw him give the Indians presents of rings and ammunition; they were told that he had released Indian prisoners (these were the decrepit neighbors of Maine settlers, who had been carried off to Boston—they were too weak to walk—as dangerous); and they agreed with the Indian who said that Sir Edmund preferred the savages to the soldiers. Provincial hatred of natives, contrasted to metropolitan tolerance of them, led easily to a belief "that Sir Edmund had hired them to fight against the English" and to the conclusion that Andros's intent "was but to serve the French Interest to the . . . Ruine to New England."[33]

Nothing was less likely. Andros himself had been the boyhood companion of Prince William. He had fought in the Dutch army. As he reminded the Bostonians, he had served in the household of that Protestant princess and English heroine, Elizabeth of Bohemia. The officers of Andros's own regiment took leading roles in lord Churchill's coup at home. The French military authorities in Canada fully expected Andros to join the coup against King James. The provincial army knew little of this and cared less. The soldiers repeatedly alleged that, like the king he represented, Sir Edmund was an agent of the longstanding, international popish plot. This plot (the popular picture of the counter-reformation) was designed to subvert the reformed religion and to eliminate civic liberty everywhere. So the provincial soldiers mutinied in Maine and, in dribs and drabs and by various routes, they returned to their home counties around the provincial capital, Boston.[34]

As Increase Mather himself concluded about the Maine mutineers, " 'tis manifest that their disbanding of themselves did *make the Revolution*." In Massachusetts as in England, it was first the military desertion from King

James and his subordinates, then the armed assault on his local governments by the disaffected, Protestant military that ended the Restoration Empire. Mather repeated that "the New-English Armies in the East" were alienated from their Indian-loving, French-speaking, militarily professional governor-general, that they hated his strategy of winter-war and interdiction, and that they were informed of the subversion at home that compelled the governor-general's hurried departure from the frontier, so "they presently (many of them) without Order went home to their Friends; and it was *this* that produced the *Revolution.*"[35]

The coup in the capital followed Sir Edmund Andros's decision to arrest the deserters and ship them back to their units in Maine. To resist the governor-general's orders required revolt. The Middlesex County deserters received from Boston the reinforcements that made revolt into revolution. Ideological arguments came from the clergy who feared for their own provincial predominance. Authoritative arguments took the form of copies of the prince's supposed "third Declaration," the spurious orders of November 28 to "immediately disarm and secure all papists whatsoever." Religiously reinforced, ordered to act against the papists, afraid of arrest for desertion, fearful of forced return to the frontier, and determined to preserve their province, God's American Israel, from the popish plot, the mutineers raised around them their parent militia companies. They found ready military support from the companies of kinsmen characteristic of militia. More news, or rather rumor, from Maine also spurred a county coup against the Abenaki war: "the Reports continually coming in from our Eastern Army now caused the Relations of those that were there perishing, here a little to bestir themselves, and so they could not forbear forming themselves here and there in the Country unto some Body, that they might consider what should be done for their poor Children, whom they thought bound for a bloody Sacrifice."[36]

The widening mutiny of the provincial army impended popular insurrection, the more so because, by April 8, 1689, word had been received in Boston (from Barbados and from Virginia) that "the Prince of Orange is now Commander in Chiefe in England." On April 16, Andros wrote to Brockholes at Pemaquid, his major military base and one from which he expected to draw assistance to meet any uprising, that "there is a general buzzing amoung the people, great with expectation of their old charter, or they know not what." The governor-general was most concerned to offset the effect of these rumors on the armed forces in Maine. He added a special caution to Major Brockholes to see "that the soldiers be in good order, and diligent to avoid surprize, and see they have provisions fitting duly served out, and, if occasion, more than ordinary allowance." The governor-general could only respond to rumors of revolt by alerts and allowances, for he felt bound by imperial military tradition to await new orders from

Whitehall before he announced any alteration in the government. It was "not . . . the Custome for Foreign Dominions to discompose their own Governments by taking notice of Reports" of political upheavals in England. Instead, proconsuls were expected to preserve the peace "according to their present grounds, until they shall receive other Directions from the Supremacy."[37]

Andros could wait to see if the friend of his youth, Prince William, with the assistance of the officers of Andros's former regiment, "Princess Anne's Horse," took command of the empire. His command was secure under either James or William. Andros's administration was anathema to the old puritan elite, and several sources suggest that these colonists intended to preempt the provincial political outcomes of the Protestant putsch. In December 1688, as soon as lord Churchill's coup was complete in London, Mather wrote to Bradstreet and the old charter magistrates "to go cheerfully to so acceptable a piece of service" as the ouster of Andros and the overthrow of the dominion. Following receipt of Mather's letter on January 10, 1689, the puritans set the people abuzz with a version of the popish plot adapted to the event of a French and Indian war to the eastward.[38]

It was essential to act if New England autonomy was to be recaptured because, as Sir Edmund expected, Prince William intended to confirm the entirety of King James's imperial apparatus (and virtually all of his absolutist policies as well, as distinct from James's Catholicizing ones). As early as January 12, the prince undertook to confirm Andros's command of the dominion. A month later, just three days after he and Mary accepted the imperial crown, William and his new privy council, Compton and Churchill prominent among them, constituted a committee for trade and plantations. They ordered it to draft despatches to the American executives to proclaim the new sovereigns, and to continue all officers (papists excepted) in their commands. But Increase Mather had managed to delay the dispatch of the orders to Andros. Waiting vainly for orders that never came, Andros wrote to his subordinate on the Maine frontier. He hoped "that all magistrates and officers will be careful not to be wanting in their duty, and particularly trust, that the soldiers be in good order, and diligent to avoid surprise." The surprise was closer to home.[39]

On April 17, Andros's orders for the arrest of the deserters from Maine were to be executed. He also issued a warrant for the arrest of the leading Congregational clergyman, Cotton Mather, son of Increase. Mather escaped but he, his Congregational colleagues, the provincial generals, and the disaffected politicians (both dominion courtiers and corporate constitutionalists) all realized that crisis of authority was at hand. The militia companies would forcibly resist Andros's orders to ship their conscript kinsmen and townsmen back to the provincial army units in Maine. All accounts agree that the elite only acted after "the Country People by any

Violent Motions push'd the Matter on so far as to make a Revolution inavoidable."[40]

Thursday, April 18, 1689, was a church meeting day, an auspicious moment for a religiously driven military coup, the more so since it was also the day on which Cotton Mather was to be arrested for preaching sedition to the provincial army. His communications from his father in London made "Young Mather" the ideological heart of the New England coup, a very Compton. Andros had also scheduled a general meeting of the dominion council for that day, indicating that he planned some extraordinary announcement. The governor-general's summons called the disaffected councilors to Boston. There they would capitalize on the impending military mutiny.[41]

At 5 a.m., twelve militia companies began to assemble in Charlestown, across the river from Boston, and at Roxbury, near the foot of Boston Neck, the isthmus that tied the provincial capital to the Massachusetts mainland. At 8:00 the Charlestown force embarked in small boats to row across the river. They were met on the Boston shore by Major General Winthrop, backed by the clubmen and apprentices of the north end mob. Simultaneously, the units assembled at Roxbury began to march up the high street, along the neck, toward the town gate, taking up the riffraff of the south end suburbs as they came on. The governor-general sent for the sheriff, who told him that the reports he had received of these two movements were false. By 8:30, both militia divisions were in Boston. Their arrival brought out the men of the Boston Regiment. They were disorganized, without their drums or company colors. These had been seized from drummers' and ensigns' homes by armed conspirators the moment that the country companies reached town, lest the Boston Regiment assemble in support of the dominion government. The regiment's newly commissioned Anglican officers were the first targets of the city coup. All were arrested in their homes by parties raised from the Boston Artillery Company by some of its officers: John Nelson, David Waterhouse, and John Foster. These three merchants were so opposed to Andros's aggression against the French and Indians in Maine, or so devoted to their own profits from trading with the enemy, that they had sent shiploads of munitions to break the governor-general's blockade and to arm the Abenaki for their assault on New England's eastern frontiers. Nelson, Waterhouse, and Foster now formed eight companies of infantry to attack the citadel, Fort Mary.[42]

Meanwhile, between 9:00 and 10:00, John George, the captain of the royal frigate on the Boston station, the *Rose*, incautiously came ashore with the ship's master and her surgeon. They were immediately arrested by the fanatical Protestant petty officer, Carpenter Robert Small (who had been absent without leave for five days, and who would be listed as a deserter on

May 17), backed by other ship carpenters from the town and by a platoon of Massachusetts militia. Captain George asked them for their warrant. They "shewed their Swords saying that was their Authority." The *Rose*, with her wavering commander, her allegedly Catholic lieutenant, her Protestant deserters, and her petty officer conspirators, was a miniature of the Channel Fleet during the coup.[43]

To demoralize the sailors and to excite the mob and the militia, the fire and fear formula of the popish plot was applied to Boston, as it was to every city of the empire. For at least six days before the coup, Carpenter Small had told his confrères, petty officers and skilled laborers, that Sir Edmund Andros "intended to fire the Town at one end and the other, and then with our Gunns from the Frigat beat down the rest, and so away in the Smoak designing for France." This invention "doubtless will be thought impossible to believe" by rational readers, as Captain George remarked at the time, but the militiamen, and many of the *Rose*'s crew, did believe it, because it was impossible. It was a fantasy perfectly designed to express their fear of Catholicism and their hatred of France.[44]

Fear and hatred, Small's fanaticism, and the credulity of artisans and militiamen meant that they hurried to do the bidding of the generals of the provincial army and the officers of the artillery company. Carpenter Small's arrest of Captain George was the first of twenty-six ordered from the town house headquarters of the coup. By midmorning there were "at least 1000 men in Arms crying one and all, Seizing and Carrying to Prison whosoever they suspected would oppose or disprove their design." These included "the Major part of ye Church of England People," the functional equivalent of Catholics in the Boston branch of the Protestant putsch. In fact, the putschists ignored the few genuine Catholics resident in Boston. Instead, they captured the Church of England leadership, for it was with Anglicans that the governor-general had replaced the Congregational elite in the militia and the magistracy. The imposition of absolutism in Massachusetts was as religiously colored as it was in England, only here it was not Catholics but rather "a little Gang . . . who went by the Name of the Church of England" who had displaced the existing, religiously exclusive, political and military elite. The arrested Anglicans included Benjamin Bullivant, founder and first churchwarden of King's Chapel, Andros's attorney general, and a captain in the Boston Regiment; Francis Foxcroft, churchwarden at King's; Sheriff James Sherlock; Samuel Ravenscroft, captain of the Artillery Company and churchwarden at King's; William White, city regiment captain; Jonathan Broadbent, tax collector; Dr. Mungo Crawford, apothecary; Thomas Larkin, marshal; and George Farewell, who had prosecuted Increase Mather for his authorship of the "Unlawfullness of Common Prayer Worship." Mather had instructed "the Common People that the Governor and all the Church of England were Papists and Idolators." Mather's work was evocative: the Boston mob stormed King's Chapel and stripped it bare, searching, they said, for the idols Anglicans were supposed to worship.[45]

As James II's Church of England officers were arrested, the former magistrates of the charter government and the leading Congregational clergy were escorted by Captain James Hill's company to the town house to reinforce the provincial army officers, Major General Winthrop, Colonel Shrimpton, and Colonel Nicholas Paige (who was himself an Anglican). "There was a great shout from the soldiers" when former Governor Simon Bradstreet appeared at the town house. At 10:00, Lieutenant Treffrey was captured. Treffrey, a kinsman of Secretary Blathwayt's and one of the original ensigns in Bath's (10th) Regiment (which would be back in Boston for the next religious and military uprising), was now the major of the Boston Regiment. His arrest, together with the confiscation of the regimental colors, concluded the first phase of the coup d'état in the capital of New England. All the dominion loyalists in Boston, save for those who had managed to join Sir Edmund Andros in the palisaded citadel on Fort Hill, were in custody. Before noon an orange flag was run up over Beacon Hill (reminiscent of the colors raised over Hull four and a half months earlier). The colors of the conqueror signaled to the 1,500 militia who had not yet crossed the Charles that the city had fallen to the cause of the Prince of Orange.[46]

Between eleven and twelve o'clock, twenty infantry companies were drawn up on parade in the market square. At midday they heard the declaration that had been previously prepared with this contingency in mind. The Boston declaration rehearsed the provincial alarm, rising for a decade, ever "since the *English* World had the discovery of an horrid *Popish Plot.*" It denounced the Catholic king's intent to extend the popish program to New England, "so remarkable for the true Profession and pure Exercise of the Protestant Religion." It complained of the illegal vacation of Massachusetts's corporate charter, the elimination of the provincial legislature, and the imposition of a royal executive, armed with a captain general's "absolute and abritrary" authority, "who besides his Power, with the Advice and Consent of his Council, to make Laws and raise Taxes as he pleased, had also Authority himself to muster and Imploy all persons residing in the Territory . . . and to transfer such Forces to any English Plantation in *America.*" Worse even than the governor-general's American military authority was its red-coated embodiment: "Several Companies of Souldiers were now brought from *Europe,* to support what was to be imposed upon us, not without repeated Menaces that some hundreds more were intended for us." These *"Standing Forces"* were hateful to puritan politics, for they were "brought a thousand Leagues to keep the Country in awe," and the redcoats also corrupted purported provincial purity. Andros's soldiers were "a crew that began to teach *New England* to Drab, Drink, Blaspheme, Curse, and Damn."[47]

Royal government and redcoats denounced, a paean of provincial protest followed, remarkably similar to that raised against King James's regime in England. Alien favorites of the viceroy—"strangers and haters of the people"—had displaced the local elite. English liberties had been denied the provincial population, who were told that "we must not think the Privileges of English men would follow us to the end of the world." Land titles had been questioned. "Popish Commanders (for in the Army as well as in the Council, Papists are in Commission)" misled the "Army of our poor Friends and Brethren" in a fruitless Indian war paid for by executive taxation. All this was, again, but a provincial "Branch of the Plot to bring us low." Therefore the Protestant putsch, Massachusetts's resistance to the popish plot, was designed to support in America "the noble Undertaking of the Prince of Orange, to preserve the three Kingdoms from the horrible brinks of Popery and Slavery." The coup in Boston, the local elite declared, had simply followed "the Patterns which the Nobility, Gentry and Commonalty in several parts of those Kingdoms have set before us."[48]

As in England, so in Massachusetts the elite had given religious and constitutional coloration to the army's initiative. Certainly the civilian and clerical leaders had "silently wished and secretly prayed" for Prince William's success, but they had "determined to await the event," news of which could not be long in coming. In any event, "the fate of New-England depended upon that of the Old . . . but the consequences of an insurrection would have been death to the principal actors" if King James had triumphed. So the clerics and civilians had caballed and propagandized but they had not acted until the soldiers, facing death on the Maine frontier and conceiving of themselves as Protestant crusaders, forced the provincial elite to ride the tiger of a military mutiny.[49]

Accordingly, at 1 p.m., the Massachusetts elite, "being surprised with the Peoples sudden taking of Arms in the first motion whereof we were wholly ignorant," summoned the governor-general to "surrender and deliver up the Government and Fortification. . . . Otherwise we are assured they will endeavour the taking of the Fortification by storm. . . ." Immediately, "armed men encompassed the Fort in great Numbers, forcing the Out-Guards to retire." Rather than surrender, Andros tried to escape to the *Rose*. As his party left Fort Mary, however, hundreds of militiamen swept around the foot of Fort Hill, captured the ship's pinnace as it touched the shore, and forced the fugitives back into the fort. The provincials re-equipped themselves with grenades and small arms taken from the boat's crew, drove the redcoats from the harbor batteries, and turned the cannon against the governor-general's palisaded post. Andros berated his sentries for not firing on the rebels but he himself did not order Fort Mary's guns to fire, much to the relief of John Nelson and his men: "they might have killed a hundred of us at once—being so thick together before the mouths of their cannon at the Fort, all loaden with small shot; but God prevented it."[50]

Instead, at 4:00, having been promised safe conduct, Sir Edmund and his suite left the fort to meet his council, as scheduled. The governor-general walked through streets "full of armed men." They saluted him. At the town house, however, Andros's aides were taken from his side and imprisoned. Alone, the governor-general confronted the town house junta. He demanded to know by what authority they had summoned him and who was responsible for "Arming the Town." The reply was "that now was the time to look to themselves, And they must & would have the Government in their own hands." Then Andros himself was arrested by a provincial captain (who afterwards became speaker of the restored Massachusetts legislature) and marched off to house arrest by "a full company of Musqueteers." He was watched, even in his bedchamber, by "another young Captain," Waterhouse, and a picked guard. Sir Edmund, and the other dominion officers arrested with him, were told that they "were prisoners of war," subject to summary execution. The dominion's military executive had now been overthrown by that of the provincial army.[51]

"By this time," late in the afternoon of April 18, 1689, "there was at least 5000 men in Armes in ye Town, most of them drawn up to the Fort, which they demanded . . . threatening to Storm it" and to put the tiny garrison "all to the Sword." Ensign Joshua Pipon commanded but one other officer "and the Main Guard in all not above fourteen men in it." Nonetheless, Ensign Pipon refused to surrender. The colonels of the coup, Shrimpton and Paige, then demanded that Sir Edmund order his ensign to surrender Fort Mary. The governor-general gave the standard captured officer's response: as a prisoner, he ought not to be asked to give orders; his subordinate would never accept a prisoner's command; Andros himself "would rather dye than give any such order." There were less professional people in the hands of the putschists. A pistol was put to the head of Secretary Randolph. He was marched up to Fort Mary and told to shout to the little garrison that the governor-general had ordered them to surrender. Randolph was not believed, but Ensign Pipon faced odds of several hundred to one and his redcoats were so few that they could not man one-fifth of Fort Mary's palisaded perimeter. So Pipon asked for, and was promised, the usual terms of honor to a capitulating garrison: he and his men could march away with bag and baggage, the officers with drawn swords, the men with bullets in their mouths, ready to load their muskets, and they would be escorted to a friendly post, but, as the regular platoon marched out of Fort Mary, they were mobbed and imprisoned. Captain John Nelson took command of the citadel. He tried to honor the terms made with Ensign Pipon, and to keep the promises of personal security that had been given Sir Edmund Andros. Nelson's sense of military honor was attributed to his being an Anglican. As soon as the military crisis was over, he was removed from command.[52]

Following the fall of the city citadel, the next objective of the provincial army was Castle Island. Its regular fortifications and batteries of cannon commanded Boston harbor. Again, Andros refused to order the garrison to surrender, despite threats to kill him if he did not and to "put all his adherents to the sword." Again, Randolph delivered false orders. Again, he was not believed. Night fell on April 18, 1689, with the Castle still holding out for King James. Besides its batteries, the other source of artillery, always decisive militarily, was the *Rose*. "Upon the tidings of the news," the man of war "put out all her flags and pennants, and opened all her ports, and with all speed made ready for fight, under the command of the lieutenant— swearing that he would die before she should be taken." Carpenter Small had the guns of Fort Mary's harbor battery trained on his former ship but the provincial gunners refused to open fire. The town house council then played with Captain George the same charade they had with Sir Edmund. They got the same professional response: the council in conscience ought not to make such a demand on a prisoner; he would not order his subordinates to surrender the king's ship, nor would his lieutenant obey any such order; if attacked, the *Rose* would resist to the death of every man aboard and the destruction of the city that lay under her guns. At dusk on April 18, the frigate too still flew the colors of England and the king.[53]

On the morning of April 19, an auspicious date for military revolts in Massachusetts, the town house council sent several of the carpenter's co-conspirators aboard their ship to persuade the rest of the crew to commit her "to Kg. Wm." The crew of the *Rose*, cut off from fresh provisions, informed that their captain "intended to Carry his Maty's sd ship into France to the late King James," and intoxicated with "the happy News of his Majestys success in delivering these Kingdoms from Popery & Slavery," turned on their loyal officers, "gave three chears and struck Yards & Topmasts," immobilizing the frigate. The Castle garrison saw the *Rose* being taken over. As "most of the Soldiers were towards the Eastwards in several Guarisons, and ye Man of War as well as the Governour [was] already in their hands, and the People very Riotous and ready to put their threats into Execution," the garrison accepted the promises of "Sevell Gentn as Indifferent persons" that they would be accorded the honors of war if they surrendered. They did, and were immediately imprisoned. Captain John Fairweather of the provincials took command of Castle Island. The coup in the capital of the dominion of New England was complete.[54]

At this moment there arrived in Boston a belated battalion of the Protestant putsch, the militiamen of Lynn, led by the redoubtable, reverend, Jeremiah Shepherd. Not enough had been done, so this militant minister declared, to save the reformed religion, the charter government, and the country itself from the chief of "those few ill Men which have been (next to our Sins) the grand Authors of our Miseries." So Shepherd and his armed flock took Sir Edmund Andros from house arrest to the common jail and chained him to the wall.[55]

Sir Edmund's hopes of rescue by the regular garrisons in Maine were disappointed when "the council of safety" at the Boston town house ordered its correspondents with the frontier forces to organize mutinies that would oust the regular officers "from their present command in the army, and send them to Boston" as prisoners of war. On May Day, the lieutenant governor, Captain Francis Nicholson, and the dominion councilors in New York, wrote to the Boston council to restore Sir Edmund Andros, or at least to allow the governor-general to come to New York. The former governor, Bradstreet, and the present general, Winthrop, replied that "it is not in our power to set any persons at liberty who are confined and kept by the soldiers." The provincial troops kept the prisoners under close guard, threatening to court martial them. The Massachusetts soldiers held the city as well: "every night they review the guard and beat tattoo as if Boston were a garrison town."[56]

The provincial army was the center of "the revolution occurring here," as the armed forces were elsewhere in Greater Britain. That revolution was completed on Sunday, May 26, when a ship made port in Boston direct from England with unimpeachable reports that William and Mary had been seated on the imperial throne. "This was the most joyful news ever received in New England." On May 29, their majesties were proclaimed in Boston. The elite, military and civil, paraded on horseback and "the regiment of the town, and many companies of horse and foot from the county, appearing in armes; a grand entertainment was prepared in the town-house, and wine was served out to the soldiers," the executors of the Protestant putsch.[57]

With all hope of his restoration in Boston apparently lost, Sir Edmund Andros escaped from the Boston jail and rode for New York. He reached Rhode Island before being recaptured. Returned to Boston under the guard of a troop of cavalry, Andros was incarcerated in a damp dungeon on Castle Island. Miraculously, he survived the winter. Finally, King William summarily commanded the coup commanders to send Sir Edmund home for judgment. The Massachusetts men, both militiamen and ministers, had acted in William's name and so they had no choice but to obey the royal command. With an awful feeling that they had exchanged King Log for King Stork, they sent Sir Edmund off in the least seaworthy vessel available. It went down within sight of England, but Sir Edmund Andros survived the wreck and was triumphantly vindicated by the privy council. He was lauded by the king. William offered to return Sir Edmund to the command of New England. Understandably, Andros chose Virginia instead.⁵⁸

By then the ironic outcomes of the Protestant putsch in the former dominion of New England had become apparent. The mutiny in Maine and the coup in Boston had deposed the professional army officers on whose discipline the campaign to defend the eastern frontiers depended and brought home the provincial soldiers. The remaining redcoats tried to defend the fortified settlements. They were killed or captured a few at a time, as the English outposts were destroyed one by one. The last to hold out was Pemaquid. There Lieutenant James Weems, with sixteen soldiers, garrisoned the fort that Andros had built to end the 1675–77 war. In that war, Increase Mather had said that faith would protect the frontiersmen from the Indians. Now the puritan governor of Massachusetts replied to desperate pleas for reinforcements "that J. C. was king of earth as well as heaven and that if J. C. did not help them, he could not." On August 2, 1689, Weems and his little garrison were attacked by hundreds of Abenakis, inspired by a French priest, armed and clothed by the French army. Blinded by an explosion, Weems had to surrender on honorable terms (which were kept). The last English outpost east of the Merrimac was lost. The provincial army, unpaid and ashamed, reassembled in the streets of Boston. The soldiers shouted "God Blesse King William God Blesse Sir Ed. Andros & Dam all pumpkin states."⁵⁹

The Protestant Putsch in New York

The second city of the dominion of New England was New York. There another officer praised by Marlborough, Captain Francis Nicholson, the young veteran of Tangier and the Sedgemoor campaign, governed James Stuart's conquest from the Dutch. As the then royal duke's personal dependency, New York had been governed absolutely. Its soldier-executives were as often Catholic as not. The last of these ducal dictators, Thomas Dongan, Marlborough's veteran comrade and fellow Stuart servant, was still resident in New York. As James Stuart's deputy, Dongan had recruited a provincial army from the New York militias, led it to the defense of Albany during the winter of 1687–88, rearmed the Mohawk and the Seneca, and reanimated them against the French and their Indian allies. Dongan's forces were designed to disappoint the French viceroy's declared intention to crush the Iroquois and celebrate Christmas in New York. It was Dongan who had informed many of Marlborough's and Blathwayt's objections to the Treaty of American Neutrality with France. Dongan had violated the intent of that treaty and the consequent order against hostilities by his aid to the Iroquois against the French. He had even won a royal order to protect both the Five

Nations and New York's voyageurs as they pushed the beaver trade west-ward. Dongan had declined to be transferred to the command of the royal artillery in Ireland (and to participate in Tyrconnel's Catholicizing schemes for Irish independence). Instead he proposed Irish resettlement in New York). Dongan's administration, bracketed by those of Sir Edmund An-dros, had established New York as the strategic center of the English em-pire in America, the heart of resistance against French aggression.[60]

Yet, in the estimation of both the largest Protestant denominations in New York, the popular and pietist part of the Dutch Reformed Church, and the puritan congregationalists of Long Island, these stalwart soldiers and British patriots (Andros was a Guernseyman and Dongan was Irish) were traitors. In large part, this was guilt by association with King James. In the eyes of New York's pietists, Dongan's Catholicism condemned him in any case. His correspondence with his co-religionist and old comrade in the armies of France, the Canadian viceroy of the grand persecutor, Louis XIV, confirmed the political malignity of Dongan's religious confession. No one but a pietist or a puritan would mistake the devout Anglican Andros for anything but a Protestant. Both did. Like Dongan, Andros was suspiciously cosmopolitan, he allied himself with Indians, and he imposed a much-resented discipline on the provincial army. Andros's malevolence was con-firmed, for those who hated established churches and absolute states, when he hosted lavish public celebrations in honor of the new Catholic prince of Wales (stories of whose illegitimacy arrived in New York together with news of his birth). Celebrated the length of New York between August and November of 1688, these loyalist street parties boasted whole roast oxen and free barrels of the best beer. Despite dominion officers' jocular remarks about jolly boors, and Councilor Bayard's genial sacrifice of his best hat and wig in a Bowery bonfire, these celebrations for a Catholic heir to James II fanned fanatics' fears of alien authority. The pietist party led by Jacob Leisler condemned Bayard for pledging the prince "although professing the Reformed Religion."[61]

Even Andros's lieutenant governor in New York, Captain Francis Nicholson, a churchman among churchmen, seemed but "a pretended protestant" to Leislerian Dutchmen and English dissenters. They assidu-ously asserted that he had been seen kneeling at Mass in King James's chapel tent in the royal army camp on Hounslow Heath. In the Protestant provincials' confounded calculus of religion, politics, and force, military professionalism seemed identical to armed absolutism and Erastian Angli-canism was indistinguishable from Roman Catholicism. All in authority under King James, "under the aparrance of the functions of the Protestant Religion, remain still affected to the Papist," or so the Leislerian pietists professed to believe. Nicholson was "popishly affected" because he did not dismiss the Catholic customs collector, or discharge all the "Souldiers in the fort, being most Papists," or dismiss the Catholic chaplain, or let Leisler destroy the religious images in the Catholic chapel. By the same token, to the pietists and the puritans, the Church of England chaplain was just "the pretended Protestant Minister." To the antiestablishmentarians, even the Quakers seemed to "encourage if not out do the Roman Catholics" in papistical inclination for they held "Mr Pen to be a person of undoubted sincerity."[62]

Strained confessional calculations moved easily to fears of militarism and dragonnades. To Jacob Leisler and company, it seemed self-evident that King James had already acquired in New York and New England what lord Churchill accused the king of seeking in England, "a pretense by Conquest" to inflict absolutism and Catholicism on free and Protestant polities. However exaggerated such fears might be in the cases of the Anglican legalists Andros and Nicholson, they found firmer foundations in the Catholic coloration of their staffs. Both of the company captains of the regulars in New York, Gervase Baxter, the commandant at Albany, and Anthony Brockholes, in charge of Pemaquid, New York's old outpost in Maine, were Catholics. So were Ensign Bartholomew Russell and his senior sergeant, commanders of the twenty-two regulars in New York's Fort James. A number of these soldiers were Irish Catholics. The garrison chaplain was Catholic. The customs collector was too. And the dissenters assumed that anyone who could work with Catholics was one. So all the officers of the dominion must be "Catholic." Most of the soldiers of the New York City Regiment, dissenters themselves, believed this and so they declared that the colony was "governed, of late, most part, by papists who had in [the] most arbitrary way, subverted our ancient privileges."[63]

That both New York's "pretended protestant" executives and its genuinely Catholic commanders would extend King James's counter-reformation overseas, from the realm to the dominions, seemed to be confirmed in November 1688. Then the dominion officers ordered every clergyman in New York to publish the royal declaration of religious indulgence. That was the order that had led the seven bishops to defy the king. On December 3, 1688, Captain Nicholson learned of the Prince of Orange's military response to King James's assault on the reformed church. Nicholson sent an express to Sir Edmund Andros, now on the Maine frontier. It was Nicholson's news, added to the royal proclamation against the impending invasion, that led to Sir Edmund Andros's January admonition against Orangist outbursts. By early February, the Prince of Orange's Dutch countrymen in New York, a great majority of the provincial population, were quick with rumors that the prince's army had invaded England. Captain Nicholson's reactions were the intemperate and unconsidered instincts of a soldier of the king. Had Prince William learned nothing from Monmouth's defeat, he asked? The prince's little army would be buried on Salisbury Plain after being cut down by the king's cavalry. Nicholson soon discovered, however, that just as the prince's invasion force was infinitely larger than Monmouth's, so the internal dissidence it excited, in America as in England, was incalculably greater. On March 1, 1689, the news of William's invasion was confirmed in New York. On March 8, Lieutenant Governor Nicholson responded to rising popular unrest by ordering the Catholic customs collector to surrender the provincial treasury. Nicholson announced that he would apply the money "towards the fortifying off this City against any fforaigne enemy." But the enemy was no longer foreign.[64]

Before the end of March, a New Yorker could report to a Bostonian that an "unnaturall Warr" (lord Churchill's coup and the prince's assault on his uncle and father-in-law) had produced "a total Revolution at home." Inspired by such reports, the Bostonians saw to it that the coup crossed the Atlantic. Ensign John Riggs was sent prisoner to Boston after the putsch reached Penobscot. Riggs actually arrived in Boston ahead of the Maine mutineers. Before he could help execute Andros's orders for their arrest, Riggs was arrested himself in the provincial army's insurrection of April 18. He escaped from Boston the following day. On April 26, Riggs reported the coup in the capital of the dominion of New England to Lieutenant Governor Nicholson. On April 27, 1689, rumors of an English declaration of war against France raced through New York. All of these developments put point to panicky Protestant stories about the governor-general's purported conspiracy with the Indians and the Jesuits and the French to "cut off" the Protestants of New York and turn over the province to Louis XIV. To try and counteract the canard, and to rally the agents of imperial authority, Captain Nicholson and the dominion councilors resident in New York announced that they had "received news of warr with France and that the French maltreated the English and the Dutch" and the executives convened "the several Justices of the Peace Leftent Coronells, Majors and Captains now in Commission" to advise and assist them in the defense of the colony from all its enemies, foreign and domestic.[65]

Unfortunately for the cause of authority, its proximate instrument, the City Regiment of the provincial army, had already been infiltrated by Orangist conspirators. Apparently directed by Captain Jacob Leisler, with the acquiesence of four other captains of the New York City Regiment, Sergeant Jost Stol (whose bar business fueled, funded, and covered his conspiracy) and other dissident noncommissioned officers "tooke out of every company of traine bands three stout . . . persons, and tould them what certaine information I had of the blessed and happy success of His Majesty King William and Queen Mary to the accession of the imperial crowne of England." These traitorous triumvirates, like their counterpart conspirators in the English army, then swore "one to another to bee faithful and true" in the coming coup. Next, each of these soldier cells set out to excite its company of the City Regiment to demand that their colonel, Councilor Nicholas Bayard (he of the burnt offering), allow the company first to join in disarming New York's "papists," as mandated by the Prince of Orange's spurious "Third Declaration," and then to take its turn in garrisoning Fort James, the city citadel.[66]

At first, neither Colonel Bayard nor Captain Nicholson would permit any of the increasingly dissident companies into Fort James. Nicholson said he'd see them hanged first. At the meeting on April 27, however, Nicholson was confronted with declarations by the City Regiment's junior officers that his regular officers were papist tyrants and that the redcoats were all Catholics and Irish (two of the refugees from Andros's companies, now added to the Fort James garrison, really were Irish Catholics). These junior officers added that Nicholson himself, having declared "that the people of New York were a conquered people and could not expect the same rights as English people, wherefore the Prince might lawfully govern them by his own will," would never admit King James's tyranny or Prince William's right. Therefore, the junior officers concluded, neither the lieutenant governor and his regular officers nor the redcoats could be relied on to defend New York's Protestants from the imminent French attack. So Nicholson and the dominion councilors were forced "to shew our Willingnesse to defend the fortt Citty and Gouverment against any common enemy" by taking the companies of the City Regiment into the citadel on a rotating basis.[67]

Letting armed locals into the king's citadel was a classic error in garrison government, avoided by a dozen English military executives in this crisis, but Nicholson felt that city security was even more menaced by the mutiny of provincial army units outside the walls of New York than by the disaffection of the City Regiment within. The "seed of sedition" blown from Boston had germinated on "the outward skirts of the province." The most fertile soil was on eastern Long Island, where the Suffolk County Regiment was recruited from the New England settlers. On May 3, Major Matthew Howell, commanding officer of the Suffolk County Regiment, learned that the lieutenant governor and his ad hoc military council had refortified the citadel, Fort James, and were rebuilding the city wall across Manhattan. Major Howell concluded that the alien city was preparing a defense against the English counties. Therefore, "for securing our English Nations liberties and propetyes from Popery and Slavery and from the Intended invasion of a foreign French design and more than Turkish crueltys," in keeping with the advice of the Boston council of safety, and following "our Country of England's example for securing our English nations liberties and property from Popery and Slavery," Major Howell assembled the Suffolk "freeholders." They resolved that the provincial regiments should seize "our headquarters of New York and Albany forts and all other fortifications" and hold them against all comers "till further order from the parliament of England."[68]

On May 4, the city and dominion officials had word of "the Revolution at the East End of Long Island." They wrote to the military commanders there to pacify the people. Instead, on May 8, the Congregationalist conspirators of East Hampton joined the coup. They voted "that the Soldiers go to New York to assist to reduce the place, that it might be better secured for the safety of the country." The revolt followed Governor-General Dongan's military organization. On May 9, veterans of Dongan's winter expedition to Albany (who had been drafted from the Suffolk, Queens, and Westchester County Regiments) assembled in arms at Jamaica, ostensibly to demand payment of their arrears. Informed of this by officers sent to the city from the Jamaica rendezvous, the New York City Regiment's veterans also turned out. Suddenly, the city streets were crowded with armed men "so possest with jealousies and feares of being sold, betrayed, and I know not what," Nicholson wrote, that they would take no orders from the existing authorities.[69]

On May 10, the lieutenant governor felt compelled to issue a proclamation against the mutiny, sedition, and rebellion he saw rising around his government. The county regiments had mustered at Jamaica, he declared, "in order [to see] if they could to make themselves Masters of this City & Fort and to Plunder (as it is feared) this City or at least such members as they would see cause to expose to the Rabble." To head off the provincial troops from the capital, the lieutenant governor ordered that the veterans units be paid their arrears, some of it in cash and the rest in certificates for the unpaid taxes of their own counties. The Long Island officers returned to Jamaica with the lieutenant governor's offer (although some of their guards remained in the city and joined the disaffected companies of the City Regiment). Apparently satisfied, the county regiments dispersed to their homes.[70]

While Captain Nicholson staved off military mutiny and menace in New York and the nearby counties, unrest reached the frontiers of the province. A captain from Connecticut with the apt appellation of "John Bull" had been stationed at Northampton by Sir Edmund Andros to protect the upper Connecticut frontier. John Bull's desertion set off the coup in Connecticut commanded by Colonel Robert Treat, but Bull himself went to Albany. There he incited the provincial companies in the garrison to seize the fort and expel its Catholic commander, Captain Gervase Baxter. Albany was the entrepôt of the Iroquois. Their habitual fears of European conspiracy, already inflamed by "libels & falsehoods from Boston" that "Sr Edmd Andros had joyn'd with the French of Canada to cutt them off," were confirmed by the Albany mutineers. The disaffection of the Iroquois would be "the utter ruine of all the English Settlements on the Continent." So wrote the troubled lieutenant governor.[71]

Captain Nicholson was concerned about the temper of the Iroquois and the menace of the French, the breakdown of imperial authority and the outbreak of war, domestic and foreign. The self-styled defenders of the city were simply frantic. On the last day of May, Nicholson awoke to find that the "most part of the Citty's melitia were in rebellion." Worse, "some of the officers ware the Instigators and Inflamers of it." The trouble had begun two days earlier. Captain Nicholson had demanded that Lieutenant Hendrick Cuyler of the City Regiment explain why his corporal had posted a sentry at the sally port of Fort James, despite the objections of the regular corporal on duty. Speaking only Dutch, Cuyler did not understand Nicholson's angry question, so he fetched a burly corporal, Hendrick Jacobie, who spoke English. Jacobie arrived carrying a naked sword in his hand. Nicholson thought the long-expected mutiny had begun. He pulled out a pistol and forced the lieutenant and the corporal from his office. The corporal then told his comrades that the lieutenant governor had exclaimed (just as Sir Edward Hales had at London and in Bristol) that he would bombard New York from the citadel rather than surrender his command of it to such ruffians.[72]

Much improved and embroidered, word of Nicholson's outburst brought the other officers of Cuyler's company to city hall the following afternoon. There "the Lieutenant Govr and Councill with all the Civill Magistrates and Military officers except Capt Liesler" had met about "allaying of all Uproar and Rebellion." When Lieutenant Cuyler and his captain, Abraham de Peyster, with other officers, demanded an explanation for Nicholson's behavior, he cashiered Cuyler. Furious, Cuyler's company officers rushed out of city hall, "the drums beat and the town [was] full of noise." The alarm assembled elements of the City Regiment. Four hundred strong, they marched on Fort James and filed in through the sally port opened to them by Hendrick Cuyler and his corporal. "In ½ hour's time the fort was full of men armed and inraged, no word could be heard but they were sold, betrayed and to be murdered, it was time to look [out] for themselves."[73]

Such had been the language of the Massachusetts military men to Governor-General Andros. It was again repeated in New York when Colonel Bayard, in Governor Nicholson's presence, mustered the men of Captain Gabriel Minviell's company (Minviell refused, then or after, to join the coup). Bayard asked the men why they had rushed into the fort. They replied that there were two hundred papist soldiers hidden on Staten Island, waiting to massacre the Protestants there, after which they would take the arms cached for them by local collaborators and attack the city. The city soldiers added that one hundred Irish Catholics from the Boston garrison were en route to join their coreligionists in the Fort James garrison. The New Yorkers were convinced that both these forces would be supported from the harbor by Colonel Dongan's armed brigantine. Colonel Bayard and most of the regimental captains then left the fort and joined the lieutenant governor and council at city hall to consider their response to the fantasies of New York's soldiery.[74]

Meanwhile the provincial guard of the fort changed. No sooner had Captain Charles Lodwick and his company entered the citadel than Lodwick's sergeant, William Churchill, took twenty men of the company to city hall. With them, he burst into the council and demanded the keys to the magazine from the lieutenant governor. To buy time, Captain Nicholson ordered Sergeant Churchill to go back and get his captain to apply in due form for the keys. Meanwhile, the councilors advised Nicholson to surrender the keys to New York's arsenal, and with them control of the capital, to the captains of the provincial companies. Without any alternative, Nicholson acquiesced. The captains then agreed that each would act as commander-in-chief of the city during his tour on guard in the fort. The majority of the captains further agreed that Captain Leisler, who had kept himself aloof from compromising councils, should replace Colonel Bayard as commander of the City Regiment. The captains declared that they would "keep and guard said fort in the behalf of the power that now governeth in England, to surrender to the person of the Protestant religion that shall be Nominated or sent by the power aforesaid."[75]

The pietist putsch in New York was apparently complete, but Captain Nicholson and Colonel Bayard tried to restore the City Regiment's allegiance to established authority. By June 2, they had recalled most of the regiment to the colors. Even half of Leisler's company responded to Colonel Bayard's commands. The next day, Captain Lodwick spread a fresh alarm. He said that an express from Long Island (no one else saw this messenger) had warned that a fleet of great ships was sailing up the sound. Then Captain Leisler, whose turn it was to command in Fort James, told the men that he knew the fleet was a French invasion force. Colonel Bayard turned out the City Regiment, determined to use the occasion of this "sham alarm" to test his authority. No enemy appeared. Colonel Bayard then dismissed the parade but Leisler activated the subaltern system, devised by his collaborator, Sergeant Jost Stol, to convince the men they had been betrayed by their officers. Panicked, the privates of the City Regiment deserted their captains and their colonel. They rushed to join Leisler in the fort to defend the city against the allegedly approaching French enemy, or the supposed Catholic conspirators in the city, or the Jesuits said to be assembled at Colonel Dongan's house on Long Island, or the invented Irish Catholic companies from Boston, or the Catholic assassins supposedly hidden on Staten Island: "the imagination of treason has gott soe deep an impression in the minds of the people that it will be hardly got out of it." Most of the captains followed their men to the fort. They feared that "if they went not in, the Commonality would pull down their Houses and they would be in danger of their lives." Captain Leisler seized the moment to force the English regular officers out of the fort. Then he disbanded their companies. The lieutenant governor now admitted that he had lost all semblance of command to "the mutinous captains." Nicholson could find "noe way to reduce them by force." He was certain that, so long as they listened to Jacob Leisler, they would not obey even King William, if he ordered them to restore the dominion officers to authority. The lieutenant governor left New York City on June 11. Shortly afterwards he sailed for England in Colonel Dongan's brigantine.[76]

On June 22, 1689, military delegates from the coup in Connecticut arrived in New York. Major Nathaniel Gould and Captain James Fitch, "having first don you that justice, noble and Loyall Captain Leisler . . . and you the other noble and courajious Captains, Leiftenants, Ensigns, Sargents, and good Soldiers in those trainbands that have been active in this affair," and given them full credit for their resistance to the papists and the "popishly affected" leaders of the dominion, advised the Leislerians to consolidate their authority by proclaiming the new sovereigns. Gould and Fitch had conveniently brought a printed copy of the English proclamation with them from Connecticut. Four of the captains of the City Regiment marched their companies from the fort to city hall. There these soldiers proclaimed William and Mary as king and queen of England and its American dominions. New York's soldiers adhered to the goals of the Protestant putsch: "the reestablishment and preservation of the true protestant Religion, liberty and property." They defied the worst efforts of the "papists who had in a most arbitrary way subverted our ancient privileges, making us in effect slaves to their will contrary to the the laws of England."[77]

Then the Leislerian soldiers purged Andros's remaining appointees from their commands in the City Regiment and installed Hendrick Cuyler as major and commander. They recruited a standing military guard to protect Leisler and execute his political orders. Sergeant Churchill was the bodyguard's lieutenant, Sergeant Stol was its ensign, and the men were paid a premium wage. Leisler then declared that all opponents of his authority were by definition "Popishly affected." To prove his point, his guard drove the dominion councilors from the customs house at knife point and took over tax collection. Taxes in New York were henceforward assessed by military requisition and levied by force.[78]

Leisler and his men then tried to oust the old order from the province of New Jersey and from the New York counties of Richmond, Ulster, and Albany by "sending messengers and letters to some of the military Officers and factious men inciting them to follow their steps." In each of these locales, the existing civil magistracy resisted the "sword rule" (and so social revolution by the lower ranks) advocated by the Leislerians. The old order relied on King William's proclamation continuing all the Protestant officers of King James in their places. Therefore Leisler had to assert a higher authority than that he derived from his council of war. He appropriated the letters addressed to Francis Nicholson by William and Mary and assumed the royal authority they conveyed as his own.[79]

Then the Leislerians demanded that the new sovereigns issue them a charter equal in authority to that they had heard was to be given "the citty of Boston." They also demanded a veto over any royal appointments in their province, and they wanted a royal commission to prosecute all of their class, religious, and personal enemies as "Rebells, Papists, and dissaffected persons." Without waiting for this commission to ethnically cleanse New York, the Leislerian council declared that all the Protestant ministers in the city were "Popish Trumpets." The clergy were arrested by Leisler's guard and jailed in Fort James (now renamed "Fort Amsterdam" as a token of the Netherlands patriotism of the Leislerians). Leisler quartered soldiers in the houses of those who denied his authority "with directions to pillage and plunder." Leisler's most prominent victim was Colonel Bayard. Leisler had Bayard arrested, jailed, and paraded around the fort chained to a chair. The deposed colonel and councilor emblemized the change of command in New York. Leisler ordered the docks patroled by "a file of musqueteers" who marched the masters and passengers of arriving vessels to the fort for public reading of their (presumably treasonable) correspondence. When legal objections were entered to the Leislerians' forcible proceedings, their commander replied *"what do you talk of a Law? the Sword must now rule."* New York's was a putsch more pietist and more revolutionary than that of the Anglican army in England, or even of the puritan army of Massachusetts, and it inspired and informed a religious and military revolt in the Chesapeake.[80]

The Protestant Putsch in Maryland

In Maryland, the echoes of 1676 continued to rebound from "the Clifts" of Anne Arundel County. There the Maryland Baconians had been hanged after the failure of the Chesapeake revolution. Their crime, like that of the Virginians and the men of Albemarle, was to complain that over-heavy taxes were levied by decreasingly representative assemblies to be misspent by ever more burdensone oligarchies on ineffectual frontier defense. Their surviving leader was that "Rank Baconist" John Coode, deacon and priest, sailor and soldier, blusterer and buffoon. Physically deformed, possessed of a "face resembling that of a Baboon," Coode was in action, appearance, and alienation the Titus Oates of the Chesapeake. Like Oates, Coode entered the witness game, endearing himself to authority by testifying to Nathaniel Bacon's revolutionary intent. For Coode, the Oatesite fanaticisms of "the Popish Plot"—anti-Catholic and antimonarchical, francophobe and xenophobe—were made to disorder Maryland. There a Catholic proprietor, his kinsmen and coreligionists, relied upon the royal prerogative for their feudal authority. There ever-growing alarms of French-inspired attacks on Protestant frontiersmen by the western Iroquois, the "Siniques," gave an edge to protests against proprietary misgovernment. These objections were further embittered by falling tobacco prices and rising tenancy. To overthrow the proprietary regime the panicked people "wanted but a monstrous head to their monstrous body," John Coode.[81]

Coode did not have to invent a "Catholic Camarilla" in Maryland, as Oates had done in England. The Maryland proprietor's council was so overwhelmingly Catholic as to excite the concern even of James II's privy council's plantations committee. And the "native" allies of the Maryland Catholic executive were closer to the frontiers of Coode's Maryland than the "native" Irish were to the shores of Oates's England. In Maryland, the proprietor's diplomacy with the Indians and his clients' fur trade gave local substance to the transatlantic fears that the Catholics and the natives would combine to "cut off" the Protestants. The ensuing imperial crisis that had crested in 1681 was given political shape by the exclusion parliaments, and it threatened another civil war. The exclusion crisis had its counterpart in every one of England's American provinces. In 1681, the general court of Massachusetts defied the crown, and its continued existence was defended by Halifax. Shaftesburian merchants and republicans impeached Sir Edmund Andros in New York and the Jerseys as a proxy for his master, James Stuart. The Jamaicans, led by that avowedly republican enemy of the royal prerogative, the Cromwellian Captain Samuel Long, rejected the "Irish Constitution" intended for America. In Virginia, this extension of Poynings's Law from Ireland to America was resisted by Major Robert Beverley and the would-be aristocrats of the "Green Spring Party." So in Maryland, in April of 1681, the insurrectionists of Charles County, "with force and armes," sought to overthrow the Catholic proprietor and his Catholic councilors for conspiring with the Jesuits (in both Maryland and Canada), the French military, and the Iroquois "to destroy all the Protestants."[82]

Coode's role in the American exclusion crisis had been to spread "false Scandalous report," to deliver "Mutinous and Seditious Speeches," and to declare to dissident, company-grade, Protestant militia officers like himself that he could raise "ten thousand Men to subvert the Government." It seemed to Coode and company that the Catholic Calverts in Maryland could hardly retain the political and military authority that the Catholic Stuarts were about to lose in England. Coode's contribution to the imperial debate was not elevated. He shouted "God Damn all the Catholic Papist

Doggs!" He tore up an order to keep the peace, saying that he cared not "a Turd for the Chancellor nor the Governor neither, No (he swore by God) nor for God Almightly neither." Then the Catholic colonel and councilor Henry Darnell and a proprietary posse broke into Coode's house, in the "dead time of the night," and carried him off to prison, still in his night-shirt. Along with his clothes, the Calverts deprived Coode of his dignity, stripping him of all his appointive offices, military and civil.[83]

Elective office, however, presented proprietary authority with insuper-able problems. After threats of jailbreaks and insurrections forced the pro-prietary officers to admit Coode to bail in 1681, he was immediately elected to the Maryland assembly. Coode and the rest of the representatives heard the proprietary clique contend that Maryland was a conquest of England. Therefore, according to Calvin's case, the people of Maryland were subject to the discretion of the king and his delegate, the proprietor (so too royal officials in the dominions of New England and of Jamaica declared that authoritarianism in America was a constitutional consequence of England's conquest of the colonies). In Maryland, the contest between proprietary prerogative and represreve government was epitomized by the proprie-tor's effort to exclude Coode from the assembly and the assembly's asser-tion that it could control its own elections, and that the voters could elect whomever they chose to represent them. Four times the proprietary execu-tive excluded Coode from the assembly. Four times the defiant voters of St. Mary's County returned him to office. In choosing John Coode, the St. Mary's electors had "made from mud a symbol of liberty."[84]

However crudely, Coode spoke for the Maryland generation of En-glish-born, English-educated, and English-connected Anglican lesser gen-try who were implicated in Maryland's exclusion crisis in 1681. Their public careers had been truncated by the Calvert imitation of "the Stuart Revenge," a royalist reaction that, in Maryland, was untempered by the im-perial constitutional compromise of 1681 (which balanced the governments of the royal colonies, neighboring Virginia among them, between executive and representative, military and civil, authoritarian and legalistic elements). As in England, so even more in Maryland, royal reaction took government down Catholic and authoritarian paths. Alarmed, the assembly accepted ex-clusionist charges that the Catholic proprietor and his closing circle of co-religionists and kinsmen were in league with the French and Indians. Fearful of this American edition of the popish plot, the Maryland com-mons, like their English counterparts, refused to underwrite any extension of the executive's military strength. In subsequent sessions, the provincial representatives, like the English commons, insisted on their right to con-trol, i.e., to forbid any increment of force if it was to be commanded by a Catholic executive. The Maryland commons also demanded that the county armories be put in Protestant hands. Finally, Maryland's "country party" reiterated a demand that dated back to the civil war, and that had been eloquently re-expressed in the "Hue and Crye" of 1676: the royalist, Catholic Calverts should be excluded from the command of the province and a Protestant officer should be appointed by English authority as "Vice Roye or Governor Generallissimo." As in England, so in Maryland, the exclusion crisis, the movement to exclude a Catholic, francophile executive, tainted by dealings with "natives" (Irish or Indian), and hostile to the Church of England, eventuated in a coup d'état by Protestant putschists.[85]

Of course, the Maryland exclusionists credited the rumors, current on the accession of James II in 1685, that the new king was "a bloody rogue, had poisoned his brother King Charles, and contrived the plan of setting fire to London in 1666." Naturally, they supported the cause of Monmouth, "the Protestant Duke" (as distinguished from the Catholic duke of York), and they declared that Maryland of right belonged to Monmouth, not to the Catholic Calverts by the favor of Catholic Stuarts. The proprietorship of Charles Calvert, baron Baltimore, in the peerage of Ireland, was doubly endangered, for he was caught between the desire of his Protestant subjects in Maryland to oust him and the plan of the English imperialists to eliminate all proprietary governments. To avoid having his province absorbed in an expanding dominion of Virginia, or truncated by Stuart grants to that complaisant Quaker, William Penn, or royalized in response to the anti-Catholic campaign orchestrated by Coode's stepson, the London merchant Gerald Slye, Calvert went home. There he successfully defended his Maryland palatinate jurisdiction until, on December 14, 1688, he was arrested by lord Churchill's Life Guards in Whitehall Palace.[86]

In the proprietor's absence, the administration of Maryland was left in the hands of eight deputy governors. The senior of these, George Talbot, was terrible to the Protestant English elite as the kinsman of Tyrconnel, the ethnic cleanser of Ireland, but Talbot quickly disqualified himself by killing the royal customs collector and was arrested by the captain of the royal station ship. To replace Talbot, Baltimore dispatched one William Joseph, "an Irish popist," to be president of the proprietary council. Joseph arrived to find Maryland politically on fire, ablaze with the news of the francophile Treaty of American Neutrality, the king's declaration of religious indulgence, and the deprivation of the American diocesan, Bishop Compton. Joseph met the Maryland assembly on November 14, 1688, a week after William of Orange and his army had invaded England. Although this was not yet known, news had already reached Maryland of King James's autumn concessions in the face of imminent invasion and anticipated coup.[87]

President Joseph nonetheless brought the restive Maryland legislators an uncompromising political message. He preached them a sermon on divine right: "there is no power but of God, and the Power by which we are Assembled here is undoubtedly Derived from God, to the King, from the

King to his Excellency the Lord Proprietary and from his said Lordship to us." Therefore the legislators were divinely bound to obey both the royal orders to prohibit the export of bulk tobacco (the poor planter's resource); to enact a general and annual thanksgiving (to be celebrated by Jesuit priests at militia musters) for that "Infinite Blessing," the birth of the "noble and Glorious" Prince of Wales; to legislate the proprietor's commands to pay increased taxes; and to immediately swear a comprehensive oath of fidelity to him. This last the assemblymen refused to do because the substitution of an oath of allegiance to the proprietor for the English oaths of allegiance and supremacy would permit papists to sit in the assembly. Here was the Maryland echo of King James's effort to enfranchise and empower Catholics in England. It was anathema to Maryland's Anglican officeholders, as it was to England's. Nonetheless, the proprietary councilors, like King James's partisans in England, personalized the issue, made it a matter of allegiance, and anticipated armed resistance. The councilors declared that, "if denyall of fidelity to your Lordsp were thus permitted Rebellion might be the next stepp."[88]

Their Maryland lordships were quite correct, but the crisis was delayed because news of the English coup and the Dutch invasion had not yet reached the province. So the Maryland representatives at last agreed to take oaths as individuals, but not as legislators. By the time the assembly was prorogued on December 8, 1688, however, "the Happy news of The Prince of Oringe's Arivall in England with considerable forces Invited thither by the Clergy, Lords, & Commons of the Nation & of his glorious undertaking of freeinge the three Kingdoms from Popery & lawless Tyraney" was current in Maryland. Reactions to the news drew another line between the proprietary party, who instantly identified the Calvert cause with that of King James, and the Protestant party, who revived the popish plot panic in an effort to incite a Protestant putsch in Maryland.[89]

Lord Baltimore was quick to send to Maryland James II's proclamation against the impending invasion and domestic subversion. His deputies were as quick to act on it. Baltimore also boasted to his colonial clients that his loyalty had moved him to raise a troop of cavalry for the defense of king and kingdom. His colonial councilors replied that even "the noise of the troubles with you in England . . . doth not altogether dismay us. First for that your Lordsp thereby had the opportunity to show the greatness of your soul by that Heroic Act of and in Raising a troop for his Majties service secondly for that our Confidence in the Almighty is such as that wee noe ways doubt but that all this is permitted by heaven for the greater Glory of God and Encrease of power and honr to the King and of welfare and happiness to your Lordsp." The Maryland councilors (like Captain Nicholson in New York) anticipated that a repetition of Monmouth's defeat would cement Stuart authoritarianism on England and in Maryland.[90]

To this end, the Calvert councilors would do what they could to defeat any Maryland mimicry of English mutiny. On the day that they wrote to lord Baltimore, January 19, 1689, the councilors recalled all county militia weapons "for repair." This repair had nothing to do with the imminent attacks of French and Indians so feared by Protestant Marylanders. Rather the weapons recall was required by "the present juncture of Affaires in England and the Invasion thereof threatened by the Dutch." Once the weapons were refitted in the proprietary arsenals in the capital, St. Mary's, and at lord Baltimore's country house at Mattapany, eight miles outside the capital, the firearms would be returned to the militia to resist a Dutch invasion, or so the proprietary council promised. As they wrote to Baltimore, however, the councilors' intent was to reissue the weapons only "into such hands as shall faithfully serve the King your Lordsp and the Country." That it was the Catholic King James and not the Protestant King William whom the proprietary government intended to serve was apparent: they decided to disarm the Maryland military only after they heard the news of James's flight and William's accession.[91]

Alarmed by their empty armories and excited by the news from England, Protestant junior militia officers on the Western Shore (the Maryland counties between the Chesapeake and the Potomac), some of whom had been implicated with Coode in the conspiracies of 1676 and 1681, began to refresh the American edition of the popish plot. They alleged that the namesake and kinsman of William Penn's lawyer and James II's electoral agent, the Catholic captain George Brent of Stafford County, across the Potomac, was in league with native war captains. The Indians had heard "that the Englishmen in England had cutt off their King's head and that there were an abundance of dutchmen coming in a great many ships." Memories of the Dutch wars were everywhere refreshed in 1688 and 1689. In the case of the council, the raid of 1673 was recalled in an effort to raise resistance to Dutch William and his invaders. The Piscataway recalled the loss of a Dutch market after 1664. Both councilors and chiefs anticipated that Anglo-Dutch events would again echo in America. So the king of the Piscataway had allegedly engaged the Senecas to "make haste and kill the Protestants before the ships come in. For after the shippes come the protestants would kill all the papists," purportedly Catholic natives included.[92]

In militia minds, the natives' strategic projections bred fearsome fantasies of the sort widespread in every American province. The "french, Northern, and all other Indians" were about to emerge from the western wilderness to join the ruling class—"Agents, Jesuits, Priests, and lay Papists"—to murder all male Protestants, make their wives concubines, and their children slaves. As in England so in Maryland, the Anglican clergy converted racial and religious fantasies into political propaganda. On the Western Shore, John Coode and John Turling converted popular Protes-

tant panic into an indictment of the proprietary regime. Across the Potomac, in Virginia's Northern Neck, "Parson Waugh" preached warnings
from his pulpit about the popish, native, executive conspiracy. Nine thousand nine hundred natives, the parson confidently affirmed, led by Jesuit
priests and French officers, were already massacring frontier families.[93]

This splendid summary of early American atavisms, complete with alleged Indian informants (who would certainly testify to the truth of these
terrors, if only they could be found), intensified popular hysteria. By March
1689, there was "all over the Country" such a "greate uproar and Tumult"
that it "will not be easily pacified." So Colonel Henry Jowles of Calvert
County wrote to the only Protestant councilor, Colonel William Digges.
Jowles had been the highest ranking militia officer among the exclusionists.
Now he led 150 men from Calvert County down to St. Mary's City and
recaptured the county's militia weapons from the arsenal. Colonel Jowles
ordered the Cromwellian veteran Captain Ninian Beale to march his rearmed company "to the Indian Fort and know their Designs." Jowles also
sent a detail of cavalry to seize the county's Catholic major, "for he is all one
the Indian." Then Jowles promoted Beale major in the Catholic officer's
place. Finally Jowles tried to recruit Colonel Digges to lead Maryland's
military coup. Digges declined, but he convinced the council to return the
remaining militia arms to the county armories and to endorse Colonel
Jowles's and Major Beale's initiatives. Digges organized frontier patrols.
Their fruitless searches for the alleged army of invasion—Waugh's 9,990
natives—finally, on March 27, 1689, persuaded the Western Shore militia
officers to sign a declaration that the purported plot was "nothing but a
sleveless fear and imaginacon fomented by the Artifice of some ill minded
persons who are studious and ready to take all occasions of raising a disturbance for their own private and malitious interest."[94]

Frontier fantasies were replaced by political realities on April 27, 1689.
The Virginia council of state proclaimed William and Mary king and
queen. The executive council ordered the civil and military authorities of
every Virginia county to follow suit on May 23. The Maryland councilors
were now unquestionably informed of the accession of William and Mary
to the imperial throne, but they refused to proclaim them. They had, they
said, received no orders to do so from lord Baltimore. The Jacobite proprietors, Baltimore and Penn, seem both to have declined to order the new
sovereigns proclaimed. At least their deputies did not act on any such orders
(perhaps being told they were pro forma). The proprietary authorities of
Maryland and Pennsylvania apparently hoped that James II would be restored in the British kingdoms by French arms in collaboration with the
Catholic, "native" Irish, just as they allegedly relied on "the great strength
of the ffrench & Kenada Indians, likely, if occation served, att the ffrench
King's Command to Invade this province & other their Majtys' protestant

Coloneys." The presumed hopes of the American Jacobites and the extraordinary fears of provincial Protestants combined to confirm the popish plot in the popular mind and so inspire a military coup in Maryland, as that plot had also done in old and New England, old and New York.[95]

On June 10, Colonel Nicholas Spencer, president of the Virginia council, wrote Secretary Blathwayt that "the Inhabitants [of Maryland] most Protestants are rageingly earnest for the Proclaiming their present Majestys and will not believe but orders have come to that government as well as to this for Proclaiming their Majesty's and that the Government have concealed the commands and are sometimes very positive they will proclaime their Majesty's without the order of the Government, which if so will unhinge the whole constitution of that Government and dissolve the whole frame of it." Given a militant English example and a Jacobite regime in Maryland, John Coode, now a self-promoted "colonel," saw his chance to execute the exclusionist program by force and so to put himself, his fellow militia officers, and their co-religionists in power.[96]

The bishop of London's clerical correspondent in Maryland (a Huguenot refugee from Louis XIV's Catholic dragonnades) told Bishop Compton that Coode's stepson in London had advised the Maryland exclusionists not to execute "the design which they had against the Papists" for the success of lord Churchill's coup in England would liberate Maryland from Catholic commanders without any need for a provincial military mutiny. A Protestant prince would name a Protestant proconsul, but he would not be a Marylander, he might not be a whig, and he would certainly not be John Coode. So, in the second week of July 1689, "Colonel" Coode raised the Protestant militiamen of Charles County. He was joined by his brothers-in-law, Nehemiah Blakiston, the royal customs collector, and Kenelm Cheseldyne, the assembly speaker, both ex officio enemies of the proprietary regime. Colonel Henry Jowles next appeared at the head of the Protestant junior officers and militiamen of St. Mary's, Calvert, and Anne Arundel counties. The proprietor's deputy governors tried to detach Jowles from the coming coup by offering to commission the colonel "general of all the forces in the Province." Jowles politely refused the promotion and led his men to Coode's camp. The proprietary deputies offered a general pardon to all who would return to their homes, but they were ignored by the rising forces of Maryland's Protestant putsch.[97]

On July 25, the Maryland putschists published their "Declaration of the reason and motive for the present appearing in arms of His Majestys Protestant Subjects in the Province of Maryland." Here was Maryland's version of the motives, legal and political, religious and military, of the Anglo-American coup. Coode and company denounced such proprietary rejections of English authority as the murder of royal customs collectors. The rebels resented the imposition of an exclusive oath of allegiance to the proprietor, an oath that would destroy the legal privileges of Anglicans. The authors of the Protestant putsch in Maryland added that the "Churches and Chapells (which by the [Maryland] Charter should be built and Consecrated according to the Ecclesiastical Laws of the Kingdom of England) to our great Regret and Discouragement of our Religion are erected and converted to the use of Popish Idolatry and Superstition. Jesuits and Seminary Preists are the only Incumbents, . . . as also the chief Advisers and Councellors in Affairs of Government." Coode, without a church or an office, had personal reason to complain that Catholicized government denied Maryland's Anglican gentry full and fair political participation. Coode concluded that Catholic executives, in the province as "at home" in England, exercised an arbitrary power to veto legislation and dispense with the law, "whereby our Liberty and Property is become uncertain." Maryland's Catholic tyrants, so the armed Protestants proclaimed, had imposed excessive fees, extorted military requisitions, and (shades of Coode's capture) seized Protestants "in their Houses, with Armed Force consisting of Papists."[98]

True religion and civil liberty were in danger, in England as in Maryland. So, said "His Majestys Protestant Subjects in the Province of Maryland," "the Hand of Providence" had selected "Our most gracious King William, to put a check to the great Innundation of Slavery and Popery, that had like to overwhelm Their Majesties Protestant Subjects in all their Territories and Dominions (of which None have Suffered more or are in greater Danger than Our Selves.)" Instead of helping Marylanders gain "a proportionable Share of so great a Blessing," lord Baltimore's deputies had prayed for "the prosperous Success of the Popish Forces in Ireland, and the French Designs against England." In England's province, Maryland, "We are every day threatened with the Loss of our Lives, Liberties, and Estates . . . by the Practices and Machinations that are on foot to betray us to the French, Northern, and other Indians . . . well rembring the Incursion and Inrode of the said Northern Indians, in the year 1681, who were conducted into the Heart of the Province by French Jesuits, and lay sore upon us, while the Representatives of the Country then in the Assembly, were severely press'd upon by our Superiors to yeild them an Unlimited and Tryanical Power in the Affairs of the Militia."

Therefore, the authors of the declaration, "looking upon our selves Discharged, Dissolved, and Free from all manner of Duty" to magistrates who had departed from their allegiance to the crown of England, "(upon which alone our Duty and Fidelity to them depends) and by their Complices and Agents aforesaid endeavoured the Destruction of our Religion, Lives, Liberties, and Properties, all which they are bound to protect," had taken up "Arms, to Preserve, Vindicate, and Assert the Sovereign Dominion, and Right, of King William and Queen Mary to this Province: To Defend the Protestant Religion among us, and to Protect and Shelter the Inhabitants from all manner of Violence, Oppression, and Destruction, that is Plotted and Designed against them. . . ."

Two days after the publication of this declaration, Colonel Coode brought up the forces of Maryland's military coup against Colonel Digges's proprietary garrison in the state house at St. Mary's City. Digges's men refused to fight and the colonel surrendered the provincial capital. Upcountry, the other deputy governors tried to raise the militia to oppose the rebels, but the men told their officers that "Cood rose only to preserve the Country from the Indians and Papists and to proclaim the King and Queen and would do them no harm." So President Joseph and the Catholic councilors took refuge in lord Baltimore's country house at Mattapany, which they garrisoned with 160 supporters. They were promptly besieged by Colonel Coode and 700 militia. The proprietary party held out until the besiegers borrowed two "great guns" and several gunners from an armed merchantman, the *Constant* of London. Cannon would put paid to proprietary palisades.[99]

Still, Coode's men hesitated to fire on fellow Englishmen, so their leader (like the Leislerians in New York) confirmed the immediacy of the crisis and the malignity of the coup with a dramatic despatch. A mounted messenger rode into the besiegers' camp shouting that "our neighbour Indians had cut up their Corn and were gone from their Towns, and that there was an Englishman found with his belly ript open." Now threatened by an hysterical militia as well as by heavy guns, on August 1 the loyalists accepted the terms offered by the rebel leaders. Coode, Jowles, and Cheseldyne were joined by that Scots Presbyterian, Cromwellian cornet, and Maryland militia captain, now major, the "Argyll" of Maryland, Ninian Beale; by John Cambell, a former militia captain who had been out with Coode in 1681, and who was now promoted major; by Captain Humphrey Warren, military leader of the coup in Charles County, of which he became colonel; and by John Turling, the Anglican minister who had also been implicated with Coode in the 1681 conspiracy. They offered the officers and men of the proprietary force at Mattapany safe conduct to their homes, on the condition that those who were Catholic leave public life, "noe papist in this province being in any Office Military or Civil as by their Majesties Proclamation and the Laws of England."[100]

In personnel and chronology, in ideology and outcome, Maryland's provincial forces had paralleled the course of lord Churchill's coup in England (and so of the coups in England's northern colonies). The insurgents now adopted the political form agreed on at Prince William's Exeter headquarters: they subscribed a Protestant Association. Given this partisan organization and their military mastery, the putschists easily dominated the August 1689 elections to the "Associators Convention," Maryland's model of the convention parliament at Westminster. The Maryland election "was in most Countyes awed by their souldiers." In Calvert, Colonel Jowles called the election, brought his own soldiers to the polls, got them drunk, and had them elect himself and three other officer associators to the convention. In Talbot County, the loyalists were disarmed before the election and dared not come to the polls. With its military officers dominating the Western Shore delegations, the associators convention met on August 22.[101]

The convention's acts reflected its members' martial ambitions and security concerns. The convention commissioned Colonel Coode as Maryland's general officer and authorized the usual cavalry troop to act as General Coode's bodyguard and his political police. The convention cashiered eight of the ten militia colonels of the proprietary regime and purged fourteen other company and field-grade officers. To their places, the convention promoted the Protestant officers dismissed by the proprietor for their involvement in the 1681 conspiracy. Then the convention ordered these "reformed" officers to instruct their men "in the art of warr or military discipline" and to use them "to suppress all homebred insurrections or foreign invasions against their Majesties Crowne and Dignity and the safety and Welfare of the Inhabitants." The convention levied a special tax to pay a bounty to the shock troops of the Maryland coup, "the souldiers late in Arms" under the command of "Capt: Coode, Coll: Jowles and Coll: Warren." The convention promotions militarily manifested a social as well as a political change of command. As their opponents said, the associators had made "the long sword in the Rables hands . . . our masters." To complete the coup, the associators elected Cheseldyne speaker of the convention, justified the coup d'état in a formal declaration, and requested that King William make Maryland a royal province. Like the convention parliament that had offered William the imperial throne, the associators convention in Maryland was an extralegal body meeting in a military environment. Legislatures were essential to lend legitimacy to the military coup of 1688–89, but they were not freely or regularly elected. The supposedly preeminent parliaments, whether of England, New York, or Maryland, were the rubber stamps of the Protestant putsch.[102]

The putsch's beneficiary, William of Orange, was focused on military crises in Ireland and Flanders, not on political developments in England or its American provinces. He had largely resigned American administration to the imperialists who had engineered lord Churchill's coup. William was pledged to protect English property rights, even those of Catholics and Jacobites. These distractions and limitations delayed and diffused all of the new king's decisions about America, save for his immediate orders to every province to make urgent preparations for war with France. Churchill and Blathwayt saw to it that William was "sensible of the great and frequent injuries his subjects daily receive from the French in apparent violation of the Treaties between the Two Crowns and particularly by the assistance that [the French] King has lately given and continues to give his enemies in Ireland and by the invading his Majesty's Territories in America." As "Commander in Chiefe of His Majesty's Forces in this Province by the order and appointment of the representative body of the whole Province," General Coode acknowledged receipt of the resulting royal military orders at "His Majesty's Garrison at Mattapany in Maryland."[103]

King William had recognized the associated officers as the interim administrators of Maryland but he could not meet their request that he royalize the province. The king's ministers could not persuade the parliament to enact a bill to resume provincial proprietaries to the crown. The king was equally disinclined to authorize an administration that anticipated lord Baltimore's restoration. The proprietor promised to put the provincial government, the Maryland militia, and the county and colonial armories entirely in Protestant hands, but Coode's coup d'état had done that already. To move as far as possible towards royalist, garrison government, without actually depriving lord Baltimore of his property rights, King William finally commissioned Colonel Lionel Copley, the captor of Hull and the client of Carmarthen (himself the godfather of Anglican empire), as the governor-general of a province all of whose undistributed soil and half of whose revenues remained the proprietor's property.[104]

Lionel Copley was transferred to Maryland because he had found the Hull government an insufficient reward for his leadership of the coup there. His garrison had been siphoned off to reinforce the partisans of the putsch in Scotland. Copley's profits were thus drastically pruned and he was deprived of the martial tools by which he had capitalized on the coup against King James. Copley had personally imposed taxes on Hull's shipping. Then, under the guise of collecting those taxes, Copley had his garrison loot local warehouses. He had interfered with the mails in personally and politically profitable ways. When the postmaster objected, Copley had him "seized by a serjeant and four musketeers, carried to the guard-room, and there tied neck and heels for more than two hours." To add insult to injury, Copley had Carmarthen arrange for the poor postmaster's dismissal. Of course, control of the mails to Yorkshire played a part in Copley's efforts to purge both the magistracy and military of Hull so as to insure Carmarthen "a place of retreat" in case of a countercoup by King James and the French. As that event seemed less likely, and Copley's corruption led to a vote of censure by the house of commons, he became a political liability. Once again eminent in imperial authority, Carmarthen had Captain Copley shipped off to Maryland, after he was jumped up from captain's rank to that of colonel, the usual rank of imperial legates in America. Colonel Copley soon died of the malarial "seasoning" common to Chesapeake immigrants.

Then, with wonderful irony, that "pretended Protestant," Colonel Francis Nicholson, who was already on record as having the utmost contempt for that "Masilino" Jack Coode and his ragbag revolutionaries, was promoted from the lieutenant governorship of Virginia to the captain generalcy of Maryland.[105]

Succession Politics in the Southern Dominions

Virginia

Nicholson had fled from the pietist panic in New York in June 1689, not knowing that his patron (perhaps his parent) the duke of Bolton, now colonel of two Williamite regiments, had gotten him a new commission as lieutenant governor of New York. The Bolton connection (which also reached out to the Leeward Islands and beyond, sponsoring at least eight colonial commanders) got Nicholson dispatched to Virginia. He arrived on May 16, 1690, determined to cauterize the "leprosye of Rebellion" produced by the provincial army coups in America. Nicholson sent military messengers home with reports from the army officers still resident in New York and New England, each a focus of imperialist allegiance. And Nicholson commissioned his own investigator, who toured the provincial capitals as far north as Boston. All these reports documented the military and administrative failures of the postcoup regimes. They argued for the reimposition of direct imperial government in the northern provinces and the elimination of all charter and proprietary jurisdictions in America.[106]

Nicholson apologized for his blunt reports and recommendations, "mostly a Souldiers Life having been my Fortune," but his suggestions were well received by the army and imperial administration. Captain Nicholson was breveted colonel and, in February 1692, named to the Maryland command in succession to Copley. He took an early opportunity to horsewhip an outrageously drunk Parson Coode out of his pulpit (the Church of England, newly established in Maryland in the wake of its Protestant putsch, had provided parishes for all the Anglican agitators). A Coode supporter complained that, while Colonel Nicholson was "furiously zealous for building of Churches and Coledges . . . he is as mad against them too that first appeared there for King William, and were principally concerned in the Revolution, calls them Rebels, threatens to try them with a Fyle of Musketeers and to hang them with Magna Charta about their necks." Nowhere in Greater Britain, as tory army officers restored imperial authority in church and state, would they willingly accept the politically liberating potential of 1689. Nicholson justified his forceful muzzling of the opposition, telling the Maryland assembly that "All Rebellions were begun In all Kingdoms and States by scandalizeing and making odious the persons in authority . . . and in Colonyes where they were Governors representing them Scandalous as for Instance the late rebellion in Virginia by Bacon etc."[107]

Virginia possessed both political extremes. It had approached revolution in 1676. Reactionaries had roughly repressed "the Plant Cutting" of 1682, a pioneering episode in the Stuart Revenge. But an anti-authoritarian outburst lacked one essential ingredient in Virginia: a surrogate for King James. The governor-general, lord Howard of Effingham, had hurried home to England the moment he learned that "the cards are come to shuffling." His withdrawal deprived Virginia's Protestant populists of a vice-regal focus for the resentments aroused everywhere in America by King James's Catholic religion, absolutist politics, francophile foreign policy, and acceptance of alien allies (in America, the awful affinity of royal executives for Indians). Effingham, like every other governor-general, had been implicated when James II apparently enthroned the popish plot. Added to that, the successive royal proclamations of neutrality and amity with France, of indulgence for dissenters, of the birth of a Catholic heir, and, finally, fatally, the king's declaration against Prince William's "specious pretences of Liberty, Property & Religion," marked the stages of widespread popular alienation from King James and his administrators in the Old Dominion, as they did everywhere else in the Restoration Empire.[108]

So the governor-general's retreat actually enhanced the effectiveness of Virginia's counciliar regime. Effingham's absence freed the provincial president and council not only from having to defend an unpopular proconsul, but also from having to respect the viceroy's loyalism and legalism. Such scruples would have hampered the councilor-colonels' practiced ruthlessness in repressing rebellion in Virginia. For a dozen years, they had put down periodic popular uprisings led by disgruntled "country" politicians. In the crisis of 1689, the councilors again played the forceful cards of prerogative politics—summary arrests of popular leaders by troops of cavalry and these opponents' imprisonment aboard royal station ships—with an assurance and skill that took both moral and political force from the leading councilors' proverbial Anglican piety. Nonetheless, as Colonel Nicholas Spencer wrote to Blathwayt on April 27, "ye late Revolutions in England made such a Influence of Affaires here, that the peace and Quiet of the Government here was some little time very doubtfull. . . ."[109]

The councilors quickly captured and isolated the country party leaders in central Virginia, but the Protestant parsons and popular politicians of the Northern Neck went some way in updating and Americanizing the popish plot as a pretense for an attack on the established authorities in church and state. These "patriots" suborned an Indian (who conveniently disappeared when the government sought to confirm his testimony) to declare that Virginia's Protestants faced attack by an unholy combination of Jesuits and

Iroquois, allegedly commissioned by the Catholic King James and led by the Catholic captain, George Brent. The resident councilor and the senior militia officers who protected Brent from the mob led by Parson Waugh were called "pretended Protestants." The Anglican agitators actually asserted that "All his Majesties Councell of this Colony, & most of the Chiefe Magistrates of each County were Papists . . . and that they conspired in the designe of Joyneing with the Indians to Cutt of[f] the Protestants." Virginia's version of the popish plot "putt the Inhabitants of those Northerne parts into restless Motions, and drawing themselves into parties upon their defence, and ready to fly in the face of ye Government. Soe that matters were very pressingly tending to Rebellion."[110]

Rebellion would unleash the poor to plunder the rich. So the Virginia elite had learned in 1676. So the gentry of Yorkshire and London had found in 1688. So the well-to-do of Boston, New York, Maryland, and Virginia as well, feared in 1689. Being rich they were considered oppressors. Oppressors, so the populace believed, must be papists. Papists had no rights that Protestants need respect. The popular equation of privilege with popery in "the mouths of the mobile" thus licensed the bigot and the bandit, the alienated and the ambitious, to "betake themselves to Armes to plunder and robb just and good men who had any estate to loose, and to be said to have an Estate had been a crime sufficient to have laid a man open to popular Rage." Such was the antisocial situation in Virginia in the spring of 1689. The fall of King James's government seemed about to carry down with it all law and order.[111]

On April 27, 1689, with the public peace still hanging in the balance, the president and council of Virginia, to their vast relief, learned that William and Mary were now lawfully presiding over the old imperial system. Virginia's councilor-colonels paraded their troops. They proclaimed the sovereignty of King William and Queen Mary, the foundation of law and order, with martial sounds: "fireing Great Guns, Sounding Trumpets, and beating of Drums." The fickle folk responded with "acclimations of Joy" and the councilor-colonels wrote home to the secretary at war and of plantations for more ammunition.[112]

Jamaica

A month to the day after the new royal champions of the old imperial order were proclaimed in Virginia, Blathwayt's deputy in Jamaica reported to the secretary at war and of plantations "the unhappy circumstances our Island at this time lies under in being governed by Sir Francis Watson and his Councill of War with arbitrary and despotical power. . . ." The islanders suffered "the oppression of being day & night in armes," Blathwayt was told. Watson "governs absolutely by ye Sword, haveing Marshalls law in force." The Life Guards officer had taken full advantage of King James's order to resist invasion and insurrection: he had declared martial law. Martial law was a Jamaican commonplace. It had been resorted to in every crisis in the colony since its conquest by Cromwell's expeditionary force in 1655.[113]

The current crisis deepened day by day during the six-month interregnum of imperial authority that followed the flight of King James. The king's last public act had been to order the imperial constitution of 1681 restored in Jamaica and the surviving champion of that constitution (and of the planter party), Colonel Hender Molesworth, recommissioned as the dominion's chief executive, but the king's flight meant that many months would pass before this last concession to the imperialists would be enforced. In the interim, Sir Francis Watson was yet more militant because, like George Churchill before him, he was obsessed with the ongoing feud between the planter and privateer parties in Jamaica. So Watson ignored both King James's last imperial act, the order to restore in Jamaica the 1681 constitution, and Prince William's first attention to empire, the confirmation of King James's order secured by Blathwayt and approved by Marlborough.[114]

Watson's waywardness was but the *reductio ad absurdum* of Albemarle's maladministration. In 1686, at the outset of his self-imposed exile to the command of Jamaica, Albemarle revived the Cromwellian privateering policies of his father, General Monck, the great patron of the Jamaica-based battle against Spanish empire in America. Albemarle had added to his aggressive inheritance an obsession with treasure hunting. That obsession was driven to mania by the duke's enormous dividends from his investment in William Phips's dive on the wreck of the *Almiranta* (the profits also paid for Phips's knighthood, his otherwise inexplicable promotion to be the marshal of the dominion of New England, and then, after his capture of Port Royal in Acadia, Phips's extraordinary elevation to be King William's governor-general in Massachusetts). To his devotion to piracy and plunder, Albemarle added a death wish, but before he drank himself to death (in spasms scientifically recorded by no less eminent a personal physician than Sir Hans Sloane), Albemarle had ripped up the imperial constitution of 1681.[115]

Albemarle esteemed all political opposition to be impudence when addressed to a duke. So he sent soldiers to the polls to beat off the freeholders who would vote for planter politicians. Then the duke enfranchised the redcoats and ordered them to vote for the Albemarle claque of Irish lawyers. Albemarle's abuses produced a legislature so subservient that, alone of all the American assemblies, it voted a permanent revenue to the royal executive. Having captured the assembly, Albemarle quickly eliminated all other opposition to his alcoholic absolutism. He dismissed judges en bloc for refusing to exact from political opponents the enormous fines that packed juries assessed for Albemarle's use. Albemarle successively sacked the secretary of state, the attorney general, the provost marshal, and, when they questioned his behavior, the planter party majority of the colonial council. To their places, Albemarle promoted the privateers. Finally, he drove from the island the privateers' great enemy, the former lieutenant governor of the island and the chief of the planter party, still the province's presiding judge, Hender Molesworth.[116]

Molesworth's last act as lieutenant governor had been to hang three pirates and one of their protectors (as he explained, an even number of victims was required to balance the yards of the royal station ship as she sailed into Port Royal harbor). Driven from the island by the piratic duke, Molesworth was followed to London by (it was said) no fewer than eight hundred wealthy and influential exiles. They fled an extremist regime that combined a tyranny militarily modeled on that of Tyrconnel in Ireland with political extremes copied from King James's English excesses. The *éminence grise* of the Albemarle regime was a Catholic priest, Thomas Churchill, sent out by King James to be the chaplain of militant Jamaica (just as the king sent priests to his English and New York garrisons to proselytize the redcoats preparatory to their dragooning the colonists). Father Churchill, a provincial Petre, conveyed to King James the duke of Albemarle's demand for all the powers Tyrconnel had as lord deputy in Ireland, on the grounds that the provincial establishment of Jamaica, like that of Ireland, must be purged of the Cromwellians and their children. Before Albemarle could obtain this untrammeled authority he drowned himself in drink celebrating the birth of the Prince of Wales. Albemarle was thirty-five. It was redundant to pickle his corpse in a hogshead of brandy for shipment home.[117]

Sir Francis Watson took over the Albemarle regime. At first, perhaps legally, Watson acted as president of the provincial council. When he heard rumors of the demise of the crown, however, Watson declared himself governor-general and carried out a military coup in Jamaica. The Life Guards officer converted the colonial council into his council of war. With their advice, Watson put the island under martial law. He called up the provincial regiments and dismissed the surviving field officers of the old elite. He commissioned in their places ambitious middle-class company-grade officers. Watson commissioned these jumped-up officers as judges in the regimental court martials, one per parish (i.e., the old regimental plantations). The military judges governed the island, acting against the old planter elite: former civil justices; the ex-officers of the Jamaican provincial army; the island oligarchy.[118]

The new field officers and military judges, so the displaced oligarchs alleged, were at best men of the "middling sorts." At worst they were "ye meanest tradesmen who are most easily imposed upon & most desirous to rule" over their elite oppressors. In Jamaica these oppressive oligarchs were the factors and clients of the Royal African Company, dealing in slaves. Anglo-American elites were always chosen from the provincially successful, the capital-connected. Their jealous juniors, here the newly promoted officers of the provincial army who took over Jamaica in the spring of 1689, were representative of that class of men who for three centuries were the heart of Anglo-American unrest. Such provincial army officers were the personnel of three British revolutions, always the enemies of the economic monopolies that supported and symbolized oligarchical authority, alike in 1641, 1689, and 1775. In 1689, the company-grade officers in the provincial armies led virtually simultaneous uprisings not only in Jamaica but also in Maryland and Virginia, New York, and Massachusetts.[119]

In the spring of 1689, Sir Francis Watson appears to have thought not only that he might take control of an imperial province by exploiting middle-class military ambitions, but also that the empire itself might revert to the partisan divisions of the 1640s and 1650s. Then the kingdoms and colonies of Greater Britain had been conquered and held by rival parties in the struggle for control of the English empire. In the present imperial Interregnum, Watson seemed to think that his command of Jamaica made him an imperial power broker. Such a conceit received some support from an Interregnum precedent. Sir Francis recalled that the last Cromwellian commander of Jamaica, Colonel Edward D'Oyley, had raised himself from council president to governor-general by the advice of his council of war. Watson observed that D'Oyley had subsequently been recognized as governor-general both by the Interregnum authorities and by the restored monarch. Watson said that he had simply emulated the colony's conqueror. In effect, he suggested that the Restoration Empire should end as it had begun, by reconstituting the institutions of Cromwellian military administration under the aegis of a new Stuart monarch.[120]

Watson frankly admitted that he had also learned state piracy from General D'Oyley's history and that of the other military colonizers who had served "under the Lord Generall Monck." Both old Cromwellians and unreconstructed Yorkists saw the Dutch as much as the Spanish as imperial enemies to be plundered. The instant that he declared martial law, Sir Francis seized an enormously valuable Dutch merchantman. He then convened an ad hoc admiralty court and had the ship condemned. There were those uncharitable enough to say that Watson had imposed martial law merely to excuse this robbery. King William's first news of Jamaica was his countrymen's protest against Watson's piratical behavior. There quickly followed the complaints of English merchant capitalists and gentry investors about Watson's attacks on the private property of their factors and correspondents, about his abrogation of civil law, and about his negation of class privilege, especially in regimental commands and military judgeships. Royal orders immediately ensued to restore the 1681 settlement and the

Lynch-Molesworth regime. These commands were too authoritative and too uncompromising for Watson to ignore. On June 3, 1689, he ordered the regimental colors cased, the provincial army to stand down, and the military courts closed. The constitution of 1681, and the entire panoply of plantocracy, was restored. Jamaica's subalterns' revolt was terminated.[121]

In September (Hender Molesworth having died before he could return to the Jamaica command), Watson was replaced by the earl of Inchiquin, one of a series of Irish officers rewarded for their British parts in the Protestant putsch. Despite his own coup credentials Inchiquin personally beat the first survivors of Monmouth's rebellion who applied to him for their freedom. Then he sent them back to their masters. Eventually there arrived King William's order to free Monmouth's men, the first opponents of King James. Among them was John Coad, who had been shot down at Philips Norton, but who survived only to be condemned by Judge Jeffreys to be hung, drawn, and quartered at his own door. Slipped instead into a slave coffle bound for Jamaica, Coad miraculously survived the voyage, and at last found himself among friends, becoming an overseer on the plantation of Colonel Beck, one of the Cromwellian conquerors of Jamaica. Puritanism still prevailed on their plantations and John Coad became a circuit-riding evangelist. Another of Monmouth's men had found a calling in America.[122]

"The Ragged Regiment"

In August, Colonel James Kendall had been rewarded for his leadership of lord Churchill's coup by being promoted to the command of Barbados. He was backed by belligerent instructions and given ample munitions to carry on the war against the French in the West Indies. The need to supply that war from the key port of Portsmouth called for the promotion of Lieutenant Colonel Gibson to be its governor. So he dropped out of the competition for command of the Leeward Islands. There, Colonel Christopher Codrington was the beneficiary of the revolt staged by Colonel Thomas Hill, and the other Protestant professionals in the island officer corps, against that veteran loyalist, Sir Nathaniel Johnson (he wound up as governor of South Carolina). The Leeward Islands officers nominated Codrington for the command. He was confirmed by King William as the only officer who could raise and direct the forces of these chaotic island colonies against the aggressive French. The imperial administrators also agreed with Codrington that the islands "should be rather treated as garisons" than as little Englands. Like the governor-general, many of the imperialists believed that the islanders "are open to no arguments but those of authority and power." Codrington's deputies included that old Life Guardsman,

Colonel Thomas Hill, who was promoted from his command of St. Kitts to be lieutenant governor of all the Leeward Islands. The other Leeward commands were restaffed by English regular officers who had played prominent roles in lord Churchill's coup. Several of them, led by Edward Nott, transferred from the 15th Foot, with its West Indian traditions and cadres, to commissions in the regiments sent out to reconquer St. Kitts and carry the war to the French islands.[123]

Secretary Blathwayt and lord Churchill had anticipated the loss of St. Kitts and the crisis in the Lesser Antilles in their American advice to both the old and the new wearers of "the imperial crown of England." Both the continuity and the significance of their imperial advice received dramatic demonstration on May 7, 1689. William III's declaration of England's war against Louis XIV and France embodied the exact language of Churchill's protest to King James against French attacks on English America. Churchill's indictment of French barbarity in Hudson Bay, and of French duplicity in simultaneously negotiating "a Treaty of Neutrality and good Correspondence in *America*," appeared in the declaration of war next to Blathwayt's oft-repeated denunciation of French aggression in the Newfoundland fisheries, New York, and the Leeward Islands. Of course, King William's declaration of war also pilloried Louis XIV's persecution of the Protestants, English as well as French, and particularly deplored the French king's armies' repeated devastation of the Palatinate. In the declaration of war, the French king's attacks on Anglo-American commerce were symbolized by the French navy's disrespect for England's ancient "Right of the Flag," the recognition of her sovereignty over the Channel. Finally, the French king's invasion of Ireland was named as the most recent and unmistakably hostile act to which the English response was war. These, then, were the imperial premises of the declaration's concluding orders to the "General of Our Forces," to the admiralty, to the lords lieutenant, and to the "Governors of Our Forts and Garrisons, and all other Officers and Soldiers under them, by Sea and Land, to do and execute all Acts of Hostility in the Prosecution of this War."[124]

A week after the declaration of war, as governor of the Hudson's Bay Company, the newly created earl of Marlborough asked the newly crowned king, William, to issue letters of marque and reprisal to the Hudson's Bay Company's ship captains; to authorize warrants for the company to recruit seamen for its ships "by beat of drum" and to protect those recruits from the royal navy's press gangs; and to grant Marlborough's deputy governors power to make alliances with the North American Indians. On June 6, 1689, the king agreed to all of Marlborough's requests. He also approved a commission to Captain Andrew Hamilton to serve in Hudson Bay as Marlborough's deputy governor. Marlborough then ordered Hamilton to proclaim William and Mary as the sovereigns of England's sub-Arctic domain.

To lend force to this refreshed imperial authority in northernmost America, as well as to fight the French at sea, Marlborough detailed one hundred royal marines to serve on the Hudson's Bay Company's ships (a long voyage to a distant destination was the fate of Littleton's last loyalists). The safe transit of the Hudson's Bay convoy drove up the price of company stock 100 percent during the ensuing year. At its annual meeting on September 27, 1690, the Hudson's Bay Company declared "a divident of 75 per cent, which has doubled their accounts. They are now the only flourishing Company in the Kingdom." Small wonder that the company directors gave Marlborough 100 guineas in gold plate (in addition to his stock dividends) as material evidence of their gratitude for their governor's martial and political efforts on behalf of the company's American enterprise.[125]

Simultaneously, the longstanding concern of Marlborough and the tory imperialists for the defense and discipline of England's American provinces won fresh military investment in America. The privy council recommended and the king accepted measures to strengthen seven royal provinces. The king and council authorized a military commander, garrison, and fortifications for Newfoundland (an outpost of special interest to Marlborough). New garrison companies were raised for New York. A regular regiment (Bolton's 2d, commanded by Major Nott) was sent to the Leeward Islands. A royal governor was named for Bermuda (not that Bermuda mattered much). More munitions were shipped to Barbados for Colonel Kendall to use in support of the Leeward Islands offensive. For that campaign squadrons of warships and troop transports were also ordered out, freighted with regular regiments for English island garrisons and for attacks on the French. Naval convoys were assigned for the trade to Virginia and Jamaica (where Inchiquin, alone of the West Indian governors-general, refused to join the offensive against the French islands). On the political front, attacks were now resumed on proprietary independence in Maryland, the Carolinas, and Pennsylvania, and the politics and administration of those provinces were substantially imperialized during the war years.[126]

By European standards, the forces sent to America from England were small. Often, as in the case of the regiment assigned to help Colonel Codrington's forces recapture St. Christopher's from the French, they were very badly equipped and shabbily uniformed. "I expect to be of the ragged regiment at the Leeward Islands," Major Nott wrote to Blathwayt from the *Mary*. Onboard under his command were companies of Bolton's 2d and the drafts Colonel Gibson had culled from the Portsmouth garrison to recruit the forces already in the islands. All the soldiers were already sickening for want of the blankets and rugs that their noble colonel, the duke of Bolton, had neglected to request from the ordnance. Nott resented that neglect the more because he, and several other officers of the 15th, after taking Berwick in the coup, had transferred to Bolton's 2d for the express purpose of joining the West Indian expedition. Few other officers, and none with such claims on the new regime, deliberately risked murderous duty in the be-plagued Caribbean provinces.[127]

Despite its officers' credit with the new regime and the unit's own importance to the balance of power in the West Indies, "never was a regiment so carelessly sent out or extremely neglected." So wrote Colonel Kendall, who was sailing out to his new command in the same fleet. Colonel Hill informed Blathwayt that, bad though the treatment of Nott's men was, and sickly as the recruits Nott brought him were, the veterans of his own independent company were worse off. They had not even been paid in seven years. Sick and hungry, ill-clothed and poorly armed, "the ragged regiment" nevertheless led the neglected regulars and provincial companies of the Leeward Islands and an entire regiment from Barbados in the hard fighting that recaptured St. Christopher's from the French. Major Nott himself survived sickness and wounds in the West Indian campaigns to join Marlborough's staff for the reconquest of Ireland. After returning to Berwick as its governor, Nott received Marlborough's imprimatur to command Virginia. Like Edward Nott, other military conspirators of 1688, the officers of the Denmark/Churchill connection, were cycled through the campaigns of King William's war to achieve independent imperial commands under the command of their princess, now Queen Anne, and her general, John Churchill, now duke of Marlborough.[128]

CHAPTER SIX

A Decade of Dissent:

1689–1698

Part One: From Walcourt to Kinsale

Walcourt

M ARLBOROUGH WAS but an earl of recent creation when, on May 13, 1689, the Hudson's Bay Company directors followed up his memorial to King William with proposals, approved by the king in council, that Marlborough's deputy governors in Hudson Bay join the native peoples to levy war against the French. Marlborough had achieved his goal: an end had been put to the Treaty of American Neutrality. Marlborough's future influence in America, however, depended upon his present achievements in Europe. If Marlborough was to further advance himself, his family, his princess, and his imperial agenda, he had first to win the victories that would confirm him in the eyes of English officers and the English public as their leading commander. So Marlborough contrasted himself to King William, the indispensable but resented and disliked Dutch conqueror of Greater Britain, and Marlborough won remarkable military victories, but then he suffered utter political and personal disgrace and he spent seven lean years leading the opposition to King William. That opposition was Marlborough's political education. Because his opposition focused on the imperial failures of King William's government, from the Lesser Antilles to Newfoundland, it qualified Marlborough to transform Anglo-American political culture, as well as providing him with the political base essential if he were to successfully succeed King William in command of the allied armies against France.

On the same day that Marlborough was authorized to make war on the French in America through his deputy governors and their indigenous allies, he himself was called away to fight in Flanders. Blathwayt informed the earl that his convoy for Holland was ready to sail and that the articles of war were complete. With these martial laws, Marlborough would discipline the eight thousand English and Scottish troops he had organized for service with the allied army in Flanders. Given full military authority to punish, pay, promote, and command the British forces in Flanders, Marlborough began to lead that transformation which eventually made the brave but brutal, undisciplined, and inexperienced English and Scottish soldiers into professional campaigners.[1]

Marlborough was hard put to join his command in Holland. He was always a bad sailor. Now his seasickness was prolonged by his ship's flight from a French privateer. The extra time at sea in bad weather killed thirty of Marlborough's horses and cost the earl himself the energy he needed to meet the problems presented by his dirty, sickly soldiers, who were short of uniforms and shoes. The bad condition of Marlborough's men reflected their own slovenly habits and their military ignorance, but it was worsened by the English government's notoriously inadequate provisioning and pay facilities and by the greed and greenness of the English officers. None were more greedy than their general.[2]

The half-dozen future governors-general who now learned their trade under Marlborough's command were concentrated in the Buffs. He made their colonel, Charles Churchill, his brigadier. The 3d of the line also numbered among its officers Edward Fox, Francis Collingwood, the absentee admiral, Sir John Berry, and an officer soon to be sacrificed in the West Indies, Henry Holt. William Selwyn commanded a battalion of the Coldstream Guards in Marlborough's division. They were disaffected, but the Royal Scots, with whom served George Hamilton (afterwards earl of Orkney, Marlborough's chief subordinate, Scots political ally, and governor-general of Virginia for almost forty years), were mutinous.[3]

Resenting Marshal Schomberg's accession as their colonel (in place of the loyalist lord Dumbarton, one of three officers to accompany King James into exile), disinclined to accept Prince William as the king of Scotland, and determined to avoid embarkation for Holland, the bulk of the Royal Scots had mutinied at the waterside. Led by their officers, 1,300 of the Scots marched north, bound for home. William was compelled to send every regiment of his Dutch cavalry and dragoons in pursuit. Before the success of the pursuit was known, the emergency inspired the parliament to pass a mutiny act. That act's immediate use was to legitimate the punishment of the Royal Scots' patriotic officers. Only in the next century did the annual passage of a mutiny act come to symbolize civilian supremacy over the military.[4]

Rounded up by the Dutch troopers (who outnumbered the Scots four to one), force-marched south and compelled to board transports bound for the Netherlands, the Royal Scots still rejected the new regime. They clung to the old with a loyalty that sprang from clan, feudal, and family alliances, all of which underlay a nascent Scottish nationalism. The Royal Scots' alle-

giances affected Marlborough's command decisions and political proposi-
tions for the next quarter of a century. Jacobite sentiment was even stronger
in the Scots corps that King James had founded for the officers who had
obeyed his summons to resign from the Dutch service. That regiment was
now commanded by Sir David Colyear, himself an outstanding recruit to
the imperial service from the Scots-Dutch brigade, afterwards Marlborough's designate as American commander-in-chief. "Le Roi Jacques est
encore trop considere parmi ces troupes," wrote the allied commander, the
prince of Waldeck, and "M. de Marlbrouck has much trouble with them."5

Much of that trouble was simply the indiscipline of raw troops new to
foreign service. At Brigadier General Churchill's corps' first halt in Holland, the local farmers brought their allies beer, bread, and cheese, but
when the Dutch peasants asked for payment, the English soldiers beat
them, broke ranks, and swarmed off "into a beautiful meadow, which was
ready for haymaking, and they made havoc of it." Now entirely out of control, the English troops smashed into the nearby houses, stole the wine
from the cellars, extorted 20 guilders from a farmer, and took a horse on
which they loaded their loot. Marlborough wrote to Blathwayt (on whom
he relied for news of the empire as well as for drill books and royal orders)
that he was determined to discipline his men. The cost was substantial. In
just two months the earl and his officers lost fifteen hundred men to illness
and desertion. But the surviving effectives, as Waldeck wrote to William,
were "so well ordered that I have admired it, and I can say that Monseiur
Milord Malbrouuck and the Colonels have shown that their application has
had a good effect."6

So did combat. It also won Marlborough the respect of his men and the
devotion of his officers that preserved his life on scores of occasions. The
first was on July 13, when a lieutenant and fifteen troopers, at the cost of
eleven casualties, saved "My Lord Malburra and several of the dutch gene-
ralls" from an ambush "by a thousand french hors." A month later, "Lieutenant General Marlbruck" demonstrated his extraordinary coolness and
calculation in combat to allies and enemies alike. On August 14/25, he was
in command of the allied army's foragers. At 9 a.m., they encountered the
French cavalry vanguard advancing on the walled town of Walcourt, ten
miles south of the River Sambre. The French attacked. Their first charge
cost the English picket thirty men from the six hundred troops of Charles
Churchill's (3d) and the Tangier veteran Colonel Robert Hodges's (16th)
regiments, who guarded the allied foragers. Commanded by Hodges, the
English outguard withdrew from hedgerow to hedgerow, fighting until the
foragers escaped. They lost another seventy men in the retreat. By 11 a.m.,
Marlborough had ordered Hodges to shelter his men in a mill and beyond
its stream. There the five hundred surviving English soldiers held off the
entire French advance. In the meantime, Marlborough ranged the whole of

his command in support on the hill east of Walcourt. Under the cover of his artillery (directed by Michael Richards, afterwards promoted by Marlborough for American service) Hodges's outpost finally "retir'd fighting" and rejoined Marlborough.[7]

At noon, the French and Swiss Guards attacked Walcourt itself. They lost heavily to Marlborough's artillery in their approach. Then the attempt of their commanders to take the place by storm left the French attackers scrabbling at the foot of Walcourt's medieval walls without either artillery or engineers. By 2 p.m. Marlborough's detachment—Selwyn's battalion of the Coldstream Guards and a German battalion—had gotten into the town and up on the walls of Walcourt. Thence they slaughtered six hundred of the French below. Finally, the French marshal ordered Walcourt bypassed and turned instead to assault the allies' main body, Waldeck's Dutch, who had now drawn up to the west of the town. This attack also failed. At 6 p.m., Waldeck ordered the allied counterattack. His Dutch infantry advanced from the west while, from the east, Marlborough led the cavalry charge of the Life Guards and the Blues, supported by the English foot. The French fell back and it was only the skill and courage of the duc de Villars (John Churchill's comrade at Maestricht and his opponent at Malplaquet) that saved them from disaster. Even so, "the six battalions of the French Guards who made the attack [on Walcourt] were ruined." The French infantry had lost 2,000 casualties to 340 English. A Scots soldier lauded "this fortunat success [which] gave great encouragement to our army and doubtless much the contrary to the ffrench it being the fflower of theyr army that was Ruffeld."[8]

The action at Walcourt was the allies' only victory of 1689. It was handsomely attributed to the English by the rather surprised prince of Waldeck: "Mons. the Colonel Hotzes and the English who are with him, have accomplished miracles, and I would never have believed that so many of the English would show such *joie de combattre* . . . M. the Count Marlbaroy is certainly one of the most gallant men I know." Indeed, the old campaigner wrote to King William that Marlborough, "in spite of his youth [Marlborough was thirty-nine, the same age as the king] saw into the Art of a General more in one Day than most [do] in a great many years." William then wrote to Marlborough, acknowledging that "it is to you that this advantage is principally owing" and formally confirmed his colonelcy of the Royal Fusiliers. Naturally, the London press touted this modest allied success as an English victory and Marlborough's preeminent place among the English commanders was reinforced by popular acclaim.[9]

"The Chief"

Marlborough came home at the end of the campaigning season and exploited his enhanced prestige in the October session of the parliament. It had been adjourned in August, at least in part so that William and Mary could avoid the humiliation of having the parliament vote a yearly allowance of £70,000 to the Princess Anne. The new monarchs were furious that the princess and her political agents (the Marlboroughs chief among them) could claim a majority of both houses of parliament in favor of an income which was both independent of the crown and double the amount that William and Mary deemed seemly. Anne, so the shaky new sovereigns thought, ought to live a retired life and show a proper sense of her subordination to her sister and her king.[10]

Instead it seemed as if the members of the Denmark / Churchill connection, the collective "interest" of the heir apparent and the embodiment of her Anglican identity, would take their natural place at the head of "the Tories and the high church men." Further uplifted by the birth of an heir, the duke of Gloucester, Princess Anne was determined to assert her rank at the court of the childless king and queen. She formed a royal household, if not a shadow cabinet of the sort her father had constructed while duke of York. Of course, that household was staffed (i.e., its places were sold) by the Churchill family. Marlborough himself proposed a ministry of moderates who would preserve the princess's position as heiress to the throne and mother of a future king. Sarah Churchill, countess of Marlborough, was the chief prop of Anne's own stubborn determination to maintain her right. Sarah identified herself with her princess. She would not have either of them mistreated. She knew that clan Churchill's greatness was measured by the princess's public position, for that would enable Anne to act on her personal favor for the Marlboroughs. Both Anne's position and her favor for the earl of Marlborough were amplified when he arrived from Flanders just in time to play off the sovereigns against the tories and so to win royal agreement for a parliamentary grant to the princess of £50,000 per annum. Sarah put it succinctly: "the success of the affair was chiefly imputed to the steadfastness and diligence of my Lord Marlborough and me, both by those to whom it was so exceedingly disagreeable, and by her to whose happiness it was so necessary."[11]

The Marlboroughs' victory was personally profitable (the princess gave Sarah £1,000 a year from the grant) but the angry sovereigns exacted a high price from the Denmark / Churchill connection. For his support of Anne's annuity in the house of commons, lord Cornbury lost the Royal Dragoons (he had already incurred the royal wrath by being one of just three members of the commons to vote against the declaration that James II had abdicated).

Captain George Churchill, deprived of royal protection, was sent to the Tower by parliament, charged with extorting bribes for assigning convoys. Prince George was denied any military command, whether by sea or by land, by King William. Queen Mary, with all the focused malignity of a limited mind, set out to force her sister the princess to dismiss Sarah, be the cost what it might. Mary's enmity was also the most obvious reason why Marlborough himself was left without a command in the spring of 1690. Of course he had been active during the winter in the dispatch of the West Indian expedition for the recapture of St. Kitts and the assault on the French Leewards, and he had ordered Colonel Gibson to reinforce Nott's and Foulke's corps for that expedition. But, come the spring, Marlborough was not sent back to Flanders nor did he accompany King William to Ireland for the decisive battle against King James.[12]

Marlborough's failure to win a field command may have owed as much to his own reluctance to attack King James as it did to Queen Mary's hatred. Repeatedly, Marlborough (like many other military conspirators of 1688) had declared that he would never endanger the person of his prince. It was the sort of scruple that King William respected. So much is suggested by his commission to Marlborough, dated June 3, 1690, as lieutenant general, commander-in-chief, and one of the nine privy councilors who were named lord justices in England during King William's absence in Ireland. Queen Mary was not pleased. She wrote of Marlborough to the king that "I can never either trust or esteem him." Nonetheless, Marlborough, as commander-in-chief, shared political power with Carmarthen (Danby) and Nottingham. He did so despite the insane jealousy of Mordaunt, now earl of Monmouth (and afterwards a designate for American command as earl of Peterborough).[13]

Insiders now referred to Marlborough simply as "the chief," but, authority and ability aside, his resources for the defense of England were small. King William had sent 48,000 men to reconquer Ireland. A nominal 6,000 were in Scotland under Mackay, being beaten up by the Jacobite clans. Waldeck had 4,500 survivors from Marlborough's former division of 8,000 in Flanders. The various American enterprises absorbed another 1,500 soldiers. Marlborough was left with just 12,000 (unpaid) men to defend England. Five thousand of them were in garrison, so that Marlborough faced French invasion with a field force of fewer than 7,000. That invasion seemed imminent because, on the last day of June 1690, off Beachy Head, Admiral Herbert (now earl of Torrington) had suffered the worst defeat in English naval history. Herbert failed to support the Dutch van, which the French then surrounded and decimated, virtually without loss to themselves. Then the French turned on the outnumbered English. Seventeen allied battleships were destroyed, ten Dutch and seven English. England was open to invasion. The convoys from America were imperiled.

The army in Ireland was cut off. In Flanders, on the same day as the disaster off Beachy Head, Waldeck's army was smashed by the French at Fleurus. No help could be had from Scotland, where the Jacobites still held the field. Left to his own devices, Marlborough called the militia from the harvest, raised private funds to recruit new regiments from the militia ranks, and moved his few serviceable regiments to defend the most likely invasion beaches on the Channel coast.[14]

From Ireland to New York

England's danger was erased in Ireland and the hopes of Jacobites as far off as Maryland, Pennsylvania, and New York were disappointed by the military ineptitude and personal cowardice of James II. On July 1, 1690, as the allied fleet fled from Beachy Head up the Thames, pulling the buoys as they passed to prevent French pursuit, the armies of the rival kings met in battle at the River Boyne. The Boyne was the ancient boundary of the English Pale in Ireland. So it was the moat of Dublin, the Irish capital where King James had reigned in person for the last fourteen months. He had reached Kinsale from France on March 12, 1689, ridden into Dublin less than two weeks later and, by April 19, 1689 (the day his viceroy was chained to the wall of the Boston gaol), King James's force, ballasted by five thousand French troops, held all of Ireland save for two ports, Londonderry at the head of Lough Foyle and Inniskilling at the narrows of Lough Erne.[15]

On July 30, 1689, two desperate strokes reclaimed Ulster from King James. After a siege of 111 days, the starving survivors of the Londonderry defense (including, it seems, Robert Hunter, the Scots volunteer in Princess Anne's escort, who was now a major) were at last relieved by the force commanded by Piercy Kirke. In fact, it was the *Dartmouth*, under the very professional captain (and Newfoundland governor) John Leake, that broke the boom across Lough Foyle, ran the French batteries, and relieved the city. On the same day, the Inniskilling irregulars—armed and officered from the English fleet—began their famous counterattack at Newtownbutler. Two thousand Inniskilling men killed between two thousand and four thousand of the six thousand Irish who had besieged them.[16]

To Protestant Ulster's southern border, Marshal Schomberg led fourteen thousand men from England during August 1689. Landing near Belfast, Schomberg's forces captured Carrickfergus before digging in at Dundalk. Schomberg refused all entreaties to advance, wasted more than two months of the campaigning season, and then announced that the Dundalk camp would be the army's winter quarters. To these winter quarters repaired Kirke and his English regiments, as well as the Inniskilling irregulars. It began to rain. The veteran Dutch, Danes, and Huguenots among the allied force "soon built good warm barracks but our English Corps,

being all new Soldiers, unacquainted with the Consequences of not Hut-
ting, neglected it till there was neither Timber nor Straw to be had; so that
in the rainy weather they died like rotten Sheep." By the end of October,
the 12th Regiment, whose serving officers at Dundalk included Captain
John Livesay (he survived these horrors only to die in a Jamaica command),
mustered only 136 effectives, having 281 sick and 363 dead. By contrast, a
well-hutted Dutch regiment lost only 11 men. Six thousand two hundred
and sixty-two of the 10,000 English troops perished before spring brought
William III across "St. George's Channel" to take command of the reconquest of England's greatest colony.[17]

At Dundalk, King William received his inspector general's assessments
of the suriving English officers. From the awful winter of an army whose
soldiers used the corpses of their comrades to weigh down their tent flaps, a
few devoted officers had emerged. The major of Princess Anne's Regiment,
the Anglo-Irish veteran Benjamin Fletcher, received high marks. The son
of a royal army officer, Fletcher had become cornet to John, Lord Berkeley,
president of Connaught (brother of the Virginia executive Sir William
Berkeley). Fletcher was promoted captain of a company of infantry in the
occupying army before being purged as a Protestant in 1685. Fletcher became a captain of Berwick's Regiment during the Portsmouth mutiny and
joined lord Churchill's coup (Fletcher was a client of the duke of Ormonde,
the preeminent Anglo-Irish officer in the conspiracy). Fletcher was promoted major when the command of "Princess Anne's Regiment" was transferred from Berwick to Beaumont, leader of the Portsmouth mutiny, and
the Regiment was shipped to Ireland.[18]

At Dundalk, at the Boyne, and in the savage guerrilla war of the Irish
reconquest, Fletcher's service was such that, as the secretary at war and of
plantations recalled, King William, "having of his own choice in consider-
ing of his Services during the whole war of Ireland," breveted Fletcher lieutenant colonel "and sent him to New York as a person very fitt to manage
the Warr in those parts." On being commissioned governor-general of
New York, on March 9, 1692, Fletcher was breveted colonel by King William. He crossed the Atlantic in company with Sir Edmund Andros, who
was outbound to command Virginia, and whose programs for New York
and the Iroquois, Fletcher adopted.[19]

On August 30, Fletcher landed in New York from HMS *Wolfe* with his
official family and a corps of Anglo-Irish officer cadets. These young officers gave a professional tone to New York's provincial units and filled gaps
in the staff of Fletcher's four regular garrison companies. While Fletcher
was en route to America, he was commissioned to take over the government
of Pennsylvania from its Jacobite proprietor. Fletcher imposed royal institutional forms on Pennsylvania government. He presided over the rise of
the assembly to supplant William Penn. He even obtained some small sup-

port from pacifist Pennsylvania to support the war in New York and to sustain the Iroquois offensive against New France.[20]

Raised in the rough school of Irish garrison government, Colonel Fletcher used his four garrison companies (and royal naval crews) to control city elections in New York. He again reflected his Irish experience (and followed King William's example) by making huge land grants to his followers. He reconstituted the provincial army organized by Governor-General Dongan. Fletcher manned these regiments with drafts from the militia of New York and the Jerseys. He officered the provincial units with his Anglo-Irish cadets, supplied them (poorly, by corrupt commissaries), and paid them with funds authorized by the New York assembly. He rewarded the legislators by conniving at their sponsorship of pirates and their illegal trade. Finally Fletcher imposed English partisan patterns on New York politics by building an Anglican party around the ideological center of Trinity Church (its present fortune stems from Fletcher's endowment, the "King's Farm" in Manhattan). When King William's war ended in 1697, the whigs got Colonel Fletcher recalled and replaced him with Lord Bellomont, another Anglo-Irish soldier, but one who fought with Fletcher's tories in New York and was actually welcomed by Boston's whigs.[21]

King William's inspector general gave a much more jaundiced estimate of the regiment at Dundalk camp in which Fletcher's lieutenant governor in New York, Richard Ingoldsby, served as the senior lieutenant. Ingoldsby's family regiment was descended (like the Jamaican redcoats) from the Cromwellian conquerors and colonists of Ireland. Its founding colonel had shown the militant flexibility of the age. He sandwiched his colonelcy of Cromwellian dragoons between royalist commands, and had the unusual distinction of being created a baronet both by Cromwell and by Charles II. Of the Ingoldsby outfit King William's inspector wrote: "colonel ill and incapable, as are almost all the other officers, who are usually absent, and are so greedy of money that the soldiers can scarce get paid, very badly clothed, and without shirts; as bad a Regiment as possible." In this disgraceful context, Richard Ingoldsby seemed so extraordinary an officer that the inspector general proposed his triple promotion to major. King William not only complied with the recommendation but, at the close of the campaign he sent Major Ingoldsby to New York as the new garrison's executive officer. By virtue of his military rank, Ingoldsby ultimately became commander-in-chief of the colony and the founder of a New York provincial dynasty.[22]

Ingoldsby began his contentious career of seventeen years in the military administration of New York with the street fighting against the forces of Jacob Leisler that ended the revolutionary regime in the province, cost the lives of such stalwart soldiers of the old regime as Major Patrick MacGregorie, and led directly to the execution of Leisler and his lieutenant,

Jacob Milbourne. On the death of his superior officer, the aptly named Colonel Sloughter, Major Ingoldsby took over the government. The provincial authorities soon complained to the secretary at war and of plantations that "the Major doth demonstrate to everyone that he hath been little acquainted with Government, preferring his pleasures and the publeq conversation of Women."[23]

It was Ingoldsby's cruelty, rather than his womanizing or the bitter partisanship that was deepened by the major's violent arrival in New York, that drove the new governor-general, Colonel Fletcher, to censure Ingoldsby as impolitic and bloodthirsty. To check desertion, Colonel Fletcher himself did not hesitate to impose court martial discipline over New York's provincial army: "Our Fusiliers Paide by ye Country." And his "Detachments" or drafts from the county militias were so resented that the assembly agreed to fund regular recruiting to replace conscription. But Fletcher disapproved when "Major Ingoldsby Catch'd one of his own Company who had Run, tri'd him, and made short work with him." When some of the Anglo-Irish soldiers who came out with Fletcher claimed that their enlistments were only for three years and mutinied to demand their discharge, the governor-general's court martial condemned the ringleaders to death, but he reprieved them on the scaffold. "In my mind," wrote the colonel, "hanging is ye worst use a man can be put to."[24]

Commanding on the remotest frontier of the empire in America, Fletcher was hungry for professional gossip, the more so as he was the head of a military family. The governor-general wrote to the secretary at war and of plantations (in terms that will be familiar to every parent) that his son "Charles is Idle, if not Graceless. Not one word from him since Parting. Hee knows how Acceptable a Short Account of the Advancements in ye Army would be to mee. Who are Alive or Dead & Advanced or Degraded. My affectione and service to him." Fletcher did his best to advance other scions of Anglo-Irish families in the imperial service. Of his three new lieutenants in the garrison companies, Colonel Fletcher wrote, "they have all been Cadets in the Irish Warr with his Maty, & two of them formerly Lts in the County Companys did behave themselves well . . . agt the french & Indians of Canada in the Mohegnes County." The geographic dimensions and personal interconnections of a military empire have seldom been so compactly put: the war in Ireland and the military families of the island's English conquerors supplied the officers and governors of New York and the commanders of the war against France on New York's Iroquoian frontiers. Much has been made of the martial seigneury of French Canada. So in New York, a class of planter-officers were introduced by the province's Anglo-Irish executives from 1684 to 1701. Their descendants and successors would command the provincial army of New York for a century.[25]

In contrast to Fletcher and Ingoldsby, other American commanders whose units served in the reconquest of Ireland were noted for *not* being with their regiments at the Dundalk camp. Kirke's regiment (the 2d, Queen's) listed among its company commanders both John Leake and Stafford Fairburne, naval captains who had been prominent in lord Churchill's coup and who were afterwards governors of Newfoundland and admirals of England. Their absence, and Kirke's corrupt clothing contracts, damaged their regiment, the senior English corps in Ireland. Nonetheless, their services at sea (Leake had broken the boom at Londonderry and Fairburne was one of the few English captains who fought at close quarters against the French at Beachy Head), as well as their political services with the fleet in 1688, made them (together with George Churchill) the leading admirals of the Churchill connection.[26]

"The Best Regt. in all the Army" at Dundalk was the 16th, Forbes's former regiment. It would become the Royal Irish at Namur, serve in all Marlborough's campaigns, and produce governors-general for New York and New Jersey, Minorca, the Leeward Islands, and Gibraltar. The regiment's fine condition in 1690 was due not only to good officers and adequate clothing but also to its soldiers being Ulstermen. "The soldiers being all of this province, the campaign is not so hard on them as others," the inspector general observed. The biological insularity of seventeenth-century populations meant that "seasoned" soldiers (and settlers) survived much more readily than new arrivals. The need to keep acclimatized troops on overseas stations led to very long postings. Long tenure led to the practice of legionary settlement in Ireland and America. So British regiments became the social skeletons of imperial provinces.[27]

The Boyne Water

The seasoned veterans of the Royal Irish mustered more men than any other British regiment when, on June 30, 1690, King William paraded his troops, thirty-six thousand strong, on the northern banks of the Boyne. The king personally pressed forward his reconnaissance of the Jacobite army as it assembled some twenty-five thousand men to the south, across the river and astride the road to Dublin. King William was closely attended by Prince George, whose futile ambition was to claim command of the allied army for England, and by the young duke of Ormonde, who was King William's candidate to displace the earl of Marlborough at the head of the English army. As the king and his staff scanned the enemy lines, William was knocked from his horse by a Jacobite cannonball. The grazing blow took coat, skin, and some flesh from his right shoulder. Remounting, the king remarked with his usual sangfroid that "it was as well it came no nearer." To hearten his troops, William concluded his inspection before he retired to his tent to have his wound dressed.[28]

The next day, Tuesday, July 1, 1690, the wounded king could not lift his sword arm but he won the decisive battle of the war. In addition to the officers already named, King William was assisted by eight future governors-general. All shared in the victory that finally secured the British kingdoms, and so the English empire, for the officer-authors of the Protestant putsch. Tactically, the battle of the Boyne was straightforward. At 6 a.m., King William threatened the fords to the left of King James's army with the seven thousand men of his right wing. The Williamite right included the veteran captain of Dutch forces in the invasion of England, now a captain in the English 5th Regiment, Thomas Handasyde. Handasyde was given the grenadier company of the 5th at the end of the Irish campaign and rose to be colonel of the 2d and 22d regiments. Marlborough's dedicated subordinate, as governor-general of Jamaica, Handasyde executed the duke's imperial policies. Next in seniority in King William's right wing was Colonel Richard Brewer's (12th) Regiment, which the colonel would take out to Jamaica. Brewer's subordinate, Captain Richard Phillips, was afterwards colonel of the 12th and founder of the 40th Regiment, the corps that shaped the infant society of Nova Scotia. Both Brewer and Phillips had been noted participants in lord Churchill's coup. Next in seniority, and standing further to the left both in imperial politics and in the line of battle, was the Anglo-Irish ensign John Nanfan of the 13th, afterwards lieutenant governor of New York and Massachusetts to his cousin Richard Coote, earl of Bellomont in the peerage of Ireland and himself a commander in the invasion of England. Thomas Stanwix, then a subaltern in the 13th and afterwards governor-general of Gibraltar, may have been present with Nanfan in the right wing of King William's army at the Boyne. Henry Worsley, another ensign of the 13th in 1689, would rise through the Guards, under Marlborough's aegis, to become governor-general of Barbados. The banks of the Boyne were the slippery and dangerous foundations of many an imperial career as the army of King William won its most important battle.[29]

Afraid that his retreat to Dublin might be cut off by the flanking movement of King William's right wing, King James detached his elite French infantry to defend the fords to the left of his position. There, for the rest of the day, the French held off the allied right and held open the door to Dublin for King James. The difficult terrain prevented an immediate allied attack on the French even after the English had forded the river under fire. Colonel Brewer described "such a bog that I thought the Divel himself could never have got through and so did [the enemy] or they had not faced us as they did for half an hour almost within musket shot."[30]

A little after eleven, as soon as he was sure that James had weakened his main body by detaching his French troops to guard the Dublin road, William ordered his Blue Guards into the Boyne at the Oldbridge ford, almost exactly opposite James's center. The Blue Guards were hard hit as they, and the Huguenot and Inniskilling regiments, waded through the river. As the survivors of the allied vanguard climbed the opposite bank of the Boyne and tried to reform their ranks, they were attacked by King James's Irish cavalry. Rallying King William's hard-pressed men, Marshal Schomberg fell, sabred by the enemy and shot from behind by his own men. With Schomberg fell the Ulster champion, Bishop Walker.[31]

Yet the Williamites were led on by lord George Hamilton. He fought on the banks of the Boyne at the head of the Inniskilling infantry regiment, having been commissioned their colonel in March. He had introduced his Anglo-Irish officers into King William's council of war and they now made good their promise to find the fords of the Boyne for King William's attack. Their survivors led the Ulster Regiment out to serve in the West Indies during much of Marlborough's heyday. Their colonel, who proved his loyalty to the new regime at the Boyne, rose to command both battalions of his uncle Dumbarton's old regiment, the Royal Scots. Hardened in the Williamite wars, Hamilton became perhaps the most able of Marlborough's British generals and the longest-serving governor-general of Virginia.[32]

After almost an hour of hand to hand combat along the banks of the Boyne between the allied center and the main body of King James's army, King William himself, at the head of the cavalry of the allied left wing, at last crossed the river and reached the enemy's right flank. Caught in the rising tide, the allied horse had to swim the river. They took time to regroup before they attacked the Jacobite right wing. In that attack, King William "expos'd himself with undaunted bravery" at the head of the Dutch, Danish, and Inniskilling cavalry (the last of which may have included Major Robert Hunter, who continued his military career as Marlborough's brigade major of the dragoons and who concluded it as governor-general successively of New York and Jamaica). When King William's cavalry charged up from the fords, they were met and broken by the Franco-Irish counterattack. King William then put himself at the head of lord George Hamilton's Inniskillings. The king "asked what they would do for him," but they misunderstood his commands. At last, William found his Blue Guards who, with the Inniskillings, followed him forward to the decisive assault. King James's Irish infantry broke and ran. So did King James. He was in Dublin by dark. At first light the following morning, James fled for the south coast. In just two days, he covered 120 miles, reached Duncannon and a French frigate, picked up a convoy at Cork, and sailed instantly into exile. James II never left France again.[33]

Ireland's threat to England's empire had passed. The threat of French invasion of England also passed in the summer of 1690. Writing from the bitter siege of Limerick, King William ordered five battalions from Flanders to join Marlborough's field force in England. Their passage was unimpeded because, at almost the moment of the Boyne, the Channel Fleet bloodied the French, who withdrew to Brest. The end of the traditional campaigning season was at hand. Substantial regular forces were now assembled encamped on Blackheath. News arrived of Codrington's success at St. Christopher's and Phips's capture of Acadia. Williamite successes were being won in the Highlands of Scotland, at Cromdale and by the construction of Fort William. Marlborough concluded both that all danger of a French invasion in 1690 was past and that there was a chance to take the offensive with the English home army he commanded.[34]

Cork and Kinsale

With characteristic foresight (and with the sagacious advice of Sir Robert Southwell), Marlborough had been planning an amphibious assault on Cork and Kinsale. Most of the French aid for the Jacobite, Catholic, nationalist Irish passed through these southeastern Irish ports. Marlborough's old master, King James, had fled from Cork. The flight of the prince, whose person Marlborough had sworn never to endanger, left the earl free for a spectacular entry into the Irish war, if only he could overcome the opposition led by Carmarthen. His timorousness, jealousy, obstruction, politicking, and military meddlesomeness drove Marlborough to despair. Incited by Carmarthen, Queen Mary and her advisors (save for that aggressive imperialist, Nottingham, and Marlborough's steadfast supporter, Admiral Russell) violently opposed Marlborough's proposal to take almost every able-bodied man from the home army to attack the Irish ports. Despite the opposition of his queen, his council, and his Dutch generals, however, King William approved Marlborough's proposal the moment it reached him in his camp outside Limerick. If Marlborough failed, the clangorous commander, who had already created an English faction to oppose Dutch dominance in the army, would be disgraced and the military units loyal to Marlborough would be decimated. If he succeeded, King William's own failure to take Limerick would be annulled and Ireland would fall.[35]

Even as King William lifted the siege of Limerick and the hearts of the Irish, Secretary Blathwayt was laying a false trail for observers of the six thousand troops Marlborough concentrated (with Governor Gibson's invaluable aid) at Portsmouth. The force, supposedly mustered for a raid on Normandy in revenge for the French burning of Teignmouth, included two regiments long associated with Marlborough: Charles Churchill's (3d) Regiment, which was among the corps recalled from Flanders to meet the French invasion threat, and Trelawney's Tangerines (the 4th or King's Own). Trelawney had been governor of Dublin until his regiment was sent back from Ireland by King William with four other English corps to join Marlborough's expedition. Marlborough's own fusiliers, as well as Princess

Anne's Regiment (with its new major, Benjamin Fletcher), were also units particularly associated with Marlborough and were therefore enlisted in his expedition. In addition, Marlborough commanded the 13th, with its corps of candidate governors-general; Hales's and Fitzpatrick's regiments, both of which ended their existence in the fever-ridden West Indies; and Sir David Colyear's Scots. The expedition also included most of two regiments of marines (one of them Carmarthen's, whose captain, Benjamin Bennett, was the governor of Bermuda), two hundred men recruited for Bolton's second battalion by Major Edward Nott, just returned from the reconquest of St. Kitts; and, finally, two hundred men whom Marlborough had drafted from Monmouth's regiment.[36]

On August 14, King William approved Marlborough's plan and shipped home the English regiments from the Dublin garrison to join the earl's expedition. The king also moved troops south to prevent Irish interference with Marlborough's operation. Colonel Brewer (who was now the governor of Dublin and who would be the commandant in Jamaica in Marlborough's time) led six regiments south to hold the line of the Shannon as a frontier against the relief or reinforcement of Cork and Kinsale by Berwick's army of seven or eight thousand men. Brewer outmaneuvered Berwick, an accomplishment seldom afterwards achieved against that brilliant tactician. In the meantime, on August 26, the earl of Marlborough left London, his wife, and their newborn child. Queen Mary wrote to the king "that this morning lord Marl. went away; as little reason as I have to care for his wife, yet I must pity her condition, having lain in but eight days; and I have great compassion on wives when their husbands go to fight."[37]

Four days later, Marlborough began to embark the troops at Portsmouth. They "went on board with all cheerfullness," Marlborough remarked. Their willingness was a tribute to their commander in an age when cavalry had regularly to force infantry onto transports. By the end of the week, the expedition was ready to sail, in eighty-two ships. Its flagship was the *Grafton* (70), commanded by the duke of that name. Grafton, Marlborough's host on this occasion, was the son of Barbara Villiers (by Charles II and not, unless the Tangier stories are true, by Marlborough himself). Their shared relation to Cleveland was perhaps a source of Grafton's devotion to Marlborough, under whose command he had fought at Sedgemoor and with whom he had conspired against King James. Grafton had voted with Marlborough for a regency. Grafton's identification with Marlborough had cost him the command of the First Guards when William and Mary attacked the Churchill connection. Desperate for distinction, Grafton had returned to his naval command. His bravery had made him the only English victor at Beachy Head. The prestige he had won could do nothing to hurry the ordnance ships to the rendezvous, however, nor could Grafton hasten the arrival of the Dutch escorts (which Marlborough thought un-

ROYAL CHARACTERS

Carolus IIdus D. G. Ang: Sco: Fra:
et Hib: Rex Fidei Defensor &c,
*W. Wissing, pinx., I. Vandervaart,
fec., E. Cooper, exe., mezzotinto
engraving from the author's collection.*

Jacobus Secundua Die Gratia Angliae,
Scotiae, Franciae et Hiberniae Rex,
*N. De Largilliere, pinx., I. Smith, fec.,
mezzotinto engraving from the author's
collection.*

Serenissima Maria D. G. Angliae,
Scotiae, Franciae et Hiberniae Regina,
*G. Kneller, pinx., I Smith, fec., mezzotinto
engraving from the author's collection.*

Guiliemus Tertius D. G. Angliae, Scotiae, Franciae et Hiberniae Rex, *G. Kneller, pinx., I. Smith, fec. & ex., mezzotinto engraving from the author's collection.*

Serenissima Maria D. G. Angliae, Scotiae, Franciae & Hiberniae Regina &c, *G. Kneller, pinx., I. Smith, fec. & ex., mezzotinto engraving courtesy of the British Museum.*

Serenissima et Potentissima
Anna D. G. Angliae, Scotiae,
Franciae et Hiberniae Regina,
*G. Kneller. pinx., I. Smith, fec.,
mezzotinto engraving from the
author's collection.*

His Royal Highness George
Prince of Denmark, *G.
Kneller, pinx., I. Smith, fec. &
ex., mezzotinto engraving from
the author's collection.*

James Welwood described King Charles II: "His face was composed of harsh features, difficult to be traced with the pencil; yet in the main it was agreeable, and he had a noble majestic main. In contradiction to all the common received rules of physiognomy he was merciful, goodnatured, and in the last twenty-four years of his life fortunate, if to succeed in most of his designs may be called so. . . . If he had any one fixed maxim of government it was to play one party against another, to be thereby the more master of both; and no prince understood better how to shift hands upon every change of the scene."

As for Charles's brother James, "He was a prince that seemed made for greater things than will be found in in the course of his life, more particularly of his reign," so bishop Burnet remarked. James "was esteemed in the former parts of his life a man of great courage, as he was quite through it a man of great application to business. He had no vivacity of thought, invention or expression; but he had a good judgement where his religion or his education gave him not a bias, which it did very often. He was bred with stange notions of the obedience due to princes, and came to take up as strange ones of the submission due to priests. . . . He was undone by them, and was their martyr, so that they ought to bear the chief load of all the errors of his inglorious reign and of its final catastrophe."

Age thirty-nine in 1672, James married the fifteen-year-old Maria Beatrice, sister of the duke of Modena, by proxy. Smitten, the proxy groom, the earl of Peterborough, wrote that his prince's bride "was tall and admirably shaped; her complexion was of the last degree of fairness, her hair black as jet, so were her eyebrows and her eyes, but the latter so full of light and sweetness, as they did dazzle and charm too. There seemed given them by nature a power to kill and a power to save; and in the whole turn of her face, which was of the most graceful oval, there were all the features, all the beauty, that could be great and charming in any human creature." Yet Mary's bigotry, even more than her beauty, helped to drive her king to the Catholic courses which incited lord Churchill's coup and excused Prince William's invasion.

"His martial inclination will naturally carry him, when he comes to the crown of England, to bear down the greatness of France," so Gilbert Burnet predicted of William of Orange, "and if he but hits the nature of the English nation right at first he will be able to give laws to all Europe. . . . But if the prince does not in many things change his way he will hardly gain the hearts of the nation. His coldness will look like contempt, and that the English cannot bear . . . and his silent way will pass for superciliousness. But that which is more important, he will be both the king of England and stadtholder. . . . and the English will hardly be brought to trust a prince that has an army of 30,000 men at his command so near them."

Prince William's claim to the imperial throne of England and its empire was that his wife, Princess Mary, was King James's elder daughter and heiress presumptive. Burnet was much her admirer. He wrote that "all that I can possibly set against this character is that she is the most reserved person alive; and that her goodness is too general, without carrying her into the particularities of friendship with any person." Certainly, as William's queen, Mary was characterized by her hatreds, chief among them both lord and lady Marlborough. Close minded and ungenerous, narrow and self-absorbed, Mary never forgave her sister, Anne, for her ambition, her fertility, or her friendship with the Churchills.

Another friend, at least of lord Churchill's, had been indelibly labeled by King Charles. He allowed that he had tried Prince George of Denmark drunk and tried him sober and found nothing in him. He was a soldier who was able to join but one military campaign in his married life (aside from the march to Salisbury in 1688), the Irish invasion under William III (who took Prince George with him to Ireland, it is suggested, to be sure of Princess Anne, and so of Marlborough). Prince George, "after thirty years living in England . . . died of eating and drinking, without any man's thinking himself obliged to him." Such is the prevalent portrait. In fact, the prince was an essential constituent of the Churchill connection. As front man for lord Churchill's coup and as Queen Anne's consort, lord high admiral, and generalissimo, the prince was of enormous importance to the Churchill commanders.

As was usually the case, the last word belongs to Sarah, duchess of Marlborough. She summed up her family's essential aegis: "Queen Anne had a person and appearance not at all ungraceful, till she grew exceeding gross and corpulent. There was something of majesty in her look, but mixed with a sullen and constant frown, that plainly betrayed a gloominess of soul and a cloudiness of disposition within. She seemed to inherit a good deal of her father's moroseness, which naturally produced in her the same sort of stubborn positiveness in many cases, both ordinary and extraordinary, as well as the same sort of bigotry in religion."

necessary, as well as a dilution of what he proposed to be an exclusively English victory). Further delays followed from English admirals' fears of equinoctial storms in the Irish Sea. Then foul winds held the fleet, and its sickening soldiers, in port until September 16 or 17.[38]

During this delay, the French forces in Ireland got wind of the impending attack. Afraid of being cut off, they evacuated the island. Still windbound in Portsmouth, Marlborough's expedition had already transformed the character of the war in Ireland. King William himself now sailed from Ireland, but he left behind him orders for a force to meet the English invaders at Cork. That force was equal in strength to Marlborough's and it was commanded by a German princeling, Ferdinand Wilhelm, duke of Württemberg-Neustadt, general of the Danish forces in Ireland. The duke would take command from a mere earl. Then King William's cabinet could give Württemberg all the credit for any success, just as they planned to "ruin" Marlborough if the expedition failed.[39]

At last, on September 21, Grafton's fleet entered the approaches to the vast bay of Cork. The next day, the English armada sailed towards shore with the flood tide, encountered hostile fire, and sent in the ships' boats. Their crews stormed the Jacobite batteries. "Resolved not to lose this good weather," Marlborough landed the entire expeditionary force in just twelve hours. The troops encamped before dark on September 23. The next morning, led by Grafton, the English overcame the half-hearted Irish resistance. "Though they lined the hedges, they were easily beat from them," Marlborough wrote. His little army advanced up the River Lee to Cork. The city was held by Irish troops who were equal in number to the English, but the vanguard of the Danes, Dutch, and Huguenots (dispatched by King William from the Limerick siege, instead of the English battalions under Kirke's command, whom Marlborough had requested so that he might retain the English complexion of the expedition and insure his own command) arrived just in time to help the English invest the city and drive the Irish defenders from its suburbs. Hales's infantry seized the Cat Fort, high on the south bank of the River Lee, overlooking the island city. This was the site from which batteries could enfilade Cork's curtain wall. Grafton supervised the construction of additional gun emplacements farther downstream. These batteries were designed to breach the city wall and open Cork to assault, always provided that assault troops could cross the tidal river in the face of the defenders' fire.[40]

At this critical moment, on September 26, Württemberg himself arrived on the north bank of the Lee with his main body. He immediately tried to take command from Marlborough. Württemberg asserted that his family's royal rank, his own continental military experience, and King William's favor (to foreigners or, conversely, his hatred of the English) justified displacing the English earl, even though Marlborough was the senior general officer and the expedition was largely English in composition. It seemed as if Marlborough was once again going to be deprived of command and credit by a favored foreigner (as he had been by Feversham at Sedgemoor). A Huguenot brigadier exercised an expatriate's tact, however, and suggested a solution that Marlborough adopted, now and often afterwards, to defuse the command pretensions of European allies. Appearances would be preserved by alternating days of command. Württemberg would preside first. But the days of action would be Marlborough's.[41]

Playing on the allies' divided command, James II's Irish governor of Cork, Roger Macelligott, won a day's reprieve. He sent a flag of truce to each of the commanders. Typically, Württemberg offered terms but Marlborough demanded unconditional surrender. The next day, Saturday, September 27, 1690, was Marlborough's day to command the allied armies. As the tide ebbed, "at one o'clock, the battalions of Churchill, Marlburrow, Collier, the granadiers of Trallany, a part of the detachment of Munmouth and Boulton" forded the south branch of the River Lee, up to their armpits in racing water and under fire. The 1,500 Englishmen were led by a "forlorne hope" commanded by leaders of lord Churchill's coup: the duke of Grafton, lord Colchester, Colonel Grenville, Stafford Fairburne, and the brigadier, Charles Churchill. Supported by the grenadiers of five English regiments and the line companies of Trelawney's battalion, these volunteers climbed the river bank, brushed aside the Irish outguards, and reached the shelter of a ditch "within pistole shot" of the city wall. Grafton was mortally wounded. His death (after eleven days of suffering), and another hundred English casualties, were the price paid for a desperate and decisive assault. It was followed up by Churchill's, Marlborough's, and Colyear's battalions, and Bolton's and Monmouth's detachments. The Danes crossed the north branch of the Lee to make a lodgement beneath the walls. Those walls were then breached by the besiegers' batteries and cleared of defenders by bomb vessels' mortars. So the allies approached the storm of Cork.[42]

Memories of the English massacre of the Irish at Drogheda and fears of what Protestant troops would do if they were first resisted and then, their blood up, set loose in a Catholic town, compelled Governor Macelligott to accept Marlborough's terms. The four thousand to five thousand men of the garrison were to be made prisoners of war (the governor himself was imprisoned in the Tower of London for seven years until, when the war was over, he was at last exchanged to join his countrymen, the famous "Wild Geese," in the French service). The Catholic clergy were to be protected. The invaders, save for the new governor-general and a garrison regiment (the 13th) were to be kept out of Cork. Cork capitulated on Sunday afternoon, September 28, just a week after Marlborough's men reached the Irish coast and only two weeks since they had sailed from Portsmouth. Such dispatch was unequaled by any other expedition in the age of sail. It bespoke the English earl's unique drive and determination, and the ability and devotion of his subordinates.[43]

Even as, on the Sunday, he concluded the surrender of Cork and named Colonel Hales as its governor, Marlborough had ordered his five hundred horsemen to ride eighteen miles to the southeast and invest Kinsale. Early on the Monday morning, Marlborough's cavalry rode into the open town and put out the fires set by the garrison in their retreat to the harbor forts. Without the shelter of the town, exposure and disease would have swept away Marlborough's men and quickly forced an end to any siege of the forts, but the early and unanticipated arrival of the allied cavalry had forced the garrison to evacuate Kinsale in a hurry, the fires had little time to spread, and the allied troopers soon smothered them. On the Wednesday, October 1, the vanguard of Marlborough's infantry reached the shelter of Kinsale. The earl himself arrived the next day with his main body. He was appalled by the strength of the Kinsale forts, one on each of the high banks of the River Brandon, reinforced as part of the Stuart seaport citadel strategy of imperial control and defense. Fort Charles alone had two hundred bronze guns mounted on five bastions and it commanded the anchorage. Marlborough said afterwards that he would never have undertaken the siege of Kinsale so late in the season if he had known its strength in advance.[44]

Daunted he might be, but Marlborough wasted no time. He ordered an immediate assault on the relatively weak "old Fort" across the river. At dawn on the Friday, a general of the Danes, the Prussian Julius Ernst von Tettau, commanded the storm of the old fort by Edward Fitzpatrick's regiment, plus volunteers, some eight hundred in all. Following such officers as Francis Collingwood and Edward Fox (who afterwards commanded the regiment in the West Indies), Fitzpatrick's men swarmed over a weak point in the wall, killed a third of the garrison on the spot, captured another third, and pursued the remnants down to the bank of the Brandon across which the surviving Jacobites escaped by boat to Fort Charles.[45]

Against that formidable fortress, Marlborough organized a siege in form. Without waiting for their heavy guns to arrive over the deep muddied tracks from Cork, the English dug parallels north of Fort Charles. The Danes dug in to the east. Then, in just five days, under cannon fire and without counterbatteries of their own, the allies sapped onto the killing field of the counterscarp. They dug to within fifteen paces of the covered way—the galleried ditch between counterscarp and curtain wall. The breaching battery (obviously, Marlborough and his engineers had studied Vauban to effect and the defenders lacked all enterprise) was excavated and waiting for the Danish guns when they arrived on October 11, despite incessant rain and marauding Irish cavalry. In four days of constant firing the Danish guns battered a "practicable breach" in the wall of Fort Charles.

Then this breach was widened by the English engineers who exploded a mine under the scarp of the fortification.

Marlborough ordered the final assault for October 15. Rather than resist it, the governor of Fort Charles and Kinsale, Sir Edward Scott (formerly James II's lieutenant governor of Portsmouth), hung out a flag of truce. Soaked by the autumn rains, which had flooded the besiegers' trenches, plunged his men "up to the middle of the leg in water," and sent the sick list soaring, Marlborough readily granted the usual, honorable, conditions. On October 16, 1690, Sir Edward Scott's coach was driven out of the fort through the breach (to demonstrate the fortress's indefensibility). The garrison of eleven thousand men followed, "with bag and baggage, drums beating, colors flying, lighted matches and bullets in mouth" (to show that they had received honorable terms). After being generously entertained by Marlborough, the defenders of Kinsale were escorted by the allies to the Irish garrison at Limerick.[46]

In twenty-five days, Marlborough had captured the keys to Ireland. James II was told, "Your Majesty has lost these two seaports with the best magazines of the kingdom." Absent Cork and Kinsale, French aid was largely cut off and the supplies stockpiled there could not be replaced. The rest of Ireland would fall to the allies in the coming campaign. The earl left his brother Charles as governor of Kinsale. His regiment, together with Princess Anne's Regiment under Fletcher's command, were the garrison. Charles, known as "the Danish Churchill" following his household service at the court of the king of Denmark, was an indispensable liaison with the Danes, the elite troops of the allied armies, not just in Ireland but in Marlborough's future continental campaigns. Marlborough put his remaining troops into winter quarters and sailed home.[47]

On October 28, just two months after he had left London, Marlborough returned to the imperial capital in triumph, "vain, that like a soldier, he had kept his word; but secretly indignant that it was not oftener put to the test." Again, invidious comparisons with King William were made. Marlborough and his English troops, Londoners remarked, had won more in a month than King William and his Dutch generals had won in a year. Given the Boyne, this was more than a little unfair, but popular and partisan opinion only recalled that the king had just abandoned the siege of Limerick. In turn, King William carefully qualified his praise of the English earl: "No General in *Europe*, that has made so few Campaigns as the earl of Marlborough could have acted [in a whole season's fighting] what he has done in a Quarter of *One*."[48]

Part Two: The Seven Lean Years

Disgrace

Fresh from his triumphs in Ireland, more than ever the imperialist, Marlborough wanted to replace the Dutch general Gedart de Ginkel, earl of Athlone, in command of the reconquest of Ireland during 1691. King William refused to give the leading English general an independent, viceregal command in Ireland. Instead the king let Marlborough know that he would have but a subordinate post, under the king's own eye, in Flanders. William also refused Marlborough the command of the ordnance. The master general's place was an office of "cabinet" rank, rich in pelf, patronage, and military power. The earl had eyed it for years and he half expected it as a reward for his coup. Now the death of Schomberg at the Boyne had opened the master generalship, but not to Marlborough. Of course the king also ignored the press agitation that he make the victorious earl a duke "in consideration of his extraordinary merits." In fact, a few cheap compliments aside, William refused to recognize Marlborough's accomplishments in Ireland, although they were "the most brilliant achievements of the war."[49]

In January 1691, his princess put aside, his connection cashiered, his wife despised, himself neglected by William and hated by Mary, Marlborough made contact with the exiled king. Marlborough merely intimated to St. Germain what every observer knew to be true, that the English army was disgusted with Dutch William and his boorish generals. In short order, he received from James II promises of pardons for what was past and of future favor for his lady and their friend, lord Godolphin (whom Marlborough now convinced to remain in the treasury commission). These pardons Marlborough promised to pay for by cultivating and coordinating military malaise. The alienated officers of the English army made Marlborough's London lodgings the headquarters of their discontent. Here centered the military politicians' efforts to realize, by pressure on King William, by the restoration of King James, or by the elevation of Princess Anne, the political power and imperial program that the Churchillian conspirators had essayed in their coup d'état.[50]

It was thus as essential to the stability of English politics as it was to the successful conduct of the war in Europe that, in the spring of 1691, King William finally achieved his aim of 1688: the substantial redirection of English military resources from control of the British kingdoms to the war against France. William left thirteen thousand troops under Ginkel in Ireland to complete the pacification of the island province. There Brewer led the frontier fighting and the counterinsurgency operations now characteristic of the Irish theatre. After Glencoe, Scotland absorbed only two thousand regulars. They regarrisoned the Cromwellian fortresses in the northern realm. William's own Dutch bodyguard held London. The king sent most of the British troops to Flanders (he hoped to get thirty-eight thousand men but the primitive English military system produced only twenty-three thousand effectives).[51]

On May 2, 1691, Marlborough took command of the British investment in King William's war. The earl landed in the Netherlands and assumed the command of the British division in the allied army: two troops of the Life Guards, whose brigadier was the duke of Ormonde; four battalions of Foot Guards, English, Scots, and Dutch; five Scots corps under Brigadier Mackay, fresh from the reoccupation of Scotland; and four English infantry regiments, brigaded under Charles Churchill. Most of the leading British generals—Kirke, Lanier, Mackay—formed Marlborough's divisional staff. These generals were veterans of conspiracy, coup, and conquest in the British Isles. Now they led into the war against France in Flanders the regimental officers who either earned here the military credentials prerequisite for imperial commands in America, or who now came to command in Europe because of promotions that they had won for American service. Consider the service battalion of the First Guards. It was officered by veterans of the Virginia expedition: captains and lieutenant colonels (for so the senior company grade officers of the Guards were ranked) Edward Rouse, John Webb, and Andrew Pitcairn-Wheeler. They now educated the governors-general of the eighteenth century: John Delavall, Thomas Povey, Christopher Codrington, and James Stanhope all were commissioned in the First Guards during the Flanders campaigns of the 1690s. William Selwyn's battalion of the Coldstream Guards included such embryo administrators as William Matthews (like Codrington the scion of a Leeward Islands family).[52]

At the right of Marlborough's line stood Bath's bluecoats (the 10th), commanded by the earl's nephew, Sir Bevil Grenville, afterwards governor-general of Barbados (Bath himself had been ordered to stay in his Plymouth government lest he encourage the army's counterrevolutionary sentiments). Captain Roger Elliot of the 10th prepared for the government of Gibraltar in Marlborough's division. Elliot brought along in his wake his half-brother, Alexander Spotswood, who would become famous as commander-in-chief of Virginia. Marlborough's own fusiliers were in his division, as were Hodges's (16th) Regiment. The 16th had been distinguished under Marlborough's command at Walcourt. Now they were leaders in the military revolution of the 1690s: the substitution of the bayonet for the pike; the replacement of line volleys by platoon firings; and the introduction of formations half as deep and twice as mobile as the old masses of pikemen and firemen. The advances in weaponry, tactics, and organization pioneered by the 16th under Marlborough's command were the military advances associated with his major victories, a decade and more afterwards.[53]

Months before he reached the front in Flanders, Marlborough had warned the allied generals that the fortress of Mons was the obvious opening objective of the French campaign and that it was ill-fortified and undermanned. Marlborough's remedies demanded haste and cash. The Dutch authorities were incapable of the first and short of the second. Mons fell to the French on April 9, months before the allies were ready to take the field. All of King William's futile maneuvering in the summer of 1691 failed to threaten the French conquest. The campaign ended almost as ingloriously as it had begun. Villars's daring cavalry raid through the fog at Leuze caught the rearguard of the retreating allies unaware. The embattled Life Guards and the hard-pressed allied infantry suffered seven hundred casualties before Marlborough could bring up "the British brigades" to their support. Reinforced, the allies withstood the final French charge, inflicted almost as many casualties as they had received, and even captured four standards.[54]

Fortunately for Marlborough's reputation, the allies' bloody nose was universally attributed to Waldeck's careless command during King William's absence. Despite such demonstrated incompetence by his Dutch generals, and despite his own relentless mediocrity as a field general, King William continued to consider British officers a lesser breed. Good judges advised William, however, that Marlborough was not just the best of the British but also the most promising allied general. The prince of Vaudemont told the king that "*Kirke* has Fire, *Lanier* Thought, *Mackay* Skill, and *Colchester* Bravery, but there is something in the Earl of Marlborough that is inexpressible. All those Virtues seem to be united in his single person." More, Vaudemont said to William, that he had no subject who "can ever attain such a Height of Military Glory as this Combination of sublime Perfections must one Day or other advance him to." In reply, William admitted only one of his English general's attributes: ambition. The earl of Marlborough, the king said to the prince, would do everything he could to verify Vaudemont's prediction.[55]

The campaign concluded, on October 19, 1691, the king and his suite landed at Margate, disappointing William's faithful Blue Guards who had marched down from London en masse to welcome him at Harwich. Instead, the windblown royal party called up the country gentlemen to escort the king and his company to London. At Shooter's Hill, an unskilled driver overturned the coach in which Churchill rode beside the monarch. "No great damage was done, only Lord Churchill complained of having his neck broken; the King told him there was little danger of that by his speaking."[56]

In William's opinion, Marlborough was speaking altogether too much. He still pressed for the master-generalship of the ordnance. William awarded that post to a remarkably unqualified and undeserving courtier. The prince and princess of Denmark begged the king to grant Marlborough a consolation prize: the order of the garter. It was a distinction that Marlborough coveted and one that William had promised him. After all, it was Marlborough who had put William in a position to grant honors. As the princess reminded her brother-in-law, "you cannot sertainly bestow it upon any one that has bin more serviceable to you in the late revolution, nor that has ventured their lives for you, as he has done ever since your coming to the crown." Prince George reminded the king that a garter for Marlborough was the only favor he had ever asked. King William denied their requests. Shortly afterwards, in December 1691, Marlborough reconciled the princess with her father, the exiled king.[57]

Simultaneously, Marlborough publicly criticized the Dutch command of the English army. He even encouraged English officers to disobey the Dutch generals. Marlborough formed "a cabal" of English officers who denounced William's preference for the Dutch (and for Germans and Danes and Frenchmen as well). Marlborough told the English officers that his campaign for command of the ordnance was designed to end William's favoritism to foreigners and to restore the government of England and command of the English army to Englishmen. Marlborough then demanded that his command of the British division in Flanders be made independent of all superiors save the king himself. If King William resisted, Marlborough told Godolphin and Russell on the night of January 9, 1691/2, he would move two resolutions in the lords: one to deny all foreign officers the right to hold English commissions; another to demand the removal of all Dutch troops from England. King William rejected every one of Marlborough's demands. Deprived of his Dutch generals and Dutch bodyguards and with Marlborough in command of the British division and the ordnance, William would be at the mercy of Princess Anne's general. For the next seven years, Marlborough pursued his xenophobic, patriotic program, to immediate disgrace and to ultimate success.[58]

Both to the king himself and in public places, Marlborough denounced William's grants of noble titles, public offices, imperial territory, and public revenues to his Dutch favorites. Marlborough warned King William, as he had King James, of impending "disaster" from "such an unpopular conduct." Outside of the king's presence, but to his certain knowledge, Marlborough compared William's Dutch favorites to James's Irish ones. After all, William had granted their estates to his favorites. These were estates that Marlborough himself might have controlled had William allowed him to complete the reconquest of Ireland. The alienation of the Irish conquest was especially offensive to English imperialists and it inspired Marlborough's most politically effective condemnation of the king he called "Caliban." William knew his Shakespeare well enough to be deeply insulted. Only his kingship, he said, prevented him from demanding of Marlborough the satisfaction of a duel.[59]

As king, William had other ways of showing that he had joined his queen in hatred of the Marlboroughs. On the same evening that the earl of Marlborough met with Russell and Godolphin to plan parliamentary opposition to Dutch dominion, Queen Mary criticized Princess Anne for her allowance to Marlborough's countess from the parliamentary grant: it demonstrated Anne's degradation, Sarah's greed, and their disrespect to their sovereigns. The next morning, January 10, 1691/2, King William permitted Marlborough to act as gentleman of the royal bedchamber and to introduce lord George Hamilton to the royal presence. Then, after speaking to Queen Mary, the king sent a secretary of state to Marlborough with orders to sell his commissions and leave the court. Presumably the disgraced earl would take his wife with him to the country.[60]

The far reaches of the empire soon learned of Marlborough's fall from favor. Bishop Compton's Virginia commissary was in London. Thence he wrote to Colonel Nicholson that "the Chief news here . . . is the disgrace of my Lord Marlborough . . . it is Said he is Suspected by the King to have made his peace with France." The royal reassignment of Marlborough's commands, the order for his lady to leave the court, Princess Anne's refusal to dismiss lady Marlborough, and the princess's own exile from the court at Whitehall to Sion House on the Thames, all were detailed to the lieutenant governor (and to the commissary's other Virginia correspondents, we may assume). Then the commissary got around to telling Colonel Nicholson that "which concerns your honour most nearly": that his former commander in the dominion of New England, King William's childhood friend, Sir Edmund Andros, would now assume control of Virginia; that Colonel Fletcher, distinguished under King William's command in Ireland, would come out to govern New York; and that Secretary Blathwayt was bound for Flanders. So the secretary at war and of plantations lost day-to-day control of the plantations office and the agenda of the privy council's plantations committee. Blathwayt no longer directed the routine rotation of troops within the British Isles and between its garrison governments, a direction always essential to the balance of political power. Colonel Nicholson's immediate response to the commissary's communication was to order that cleric to pay the respects of the lieutenant governor of Virginia to Princess Anne. The gesture was aimed to express Colonel Nicholson's Anglican imperial enmity to those who would "swear down our English Dominion."[61]

But the armed center of Anglican imperialism was indeed being sworn down. On May 1, 1692, the king's Dutch favorite was anonymously informed that Marlborough had vouched for the loyalty of more than one hundred army officers to the exiled King James II. The earl's name, at the head of a list of those imperial proconsuls, Lanier, Trelawney, Hales, Brewer, and Billingsly, testified both to the disaffection of English professional officers from alien, overbearing, and incompetent Dutch commanders and to Marlborough's continuing preeminence among these veteran king breakers and makers. According to the information given Portland, these officers swam in swirling political currents that scoured the most distant banks of the English empire. Led by their major, William Matthews, the West Indian satrap, the Coldstream Guards were still allegedly plotting King James's restoration. The new regime resorted to massive arrests of the dissident officers. Colonel Hales (Marlborough's aide and his governor of Cork, whose regiment was being sacrificed to its colonel's politics and to American diseases in the West Indies) was the first of the regimental officers apprehended by Queen Mary's order.[62]

Colonel Hales found the leader of the alleged military conspiracy already closely confined in the Tower. Marlborough was arrested on a charge of treason on May 4, 1692. The official evidence against him had been fabricated by the court since his disgrace. The "Flower Pot" informers intended not only to implicate the earl himself but to involve in treason charges other military members of the Denmark / Churchill connection, such as lord Cornbury, who could plausibly be alleged to have acted for Princess Anne. Thus the queen and her advisors hoped to surround the princess with allegations that she had treasonably sought her own ascendancy, through her father's restoration, to be achieved by another of Marlborough's coups. Queen Mary also insisted that the evidence against Marlborough implicated his brother George. Captain Churchill had already been driven from the admiralty. He was now at sea in Admiral Russell's Channel Fleet. The admiral resisted the queen's call for George Churchill's removal from command. Moreover, Admiral Russell reminded King William that Marlborough had "set the Crown upon his Head." Russell flatly told William that he must produce some very weighty reasons for such remarkable ingratitude as he had shown in his disgrace and imprisonment of Marlborough.[63]

On June 15, Marlborough was finally bailed but the royal animus extended to his sureties, among them the former Jamaica viceroy Carberry (Vaughan) and two privy councilors, Halifax and Shrewsbury. They had accepted Marlborough's assurances that the evidence against him was forged. They agreed with him that the prosecution was "a reproach to the government as well as an injustice to him." On standing bail for him they were immediately deprived of all their places under the crown. Contemporaries remarked that these dismissals were intended to show English army officers and politicians the price of joining Marlborough in opposition to the government. When the parliament reassembled in November, however, the lords refused to consider the king's opening speech until he erased the breach of their privilege as peers in the earl of Marlborough's arrest without significant evidence and his being kept in bail while their house was in session. To terminate the attack on his government, and in particular on the queen and her advisors (whose hatred of the Marlboroughs was seen to lie at the root of the entire episode of allegations and arrests), King William was forced to order Marlborough's bonds canceled and to certify to the lords that he had been unconditionally released.[64]

Opposition

While Marlborough was under arrest, on July 24, 1692, the English army was sent to the slaughter at Steinkirk by Solms, the most vindictive and imbecilic of King William's Dutch generals. This murderous engagement combined with the royal certification of Marlborough's innocence to make him the lost leader of an outraged English army, the patriotic spokesman of a deeply wounded national pride, and the voice of a refreshed racial prejudice against the Dutch. A militant and xenophobic nationalism was the powerful political impulse that Marlborough manipulated for the rest of the war. Its first fruit was the lords' insistence that Marlborough's replacement in Flanders should be a native Englishman, that English officers should succeed to every vacant post in both the army and the ordnance, and that all the garrisons of England should be English soldiers under English governors.[65]

William paid no attention to the lords. Then, in 1693, two more military disasters almost exhausted the political nation's capacity for outrage. In June, the main French battle fleet, having got out before the English could blockade Brest, set an ambush in Lagos Bay. There they intercepted the great convoy bound for Smyrna, Turkey, and the Levant. Sir George Rooke, in command of the escort, fifteen English and eight Dutch men-of-war, conducted a clever and courageous defense. Nonetheless, the French destroyed three Dutch warships, ninety-two allied merchantmen, and cargo worth more than £1,000,000. Then the ill-fated Sir Francis Wheeler went out to try and save the survivors, scattered in the Iberian ports. His ship was lost with all hands in an epic storm that drowned 1,500 English sailors. The disaster in Lagos Bay was but the greatest of a series of French raids that seemed about to cut England off from her empire, to eviscerate allied commerce, and to curtail the customs revenue that financed the war with France.[66]

Of yet more awful human consequence was the botched battle of Landen. William III, demoralized by his own military defeats and distracted by his concern for the Mediterranean convoy, allowed himself and the allied army of fewer than fifty thousand men to be surprised in a crowded camp with their backs to the morass of the Little Gheete by more than sixty-six thousand French. Having refused advice to retreat across the river while there was still time, William posted the British brigades in the most exposed sectors of the defense, as usual. Together with a brigade of Brandenburgers and one of Hanoverians, on a sunny and hot day, July 19, 1693, the British fought hand to hand in the village streets of Neerwinden against overwhelming numbers of the enemy. Again, as at Steinkirk, they were not reinforced or rescued, although for a time William himself fought with them. The king joined the fight first in Neerwinden and then he was engaged in two hours of hand to hand combat in the adjacent post of Neerlanden. There, William fought at the head of Brigadier Selwyn's new command, the 2d of the Line, and the rest of his brigade. One musket ball passed though the king's hat and deafened him temporarily. A second shot went through his coat sleeve. A third cut the knot off his scarf of office and grazed his side. The French attack was led by the duke of Berwick. As it was driven back, Brigadier Churchill personally captured his nephew (and Marlborough's). Then, to the undisguised delight of the English troops, Count Solms lost a leg to a cannonball and died, shrieking. Neerwinden was captured three times by the French. The British drove them back out of it twice. Finally the defenders were overcome by three simultaneous assaults, each at odds of three to one. The islanders fell back, after eight hours of fighting, having lost 135 officers.[67]

Once the British were beaten, all the allies ran for the river crossings. The fleetest of the English, so his enemies said, was the secretary at war and of plantations. Secretary Blathwayt "was so careful of his papers yt, for feare of loosing them, he never stopt till he came to Breda." No historian of England in America can be anything but approving of Blathwayt's care to preserve the records, especially as the allies left so much else behind. Sixty guns of the army's artillery train, all of its field equipment, and six thousand casualties, including the duke of Ormonde, were abandoned by the fleeing army. But King William's apologists had learnt of long necessity how to make his defeats into victories. They pointed out that the French could not afford many more such bloodlettings. The public relations impact of this was a bit diminished, however, when the clergy thanked God for the king's deliverance from them that "were too many and too mighty for him."[68]

Suddenly, however, at the end of August 1693, the church bells of London ("wch have all this summer been very silent") began to ring for "the great news" that Queen Mary and Princess Anne were reconciled, and that "my Lord Churchill hath (as report saith) effected it, and yt for his reward he is to be declared General of ye forces here." This would have been a politic as well as a popular development. King William was about to open parliament with a speech of "regret for ye disadvantages ye armies received this year at land and ye great miscarriages [that] befell ye navies at sea." These military failures might be mitigated in the eyes of an English parliament if the royal government could announce the reappointment of the best English general, Marlborough, and his belligerent brother, the admiral. Within the week, however, all hopes of reconciliation and restoration were disappointed. The sisters' estrangement and the Churchills' unemployment continued through 1694.[69]

That year's most excoriating episode was the English attack on the French fleet's base at Brest. Unemployed though he was, Marlborough has been blamed for the tragedy. In April, seven thousand English soldiers were mustered in and around Portsmouth. On May 4, Marlborough gave a Jacobite colonel a letter for King James. Marlborough reported that he had just discovered that the troops at Portsmouth were aimed at Brest. On May 5, Admiral Russell sailed to reconnoitre Brest and returned to declare that the port was relatively undefended. On June 2, the expedition sailed from Portsmouth. Under the date of June [4/] 14, however, the official *London Gazette* published details of the massive defensive preparations by the French at Brest. Presumably this information was in the hands of Thomas Tollemache, commander of the land forces, before the fleet sailed from Spithead. On June 7, the English fleet entered Camaret Bay, the approach to Brest, and immediately encountered heavy fire from shore batteries. Nevertheless, on the morning of June 8, General Tollemache led the first wave of English infantry ashore. He and they were killed on the beach by artillery fire and musketry from the French entrenchments. By June 12, the English fleet, with the remaining troops onboard, was back in Portsmouth.[70]

That Marlborough told anyone of the expedition is disgraceful, much less that he wrote for enemy information. As was clear even at the time, however, Louis XIV had long since been fully informed of the intended attack by his own spies. On April 4, exactly a month before Marlborough contacted the clandestine colonel, King Louis had ordered his chief engineer, Vauban, and twelve thousand troops, to reinforce Brest. They arrived at the port, and, as the *London Gazette* made clear prior to the event, the English expedition was doomed, a month before Marlborough's message reached the exiled court of James II at St. Germain (it had then to be decoded, transcribed, and sent to Versailles). As was his wont, Marlborough had deceived King James, this time with important-sounding but entirely outdated information. His was a political ploy, not a betrayal of his comrades. Marlborough had made an overdue payment on an unsavory insurance policy.[71]

On the return of the broken Brest expedition, and in light of King William's unbroken string of military failures, Marlborough offered his services to the king. Secretary Shrewsbury reported from London to William "what is here become a very general discourse, the probability and conveniency of your majesty's receiving my lord Marlborough into your favor."

Shrewsbury reminded William that he had all along admitted Marl-borough's military skill and that it was the king's personal prejudice that had kept Marlborough in disgrace. If only because "it is so unquestionably his interest to be faithful," it would be safe for King William to return the earl of Marlborough to military command. Shrewsbury was seconded by Admiral Russell, but to no avail. The king flatly replied: "I do not think it for the good of my service to entrust him with the command of my troops."[72]

The first prerequisite of Marlborough's return to office was the death of Queen Mary. This occurred suddenly, from smallpox, on December 18, 1694. Mary's sister, Marlborough's aegis, Princess Anne, was now not only the heiress apparent to the imperial throne, she was, by right of birth—assuming her father to have abdicated and her brother to be supposititious—queen. She had only set aside her claim to succeed her elder sister, Queen Mary, in 1689, when faced by the fact of William's military might and his personal determination to rule. Now, as Sarah said, King William "had sense enough to know that it would be impossible to continue any longer on open difference with the Princess and he was well aware that everybody who had a mind to show they did not care for him would certainly do it by making their court to her." As they did. The Denmark residence, so long shunned by courtiers, was suddenly full with "crowds of people of all sorts flocking to Berkeley House to pay their respects to the Prince and Prin-cess." The Guards once again saluted and escorted the royal pair (although, to remind Anne and George where the real power lay, their Guards were Dutch Blues). Soon the princess returned to St. James's, residing in the palace "as if she were a crowned head."[73]

The king did not restore the princess's champion and the leader of the military opposition to command. Nonetheless, Marlborough, much against his wife's inclination (for, as Sarah said of Anne, "I could not endure to have her do anything that I would not have done in her place"), saw to it that the princess "omitted no opportunity to shew her zeal for his majesty and his government." As Shrewsbury wrote to Russell of Marlborough, "our friend, who has no small credit with her," kept Anne to the mark of con-ciliation "as the only thing that can support her or both. I do not see he is likely, at present, to get much by it, . . . but his reversion is very fair and great."[74]

Sarah was bitterly opposed to any reconciliation, "but I was never the councillor upon such great occasions." Marlborough had Princess Anne convey formal congratulations to William for his only continental victory as king of England, the successful siege of Namur in 1695. To Sarah, the princess's letter "served no other purpose but to give the King an opportu-nity for showing his brutal disregard for the writer; for he never returned any answer to it, not so much as a civil message." Marlborough responded with his habitual diplomacy to William's equally characteristic incivility. He inquired privately of the king's favorite if perchance the princess's letter had been lost at sea. Despite the king's choice of the duke of Ormonde as his English aide and his obvious intent "one Day [to] confide the leading of his Armies" to Ormonde rather than to Marlborough, the earl did nothing to denigrate the king's logistical, operational, and technical accomplishments before Namur at the head of an army of 124,700 men. Indeed, Marlborough particularly valued the valor and discipline of the British vanguard at the siege.[75]

On September 1, 1695, after a defense that had lasted eight weeks, 5,442 survivors from the original French garrison of 18,000 marched out of the citadel of Namur to join the French field army, which then retired, discomfited, having been unable to raise the allied siege. Twenty battalions of the allies marched into the citadel. King William had won his first and only continental victory. He had recaptured "the key to the Netherlands." He now admitted, for the first time, that the British troops were the best he had ever commanded. His triumph, and theirs, was a consequence of William's daring invasion of the British Isles and of a domestic coup that had brought England and its empire into the war against Louis XIV's aggression. William's initiatives and lord Churchill's coup combined to compel the British regiments into the combat from which they had emerged as the finest troops in Europe.[76]

The imperial economy, however, could no longer sustain the cost of the war. In 1696, English credit, commerce, and currency collapsed. The government had long failed to pay its soldiers their arrears. Now it failed the rest of its creditors. Government paper was discounted 40 percent and foreign exchange rose to 47 percent. Commerce was crippled by the war at sea and eviscerated at home. The coinage had been debased. Recoinage deepened a dreadful deflation. The specie shortage caused by clipping and recoinage was exacerbated by subsistence payments to about ninety thousand soldiers overseas, payments in excess of £200,000 per annum. Yet a moment's failure to remit subsistence would dissolve the field force fighting France. King William wrote to his English ministers that he could find "no resource which can prevent the army from mutiny or total desertion; for it is more impossible to find here than in England money for their subsistence; so that if you cannot devise expedients to send contributions, or procure credit, all is lost, and I must go to the Indies."[77]

The national debt had now reached the unprecedented depths of three years' peacetime revenue. The American commerce that provided between a quarter and a third of that revenue was ruined by the war. The fivefold increase in the price of sugar on the London exchange was a measure of the impact of French raids on the West Indies and on American convoys. Another gauge of transatlantic distress was that American imports had fallen by a third since the outbreak of war. These commercial and fiscal shortfalls inspired a creative compensation. Instead of declaring bankruptcy, as the royal government had done as recently as 1672, the national debt was both consolidated and funded on a long-term basis. Ultimately the funded debt, bearing interest guaranteed by taxes hypothecated by parliament, would provide an instrument of political as well as fiscal stability. The owners of capital invested in the national government. So the emerging capitalist class married monarchy. For the moment, however, the debt could not be serviced, nor could the currency crisis be resolved, without peace. The English situation was debilitating. The French situation was desperate. After both empires' exhaustive efforts at Namur, economic collapse could no longer be ignored. Louis XIV sought a truce in the war with England for Atlantic empire.[78]

Demobilization

In May 1697, peace negotiations were renewed. In September the Treaty of Ryswick was signed. In it, Louis XIV recognized William III as king *par la grâce de Dieu*, and there was a mutual return of West Indian conquests, but none of the American continental causes of the war were addressed. The French retained most of the Hudson Bay posts; they did not recompense New England fishermen; and they did not recognize the Iroquois as English subjects. The king ignored the protests of Blathwayt and the Marlborough circle. King William had defeated King Louis at Namur, but a failed peace made him doubly vulnerable in England. Outraged imperialists joined the county opposition to attack the military foundation of William's power. The end of the war meant demobilization. Most exposed were the Dutch Guards, governors, and generals who had kept King William on the imperial throne. They had been the object of Marlborough's parliamentary attack since January 9, 1692. If, at last, after a decade of Dutch occupation, the foreign forces could be removed from England, Marlborough and the English army could resume something of the political power and all of the military monopoly that they had expected to win in lord Churchill's coup.[79]

The danger was that the Jacobites and the commonwealthmen, the least and the most liberal of Englishmen, would combine not just to oust the Dutch army but to eradicate the English army as well. That army was Marlborough's power base. More largely, the army was the forceful and administrative foundation of the nation-state and its American empire. The emissaries of nostalgia saw the standing army as the ultimate obstacle both to reactionary plots and to arcadian ideals. Consistent in their opposition to the army and to the state at least since 1628, the "country" party tried to capitalize on the imperial economic crisis, universal war-weariness, and a general hatred of the military as the symbol and the instrument of the administrative class and the armed state. The agents of arcadia sought to shrink the professional army by nine-tenths. A national army and an imperial administration would be reduced to royal bodyguards and outport garrisons. Such were the military's usual roles between the raising of the Guards at the Restoration and the return of the Tangier garrison in 1681.[80]

At the peace of Ryswick, 87,440 officers and men, horse, foot, and dragoons, were in English pay. Staff, artillery, engineers, commissary, transport, and hospital personnel brought the army's numbers to more than 90,330. The navy employed another 45,000. The ratio of English armed forces to total population was equal to that of the most militarized states in Europe. Of course the "English" army was cosmopolitan, as were most European forces. The English taxpayer supported 94 troops of Dutch cavalry and 154 companies of Dutch infantry as well as 4,000 Scots and smaller numbers of Danes, Huguenots, and Germans. On the other hand, 12,030 English troops were Irish for budgetary purposes and there were at least five regiments, plus garrison companies, stationed in English America. So that the usual figure of 87,500 "English" officers and men is accurate enough to assess the relative size of the peacetime force of 35,000 that Marlborough advocated in the lords (and of 8,000 proposed by the country party in the commons).[81]

The earl of Marlborough proposed that the first step in a 60 percent reduction in force be to make the "English" army truly English. King James's plans to the contrary had been a major cause of that military disaffection on which Marlborough had played to incite the army coup. King William's occupation of London by the Dutch Guards and his subordination of English officers to Dutch (and German and Huguenot) generals had lain at the heart of Marlborough's opposition to William's government, even before the king disgraced him. For the ensuing seven years, resentment of the Dutch military command of Englishmen and of the Dutch occupation of London had underlain Marlborough's political agitation among the English officers. Marlborough saw "the standing army crisis" as the climax of his campaign to rid the English army of its foreign generals, to restore the army's ethnic integrity, and, by turning the Dutch garrison out of England, to reassert the English army's political power.

The so-called "standing army crisis" was as much the culmination of a decade of effort by Anglican officers to make the army English as it was the work of the country party who sought to reduce the army to impotence. The military motives that drove the "standing army crisis" were as much imperial as they were Anglican. The imperial impulse appeared in the second stage of Marlborough's plan to reduce the army. Not only would he make the army English but he would also disperse about half of it to the imperial garrisons in Ireland and America. This plan would leave in Marlborough's hands a nationalized army in England, able to secure Princess Anne's succession to the imperial throne. Garrisons in America would be sufficient to protect the existing empire and to add to it a full share of the Spanish American inheritance. The reserves garrisoned in Ireland could be mobilized against Louis XIV's plans to add Spain itself to France.[82]

Marlborough's plan for an English imperial army had some chance of succeeding despite the anti-army majority in the commons and despite King William's sullen refusal to make the army's case. On December 11, 1697, the commons resolved that the army should be reduced to its size as of Michaelmas (September 29) 1680, that is, to about ten thousand officers and men. Three thousand marines were added to this total subsequently. As in 1679, however, reductions were more easily resolved than financed. The troops were owed their arrears of pay on disbandment, but the rapidly shrinking military budget (it fell from £2,709,713 in 1696 to £360,000 in 1700) could not pay off the troops. Indeed, it was estimated that more than £2,000,000 was owed the army for arrears that dated back to 1689. If only because parliament would not enable the king to meet the public obligations to the soldiers, King William still had more than forty thousand men in his army in the British Isles and in America, a year after the commons had resolved reduction to thirteen thousand.[83]

Because there was no way for parliament to pay their arrears without sustaining wartime taxation, the officers received a significant concession. The commons resolved in January 1698 and April 1699 that if disbanded officers were native-born subjects, commissioned in a British regiment, and if they were available for future service with the colors, they would receive half the pay of their military rank (but not their arrears of back pay). These momentous resolutions were adopted out of pure parsimony but they were far more significant for the future of the army and the empire than the partisan rhetoric of the much-studied standing army debate. The commons had authorized a permanent military profession in England and its empire. The legislature had resolved to retain the entire English officer corps, risen to corporate self-consciousness and self-confidence in a decade of conspiracy, coup, and war, all around the Atlantic world.[84]

That resolution kept 1,500 officers on half-pay. As King William wrote, having those officers on call "will enable me to have the regiments speedily reassembled in case of need." Half-pay, together with the permanent organization of fifty-seven regiments in the British kingdoms (as well as four marine regiments, the American garrisons, the artillery, engineers, and staff, and half a dozen British regiments in Holland), perpetuated the military profession as the *ultima ratio* of English politics, a place it had occupied in practice at least since 1641. Disbandment of the men meant "that we had an army of officers." Their half-pay (and the disproportionate retention of noncommissioned officers in the standing, senior, regiments) insured unbroken careers for the veteran cadres of a British army. In effect, although assuredly not in intent, half-pay was parliament's permanent reinforcement of the military bureaucracy that administered the Anglo-American empire.[85]

On December 16, 1698, confronted with reports that the army was still 40,000 strong despite parliament's declaration that it should be but 13,000, the commons, followed by the lords, resolved to reduce the English army establishment to 7,000 officers and men (plus the 2,000 or 3,000 marines championed by George Churchill), the Irish establishment to 12,000. The dispatch of three regiments from Scotland to Holland pushed the establishment of the northern kingdom of the empire below 4,000. In America, military numbers nominally fell to perhaps 1,058 (a thin regiment in the West Indies, four independent companies in New York, two each in the Leeward Islands and Newfoundland, and one in Bermuda).[86]

King William was appalled at parliament's resolution to further reduce the army. He threatened to abdicate, a threat no one took seriously, or to abandon England to a regency, a bait the king actually cast before Marlborough "(which one would wonder at, almost as much as the thing itself)." Marlborough can have seen nothing but disaster in an abdication or withdrawal by King William in 1698. It threatened Anne's orderly succession, England's alliances against France, and the prospects of English empire. And the three were one. The Dutch had guaranteed military support for the English succession in return for the English army's assistance against France; the English and the Dutch were joint guarantors of and potential benefactors from the proposed partition of the Spanish empire. These facts elicited Marlborough's best efforts not only to persuade William to stay on as king, but his support for the king's diplomatic and military programs. Marlborough's backing was so self-interested and so sincere (now that the king's Dutch Guards and garrisons were to be sent home) that it could not be long before William himself took Marlborough back into office, as he had already taken him back into his confidence.[87]

As Marlborough could recall from the imperial army's previous disbandment in 1679, there were expedients by which to alleviate even the most draconian resolves of the commons to reduce the army in England. The Channel Islands absorbed a regiment. Orkney's two-battalion regiment was transferred to the Irish establishment. These Royal Scots exemplified another imperial fact. Because the "natural born subjects" of parliament's half-pay resolve included Scots and Irish as well as English, the British nature of King William's army was preserved into Marlborough's military as a force for union. So the Royal Scots were maintained in Ireland as the senior line regiment of the English army. To save them from disbandment, King William also agreed to send "four or five regiments to Jamaica under pretence of defending our possessions in those parts." Their real mission was to take military advantage of the impending partition of the Spanish empire. That is, the regiments in America were to "make themselves masters of the Spanish possessions in the West Indies, without France being able to hinder them," at the demise of the Spanish king. It was suggested that the imperial agenda could be further advanced by shipping ten to twelve additional regiments to the American continent for disbandment and military settlement. This extension to the American mainland of Romanesque legionary colonization, previously essayed in Ireland and Jamaica, would be modestly realized during the next seventy years, but even in 1698 it appealed to the tory imperialists in parliament.[88]

In pursuance of these plans, Collingwood's regiment was shipped out to the Leeward Islands in 1698. Its colonel was commissioned lieutenant general and lieutenant governor to the new governor-general, Christopher Codrington the younger. He was a Leeward Islands native, a Guards captain and colonel distinguished at Namur. Colonel Codrington now succeeded his father in the Leeward Islands command now reinforced by Collingwood's corps. As usual, garrison duty in the islands was more deadly than any battle, but it had the same result, the rapid promotion of the surviving subordinates. Within the year, Colonel Collingwood, his wife, their daughter, and half his men were dead of disease and the colonel was succeeded in both the regiment and the government by his lieutenant colonel, Edward Fox.[89]

New Found Land, and Office

The only imperial service that was as much feared as the Caribbean was Newfoundland. There cold replaced heat and neglect supplanted disease as the chief killers of redcoats. Yet, to the empire, fish was as commercially valuable as sugar, and seamen trained in the fisheries manned both the navy and the merchant marine. Therefore, Newfoundland was early the object of imperial regulation. One of the first provided that every fishing crew must contain a proportion of landsmen for training. At least since Sir John Berry's recommendations in 1676, the imperial authorities had also sought to establish a military governor and garrison to displace the rough rule of the "fishing admirals" (the captain of the first English vessel to anchor each spring at St. John's traditionally presided over the shore fishery and drying stages). Resident redcoats would make permanent the imperial authority periodically represented by the commodores of the royal navy's Newfoundland convoy. Garrison government would substitute a permanent settlement and a fortified port for a seasonal occupation of scattered shoreline sites.[90]

In November 1696, the latest of these efforts to make Newfoundland "a plantation" had fallen prey to a French raid. In March 1697, Colonel

Gibson's latest offer to lead an American expedition was accepted. He and his Portsmouth garrison regiment (whose major was Thomas Handasyde, governor-general of Jamaica under Marlborough, and whose artilleryman was Michael Richards, twice wounded at Namur, soon to be lieutenant governor of St. John's, Newfoundland) received the royal orders (written by Blathwayt) to recapture, garrison, and govern Newfoundland. Their naval transport and support were the fifteen ships commanded by Commodore John Norris. For their encouragement, the soldiers and sailors were to keep everything they could plunder from the French by land or by sea, munitions excepted.[91]

With that kind of license, the sailors chased every ship they saw. The English fleet did not begin to straggle into St. John's until June 6, 1697, its decks crammed with the plunder taken from French merchantmen. By then, there was nothing left of St. John's to recapture. The town had been burnt by the French, the fortifications were leveled, and those of the settlers who had not been killed by the Indians and the French had been taken off as captives. Gibson and his regiment went ashore to rebuild the ruined fort. "Fort William" was designed to shelter a permanent garrison in its barracks and their supplies in its storehouses, as well as to command the harbor entrance. While the soldiers fortified St. John's, Norris's sailors again dispersed to raid the French fishermen on the Grand Banks, leaving boat crews to fish along the coast.[92]

The English fleet had reassembled at St. John's when, on July 21, a few French warships were seen in the offing. The tween-decks of the English warships were full of merchandise. Their boats were out fishing and their spare sails covered the fish stages. Their crews were paralyzed with fear that the Frenchmen were the vanguard of the fleet that had set out from Brest in pursuit of the Gibson-Norris expedition. On the shore, Gibson and his officers were equally alarmed by patently false reports that five thousand French and Indians were advancing against them from Placentia. They demanded to be taken back onboard the fleet. The army officers made up the majority of the council of war that decided to shelter the fleet behind a boom across the harbor mouth rather than go out to engage the enemy. Despite their later protestations, however, the naval officers were no more anxious to fight than the military men were. Captain Charles Desborough came back from scouting to report that the French ships were only five fever-ridden, but treasure-filled, survivors of the fleet that had captured and looted Cartagena. Commodore Norris and his captains refused to believe him. Desborough insisted that their timidity was wasting the chance of a lifetime. The cowardly naval captains were so incensed that they court-martialed Desborough, cashiered him, and left him on the beach when they sailed for England. This they did as soon as the coast was clear. With Desborough at St. John's were left Major Handasyde and three hundred soldiers of Gibson's regiment to hold Fort William and rebuild St. John's. Two hundred and fourteen of the garrison were dead before spring brought relief from England, but the army had begun another permanent plantation in America. Meanwhile, Desborough escaped from St. John's in a fishing boat. It foundered off Ireland but Desborough built a raft and, after many adventures, reached London to denounce Commodore Norris, Colonel Gibson, their cowardly officers, and all their works, to an utterly unsympathetic admiralty.[93]

The fiasco at St. John's would have been covered up, like so many other discreditable episodes of empire, save that in May 1698, when Desborough protested to parliament about Norris's looting and avarice and abuse of military justice and about the council of war's refusal to attack the weakly manned French treasure ships, his cause was taken up by the leading critics of the military failures of King William's government, "the friends of Princess Anne." With Marlborough as their teller, a majority of the lords voted to compel every officer from the Newfoundland expedition then in England to testify about the shameful episode.[94]

The upshot of the Newfoundland hearings was an address to the king that called for the reinstatement of Desborough, the censure of Norris, the separation of future councils of war into naval and military entities, and the regularization of court martial proceedings, dispositions, records, reviews, and appeals. Besides criticizing the court and improving military justice, Marlborough had refreshed his oft-expressed interest in the army's administration of Newfoundland, in opposition both to the French empire and to the English merchants. Beginning with Major Handasyde, Marlborough reviewed the service of every army officer who commanded Newfoundland, discountenanced the culpable and the cowardly, and promoted the courageous and the devoted. The English future of Newfoundland was Marlborough's doing. He made possession of the province, in which so many English soldiers were already buried, an imperial war aim in the alliance negotiations of 1700. In 1709, Marlborough wrote England's claim into the preliminaries of the peace negotiations with France. So, in 1714, the French at last conceded Newfoundland to the English empire.[95]

Marlborough's Newfoundland investigation embarrassed the king's government. Nonetheless, on June 19, 1698, the king added the earl to his privy council and invited him to sit in the inner "cabinet council." At the meeting of the cabinet the next day, King William named Marlborough governor of Princess Anne's son and heir, the duke of Gloucester, saying, "My Lord, teach him but to know what you are, and my nephew cannot want for Accomplishments." King William pointed his compliment and extended the special relationship of the Churchills to the Stuarts into another generation by approving the appointment of Marlborough's son and heir, John, marquess of Blandford, as the duke of Gloucester's master of horse.

As these appointments suggest, King William had put Marlborough at the head of a new royal household, the first formed in England since the Churchills had enlisted in the ménage of Princess Anne sixteen years before.[96]

In returning Marlborough to favor, the king had given way to Princess Anne's importunities, Sunderland's persuasions, and the advice of Arnold Joost von Keppel, earl of Albemarle, who had displaced Marlborough's old enemy, Portland, as King William's favorite. All of them could point to the conciliatory course Marlborough had followed since Queen Mary's death; to his obvious institutional, physical, and political power as the leader of the army Anglicans; to Marlborough's eminence among the moderate "men of business"; and to Marlborough's preeminent position with Princess Anne. Once the ice was broken, King William moved with speed to bring Marlborough back to the center of the government and into the heart of the negotiation of what was to become the Grand Alliance against Louis XIV's attempt to seize the Spanish empire, and with it the mastery of the Atlantic world. On July 16, William named Marlborough one of the council of regency that would govern England during the king's absence at The Hague. To make Marlborough's role as regent clear, the king restored him to his military rank as lieutenant general of the English army and colonel of a regiment.[97]

In the coming year, King William reappointed the entire Churchill connection to office. In October 1699, George Churchill returned to the admiralty. Charles Churchill was commissioned as a major general in the army and nominated governor of Hull (a distinct snub to Carmarthen). Colonel Godfrey (Marlborough's brother-in-law) was named master of the jewel house. Now even distant Churchill connections were introduced to careers in the royal household that would affect America and the empire. A remote cousin of lady Marlborough's, one Jack Hill, was promoted from a page's place in the Denmark household to become a gentleman of the duke of Gloucester's bedchamber. Jack's sister, Abigail, rescued from destitution by Sarah Churchill, took charge of the Gloucester laundry. Ultimately, Abigail Hill would wash in public the dirty laundry that disgraced her benefactors and Jack Hill would mislead an American expedition designed to outshine Marlborough's European victories.[98]

So great was the ascendancy of the Churchills that even Sunderland begged for a family alliance. Perhaps because their mothers were close friends, Anne, the Marlboroughs' second daughter and her father's favorite, married Sunderland's heir, the prig whig widower Charles Spencer. For all her loathing of Spencer's republicanism, Princess Anne contributed £5,000 toward her namesake's dowry. In return, the bridegroom's father promised that Charles would always do the earl of Marlborough's bidding "in everything, public and private" and so spare the future queen's sovereign, Stuart, sensibilities. This, like all of Sunderland's assurances, was false. Consummated in 1700, the Spencer-Churchill marriage would reshape imperial politics a decade later. It affects the English throne today.[99]

All of these arrangements obviously looked beyond King William's reign to Anne's accession and Marlborough's ascendancy. The king still hated the earl. William would continue to thwart Marlborough professionally and politically whenever he could do so without damaging their shared preparations to meet the impending succession crises, English and Spanish. But the coming conflict compelled King William to call upon all of Marlborough's diplomatic and logistical skills, as well as on his political and military capacity to commit Princess Anne and the English army to the grand alliance. Grumbling as he did so, the king had paid the patronage price that Marlborough's services commanded. So, before his reign came to its sudden end, King William had poised the earl of Marlborough to outdo the accomplishments in Europe of every English subject known to history and to permanently alter American politics, culture, and empire.[100]

Marlborough could at last anticipate achieving his agenda for the coup d'état he had constructed and led. A world arena was about to open to him. In it his courtly charm, his political ruthlessness, and his military genius would finally win him the rewards he had expected for his overthrow of King James: the order of the garter, the master-generalship of the ordnance, ministerial power, ducal rank. Eighteen years earlier, Marlborough had taken long odds in the succession sweepstakes. The bet he had then made on Princess Anne's regal prospects, and the consequent gamble on her behalf that underlay lord Churchill's coup, were about to pay off.

Anne was the Anglican princess. Every aspect of the Anglican and imperial policy that had propelled John Churchill towards the coup of 1688 would bask in the "the Sunshine Day" of Anne's accession, if it could be achieved. For this the army was essential. The whigs, the party of dissent and of oligarchy, already looked past that most Anglican and monarchical figure, Anne Stuart, toward the Protestant princelings of Hanover. But Churchill's military organization, under Anne's aegis, for the coup of 1688, his postputsch purge of the English army, and his long years at the center of opposition to Dutch military dominion meant that Marlborough could command the English army to insure Anne's accession.

Himself ascendant over both Queen Anne and the royal army, Marlborough could implement the imperial strategy that had been the third objective of lord Churchill's coup: he could win America from France in Europe. The declaration of war against France in 1689 had condemned the American aggressions of Louis XIV in the very words with which John Churchill had so strongly objected to the Treaty of American Neutrality, but the subsequent seven years of war had dreadfully indicted England's inability to recapture the American initiative from France. The eloquent silences of the Treaty of Ryswick were proof of that. Among Marlborough's closest military aides were survivors of the failed amphibious expeditions of the 1690s. None of them would willingly reinvest in the bad planning and poor provisioning, or face the yellow fever, interservice rivalries, and colonial unpreparedness that had combined to eviscerate expeditions to America. Rather, they would realize the imperial program of "the friends of the governors" by strengthening the imperial executive to discipline and to defend England's provinces in America. Marlborough would commission his own aides as governors-general, the linchpins of the imperial system. He himself, as England's plenipotentiary to the grand alliance against France, placed the American agenda he had developed in the 1680s at the center of the allied war aims. So the finest English military moment in centuries, Marlborough's victories in the War of the Spanish Succession, led, as they were designed to lead, to the realization of the American aims of lord Churchill's coup.

Epilogue

THE RESTORATION EMPIRE was underdeveloped. Riven by religion, it was ruled by an army. During the Restoration, the parliament was concerned to protect the Church of England and to eliminate the royal army, almost to the exclusion of all other subjects, especially James Stuart, duke of York. Because religious truth is singular, there could be no compromise between the Anglican political nation, which identified Protestantism with public liberty, and the Stuart monarchs, who identified Catholicism with the authoritarian state. The restoration of the old religion by the restored monarchy would menace every Anglican interest, political as well as confessional, landed as well as professional.

The professional instrument of absolute monarchy was the standing army. The very existence of both the modern state and its mercenary army was anathema to the representatives both of agrarian aristocrats and urban elites. They focused their fears on the Catholic heir to the throne. But the conundrum of a Catholic (and, therefore, francophile) king as defender of the Anglican church and commander of the national army could not be politically resolved. The English polity had not yet achieved the hallmark of constitutional maturity: the capacity for compromise requisite to the peaceable transmission of executive authority. In every change of executive in John Churchill's lifetime, the army enthroned the new leader. For the army was England's most powerful administrative institution.

Throughout the period the army of England was militantly Protestant. The crisis of 1688 occurred because the Protestant army found itself commanded by a Catholic king. The army knew from the example of Ireland that it was about to be purged of Protestants. The miraculous birth of the prince of Wales also meant that the army would be ordered to insure the hereditary succession of a Catholic prince. That the king was, and that the prince would be, a creature of Louis XIV added patriotic energy to religious anxiety. Together with professional fear, love of church and country propelled Anglican officers, led by lord Churchill, towards a coup d'état.

The dominion of religion and the military in the Restoration Empire, and the resolution of its most pressing political problem by a coup of black coats and red coats, was to be expected. For Restoration England was an immature state. Its political class was unrepresentative, factionalized, and irresponsible, even feudal in its loyalties to family and locality. From that class, a selfish sovereign selected a kaleidoscopic cast of corrupt ministers. The church and the army alone provided ideological and administrative footing for the feckless monarchs and their apprentice statesmen.

To execute an economic strategy—the vaunted mercantilism—was impossible. The stop of the exchequer in 1672 broadcast the fiscal failures of a government as yet without effective instruments of taxation or accounting. Commerce was crippled by a clipped currency. England's staple crop economy was still dominated by wool. The new, vital, re-export market from America had to be serviced by ships captured from the Dutch because England did not have the capital, the industry, or the designs with which to build its own merchant fleets. Only the trading and colonizing corporations promised to focus capital and enterprise overseas, but those that survived the quo warranto campaign were the stock-jobbing monopolies of royal favorites. The Hudson's Bay Company was a good example.

Underdevelopment was equally apparent in the predisposition of the English, on both sides of the Atlantic, to riot and rebellion. In the metropolis, in ports and colonies, in country parishes and frontier counties, public order still depended primarily on the church and the military. An Erastian clergy—Anglican, Congregational, or Reformed, depending on the location—usually exhorted the faithful to passive obedience. The king's bodyguards and garrisons regularly policed population centers. The select militias of the county magnates patrolled the countryside in times of turbulence. The church, the army, and the militias were commonly dedicated to the suppression of dissent, religious or political.

The provinces of the Restoration Empire exaggerated the rebelliousness characteristic of English underdevelopment. They did so by design. Even after 1660, the provinces in America continued to be what the first generation of inchoate English colonies had been: social laboratories. In these American experiments, religio-political ideals still competed for dominion. The emerging mercantile and metropolitan elites fought with established agrarian provincial families. Both of these oligarchies struggled with the state executive. As the English elites resisted the fiscal impositions and foreign policy adventures of the monarchy, so their provincial kinsmen and counterparts struggled with the governors-general for control of staple-crop economies and frontier land development. In these American experiments, English divisions were pushed to logical, violent, extremes.

The first-generation colonies, puritan Massachusetts, Catholic Maryland, materialist Barbados, its savage offshoots in the Leeward Islands, and Anglican Virginia, were joined in the Restoration Empire by officially tolerant New York, Erastian Jamaica, agnostic Carolina, Quaker Pennsylvania, and the dissenting New Jerseys. Each of these provinces had the political complexion appropriate to its religious confession. Puritan Massachusetts remained defiantly republican. Anglican Virginia was misruled by the Gloucestershire gentry of Bruton Parish. Catholic Maryland was exploited by Anglo-Irish landlords. Religious toleration underlay apprentice absolutism in James Stuart's New York. The forms of the Church of England publicly blessed the arms of the conquerors and the garrison of the governor-general in Jamaica (although much of the old Commonwealth and Protectorate army elite remained privately Independent). Mammon was the god of Barbados. There, cavalier command had passed to a factor of the Royal African Company, exemplifying the identification of corporatism with absolutism under James Stuart. That identification was dreadfully dramatized by the enslavement of Monmouth's rebels. The Leeward Islands were little Irelands in America. A Catholic governor-general, an Anglican planter class, and Irish slaves expressed their hatred for one another, even as they were overshadowed by their more powerful French neighbors. In Carolina, passive Protestantism permitted the privy council to preside over a Harringtonian experiment, a sort of postmedievalism. William Penn paid James Stuart for Pennsylvania with supreme sycophancy. Inside his proprietary Penn found that Episcopalians and dissenters alike wanted to seize his princely prerogatives and connived to that end with the imperial bureaucracy. Across the river in New Jersey, the most murderous plotters against the Stuarts planned a yeoman utopia of dissent, religious and political.

Far from being insulated by the Atlantic from English political conflict and religious strife, the American provinces of the Restoration Empire were the social containers in which mediums of unassimilated emigrants nourished potential English developments. Throughout the Restoration, this fact was obvious to every element in the political nation. Therefore American rehearsals of metropolitan debates acquired a prominence at home out of all proportion to the numbers of persons involved or to the problem's immediate economic, fiscal, or religious impact.

In 1676, the army, as organized by James Stuart's household, was shipped, in a squadron commanded by the duke's fleet captain, to repress revolution in Virginia. So the military response to Bacon's revolution warned the English parliament of the authoritarian implications of Danby's imperial program. In 1681, the privy councilors debated the constitutional fate of Jamaica and Virginia. As Halifax warned, if Poynings's Law was extended from Ireland to control legislatures in those two American dominions of the crown, the like restrictions on the English parliament could be anticipated. In 1683, Louis XIV argued that lord Halifax's defense of New England's right to a government of law (rather than rule by military and monarchical decree under the proposed dominion of New England) demonstrated Halifax's disloyalty to the authoritarian intent of the English crown. When he came to the crown in 1685, James II dismissed Halifax and imposed a third dominion, the dominion of New England. In 1686, lord Churchill's opposition to the entente between James II and Louis XIV was premised on the danger that French expansion in America would deprive the Protestant powers of England and the Netherlands of the maritime and material resources with which they defended religious and political liberty.

So it was that the attention of the English elite to Jamaican cacao, Barbadian sugar, Carolina cypress, Chesapeake tobacco, Pennsylvania land, New York and Hudson Bay furs, and Newfoundland fish, had political as well as pecuniary, religious as well as economic, military as well as mercenary implications for the generation in which John Churchill progressed from junior subaltern to senior general. First in the matter of his own assignments, then as a senior officer in James Stuart's service, Churchill himself was repeatedly involved in the competition of army officers for American commands, and in the contests of navy officers with army officers for influence in America.

American investment, political and material, was universal among the "new class" of professional administrators but Churchill's transatlantic concerns were unusually important because his ascent to military and political power made his American interests matters of state. As governor of the Hudson's Bay Company, he placed the struggle with France for America in a European political context. The coup that he engineered eventuated in the constitutional reform of the empire. And Churchill's contribution to the consequent declaration of war defined the struggle with France as a contest for America.

The first effects of military coup and imperial combat in English America were wholly destructive. As Marlborough had been warned by his imperial associate, William Blathwayt, the copycat coups in the American provinces devastated imperial administration as well as the provinces themselves, now subject to further French attacks on the Iroquoian allies of the English, and on the English themselves in New England and New York, in the Leeward Islands and on Jamaica, in Newfoundland and Hudson Bay; English resistance to the French was feeble because, as Blathwayt feared, the coup against the king that he had helped Churchill effect inspired the republicans in America, in New England especially, to reclaim that provincial autonomy which was the eternal enemy of English empire. The coup also reempowered English parliamentarians devoted to provincial self-government. Yet the revolutionary potential of the Protestant putsch was short-circuited. The elimination of King James exposed the empire to the power of the state in the hands of King William. The Leviathan's maw of war with France swallowed up most libertarian advances beyond the status quo of 1681.

The fight with France for America was the consequence if not the cause of lord Churchill's coup. So in 1689 began a hundred years of imperial war. During America's ancien régime the prerogative politics long practiced by the governors-general were fueled by a series of wars with France. Each war enabled the imperial executive to further strengthen an anglicized ruling class in every royal province with military commissions and supply contracts. So the royal governors-general married emergent American oligarchies to state finance, armed authority, and polite culture. Indeed, everywhere in Greater Britain, force, finance, and finesse apparently overwhelmed provincialism. In John Churchill's lifetime, 1650–1722, Protestant imperialism, a militarized state structure, war-required capitalist institutions, and cultural anglicanization, all came to maturity. Underdevelopment was expunged in Greater Britain. In America the religious, militant, and exploitative values exemplified by John Churchill in the Restoration Empire were imposed by his subordinates on frontier provinces at war in the age of Anne. Unending conflict so deeply implanted Churchill's imperial constructs in American constitutions and consciences that they were not displaced even by the American Revolution.

Indeed, the first stages of the American Revolution recapitulated the coup of 1688. Protestants, professionals, and constitutionalists in the provincial armies conspired against an imperial executive whom they saw as religiously suspect, militarily restrictive, and politically tyrannical. The consequence, seven years of civil war, impelled a political and social revolution. Real revolution provoked profound reaction. Under a constitution that harked back to 1681, the government of the United States in the 1790s explicitly copied the executive, capital, and military developments of the 1690s in England. Such anglophile officers as Colonel Alexander Hamilton recognized that the army, the bank, and the executive had been the bases of British dominion. So they could be the foundations of American empire. Marlborough's America was succeeded by Washington's. The imperial foundations of the United States, at least to the close of the second millennium of the Christian era, remained those exemplified by the protagonists of lord Churchill's coup.

Appendix:
Inglorious Revolution:
The Channel Fleet in 1688

We are an Island, and as I may say one great Garrison
or Fortress of Nature's own fortifieing,
and tho' it be true We have a good Ditch Between Us and Danger,
yet if Our Outwarks, which are Our Navy shou'd be once Gained,
'twill be a great step towards Our Expurgation.

[*Sir Henry Shere*], Naval Reflections (1690)

THE PROTESTANT WIND was the gift of God to the believers in the reformed religion, but the chaos in the Channel Fleet had secular sources. The first of these was the steady stream of officer desertions from King James's service to that of the Prince of Orange. Charles, lord Mordaunt (afterwards famous as the third earl of Peterborough, and, under John Churchill's aegis, commissioned governor-general of Jamaica and commander-in-chief in America), had taken the occasion of Dykvelt's mission to remark on the obvious: that Prince William's armed support of the Anglican opposition to James II might win English military resources for William's struggle with Catholic France. More particularly, Mordaunt was said to have been the first English nobleman to go over to William at The Hague in order to press the prince "to undertake the business of England."[1]

Prince William did not need lord Mordaunt to tell him that King James's imperial accommodations with France had alienated the Anglican imperialists. The prince was informed more particularly of the duke of Albemarle's revulsion at Russell's execution as well as his disgrace after Monmouth's rebellion. The prince knew that the duke's double disaffection might be expected to be widespread in the American colonies. There Albemarle had retreated to console himself with alcohol, treasure hunting, the government of Jamaica, and the command of all American land forces. Albemarle was widely interested in America, being a proprietor in both the Bahamas and the Carolinas. Perhaps to test both Albemarle's loyalty and American sentiment, William commissioned Mordaunt as commander of a Dutch naval squadron bound for the West Indies. At the end of 1687, Mordaunt's flagship, the *North Holland* (48) rendezvoused on the Bahama banks with the Jamaica squadron, commanded by Sir John Narborough in the *Foresight* (48). Narborough had begun his career on the Jamaica station, as a protégé of Sir Christopher Myngs, a conqueror of the colony. Narborough had been fascinated with Hispaniola ever since he had raided it under Myngs's command. So the admiral had invested £300 in Phips's treasure hunt. It brought him £32,000. Wealth made Narborough even more influential among his peers in the navy, well worth William's sounding out.[2]

Narborough's squadron was supposedly executing Albemarle's treasure-hunting commission from King James, but "they were wholy unprovided to work the wreck." Something other than the remains of the Spanish treasure (which had already had its effect on the Anglo-American empire in the careers of Sir William Phips in Massachusetts, of Albemarle in England and Jamaica, and in the illicit enrichment of innumerable Bahamians, Antiguans, Nevismen, Jamaicans, New Yorkers, and Bostonians) brought Narborough's squadron to the Bahama banks. Mordaunt's squadron did have divers aboard. He himself was a partner in a treasure-hunting syndicate organized by the conspiratorial naval captain and Churchill associate, William Constable. Knowing this, King James sent an express to Albemarle warning that Mordaunt's squadron was under orders to attack the English treasure hunters and seize their trove. This was the king's ploy to block Mordaunt's presumed mission: "to try the temper of the English colonies and their attachment to the reigning sovereign." How much the naval officers, gathered from several American stations, reported about provincial unhappiness with King James's francophile and Catholic policies, in particular the Treaty of American Neutrality with France, is unclear. Neither can it be ascertained what messages Phips—who sailed away from the Bahama rendezvous for Boston on May 10, 1688—carried to his Mather mentors. Yet the amicable meeting of the Dutch and English naval officers with crews from thirty-two vessels hailing from five American colonies on the Bahama banks for seven days in February 1688 (and in kaleidoscopic contacts at Samana Bay, Hispaniola, for weeks afterwards) was the sort of transatlantic communication which must have underlain the combined operations by the maritime powers and American provinces that first brought down King James and then altered the balance of sea power in the Atlantic world.[3]

Perhaps begun on the Bahama banks, already embracing elements of the English military in America, the incipient Anglo-Dutch naval alliance against the king and the French was facilitated by the arrival at The Hague of Captain Edward Russell. The representative of a great house savaged by King James, Russell had served for eleven years under Narborough and Dartmouth. He was well placed to coordinate naval disaffection from King James, but Russell was no admiral and he had never had a flag officer's opportunity to build a service following. King James knew that "there were those in Holland who gave themselves some hopes of seeing English Lords at the head of some of their squadrons." That would make a Dutch invasion more palatable to the English navy. So much King James said when he denied Danby's son and heir, the naval officer lord Dumblane, permission to go to The Hague. After Arthur Herbert, the courtier-admiral, Churchill confrère, and colonel of the 15th Regiment, was cashiered by King James (when he refused to assent to the repeal of the Anglican tests), he was served with a *ne exeat regnum*. To forward the military conspiracy against the Catholic king, Herbert had to escape from England disguised as a common sailor aboard the packet vessel maintained by the conspirators. With him, the incognito admiral carried the invasion invitation to William. The prince immediately commissioned Herbert as his "Lieutenant-Admiral-General" in command of the Dutch fleet for the invasion of England.[4]

Herbert's simultaneous commissions in both the army and the navy were characteristic of an age that had yet to sharply distinguish military commands at land from those at sea. The secretary of the navy, Samuel Pepys, complained bitterly to the king of the delays in readying the fleet in the early autumn of 1688 because "gentlemen are allowed to hold ships at sea, in commendam with troops and companies ashore, at a time when there is an equal necessity for their attendance upon both." Pepys's examples were two naval captains central to the conspiracy, "Colonel Delavall" and "Colonel Hastings." They (and their courier to the councils of the military conspiracy, the army and navy lieutenant George Byng) had been encamped on Hounslow Heath well into October. These officers, instrumental in the coming coup, had fully engaged themselves in the army's intrigues before they finally joined their naval commands, another indication of the army's primacy in lord Churchill's coup.[5]

Of the eight battleship captains at the heart of the coming coup, six were officers in both services. Their regiments were the most disaffected units in the army and they themselves were members of the Churchill connection. For example, lord Berkeley, captain of the *Montague*, was lord Churchill's major in the Horse Guards. George Churchill of the *Newcastle* retained his troop in his brother's dragoons, now lord Cornbury's command. Matthew Aylmer of the *Swallow* was a former Tangier Regiment subaltern, like so many of the conspirators, and, like them, Aylmer was close to lord Churchill. Aylmer was now a captain in Lumley's cavalry, and Lumley had signed the invasion invitation that Herbert had carried to Prince William.[6]

The Tangier foot (2d, Queens) mustered three naval officers (all conspirators), William Davies, George Byng, and Richard Carter. Sir Francis Wheeler of the *Centurion* had been a First Guards officer since his return from the punitive expedition to Virginia in 1676. Ralph Delavall of the *Yorke* was, like Wheeler, a captain and lieutenant colonel in the First Guards. The colonel of the First Guards, the duke of Grafton, Churchill's coadjutor in the coup, retained the naval interest he had built up during his service at Tangier in 1679–81, his command of the *Grafton*, and his tenure as vice admiral of England. Grafton's political position in the navy was only just less influential than those of Herbert and Dartmouth. Of the key naval conspirators, Cloudesly Shovell and Anthony Hastings were Grafton's clients.[7]

Perhaps most important to the navy's share in the coup against King James, as well as the naval officer with the widest and most responsible share in American administration, was Admiral Sir John Berry, captain of the *Elizabeth* and rear admiral of the Channel Fleet during the invasion crisis. Berry was also a captain in the Holland Regiment (3d, Buffs), with its covey of imperial administrators. All these captains of ships of the line thus had double service links to lord Churchill's coup and they all had that extensive American experience that had sensitized them to the imperial liabilities of King James's francophilia and Catholicism. Indeed, Admiral Herbert himself was linked with Churchill and Blathwayt among "the friends of the governors," the court connection of the American viceroys.[8]

It may be that their crews shared these commanders' hostility to the king's anti-Protestant and unpatriotic courses. Certainly the common sailors hated Catholicism, both in itself and because the sailors were threatened by Irish Catholic replacements just as the soldiers were. Religious hatred found its first expression in the Channel Fleet when some of the Catholic chaplains introduced by its admiral, Sir Roger Strickland, were thrown overboard. The rest were withdrawn by the king, with a personal apology to the fleet. The antipapist phobia so virulent on the lower deck of the Channel Fleet was bred in the dissenting communities of Thameside, the fleet's recruiting base in 1688. Anti-impressment riots in the East End of London were exalted as Protestant resistance to a Catholic king's inimical service.[9]

Of course, hostility to the king's service also had material motives. Besides the threat of commissions to Catholics, arrears of officer pay dated back to the reign of Charles II. Sailors anticipated pay pauses in any extended action against the Dutch because parliament had made no provision for a foreign war. For the same reason, provisions and naval stores were in short supply. What material there was to distribute was even more than usually mishandled by alienated officers. For example, Sir John Berry, as a commissioner of the navy, impeded preparations in a way quite out of character in that able officer, but King James could not in his navy, any more than in his army, dispense with Anglican officers (or Protestant crews). So the king could not prevent the religious and political disaffection of his key military units, whether they were regiments, garrisons, or capital ships.[10]

In the fleet as in the army, Anglican officer alienation was the key to the coup against King James. Religion justified and focused disaffection founded in Protestant officers' particular professional grievances and personal hatreds. Take a leading example. The king had not continued in command Sir John Berry's naval protégé, the duke of Grafton, after Grafton returned from the Mediterranean in March 1688. Instead, the king turned to Sir Roger Strickland. Strickland had been unemployed at sea for five years prior to King James's accession. Immediately following his public adherence to Catholicism (allegiance to the old religion was traditional in his family), Strickland was given commands by King James, first as Grafton's vice admiral in the Mediterranean, and then, in June 1688, of the Channel Fleet. The command was available to Strickland because the king canceled Grafton's commission as vice admiral of England and then cashiered Admiral Herbert for refusing to support parliamentary repeal of the test which prohibited the king's military employment of his Catholic coreligionists. To make his point quite clear to all his naval officers, the king gave the Catholic Strickland the Protestant Herbert's flag as rear admiral of England. Strickland then proceeded to promote the Catholic converts from among his own officer following. Concentrated in the Channel Fleet, Strickland's followers constituted the bulk of the Catholic 10 percent of officers in the navy.[11]

The Catholic king himself, still lord high admiral, sailed down to the fleet to "consult with the flags and other officers, what was most advisable to be done to intercept the Prince of Orange," and to try to quiet what even King James recognized as "disaffection." An admiral since the age of four and a victorious commander in the previous Dutch wars, King James knew how to cosset sailors. He "went on board most of the ships in the fleet, not only to view their condition but likewise to ingratiate himself with the officers and seamen, behaving with great affability and taking notice of every perticular officer." But the king wanted those officers to act against the coming invasion much more vigorously than they proposed to do.[12]

On his return to Whitehall, the king rejected the plan put forward by Strickland's council of war. They proposed that the Channel squadron take station at the Gunfleet, the anchorage inside the sands just west of Harwich. King James objected that easterly winds and westerly tides might combine to prevent a sortie from the Gunfleet against the Dutch invasion armada as it sailed down Channel. Instead, the king ordered the squadron to take station outside the sands of the Thames estuary. Cruising on a north-south course between the Kentish Knock and the North Sand Head, Strickland's twenty-six ships could intercept the Dutch whenever they might come out and toward whatever landing they might steer, whether the North Sea ports or the Channel coast.[13]

The king's choice of station was correct but it could not long be kept by a fleet poorly manned, inadequately provisioned, and tardily reinforced. Whether because of Sir Roger Strickland's newly publicized Catholicism, his lack of naval reputation, or the lateness of the season (it was the end of August before the admiral acknowledged the manpower crisis and called for army drafts that were then unaccountably delayed), Strickland had not been able to enlist sufficient sailors to man the fleet. The manpower crisis deepened as the fleet size was doubled during the autumn. As the refitted ships came out of the dockyards they assembled at the buoy of the Nore, in the mouth of the Thames. There they were joined by Strickland's squadron, come in from its sea station to recruit its ships' scanty crews and resupply their short provisions. There the admiral was superseded.[14]

On September 24, 1688, the king commissioned George Legge, lord Dartmouth, to command the combined fleet. In terms of court rivalries, Dartmouth was an apt choice. He was Churchill's chief competitor among the military courtiers. He hated Churchill's friend Herbert so much that Dartmouth had recently challenged him to a duel. He was a good friend of Strickland, who would cheerfully serve under his command. Ideologically too, Dartmouth was a good choice. He was on public record as a devout Anglican and a dedicated royalist. He might recall like-minded officers to the king's cause (but, in the navy, the chief of such officers was the duke of Grafton and he was so offended by the king's promotion of Dartmouth over him that Grafton immediately crossed the Channel to consult, on his own behalf and that of the navy, as well as for Churchill and the army, with William of Orange). However well advised personally and politically Dartmouth's promotion to command the Channel Fleet might be, the admiral had a fatal military flaw: Dartmouth chose the famous *Resolution* as his flagship but the admiral himself was utterly irresolute.[15]

Lord Dartmouth's first problem was whether to take the fleet back to a station outside the sands, ready to intercept the Dutch invasion fleet, running in no farther than was absolutely necessary to escape the equinoctial storms, or to anchor well inside the sands, at the buoy of the Nore, off the naval yards at Chatham and Sheerness. The king wanted his fleet at sea, ready to intercept the invasion but the admiral's abilities were administrative (he was also the master general of the ordnance). To bring the fleet up to strength, Dartmouth concluded that he must stay at the Nore. The king peppered Dartmouth with admonitions to get the fleet out to sea. "I need not mind you to lose no tyme to gett out from amonge the sands as fast as you can," King James wrote to Dartmouth on October 5, 1688. Anchored there, the English fleet would be helpless to intercept the Dutch invaders. Yet the king could not force an aggressive course on an admiral who never thought his fleet strong enough to meet the enemy. Dartmouth always exaggerated the Dutch strength. His overcaution was encouraged by his council of war, many of whose members were determined to prevent any action against the Dutch.[16]

To reinforce Dartmouth's resolution, the king commissioned as rear admiral of the fleet a battle-hardened veteran, Sir John Berry. Sir John had rescued James at Solebay. He had been James's own flag captain. Berry was James's choice to investigate the governments of Newfoundland and New England and to command the expedition to Virginia. He had been James's captain aboard the ill-fated *Gloucester*, mention of which recalls Berry's long and intimate association with lord Churchill as one of the most determined enemies of French imperial aggression. King James had complete confidence in the loyalty of his longtime subordinate, however, even though Berry was so resolute a Protestant as to refuse the king's command that he join the jury for the trial of the seven bishops. Berry had material reasons for his Anglican abstention: he held former abbey lands, likely forfeits to a Catholic restoration. Berry was forward enough to warn King James that, if he commissioned any more Catholic officers to the Channel Fleet, "the seamen would knock them in the head." Yet, as a commissioner of the navy, Berry was essential to building up the fleet. He was the senior officer associated with the Thames pilots of Trinity House, so Berry was the senior officer best informed to advise the movements of the fleet from the buoy of the Nore. The king also put great weight on Berry's hatred of Herbert, now commander of Prince William's invasion fleet.[17]

On Friday, October 19, 1688 (old style), William of Orange's expedition put out to sea. "Never sail on a Friday." A great northwesterly storm drove the invasion armada back to the Netherlands ports before the English even knew Prince William's expedition had sailed. Not until October 24 did Dartmouth's fleet sortie from the buoy of the Nore. Thirty-one battleships and fourteen fireships rode the ebb tide for four hours, moving north and east to the "Shipwash" anchorage off Harwich, bounded by the sands of the Gunfleet and the West Rocks. George Churchill's *Newcastle* was not among them. Captain Churchill had written to the navy commissioners that his ship's beef and pork had been delivered to the admiral by mistake. Reasonable men might, and did, suggest that Churchill follow the admiral to the Gunfleet and collect his supplies there. Churchill refused, writing that as "for the notion that I should sale to look for them, I shall ask your pardons, for I will not saile for any man's pleasure, without my provisions." Of course, Churchill's problem was more political than logistical, just as Dartmouth's problems were more political than tactical. The admiral made it clear that he had not shifted anchorages to oppose a Dutch invasion, for (as King James had often observed to his admiral) any wind and tide that would serve the invader's fleet would trap an English squadron in the Gunfleet. Rather, Dartmouth moved the Channel Fleet from the mouth of the Thames to keep his captains "aboard their own shipps and not liable to be caballing one with another, which, lieing idle together they may be apt as Englishmen naturally do to fall into, especially being in the way of dayley pamphlets and newes letters."[18]

The loyalist publicist and politician William Penn wrote to Dartmouth to warn the admiral that the Prince of Orange's agents, "dealing with the King's officers of his army to revolt," had contacted the navy. Penn also passed on the king's latest intelligence report, that the prince had refitted his invasion fleet and intended to sail again at the first opportunity of wind and weather. Finally Penn exposed the dynastic and legal issues behind the Orangist military conspiracy and invasion. He both assured Dartmouth of the legitimacy of the baby prince of Wales and (falsely) reported the willingness of such moderates as the earl of Halifax to serve the king, now that James had offered to restore corporate charters. But Penn's news did not reinforce the loyalty of the officers of lord Dartmouth's fleet.[19]

Instead they were excited by the news that "Mr Russell is gone for Holland." This was reported to the dissident officers by the duke of Grafton in person; he had just returned from his own conference with Prince William. "The Duke of Grafton was down here a little after my comeing tho' he would not let me know it," Dartmouth complained to the king. Grafton's chief agent in the fleet was Captain Matthew Aylmer. After Grafton left the fleet to cabal with lord Churchill at Whitehall, the link between Grafton and Aylmer was George Byng, now first lieutenant of the *Defiance*.[20]

Byng's first voyage had been to Newfoundland in 1679. Thence he sailed with the fishing trade to the Mediterranean. There Byng fought in defense of Tangier, and he only narrowly escaped capture by the Moslem besiegers. In the summer of 1681 he returned to Tangier, where his uncle was a colonel in Kirke's garrison. Colonel Johnson secured the governor-general's orders to appoint George Byng a cadet in Kirke's own grenadier company. Byng learned his new trade quickly. Soon he was "esteemed in the garrison as one of the best martinets there." After six months' service, Byng was commissioned by Kirke as ensign of his own company in "the Lambs." On the eve of his departure from Tangier in 1683, Kirke promoted Byng over the heads of all the other ensigns to be lieutenant of Charles Churchill's company. Byng had served for two years under Kirke and Churchill (with intervals acting as lieutenant of various naval vessels on the Tangier station) when lord Dartmouth arrived with the fleet to evacuate the garrison and demolish Tangier. Kirke advised Byng that continued imperial service was essential to his military advancement and so secured his transfer back to the navy. In February 1684, lord Dartmouth duly commissioned Byng as a lieutenant in his fleet, but Byng did not resign his commission in Churchill's company.

No sooner did the evacuation fleet reach England from Tangier than Byng's ship, the *Phoenix*, was ordered to Newfoundland. As the outbound Newfoundland convoy touched at Plymouth for orders, the *Phoenix* was diverted to India, "for the better reducing to a due obedience to His Majesty's inhabitants of the Island and Fort of Bombay, lately revolted from the government there established by his Majesty, and for the better securing the trade granted by charter to the East India Company against the interlopers complained of by them and against pyrates. . . . " In Byng's extraordinary service on the Malabar coast, he survived disease and shipwreck, battles and wounds, and won the favor of both the king's governor, Sir John Wynbourn, and Sir John Child, the East India Company's factor. Their warm recommendations accompanied Byng back to England. There, at the end of 1687, the *Phoenix* was paid off and Lieutenant Byng "went to his duty in the land service, in Trelawney's regiment, as leftant to Capt. Churchill, now in their quarters at Bristol." In the spring of 1688, Byng's "interest" won him nomination to be Sir Roger Strickland's flag captain, but Byng refused to serve under a Catholic. Instead, he became first lieutenant of John Ashby's *Defiance*.[21]

At a meeting of the conspirators in London on the eve of the fleet movement to the Gunfleet, "upon mentioning who of the fleet could be trusted, Kirke had recommended Mr. Byng as a person he would answer for." Captain Matthew Aylmer (like Kirke, a Tangerine and close to Admiral Herbert since their shared service at Tangier) was ordered to approach Byng. Aylmer followed the recruiting pattern already established by the Churchill connection. First, Aylmer had Byng promise not to betray what he was about to hear. Then, Byng was told that Aylmer himself, Kirke, Russell, "and other perticular persons were going over to the Prince of Orange" when his army landed. Finally, implicated in the conspiracy and impressed by its membership, the young officer agreed to join the coming coup. Byng then arranged a meeting between Aylmer and his own captain, John Ashby. Next, Byng induced Captain Wolfran Cornwall (who was himself a lieutenant of Horse Guards and whose brother was a comrade of Byng's in Trelawney's regiment) to listen to Aylmer explain the conspirators' intentions. These three officers proceeded to recruit additional commanders, first pledging them to secrecy, then telling the captains that "the chiefest and most considerable" officers of the Channel Fleet were already of the prince's party, and at last opening "the necessity there was to free themselves from popish oppression." So officer after officer promised to participate in the impending putsch.[22]

Presumably these conspirators circulated copies of the Prince of Orange's letter of September 29 to "Gentlemen and Friends in the English Fleet." The prince pointed out to the Channel Fleet's Protestant crews that his expedition was designed only to prevent "the totall ruine of your Religion being as much designed by the Papists in England, as it is already accomplished in France." The prince played on English xenophobia as well. He warned the seamen that "you are only made use of as Instruments to bring both Yourselves and Your Country under Popery and Slavery by the means of both the Irish and the Foreigners. . . ." The prince fully endorsed Admiral Herbert's covering letter to his old comrades and clients. "I as a true Englishman and your Friend," Admiral Herbert exhorted the navy, "to join your arms to the PRINCE for the Defence of the Common Cause." "The best part of the Army as well as the Nation," Herbert wrote, was pledged to support the Prince and, " . . . as the Kingdom has always depended on the Navy for its defence," so now the sailors should act for "the protection of its Religion and Liberties." If they opposed the prince and prevailed, Herbert told his colleagues, it would be "by your means the Protestant Religion was destroyed, and your Country deprived of its Ancient Liberties." Such naval captains as George Aylmer (Matthew Aylmer's brother), Francis Wheeler (Sir Charles's son), Anthony Hastings, Cloudesly Shovell, and Charles Kirke (Piercy's brother) were inclined to agree with Herbert. They (and their relatives in the service) had been his clients on the Tangier station (where George Churchill had been Herbert's favorite lieutenant). Now they refused to accept the king's characterization of Herbert's reaction to being cashiered for conscience's sake as desertion and "ingratitude."[23]

During long, alcoholic "suppers" in the great cabin of Rear Admiral Berry's flagship, the *Elizabeth*, more and more captains were drawn to the position that, although honor forbade outright betrayal of their king, still they would see to it that the fleet did not act to obstruct the prince's landing. So it was that Dartmouth's council of war concluded that the fleet, rather than returning to offshore patrol, or sailing to Holland to interdict the Prince of Orange's expedition, should remain anchored at the Gunfleet: "this was a point artfully gained by those that were industrious to possess the fleet in favour of the Prince of Orange, and in ridiculing all the measures taken to prevent his designs." Many years later, the secretary of the navy, writing under the direction of the former captain Matthew Aylmer, now lord Aylmer, vice admiral of Great Britain, put the conclusion of these Gunfleet conferences concisely: "Matters were so concerted and agreed among the Commanders (who had frequently private Meetings to Consider the Circumstances of Affairs) that had the Admiral [Dartmouth] come fairly up with the Dutch, it would not have been in his Power to have done them much Damage. . . ."[24]

Having repaired the storm damage, the prince's fleet sailed again on the afternoon of October 30. At dawn on Saturday, November 1, 1688, thirteen ships of the Dutch armada were in sight from the English anchorage northeast of the Gunfleet. Despite gale-force winds, three of Dartmouth's lighter ships set up their topmasts, crossed their yards, slipped their cables, and got out to sea. They signaled that the entire enemy fleet was passing westward and they seized a disabled transport. Aboard this flyboat was part of the Anglo-Dutch brigade under the command of Major Ventris Columbine. Columbine told his jailor, Sir Charles Littleton, the veteran viceroy (who reminded the king that he is "the oldest [most senior] Colonel in His Dominions"), that the Dutch escort squadron was twice its actual strength. Passed on to the Channel Fleet, this information paralyzed Dartmouth's pursuit of Prince William's armada (William would reward Columbine with command of the regiment at whose head he died in the West Indies). The English pursuit was more immediately delayed because the ebb tide, essential to get the main body of the English ships out of the Shipwash and away from the Gunfleet, was almost spent. The east-southeast gale that was driving the Dutch invasion fleet down the Channel meant that, even if the English cleared the Gunfleet, their heavy units might not weather the Long Sand and the Kentish Knock. It was a Protestant tide as well as a Protestant wind that declared for the Dutch invaders.[25]

Not until first light on November 4 was the English fleet able to get clear of the sands. Given a full day's head start, the prince's squadrons were already west of Wight, steering for Torbay. Their warships outnumbered the distant English pursuers, or so the English believed, by better than five to three. That supposed superiority was due in part to Captains George Churchill, Arthur Hastings, Stephen Ackerman, and perhaps a fourth officer, William Constable. After the meeting of the conspirators at the Gunfleet, these captains had used "the Protestant wind" to sail their capital ships down the King's Channel, past the buoy of the Nore and far up the Thames, beyond the Long Reach, on the excuse that they needed to provision. Close to London, they "suffered" (i.e., permitted) massive desertions. Then they pled the need to recruit their crews as an excuse to stay longer in the Thames. Captain Churchill actually came up to town to consult with his brother. The Dutch ambassador reported that "the king has spoken very seriously to lord Churchill about his brother in this respect, and many are very anxious as to the result of this."[26]

At daybreak on November 5, the van of the invaders' fleet discovered that they had fatally overshot their objective at Torbay. Russell told Burnet to pray. At that moment, the wind first died then veered south and west. Five hours later, Hugh Mackay led the Anglo-Dutch and Scots-Dutch brigades ashore. The wind shift found the English off Beachy Head, well to the east. There they hove-to while lord Dartmouth called a council of war. It unanimously advised the admiral that (as the conspirators had agreed at the Gunfleet) the Dutch should not be attacked "if in honour it could be avoided." The managers of the council insisted that the Dutch battlefleet was "very much superior in both number and quality" to the English. Several captains said that they (somehow) knew that the Dutch had already emptied their three hundred transports at Torbay and so had relieved the escort to form up as a single fighting force. All things considered, the council of war concluded that an attack would foolishly endanger the king's ships. For Dartmouth, the crucial fact was that "I am wanting a very considerable part of the fleet. . . ." Already reduced to twenty-eight battleships by Churchill's detachment, Dartmouth's numbers were further reduced when two ships, both commanded by captains of "the faction," fell foul of each other in the calm and fog and were disabled. Then Matthew Aylmer reported that the *Swallow* had sprung a leak and was on the verge of sinking. Before the fleet, outnumbered and crippled, becalmed and fog-bound, sought out the Dutch, the council of war said that the admiral should obtain the king's explicit orders to attack.[27]

By the afternoon of November 6, the light southerly wind had gotten some west in it. By dawn of November 7, it was blowing a full gale. Dartmouth's smaller vessels flew distress signals. The frigate *St. David* sank, and all the ships of her rate were severely damaged. Even the flagship sprung her foremast. The admiral ordered the fleet to run for shelter. The English ships were driven east, past Dover. They anchored in the Downs before dark. Here the admiral heard confirmation "that the Dutch Fleet had landed the Prince of Orange and his army in Torbay." Only now was word received that Churchill's detachment had at last sailed from the Thames. Before they could arrive in the Downs, Dartmouth's fleet was further reduced: Sir Francis Wheeler's *Centurion* went aground. Hauled off, she sailed for the Thames dockyards. There Wheeler's crew promptly deserted. At last, on November 12, Churchill's ships rejoined the Channel Fleet but Churchill immediately told Dartmouth that the *Newcastle* had sprung an incredible leak ("23 inches of water a glass," i.e., almost two feet in every thirty minutes). His consort, the *St. Albans*, reported damage from grounding on the North Sands Head in approaching the Downs. Then the "dissaffected" captains of the two ships damaged in the calm declared that their vessels could not proceed to windward. With five battleships disabled, Dartmouth could not sail westward as he had planned to do on November 13.[28]

On that day, Russell wrote from the prince's headquarters at Exeter to Herbert, in command of the invasion fleet at Torbay. Presumably informed by Grafton (who had left the fleet in the Downs on November 3 and had come up to join lord Churchill) of the upshot of the Gunfleet council, Russell reported that the naval "Capts was Resolved to Salute my lord Dartmouth and come over to us" in the event of a battle. Russell named as the leading naval conspirators Sir John Berry, Deane, Arthur Hastings (Grafton's subordinate in the Guards and his host during Grafton's subversive "visit" to the fleet), "Admarall" George Churchill, Matthew Aylmer, Cloudesly Shovell, and John lord Berkeley. Berkeley justified his place on this list by allegedly plotting with Sir John Berry to seize Dartmouth and turn over command of the fleet to Grafton (a plot suspiciously reminiscent of lord Churchill's supposed plan to seize King James and carry him to Prince William's army). When Dartmouth took alarm, Berkeley wrote to Dartmouth (on November 13) that the condition of the *Montague* was such that he could not accompany his admiral in the long-delayed attack on the Dutch, this despite Dartmouth's harsh warning that Berkeley's reputation for public honor and personal courage were both at stake.[29]

At 3 p.m. on November 16, perhaps emboldened by an analysis that his fleet's strength was not much inferior to that of the Dutch and authorized by King James to act on this intelligence, Dartmouth got the Channel Fleet under sail, "being bound for Torbay to fight the Dutch." Although he was deserted by the *Montague* and the *Constant Warwick* on November 17, Dartmouth held to his course. This was his last chance, the royal navy's last chance, to fight for the king, their liege lord and commander-in-chief. The tide of desertion was such the admiral knew he could never get a fleet to sea again. And "the season of the year is intollerable," Dartmouth wrote, "sixteen hours night to eight hours day with lea shoares in the Channel is harder working then any battle." As Dartmouth stood westward, night came on November 18. In the darkness the wind rose "harder and harder to a violent storme." The next morning, the fleet was reduced to twenty-four sail. Sir John Berry's entire division had disappeared to the east, running before the rising gale. Still, Dartmouth stood inshore toward Torbay. On the afternoon of November 19 he had the Dutch fleet once again in sight. Ever irresolute, Dartmouth sent a scout ship in to count the enemy. Before its captain could report, the storm veered to the west and drove the Channel Fleet eastward before it. On the morning of November 20, 1688, "very much shaken and shattered," Dartmouth's fleet anchored alongside Berry's squadron in Spithead and St. Helen's. By then, Captain Churchill and the *Newcastle* had also disappeared. The explanation was not long in coming. No sooner had the *Resolution* come to her anchors than Dartmouth learned of lord Cornbury's desertion with the king's advance guard of cavalry. On November 22, he wrote to his royal commander that "I am sorry to heare any have proved false to your Majesty in the army; I not only wish, but will be watchful that it may have noe influence here. The Prince of Wales I am told is at Portsmouth, and tomorrow I will venture your Majesty's leave to pay my duty to him. . . ."[30]

The presence of the baby prince, the king's heir, at the gateway to France could only mean that King James would order his admiral to escort his family across the channel to Louis XIV. King James confirmed that conclusion three days later. He wrote to Dartmouth that because "Lord Churchill and the Duke of Grafton are gone over to the enemy with some others," he was returning to the capital from Salisbury. He had ordered his army to defend the line of the Thames, and he now ordered lord Dartmouth to provide Sir Roger Strickland, the Catholic admiral, with ships and crews to convey the prince of Wales to France.[31]

With his letter to lord Dartmouth, the king enclosed an order for the arrest of George Churchill and an account from Secretary Pepys reporting the failed attempt to arrest lady Churchill and the consequent "withdrawing of the Princess of Denmark." It was clear now to the admiral that lord Churchill had not only deserted to the Prince of Orange, but that he had also taken the professional heart of the army with him, and that he had even arranged for Princess Anne to flee from her father's capital. So Dartmouth reported that it was impractical to send a ship to Plymouth to arrest George Churchill and retake the *Newcastle*. The admiral waited until December 2 to admit that he had received the royal orders for "sending away the prince of Wales." He did not actually reply until December 3, by which time he was unable to act without the conspiratorial captains' approval.[32]

This was made clear when the duke of Berwick returned to the command of Portsmouth from the king's retreating army. He came on board the *Resolution* to get help to hold the port but lord Dartmouth told Berwick that "he was no more master of the fleet than I was; that in reality he was a prisoner there, though to appearance all honours due an Admiral were paid him; that it was Sr J: Berry, his Rear Admiral, who really comanded, and therefore, that the best advice he had to give me was not to come on board any more, lest I should be made prisoner." Deprived of help from the Channel Fleet, Berwick could not defend Portsmouth for his father, King James. He had three thousand men in garrison but, as the Portsmouth mutiny had demonstrated, they were divided by religion and nationality as well as by politics, and they had no reserves of food. Before they left Salisbury, Berwick had moved the king to order provisions shipped to Portsmouth, "but Sir J. Berry had seized upon it, on pretence that the fleet was in want." Berry's seizure left the Portsmouth garrison dependent upon daily purchases of food from the farmers' market, but Colonel Edward Norton, an old Cromwellian, a conspirator in 1681, a rebel in 1685, and the senior partner in the republican refuge and political experiment in West New Jersey, had emerged from hiding to rally the county militia on Portsdown and to take control of the approaches to Portsmouth. The farmers' market was at Norton's mercy. Rather than be starved into surrender, Berwick was "obliged to agree with Norton, that I would commit no act of hostility, provided he would permit the country people to come to market. . . ." The conspirators at sea in the fleet and the Cromwellians encamped on Portsdown between them had neutralized the greatest garrison and the most strategic port in the empire, London itself excepted. On December 16, by King James's order, Berwick surrendered Portsmouth to the duke of Grafton and the purged First Guards.[33]

Meanwhile, aboard the fleet in Portsmouth harbor, both the conspirators "and even some that were timorous and silent hitherto," when they learned that the prince was marching on London, felt it was high time that they assured "his highness of their assistance and readiness to obey his orders." The conspirators decided to send Lieutenant Byng to the prince. Byng got family leave from lord Dartmouth, and set off, disguised, through the troubled west country. Byng escaped the patrols of both sides, learned of General Kirke's arrest, and fortuitously met his army uncle, who had just deserted King James and who helped Byng on his perilous way. At last, on November 28, 1688, Byng walked into the prince's headquarters: "the first person he met with that knew him was my Lord Churchill, who was that day come with the Prince of Denmark; and from the stair head asked him what he did there." Churchill took Byng to Russell and both of them introduced the lieutenant to the prince. Delighted at Byng's news, William immediately promoted Byng to succeed Charles Churchill as a captain in Trelawney's regiment (Churchill becoming a colonel). Promotions were quick in lord Churchill's coup.[34]

On November 29, the prince sent Byng back to the fleet with his orders to the officers and a letter to lord Dartmouth. "The Protestant religion and the liberties of England being at Stake," the prince invited the admiral to unite the English fleet with the Dutch armada and to declare for the coup. It was a matter of some difficulty to get the message to Dartmouth without exposing the messenger (and Byng's caution suggests that the coup was far from concluded). At last Byng gave the prince's letter to Captain Aylmer who "one morning took an oppertunity privately to lay it upon his toilet." Dartmouth's dressing room reading was reinforced by his realization that, for the first time, conspirators outnumbered loyalists in his council of war. The admiral did not immediately declare for the Prince of Orange but, on December 1, 1688, lord Dartmouth signed his officers' address to King James for a free parliament and he wrote to his royal master in support of it. He also ordered Captain Cornwall and Lieutenant Byng to keep watch over the prince's lodgings to warn of any escape attempt, and the admiral accepted the plan of Captains Aylmer, Hastings, and Shovell to intercept the prince's yacht (which Sir Roger Strickland had agreed to command).[35]

Byng was sure that Dartmouth warned the prince's party that they would be captured if they put to sea from Portsmouth. So they fled by land, first back to London and then, with the faithful Sir Roger Strickland, sailed from a quiet cove for France. On December 11, 1688, the king himself followed his family. He wrote to his admiral that, "Having been basely deserted by many officers and souldiers of my troops, and finding such an infection gott amongst very many of those who still continue with me on shore, and that the same poysone is gott amongst the fleet . . . , I could no longer resolve to expose myself to no purpose to what I might expect from the ambitious prince of Orange and associated rebellious lords, and therefore have resolved to withdraw till this violent storme is over." The king ordered the admiral to send what ships he could to Ireland, "where there are still some that will stick to me." King James concluded his last order with a final denunciation of the military coup: "never any Prince took more care of his sea and land men as I have done and been so very ill repayd by them."[36]

It remained to Dartmouth only to surrender the king's fleet to the prince. This he did "out of my duty to the Reformed religion of the Church of England (of which as I am, I have always professed myself a true son)." The admiral sent his surrender to the prince in a letter of December 12, 1688. It was carried to William by Captain Matthew Aylmer, who took Hastings and Byng with him. After delivering the document with difficulty (the traitorous triumvirate had to pass through a countryside convulsed by the Irish fright), they returned to Portsmouth on December 19 with the prince's congratulations to Dartmouth that he had remained firm to the Protestant religion and the liberties of England, "to which not only the fleet, but the army, and the nation in general, have so frankly concurred." The prince ordered lord Dartmouth to take the bulk of the battlefleet back to the Nore, to promote Sir John Berry vice admiral in Strickland's stead, and to put Berry in command of a squadron of the prince's partisans to begin the war against the French.[37]

Lord Dartmouth obeyed the prince. He promoted and detached Sir John Berry, took the remnant of his fleet around from Portsmouth to be mothballed in the Thames yards, and went up to London to see if John Churchill would make his case with William the Conqueror. Lord Churchill had promised lady Dartmouth to use his good offices with the prince, presumably if the admiral cooperated in the coup. Through Churchill, Dartmouth asked William to continue him as master general of the ordnance, a reward for his refusal to assist the escape of the prince of Wales. William was informed, however, that, following news of lord Churchill's desertion, Admiral Berry and the Channel Fleet conspirators had left Dartmouth no choice in the matter. He denied Dartmouth's request to remain in office. Lord Dartmouth's regiment of fusiliers became lord Churchill's personal command. Churchill's distant cousin, sometime friend, and longtime fellow servant of James Stuart, left the stage of armed force and imperial administration, soon to die in the Tower of London. The disgrace and death of its irresolute admiral was a fitting conclusion to the ignominious history of the Channel Fleet in lord Churchill's coup.[38]

Note on Dates

Two calendars were in use in this period, the Julian, or Old Style Calendar, under which the year began on March 25, and which was ten or eleven days behind the Gregorian or New Style Calendar, under which the year began on January 1. In the Restoration Empire, dates between January 1 and March 25 were dated to both the Old Style and the New Style years, as February 2, 1676/7. The dating of the original document is retained in these notes. In the text, the year is taken to have begun on January 1, and the day is written as it appears in the source.

Note on Documentary Citations

Two sets of documents are here cited doubly.

The first of these are the Blenheim Palace Papers. I reviewed this archive in the Muniment Room and the Long Library of Blenheim Palace from 1966 to 1968. In 1973, the collection was acquired by the nation. Virtually all of the Blenheim Palace Papers cited in this volume are now in the Additional Manuscripts of the British Library. Unfortunately, no correspondence list was made of the relation of the Blenheim Palace shelf marks to the Additional Manuscript numbers when the collection was rearranged and recatalogued. Some items I saw at Blenheim I have not located in the British Library. They have Blenheim Library citations only. Most items I have seen in both archives. For these items, both the Blenheim shelf mark and the Add. Ms. number are given. Items that I have seen only in the British Library are cited to the Add. Ms. only. The duke of Marlborough has asked me to remind researchers that the Blenheim Palace Papers here cited are now to be found only in the British Library.

It has been brought to my attention that the edition of Sir John Dalrymple, Bt., *Memoirs of Great Britain and Ireland* . . . 3 vols. (4th ed., Dublin, 1773), which I first used, is not readily available, so I have added citations to a more accessible edition, in 2 vols. (2d ed., London, 1773), for items that appear in both editions.

Notes

Abbreviations

ADD. MS.	Additional Manuscripts, B.L.
ADM	Admiralty Manuscripts, P.R.O.
AHAR	*Annual Report of the American Historical Association*
AMD	William Hand Browne, et al., eds., *The Archives of Maryland* (Baltimore, 1883–present)
BIHR	*Bulletin of the Institute for Historical Research*
B.L.	British Library, London
CHR	*Canadian Historical Review*
CJ	*Journals of the House of Commons* (London, 1803–present)
C.O.	Colonial Office Group, P.R.O.
CSPC	W. Noel Sainsbury, et al., eds., *Calendar of State Papers, Colonial Series, America and West Indies* (London, 1860–1969)
CSPD	Mary Anne Everett Green and F. H. Blackburne Daniell, et al., eds., *Calendar of State Papers, Domestic Series* (London, 1860–1938)
CTB	William A. Shaw, ed., *Calendar of Treasury Books* (London, 1904–1969)
CWWB	William Blathwayt Papers, Colonial Williamsburg
DHNY	Edmund B. O'Callaghan, ed., *Documentary History of the State of New York* (Albany, 1887)
DNB	Leslie Stephens and Sidney Lee, eds., *Dictionary of National Biography* (London, 1885–1903)
EHD	Andrew Browning, ed., *English Historical Documents*, Volume 8: 1660–1714 (New York, 1953)
EHR	*English Historical Review*
EJC	H. R. McIlwaine, ed., *Executive Journals of the Council of Colonial Virginia* (Richmond, 1925)
ESR	*European Studies Review*
HJ	*The Historical Journal*

HMC	Historical Manuscripts Commission, *Reports*
HMPEC	*Historical Magazine of the Protestant Episcopal Church*
HT	*History Today*
JBS	*Journal of British Studies*
JEH	*Journal of Ecclesiastical History*
JHI	*Journal of the History of Ideas*
JMH	*Journal of Modern History*
JSAHR	*Journal of the Society for Army Historical Research*
JSH	*Journal of Southern History*
MFQ	Military Maps and Plans Group, P.R.O.
MHM	*Maryland Historical Magazine*
MHSP	*Proceedings of the Massachusetts Historical Society*
NEQ	*New England Quarterly*
NYCD	Edmund B. O'Callaghan, and Berthold Fernow, eds., *Documents Relative to the Colonial History of the State of New York* (Albany, 1853–1887)
NYHSC	*New-York Historical Society Collections*
P.R.O.	British Public Record Office, London
S.P.	State Papers Group, P.R.O.
T.	Treasury Papers Group, P.R.O.
VMHB	*Virginia Magazine of History and Biography*
WMQ	*William and Mary Quarterly*, Third Series
W.O.	War Office Group, P.R.O.
YAJ	*Yorkshire Archaeological Journal*

Preface

1. The quotation is from John M. Murrin, "Political Development," in Jack P. Greene and J. R. Pole, eds., *Colonial British America* (Baltimore, 1984). The idea was first expressed by Edmund S. Morgan, *New York Review of Books*, Dec. 4, 1980.

2. The quoted observation is that of Pauline Maier, "Second Thoughts on Our First Century," *The New York Times Book Review*, July 7, 1985, 1, 20.

3. I quote William S. McFeeley, "Realpolitik in Colonial New England," *The New York Times Book Review*, June 24, 1984, 13.

4. The estimate is Charles M. Andrews's, in *The Colonial Background of the American Revolution* (New Haven, 1924), 98, still the palimpsest of our past.

Introduction

Apart from the sources cited in the acknowledgments and in the text, this introduction has been informed by John Miller, "The Potential for 'Absolutism' in Later Stuart England," *History* 69 (1984): 187–207; James Daly, "The Idea of Absolute Monarchy in Seventeenth-Century England," *HJ* 21 (1978): 227–50; three chapters in Trevor Aston, ed., *Crisis in Europe 1550–1660* (London, 1965): E. J. Hobsbaum, "The Crisis of the Seventeenth Century," H. R. Trevor-Roper, "The General Crisis of the Seventeenth Century," and V. G. Keirnan, "Foreign Mercenaries and Absolute Monarchy"; and two articles in the *HT* special issue on 1688 (38: July 1988), John Morrill, "On Second Thoughts . . . ," and Bill Speck, "Religion's Role in the Glorious Revolution." King James is quoted on page 159. Lord Churchill's letter to the king is printed on page 75.

Book I: A Soldier's Schools
epigraph: Bonamy Dobree, ed., *The Letters of Philip Dormer Stanhope, 4th Earl of Chesterfield* (New York, 1932), #1837.

Chapter One: The "Handsome Englishman," 1667–1679

1. Major P. R. Adair, "The Coldstream Guards, c. 1680," *JSAHR* 40: 111–13, and see H. Oakes-Jones, *ibid.* 13: 64–65. Hendrick Danckert's picture of this scene is in the collection of the duke of Roxburghe at Floors Castle. On the royal walks, see Antonia Fraser, *Royal Charles* (New York, 1979), 291–92, 339.
2. *The Lives of the Two Illustrious Generals, John, Duke of Marlborough, And Francis Eugene, Prince of Savoy* (London, 1713), 7–8; [Francis Hare,] *The Life And Glorious History of John Duke of Marlborough . . .* (2d ed., London, 1707), 7, 8–9. The provenance of this work is established by Robert D. Horn, "Marlborough's First Biographer, Dr. Francis Hare," *Huntington Library Quarterly* 20 (1956): 145–62, esp. 150. Thomas Lediard, Gent., *The Life Of John, Duke Of Marlborough, Prince of the Roman Empire* (London, 1736), 1: 20, 21; S.P. 44/20, 179, P.R.O. Charles Dalton, ed., *English Army Lists And Commission Registers 1661–1714* (London, 1892–1904, 1960), 1: 91. See also, John Childs, *The Army of Charles II* (London, 1976), 40.
3. See the establishment of 1661 and illustrations of the garrison fortifications in *JSAHR* 9: passim; Stephen Saunders Webb, *The Governors-General The English Army and the Definition of the Empire, 1569–1681* (Chapel Hill, 1979, 1987), Ch. 2; Webb, " 'Brave Men and Servants to His Royal Highness': The Household of James Stuart in the Evolution of English Imperialism," *Perspectives in American History* 8:61–62, n.7. Figures for the armies of Charles II are in David Ogg, *England in the Reign of Charles II* (Oxford, 1932), 2: 253–54; J. R. Western, *Monarchy and Revolution: The English State in the 1680s* (London, 1972), 123–24, 136–37, and in sources analyzed in Webb, "The Data and Theory of Restoration Empire," *WMQ* 43 (1986): 444–49.

4. Robert Latham and William Matthews, eds., *The Diary of Samuel Pepys* (Berkeley, 1970–83), 8: 332, n. 2; [Hare,] *Marlborough*, 5–6.

5. John Heath, ed., George [Monck], duke of Albemarle, *Observations upon Military and Political Affairs* (London, 1671), n.p.; Colonel [Daniel] Mackinnon, *Origin and Services of the Coldstream Guards* (London, 1833), 1: 196–97, 201–02; Lieut. Gen. Sir F. W. Hamilton, *The Origin and History of the First or Grenadier Guards* (London, 1874–1877), 1: 43, 66–69; Webb, *Governors-General*, 60; Sir Charles Firth and Godfrey Davies, *The Regimental History of Cromwell's Army* (Oxford, 1940), 534–46; [Hare,] *Marlborough*, 6.

6. Lawrence Echard, *The History Of England* (London, 1718), 3: 195, 198; Captain Sir George Arthur, Bart., *The Story of the Household Cavalry* (London, 1909), 1: 89–91; Field Marshal Viscount Wolsey, *The Life of John Churchill Duke of Marlborough to the accession of Queen Anne* (4th ed., London, 1894), 1: 42, 51–52; Latham and Matthews, eds., *Pepys*, June 13–14, 1667; *CSPD*, 1666–1667, 196, 206–207; John Miller, "Catholic Officers in the later Stuart army," *EHR* 88: 43; Privy Council 2/59, 26–27, 586–87, P.R.O.; Webb, *Governors-General*, 80.

7. Hamilton, *First Guards* 1: 67, 78–82, 90, 92–93.

8. *Two Illustrious Generals*, 6; Churchill, *Marlborough*, 1: 26–36.

9. "A Declaration of His Highness," Samuel Rawson Gardiner, ed., *Commonwealth and Protectorate* 3: 184, quoted by Keith Feiling, *A History of the Tory Party* (Oxford, 1924), 84.

10. *Ibid.*, 31, 60, 64. Webb, *Governors-General*, #27.

11. Ronald G. Bell, "The Shetland Garrison, 1665–1668," *JSAHR* 43: 5–26; Childs, *Army of Charles II*, 17, 41–42.

12. Webb, *Governors-General*, 4, 468, 486, 510; #5, 69, 189–97; Dalton, ed., *Army Lists*, 1: 37, 91; Hamilton, *First Guards*, 1: 55, 79–80, 118, etc.

13. That Churchill's posting to Tangier, and his first decade of service, were typical of his professional generation's careers appears in Childs, *Army of Charles II*, 30–37. Note, however, that that exemplary professional, Harry Norwood, was not "an old Cromwellian officer," as he is libeled in *ibid.*, 31. See P. H. Hardacre, "The Further Adventures of Henry Norwood," *VHMB* 57: 271–82; Webb, *Governors-General*, #35, 176, 178. See generally Sir Julian S. Corbett, *England in the Mediterranean: A Study of the Rise and Influence of British Power Within the Straits, 1603–1713* (London, 1904).

14. *Ibid.*, 2: 17, 33, 46; the earl of Castlemain to the earl of Arlington, March, 1670, S.P. 94/56, f. 94v, quoted in Winston S. Churchill, *Marlborough, His Life and Times* (London, 1933, 1934, 1947), 1: 56. [Richard Cannon], *Historical Record Of The Second, Or Queen's Royal Regiment Of Foot* (London, 1837), 8–9, 11, 15, 21, 25, 28.

15. Stephen Saunders Webb, *1676: The End of American Independence* (New York, 1984, Cambridge, Mass., 1985), 312–21; Webb, *Governors-General*, Appendix #27, 30, 116, 148, 201.

16. S.P. 44/24, 35; C.O. 1/21, 35, P.R.O.; Egerton Ms. 2395, 123, B.L.; Childs, *Army of Charles II*, 152; Lediard, *Marlborough*, 1: 21.

17. Lediard, *Marlborough*, 1: 16–17; Churchill, *Marlborough*, 1: 47–48, 115, 165–166; Anthony Hamilton, *The Memoirs of Count Grammont*, ed. Sir Walter Scott (London, 1902), 329–30, 337–38, 373–75; H. C. Foxcroft, ed., *A Supplement to Burnet's History of My Own Time* (Oxford, 1902), 291; *Memoirs of the Duke of Berwick, with a panegyric by President Montesquieu* (London, 1708), xi.

18. William Coxe, *Memoirs of John Duke of Marlborough With His Original Correspondence . . .* (London, 1820), 3: 262; P. H. Hardacre, "The English Contingent in Portugal 1662–1668," *JSAHR* 38:112–13, 124–25; *ibid.* 1: 18n; Latham and Matthews, eds., *Pepys*, 5: 185–96, June 21, 1664; E. M. G. Routh, *Tangier: England's Lost Atlantic Outpost, 1661–1684* (London, 1912), 315; C. T. Atkinson, *History of the Royal Dragoons, 1661–1934* (Glasgow, 1934), 21, but see Lt. Col. John Davis, *The History of the Second, Queen's Royal Regiment* (London, 1887), 1: 93, 95. See also note 13, above.

19. Routh, *Tangier*, 123; Egerton Ms. 2395, 652–60; Davis, *Second, Queen's*, 1: 94–96n., 97; Webb, *Governors-General*, #35, 176, 178, and index; Webb, *1676*, 151–54; Latham and Matthews, eds., *Pepys*, 9: 392–93, Dec. 14, 1668; Norwood to Ormonde, Dec. 10, 1668, HMC, *Ormonde Ms.*, n.s., 3: 288; Norwood to Legge, Nov. 10, 1668, HMC, *Dartmouth Ms.*, 1: 16.

20. Laws and Ordinances of War, printed in Davis, *Second, Queen's*, Appendix C, 1: 283, 284.

21. An Abstract of the state of the Citty and Garrison of Tangier 30 Dec. 1676, By John Bland, printed in *ibid.*, 1: 114. Pepys was no prude, but his shock (or jealousy) is recorded in Edwin Chappell, ed., *The Tangier Papers of Samuel Pepys*, Publications of the Naval Records Society, 73 (1935), 90, although the editor has expurgated all of Pepys's sexual observations.

22. Colonel L. I. Cowper, *The King's Own . . .* (Oxford, 1939), 7–8; Davis, *Second, Queen's*, 1: 94, 96, 114; *JSAHR*, 6: 51–53; Webb, *Governors-General*, Appendix #37, 206.

23. S.P. 44/20, 90, 93; Henry Norwood, "A Voyage to Virginia," Peter Force, ed., *Tracts and Other Papers, Relating Principally to the Origin, Settlement, and Progress of the Colonies in North America* (Washington, D.C., 1836–1844), 3: #10. Norwood's analysis of the Virginia conflict is in C.O. 1/21, 156–58 and see Webb, *1676*, 204; Webb, *Governors-General*, 341.

24. See the letters of Sir William Berkeley and Colonel Richard Nicolls about Norwood and Tangier, 1666–1668, in the Blathwayt Papers, Huntington Library; Webb, *Governors-General*, 333–34n; Webb, *1676*, 204; Routh, *Tangier*, 113.

25. Henry, earl of Peterborough's commission as captain general of all the forces at Tangier, adjacent dominions and conquests, 6 7br, 18 C.II, S.P. 44/4, 1–3, printed in Davis, *Second, Queen's*, 1: 15–17. The forms here established were intended to be applied to the command of all royal dominions, *ibid.*, 54. See also, *ibid.*, 82.

26. Davis, *Second, Queen's*, 1: 91, 97–98, 100–101; Routh, *Tangier*, 98–99, 125n–127.

27. Laws and Ordinances of War, printed in Davis, *Second, Queen's*, Appendix

C, 1:283–96. The best account of Tangier training and professional soldiering is "The Diary of Sir James Halkett," ed. Capt. H. M. McConce, *JSAHR* 1: Special Number.

28. S.P. 63/327, 54–55, printed in Churchill, *Marlborough*, 1: 56–57; Wolsey, *Marlborough*, 1: 110–111. On O'Brien, see, Routh, *Tangier*, 146 n.; Davis, *Second, Queen's*, 1: 159 n. See also, Webb, *Governors-General*, #61, 134, 56, 181.

29. Coxe, *Memoirs*, 1: 5; Routh, *Tangier*, Ch. 8, "The Pirates of Algiers, 1667–1679," esp. 141–142; Lt. Col. R. L. Playfair, *The Scourge of Christendom* (London, 1884), 107–109. Each of Allin's ships carried twenty-five marines above complement, necessitating a number of subalterns, preferably with shipboard experience, such as Churchill's.

30. Martin Joseph Routh, ed., *Bishop [Gilbert] Burnet's History Of His Own Time* . . . (Oxford, 1833; Hildesheim, 1969), 1: par. 264, p. 484; Graham Greene, *Lord Rochester's Monkey* (New York, 1976), 101–102; Churchill, *Marlborough*, 1: 58–59; Lediard, *Marlborough*, 1: 22.

31. Routh, ed., *Burnet's History*, 1: 484–85 and Dartmouth's n.; Lediard, *Marlborough*, 1: 22. Churchill, *Marlborough*, 1: 60, effectively disputes the dating of this gossip, but its essence is insisted on in all accounts. A variant was current in Tangier, where garrison officers said that Cleveland's front door was locked and that Churchill escaped through the back door, Helen Andrews Kaufman, ed., *Tangier at High Tide: The Journal of John Luke, 1670–1673* (Geneva and Paris, 1958), 201. The story has a marked resemblance to one told of the duchess of Norfolk (Mordaunt's sister) and a Dutchman, in Mary R. Geiter and W. A. Speck, eds., *The Memoirs of Sir John Reresby* . . . (2d ed., London, 1991), 392, and may be a stock tale about mésalliance.

32. HMC, *Dartmouth Ms.*, 1: 56; Add. Ms. 47128, 1077A; Bonamy Dobree, ed., *The Letters of Philip Dormer Stanhope, 4th Earl of Chesterfield* (New York, 1932), No. 1262; and see Churchill, *Marlborough*, 1: 60–64.

33. [Hare,] *Marlborough*, 8; Dartmouth quoted in Routh, ed., *Burnet's History*, 5: 416.

34. The anecdote is attributed to Prince Eugene by the author of the *Two Illustrious Generals*.

35. David M. Vieth, *The Complete Poems of John Wilmot, Earl of Rochester* (New Haven, 1968), 68; Sir Charles Littleton to Christopher, lord Hatton, August 21, 1671, March 22, 1671/2, Add. Ms. 29577, f. 87, 109–10. The latter letter is printed in Edward Maude Thompson, ed., *Correspondence of the Family of Hatton*, Camden Society, New Series 22, 1:66. Note that this published correspondence is but a tiny selection from the vastly informative collection in B.L., and is not always either accurate or representative. Routh, ed., *Burnet's History*, 1: par. 307, pp. 562–63; C. T. Atkinson, *Marlborough and the Rise of the British Army* (New York, 1921), 39; The Journal of Sir J[oseph] Williamson, March 17: "Lieut. Churchill and Capt. Legg arrived from the Downs with an account of the engagement," *CSPD 1671–1672*, 71, 609; Keith Feiling, *British Foreign Policy, 1660–1672* (London, 1930, 1968), 278–79, 338, 341–43, 364; Alexander B. Grosart, ed., *The Complete Prose Works of Andrew Marvell, MP* (London, 1875; New York, 1966), 4: 326. On the imperial dispute over Surinam, see

Routh, ed., *Burnet's History*, I: 558; Feiling, *Foreign Policy*, as cited above, n. 28, and see 304, 313, 346, 348.

36. Atkinson, *Marlborough*, 42–43; Captain Alfred Thayer Mahan, *The Influence Of Sea Power Upon History, 1660–1783* (New York, 1890, 1957), 126–31; James MacPherson, ed., *Original Papers Containing The Secret History Of Great Britain From The Restoration To The Accession Of The House of Hanover . . .* (London, 1775) 1: 61.

37. Haviland to Hatton, June 3, 1672, Add. Ms. 29553, 444; Webb, "Brave Men," *Perspectives*, 8: 65, 68–69; Webb, *Governors-General*, 351; Routh, ed., *Burnet's History*, 1: 591–93 denigrates the duke but Burnet's reflections are contested in the notes; Churchill, *Marlborough*, 1: 81–82; MacPherson, ed., *Original Papers*, 1: 62, 63–67; Littleton to Hatton, June 14, 18, 1672, Add. Ms. 29577, 101–101b; 119, 120; John Charnock, *Biographia Navalis . . .* (London, 1794–1798), 149–150.

38. S.P. 44/35A, 41, Commissions signed for the Admiralty Regiment, 10 June 1672; Dalton, ed., *Army Lists*, 1: 127–28; *CSPD 1671–1672*, 218, 222, "by the duke's order"; Churchill, *Marlborough*, 1: 83, 84; Littleton to Hatton, June 14, 1672, Add. Ms. 29577, 119–20; Thompson, ed., *Hatton Correspondence*, 1: 92; Hamilton, *First Guards*, 1: 66; Wolsey, *Marlborough*, 1: 113; Lediard, *Marlborough*, 1: 22–23. "Caesar's Ghost" is quoted in Add. Ms. 47128, 51b.

39. J. W. Fortescue, *A History of the British Army* (London, 1910), 1: 316–24.

40. Hamilton, *Memoirs of Grammont*, 277, 246; Dalton, ed., *Army Lists*, 1: 228; Webb, *Governors-General*, 373n. It is regrettable that this famous regiment, ancestor of the Royal Marines and for the whole of the Restoration the second of the line, has no historian, having been dissolved in 1689 for its colonel's loyalty to James II (and his reluctance to take orders from his former subordinate, now immeasurably his superior, John Churchill).

41. [Sir] Winston Churchill to the duke of Richmond, Mintern, 25 Oct. [16]72, Add. Ms. 21948, 381; the author of *Two Illustrious Generals*, 9, states that the decision was wholly professional. Vaughan, the captain Churchill replaced, was his cousin.

42. Webb, *Governors-General*, 135; Add. Ms. 29577, 141–42, 145; S.P. 44/35A, 57; Atkinson, *Marlborough*, 45; Atkinson, "Charles II's Regiments in France 1672–1678," *JSAHR* 24: 55, 56n. Recruiting also went forward in the spring of 1672 for the Barbados Dragoons (by its senior officer, Major Edmund Andros) and for the Tangier corps of Governor John Fitzgerald. Routh, ed., *Burnet's History*, 1: par. 301, p. 549–52.

43. Atkinson, "Charles II's Regiments," *JSAHR* 24: 60–61; H. T. Dickinson, "The Richards Brothers: Exponents of the Military Art of Vauban," *ibid.* 46: 76–77; David Chandler, *The Art of War in the Age of Marlborough* (London, 1976), ch. 15 and Appendix #4.

44. Roger Earl of Orrery, *A Treatise of the Art of War: Dedicated to the Kings Most Excellent Majesty* (London, 1677), 15; Osmund Airy, ed., *Essex Papers* (Camden Society, 1890), 250–52; Routh, ed., *Burnet's History*, 1: 498; 2: 99–102; Childs, *Army of Charles II*, 63.

45. *Two Illustrious Generals*, 11; Lediard, *Marlborough*, 1: 25–28; Arthur, *House-*

hold Cavalry, 1: 109n; Wolsey, *Marlborough*, 1: 122–24; despatches of June 12, 17, 1673, *London Gazette*, #789; S. P. 78/137, 142, 146, 194, 225.

46. Lord Alington to Sec. of St. Lord Arlington, Maestricht, June 26, [1673], S. P. 78/137, 146, cited as 142 and printed in Churchill, *Marlborough*, 1: 90–91; Arthur, *Household Cavalry*, 110–113. One of the volunteers was Captain [Francis] Godfrey, afterwards Churchill's brother-in-law and coconspirator.

47. Charles Hatton to Christopher, Lord Hatton, June 26, 1673, Thompson, ed., *Hatton Correspondence*, 1: 108–109; [Hare,] *Marlborough*, 9–10; Lediard, *Marlborough*, 1: 27–28; alternate wording in Churchill, *Marlborough*, 1: 92.

48. The bibliography of Godefroid-Charles-Henri, Vicomte de Turenne, son of the duc de Bouillon, and his influence on the English army in the person of his devoted pupil, James, duke of York, is sketched in part by A. Lytton Sells, ed., *The Memoirs of James II: His Campaigns as Duke of York, 1652–1660* (Bloomington, 1962), 43–47. Quotation from Halifax's memoranda, Add. Ms. 51511, 15. Naturally, Turenne educated even more French imperial administrators than he did English governors-generals. On the American services of one of them, the comte de Blenac, and the model his administration provided for his English counterpart, see especially, Sir William Stapleton to William Blathwayt, Feb. 19, 1683/4, CWWB 37 #4.

49. *Two Illustrious Generals*, 10, paraphrased by Lediard, *Marlborough*, 1: 25; Coxe, *Memoirs*, 1: 6; Atkinson, "Charles II's Regiments," *JSAHR* 24: 61–62.

50. W. D. Christie, ed., *Letters Addressed from London to Sir Joseph Williamson . . .* (Camden Society, 1874), 1: 186; 2: 88; Atkinson, *JSAHR*, 24: 62–63; Routh, ed., *Burnet's History*, 2: par. 345–52; John Miller, *James II: A Study in Kingship* (Hove, 1977), 70–71; Wolsey, *Marlborough*, 1: 126–27; *EHD*, #143; E. S. De Beer, ed., *The Diary of John Evelyn* (Oxford, 1955), 4: 12–13n, June 1, 1673; Add. Ms. 29554, 192.

51. Littleton to Hatton, June 24, 1673, Add. Ms. 29577, 145; Add. Ms. 28042, 28; Browning, *Thomas Osborne, earl of Danby and duke of Leeds, 1632–1712* [Glasgow, 1944–1951], 1: 91–92, 102; Webb, "Brave Men," *Perspectives*, 8: 60; Routh, ed. *Burnet's History*, 2: 30, 76; Miller, *James II*, 62–63; Lord Macaulay, *The History of England from the Accession of James the Second*, ed. Charles Harding Firth (London, 1913), 1: 313. For an additional example of the limitation of the Test Act to English office, see Add. Ms., 29554, 170b. On the British professional troops in foreign service as an English royal army reserve, see also John Childs, *Nobles, Gentlemen, and the Profession of Arms in Restoration Britain, 1660–1688: A Biographical Dictionary of British Army Officers on Foreign Service*, Society for Army Historical Research Special Publication No. 13 (1987), x–xi.

52. HMC, *Le Fleming Ms.*, 104, 107; Atkinson, "Charles II's Regiments," *JSAHR*, 24: 63ff; Christie, ed., *Letters to Williamson*, 2, 11, 21, 26; Childs, *Army of Charles II*, 170–171.

53. Webb, *Governors-General*, 263–75; HMC, *Le Fleming Ms.*, 107; Atkinson, "Charles II's Regiments," *JSAHR*, 24: 64. Ian Steele, "Governors or Generals . . . ," *WMQ*, 46 (1989): 308, reviews the evidence regarding Howard's possible service in two other regiments.

54. HMC, *Le Fleming Ms.*, 108; Coxe, *Memoirs*, 1:7; Churchill, *Marlborough*, 1: 99.

55. General Max Weygand, *Turenne, Marshal of France*, tr. George B. Ives (New York, 1930), 213–232; Orrery, *Art of War*, 15; Atkinson, *JSAHR* 245: 64, 129; Wolsey, *Marlborough*, 1: 135. Add. Ms. 9731, 95 officially summarizes Handasyde's career in the Netherlands, the Revolution, and in Newfoundland, in support of his promotion to regimental lieutenant colonel. See also, Frank Cundall, *The Governors of Jamaica in the First Half of the Eighteenth Century* (London, 1937), 12; *An Historical Account Of The British Regiments . . .* (London, 1794), 50, 52–54; James Ferguson, ed., *Papers Illustrating the History of the Scots Brigade . . .* (Edinburgh, 1899), 1: 11n, 474–476, 478n, 481, 567, 568. For the careers of imperial officers in the British brigades in the service of the states general, see also Childs, *Dictionary*, 36, 41, 53, 110–11; Ventris Columbine or Collambine (18), Edward Dutton Colt (19), David Colyear (19), Sir Richard Dutton (29); Henry Erskine, Lord Cardross (30), John Foulkes (35), Robert Godwyn (36), Geoffrey Lloyd (54), William Meoles (61), Guy Molesworth (62), and see Childs, *Army of Charles II*, 240–243, on William, earl of Craven.

56. Coxe, *Memoirs*, 1: 8n.; Churchill, *Marlborough*, 1: 100; Atkinson, "Charles II's Regiments," *JSAHR* 24: 129–31; Weygand, *Turenne*, 250–51; [Hare], *Marlborough*, 6.

57. Atkinson, "Charles II's Regiments," *JSAHR* 24: 129–31; Churchill, *Marlborough*, 1: 101; Wolsey, *Marlborough*, 137; Weygand, *Turenne*, 204–205.

58. John Churchill to the duke of Monmouth, The Camp within a League of Strasburg, Sept. 25/ Oct. 5, 1674, *CSPD 1673–1675*, 367–68. The full account of the same date, only mentioned in *ibid.*, 368, as "Lord Duras to His Royal Highness" [the Duke of York], is edited by Captain C. T. Atkinson as "Feversham's Account of the Battle of Entzheim—1674," *JSAHR* 1: 33–43, and see Atkinson, *Marlborough*, 55. Feversham's aide at Entzheim, or Waldheim, as Churchill called it in his despatch, was Sir Richard Dutton, then lieutenant of the duke of York's troop of the Horse Guards and afterwards governor-general of Barbados, S.P. 44/35A, 49b.

59. Churchill's despatch, *CSPD 1673–1675*, 367; Atkinson, ed., "Feversham's Account," *JSAHR* 1: 43; Atkinson, "Charles II's Regiments," *ibid.*, 24: 133.

60. Churchill's despatch, *CSPD 1673–1675*, 368; Atkinson, ed., "Feversham's Account," *JSAHR* 1: 43. Among Churchill's subordinates was Charles Trelawney, afterwards colonel of a Tangier regiment (the 4th or King's Own), and a key coconspirator of Churchill's in 1688.

61. Churchill's despatch, *CSPD 1673–1675*, 368; Dalton, ed., *Army Lists*, 1: 323; Sir W. Lockhart to Sec. Coventry, Oct. 10, 1674, HMC, *Bath Ms.*, 238; HMC, *Verney Ms.*, 492; Atkinson, "Charles II's Regiments," *JSAHR*, 24: 133; Add. Ms. 29577, 89b, 92.

62. Churchill's despatch, *CSPD 1673–1675*, 368. Atkinson, ed., "Feversham's Account," *JSAHR* 1: 43; Atkinson, *Marlborough*, 57.

63. *Ibid.*, 58–59; Atkinson, "Charles II's Regiments," *JSAHR* 24: 134–36;

HMC, *Bath Ms.*, 240; duke of Monmouth to Col. Churchill, Whitehall, November 2, 1674, S.P. 44/11, 11 and *CSPD 1673–1675*, 393–94.

Chapter Two: In James Stuart's Service: 1675–1683

1. Dalton, ed., *Army Lists*, 1: 180, 196; *CSPD 1673–1675*, 519, dates this January 5; S.P. 44/29, 120, 341; Clarendon to Rochester, Dublin Castle, Oct. 23., 1686, Samuel W. Singer, ed., *The correspondence of Henry Hyde, earl of Clarendon, and of his brother Laurence Hyde, earl of Rochester, with the diary of Lord Clarendon* (London, 1828), 1: 38. Of course, the commission was King Charles's. Louis XIV's recommendation had a weight made ironic by its promotion of an officer who would defeat him in due time: *Two Illustrious Generals*, 11.

2. S.P. 44/29, 120, 140, 148, 190, 210; S.P. 44/164, 24; Lediard, *Marlborough*, 1: 10–15.

3. S. v. "Admiralty Regiment" in regimental index of Webb, *Governors-General*, 540; HMC, *Fitzherbert Ms.*, 108.

4. Hamilton, *First Guards*, 1: 195; *CSPD 1673–1675*, 527, 603; Webb, *Governors-General*, Appendix #147; Webb, *1676*, 334; HMC, *Le Fleming Ms.*, March 2, 9, 1675, p. 117.

5. Webb, " 'Brave Men' . . . ," *Perspectives*, 8: 55–80.

6. Churchill had been trying to buy the robes place since 1672, William Durrant Cooper, ed., *Savile Correspondence . . .* (Camden Society, 1858), 30; Lediard, *Marlborough*, 1: 29; Wolsey, *Marlborough*, 1: 118; Ormonde to Arran, Jan. 24, 1677, HMC, *Ormonde Ms.*, n.s. 4: 102. In abbreviated, but authoritative fashion, this is confirmed by [Hare,] *Marlborough*, 10–11.

7. Browning, *Danby*, 160–61, 177, 256; Childs, *Army of Charles II*, 176–78; Atkinson, "Charles II's Regiments" *JSAHR* 24: 163–64; Clement Edwards Pike, ed., *Essex Papers*, Camden Third Ser., XXIV (London, 1913), ix, Appendix # VI, VII; Feiling, *Tory Party*, 159–60, 167. This consolidation may have been delayed until the English regiments were decimated in their great rear guard action at Altenheim in July: Weygand, *Turenne*, 237–40.

8. Atkinson, *Marlborough*, 65–66; Churchill, *Marlborough*, 1: 113–14; Warrant from Danby, Oct. 8, 1675, *CTB 1672–1675*, 830.

9. *Two Illustrious Generals*, 14; Sarah, quoted by A. S. Turberville, *English Men and Manners in the Eighteenth Century* (New York, 1957), 110.

10. Coxe, *Memoirs*, 1: 11; Churchill, *Marlborough*, 1: 114, 118; Wolsey, *Marlborough*, 1: 135, 147–48; David Chandler, *Marlborough as Military Commander* (London, 1949), 8; Allen Andrews, *The Royal Whore Barbara Villiers Countess of Castlemaine* (London, 1971).

11. S.P. 44/29, 185; *CSPC, 1677–1680*, #185; Hamilton, *First Guards*, 1: 202; Mackinnon, *Coldstream Guards*, 1: 155–56; Webb, *Governors-General*, 349–59 and Appendix #189–97; Webb, *1676*, Book One. On the duke's continuing influence, see Routh, ed., *Burnet's History*, 2: 14–15.

12. On Virginia's "paramilitary politics" and absolutism's English face, see Webb, *Governors-General*, 94, 96, 57–69, 79–87, 123–48, as treated by John Childs, "1688," *History*, 73: 401–402, 404.

13. See n. 11, and Dalton, ed., *Army Lists*, 1: 186; Webb, "Brave Men," *Perspectives*, 8: 69–70, 72n.

14. S. P. 44/29, 173–83, 290; Petition of Edw. Rous to the king, [Dec. 17, 1678, Jan. 1679,], C.O. 1/43, 14, 15; Dalton, ed., *Army Lists*, 1: 130, 186, 242; 2: 51, 114; 3: 306; 4: 159; Webb, *Governors-General*, 510; Hamilton, *First Guards*, 1: 266, 277, 288, 293, 368, 427; 2: 2. Colonel Rouse died in 1703.

15. Atkinson, "Charles II's Regiments," *JSAHR* 24: 161–70; Pike, ed., *Essex Papers*, 119; CII Proc. 3/335; S.P. 393/14; John Miller, "Catholic Officers," *EHR* 88: 36.

16. Andrew Marvell, "An Account of the Growth of Popery and Arbitrary Government" (London, 1677), in Grosart, ed., *Works of Marvell*, 4: 263. See this MP's denunciation of the underhand supply of English men and munitions to France, *ibid.*, 319, and his support of the proposed act of parliament against it in 1677, *ibid.*, 402.

17. Lediard, *Marlborough*, 1: 32–33. An apparently more important role was that of a future governor-general: see Estelle Frances Ward, *Christopher Monck: Duke of Albemarle* (London, 1915), 102–105. Sir Charles Littleton to Lord Hatton, London, Oct. 25, 1677, Add. Ms. 29577, 167 and Thompson, ed., *Hatton Correspondence*, 1: 153. See Add. Ms. 29556, 220, 284: "we are now talking of Nothing but War with France And Ruyneing our Papists at home. . . ." Routh, ed., *Burnet's History*, 2: 120–24. HMC, *Ormonde Ms.*, n.s. 4: 396; Browning, *Danby*, 1: 256, 282–83, 311. The head of C.O., Sir Robert Southwell (and his assistant, Blathwayt) traced the fluctuations of royal opinion concerning French imperial aggression in Europe and America, and testified to his own constant opposition to it everywhere to his American correspondents. See Southwell to Stapleton, June 11, 1678, CWWB, 39 #1. See also Bentinick to Blathwayt, de la Haye, Jan. 3, 1679, Add. Ms. 9735, 6–7.

18. Andrew Browning, ed., *The Memoirs of Sir John Reresby . . .* (Glasgow, 1936), 131, for Jan. 30, 1677/8; HMC, *Ormonde Ms.*, n.s. 1: 399–400, 403, 409, 410, 419, 432. *CSPD 1677–1678*, 632; *ibid.*, 1678, 23.

19. Sir Robert Southwell to Ormonde, Jan. 19, 1677/8, HMC, *Ormonde Ms.*, N.S. 1: 395. Feiling, *Foreign Policy*, 275–76. See also the discussion by J. R. Jones, *Britain and Europe in the Seventeenth Century* (New York, 1966), 60–66, and *Britain and the World (1649–1815)* (Brighton, 1980), 57–59. The Dutch option—Protestant and parliamentary, commercial and colonial, and francophobe—was the moderates' foreign policy, defined by Sir William Temple and, with military and imperial accents, accepted by his former clerk, Blathwayt (who was sworn a clerk of the privy council at this juncture as a reward "for the pains he has taken in the Plantation business"), and by such associates as Churchill. Blathwayt sent copies of the Nimwegen agreement to the governors-general "as it has a relation to the present posture of Affairs in Europe and consequently those of America" (Blathwayt to Culpepper, April 5, 1680, CWWB, 17 #1; same to Stapleton, Mar. 27, 1679/80, *ibid.*, 37 #2) "for the greatness of France . . . threatens all." Blathwayt's hopes for an anti-French alliance are detailed in his letter to the Life Guards officer in Jamaica, Sir Francis Watson, July 6, 1680, *ibid.*, 27 #4. Temple's page was Ventris Columbine, who ended his career in command of an allied force in America. Another symbol of the program for winning America in Europe in alliance with the Dutch was Captain William Meoles of the Holland Regiment and the Virginia battalion. He returned from Virginia in 1678, joined Churchill in Flanders, and remained abroad in the Anglo-Dutch Brigade, being promoted lieutenant colonel in 1688, Childs, *Dictionary;* Childs, *Army of Charles II,* 241; Dalton, ed., *Army Lists,* 1: 50, 68, 161, 186; Webb, *Governors-General,* #194 is here modified.

20. [Hare,] *Marlborough,* 11; Wolsey, *Marlborough,* 1: 201n., 211; S.P. 44/44, 67; S.P. 44/52, 1–12, 17–26, 31ff.; Hamilton, *First Guards,* 1: 215, 219; Littleton to Hatton, Bruges, May 18, 1678, Add. Ms. 29577, 175 and Thompson, ed., *Hatton Correspondence,* 1: 161–62. S.P. 44/29, 273. At the same time, a regiment was organized to defend the Leeward Islands from France, S.P. 44/11, 128–29.

21. James to William, London, April 2, 1678, Sir John Dalrymple, Bt., ed., *Memoirs of Great Britain and Ireland . . .* (4th ed., Dublin, 1773), 2: 186–97; *ibid.,* (2d ed., London, 1773), 2: 153; Childs, *Army of Charles II,* 187; Wolsey, *Marlborough,* 1: 204–205, 211; Churchill, *Marlborough,* 1: 134–36; Dobree, ed., *Chesterfield Letters,* #1748, 1837.

22. Hamilton, *First Guards,* 1: 210–11; Browning, *Danby,* 1: 249–55; 2: 432, 458; Webb, *1676,* 179–80, 196–99.

23. Churchill was here Danby's errand boy, and he could never afterwards accept Churchill as a peer. Observe William's pressure on James's household officers: Singer, ed., *Clarendon Correspondence,* 1: 32; Dalton, ed., *Army Lists,* 1: 201–50; Add. Ms. 10115, 81–84; Wolsey, *Marlborough,* 1: 205, 207; John Childs, "Monmouth and the Army in Flanders," *JSAHR* 52 (1979), 3; Childs, *Army of Charles II,* 186–87. Churchill here began that enormously profitable association with the bread supply of English troops in Flanders that fed but did not satisfy his insatiable avarice. So too his men's hunger. See the letter printed in *ibid.,* 212, and see 207, 211–13; Macaulay, *History,* 1: 408, 410; Add. Ms. 10115, 81–84. The governors-general in America were warned, as Blathwayt put it to Carlisle on July 19, 1678, that "all things and persons seem more disposed to War than ever," CWWB 22 #1.

24. Dalton, ed., *Army Lists,* 1: 201–20; Childs, "Monmouth," *JSAHR* 52: 3; Childs, *Army of Charles II,* 185ff.; De Beer, ed., *Evelyn Diary,* 4: 136–37, June 29, 1678; Miller, "Catholic Officers," *EHR* 88: 43; Monmouth to Feversham, Sept. 2, 1678, S.P. 44/20; Capt.-Gen. the earl of Monmouth to Col. Churchill, W[hitehal]l, 3 Sept. 1678, Add. Ms. 61336, 162, Blenheim, F 1–12.

25. Hamilton, *First Guards,* 1: 215, 223, 224; Mackinnon, *Coldstream Guards,* 1: 160; S.P. 44/44, 99; [Richard Cannon], *Historical Record of the Third Regiment of Foot or The Buffs . . .* (London, 1839), 123; Dalton, ed., *Army Lists,* 1: 221.

26. See HMC, *Ormonde Ms.,* n.s. 4: 446–47 on William's victory, at the cost of the Anglo-Dutch regiments, and note that the 2d duke of Albemarle, afterwards Jamaican viceroy and American commander-in-chief, was on Monmouth's staff. Add. Ms. 29577, 239, 357, 363, 394.

27. S.P. 44/43, 84, 234, 237; Ormonde to Coventry, Aug. 16, 1678, HMC,

Ormonde Ms., n.s., 4: 185 and see *ibid.*, 228–29, 231, 232, 237, 238–39, 240, 245; N.S. 1: 444, 448, 449; Add. Ms. 9735, 12–13; Dalton, ed., *Army Lists*, 1: 209; Miller, "Catholic Officers," *EHR* 88: 43.

28. Southwell to Ormonde, Dec. 23, 1679, HMC, *Ormonde Ms.*, n.s., 4: 569; Francis Gwyn to Ormonde, Feb. 10, 1679/80, *ibid.*, 5: 273; Henry Savile to Visct. Halifax, Paris, June 5, 1679 and reply, June 2/12, Cooper, ed., *Savile Correspondence*, 92, 97. S.P. 44/44, 104–105; Coventry to Dongan, Sept. 27, 1679, Add. Ms. 25120, 149; Blathwayt to Stapleton Mar. 27, 1680, CWWB, 37 #2; Blathwayt to Culpepper, Aug. 26, 1680, *ibid.*, 17 #1, on Inchiquin's disgrace. See also Blathwayt to Carlisle, July 9, 1680, *ibid.*, 22 #3, and Littleton to Hatton, July 13, 1680, Add. Ms. 29577, 260–70. For Dongan's despatch to New York by the duke of York's household commissioners, see Add. Ms. 24927 and O'Callaghan, ed., *NYCD* 3: 460.

29. Miller, "Catholic Officers," *EHR* 88: 42; Hamilton, *First Guards*, I, 235–36; Routh, ed., *Burnet's History*, 2: 235, 237; Cowper, *King's Own*, 6–13; Dalton, ed., *Army Lists*, 1: 269; S.P. 44/164, 57.

30. R. L[anghorne] to Hatton, Jan. 13, 1678[/79], Add. Ms. 29556, 409; the correspondence of James to William, esp. Jan. 10 [1678/79], HMC, *Foljambe Ms.*, 127; An Account of the Popish Plot, Oct. 31, 1678, HMC, *Kenyon Ms.*, 105–109; *EHD* 8:#33. The hysterical fears of Catholicism and James are strikingly portrayed in W. A. Speck, *The Reluctant Revolutionaries* (Oxford, 1988), Chapter 8. The best contemporary accounts are Southwell's despatches to Ormonde HMC, *Ormonde Ms.*, n.s. 4, 457–61, etc.; 5: 8.

31. Newsletter, March 4, 1679, HMC, *Le Fleming Ms.*, 156–57; Charles R to the duke, Feb. 28, 1678/9, Add. Ms. 29577, 192–192b; Sir Charles Littleton and Charles Hatton to Lord Hatton, March 4, 1678/9, Thompson, ed., *Hatton Correspondence*, 1: 176, 177; Wolsey, *Marlborough*, 1: 217. See Sir Robert Southwell's prescient memorandum to Ormonde, April 19, 1679, HMC, *Ormonde Ms.*, n.s. 4: xvii–xix. *CJ*, IX, 608. Leave for an entire session was most unusual. S.v. "Churchill, John II," B. D. Henning, ed., *The Commons 1660–1690* (London, 1983). For the Popish Plot and the exclusion crisis in American settings, see Chapter Five, below.

32. James to Legge, May 28, 1679, HMC, *Dartmouth Ms.*, 1:33–34; James—William. May 11, 17, June 1, July 3 [1679], HMC, *Foljambe Ms.*, 129, 130, 131, 133; Add. Ms. 18447, 8; *EHD* 8: #96.

33. James to William, June 8 [1679], HMC, *Foljambe Ms.*, 132; James to Legge, Dec. 14 [1680], HMC, *Dartmouth Ms.*, 1: 55; James Stanier Clarke, ed., *The Life of James The Second* (London, 1816), 1: 560; James to L. Hyde, July 24, 1679, "I will never try that way you mentioned in yours to Churchill," Singer, ed., *Clarendon Correspondence*, 1: 45; Robert Beddard, *A Kingdom without a King* (Oxford, 1988), 14; Edward B. Powley, *The English Navy in the Revolution of 1688* (Cambridge, 1928), 5, n. 2.

34. Wolsey, *Marlborough*, 1: 217; James to William, July 6 [1679], HMC, *Foljambe Ms.*, 134; Beddard, ed., "The Loyalist Opposition in the Interregnum: a letter of Francis Turner," *BIHR* 40 (1967), 1029; s.v. DNB, Agnes Strickland,

The Lives of the Seven Bishops . . . (London, 1866), 150–235. Like Churchill, Turner was the child of royalist courtiers, broken in the civil war, impoverished in the Interregnum.

35. *Two Illustrious Generals*, 13; Sir Lionel Jenkins to the lord high chamberlain, July 28, 1687, S.P. 44/62, 230; Churchill, *Marlborough*, 1: 28–33; Coxe, *Memoirs*, 1: 20; John Kenyon, *The Popish Plot* (New York, 1972), 155–56; Kenyon, *The Nobility in the Revolution of 1688* (Hull, 1963), 19; John Miller, *Popery and Politics in England 1660–1688* (Cambridge, 1973), 169–71.

36. *Two Illustrious Generals,* 13, suggests that the royal illness was prearranged with the duke to bring him home, a possibility reinforced by Raymond Crawfurd, *The Last Days of Charles II* (Oxford, 1909), 17ff., who diagnosed Charles II's "fit" as a recurrence of malaria. James to William, Sept. 6 [1679], HMC, *Foljambe Ms.,* 137 and Dalrymple, ed., *Memoirs,* 2: 303; Routh, ed., *Burnet's History,* 2: 237–38; H. C. Foxcroft, *The Life and Letters of Sir George Savile, Bart., First Marquis of Halifax* (London, 1898), 1: 189; F. C. Turner, *James II* (London, 1948, 1950), 166–68; Wolsey, *Marlborough,* 1: 219; Clarke, ed., *James the Second,* 1: 565–68; Thompson, ed., *Hatton Correspondence,* 1: 291–92, 297; Churchill, *Marlborough,* 1: 240; Lediard, *Marlborough,* 1: 35–36. Churchill's own company had moved up from the Portsmouth garrison to the Tower, S.P. 44/60, 23. Blathwayt reported the crisis to Sir Edmund Andros at New York, Aug. 29, 1679, CWWB, 3 #1; see also same to Culpepper for the information of Virginia's administrators, Aug. 26, 1680, CWWB, 17 #1.

37. James to William, Sept. 12, 16, 23 1679, Dalrymple, ed., *Memoirs,* 2: 303, 304, 306, *ibid.,* (2d. ed., London, 1773) 2:248–49; HMC, *Foljambe Ms.,* 137; Coxe, *Memoirs,* 1: 19; Wolsey, *Marlborough,* 1: 222; S.P. 44/164, 25, 31; Ward, *Albemarle,* 112–14, 119; Arthur, *Household Cavalry,* 141–42; Hamilton, *First Guards,* 1: 234; Thompson, ed., *Hatton Correspondence,* 1:196; HMC, *Ormonde Ms.,* n.s. 5, 211, 536–37. Monmouth lost control of the Guards when he returned to London in November 1679, without leave, to protest that he had not tried to mount a military coup: *ibid.,* 562; Add. Ms. 29577, 209b–210. Blathwayt reported to Culpepper on Aug. 26, 1680, the duke's involvement in the Tangier relief and the change of command there, CWWB, 17 #1.

38. Coxe, *Memoirs,* 1: 21; H. C. Foxcroft, *A Character of the Trimmer* . . . (Cambridge, 1946), 133, 144, 149, 153; Churchill, *Marlborough,* 1: 161; Cooper, ed., *Savile Correspondence,* 124, 128, 129; James to Louis, Sept. 4, Oct. 18, and James to M. de Pompone, Sept. 4, 1679, Dalrymple, ed., *Memoirs,* 2: 293–96; *ibid.,* (2d ed., London, 1773), 2: 239–40.

39. Sir Charles Littleton predicted this outcome Sept. 20, 1679, and noted that Monmouth's commission as general in Scotland had been canceled, leaving York a clear field, Add. Ms. 29577, 197, Thompson, ed., *Hatton Correspondence,* 1: 194, 195–96; Hamilton, *First Guards,* 1:233; HMC, *Ormonde Ms.,* n.s. 5: 540–42; Foxcroft, *Halifax,* 1: 181.

40. To Hatton, Oct. 2[6], 1679, Add. Ms. 29577, 205–205b, Thompson, ed., *Hatton Correspondence,* 1: 197–98; James to William, Sept. 12 [1679], HMC, *Foljambe Ms.,* 137–38; Turner, *James II,* 168; S.P. 44/68, 167, 168–69; HMC,

Ormonde Ms., N.S. 5: 546, 552; Blathwayt to Stapleton, Oct. 21, 1679, CWWB, 37 #1.

41. James to William, Oct. 14 [1679], HMC, *Foljambe Ms.*, 139–40; same to Legge, Dec. 13, [1679], HMC, *Dartmouth Ms.*, 1: 41; S.P. 44/164, 74.

42. James to Legge, Jan. 16 [1679/80], HMC, *Dartmouth Ms.*, 45–46; HMC, *Ormonde Ms.*, n.s. 5: 571.

43. *Ibid.*, 580, Add. Ms. 29577, 237. Blathwayt to Andros, Feb. 21, 1679/1680, CWWB, 3 #1. May 29, 1680, HMC, *Ormonde Ms.*, n.s. 5: 329–30 and see Webb, *Governors-General*, #6; Littleton to Hatton, May 22, 1680, Add. Ms. 29577, 265. For a previous proposal to exchange command of the duke's regiment for that of Barbados, see Littleton to Hatton, June 24, 1673, *ibid.*, 146b, and various other proposals to promote Churchill and Legge are discussed by the same correspondents, Dec. 26, 1679, *ibid.*, 217. Littleton's delight in the Sheerness government was multiplied by "a very gracious letter from ye Duke ... to tell me he was glad I had it," *ibid.*, 233. Blathwayt to Culpepper, Aug. 28, 1680, CWWB, 17, #1.

44. Blathwayt to Carlisle, July 9, 1680, *ibid.*, 22 #3. Instructions and commission to Dutton, Oct. 22, 1680, Hyde Papers, Add. Ms. 15898, 26–48.

45. Littleton to Hatton, June 21, Aug. 3, 21, 1680, Oct. 2, 1683, Add. Ms. 29577, 267, 273, 279b, 549b.

46. Geiter and Speck, eds., *Reresby*, 294. Class feeling did not keep Reresby from cultivating Churchill, *ibid.*, 191–92. On *The New Class*, see Milovan Djilas's (1957) work. "Greater Britain" is the coinage of J. R. Seeley, *The Expansion of England* (1884, 1971), 12, revitalized by J. G. A. Pocock, "The Limits and Divisions of British History," *The American Historical Review* 87 (1982): 311–36, and tied to the themes of this work, *ibid.*, 326–29.

47. [Halifax,] A Rough Draft of a New Model At Sea, Mark K., Brown, ed., *The Works of George Savile Marquis of Halifax* (Oxford, 1989), 1: 304.

48. Add. Ms. 29577, 297; Blathwayt to Stapleton, Oct. 22, 1680, CWWB, 37 #2; Turner, *James II*, 180, 182; James to Legge, Nov. 22, Dec. 14 [1680], HMC, *Dartmouth Ms.*, 1: 54, 55, but Legge did not actually take command as master general of the ordnance until June 29, 1681, Add. Ms. 29577, 345, 368; J. H. Leslie, "Old Printed Army Lists," *JSAHR* 3: 87. On the parliamentary debate over the government of Portsmouth, see esp. HMC, *Ormonde Ms.*, N.S. 5: 8. On the opposition's campaign of petitions for (an exclusionist) parliament, "the Protestant Duke" of Monmouth's tour through the puritan west, accompanied by lord Culpeper, the Virginia proprietor, the stockpiling of arms and the resulting American fears of another English civil war, see S.P. 44/62, 43–47, 50, 51, 69, 79, 87; S.P. 44/64, 20, 67. In the eyes of the duke's military servants, all this was indeed the groundwork for a rebellion: Add. Ms. 29577, 213, 215, 217, 221–29, and see 277, 281. York's exile and Monmouth's parliamentary campaign were reported to the governors-general by Blathwayt. The reply of the veteran Sir William Stapleton characteristically condemned "ye Indeavours of such restless spirits against his R. H. [York] who has so often ventured his life fore the Nation," Oct. 22, 1680, CWWB 38 #1. See also *ibid.*, 37 #2.

49. Cowper, *King's Own*, 6–13; Dalton, ed., *Army Lists*, 1: 269; S.P. 44/164, 57; Mackinnon, *Coldstream Guards*, 1: 348n; James to lord Hyde, Edinburgh, Dec. 2, 1682, Singer, ed., *Clarendon Correspondence* 1: 81, also pushed the command pretensions of Churchill's colleague on the Flanders general staff, Sir Palmes Fairburne.

50. Foxcroft, *Halifax*, 1: 246–47; Foxcroft, *Character*, 116–17; Clarke, ed., *James the Second*, 1: 614, 618; Routh, ed., *Burnet's History*, 2: 252. James himself had explicitly threatened to use his power in the dominions and his party in England, Scotland, and Ireland to fight a civil war, if he were denied his royal inheritance: Barrillon to Louis, Oct. 31, Dec. 30, and reply, Nov. 8, 15, 1680, Dalrymple, ed., *Memoirs*, 2: 330–40, *ibid.* (2d ed., London, 1773), 2: 269–77. See also, James to L. Hyde, Dec. 14, 1680, Singer, ed., *Clarendon Correspondence*, 1: 47. The refusal of the commons to further finance Tangier was based on this threat, *ibid.*, 620–21.

51. James to Legge, Dec. 13 [1680], HMC, *Dartmouth Ms.*, 1: 40–41; Clarke, ed., *James the Second*, 653, 661, 677–83, 698–99, 718–19, 728; Beddard, "Ecclesiastical Promotions, 1681–1684: An Instrument of Tory Reaction," *HJ* 10 (1967): 36–37; James to Legge, Aug. 14 [1681], HMC, *Dartmouth Ms.*, 1: 66: "Churchill has confirmed me in the good opinion I have of Lord Halifax. . . ." Legge said that his feud with Churchill began when the colonel revealed their conversations with Hyde, Add. Ms. 51511, 9.

52. Clarke, ed., *James the Second*, 659–60, 668; *EHD*, 8: 186; Barrillon to Louis XIV, Feb. 3, 1681, Dalrymple, ed., *Memoirs*, 2: 358–65, *ibid.* (2d ed., London, 1773) 2:295–96; Wolsey, *Marlborough*, 1: 238–39; Turner, *James II*, 194–95.

53. Barrillon au Roy, 3 Fevier 1681, Dalrymple, ed., *Memoirs*, 2: 362, *ibid.*, (2d ed., London, 1773), 2: 295; James to Legge, July 16, 1681, HMC, *Dartmouth Ms.*, 1: 65.

54. Sir Charles Littleton to Lord Hatton, Aug. 1681; same, Sept. 14, 21, 1680, Add. Ms. 29577, 363, 288–288b, 289. See also Routh, ed., *Burnet's History*, 2: 276; Clarke, ed., *James the Second*, 1: 659–61, 664–65; Feiling, *Tory Party*, 185–86.

55. York to Barrillon, received March 1, 16, 1681, Dalrymple, ed., *Memoirs*, 2: 366–68, *ibid.*, (2d ed., London, 1773), 298–301.

56. Clarke, ed., *James the Second*, 1: 664–65, 667–68, 673, 730; Turner, *James II*, 206; Wolsey, *Marlborough*, 1: 229–30; Barrillon's despatch of May 22, 1680, printed in Churchill, *Marlborough*, 1: 149; H. Savile to Halifax, Nov. 8, Dec. 16, 1679, July 8/18, 1680; Halifax to Savile, Oct. [*sic* for Nov.] 13/23, 1679, Cooper, ed, *Savile Correspondence*, 124, 128, 129, 162; Conway to Blathwayt, Mar. 23, 1682/3, Add. Ms. 37990, 30; Routh, ed., *Burnet's History*, 3: 280. James to L. Hyde, Dec. 14 [1680], Singer, ed., *Clarendon Correspondence*, 1: 51. Littleton to Hatton, July 23, 1681, Add. Ms. 29577, 357b, reported that both Churchill and Albemarle used the occasion of William's visit to solicit from him the Anglo-Dutch command. In addition to n. 49, see Dalrymple, ed., *Memoirs*, 2: 364, 369; Ward, *Albemarle*, 120–23.

57. Littleton to Hatton, July 19, 1681, Add. Ms. 29577, 353. John Childs, "The Army and the Oxford Parliament," *EHR* 94 (1979): 580–87; Childs, "1688,"

History 73: 411. The political impact of the Oxford parliament quickly reached the far corners of the waiting empire and, in Jamaica, confirmed the imperial constitution of 1681. Powell to Blathwayt, Jamaica, May 18, 1681, CWWB, 27 #3.

58. Barrillon's comment is in Dalrymple, ed., *Memoirs*, 2: 363; *ibid.*, (2d. ed., London, 1773), 2:296; Clarke, ed., *James the Second*, 1: 660, 683–84, 694–97.

59. Routh, ed., *Burnet's History*, 2: 73–74, 212, 305–306, 309–12, 320. Littleton asserted (to Hatton, Jan. 8, 1681, Add. Ms. 29577, 419) that Argyll was "not much pitied" in London circles, for he was seen as violently unjust himself, and as an old enemy of the crown. A more recent assessment of the duke as a characteristically oppressive and fractious Scots noble is by Kathleen Mary Colquhoun, "Issue of the Late Civil Wars": James, Duke of York and the Government of Scotland, 1679–1689, Ph.D. Dissertation, U. Illinois (Urbana, 1993), 174–205. *EHD* 8: #245, 246; Lediard, *Marlborough*, 1: 43, 44. York to lord Hyde, May 13, 1682, Singer, ed., *Clarendon Correspondence*, 1: 74; Clarke, ed., *James the Second*, 1: 704, 706, 707–13; Wolsey, *Marlborough*, 1 240–41. A sagacious summary of James's Scots experience is in J. R. Jones, *The Revolution of 1688 in England* (New York, 1972), 56–57. On the hereditary hostility of the Stuarts and the Campbells, see Routh, ed., *Burnet's History*, 1: par. 125. The view that Churchill consistently moderated James's behavior in Scotland, saving many dissenters from Episcopal persecution, was put forward in 1713 by Churchill's first biographer and has been consistently adopted by his successors: Wolsey, *Marlborough*, 1:246n; Churchill, *Marlborough*, 1: 153–54, who reconstructs his ancestor's letter to Sir John Werden, the chief of the duke's household staff in London, advocating a royal pardon for Argyll; and Maurice Ashley, *Marlborough* (New York, 1939, 1956), 20. The evidence here used is Werden to Churchill, St. James's, 22 Dec. [1681], Add. Ms. 61363, 4. For the persecution in Scotland, see Swift, comp., "Memoirs of Creichton," in Davis, ed., *Works of Swift*, 5: 130–35, etc. See also, Miller, *James II*, 108–109. The crown's position on Argyll is given by [Bp. Thomas Sprat,] *A True Account And Declaration Of The Horrid Conspiracy Against The Late King . . .* (London, 1685), 10–13, 25, 31–32, 63–65, 71, 74, 77–79, 82–94. This is presumably the "booke of the late Presbyterian Plott," which Effingham received from Blathwayt to warn the Virginians against seditious meetings and of the liabilities of rebellion, Nov. 14, 1685, CWWB, 14 #4.

60. Colonization, authorized by royal charters that permitted the arming of provincial garrisons and fortresses and the collection of capital funds (for the Carolina case, see S.P. 44/29, 34, 53) was an ideal cover for conspiracies against the crown, from 1619 to 1776. On this occasion, see [Sprat,] *A True Account*, 19, 22, 25–26, 27, 57–58, 64–65, 80, 81, 91, 93, 94, 101, 106, 100, 116, 130; Clarke, ed., *James the Second*, 1: 743; G. M. Waller, *Samuel Vetch, Colonial Enterpriser* (Chapel Hill, 1960), 8–12.

61. See also n. 87, 91, Ch. 3, below. Both whigs and tories tried "to bring in the New World to redress the balance of the Old." The legitimate emigration of French Huguenots, recruited in Paris by Shaftesbury's agents, and of Englishmen, enlisted by the proprietors at their weekly meeting at the Carolina Coffe

House, as well as of Cardross's Scots, are noted by Kenneth H. D. Haley, *The first earl of Shaftesbury* (Oxford, 1968), 706–707. S.v. "Erskine, Henry, and "John" in Childs, *Dictionary*.

62. Littleton gives a formulation almost identical to Burnet's (quoted here), but adds that it was "made use of by those who don't love him," i.e., James, Add. Ms. 29577, 419. See also *ibid.*, 372. Beddard, "Ecclesiasticial Promotions," *HJ*, 10: 26, 30; Strickland, *Lives of the Bishops*, 163; *Two Illustrious Generals*, 15; Routh, ed., *Burnet's History*, 2: 323. Churchill, *Marlborough*, 1: 155, 173–74.

63. Foxcroft, *Character*, 141; Routh, ed., *Burnet's History*, 2: 312; Clarke, ed., *James the Second*, 1: 626–29, 657–58, 699–701; James to Legge, Sept 11 [1681], HMC, *Dartmouth Ms.*, 1: 67.

64. Churchill to Legge, Sept. 12, [1681], *ibid.*; see also *ibid.*, 49 and Sir Charles Littleton to Lord Hatton, July 12, Oct. 14, 1681, Add. Ms. 29577, 351b, 384; Barrillon to Louis, Oct. 14, 1680, Dalrymple, ed., *Memoirs*, 2: 340; Add. Ms. 51511, 9v. As of this date, Feiling, *Tory Party*, 181, 192, 197, ranks Churchill as on a par with Laurence Hyde (already in charge of the treasury) as a statesman, and puts Churchill just below that eminence, Danby. All of these moderates joined "in opposition to despotism, to Popery, and to France."

65. James to Legge, Dec. 14 [1697]; Churchill to Legge, Sept. 12, 1681, HMC, *Dartmouth Ms.*, 1: 41, 67; Littleton to Hatton, Mar. 11, 1681, Add. Ms. 29577, 321b. Note that the report exonerating Andros was signed by Sir John Churchill, cousin of his namesake, the colonel. Sir John had been the duke's attorney-general since 1674. s.v. *DNB. EHD* 8: 188–90; Webb, " 'The Peaceable Kingdom:' Quaker Pennsylvania in the Stuart Empire," Richard S. Dunn and Mary Maples Dunn, eds., *The World of William Penn* (Philadelphia, 1986), 173–94; Webb, "The Trials of Sir Edmund Andros," James Kirby Martin, ed., *The Human Dimensions of Nation Making* (Madison, Wisc., 1976), 23–55; Add. Ms. 29577, 321b; Blathwayt to Culpepper, Aug. 20, 1680, CWWB, 17 #1.

66. HMC, *Dartmouth Ms.*, 68–69; Webb, *Governors-General*, 281–312. While in Edinburgh, Stapleton recalled to Blathwayt (June 18, 1682, CWWB, 38 #2) that the duke also attended to the affairs of the Royal African Company. S.P. 44/62, 72–73, 76. See the Lynch-Blathwayt correspondence (CWWB, 24 passim) and note George Churchill's involvement.

67. Barrillon to Louis XIV, Dec. 7, 1684, *A Translation of the French Letters in the Appendix of Mr. Fox's History* . . . (London, 1808), 2. Louis replied, "the reasonings of Lord Halifax upon the mode of governing New England ill entitle him to the confidence which the king reposes in him," *ibid.*, 3.

68. Clarke, ed., *James the Second*, 1: 702, 724–30. The whiggish Colonel John Russell, after twenty years in command of the Guards, was replaced by Grafton, early in December 1681: Dalton, ed., *Army Lists*, 1:7; Add. Ms. 29577, 407; Hamilton, *First Guards*, 1: 219–52, 253; Mackinnon, *Coldstream Guards*, 1: 348n; York to Hyde, Dec. 7, 1682, Singer, ed., *Clarendon Correspondence*. 1: 81; Routh, ed., *Burnet's History*, 2: 281n., 300–301, 323, 326n; Wolsey, *Marlborough*, 1: 213–14; Turner, *James II*, 212; Churchill, *Marlborough*, 1: 156–57; HMC, *Dartmouth Ms.*, 1: 69; Add. Ms. 29577, 380, 398, 399, 401, 404, 427,

433, 447b. Blathwayt was a prominent witness for the prosecution against Shaftesbury, testifying that he found in Shaftesbury's papers "A Scheme to form A Rebellion & Change the Government by seizing the K[in]gs person & associating in Armes." Haley, *Shaftesbury*, 631–32, 667–68, 670, 677, 678.

69. Blathwayt also recorded the confession of Monmouth's colonel, Nathaniel Wade, Oct. 4, 1685, which revealed the conspiratorial connection with West New Jersey. James II's interest in his former property was aroused and, on Oct. 11, Blathwayt secured from Wade the names of the interlocking directorates of the Shaftesburean King's Head Club and the West Jersey proprietors, Harleian Ms. 6485, 267, 282, BL. On Maryland in 1681, see below, chapter five.

70. Blathwayt to Lynch, March 1, 1681/2, May 20, 1682, CWWB, 23 #1; same to Stapleton, March 20, 1681/2: "the most welcome news we have is the Duke's return into England . . . ;" and same, Sept. 26, 1681, *ibid.*, 37 #3.

71. Lediard, *Marlborough*, 1:40–42; Chappell, ed., *Tangier Papers of Pepys*, 208, 209, 248–50. The pilot, James Aires, had recently returned from American service. He held to the fatal course against the advice of the *Gloucester*'s experienced North Sea sailors, M. Cowburn, "Christopher Gunman and the Wreck of the Gloucester," *The Mariners' Mirror*, 42 (1956), 115–26.

72. Singer, ed., *Clarendon Correspondence*, 1: 67–73 includes Berry's Journal and Pepys's Account. MacPherson, ed., *Original Papers*, 1: 61n., casts doubt on the Sandwich episode.

73. *Two Illustrious Generals*, 15; Legge's account in Singer, ed., *Clarendon Correspondence*, 68; Wolsey, *Marlborough*, 1: 24; Dalrymple, *Memoirs*, 1: 79; Turner, *James II*, 213–14.

74. Singer, ed., *Clarendon Correspondence*, 1: 67, 68; Turner, *James II*, 214. Most sources say 130 of the ship's company of 300 were drowned. Churchill, *Marlborough*, 1: 157, makes the number 260. Sir James Dick, a survivor, writing to Mr. Patrick Ellis, from Edinburgh, May 9, 1682, appears to count more than 200 casualties, Dalrymple, ed., *Memoirs*, 2: 83–86; *ibid.* (2d ed., London, 1773), 2: 68–71. See also, Clarke, ed., *James the Second*, 1: 731. On Wynbourne, who was knighted after this episode, see Webb, *1676*, 224–27, and Edward Cranfield to Blathwayt, writing from Portsmouth, Feb. 20 1682/3, on "our friend now on the coast of Ireland" whose frigate could coerce the New Englanders, CWWB, 1 #1.

75. "Narrative from Sir John Berry, Knt., 4–6 May 1682," Singer, ed., *Clarendon Correspondence*, 1: 73; Proceedings of the court martial, June 6, 13, 1682, HMC, *Dartmouth Ms.*, 1: 74–75. Berry's next voyage was to convey Cranfield to New Hampshire as governor, S.P. 44/63, 43–45. The language condemning James is Sarah's, quoted in Churchill, *Marlborough*, 1: 158, and is discussed, together with all the other accounts, in Cowburn, "Wreck," *Mariners' Mirror*, 42: 113–26, 219ff.

76. T. Deanes to Lord Preston, Feb. 26, 29; 1693, HMC, *Graham Ms.*, 363, 375; Laurence Echard, *The History of England* (London, 1718), 3: 665–66; Add. Ms. 29577, 253b, 521–22. Sunderland succeeded Conway early in 1683, as Blathwayt told Culpepper, Feb. 10, 1682/3, CWWB 17 #2. Godolphin's replacement of Jenkins and Sunderland's promotion to first secretary (and so to supervision of the colonies) took place in the spring of 1684, as Blathwayt wrote to Lord Howard of Effingham (now in command of Virginia), April 3, 1684, *ibid.*, 14 #1. These changes delighted such a Yorkist, and a member of the Blathwayt-Churchill circle, as Sir Thomas Lynch, writing to Blathwayt, June 26, 1684, *ibid.*, 24 #6.

77. Blathwayt to Preston, Jan. 15, 1682/3, Dec. 17, 1683, HMC, *Graham Ms.*, 362–63 and see HMC, *Dartmouth Ms.*, 1: 81. On Blathwayt's imperial career, see Webb, "William Blathwayt, Imperial Fixer," *WMQ* 25: 3–21, 26: 373–415, and works cited therein. On the French forms, and their adoption by the English Guards and garrisons, see Add. Ms. 38694, esp. 19, 76, 91b–96. These are the missing sections of W.O. 1.

78. "Minutes of Proceedings of the Commissioners of Revenue etc, of James, Duke of York, 1682–1683, 1684–1685," Add. Ms. 24927, 4, 9–11, 14, 15, 45. William Harper Bennett, *Catholic Footsteps in Old New York* (New York, 1909), 82–111, 147, 196 (I owe this citation to David William Voorhees). See also *NYCD*, 4: 166. It may be that even Alexander James, commissioned chaplain of the New York garrison April 20, 1686, was a Roman Catholic. For further Catholic commissions see S.P. 44/164, 39. In 1681, in formal trials (paralleling those in Jamaica), the New York opposition had protested James's prerogative plans. Their correspondents in the metropolis kept public opinion (to say nothing of such insiders as Churchill) fully aware of the progress of exclusion in the province. For New Yorkers' local application of the popish plot, see Webb, "Trials," in Martin, ed., *Dimensions*, 33–41 and chapter five, below.

79. Webb, "Peaceable Kingdom," Dunn and Dunn, eds. *Penn*, 174. An especially well-balanced picture of the religious and political relations of Penn with James Stuart is J. R. Jones, "A Representative of the Alternative Society of Restoration England," *ibid.*, 55–69.

80. Peter Earle, *The Wreck of the Almiranta, Sir William Phips and the Search for the Hispaniola Treasure* (London, 1979), 123, 129–30; and see the Appendix to this volume, "Inglorious Revolution: The Channel Fleet in 1688."

81. Lynch to Blathwayt, Jan. 24, 1681/2, June 12, 1682, CWWB, 23 #1; Blathwayt to Lynch, Nov. 26, 1682, *ibid.*, #3. Lynch to Blathwayt, May 29, 1684, recalls Halifax's role in formalizing the imperial constitution, and also memorializes the Hyde family's concern for the colony, *ibid.*, 24 #5.

82. Lynch to Blathwayt, Oct. 8, 1682, *ibid.*, 23 #3. Blathwayt to Lynch, Mar. 5, 1682/3, *ibid.*, #4; June 30, 1683, *ibid.*, 24 #1; Mar. 3, 1683/4, *ibid.*, #4; Lynch to Blathwayt, Aug. 13, 1684, *ibid.*, #6. Note that Clarendon, Littleton, Blathwayt (as the beneficiary of a huge bribe from Lynch), Albemarle, and Stapleton were all major landowners in Jamaica. See, for example, Blathwayt to Lynch, Nov. 1, 1682, *ibid.*, 23 #3. On Vaughan, see Webb, *Governors-General*, 263–75, #49.

83. On the Jamaican political parties, and the military government of Port Royal, see Lynch to Blathwayt, Dec. 18, 1682, CWWB 23 #3. Lynch was now married to Littleton's sister, Philadelphia. "Philly" was also related to Admiral Herbert. See Lynch to Blathwayt, May 29, 1684, *ibid.*, 24 #5, and the Littleton-Hatton correspondence on the subject, esp. Sept. 8, 1684, Add. Ms. 29578, 30.

84. Lynch to Blathwayt, Mar. 3, 1682/3, CWWB, 23 #4; Lynch to Blathwayt, May 10, 1683, *ibid.*, 24 #1; Blathwayt to Lynch, July 18; Lynch to Blathwayt, Oct. 6, 21, 1683, *ibid.*, #2; Blathwayt to Lynch, March 3, 1683/4, *ibid.*, 24 #4. Of course, army salaries for the governors-general were the norm: Webb, *Governors-General*, 94, 120–21, 169, 175–76, 200, 214, 229, 276, 305, 321, 381, 384–85, 398–400. Lynch to Blathwayt, Nov. 9, 1683, CWWB, 24 #3. Lynch's speech is in Add. Ms. 12429, 135–39. See also Hender Molesworth to Blathwayt, Dec. 29, 1687, CWWB, 25 #6. For the government's account, see [Sprat,] *Account and Declaration*, as cited in notes 59 and 60, above.

85. Lynch to Blathwayt, Nov. 9, 1683, CWWB, 24 #3; Blathwayt to Lynch, Mar. 3, 1683/4, *ibid.*, #4.

86. Recall that Sir Philip Howard of the Life Guards held a reversion to the Jamaica government, and that the duke of Grafton, colonel of the First Guards, was now lobbying for the command. Lynch to Blathwayt, April 15, 1683, *ibid.*, 24 #1; Lynch to Blathwayt, Nov. 9, 1683, *ibid.*, #3. What Lynch wanted Captain Churchill to say was that only the governor-general's vice admiralty authority sufficed to supply the frigates, the naval ships essential to protect trade and repress piracy, with island provisions of food, timber, and men. Lynch to Blathwayt, Dec. 15, 1683, *ibid.*, #4. On Craven's connection, see Blathwayt to Lynch, March 3, 1683/4 and Lynch to Blathwayt, June 2, 1684, *ibid.*, #5; Blathwayt to Lynch, June 28, 1684, *ibid.*, #6. Lynch also complained to Blathwayt, Oct. 6, 1683, *ibid.*, #2, that the pirates he pursued fled to shelter in Carolina and New England. Add. Ms. 12429, 135–39; Lynch to Blathwayt, Nov. 9, 1683, CWWB, 24 #3.

87. "Reflections on a Paper Concerning America," B.L. 416, Blathwayt Papers, Huntington Library, printed in Barbara Cresswell Murison, William Blathwayt's Empire: Politics and Administration in England and the Atlantic Colonies, 1668–1710, Ph.D. dissertation, University of Western Ontario (London, Ont., 1981), 238–40.

88. Dalton, ed., *Army Lists*, 1: 270; John Cordy Jeaffreson, ed., *A Young Squire of the Seventeenth Century. From the Papers (A.D. 1676–1686) of Christopher Jeaffreson* [London, 1878], 2: 9, et seq. On Capt. Jeaffreson's agency, and for Col. Hill's career in the islands, see the correspondence of Capt. Jos. Crispe with Blathwayt, July 18, 1682, CWWB, 39 #1 and Hill to same, *ibid.*, #2, #4; Webb, *Governors-General*, 475, 490, #73, 110.

89. Add. Ms. 24927, 24928; Clarke, ed., *James Second*, 1: 399, 400; K. G. Davies, *The Royal African Company* (London, 1957), 103–104, 156, 180, 266; George Bryce, *The Remarkable History of the Hudson's Bay Company* . . . (Toronto, 1904; New York, 1968), 29; Webb, "Brave Men," *Perspectives*, 8: 63–64. In the summer of 1683, the duke approved Effingham's appointment to command Virginia. See Effingham's retrospective remarks in his letters to Blathwayt, Apr. 26, 1685, Aug. 26, 1687, CWWB, 14 #3, #6. Effingham also received a vice admiral's commission from the duke, as he called on the former York household secretary to witness: same, July 6, 1688, *ibid.*

90. Hen. Fanshaw to lord Hatton, June 19, 1683, Add. Ms. 29560, f. 39b; Littleton to same, June 1, 1683, Add. Ms. 29577, 531; Capt. G. Littleton to same,

July 25 and William Longueville to same, July 28, 1683, Add. Ms. 29560, 68, 70. O. Wynne to Preston, June 14, July 9, 1683, HMC, *Graham Ms.*, 364, 364; Blathwayt to Conway, June 12, 1683, *CSPD 1683*, 311; letter of Mar. 12, 1679/80, CWWB, 37 #2.

91. See Routh, ed., *Burnet's History*, II, 391, Turner, *James II*, 244, and Edward Gregg, *Queen Anne* (London, 1980, 1984), 32, on the initiative of Louis XIV and on the marriage as an effort of James to challenge William's influence in England. Note that Bishop Turner (Marvell's "Mr. Smirke, or the Divine in Mode") was close enough to Princess Anne to ask the king for clerical patronage in her name. Turner's role was the larger because Compton "was so burdened with, and so engaged to those whom he hath sent abroad in the ships and into the Plantations. . . . All the ministers that were at Tangier, besides many others, now hang upon him," Beddard, *HJ* 10:31–32, 36; *DNB*.

92. Anne to Mrs. Churchill, 1683, Beatrice Curtis Brown, ed., *The Letters and Diplomatic Instructions of Queen Anne* (New York, 1935, 1968), 12, Coxe, *Memoirs*, 1: 27; Helen C. Foxcroft, ed., *Supplement to Burnet's History of My Own Time* (Oxford, 1902), 29, and see note 94. The origins of the relationship of Anne and Sarah, quite representative of the passionate female friendships of young women at court in this period, is handled with insight and economy by Bonamy Dobree, *Three Eighteenth Century Figures* (London, 1962), 11–16. Sarah herself seems to say that her husband, lord Churchill, arranged her post with the princess: David Green, *Sarah Duchess of Marlborough* (New York, 1967), 41. See also, Gregg, *Anne*, 28, 33.

93. Anne to Mary, Jan. 10, 1687/8, Dalrymple, ed., *Memoirs*, 3: 221 Add. Ms. 15897, 54; *ibid.*, 29560, 70; *ibid.*, 15897 (Hyde Papers 3), 54; "Servants Belonging to Prince George of Denmark," Singer, ed., *Clarendon Correspondence*, 2: 250–51 and see *ibid.*, 1: 19n. Coxe, *Memoirs*, 1: 27; *An Account of the Conduct of the Dowager Duchess of Marlborough* (London, 1742), reprinted in William King, ed., *Memoirs of Sarah, Duchess of Marlborough* (London, 1930), 7–11; Webb, *Governors-General*, Appendix, #155, 204. Add. Ms. 29577, 531–531b reports Dartmouth's discontent at being left out of these arrangements.

94. Foxcroft, ed., *Supplement*, 291–92. See n. 1, above, and Coxe, *Memoirs*, 1: lviii–xlix.

95. For Charles Churchill's early career, see Dalton, ed., *Army Lists*, 1: 178, 184, 223, 255, 263, 295, 323, and Lediard, *Marlborough*, 1: 14.

96. Charnock, *Biographia Navalis*, 2: 42–47. For George Churchill's military commissions, see Dalton, ed., *Army Lists*, 1: 187, 225. Note also that Sarah's brother-in-law, Colonel Edward Griffith, was named Prince George's secretary as a result of lord Churchill's manipulations, Gregg, *Anne*, 35.

97. See Anne to Mary, December 29, 1686, Brown, ed., *Letters of Anne*, 20–21.

98. Compton, in Burnet's famous phrase (Routh, ed., *Burnet's History*, 2: 91), "was a property to lord Danby, and was turned by him as he pleased." For a contrary view, see Lawrence L. Brown, "Henry Compton," *HMPEC*, 25 (1956): 5–71, esp., 51–54, who also records Compton's activities in church government in the Leeward Islands, Jamaica, Maryland, and Pennsylvania, as well as in the composition of instructions to the governors-general. And see J. H.

Bennett and Anthony H. Forbes, "English Bishops and Imperial Jurisdiction,", *ibid.*, 32: 176–88, which adds instances of Compton's involvement, in Barbados and Virginia.

Book II: Lord Churchill's Ingratitude

epigraph: Draft in Blenheim Ms. B.2.31, now Add. Ms. 61101, ff. 1–2, British Library. Printed [Francis Hare], *The Life and Glorious History of John Duke of Marlborough* (2d ed., London, 1707), 14–15; "Corrected," by Winston S. Churchill, *Marlborough, His Life and Times* (London, 1933, 1934, 1947), 1: 263–64.

Chapter Three: Rebellion and Empire: 1683–1687

1. For Dartmouth's prior connection with Tangier administration, see his correspondence with the governor-general, Kirke, and the master gunner, Povey, in HMC, *Dartmouth Ms.*, 1. For his brief command there, see *ibid.*, and, on Berry and naval administration see Chappell, ed., *Tangier Papers of Pepys*. Grafton expected the Tangier command and, so Sir Charles Littleton wrote on Aug. 14, 1683, the duke was "the most mortified creature in the world" when he lost it to Dartmouth, Add. Ms. 29577, 545. Both Grafton's interest in Tangier and his hostility to Dartmouth bore fruit in 1688. See Appendix: "Inglorious Revolution: The Channel Fleet in 1688," below. See also: Cowper, *King's Own*, 28–29; Davis, *Second, Queen's*, 1, passim and esp. App. E. Nonetheless, Childs, *Army of Charles II*, 231, states that "the army itself was never a political force" and that the standing army debates were only conceptual and "emotive." Contrast Childs, "1688," *History*, 73: esp. 412–13.

2. Dartmouth [to Jenkins,] Tangier, Oct. 19, 1683, C.O. 279/32, 276.

3. Corbett, *England in the Mediterranean*, 2: 122–23, 128–39; Routh, *Tangier*, 239–44. On the cost of the evacuation to English empire, see *ibid.*, 270–71. See also, Routh, ed., *Burnet's History*, 2: 427. King Charles's characteristic reaction, on being told in July 1680, that Tangier was indefensible, was that "he was in ye condition of a man that had lived several years with a wife who had preserved her fame & at last one telling him he took one a'bed with her, he could not tell how to give credit to," Add. Ms. 29577, 271. See also *ibid.*, 273–273b, 283. On the royal economic disappointment, see Sec. Coventry to Sir Palmes Fairbourne, Jan. 12, 1676/7, Add. Ms. 25120, 106–107. And See HMC, *Ormonde Ms.*, n.s. 5: 527.

4. Edwyn Stede to Blathwayt, Barbados, 18 Dec. 1683, 3 June 1687, CWWB, 32, #3. The fullest account of the plot is that by the former Jamaica commander, Sir Charles Littleton, 30 June [16]83, Add. Ms. 29577, 535–39. Haley, *Shaftesbury*, 706, gives a tangential reference to the Carolina connection, and Wilkinson became a particular target of the crown, *ibid.*, 674, 678. Dartmouth sailed ca. August 6: S.P. 44/68, 293; HMC, *Graham Ms.*, 363, 365; Routh, ed., *Burnet's History*, 2: 354–91; S.P. 44/64, 76; Davis, *Second, Queens*, 1: 261; C.O. 279/33, 273–76; Add. Ms. 15897, 71; Add. Ms. 29560, 161b. An odd adjunct to

the plot was Captain William Blagge, technical advisor for the new class of galley frigates (Webb, *1676*, fol. p. 104) who put off his voyage for New York to plan an attack on the Tower of London: Davies, "Navy," *HJ* 36: 285–86.

5. The members of the duke's household hoped that the New Englanders "Probably will be brought to reason by psecution of the Quo Warranto wch is brought agt them," Add. Ms. 24927, 49. Webb, "The Strange Career of Francis Nicholson," *WMQ*, 3d Ser., 23 (1966). Note that Nicholson's passage was in the *Deptford Ketch*, Captain John George, afterwards captain of the *Rose* on station at Boston in 1688–89, Chappell, ed., *Tangier Papers of Pepys*, 179; Barrillon to Louis XIV, London, Dec. 7, 1684, *Translation*, 1. Littleton to Hatton, Nov. 3, 1684, Add. Ms. 29578, 37; Jeaffreson to Hill, Nov. 11, Dec. 6, 1684, Jeaffreson, ed., *Young Squire*, 2: 150, 153; Foxcroft, *Character*, 204–205; S.P. 44/56, 111; Feiling, *Tory Party*, 199.

6. Blathwayt to Lynch, Nov. 1, 1682, CWWB, 23 #3.

7. C.O. 279/32, 275ff.; Cowper, *King's Own*, 33–34; Add. Ms. 29560, 202–202b.

8. Dartmouth to [Jenkins,] Tangier, Oct. 19, 1683, C.O. 33/279, 273–76, is partially printed in Davis, *Second, Queen's*, 1: 300–304. As it happened, the second battalion of Dumbarton's Scots marched home and Trelawney's first battalion replaced them. The junior companies of each of the Tangier battalions went off to garrison in Ireland. The Tangier battalion of the Guards reentered the ranks of their parent corps and the Tangier grenadiers reinforced their regiments in the outport garrisons. W.O. 4/1, 5–6. The duke of York took this opportunity to concentrate his own marines, under Sir Charles Littleton, in the Tower and in the Thames forts. A battalion of Dumbarton's veterans garrisoned Portsmouth and were replaced in the French service by a new Scots battalion, the king not being willing to lose any of his recently domesticated professional units: Add. Ms. 29577, 555, 557. On the concentration of regimented companies from the garrisons, see *ibid.*, 557.

9. Littleton to Hatton, Nov. 5, 18, Dec. 17, Add. Ms. 29577, 533, 555, 557. Dartmouth as reported by Pepys, Chappell, ed., *Tangier Papers of Pepys*, 311. To Laurence Hyde, Dartmouth denounced "all the ill practices and arts of Churchill," Dec. 29, 1683, Singer ed., *Clarendon Correspondence* 1: 92.

10. C.O. 32/279, 276. Cornbury's commission as Churchill's lieutenant colonel was also reported by Littleton to Hatton, Nov. 5, 1683, Add. Ms. 29577, 533. Trumbull arrived from Tangier with Dartmouth's despatches Nov. 18, *ibid.*, 555. HMC, *Downshire Ms.*, 1, *Trumbull Ms.*, Pt. I: 52, 53. The history of the dragoon in C. T. Atkinson, *History of the Royal Dragoons, 1661–1934* (Glasgow, 1935), 36–37, omits the Barbados Dragoons, who introduced the bayonet into England, S.P. 44/35A, 28b–29, 37. As usual, the most trenchant definition of the military type is in Firth and Davies, *Cromwell's Army* 125. Note that Churchill's formative English service was mostly in regiments—the marines and the dragoons—which, though they might fight as infantry, did not have pikemen, a type that Churchill ultimately eliminated from English fighting forces. HMC, *Dartmouth Ms.*, 1:85. For the Barbados Regiment's imperial service, and on Andros's transformation of New York from colony to province, see Webb, *1676*, 303–54.

11. S.P. 44/164, 101; Dalton, ed., *Army Lists*, 1: 301; [Charles Philip] De Ainslie, *Historical Record of the First or the Royal Regiment of Dragoons* (London, 1887), 15. Appropriately, the orders protecting Churchill's dragoons against civil jurisdiction appear in the same register as those expelling John Locke from his studentship at Christ Church: S.P. 44/56, 123. See also, S.P. 44/69, 72, 141.

12. S.P. 44/69, 73–74; DeAinslie, *First Dragoons*, 15–17; McCance, ed., "Halkett Diary," *JSAHR* I: 16–19.

13. Establishments, Add. 61316, 7b, still in its Blenheim binding with the double eagle crest. Nathan Brooks, comp., "A General And Compleat List Military Of Every Commission-Officer Of Horse And Foot Now Commanding His Majesties Land-Forces Of England (Excepting the Unregimented Companies)," (London, 1684), ed. Lt. Col. J. H. Leslie in *JSAHR*, 1:145; Atkinson, *Royal Dragoons*, 35; S.P. 44/164, 101; Dalton, ed., *Army Lists*, 1: 301; Bryan Little, *The Monmouth Episode*, (London, 1956), 120.

14. Add. Ms. 61316, 7b. Churchill drew £273/15s p.a. as colonel and £200/15s p.a. as captain, including allowance for six horses. Brooks, ed., "Army List," *JSAHR*, 1: 145; Andros to Blathwayt, Oct. 18, 1686, CWWB, 3 #2. As early as June 1684, Churchill could offer the duke of Hamilton £11,000 for a manor, Add. Ms. 61363, 5.

15. Dalton, ed., *Army Lists*, 1: 323; Dartmouth to Preston, Tangr Roads, Feb. 11, 1683/4, HMC, *Graham Ms.*, 369; Jeaffreson, ed., *Young Squire*, 2: 150. In this same summer, the American executives were informed that the duke had formally resumed control of the admiralty and had been readmitted to the privy council, Blathwayt to Effingham, July 28, 1684, CWWB, 14 #2; same to Lynch, June 28, 1684, *ibid.*, 24 #6. Add. Ms. 29578, 32, 34; Brooks, comp. "List Military," *JSAHR*, 1: 6–9, 56–99, 142–45; 2: 164–67; 3: 22–25, 85–89. In rank order, the governors-general listed in the October 1684 muster were: Christopher, duke of Albemarle, captain and colonel of the king's troop, Horse Guards, eldest colonel of cavalry; Sir Philip Howard, captain and colonel of the queen's troop; George lord Dartmouth, master general of the ordnance; Captains William Selwyn and John Seymour of the Foot Guards; Lieutenant Colonel Edward Sackville, Captain James Kendall, and Ensign William Matthews of the Coldstream Guards; Lord George Hamilton (afterwards earl of Orkney) captain in Dumbarton's (the Royal Scots); Colonel Piercy Kirke of the Queen's; Colonel Sir Charles Littleton and Captain Edward Nott of the Admiral's; Captains Sir John Berry and Francis Collingwood, and Lieutenant Edward Fox of the Holland Regiment (the Buffs); and Lieutenant Francis Nicholson of the duchess of York's.

16. S.P. 44/56, 149; Macaulay, *History*, 1: 280–88; DeAinslie, *First Dragoons*, 20; Atkinson, *Royal Dragoons*, 38–40.

17. Littleton to Hatton, [Feb. 3, 1684/5]; William Longueville to Hatch, Feb. 7, 1685, Thompson, ed., *Hatton Correspondence*, 2: 51–52, Add. Ms. 29578, 46–46b, 54; Barrillon to the king, Feb. 26, March 5, 1685, *Translation*, 30, Dalrymple, ed., *Memoirs*, 2: 137, 139; *ibid.* (2d ed., London 1773), 106–113, 116; same, Feb. 18, 1685, *ibid.*, 90–98. Routh, ed., *Burnet's History*, 2: 446–76, 3: 7; Crawfurd, *Last Days*, 14–15; Foxcroft, *Character*, 202–204; Sunderland to the garrison governors, Feb. 7, 1684/5, S.P. 44/169, 127; S.P. 44/56, 159–66; *CSPD 1685*, #11, 12–14; Blathwayt to Reresby, Feb. 14, 1684/5, W.O. 4/1, 6–7; Miller, *James II*, 120; Jeaffreson, ed. *Young Squire*, 2: 24. Effingham to Blathwayt, Apr. 26, 1685, noted, for Virginia and Nevis, that the first concern of the colonists was that King James "would maytaine ye Laws & Religion of England," CWWB, 14 #3. Spencer to Blathwayt, May 15, 1685, *ibid.*, 16 #3, rejoiced in James's "peaceable succession to the Imperial Crowne," and promised Virginia's obedience to his government.

18. Lediard, *Marlborough*, 1: 49; Barrillon to Louis XIV, Feb. 19, 26, 1685, *Translation*, 12, 26, and see 49; Dalrymple, ed., *Memoirs*, 2: 137; *ibid.* (2d ed., London, 1773), 100–113. Routh, ed., *Burnet's History*, 3: 12, 282, but see Lediard, *Marlborough*, 1: 73. For the prescience of Halifax and Churchill, see Feiling, *Tory Party*, 203. S.v. "Turner, Francis," *DNB*.

19. Coxe, *Memoirs*, 1: 30; Capt. H. Oakes-Jones, ed., "The King: His Ancient Royal Body Guards, Horse and Foot," *JSAHR* 16 (1937): 71–85, prints Francis Sandford, *Lancaster Herald*, "The History of the Coronation of . . . James II, etc." (London, 1687); Childs, *The Army, James II and the Glorious Revolution* (Manchester, 1980), 110.

20. C.O. 135/1; Wolsey, *Marlborough*, 1: 342; Churchill, *Marlborough*, 1: 414–15; Bryce, *Hudson's Bay Company*, 24–25, 30–31. For the details of Churchill's investments, see the magisterial study by E. E. Rich, *The History of the Hudson's Bay Company 1670–1870* (London, 1958), 1: 173 (it would be interesting to know if Churchill bought this stock "ex-dividend," for the March premium was £50!), 177, 240, 273–74, 283.

21. E. E. Rich, ed., *Letters Outward, 1679–1694* (Toronto, 1957), *1688–1696* (London, 1957), passim. It is also fairly clear (Rich, *Hudson's Bay Company*, 1: 229) that Churchill was expected to eliminate Shaftesbury's partisans from the board.

22. Sir Lionel Jenkins to Preston, March 10, 1683/4, HMC, *Graham Ms.*, 369.

23. [Hare,] *Marlborough*, 11; Barrillon to Louis XIV, Feb. 9, 1685, *Translation*, 12–13; Kenyon, *Nobility in 1688*, 6–7; Littleton to Hatton, March 18, 1685, Add. Ms. 29578, 53b; Lediard, *Marlborough*, 1: 50, 72; Dumbarton to James II, May 1685, HMC, *Stopford-Sackville Ms.*, 1: 1; Browning, ed., *Reresby*, 326. On Argyll's botched expedition, see Swift, comp., "Creichton," *Prose Works*, 5: 158–60.

24. Sunderland to the lt. govr. of Berwick and the dep. lts. of the Borders and the western shires, May 10, 1685, to disarm the disaffected, secure the militia arms, etc., S.P. 44/56, 198, and see 201–202, 205; S.P. 44/164, 210, 211; The Declaration of James Duke of Monmouth, [in] An Exact Relation of . . . the late James Duke of Monmouth's Proceedings . . . Lyme Regis, Dorset, Harleian Ms. 6845, 256–57. Note that John Locke contributed (besides ideas) £400 or £500 to Monmouth's invasion and £1,000 to Argyll's, according to Nath. Wade's Confession, Oct. 4, 1685, *ibid.*, 270, 272. Locke's clandestine activities

are neglected by his biographers. Singer, ed., *Clarendon Correspondence*, 1: 132.
King Charles's death occurred fortuitously for James, for the king was about to
send the duke back to Scotland (Barrillon to Louis XIV, Dec. 7, 1684, *Translation*, 2), and the demise was surprising, for Charles had been in good health and
spirits, so that foul play was instantly alleged, but Crawfurd, *Last Days*, 13–16,
20, concludes that the king died of Bright's disease. On mass arrests, see Peter
Earle, *Monmouth's Rebels* (New York, 1977), 62; Barrillon to Louis XIV, July 16,
1685, *Translation*, 109–10; *CSPD 1685*, #852–61.

25. A Journal of the Proceedings of ye D. of Monmouth . . . by Mr. Edward
Dummer, then serving in the Train of Artillery . . . , Add. Ms. 31596 (III, 26),
1–2. S.P. 44/164, 186, 193, 200, 205–12, 217, 221; Jeaffreson, ed., *Young Squire*,
1: 324, 2: 9, 220; S.P. 44/42, 18–19; S.P. 44/44, 17; S.P. 44/56, 227, 228–32;
Dalton, ed., *Army Lists*, 2: 14, 19. Andros's commissions, *CSPD 1685*, #928,
937; Stapleton's, *ibid.*, 929, 940, 941.

26. In addition to the material on the Royals in note 25, above, see Churchill,
Marlborough, 1: 185; Wolsey, *Marlborough*, 1: 276; Frank Taylor, *The Wars of
Marlborough, 1702–1709* (Oxford, 1921), 2: 406; Barrillon to Louis XIX, June
13, 16, 1685, *Translation*, 97, 103; Sunderland to Albemarle, June 11, 13, 14,
1685, S.P. 44/56, 211–16; Add. Ms. 31596, III, 26, 1.

27. W. MacDonald Wingfield, *The Monmouth Rebellion* (Bradford-on-Avon,
1980), 34–35. Atkinson, *Royal Dragoons*, 1: 176–77, 179, reports that Albemarle's excuse for his inaction, as of 21 June, was that "my Ld Churchill
having not yet joyned me, and I having no orders to attack the enemy without
him, would not attempt it." Albemarle's orders were not to attack "except at
great advantage," S.P. 44/56, 214.

28. Sunderland "to Lord Churchill, to Command the Forces at Salesbury,"
June 15, 1685, S.P. 44/52, 216, and Add. Ms. 61336, 164; S.P. 5/1, 40–44;
James to William, June 15, 19, 1685, Dalrymple, ed., *Memoirs*, 3:8, 10; Churchill to the king, HMC, 9th Report, *Northumberland* Ms., 3:97–99; Ward, *Albemarle*, 195–208; Albemarle [to Sunderland], June 18, 1685, HMC,
Stopford-Sackville Ms., 2–3; Wolsey, *Marlborough*, 1: 290.

29. See also Davis, *Second, Queen's*, 2: 46 and, on Taunton's "mutinous" temper, the king to lord Paulet and deputy lieutenants of Somerset, Oct. 3 [1662],
S.P. 44/3, 94; Sunderland to the mayor of Taunton, June 4, 1685, S.P. 44/56,
204. Harleian Ms. 6845, 167, 176, 182; Davis, *Second, Queen's*, 2: 15–17, 22, 46;
Coxe, *Memoirs*, 1: 31; Atkinson, *Royal Dragoons*, 40; Wolsey, *Marlborough*, 1:
294; Routh, ed., *Burnet's History*, 2: 372, 412n; J. N. P. Watson, *Captain-General and Rebel Chief, The Life of James, Duke of Monmouth* (London, 1979), 153–
54; Clifton, *Last Popular Rebellion*, 139, 140, 156, 160, 166, 168; Little,
Monmouth, 33, 59–60, 65, 78; S. P. 44/3, 63–64; David Chandler, *Sedgemoor*
(New York, 1985), 19–22.

30. Atkinson, *Royal Dragoons*, 40, but see Wingfield, *Monmouth Rebellion*, 42;
Add. Ms. 31596, 1–3, partly printed in Davis, *Second, Queen's*, 2: 46; Lediard,
Marlborough, 1:51. Wade's Information, Oct. 4, 1685, Harleian Ms. 6845, 272;
Chandler, *Sedgemoor*, 22–24, 25, 27, 119–20. Albemarle was condemned as a
traitor by "King James's" proclamation, but offered pardon if he submitted.

The duke denounced both proclamation and pardon: Clifton, *Last Popular Rebellion*, 169. It had been announced to Albemarle et al. that Piercy Kirke would command (S.P. 44/56, 212), but the next day (June 14) Churchill was named instead (*ibid.*, 216) and Churchill's commission as brigadier finally appeared June 19, 1685, S.P. 44/164, 203; S.P. 44/69, 139; Davis, *Second, Queen's*, 2: 17ff.; S.P. 44/56, 259; S.P. 44/164, 209; Add. Ms. 31596, 3. Note that the royal navy arrived off Lyme on June 20, took two rebel vessels with arms for four to five thousand men, and cut off Monmouth's retreat, Add. Ms. 31596 (III, 26), 3. On the 10th, see Richard Cannon, *Historical Record of the Tenth* ... (London, 1847), Albert Lee, *The History of the Tenth Foot* (London, 1911), and note that its first ensigns included Thomas Treffry, promoted lieutenant to Andros's independent company and major of the Boston Regiment. See below, chapter five.

31. HMC, *Stopford-Sackville Ms.*, 1: 3; Davis, *Second, Queen's*, 2: 21; Blathwayt's impression of the Scots is in his letter to Albemarle, July 4, 1685, W.O. 4/1, 9–10, and see same to Effingham, July 8, 1685, CWWB, 14 #4; *London Gazette*, #2044, June 18–22, 1685; Davis, *Second, Queen's*, 2: 23; Churchill to Somerset, Chard, June 21, 1685, HMC, *Northumberland Ms.* 97. Earle, *Monmouth's Rebels*, 88, 111 gives both the high (7,000) and low (5,000) estimates of Monmouth's numbers, but Clifton, *Last Popular Rebellion*, 246, uses the "Constables' List" of those out in rebellion to arrive at a figure of about 3,000 rebels, most of whom were recruited from artisans in the towns along Monmouth's line of advance from Lyme Regis to Taunton, (*ibid.*, 248, 252), recruiting elsewhere being prevented by the militia (*ibid.*, 249). Kirke's five companies, nominally 500 strong, were also under Churchill's command. *CSPD 1685*, 210 219 206, 237, 197ff.

32. Dummer's Journal, June 22, 23, Add. Ms. 31956 (III, 26), 3–4; Lediard, *Marlborough*, 1: 51–52; Little, *Monmouth*, 31–32, 126–27, 135; Earle, *Monmouth's Rebels*, 93; Henry Shere to Dartmouth, July 1, 1685, HMC, *Dartmouth Ms.*, 1:126.

33. Add. Ms. 31956 (III, 26), 3; Harleian Ms. 6845, 278.

34. Chandler, *Sedgemoor*, 29–30, 102. Taylor, *Marlborough*, 2: 425. There is disagreement as to whether King James's order to the indecisive lords lieutenant and the dilatory Feversham to destroy the bridge at Keynsham was obeyed. Again, Earle has both versions, unreconciled: *Monmouth's Rebels*, 94, 96. Clifton, *Last Popular Rebellion*, 181, contradicts *ibid.*, 194, on the bridge question. Monmouth's fatal expectation is discussed by *ibid.*, 152, 169–70, 181. Add. Ms. 31956, III. 26, 2–4; HMC, *Northumberland Ms.*, 2. Sir Almerick Fitzroy, *Henry Duke of Grafton 1663–1690* (London, 1921), 28, relying on a Ms. from Drayton House, says Monmouth took the bridge, but did not cross because of attacks by Oglethorpe's and Churchill's cavalry. Monmouth's council of war is quoted from Wade's Further Information, 11 Oct. 1685, Harleian Ms. 6845, 279.

35. Clifton, *Last Popular Rebellion*, 129; Effingham to Blathwayt, Nov. 14, 1685, T. 64/88, 95b; same, Feb. 6, 1685/6, Blathwayt Papers, 14 #4. *CSPC 1681–1685*, #461, and see #563, p. 151; *1685–1688*, #378, 533, 563, 591, 596, 863, 1898 xxiii, xxvi; Charles M. Andrews, *The Colonial Period of American History* (New Haven, 1934), 1: 246n.

36. Edward Randolph to Blathwayt, Nov. 16, 1685, CWWB, 4 #3; William

Dyre to same, 9br 16, 1685, *ibid.*, 4 #2. For the rumors in New York, see John
Sprague to same, Oct. 3, 1685, *ibid.*, 10 #3, and, on the "damnable reports from
Boston & New England," see Dongan to same, Sept. 18, 1685, *ibid.*, 11 #1, and
see same to the lord president, Sept. 18, 1685, O'Callaghan, ed., *NYCD*, 3 364.
See *ibid.*, 391 on fortifications against civil unrest. See also S.P. 44/164, 214.
37. *CSPC 1685–1688*, #183 I, 246, 253, 378, 382.
38. Sunderland to Churchill, June 17, 19, 1685, S.P. 44/56, 224, 228–29, 232;
S.P. 44/164, 214, 263; Davis, *Second, Queen's*, 2:21; Lediard, *Marlborough*, 1: 53;
Sunderland to the mayor and aldermen of Bristol, Dec. 9, 1684, S.P. 44/56, 149
and see S.P. 44/68, 113; Beaufort to Clarendon, Bristol, June 19, 1685, Singer,
ed., *Clarendon Correspondence* 1: 132. Dummer, Add. Ms. 31956, 4, has Feversham joining Beaumont in Bristol on June 24.
39. *Ibid.*, June 24, 26, p. 4–5; Lediard, *Marlborough*, 1:52–53; Wolsey, *Marlborough*, 1: 297–99; HMC, *Stopford-Sackville Ms.*, 2; Fitzroy, *Grafton*, 28–29;
Oglethorpe's capacity and conduct is much criticized by Taylor, *Marlborough*,
2: 428, and Wolsey, but see Clifton, *Last Popular Rebellion*, who concludes, 184,
that "Monmouth was defeated at Keynsham not by his own mistakes, but by a
modern standing army's speed of deployment, which, as much as its superior
fighting skills, was making military victory impossible for popular revolts by the
later seventeenth century. The duke was defeated, too, by the strategic grasp of
James II, who saw, more clearly than his commander in the field, that Bristol
was the key and rushed troops up to defend it." Chandler, *Sedgemoor*, 30–31,
and the rebel account printed in *ibid.*, 121–23. Wingfield, *Monmouth Rebellion*,
49–51.
40. Dummer's Journal, Je. 26, 1685, Add. Ms. 31956, 5; Wade's Information,
Harleian Ms., 6845, 279; Hamilton, *First Guards*; S.P. 44/164, 145, 146; James
to William, June 19, 1685, Dalrymple, ed., *Memoirs*, 2:10; *ibid.* (2d ed., London,
1773), 2: 130; S.P. 44/69, 143–44.
41. Barrillon to Louis XIV, Je. 16, 1685, *Translation*, 103, 108; Sunderland to
Churchill, same to lords lieutenant, June 19, 1685, S.P. 44/56, 230, 232;
Churchill to Clarendon, July 4, 1685, Singer, ed., *Clarendon Correspondence*, 1:
141; James to William, June 23, 1685, Dalrymple, ed., *Memoirs*, 3: 11; *ibid.* (2d
ed., London, 1773), 2: 130–31; Add. Ms. 31956, 5. John Coad, *A Memorandum
of the Wonderful Providences of God . . .* (London, 1849), 5. For James's devotion
to Feversham and on the source of Feversham's slowness, see James to William,
Jan. 28, [1678/9,] HMC, *Foljambe Ms.*, 128. And see Clifton, *Last Popular Rebellion*, 185. The governor-general of *Africa Nova*, Gaius Sallustins Crispus, is
quoted from the translation of *The Jugurthine War* by S. A. Handford (Baltimore, 1963), 118.
42. Add. Ms. 31596, 5, June 27, 1685; Harleian Ms., 6845, 279–80; Feversham
to James, June 28, 1685, HMC, *Stopford-Sackville Ms.*, 7–8; Feversham's march
is recorded in *ibid.*, 14–15; Davis, *Second, Queen's*, 2: 26–27; S.P. 44/164, 238.
Blathwayt to Albemarle, July 4, 1685, W.O. 4/1, 5–6; Churchill [to Clarendon,]
July 4, 1685, Singer, ed., *Clarendon Correspondence*, 1: 146; Wolsey, *Marlborough*, 1:306; Fitzroy, *Grafton*, 30–35. On Matthews, see Phineas Pett to Hy.
Gasgoine, July 1, 1685, G. Davies, ed., "Three Letters on Monmouth's Rebel-

lion, 1685," *EHR* 35 (1920), 114. The fullest details, and helpful maps, are in Chandler, *Sedgemoor*, 32–37, and see Wingfield, *Monmouth Rebellion*, 52–56.

43. Sheres to Dartmouth, June 30, July 1, 1685, HMC, *Dartmouth Ms.*, 1: 126; Davis, *Second, Queens*, 2: 28; John to Sarah, June 30, 1685, in Churchill, *Marlborough*, 1: 197. See also S.P. 44/164, 121; Dalton, ed., *Army Lists*, 1: 323.

44. Account of Monmouth's officer, printed, Chandler, *Sedgemoor*, 125; Dongan's Report, *NYCD*, 3: 408; Wade's Further Information, Harleian Ms., 6845, 280, 290, in Blathwayt's hand.

45. Add. Ms. 31596, 7, July 5, 1685; "The King's Account of the Battle of Sedgemoor," printed Chandler, *Sedgemoor*, 111, gives the royal forces as 1,800 foot and 700 horse and dragoons. Wolsey, *Marlborough*, 1: 318–19; HMC, *Stopford-Sackville Ms.*, 1: 12, 16, 19; *London Gazette*, #2048, #2049, July 6, 7, 1685; Lediard, *Marlborough*, 1:54; Davis, *Second, Queen's*, 2: 46. James to William, July 7, 1685, Dalrymple, ed., *Memoirs*, 3: 14, *ibid.* (2d ed., London, 1773), 133–34, estimated his force as 2,000 foot in 6 battalions; 700 horse and dragoons, and 18 small field guns. The rebels may have numbered more than 7,000 at Bridgewater; Fitzroy, *Grafton*, 36; Chandler, *Sedgemoor*, 52, and see 108.

46. *Ibid.*, 60–63; Dummer's Journal, July 5, 6, 1685, Add. Ms. 31956 (III, 26), 7–8, Davis, *Second, Queen's*, 2: 48; Arthur, *Household Cavalry*, 1: 190;. Earle, *Monmouth's Rebels*, 107, quotes Churchill's estimate and, 124–25, gives the strength of Monmouth's attack as about 4,500 men. Clifton, *Last Popular Rebellion*, despite his estimate that Monmouth had only 3,000 men at his high point, has him bring 3,600 to this attack. Compare p. 246 with p. 209.

47. Andrew Paschall's and King James's accounts printed in Chandler, *Sedgemoor*, 109, 114; The rebel horse may have passed the Scots' position claiming to be Albemarle's militia, but the Foot Guards fired on them. Harleian Ms., 6485, 292–93; *Two Illustrious Generals*, 17.

48. See also, Jeaffreson, ed., *Young Squire*, 2: 221–24, who states that there were few other officer casualties, and that the victory was owing to the rank and file of Dumbarton's and of the Guards. Lord George Hamilton, afterwards a leading member of Churchill's staff and governor-general of Virginia, had been commissioned a captain in his Uncle Dumbarton's regiment Feb. 11 previous, S.P. 44/164, 119; S.P. 44/69, 143. Feversham's casualty estimates are in: HMC, *Stopford-Sackville Ms.*, 1: 21; Chandler, *Marlborough*, 19; Earle, *Monmouth's Rebels*, 125; Clifton, *Last Popular Rebellion*, 202; Paschall's account, and the king's, printed in Chandler, *Sedgemoor*, 110, 115.

49. For Monmouth's officers on leave from the Anglo-Dutch brigade, s.v. "Foulkes, John," "Fox, James," and "Venner, Samuel" in Childs, *Dictionary*. The best account from the rebel side is still Sir Arthur Conan Doyle, *Micah Clarke* (London, 1889). See Harleian Ms. 6485, 291; Chandler, *Sedgemoor*, 123; Wingfield, *Monmouth Rebellion*, 121; Atkinson, *Royal Dragoons*, 43; Dalton, ed., *Army Lists*, 2: 144; Childs, *Army of James II*, 125; Add. Ms. 31956, 8; Fitzroy, *Grafton*, 39. The official despatch, *London Gazette*, #2049, July 6–9, 1685, has Feversham fully informed of the rebel intent to attack, on the scene from the outset, and in complete command throughout.

50. *Ibid.* Most authorities have Churchill leading the cavalry charge in person. Atkinson, *Royal Dragoons*, 46, says "Churchill's charge on the rebel guns had been the decisive incident of the day." There is no evidence for this. It is unlikely that Churchill would have left his duties as general of the day, directing the whole defense. After moving the Tangerines to the right of the line, Churchill did order a cavalry charge and he did lead the infantry assault, King James's Account, Harleian Ms. 6845, 295, printed in Chandler, *Sedgemoor*, 116; Add. Ms. 31956, 8–9, July 6, 1685. See also, Arthur, *Household Cavalry*, 1: 191; Geo. Roberts, *Life of Monmouth* (London, 1844), 2: 83. See HMC, *9th Report*, p. 18, and Clifton's interpretation of it (*Last Popular Rebellion*, 218) for Churchill's control of the battle, and Pett's Account, at 7 a.m. on July 6, 1685, Davies, ed., "Three Letters," *EHR* 35: 115.

51. "Feversham's March," HMC, *Stopford-Sackville Ms.*, 1: 17, brings Feversham to the battle in command of the cavalry just after Monmouth's arrival, say 3 a.m., but see Wolsey, *Marlborough*, 1: 332, and Chandler, *Marlborough*, 20. See Childs, *Dictionary*, on Feversham, and see Chandler, *Sedgemoor*, 66, which has him on the scene at 3: 35. Colonel Kirke had also slept away from the camp, at the vicarage in Weston Zoyland, *ibid.*, 108. Churchill's challenge to the fallen Holmes is in Harleian Ms. 6845, 294–95. Much of the confusion about the royalist command at Sedgemoor stems from its division between Churchill, who commanded the dragoons, infantry, and artillery, and encamped with them, and Feversham who, as senior officer, commanded the cavalry and quartered with them in Weston. Until daybreak, Feversham limited his orders to the cavalry. On the pursuit and the killing, see Henry Elliott Malden, ed., *Iter Bellicosum Adam Wheeler: His Account of 1685*, Camden Miscellany, XII (London, 1910), 157 (who gives 1,384 rebels killed on the battlefield, "besides many more they did believe lay dead in the Corne," *ibid.*, 164); Harleian Ms. 6845, 281; Wolsey, *Marlborough*, 1: 336; Sir James Mackintosh, *History Of The Revolution In England In 1688* (London, 1834), 13. *EHD* 8: #306. Routh, ed., *Burnet's History*, 3: 51, gives round numbers: 1,000 rebel casualties, 1,500 prisoners. Feversham's despatch by Oglethorpe estimated 1,500 rebels killed, 200 captured, Fitzroy, *Grafton*, 39. Chandler, *Sedgemoor*, 71, gives the royalist casualties as 80 killed, 220 wounded; the rebels as 1,000 killed and 500 captured, but, on p. 173, has 1,400 rebels killed. For variant estimates, see Webb, "Brave Men," *Perspectives*, 8: 78–79. S.P. 44/56, 260 officially acknowledged the massacre. The promotions of the wounded royalists are listed in *ibid.*, 44/164, 252, and see note 55, below.

52. *Persecution Expos'd in Some Memoirs Relating to the Sufferings of John Whiting, and Many Others of the People called Quakers* . . . (London, 1715), 143–44.

53. Davies, ed., "Three Letters," *EHR* 35: 115, 116; Wheeler, *Camden Misc.*, 12: 165 reported that, at Glastonbury, six prisoners were hanged on the signpost of the White Hart, "who after as they hung were stripped naked, and so left hanging there all night" and for days afterward. Taylor, *Marlborough*, 2: 427; Lediard, *Marlborough*, 1: 56; Wolsey, *Marlborough*, 1: 342. The King's Account, Harleian Ms., 6845, 294, while noting that, in a night action, it was hard to allocate credit, gives it all to Feversham. For Buckingham's "The Battle of

Sedgemoor: A Farce," see Ward, *Albemarle*, 213. HMC, *Stopford-Sackville Ms.*,
19; Dummer's Journal for July 11, 1685, Add. Ms. 31956 (III, 26), 9, sends
Churchill up to London with Feversham and Grafton, and consigns the western command to Sackville of the Guards (afterwards Churchill's conduit to St.
Germain), but the author was with the artillery, which by then had separated
from the army to return to the Tower via Portsmouth. The London newslet-
ters gave full credit for the victory to Churchill and, under him, to Grafton,
whose biographer (Fitzroy, 42), sees them linked for life from this moment.
Arthur, *Household Cavalry*, 1: 194–95; James to William, July 10, 1685, Dalrymple, ed., *Memoirs*, 3: 15; *ibid*. (2d ed., London, 1773), 2:134. On Feversham's
eclipse, see Routh, ed., *Burnet's History*, 3: 49n–50.

54. Mackintosh, *The Revolution*, 17, 22, 23; Jeffreys to James, Taunton, Sept.
19, same to Sunderland, Bristol, Sept. 22, 1685, *ibid*., Appendix, 686–88; *CSPD
1685*, 332–33, #1644. Little, *Monmouth*, 221, gives the total number of executions as "perhaps 230." Coad, *Wonderful Providences*, 14, has 600 men condemned in a single lot. The best informed account is Chandler's *Sedgemoor*,
Appendix C, on Jeffreys's sentences, and miscellaneous executions. Chandler
counts 324 persons condemned to be executed at fifty-two sites. The descrip-
tion is Whiting's *Persecution Expos'd*, 144. Macaulay's figure of 320 (*History*, 1:
645) is supported by E. S. DeBeer, "Executions Following the 'Bloody Assize',"
BIHR, 4 (1926), 369. Roberts, *Monmouth*, 218, 242, 262–66, totals 331 executed, 849 transported, 33 fined or whipped.

55. S.P. 44/164, 246, 255, 257, 276. Jeaffreson, ed., *Young Squire*, 223–24, reported this to the Leeward Islands. Feversham and Churchill were promoted
major general, Sackville and Kirke brigadiers general; William Matthew was
comissioned captain of grenadiers in the First Guards; and E. Rouse promoted
captain, Dalton, ed., *Army Lists*, 2: 50, 52, 53. Geiter and Speck, eds., *Reresby*,
390. Sunderland to Albemarle, June 27, July 14, 1685, S.P. 44/56, 246, 258;
same to the lords committees of trade and plantations, May 31, 1686, *ibid*., 337;
Dummer's Journal, June 26, 28, 29, July 1, Add. Ms. 31596, Davis, *Second*,
Queen's, 47–48. Narcissus Luttrell, *A Brief Historical Relation of State Affairs from
September 1678 to April 1714* (Oxford, 1857; Farnborough, 1969), Sept. 7, 1685,
April 14, 1686, 1: 356, 374. The governor-generalship of Jamaica became open
on the death of Sir Philip Howard. He had exchanged a troop of the Life
Guards for the reversion to this colonial command in November 1680, Add.
Ms. 29577, 299. Albemarle had been an unusually negligent colonel. James II's
personal drill of the Life Guards found him out: Ward, *Albemarle*, 187; Arthur,
Household Cavalry, 1:198–99. When, after delaying almost two years (S.P. 44/
56, 337, 381), Albemarle reached his government, he made his Life Guards
quartermaster, Sir Francis Watson, his chief aide, *ibid*., 44/29, 273; S.P. 44/56,
335, 381–82; William Chapman to Blathwayt, Jan. 4, 1687/8, CWWB, 22 #1.
Webb, *Governors-General*, see index s.v. "Watson"; Arthur, *Household Cavalry*,
1: 49. Long a Jamaica agent in London, occasionally an officer in the island's
military administration, and a candidate for the New England command, Watson succeeded Albemarle in command of Jamaica, and tried to set up for himself in 1688–89. See chapter five below and Ward, *Albemarle*, 216–25, 233–43,

257–58 and on the treasure hunting syndicate with Phips, Nicholson etc., see also Thompson, ed., *Hatton Correspondence*, 2: 67–68; S.P. 44/56, 395, 427; T. 64/88, 126b–127b; Cyrus H. Kanacker, "Spanish Treasure," *JMH* 5 (1933): 305–307, and the Appendix, "Inglorious Revolution: The Channel Fleet in 1688." Turner, *James II*, 284–85n (as does Charles Chenevix Trench, *The Western Rising* (London, 1969), 262), sees Albemarle's resignation as "the first open defection from James," the warning to Protestant officers of the danger to their careers; but see, Webb, "Brave Men," *Perspectives*, 8: 75n. Certainly, Clarendon had warned Churchill that he was a marked man. In reply, Churchill wrote that, "as for my obedience, I am sure Mr. Oglethorp is not more dutyfull than I am," Singer, ed., *Clarendon Correspondence*, 1: 141. On the system of these promotions, see Rochester to Clarendon, Aug. 1, 1685, *ibid.*, 149. On Albemarle's military misjudgments and maladministrations, see Clifton, *Last Popular Rebellion*, 192–93, 289. On Churchill's unease, see *Two Illustrious Generals*, 18.

56. Russell's new troop escorted Monmouth to London for execution. Francis Turner was assigned to prepare him for death. Five strokes of the bumbling executioner's axe were required to sever Monmouth's head, and Jeaffreson, ed. *Young Squire*, 2: 207–11, reported to his Leeward Islands correspondents that knife work was required to sever the head completely. Atkinson, *Royal Dragoons*, 47; Blathwayt to Cornbury, Jan. 1, 1685[/6], W.O. 4/1, 26; same to Bath and Albemarle, July 17, 1686, *ibid.*, 34. Blathwayt to Shackerley, Nov. 28, 1685, W.O. 4/23. Contrast this punitive assignment with Sunderland's official indignation at the infantry's behavior in Wiggan, S.P. 44/56, 291–93. The ensuing court martial gave Edward Nott his step to major in the marines. See Robert J. Jones, *A History of the 15th (East Yorkshire) Regiment (The Duke of York's Own) 1685 to 1914* (Beverley, 1958), 10–11, 12. On quartering, see also S.P. 44/56, 304, 306; Blathwayt to Heyford, Sept. 15, 1688, W.O. 4/1, 99 and, on Cornbury's dragoons, Sunderland to Cornbury, Dec. 3, 1685, S.P. 44/56, 303, and same to j.p.s of Devonshire, *ibid.*, 313; Blathwayt to Cornbury, Jan. 13 1685[/6] and same to Bath and Albemarle, Jan. 13, 1685[/6], W.O. 4/1, 26, 34; Sunderland to Bath and Albemarle, Jan. 16, 1685, deploring the excesses of Cornbury's dragoons, S.P. 44/56, 316–17; Webb, "Brave Men," *Perspectives*, 8: 77n. The whig comment is Routh, ed., *Burnet's History*, 3: 58, and the tory one is Littleton's, to Hatton, from Taunton, Oct. 7, 1685, Add. Ms. 29578, 67; see also *ibid.*, 82. Cornbury was a notorious abuser of false musters, W.O. 4/1, 53; Childs, *Army of James II*, 50. On renewed repression and rebel bands, see S.P. 44/56, 306, 310, 319, 326; S. P. 44/69, 172; HMC, *Downshire Ms.*, 1: part 1: 69, 70, 109, 131, 134; Atkinson, *Royal Dragoons*, 50–51.

57. Sunderland to Kirke, July 14, 25, 28, 1685, SP 44/56, 260, 266, 268; Luttrell, *Brief Relation*, July 15, 1685, 1:354; Routh, ed., *Burnet's History*, 3: 58–59; Blathwayt to Kirke, July 21, 1685, W.O. 4/1, 12–13; Littleton to Hatton, Aug. 11, 1685, Add. Ms. 29578, 62–63. Earle, *Monmouth's Rebels*, 138–40, has a variant interpretation of Kirke's behavior, and see Chandler, *Sedgemoor*, 74. Jeaffreson, ed., *Young Squire*, 2: 159–60, 302, reflects the intense interest provincials took in this extension of garrison government.

58. The contortions of New England opinion are given by Dyre to Blathwayt, 16 9br 1685, CWWB, 4 #2. Andros's commission was dated July 30, 1685, S. P. 44/164, 250, and see 347. The intended shape of garrison government in Massachusetts, and an informed recollection of the colony's origins as a military plantation, appear in the order to Dartmouth to supply Edward Randolph with royal flags for Boston castle and fort, and for forts at Piscataqua, Salem, and Charlestown (Cambridge), *ibid.*, 272, and see 357–61. Andros's military establishment is authorized in part (two companies of infantry, surgeon, armorer, and chaplain) in T. 64/88, 103.

59. Wm. Dyre to Simon Bradstreet, May 15, 1684/5, CWWB, 4 #2.

60. Childs, *Army of James II*, 88; Jeffreys to James II, Taunton, Sept. 19, 1685, in Mackintosh, *History of the Revolution*, Appendix, 686–88; Littleton to Hatton, At Taunton, Oct. 7, 1685, Thompson, ed., *Hatton Correspondence*, 2: 60, Add. Ms. 29578, 67, 69; Singer, ed., *Clarendon Correspondence* 1: 159–60. [Sprat,] *Account and Declaration*, 19; James to William, Sept. 10, 1685, Dalrymple, ed., *Memoirs*, 3: 56, *ibid.*, (2d ed. London 1773), 2: 165. See note 54, above. Chandler, *Sedgemoor*, App. C, gives Jeffreys's sentences for 849 transportations. The largest single consignment was 200 to Sir Philip Howard, governor-general designate of Jamaica (33 escaped en route to embarkation). Stapleton received 100 for his Leeward Islands, but Barbados, as the wealthiest colony, took 423 of Monmouth's men. They, with former Cromwellian soldiers and subsequent Highland transportees, formed a distinct community, the "Redlegs," which still survives: Wingfield, *Monmouth Rebellion*, 87, 90–91, 94, 102–104; Jill Shepherd, "Redlegs—Myth and Reality," *The West Indies Chronicle*, 89 (1974): 144–45. Of the condemned, 750 lived to reach the New World. Their shipment covered substantial kidnapping, *CSPC 1685–1688*, #380, 381, 402, 403, 418, 420–24, 441, 442, 540, 561–62, 610, 768, 2,114, 2,121, 2,124, 2,125.

61. See also: Sunderland to [Jeffreys,] Windsor, Sept. 15, 1685, in Mackintosh, *The Revolution*, Appendix, 686–87; Sunderland to [Jeffreys]; Sept. 14, 1685, S.P. 44/56, 284–85. The search for rebel convicts' labor can be most easily followed in Jeaffreson, ed., *Young Squire*, 2: 9, 16, 42–44, 58, 61, 73, 124, 162–64, 170, 195–97, 224, and see Howard of Effingham to Blathwayt, Feb. 6, 1685/6, CWWB, 14 #4; Webb, "Brave Men," *Perspectives*, 8: 79n; Little, *Monmouth*, 224–48; Coad, *Wonderful Providences, CSPD 1685*, 329. William Penn to James Harrison, Oct. 25, 1685, Mary Maples Dunn and Richard S. Dunn, eds., *The Papers of William Penn* (Philadelphia, 1981-), 3:65–67. Vincent Buranelli, "William Penn and James II," APS *Proceedings* 104 (1960), 38–39, cites this to demonstrate that "Penn convinced James that some of the penalties imposed by Jeffreys were exorbitant," rather than that Penn sought to profit from them.

62. "A Relation of the Great Sufferings and Strange Adventures of Henry Pitman, Chirgeuon to the late Duke of Monmouth, 13 Je 1689," C. H. Firth, ed., *An English Garner: Stuart Tracts 1603–1693* (Westminster, 1903), 436; William Orne, ed., *Remarkable Passages in the Life of William Kiffen . . .* (London, 1823), 147, rewritten by Macaulay, *History*, 1: 317; Ducket, ed., *Penal Laws*, 136; Wingfield, *Monmouth Rebellion*, 92, etc. Jeffreys to James II, Sept. 19, 1685,

CSPD 1685, 332–33, #1644. See Clifton, *Last Popular Rebellion*, 238–39, on King James's insistence on a second and increased round of executions.

63. Dalton, ed., *Army Lists*, 2: 5–9, 11–12, 28–36; C. T. Atkinson, "James II and His Army . . . ," *JSAHR*, 14 (1935): 1–11; Arthur, *Household Cavalry*, 1: 200; Van Citters to the states general, July 18/28, Add. Ms. 32512, 23–24, and see Van Citters to the states general, May 28/June 7, 1686, *ibid.*, 34; HMC, *Dartmouth Ms.*, 1: 171, gives 34,320 English, 2,981 Scots, and 2,816 Irish soldiers in England on Oct. 26, 1688, a total of 40,117, confirming Secretary Blathwayt's figure.

64. Jeaffreson, ed., *Young Squire*, 2: 223; Turner, *James II*, 284–85n; Dalton, ed., *Army Lists*, 2: 9.

65. Webb, *Govenors-General*, #9, 30, 55, 155, 158. The sale of Andros's lieutenant colonelcy and troop are detailed in his letter to Blathwayt, "Re'd 18 Oct 1686," from the *Kingfisher* en route to Boston. All the habiliments and accounts of a typical troop are given here: clothing contracts, quarters allowances, subsistence payments, musters, colors. Blathwayt settled this account with Andros in May 1687, CWWB, 3 #3. See also W.O. 4/1, 38, and note that Churchill's subordinate and associate Langston succeeded Andros.

66. Webb, *Governors-General*, #88. Memls. of Capt. Tho. Fowk to Marlborough [1705], Add. Ms. 61287, 163, 165. The only other imperial officer who rose to American command from one of James II's new regiments was Richard Brewer, an officer in the regiment raised by the Catholic colonel Sir Edward Hales. Hales's collusive case, the colonel's religion, and the dispersion of its companies to the garrisons, all retarded the regiment's formation, Add. Ms. 29561, 223, 276, 305; *ibid.* 29563, 129; *ibid.* 29578, 108. Perhaps these impediments reflected the resistance of the older, Protestant, establishment to this avowedly Catholic corps. In the summer of 1685, as part of the army's expansion and reorganization, the regiments of the line (i.e., not the household troops), were assigned a rank independent of the seniority of their colonels: Singer, ed., *Clarendon Correspondence*, 1: 156; H. M. order, Aug. 3, 1685, Add. Ms. 38694, 56–57a. Routh, ed., *Burnet's History*, 3: 97; *EHD* 8: 315; S.P. 44/69.

67. Jones, *15th*, 12: "on the 26th November [1685] . . . Lt. Col. James Cotter . . . was succeeded by Lt. Col. Rupert Billingsly of . . . the Irish Army, who had served with Lt. Col. Cotter in the West Indies as lieutenant of his company in the Barbados Regiment." For Billingsly's efforts to reunite the regiment in garrison at Yarmouth, see W.O. 4/1, 59. Supposedly the Barbados Regiment had purged its officer ranks of Roman Catholics in 1676 (see the petition of Capt. James Benett, Oct. 25, 1676, Blathwayt Papers, Huntington Library), and they dispersed to service in France, Tangier, and New York (s.v. "Roch, Maurice," in Childs, *Dictionary*). Robert John Jones, the regimental historian of the 15th was especially sensitive to the imperial regimental connection because he himself had enlisted in the 15th in Barbados in 1887. In twenty-one years of service, he saw action in South Africa, Egypt, India, and Burma. Retiring as the senior sergeant of the 15th, he was as much a centurion of the second British Empire as the founders of the 15th had been of the first. On the Nottingham tradition, see Webb, *Governors-General*, 24–31, and on Rupert's example, Webb, *1676*, fol. 196, pp. 324–25.

68. Childs, *Dictionary*, 78, has Cotter as a Roman Catholic, even after the purge. Jones, *15th*, 17n.2; Webb, *Governors-General*, 487–88; C.S.S. Higham, *The Development of the Leeward Islands under the Restoration, 1660–1688* . . . (Cambridge, 1921), 219. The leave given Captain Thomas Foulke to go to the West Indies on private business after Sedgemoor reinforces the evidence that he was a property owner in Antigua before he was commissioned as the island's lieutenant governor, S.P. 44/164, 392. For another governor-general's plans for a family plantation, see Add. Ms. 29577, 549b.

69. Jeaffreson, ed., *Young Squire*, 1: 212. For the Roman principles, as they were understood in 1677, see Orrery, *Art of War*, 14. For examples prior to that date, see Webb, *Governors-General*, and Webb, *1676*, s.v. the colony in question. For Russell's regiment and Barbados society, see Capt. Jos. Crispe to Blathwayt, Rec'd Aug. 3, 1697, CWWB 39 #1.

70. Add. Ms. 28103, 68; Atkinson, "James II and His Army," *JSAHR* 14: 7; Jones, *15th*., 6–8.

71. Barrillon to Louis XIV, Nov. 5, 9, 1685, *Translation*, 129, 132.

72. Four of the new regiments' first colonels were Catholic. On the issue of Catholic officers, see John Miller, "Catholic Officers," *EHR* 88 (1973): 40 (where he makes the number eighty-five), 42, 45, 46; Childs, *Army of James II*, 2; *The Several Debates Of The House of Commons Pro & Contra Relating to the Establishment of the Militia, Disbanding the New Raised Forces, and raising a Present Supply for His Majesty* (London, 1686) was published as a pamphlet and pp. 4 and 5 are quoted here. See *EHD* 8: #14; HMC, *Downshire Ms.*, I: 78; Jeaffreson, ed., *Young Squire*, 2: 281–82, 285, 294–95; Routh, ed., *Burnet's History*, 3: 88.

73. *The Several Debates*, 6, 13, 20. Blathwayt was the government spokesman. He insisted that martial law, free quarter, and plunder all had ceased by the king's order, that soldiers abusing subjects would be punished, and that the amount of money sought by the government for the army was far too small if England was to stand with the European powers, *ibid.*, 20–21, 22.

74. Sir T[homas] C[larges,] in *The Several Debates*, 9, also defended Albemarle's conduct; Ward, *Albemarle*, 23, 63, 76, 227. Routh, ed., *Burnet's History*, 3: 69, 79, 88; Geiter and Speck, eds., *Reresby*, 400. See also Barrillon au Roy, July 30, 1686, Dalrymple, ed., *Memoirs*, 3: 62; Jeaffreson to Hill, June 4, 1686, Jeaffreson, ed., *Young Squire*, 2: 294–95.

75. *The Several Debates*, 22–23; Barrillon to Louis XIV, Nov. 26, 1685, *Translation*, 137; Jeaffreson to Col. Hill, Dec. 9, 1685, Jeaffreson, ed., *Young Squire*, 2: 244; Miller, *James II*, 147; HMC, *Leybourne-Popham Ms.*, 263. The new imposts damaged trade especially in the dominion of New England, as Andros complained to Blathwayt, Aug. 12, 1687, CWWB, 3 #3.

76. Routh, ed., *Burnet's History*, 3: 92n, and note 63, above; Dalton, ed., *Army Lists*, 2: 21; Webb, *Governors-General*, Appendix #8; S.P. 44/164, 47. Geiter and Speck, eds., *Reresby*, 402–403, lists the ousted officers, beginning with the paymaster of the army, 3 Berties (Danby's clients, all with extensive Barbadian interests), all captains of horse, and three infantry officers, plus Kendall.

77. Routh, ed., *Burnet's History*, 3: 69, 71–72, 90–91; Luttrell, *Brief Relation*, 1: 368, Dec. 18, 1685; Carpenter, *Protestant Bishop*, esp. 256–57. Reresby ascribed Compton's disgrace to "his being industrious to preserve the Princess Anne of Denmarke in the Protestant religion," Geiter and Speck, eds., *Reresby*, 405. Turner, *James II*, 294–95, 297; Feiling, *Tory Party*, 209–12. Halifax's memo, Add. Ms. 51511, 44, has Sunderland elevating Feversham's troop to the lords. The anecdote is suspect, but Churchill led the list of the "Queen's Friends" organized by Sunderland, Geiter and Speck, eds., *Reresby*, 401.

78. *Ibid.*, 406–408; Barrillon au Roi, March 26, 1685 Dalrymple, *Memoirs*, 2: (2d ed., London, 1773), 141–52. T. B. Howell, comp., *A Complete Collection of State Trials*, XI, A.D. 1680–1688 (London, 1811), 510–600. The full number of thirty-three triers did not appear, the dukes of Ormonde and Albemarle being in command overseas. All were officeholders. To no avail, Delamere pled his right to be tried before the whole house, *ibid.*, 520–21; Luttrell, *Brief Relation*, 1: 369, Jan. 13, 1685/6. Routh, ed., *Burnet's History*, 3: 95–96; Atkinson, *Marlborough*, 84. A much different view of the Delamere trial is given by the loyalist Thomas Bruce, *The Memoirs of Thomas Bruce, earl of Ailesbury* (Westminster, 1890), 134–35: that James knew the evidence would not stand up, and anticipated the not-guilty verdict as an example of his justice. Ailesbury has the first vote being cast by Ormonde's brother, Lord Butler of Weston.

79. James to [Legge,] Edinburgh, Jan. 26, 1679/80, HMC, *Dartmouth Ms.*, 1: 48; Luttrell, *Brief Relation*, 1: 367, Dec. 13, 1685; Littleton to Hatton, Mar. 12, 22, 1686, Add. Ms. 29578, 93, 95, and Thompson, ed., *Hatton Correspondence*, 2: 61; HMC, *Downshire Ms.*, 1: 78–79, 166, 173; Littleton to Hatton, Mar. 27, 1686, Add. Ms. 29578, 97, 102; Dalton, ed., *Army Lists*, 2: 29; Routh, ed., *Burnet's History*, 3: 68–69, 93; Miller, "Catholic Officers," *EHR*, 88: 40, 47, 49, and see Childs, *Army of James II*, 101.

80. Thomas Windsor, earl of Plymouth, to Sir William Trumbull, Hounslow Camp, June 24, 1686, HMC, *Downshire Ms.*, 1:187. Note the hostility to the introduction of Roman Catholic privy councilors that Princess Anne expressed to lord Churchill, Coxe, *Memoirs*, 1: 33. The privy council stood between the king and the generals in the garrison government's chain of command, S.P. 44/164, 8.

81. Van Citters to the states general, June 1/11, 1686, Add. Ms. 31512, 36; Blathwayt to Effingham, Jan., 27, 1687, CWWB, 14, #5.

82. [Hare,] *Marlborough*, 12; Christopher Jeaffreson to Colonel Hill, London, Jan. 20, 1685/6; n.d.; June 4, Aug. 3, 1686, Jeaffreson, ed., *Young Squire*, 2: 260, 281, 294, 303; Christopher Jeaffreson to Capt. James Phips, Jan. 28, 1685/6, May 3, 1686, *ibid.*, 265–66; Christopher Jeaffreson to Major Crispe, Jan. 30, 1685/6, *ibid.*, 271; Routh, ed., *Burnet's History*, 3: 79–88. The tale was amplified in Anglican pulpits, Singer, ed., *Clarendon Correspondence* 1: 282. The chief of these diplomats was Churchill's friend Sir William Trumbull, whom he had persuaded the Hudson's Bay Company directors to wine and dine on the eve of Trumbull's departure for Paris, a preface to Sir William's presentation of the HBC protests against French aggression in the Americas, Rich, ed., *Letters Outward*, 154–55, 157–60.

83. R. H. Whitworth, "1685—James II, The Army and the Huguenots," *JSAHR*, 63(1985): 130; Ailesbury, *Memoirs*, 1: 130–31; Arthur, *Household Cavalry*, 1: 202; [Hare,] *Marlborough*, 12.

84. Not only the Guards' barracks (the former royal mews at Whitehall, the Savoy Palace, and Somerset House) but the enlarged barracks for the Tower garrison (in meeting houses seized from dissenters) belie the usual assertion that the English army had no barracks. S.P. 44/164, 301–17. In this connection, note also the purpose-built barracks in each of the new seaport citadels in England and America. Dalton, ed., *Army Lists*, 2: 89; W.O. 4/1, 7; [Cannon,] *Queen's Royal Regiment*, 18; Cowper, *King's Own*, 46; Dr. George Clarke, the advocate general of the army, in HMC, *Leybourne-Popham Ms.*, 265; Van Citters to the states general, June 1/11, 1686, Add. Ms. 31512, 37. As late as "11 xbr 1688," Sir Edward Scott, the (Catholic) deputy governor of Portsmouth, wrote Blathwayt for permission to execute martial law, Add. Ms. 38695, 101.

85. Cowper, *King's Own*, 44–49; Hamilton, *First Guards*, 1: 281–85; Ailesbury, *Memoirs*, I: 110, 121, 150.

86. Van Citters to the states general, June 1/11, 1686, Add. Ms. 31512, 35. Chapter Five, below. Ailesbury, *Memoirs*, 150; Routh, ed., *Burnet's History*, 3: 163.

87. *Ibid.*; Jeaffreson to Hill, June 4, 1686, Jeaffreson, ed., *Young Squire*, 2: 297–99; Terrisi is quoted in Turner, *James II*, 364; Cowper, *King's Own*, 28–29, 35.

88. Lediard, *Marlborough*, 1: 63–64; Hamilton, *First Guards*, 1: 286, dates this in November 1686, but the sentence was passed in June: HMC, *Downshire Ms.*, 1: 185. Miller, *Popery and Politics*, 256; Luttrell, *Brief Relation*, 1: 381–82, June 21, 1686. Samuel Johnson, "Address to All the English Protestants in the Army," *A Compleat Collections of Papers* (London, 1689).

89. Compton himself reported this to Effingham, Nov. 19, 1686, Effingham Papers, Library of Congress. Effingham deplored this degradation, Warren M. Billings, ed., *The Papers of Francis Howard, Baron Howard of Effingham 1643–1695* (Richmond, 1989), 274, 282. Jeaffreson to Hill, Aug. 3, Sept. 8, Jeaffreson, ed., *Young Squire*, 2: 303, 311–14; Jeaffreson to Crispe, Sept. 8, 1686, *ibid.*, 306; HMC, *Downshire Ms.*, 1: 185–86; Routh, ed., *Burnet's History*, 3: 107–12; Arthur, *Household Cavalry*, 1:205; Van Citters to the states general, Sept. 7/17, 1686, Add. Ms. 31512, 51. Compton was silenced, but not deprived and, in the coming year, he led his clergy to "carry on their opposition to popery by wch. they have raised a spirit against it all over the Nation," Add. Ms. 34515, 37–38. For Compton's removal from ecclesiastical authority in America by King James, see also *NYCD* 3: 368, 372, and, for his restoration by King William, *ibid.*, 688.

90. Jeaffreson, ed., *Young Squire*, 2: 269–66; J. D. Davies, *Gentlemen and Tarpaulins, The Officers and Men of the Restoration Navy* (Oxford, 1991), 201; Turner, *James II*, 382–87; Routh, ed., *Burnet's History*, 3: 72, 118, 119–120n, 459–61; Sir Charles Petrie, *The Great Tyrconnel* (Cork, 1972), 143–55; Miller, *James II*, 216–19; J. G. Simms, *Jacobite Ireland* (London, 1969), 23, 24–25, 32; Mackintosh, *The Revolution*, 381, 400n, 402; Singer, ed., *Clarendon Correspon-*

dence, 1: 38, 184; 2:125. Tyrconnel's displacement of Clarendon was a signal to the empire of the regime's shift to extreme measures: Blathwayt to Effingham, Jan. 2, 1687, CWWB, 14 #5.

91. HMC, *Ormonde Ms.*, 1st Ser., 1: 204, 335, 402–403, 406; W.O. 26/4; 282; *ibid.*, 5: 57; Add. Ms. 15897, 69; *Clarendon Correspondence*, op. cit. and 2: 135–37; Webb, *Governors-General*, #152, 156; Childs, *Army of James II*, 70–71. Dongan refused Tyrconnel and resisted Penn's machinations against him as well: *NYCD*, 3: 492, 422–24. The French reported that King James was recalling Dongan to become "general of the artillery" (*ibid.*, 488), and that Dongan himself would be succeeded by Lord Granard (on whom see below, chapter four, note 85).

92. Ormonde to Capt. Matthew, Feb. 5, 1686/7, HMC, *Ormonde Ms.* N.S., 7: 483; Feiling, *Tory Party*, 215. On Ormonde's household as a military academy (and so the comradeship of the second duke, a key figure in 1688, with the Anglo-Irish Protestant professionals), see Captain Robert Parker, *Memoirs of The Most Remarkable Military Transactions From The Year 1683 To 1718 . . . In Ireland And Flanders . . .* (Dublin, 1746), 2–3; see also 5–8. HMC, *Downshire Ms.*, 1: 195; HMC, *Ormonde Ms.*, 1st Ser., 1: 402, 414, 415, and Add. Ms. 9762, 1–3, on the Irish army commissions, and cashiering, of Rupert Billingsly, Toby Caulfield, Benjamin Fletcher, George Sloughter, and John Corbett (afterwards named by Marlborough to command Maryland). A general account is in Patrick Kelly, "Ireland and the Glorious Revolution: From Kingdom to Colony," Robert Beddard, ed., *Revolutions of 1688* (Oxford, 1991), esp. 176.

93. "The son of such a father should find some favor, at least not severity," Clarendon wrote of Captain Coote, to Rochester, Dublin Castle, Jan. 23, 1685/6, Singer, ed., *Clarendon Correspondence*, 1: 221 and, to previous citations, add, *ibid.*, 236–37, 240, 263, 272, 294, 298, 305, 341, 401, 431–47, 453, 464, 469, 476, 482–83, 485, 543; 2: 26, 30, 93, 114–15. On Toby Caulfield, see *ibid.*, 1: 506, 2: 56. On the Dongan–Tyrconnel connection, see *ibid.*, 1: 343, 556–57, etc.; 2: 512. Add. Ms. 15897, 68; Webb, *Governors-General*, #123; Childs, *Army of James II*, 62, 75; Parker, *Memoirs*, 1–8; Anne to Mary, March 26, 1688, Dalrymple, ed., *Memoirs*, (2d ed., London, 1773), 2: 301. James was furious with Mary for taking Coote "into her family." On the restoration of Catholic lands, see also Van Citters to the states general, 4/14, 1687, Add. Ms. 31512, 63.

94. Coote to Middleton, Hague, Aug. 12, 1687, Add. Ms. 48820, 273; A List of Officers Coming with the Prince of Orange, Add. Ms 48822, 230.

95. John Mackay of Rockford, *Life of Lt. Gen. Hugh Mackay of Scoury* (Glasgow, 1836), 12; Major General Hugh Makay (of Scoury), *Memoirs of the War Carried on in Scotland and Ireland* (Edinburgh, 1833), xiv–xv; Van Citters to the states general, Jan. 14/24, 1686/7, Add. Ms. 31512, 56–57; Feb. 24, 1688, Add. Ms. 34510, 118; Barrillon to Louis XIV, June 13, 1685, *Translation*, 97–98.

96. Churchill, *Marlborough*, 1: 217; Earle, *Monmouth's Rebels*, 109; Jeaffreson to Crispe, London, Mar. 11, 1683/4, Jeaffreson, ed., *Young Squire*, 2: 109–10.

97. James to William, Jan. 17, 1687/8, Dalrymple, ed., *Memoirs* (2d ed., London, 1773), 2: 265, and see 139–141. Van Citters to the states general, Mar.

16/26, 1688, Add. Ms. 31512, 75; Van Citters to the states general, Jan. 24/Feb. 5, 1688, *ibid.*, 68–69; Childs, *Army of James II*, 133–34; Turner, *James II*, 348–51; Mackintosh, *The Revolution*, 402n–406.

98. Van Citters to the states general, 16/26 March, 24 Jan./5 Feb. 1688, Add. Ms. 31512, 75, 68–69.

99. *Ibid.*, 68b. For William's plants, see Childs, *Dictionary*, s.v. "Bonfoy, Samuel," "Colt, Edward Dutton," "Wolfe, Edward." And for other Anglo-Irish officers who fled from Tyrconnel and returned with William, see *ibid.*, s.v. "Courtney, Richard," "Echlin, Robert," "Slater, John."

100. Frances Gardiner Davenport, comp., *European Treaties Bearing on the History of the United States and Its Dependencies* (Washington, 1929), 2: #79, and, on Churchill, see p. 326. Ratifications were exchanged 6/16 Nov. 1686. "Commissioners appointed for adjusting all differences . . . between both Nations in America and particularly for the Better execution of the late Treaty of Neutrality between both Crowns in those Parts," were named, 1/11 Dec. 1687. The governors-general were ordered to suspend hostilities *NYCD* 3: 504–506; C.O. 1/135, 42. See also note 82, above.

101. Churchill, Governor, for the Hudson's Bay Company, to the King, Hudson's Bay House, Noble Street, London, May 13, 1687, C.O. 135/1, 43–49. This is dated May 18, in *CSPC 1685–1688*, #1257. Miller, *James II*, 131, 160, 161, 168; HMC, *Downshire Ms.*, 1: 181–82, 247, 277. See the correspondence of Bonrepaus with Seignelay, summarized by Donald G. Pilgrim, "France and New France: Two Perspectives in Colonial Security," *CHR* 55(1974): 405; W. J. Eccles, *Canada Under Louis XIV* (London, 1964), 147–48.

102. The origins of the treaty in Stapleton's initiative appear in Blathwayt to Stapleton, June 1, 167[8], June 28, July 25, 1679, CWWB 37 #1; Stapleton to the lords of the committee [for plantations], July 20, 1678, *ibid.*, 38 #1; lords to the king, May 17, 1677, Blathwayt Papers, Huntington Library. The Leeward Islands truce, with proposals to extend it to Jamaica and Barbados, is in Davenport, comp., *Treaties*, 2; #72, and see pp. 310–11. The idea was extended to the American continent, *CSPC 1685–1688*, #497, 521, 522; Denonville to Dongan, (June 5, 1686, *ibid.*, #694; *NYCD*, 3: 457) also denounced Monmouth, recalled shared service at Maestricht, and expressed the admiration of French soldiers for James. See also *ibid.*, 475.

103. On these themes, see Van Citters's despatches, esp. May 28/June 7 and Sept. 7/17, 1686, Add. Ms. 31512, 34, 45.

104. Jeaffreson, ed., *Young Squire*, 2: 265–67, 283, 302. On Scottish dissenters' migration to New York and New Jersey, see *NYCD*, 3: 399, 408. Marlborough for the Governor & Company of Hudson's Bay to the King, referred to the privy council plantations committee, Apr. 25, 1689, C.O. 135/1, 69, p. 124; *CSPC, 1685–1688*, #1257, 1258, 1324; Don Pedro Ronquillo to Sir William Trumbull, London, June 12, 1686, HMC, *Downshire Ms.*, 1: 182. See also Dongan to Sunderland, Albany, Feb. 19, 1687/88, *NYCD*, 3: 510–11.

105. C.O. 135/1, f.47, the protest of Feb. 17, 1687, signed by Churchill, spoke of the prior discovery by "the subjects of the Imperiall Crown of this Kingdome," their settlements, trade, and investment, the cruelty of the French, and the royal assurance of redress. Sir Edw. Dering to Ld. Churchill May 11, 1687, Rich, ed., *Letters Outward*, 226–27; Davenport, comp., *Treaties*, 2: #80, and see p. 326. See also the French replies, *CSPC 1685–1688*, #1324, 1325; a second set of exchanges, #1368–1369, 1381, 1418, 1489, and see #1504. To rebut the French reply, Churchill introduced the HBC directors to King James and declared that "your petitioners at their own great charge have encountered with Interlopers of Old England & New England, but the power of Canada they cannot withstand, without your Majesty's Royal Assistance . . . (*ibid.*, 168–69). Churchill's pressure compelled the King's conciliatory reply, Rich, *Hudson's Bay Company*, 1: 207–208. On the posts, see *ibid.*, 1: 210–17, 228; Eccles, *Canada Under Louis XIV*, 147, 160, where the HBC losses are estimated at £500,000 in the forts and £20,000 p.a. in lost trade.

106. See also C.O. 135/1, f. 47, p. 81, f. 57–59, p. 101–103, 105. Rich, ed., *Letters Outward*, 218, 220–22 (App. 3); Rich, *Hudson's Bay Company*, 1: 223.

107. The Treaty of Peace between England and France, concluded at Breda, July 21/31, 1667 (Davenport, comp., *Treaties*, 2 #58) restored the status quo as of Jan. 1 1665. The French were to return to the English part of St. Kitts and the islands of Antigua and Montserrat in exchange for "Acadia." The two crowns were secured in their other American possessions as of this date. The issues in dispute in 1687 and 1688 were contentious because the Hudson's Bay Company did not yet exist in 1667 and because the Mohawks, whose territory had been invaded by the French in 1666 and 1667, were not recognized as English subjects by the French.

108. C.O. 135/1, f, 57b; Miller, *James II*, 173; HMC, *Ormonde Ms.*, New Ser., 7: 483; Haley, *Shaftesbury*, Ch. XII. See M. Eugene Sirmans, *Colonial South Carolina . . .*, (Chapel Hill, 1966), 35–37, on Craven's succession to Shaftesbury as the dominant Carolina proprietor, and on schemes for settlement with Protestant dissenters; Verner W. Crane, *The Southern Colonial Frontier, 1670–1732*, (Ann Arbor, 1929, 1956). See especially 20, 25–32, on lord Cardross's settlement of Covenanters in 1684, inspired by Shaftesbury as he contemplated the possibility of his own exile to Carolina. L. F. Stock, *Proceedings and Debates of the British Parliaments Respecting North America*, 1924), 1: 451.

109. C.O. 135/1, f. 57, p. 102. J. R. Jones, "Representative of the Alternative Society . . .," in Dunn and Dunn, eds., *World of Penn*, 63–66; J. R. Jones, *Charles II Royal Politician* (London, 1987), 80, 184; J. R. Childs, "1688," *History*, 73 (1988), 403; Vincent Buranneli, *The King and the Quaker*, (Philadelphia, 1962), 99–101. Routh, ed., *Burnet's History*, 3: 139–40.

110. Van Citters to the states general, Windsor, August 4/14, 1687, Add. Ms. 31512, 63; John Paget, *The New "Examen"* (London, 1934), 163, 211–12; Roger Thomas, "The Seven Bishops and Their Petition, 18 May 1688," *Journal of Ecclesiastical History* 12 (1961), 57.

111. C.O. 135/1, f. 70b; Singer, ed., *Clarendon Correspondence*, 1: 87–89, 117–18; Rich, *Hudson's Bay Company*, 1: 224.

112. Blathwayt met with Churchill and his deputy governor of the Hudson's Bay Company on Nov. 3, 1687, to prepare the Memorial of Nov. 16, 1687. Their agenda, and the memorial, are in Blathwayt Papers, Huntington Library.

Shorter versions are in *NYCD*, 3: 509; *CSPC 1685–1688*, 468–469; S. P. 44/ 164, 97. Presumably, the vessels in question were the eight New England ketches taken on the Grand Banks in 1685 and "carried to Rochelle." This was the proximate incident both for the formation of the dominion of New England and the Treaty of Whitehall. Randolph to the privy council committee, May 29, 1689, *CSPC 1689–1692*, #152.

113. Memorial, Nov. 16, 1687, Blathwayt Papers, Huntington Library. See also Webb, *1676*, 284. Note the exchanges between the English and French commissioners, *CSPC 1685–1688*, #1491, 1504, 1505–1506, 1660. On the centrality of the Iroquois, see Dongan to Blathwayt, Aug. 11, 1685; same to the lord president, n.d.; James II to Dongan to protect the Five Nations as English subjects, Nov. 10, 1687, *NYCD*, 3: 363, 428–30, 503–504, and, on Patrick MacGregorie, *ibid.*, 395n, 516, 472; Effingham to Blathwayt, Feb. 16, 1687/88, CWWB, 14 #6; Andros to same, Aug. 17, 1687, *ibid.*, 3 #3; Cadwallader Colden, *The History of the Five Indian Nations Depending on the Province of New York in America* (London, 1827, 1847; Ithaca, 1958), Pt. 1, Ch. 4.

114. Dongan to lord president, Mar. 2, 1686[/7]; same to James II, Oct. 24, 1687, *NYCD*, 3: 423, 492 and see Dongan's report, *ibid.*, 394, 396, 428–29; instructions for same, Sept. 8, 1688, *ibid.*, 476–77; P. Schuyler to Dongan, Sept. 2, 1687; intelligence from Anthony L'espinard, Sept. 15, *ibid.*, 479, 488; Dongan to Denonville, Oct. 25, 1687, *ibid.*, 514 (n.b. Churchill's parallel language in C.O. 135/1); Effingham to Blathwayt, Mar. 7 1687, CWWB, 14 #5; Pilgrim, "Security," *CHR* 55: 381–407.

115. Dongan to Blathwayt, Albany, Feb. 21 1687[/8], CWWB, 11 #1; same to lord president, Feb. 19, 1687/8, *NYCD* 3: 511; Five Nations' response, *ibid.*, 533–36; Dongan to Denonville, Feb. 17, 1688, *ibid.*, 519. Dongan's observation about the French text is borne out by "Traité de neutralité conclu à Londres, entre les Rois de France et l'Angleterre touchant les limites des Pays dedeux Rois en Amerique, Nov. 16, 1686," *EDITS, ORDONNANCES ROYAUX, Et Arrets du Conseil d'Etat du Roi, Concernant le Canada*, (Quebec, 1803), 1: 269.

116. Memorial from the French Commissioners to the English, Nov. 7, 1687; English commissioners to the king, Nov. 16, 1687; royal warrant, Nov. 10, 1687, *NYCD* 3: 506, 509, 503–504, and see 537–43; Effingham to Blathwayt, Feb. 16, 1687/8, CWWB, 14 #6. On Andros and the Iroquois, see Webb, *1676*, Part III.

117. Dongan to Denonville, Oct. 31, 1687, *NYCD* 3: 516, and see 475–77; Andros to the privy council committee, Boston, Apr. 4, 1688 and abstract of Dongan's letter, C.O. 905/62, pp. 15, 18, and *NYCD* 3: 475–77.

118. Memorial, Nov. 16, 1687, Blathwayt Papers, Huntington Library; C. S. S. Higham, *The Development of the Leeward Islands Under The Restoration . . .* (Cambridge, 1921), 118–20; John Romeyn Brodhead, *History of the State of New York* (New York, 1871), 2: 379, 393, 394.

119. Davenport, comp., *Treaties*, 2: #58, 64, 79, p. 322–23; Thomas Spencer, "A True and faithful Relation of the proceedings of the forces of their Majesties . . . under Colonel Codrington, 1689–1690," *Harleian Miscellany*, 2: 564–75.

120. Davenport, comp., *Treaties*, #80; C.O. 135/1, passim; the English commissioners (the two secretaries of state, Sunderland and Middleton, and lord Godolphin) to the king, Nov. 16, 1687, *NYCD* 3: 509; the French proposals, *ibid.*, 506–507. For an example of the critiques, see Blathwayt to Dongan, enclosing copies of the treaty, March 4, 1686/7 and Dongan's reply, Feb. 21, 1687[/8], CWWB, 11 #1. All the governors-general were sent copies of the treaty (*CSPC 1685–1688*, 302) and letters to suspend hostilities with the French for a year and then until further notice, Jan. 22, 1687[/8], C.O. 135/1, f. 67, p. 121. James's remark to Van Citters is quoted by Powey, *English Navy*, 5, n.1. See note 104, above. See also Robert Livingston to Robert Ferguson ("the Plotter," Monmouth's lieutenant), Boston, Mar. 27, 1690, *NYCD* 3: 698–99, rejoicing in "in the particular Notice taken in His Majtyes declaration of War against the French King," of French aggression against the Iroquois and New York trade. For William's declaration, see Lediard, *Marlborough*, 1: 88–92.

Chapter Four: Lord Churchill's Coup: 1686–1688

1. Routh, ed., *Burnet's History*, 3: 139–42. The most favorable view of Penn's motives and consistency is J. R. Jones, "James II's Whig Collaborators," *HJ* 3 (1960), 65–66, J. R. Jones, "Alternative Society," Dunn and Dunn, eds., *World of Penn*, 63–66; J. R. Jones, *Revolution of 1688*, 219; and see J. R. Western, *Monarchy and Revolution The English State in the 1680s* (London, 1972), 205. Penn's June exemption from the quo warranto proceedings against private jurisdictions in America was a quid pro quo. See S.P. 44/56, 337, 356, and 360. James Muilenburg, "The Embassy of Everaard Van Weede, Lord of Dykvelt, To England In 1687," *The University Studies of The University of Nebraska*, XX (Lincoln, 1920), 91, 104, 117, 129.
2. *Ibid.*, 108; Turner, *James II*, 352–55; Routh, ed., *Burnet's History*, 3: 173, 180–81; Churchill, *Marlborough*, 1: 209–13; Feiling, *Tory Party*, 224–25.
3. Van Citters to the states general, Jan. 14/24, 1687/8, Add. Ms. 31512, 56–57.
4. *EHD*, 8: 1146; Routh, ed., *Burnet's History*, 3: 184, 224–25. For Brent, see Jones, "James II's Whig Collaborators," *HJ* 3: 67068, 71. On Virginia's response to the declaration, see Effingham to Blathwayt, Feb. 16, 1687/8, CWWB 14 #6.
5. Churchill to William, May 17, 1687, Dalrymple, ed., *Memoirs*, 3: 88–89; see also *ibid.*, Appendix to Book V, 62; *ibid.*, (2d ed., London, 1773), 190–91; and Coxe, *Memoirs*, 1: 34.
6. Richard Lumley, who had lost his cavalry regiment to a Catholic (Luttrell, *Brief Relation*, 1: 393, Feb. 1, 1687/8, and see 396), as reported to Effingham by Blathwayt (Jan. 22 1686/7, (CWWB 14 #5) should also be noted among the opponents. In addition, see Jones, *Revolution of 1688*, 221; Wolsey, *Marlborough*, 1: 380–83; Routh, ed., *Burnet's History*, 3: 100–1, 180–81; Jones, *15th*, 23, and see the remark of the continuer of Mackintosh, *The Revolution*, 390, that Churchill's behavior "has left the name of *Marlborough*, like that of Bacon, a perpetual memorial to mankind of the excellence of human capacity, and [the] infirmity of human nature." Van Citters to the states general, Sept. 7/17, 1686, Add. Ms. 31512, 151.

7. The correspondence between James and William on these subjects is in HMC, *Dartmouth Ms.*, 1 and Dalrymple, ed., *Memoirs*, 3. Muilenberg, "Dykvelt," *Nebraska Studies*, 20: 135–36, argues that "Churchill's letter to the Prince of May 17, 1687, is treasonable."

8. Jones, "Collaborators," *HJ* 3: 71–72; Add. Ms. 34512, 77; John Miller, "The Militia and the Army in the Reign of James II," *HJ* 4 (1973): 664; Van Citters to the states general, Dec. 12, 1687, Add. Ms. 34510, 64–66; *Two Illustrious Generals*, 18. See the whimsical account of the advocate general's flight to avoid the three questions, HMC, *Leybourne-Popham Ms.*, 263–65. On closeting and cashiering, see Add. Ms. 29578, 102b, and for corporate purges, *ibid.*, 127. See also, Turner, *James II*, 332–34. Feiling, *Tory Party*, 218–19, and see note 68 below and, for Kirke's rejoinder, Childs, *Dictionary*, 48.

9. J. R. Bloxam, ed., *Magdalen College and King James, 1686–1688* (Oxford, 1886), esp. #122, 124, 129; Macaulay, *History*, 2: 948, revised by Sir Charles Firth, *A Commentary on Macaulay's History of England* (London, 1938), 270–71; Padget, *The New "Examen,"* 169–85.

10. Randolph to Blathwayt, Mar. 29, 1688, CWWB, 1 #5; Johnson, *Adjustment to Empire*, 137–40; Randolph to the lords committee, May 29, 1689, *CSPC 1689–1692*, #152, and chapter five below.

11. For the campaign, see Sir George Ducket, Bt., ed., *Penal Laws and Test Act. Questions Touching Their Repeal Propounded in 1687–8 By James II . . . From the Original Returns in the Bodleian Library . . .* (London, 1883). Van Citters to the states general, Jan, 6/13, Feb. 17/24, Apr. 20/27 1688, Add. Ms. 34510, 83, 112, 140, 144, 147, are a litany of refusals and dismissals. See also Add. Ms. 6977, 82. On Sawyer's services for Andros, see Webb, "Trials of Andros," Martin, ed., *Nations Making*, 46–50.

12. *Two Illustrious Generals,"* 19, rephrased by Churchill, *Marlborough*, 1: 214–15; Routh, ed., *Burnet's History*, 3: 282. On touching, and popular disapproval, see Add. Ms. 29578, 78, but see *ibid.*, 123.

13. The author of the *Two Illustrious Generals*, 21, claims to have witnessed most of the Winchester episode and to have overheard Churchill's own account of his conversation with the king. This source is variously adapted by Coxe, *Memoirs*, 1: 35–36; Wolsey, *Marlborough*, 1: 386–87, and Churchill, *Marlborough*, 1: 214–15. See also Goldie, "Anglican Revolution," Beddard, ed., *Revolution of 1688*, 113; HMC, *Portland Ms.*, 3: 403.

14. Turner, *James II*, 405–6; Jones, *Revolution of 1688*, 35.

15. Add. Ms. 34515, 32, and see 33. Van Citters to the states general, Dec. 12, 1687, Add. Ms. 34510, 65: "the King seems determined to turn out of their Situations all those who hold employments and will not declare themselves . . . conformable to his wishes." Taylor, *Marlborough*, 2: 437; Churchill, *Marlborough*, 1: 217, 221, and, to the contrary, Lucile Pinkham, *William III and the Respectable Revolution*, (Cambridge, Mass., 1954) 51, but her evidence is from citations of Mackintosh that do not appear to collate with that source. Anne to Mary, Dec. 29, 1687, Dalrymple, *Memoirs* (2d ed., London, 1773), 2: 297–98. Routh, ed., *Burnet's History*, 3: 172.

16. *Ibid.*, 240–41; Add. Ms. 29563, 172; D'Estrees to Louvois, Dec. 18, 1687,

Dalrymple, ed., *Memoirs*, 3: 150–54; *ibid.*, (2d ed., London, 1773), 246–47; Shrewsbury et al. to William, June 30; Nottingham to William, July 27, 1688, *ibid.*, 146, 136–39. See also Herbert to William, May 24 and Russell to William, July 28, 1688, *ibid.*, 131, 147; *ibid.* (2d ed., London, 1773), 228–31, 236–37, 225, 238; Add. Ms. 29578, 151.

17. On the "dragooning system," see Van Citters to the states general, May 1/11, 18/28, 1688, Add. Ms. 31512, 78–81; Van Citters to the states general, Apr. 27, May 29/June 8, 1688, Add. Ms. 31150, 114, 117. For the three questions, see Duckett, ed., *Penal Laws and Test Act*, and the analysis by David Ogg, *England in the Reigns of James II and William III* (Oxford, 1955), 186–189.

18. Routh, ed., *Burnet's History*, 3: 241n., 277–79. Burnet's revision lists the chief officers as Churchill, Kirke, and Trelawney, Foxcroft, ed., *Supplement to Burnet's History*, 290–92. Childs, *Army of James II*, 48–49, n. 125; Dalton, ed., *Army Lists*, 2: 26; Turner, *James II*, 360–61; and see William to Danby, April 30, 1688, HMC, *9th Report*, Appendix, 460.

19. Ailesbury, *Memoirs*, 1: 184; Churchill, *Marlborough*, 1: 236. Van Citters to the states general, Jan. 21/31, 1687/8, Add. Ms. 31512, 58b. The grub worker of this conspiracy appears to have been Churchill's Life Guards clerk, Davis, *Second, Queen's*, 2: 74. Special alarm was caused the conspirators by the news of May 10, 1688, that the Irish would displace the English garrrison at Chester and by Tyrconnel's proposal that the new garrison fortify the port to secure access to England for the Irish army, just as the Irish occupation of Portsmouth had supposedly opened England to the French: Add. Ms. 29563, 149; Add. Ms. 29578, 124.

20. Routh, ed., *Burnet's History*, 3: 282–83; *Memoirs of Lord Balcarres*, Somers Tracts, 11; Macintosh, *The Revolution*, 501–502. From the end of May 1687, such court and army observers as Littleton began to report Princess Anne's movements on a daily basis. See Add. Ms. 29578, 106 et seq.

21. Routh, ed., *Burnet's History*, 3: 283 n; Foxcroft, ed., *Supplement*, 291. The young duke of Ormonde did not succeed to the title until July 21, 1688 (Add. Ms. 29578, 181), but contemporaries, recalling the conspiracy, always thus refer to him. Dalton, ed., *Army Lists*, 2: 26, 78, 133; Add. Ms. 29578, 215–216b; Add. Ms. 38695, 146–48.

22. Davis, *Second, Queen's*, 2:67, 70–71; Cowper, *King's Own*, 1: 52; Peter Le-Fevre, "Tangier, the Navy and its connection with the Glorious Revolution of 1688," *Manner's Mirror* 73 (1987), 187–90.

23. Hamilton, *First Guards*, 1: 306; Jeaffreson, ed., *Young Squire*, 265–66; S.P. 44/69, 102, 103, 108, Webb, *Governors-General*, Appendix #58, 119, 78, 115.

24. In addition, see John Mackay, *Life*; 5, 13; Childs, *Army of James II*, 147; Routh, ed., *Burnet's History*, 274–84; Childs, *Dictionary* s.v. these names; Feiling, *Tory Party*, 227.

25. *EHD* #17; *Two Illustrious Generals*, 23; Western, *Monarchy and Revolution*, 229–35; Routh, ed., *Burnet's History*, 3: 224–228n, 232; Turner, *James II*, 399; Add. Ms. 29563, 130–31; Add. Ms. 29578, 165, 171; Van Citters to the states general, May 22/June 1, 1688, Add. Ms. 31512, 81–82; June 18, 1688, Add. Ms. 31510, 168.

26. See also, Thomas, "The Seven Bishops," *JEH* 12: 57–58, 60, 61, 69; *A Compleat Collection*, I, #1.

27. Captain Hugh O'Donnell, *Historical Records of the 14th* (Devonport, 1893) says nothing of the Tower episode, but see Hamilton, *First Guards*, 1: 295; Dalton, ed., *Army Lists*, 1:18, 2: 35, 144; Cowper, *King's Own*, 1: 51; Routh, ed. *Burnet's History*, 3: 228n; Geiter and Speck, ed., *Reresby*, 500; Webb, *Governors-General*, #57, and see p. 471, #8.

28. Routh, ed., *Burnet's History*, 3: 232; Clarke, ed., *James Second*, 2: 160–61; Add. Ms. 29578, 173; Van Citters to the states general, Oct. 4/14, 1687, Add. Ms. 31512, 63; June 22, 1688, Add. Ms. 31510, 127; Jones, *Revolution*, 125; Miller, *James II* (Hove, 1977), 186; Ogg, *James II and William III*, 201; but Turner, *James II*, 405, dates the birth July 10.

29. Van Citters to the states general, June 29/July 9, 1688, Add. Ms. 31512, 87–89.

30. *Ibid.*, 89.

31. Routh, ed., *Burnet's History*, 3: 233, 236–37; Add. Ms. 29578, 112; Clarke, ed., *James Second*, 2: 165; T. B. Howell, *State Trials*, 12: 422–26; Turner, *James II*, 404; Van Citters to the states general, July 13, 1688, Add. Ms. 31510, 138–39.

32. June 30, 1688 invitation to the prince, in Macintosh, *Revolution*, Appendix, 690–92; Dalrymple, ed., *Memoirs*, 3: 136–39; *ibid.*, (2d. ed., London, 1773), 2: 228–31; Jones, *Revolution of 1688*, 230; *EHD* 8, #39; Add. Ms. 29578, 177, 179; Routh, ed., *Burnet's History*, 3: 164, 261. The bishops' acquittal and the army's reaction "makes the nation considerably more resolute," Van Citters wrote to the states general, July 13, 1688, Add. Ms. 31510. Three days later he hurried home to report what he could not write (plans for the putsch, presumably).

33. Routh, ed., *Burnet's History*, 240; John Trenchard, *An Arguement, Shewing that a Standing Army is inconsistent with A Free Government . . .* (London, 1697), 13.

34. Add. Ms. 29578, 185; John, Baron Churchill to the Prince of Orange, Aug. 4, 1688, HMC, *Morrison Ms.*, 460; Dalrymple, ed., *Memoirs*, 3: 149; *ibid.*, (2d ed., London, 1773), 239; holograph facsimile, Churchill, *Marlborough*, 1: f. p. 240; *Two Illustrious Generals*, 23.

35. See also, Van Citters to the states general, Nov. 23, 1688, Add. Ms. 31510, 174–75.

36. *The Art of Complaisance or the Means to Oblige in Conversation* (London, 1677); *An Essay in Defense of the Female Sex* (London, 1696). I am indebted to Dr. Peter S. M. Webb for these citations. Hamilton, *First Guards*, 1: 296. Note the operations of the Association of Protestant Officers at the camp. Childs, *Army of James II*, 158–59; Miller, *James II*, 200; Routh, ed., *Burnet's History*, 3: 286–87; HMC, *Dartmouth Ms.*, 1: 220; E. J. Priestly, "The Portsmouth Captains," *JSAHR* 55 (1977), 153–64; Blathwayt to Langdale, Sept. 8, 1688, W.O. 4/1/95.

37. Childs, *Dictionary*, 7; Van Citters to the states general, Dec. 12, 1687, Feb. 13, Sept. 17, 28, 1688, Add. Ms 31510, 83, 142, 143, 145.

38. See also, same, Sept. 11/21, 1688, Add. Ms. 31512, 89b. See Childs, *Dictio-*

nary, 6, on Beaumont: a captain in the Anglo-Dutch brigade, second son of the viscount Beaumont, and m.p. for Nottingham. Geiter and Speck, eds., *Reresby*, 509–10. On Beaumont see also Ducket, ed., *Penal Laws*, 88, 100, 106, 126, 238; Dalton, ed., *Army Lists*, 2: 138. William III rewarded Beaumont with the command of this senior (8th) regiment and commissioned him governor of Dover Castle. Despite his loyalty, Reresby insisted on recruiting his own company, the grenadiers, in Beaumont's regiment, Geiter and Speck, eds., *Reresby*, 542, 543, 544.

39. Van Citters to the states general, Sept. 21/Oct. 1, 1688, Add. Ms. 31512, 98, adds that there was also published a print of "the officer who caused the Mayor of Sherborne to be well beaten by his soldiers for having pressed the preacher . . . to proclaim the act of tolleration in the church."

40. W. O. 4/1, 93–94; Blathwayt to Langdale, Windsor, Sept. 8. 1688, *ibid.*, 95–96, printed as #158 of Godfrey Davies, ed., "Letters on the Administration of James II's Army," *JSAHR* 29 (1951), 79; *Publick Occurances Truly Stated*, 132, Sept. 25, 1688; Childs, *Army of James II*, 151, 154; Feiling, *Tory Party*, 228; Clarke, ed., *James Second*, 2: 168–69; HMC, *Leybourne-Popham Ms.*, 266–67; Turner, *James II*, 410; Routh, ed., *Burnet's History*, 3: 164; Jones, *Revolution of 1688*, 230; Van Citters to the states general, Sept. 11/21, 14/24, 1688, Add. Ms. 31512, 95–96. [E. Bohun,] *The History Of The Desertion* (London, 1689), 7, declares that the attempt to make Protestant military martyrs (which severity Sunderland afterwards claimed as his own idea) was so transparent that Barrillon prevailed with James to reduce the punishments to cashiering.

41. Blathwayt to Oglethorpe, Sept. 12, 1688, W. O. 4/1, 98. Oglethorpe had been dispatched to Bath to report the birth of the Prince of Wales to the Princess Anne, Van Citters to the states general, June 22, 1688, Add. Ms. 31510, 127; Sept. 21/Oct. 1, Oct. 2/12, 1688, Add. Ms. 31512, 98, 106–107; Oct. 19, 1688, Add. Ms. 31510, 152; Sept. 25/Oct. 5, 1688, Add. Ms. 31512, 102–105; Davies, ed., "Army Administration," *JSAHR* 29, 127; HMC, *Downshire Ms.*, 1: 300.

42. Lt. Col. John Beaumont to Bridget Bosville, Sept. 25, 1688, W.O. 4/1, 104 printed in Priestly, "Portsmouth Captains," *JSAHR* 55: 160–61, and see Add. Ms. 29578, 188, 190. The lifting of Compton's suspension was the lead item in the *London Gazette* of Sept. 17–Oct. 1, 1688 (#2386), prefacing the king's proclamation of Sept. 28, 1688, warning of the impending invasion and conspiracy. On Sept. 28, *Publick Occurances* 133 reported "the Present Hottest News" was that "a Bold Neighbour" was "now Crossing the *Herring Pond* to make us a Bolder Visit" called "the Protestant Invasion" and that King James had rejected French aid.

43. James's army, on the invasion eve, actually numbered 40,235, of whom 3,763 were Scots and 2,818 were Irish. The Irish Guards, 1,500 strong, landed in the first days of December. Numbers naturally vary: compare HMC, *Dartmouth Ms.*, 1: 171; Clarke, ed., *James Second*, 2: 186–87 (from which the king is quoted); and Littleton's estimate of the king's field force as 30,000, Add. Ms. 29578, 198. On the southward march of the Scots, much delayed by Williamite officers, see Swift, comp., "Memoirs of Creichton," in Davis, ed., *Prose Works of*

Swift, 5: 161–67, and Geiter and Speck, eds., *Reresby*, 518–29 (who numbers the royal army as 6,000 horse and 38,000 foot, and observed that it was "impossible that the Prince durst attack England with an army of under 20,000 men if he expected not very good helpe in England," *ibid.*, 525. Van Citters to the states general, Oct. 19, Nov. 2, 9, 1688, Add. Ms. 31510, 132–33, 158, 161.

44. Buckley, ed., *Ailesbury Memoirs*, 131, 150, 184; Clarke, ed., *James Second*, 1: 191; HMC, *Dartmouth Ms.*, 1: 140; Van Citters to the states general, Oct. 16/ 26, 1688, Add. Ms. 31512, 114–15. Same, 117, notes that, even after James II published his declaration for the restoration of corporate charters and of the Magdalen fellows on Oct. 19, Halifax and Danby declined to kiss his hand.

45. Priestly, "Portsmouth Captains," *JSAHR* 55: 160; Hamilton, *First Guards*, 1: 302–303; Van Citters to the states general, Nov. 12, 1688, Add. Ms. 31510, 105. For officer-couriers, s.v. "Lantham, Humphrey," and "Makay, Aneas," Childs, *Dictionary*.

46. Davis, *Second, Queen's*, 2: 67, 171; Dalrymple, ed., *Memoirs*, 3: 241–47; Parker, *Memoirs*, 10; Childs, *Army of James II*, 174; Routh, ed., *Burnet's History*, 3: 299, 304, 337; "Correspondence of Admiral Herbert," *EHR*, 1 (1886): 522–36; HMC, *Dartmouth Ms.*, 1: 185, 193, 203, 213; Buckley, ed., *Ailesbury Memoirs*, 1: 220–21; Littleton to Hatton, Nov. 6, 1688, Add. Ms. 29578, 194; Jonathan I. Israel, "The Dutch Role in the Glorious Revolution," in Israel, ed., *The Anglo-Dutch Moment* (Cambridge, 1991), 124–25.

47. [Bohun,] *Desertion*, 40; Miller, "Militia and Army," *HJ* 4: 672; John Stoye, "Europe and the Revolution of 1688," in Beddard, ed., *Revolutions of 1688*, 196–197. The exaggerated numbers (22,000) given by [Burnet], "The Expedition of His Highness . . . ," *Harleian Misc.* 1 (London, 1808), 449, and by the author of the "Further Account," *ibid.*, 453 (30,000 men), were partisan propaganda.

48. S.v. many of these names in Childs, *Dictionary*, and add, as examples of the imperial administrative talent in William's invasion force, the officers and governors John Farwell, James Ferguson, James Fox, Emanuel Scrope Howe, Edward and Godfrey Lloyd, William Jephson, Hugh Mackay, the Hon. John Stanley, and Thomas Talmash. On William Vetch, who had left his studies at the University of Utrecht to join William and was promoted by him captain of the new Scots dragoons, see Vetch to Blathwayt, May 25, 1702, Blathwayt Papers, Huntington Library. For Cardross, see Bruce C. Lenman, "The Scottish Nobility and the Revolution of 1688–1690," in Beddard, ed., *Revolutions of 1688*, 158. On Lillingston and Columbine, see Dalton, ed., *Army Lists*, 2: 228, and for David Colyear, see *ibid.*, 232. On Cutts's mission, see J. R. Jones, *Revolution of 1688*, 221, 231.

49. Van Citters to the states general, Nov. 23, 1688, Add. Ms. 34512, 173; *JSAHR* 44: 152–53; Robert Beddard, *A Kingdom Without a King* (Oxford, 1988), 19; Childs, *Dictionary*, 19.

50. Webb, *Governors-General*, Appendix #167; Captain R. H. Raymond Smythies, *Historical Records of the 40th (2d Somersetshire) Regiment . . .* (Devonport, 1894), 496; [Bohun,] *Desertion*, 73–74; Macintosh, *The Revolution*, 465,; *ibid.*,

Appendix, 692–792; Clarke, ed., *James Second*, 2: 215–16; Beddard, *Kingdom*, 145.

51. S.P. 44/165, 135; W.O. 4/1, 109a–110; Van Citters to the states general, Nov. 26, 1688, Add. Ms. 31510, 177; Anthony Hewitson, ed., *Diary of Thomas Bellingham* (Preston, 1908), 29–30. On Lovelace's rescue from the Gloucester jail by Dutton and his cavalry, see *The Universal Intelligence*, #1, Dec. 11, 1688. Routh, ed., *Burnet's History*, 3: 331n; Dalrymple, ed., *Memoirs*, 2: 342.

52. Interestingly, the relevant marching orders were not entered by the meticulous and methodic Blathwayt. W.O. 5/3, ends on Nov. 8. W.O. 5/4 begins on Nov. 16, 1688. On Blathwayt's orders to Cornbury, see Gertrude Ann Jacobsen, *William Blathwayt* (New Haven, 1932), 234–236; Berwick, *Memoirs*, xiii, 27–28, 29. Cornbury's desertion was described by Van Citters to the states general, Nov. 26, 30, 1688, Add. Ms. 31510, 177–78, 181. Feiling, *Tory Party*, 233–34, speaks of "Clarendon's unbalanced heir Cornbury." Hamilton, *First Guards*, 1: 305; Childs, *Army of James II*, 159 n.64.

53. [Bohun,] *Desertion*, 43; Berwick, *Memoirs*, 28; Routh, ed., *Burnet's History*, 3: 331–32. Burnet to Herbert, Nov. 16/26, 1688, Foxcroft, ed., *Supplement*, 520 and Egerton Ms. 2621, f.51–52, lays the final failure to "Sir Francis Compton's want of head or heart together with the vigour of some Popish Officers." Hewitson, ed., *Bellingham Diary*, 30 (Nov. 20, 1688); Macintosh, *The Revolution*, 486–87; HMC, *Graham Ms., 7th Report*, Appendix, 417.

54. "O God, that my son should be a rebel!" Diary of Henry, earl of Clarendon, Nov. 15, 1688 and the princess's reply, Nov. 20, 168, Singer, ed., *Clarendon Correspondence*, 1: 204, 205.; Routh, ed., *Burnet's History*, 3: 332; Beddard, *Kingdom*, 21; Feiling, *Tory Party*, 233. Russell to Herbert, Exeter, 13 8br 1688, Egerton Ms. 2621, 47. Herbert's letter of Nov. 16, 1688, *EHR*, 1: 528, reported relief that "the Newes that we have of the Intentions of the Army . . . make levies here less necessary." Clarke, ed., *James Second*, 2: 215, 217.

55. Middleton to Preston, Nov. 24, 25, 1688; HMC, *Graham Ms.*, 418; Nottingham to Hatton, Nov. 15, 1688, Thompson, ed., *Hatton Correspondence*, 2: 102–103, but see the more accurate account by the leading imperial engineer, Thomas Phillips, to Dartmouth, Nov. 16, 1688, HMC, *Dartmouth Ms.*, 1: 204. Van Citters to the states general, Nov. 26, 1688, Add. Ms. 31510, 177. Berkeley took care to inform the fleet of the desertion (*ibid.*, 210–11 and see 222–23). He noted in particular the decisions of Cornbury, Richard Brewer, and Frank Russell, as they made crucial steps toward imperial command. See also, Dalton, ed., *Army Lists*, 2: 114. Clarke, ed., *James Second*, 2: 215, 217, 218, and see 225–26.

56. *Ibid.*, 218, 219; Beddard, *Kingdom*, 23; Van Citters to the states general, Nov. 28, 1688, Add. Ms. 31510, 178; Fitzroy, *Grafton*, 64; Feiling, *Tory Party*, 232. Bishop Turner was also prominent on this occasion, the Nov. 12 petition of the Protestant peers who, "in deep sense of the miseries of war," and "bound in conscience and out of the duty they owed to God and their holy religion" called for "a Parliament regular and free in all respects," *A Compleat Collection*, I, #4.

57. Clarke, ed., *James Second*, 220, 222; Anne to William, Nov. 18, 1688, Dalrymple, ed., *Memoirs*, 3: 365; *ibid.*, (2d ed., London, 1773) 333–34; Van Citters to the states general, Oct. 19, 1688, Add. Ms. 31510, 133; William L. Sachse, "The Mob and the Revolution of 1688," *JBS* 4 (1969), 26; Miller, "Militia and Army," *HJ* 4: 674–75.

58. Macintosh, *The Revolution*, 489, 495, 497, 509; Routh, ed., *Burnet's History*, 3: 333; Halifax's memos., Add. Ms. 51511, 35, 66b; *Two Illustrious Generals*, 25; Churchill, *Marlborough*, 1: 261; Clarke, ed., *James Second*, 2: 218; Hamilton, *First Guards*, 1: 307; Davis, *Second, Queen's*, 2: 72; Van Citters to the states general, Oct. 19, Nov. 30. 12688. Add. Ms. 31510, 133; 179–80; Thompson, ed., *Hatton Correspondence*, 2: 103. Middleton to Preston, Salisbury, Nov. 24, 1688, HMC, *Graham Ms.*, 418; Swift, comp., "Creichton Memoirs," Davis, ed., *Works of Swift*, 5: 162; Fitzroy, *Grafton*, 62.

59. Clarke, ed., *James Second*, 2: 222–23; Berwick, *Memoirs*, 1: 31; Davis, *Second, Queen's*, 2: 74. In support of Clarke and Berwick, note that the purported plan for the Warminster abduction was current in London as early as Nov. 26/Dec. 6, 1688, Van Citters to the states general, Dec. 6, 1688, Add. Ms. 31510, 189. Reresby (*Memoirs*, Geiter and Speck, eds., 534) reported it under the date of Nov. 28. Reresby added that "this ungrateful Lord Churchill was raised from page to the King to the degree of a viscount of England, and had a great estate with it by the Kings bounty." Churchill took the first opportunity, on Dec. 3, 1688, to deny to King James's envoys that he had intended to capture the king, he vowed always to protect James's person, and insisted "that he had never left him but he saw our religion and country even in danger of being destroyed," Singer, ed., *Clarendon Correspondence*, 2: 214. Beddard, *Kingdom*, 23–24.

60. *Two Illustrious Generals*, 25; Clarke, ed., *James Second*, 2: 224, 225, 226–27; HMC, *Leybourne-Popham Ms.*, 267; Burnet to Herbert, Dec. 9, 1688, Foxcroft, ed., *Supplement*, 533, Egerton Ms. 2621, f. 69–70; Halifax memo., Add. Ms. 51511, 28; Middleton to Preston, Salisbury, Nov. 24, 1688, HMC, *Graham Ms.*, 418. Some of Churchill's closest conspirators pretended to pursue his party. Churchill, *Marlborough*, 1: 256, 259, 263n.; Hamilton, *First Guards*, 1: 308, 310; Davis, *Second, Queen's*, 2: 73–74; Thompson, ed., *Hatton Correspondence*, 2: 113, 118–119, 120–21; Edmund Packe, *An Historical Record Of The Royal Regiment Of Horse Guards or Oxford Blues* . . . (London, 1851), 50n; Add. Ms. 29563, 340. On the retreat, see Blathwayt to Kirke, Salisbury, Nov. 23, 1688, W.O. 4/1, 110–11. Sir John Reresby summed up (Geiter and Speck, eds., *Reresby*, 535): "The number of thos that revolted was not yet 1000 in all as yet, but everyone was soe jealous one of another that they knew not who to trust; soe the army and artillery marched back towards London, and the King came there on the 26th." See the reflections of Childs, "1688," *History* 73: 412–13.

61. [Hare,] *Marlborough*, 13, 16; Routh, ed., *Burnet's History*, 3: 282; Foxcroft, ed., *Supplement*, 291. *Ibid.*, 290n, observes that this revised estimate of lord Churchill's limited betrayal of King James followed Burnet's twelve years of exposure "to the fascinating influence of the most seductive intellect in Europe."

62. For Churchill's plan for the Tangerines' desertion, see Burnet to Herbert, Nov. 29, 1688, *EHR* 1: 532; Egerton Ms., B.L., 2621, 63–68v; Montesquieu's panegyric, Berwick, *Memoirs*, xiv, and see *ibid.*, 29, on the desertions. *EHR* 1: 520–21; Thompson ed., *Hatton Correspondence*, 2: 112–13; HMC, *Leybourne-Popham Ms.*, 268; Jones, *Revolution of 1688*, 297, 299; Miller, "Militia and Army" *HJ* 4:673.

63. Routh, ed., *Burnet's History*, 3: 333; Parker, *Memoirs*, 9–10; Clarke, ed., *James Second*, 2: 223–24, 229, 242. Lord Churchill [to King James, Nov, 23, 1688], Blenheim Ms., B.2.31; Add. Ms. 61101, 1–2; Churchill, *Marlborough*, 1: 263–64; *Two Illustrious Generals*, 24. See the like language of Prince George to the king, denouncing the "restless enemies of reformed religion, backed by the persecuting power of france," a power which must be resisted by all Protestant princes. Prince George summoned King James to return his government to "the only secure foundation that of the love and interest of your subjects." That this invocation of religion and constitutionalism emerged from the Churchill chancery is emphasized by the copy's place in Blenheim Ms. B.2.31, now Add. Ms. 61101, f. 3. See also Macintosh, *The Revolution*, 496, 501, and 489; Hamilton, *First Guards*, 1:308. Churchill's letter and his rationale for this decision, "the most important he took in the whole course of his life," are analyzed by Jones, *Marlborough*, 36–40. Churchill's draft is printed on p. 75, above. Note that Churchill's position follows precisely the positions developed by Bishop Turner. These appear in Feiling, *Tory Party*, 222, 224, 229–30.

64. Samuel Pepys to Dartmouth, Nov. 26 (1688), 11 at night, Admiralty, HMC, *Dartmouth Ms.*, 1: 214. See also *ibid.*, 215, and J. R. Tanner, ed., *EHR* 8 (1893): 740–41; Princess Anne to William, Nov. 18, bishop of London to same, Dec. 2, 1688, Dalrymple, ed., *Memoirs*, 3: 265–66; *ibid.* (2d ed., London, 1773), 333–34; Luttrell, *Brief Relation*, 1: 484. The sequence of events, in particular the arrival of the guards, is reported differently in David H. Hosford, *Nottingham, Nobles, and the North* (Hamden, Ct., 1976), 101–103. See bishop Compton to Danby, HMC, *9th Report*, 2: 461. I have resolved some of these inconsistencies by reference to Van Citters's despatch to the states general, Dec. 6, 1688 (n.s.), Add. Ms. 31510, 185–87; Dec. 7, 1688, *ibid.*, 191. Van Citters thought that Queen Mary, a devout, francophile foreigner, was the uxorious king's evil genius. See also his despatch of Nov. 9, 1688, Add. Ms. 31510, 162. Ailesbury (Buckley, ed., *Memoirs*, 1: 191) alleges that lady Churchill and Mrs. Berkeley "obliged" Princess Anne "to rise out of bed in nightgown and slippers, making her to believe that the Queen . . . would send her to the Tower." The importance of the northern rising was more moral than military. As Devonshire wrote to William on Dec. 2, "Our officers are unexperienced and our men new raised," *ibid.*, 266. Agar, ed., *Ellis Correspondence* (London, 1829), 4: 177–78; *The Universal Intelligence*, #1, Dec. 11, 1688; Compton to Danby, Nottingham, Dec. 2, 1688, HMC, *9th Report*, Appendix, 461; same, Dec. 5, 1688, notes that professional officers were so few at Nottingham that the bishop himself dominated the council of war (see Evans, "Yorkshire and the Revolution of 1688," *YAJ*, XXXIX, 279). Bishop Compton even became colonel of a regiment. William to Compton, Salisbury, Dec. 5/15, 1688, *ibid.*, 460–61; Routh, ed., *Burnet's History*, 3: 285, 335n–336; Add. Ms. 29563, 348; Singer, ed., *Clarendon Correspondence*, 2: 207.

65. Hosford, *Nottingham*, 94, #54, p. 150. Nottingham's was a limited contribution to Boston's declaration. See Ian K. Steele, "Origins of Boston's Revolutionary Declaration of 18 April 1689," *NEQ* 62 (1989), 79–80, but contrast the "Declaration of the Nobility, Gentry, and Commonality at the Rendezvous at Nottingham, Nov. 22, 1688 (Ducket, ed., *Penal Laws*, 113–15; #185, in the Collection of T[racts]. 100x.65, BL), and Samuel Greene's Boston edition (Evans #465), with the Boston Declaration (W. H. Whitmore, ed., *The Andros Tracts* . . . [Boston, 1868–1874], 1: 11–19), which repeats little more than the authorship phrase in the title of the Nottingham Declaration. See also chapter five, note 48.

66. Van Citters to the states general, Nov. 30, Dec. 3, 6, 1688, Add. Ms. 31510, 182, 184, 187, and, on the limited objectives of the northern rising, see note 76 below. Webb, *Governors-General*, 22–31; see chapter two, above.

67. S.P. 44/164, 426; Dalton, ed., *Army Lists*, 2: 81, 94, 99, 111, 112.

68. *Ibid.*, 1: 12, 76; 2: 31, 38, 91, 140; Major F. W. Pfiel, "The Royal Citadel of Plymouth," *JSAHR* 12: 91, 92; S.P. 44/20, 90; Routh, ed., *Burnet's History*, 3: 16; S.P. 44/56, 360, 457; Van Citters to the states general, Apr. 13, 1688, Add. Ms. 31510, 112; Bath to Dartmouth, Oct. 3, 1688, HMC, *Dartmouth Ms.*, 1: 139; "King's Agents Reports . . . approved by the Board of Regulators," Ducket, ed., *Penal Laws*, 213–17, 269–70, 286, 307n. In 1685, Bath had made his regimental officers freemen of forty-four corporations so as to be sure of Cornwall. They had returned "Sir Bevill Grenville" for Fowey and he was proposed for 1688. So too the Trelawneys, Col. Charles (also a deputy lieutenant and 1st j.p.) being returned with John Kendall (j.p.) for Eastlowe, and Capt. Henry Trelawney (j.p.) for Westlowe, joined the Grenvilles in "makeing the Regulation." All were "Gentlemen to be enquired of from the earle of Bath." Now they all promised to vote for repeal but only if the parliament were offered some "reasonable expedient" in its place. In 1686, the king had followed Bath's example and declared that all field-grade officers should be j.p.s (justices of the peace) in the counties where their units were quartered.

69. Routh, ed., *Burnet's History*, 3: 327, 336–37; Clarke, ed., *James Second*, 2: 230; Pfiel, "Plymouth," *JSAHR*, 12: 89; Mackintosh, *The Revolution*, 483–84, 507. Sir Ed. Seymour to Halifax, Add. Ms. 51511, 70; Orange to Herbert, Exeter, Nov. 13/27, 1688, Egerton Ms. 2621, writes that Bath had promised him Plymouth in two or three days. On Seymour and Gibson, see Burnet to Herbert, Th. Nov. 29 [1688], Egerton Ms. 2621. Seymour had been ousted from King James's privy council for saying that "he saw popery come on so fast, he cd. doe notheing to oppose it," Add. Ms. 29577, 449. As usual, imperial factions paralleled English ones, Seymour being a patron of Jamaica's planter party, whereas Bath, and Albemarle, supported the privateer party, their inheritance from George Monck. See Lynch to Blathwayt, Feb. 25, 1683/4, CWWB, 24 #4. John Miller, "James II and Toleration," Eveline Cruickshanks, ed., *By Force or By Default?* (Edinburgh, 1989), 22, and Cruickshanks, "The Revolution and the Localties," *ibid.*, 31; Singer, ed., *Clarendon Correspondence*, 2: 238.

70. Bath to the Prince of Orange, Nov. 18, 1688, Dalrymple, ed., *Memoirs*, 3:267; *ibid.* (2d ed., London, 1773), 338; Davis, *Second, Queen's*, 2: 75n.; Lee,

Tenth, 34–36; Pepys to Dartmouth, Nov. 28, 1688, HMC, *Dartmouth Ms.*, 1: 216; "Expedition of His Highness," *Harleian Misc.*, 1:452. See Kenyon, *Nobility in 1688*, 14–17, on the important defection of one of the "few Englishmen— outside the army—who could help James. . . ."

71. Pepys to Dartmouth, Oct. 26, HMC, *Dartmouth Ms.*, 171, and see 181, 210, 212, 215. Churchill's fellow naval conspirator, Berkeley, also pled leaks as his excuse for deserting the fleet. Churchill to Dartmouth, Plymouth, Nov. 20, 1688, *ibid.*, 210; Powey, *English Navy*, 133. Davies, "James II . . . & the Admirals," Cruickshanks, ed., *By Force*, 96–97, accepts Churchill's protestation at face value, but note William's particular reward to the crew of the *Newcastle*. Churchill tried to authenticate his plea by entering claims for repairs to the navy commissioners for Plymouth, Dec. 20, 1688, ADM 106/383. It is suggestive of prior planning that the Dutch ambassador, drawing on captains' letters circulated on the royal exchange, reported a rumored coup at Plymouth just as Churchill was expected to arrive there: Van Citters to the states general, Nov. 30, 1688, Add. Ms. 31510, 181.

72. HMC, *Dartmouth Ms.*, 1: 216; Thompson, ed., *Hatton Correspondence*, 2: 117; *The English Currant*, 11, Dec. 12, 1688; Clarke, ed., *James Second*, 2: 230. Burnet to Herbert, Nov. 16, 1688, Foxcroft, ed., *Supplement*, 530, Egerton Ms. 2621, f. 51–52, reported that "Cherry" (identified as George Churchill, Dalrymple, ed., *Memoirs*, V, Pt. II, Book VI, App. p. 25) "is just now gone to plimouth upon an advice we had yesterday that it will be delivered to us."

73. Bentinck to Herbert, Nov. 26/ Dec. 6, 29 Nov., 1688, *EHR*, 1: 529, 530; Berkeley to Dartmouth, Dec. 3, 1688, HMC, *Dartmouth Ms.*, 1: 222; Routh, ed., *Burnet's History*, 3: 338; Clarke, ed., *James Second*, 2: 230; Lee, *Tenth*, 33– 40; Ber. Ellis to Hatton, Plymouth, xbr 6th, 1688, Add. Ms. 29563, 353. Sydenham makes the Dutch fleet two hundred transports, forty-nine warships, and a variety of small craft, *HT*, 12: 716.

74. HMC, *Dartmouth Ms.*, 1: 41; S.P. 44/69, 8–10, 28; S.P. 44/164, 74, 154, 155, 156. For the Boston analogies, see Randolph to Blathwayt, Aug. 5, 1687, CWWB, 1 #4; Andros to Blathwayt; June 4, Nov. 8, 1688, *ibid.*, 3 #3, 3 #4.

75. S.P. 44/68, 267, 288, 291, 349; S.P. 44/164, 426; Add. Ms. 29559, 310b; Add. Ms. 29560, 183; Add. Ms. 29577, 558; Add. Ms. 19278, 136; Dalton, ed., *Army Lists*, 2: 94, 111, 141; Clarke, ed., *James Second*, 2: 41–42. Geiter and Speck, eds., *Reresby*, 437 n; John Stoye, "Europe and the Revolution," Beddard, ed., *Revolution*, 203.

76. Clarke, ed., *James Second*, 2: 231–32; Macintosh, *Revolution of 1688*, 498. Geiter and Speck, eds., *Reresby*, Nov. 22, 1688, 528–33, notes Belasyse's recent arrival from the Anglo-Dutch brigade and his professionalism at the moment of the York coup. *The Universal Intelligence*, #1, Dec. 11, 1688; W.O. 4/1, 104– 105, 108; Childs, *Army of James II*, 159; HMC, *Dartmouth Ms.*, 1:178, 183–84; Routh, ed., *Burnet's History*, 3: 303; David H. Hosford, *Nottingham*, 34–38, 87, associates all of the leaders of the northern risings, save for Danby (who had his own direct links to Orange), with "the circle of conspirators associated with Lord Churchill . . . a circle marked by strong connections with the household of the Prince and Princess of Denmark." The decisive point is Kenyon's, *Nobility*,

14, that it was the south, not the north, and the army, not the nobility, that would conclude the coup. On the reliance of both James and William on their professional officers, see *ibid.*, 18. The implication of Evans, "Revolution," *YAJ*, 29: 258–85, esp. 278–79, is that Danby had subverted the militia and seized York so as to become a makeweight in a crisis to which he was not otherwise central. Browning, *Danby*, ch. 17, is a full account that stresses the strength of the royal garrisons in the north.

77. Danby to Hanmer, Nov. 30, 1688 (HMC, *Leeds Ms.*, 27, and Browning, *Danby*, 2: 142–43), offered £5,000 for the surrender of Hull and wrote that "divers of the best quality have set you the example, as particularly the earl of Bathe, who has declared for the Prince at Plymouth, the Duke of Grafton, the Lord Churchill, and twenty others, men of the first ranke." As Browning makes clear, however, the Hull coup was accomplished before Hanmer received Danby's letter, *ibid.*, 1: 409n; Danby to his countess, Dec. 5, 1688, *ibid.*, 2: 148. Devonshire, on Dec. 3, 4, expected hourly to hear of Hull's surrender, and noted that the arrival of Princess Anne had brought in the north, *ibid.*; *The English Currant*, Dec. 12, 1688. Geiter and Speck, eds., *Reresby*, 535–36, gives all the credit to Copley and notes that after "that considerable garrison . . . one of the strongest in England" was taken, the York rebels were notified. Evans, "Revolution," *YAJ*, 29: 273–74.

78. In addition, see S.P. 29/145, 156–57. Browning, *Danby*, 1: 409n, prints an alternative account of the coup, in which Copley, informed of the Catholic officers' intent to seize him "and all the Protestant officers and souldiers in garrison," planned a surprise with the aid of the town fathers. At Tattoo, the Catholic force of four hundred was confronted by Copley and his company in a suddenly illuminated town. Copley disarmed all the Catholics, imprisoned the officers, and put the men out of town, while seamen seized the unguarded citadel, the whole episode being concluded "in two hours time." See also Hanmer to Danby, Dec. 4, 1688, ibid., 2: 147n. Macintosh, *Revolution*, 508; Clarke, ed., *James Second*, 2: 230; Sachse, "Mob," *JBS*, 4: 35. Note that the Hull coup was only possible because the Scots Guards were somehow diverted from entering the garrison, Blathwayt to Langdale, Aug. 21, 1688, W.O. 4/1, 92.

79. Clarke, ed., *James Second*, 231; *The Universal Intelligence*, #1, Dec. 11, 1688; Geiter and Speck, eds., *Reresby*, 365, 571; *CSPD 1689–1690*, p. 137; Dalton, ed., *Army Lists*, 2: 37, 39; Webb, *Governors-General*, #115. For lady Baltimore's detention, with her daughter and their priest, in the town of Bromley, Kent, see Beddard, *Kingdom*, 193n.

80. Add. Ms. 9759, 5. Billingsly to Sir Charles Porter, HMC, *Leeds Ms.*, 28–29, #53; Jones, *15th*, 26. Following Browning, *Danby*, 1: 417, Evans, "Revolution," *YAJ*, 29: 277–78, asserts that Widdrington surrendered to a letter written by Danby on December 15, conveying William's order to turn the garrison over to Danby's nominee. On the same weekend, Tynemouth's lieutenant governor, Capt. Henry Villiers, took control of the port, fort, and garrison in the prince's name, Browning, *Danby*, 1: 417.

81. Berwick was taken over by Philip Babbington, Belasyse's lieutenant colonel in the Anglo-Dutch brigade (see Childs, *Dictionary*) and his regiment, whose cadres were also veterans of the Netherlands service. Their displacement of the 15th from Berwick was another example of William's purge of the English army from every important post. ˙

82. Browning, *Danby*, 1: 417–18. James II's remarks were reported by Van Citters to the states general, Dec., 7, 1688, Add. Ms. 31510, 192. At the other end of the Scots border from Berwick was Carlisle. In part, the coup at Carlisle, also on Dec. 15, was one more episode in the ancient feud of the Howard, Lowther, and Musgrave families (Webb, *Governors-General*, 69–93; Howard S. Reinmouth, Jr., "A Mysterious Dispute Demystified: Sir George Fletcher vs. the Howards," *HJ* 27 (1984): 289–307), but that feud paralyzed the gentry and the coup at Carlisle was engineered by a professional soldier, Jeremiah Bubb, the senior officer in the Carlisle garrison, whom William commissioned governor a year later (Dalton, ed., *Army Lists*, 2: 30; 3: 100, 128). He also named Bubb his gentleman usher. Bubb was duly elected Carlisle's m.p. (Luttrell, *Brief Relation*, 2: 372) before he died on Mar. 1, 1692.

83. James to Dartmouth, Oct. 14, 20. 1688, HMC, *Dartmouth Ms.*, 1: 158, 169, 171, 219; Thompson, ed., *Hatton Correspondence*, 2: 112, 113, 114; Clarke, ed. *James Second*, 2: 224, 225; *CSPD 1687–9*, #1552; Van Citters to the states general, Dec. 7, 1688, Add. Ms. 31510, 190; The Route of Col. Wachopes Regimt from Preston (15 Oct.) to St. Albans (1 Nov.), Add. Ms. 29878, 37; Turner, *James II*, 409n; but see, Miller, *Popery and Politics*, 199.

84. Clarke, ed., *James Second*, 2: 224, 249; *The Universal Intelligence* #2, Dec. 15, 1688; *The London Courant* #1, Dec. 12, 1688; *The English Currant* #1, Dec. 12, 1688, 12, Dec. 14, 1688; *The London Mercury or Moderate Intelligencer* #1, Dec. 15, 1688; W.O. 4/1, 110, 113; Hamilton, *First Guards*, 1: 313–17; Thompson, ed., *Hatton Correspondence*, 2: 122; HMC, *Dartmouth Ms.*, 1: 228; HMC, *9th Report*, Appendix, 460–61; Routh, ed., *Burnet's History*, 3: 351n; Mackintosh, *The Revolution*, 525; Dalrymple, ed., *Memoirs*, 3: 274; Van Citters to the states general, Dec. 9/19, 1688, Add. Ms. 31510, 195; Fitzroy, *Grafton*, 64.

85. Parker, *Memoirs*, 9–13; Lt. Col. G. Le M. Gretton, *The Campaigns and History of the Royal Irish Regiment* (Edinburgh, 1911), 1–4; Childs, *Army of James II*, 65–66; Webb, *Governors-General*, #137; Mackintosh, *The Revolution*, 531; but see Dalton, ed., *Army Lists*, 2: xx, 221; 3: 6, and Swift, comp., "Creichton Memoirs," Davis, ed., *Prose Works*, 5: 165–66, on Forbes's own refusal to act against King James and his consequent loss of the colonelcy. When Ormonde put Forbes's name forward to the peers as an officer who could reform the duke's own regiment, Churchill, always beforehand with Ormonde, reported that he had already seen to it, Beddard, *Kingdom*, 154. See *ibid.*, 167, on the fate of Forbes's Irish cadres. Some tried to seize the rich Indiaman *Asia* and escape. Running aground, they were secured by the Virginia and Newfoundland veteran, Sir Francis Wheeler of the Guards, in command of the *Kent*, *ibid.*, 81, 193n; Van Citters to the states general, Dec. [14/]24, 1688, Add. Ms. 31510, 200; Webb, *Governors-General*, #197. Note that Forbes's father, then colonel of the regiment, had been named as Dongan's replacement in New York, if Dongan had accepted a recall to Irish command, Effingham to Blathwayt, March 7, 1667, CWWB, 14 #5.

86. Van Citters to the states general, Reading, Dec. 1/10, 9/19, Add. Ms. 31510, 192, 197–8; Clarke, ed., *James Second*, 2: 240–41.

87. W.O. 4/1, 117; Recit Du Depart Du Roi Jacques II, Mackintosh, *The Revolution*, Appendix 703, dates this Dec. 8, but see Clarke, ed., *James Second*, 2: 251; Beddard, *Kingdom*, 24; Buckley, ed., *Ailesbury Memoirs*, 1: 196. Pepys to Dartmouth, Dec. 10, 1688, HMC, *Dartmouth Ms.*, 1: 227–28.

88. Mackintosh, *The Revolution*, 526; *The English Currant*, #2, Dec. 12–15, 1688. For a less colorful narration, see Roger Morrice's account, printed by Beddard, *Kingdom*, 170, and analyzed 32–34. *Ibid.*, 170, 193n., which has Jeffreys taken from a ship at Wapping, perhaps with Baltimore, as does Browning, ed., *Reresby*, Dec. 10, 1688, p. 539. The king's departure by land is detailed in Llewelyn Powys, *The Life & Times of Anthony a'Wood* (London, 1932), 270–72. See also Van Citters to the states general, Reading, Dec. 11/21, 1688, Add. Ms. 31510, 197. Reresby (Geiter and Speck, eds, 537) has the great seal taken by the chancellor, but sees the same result: a chaos that called in the prince to govern. For the view that the terrified tyrant simply panicked, see A. A. Mitchell, *HT* 15 (1965): 503–504.

89. Whitehall, Dec. 10, 1688, HMC, *Dartmouth Ms.*, 1: 226, and the parallel account by Van Citters, Dec. 10/21, 1688, Add. Ms. 31510, 197, which has the king, "seeing that he would not have been able to bring Parliament to moderation, and to fight was impossible, as he could not depend on his troops," fleeing to France. See also, Clarke, ed., *James Second*, 2: 249. Ailesbury, *Memoirs*, 1: 195; Turner, *James II*, 443–44.

90. Clarke, ed., *James Second*, 2: 249–51; *The English Currant* #2, Dec. 14, 1688; Feversham to the Prince of Orange, Dec. 11, 1688, HMC, *Dartmouth Ms.*, 1: 229–30, and see 232, 233; Turner, *James II*, 442. Geiter and Speck, eds., *Reresby*, 538–39, 541. The furious prince had Feversham arrested, Routh, ed., *Burnet's History*, 3: 345n. The prince had sent orders, even to the royalists, to keep the regiments together the moment he knew of James's flight, Mackintosh, *The Revolution*, 534–35, 582; Van Citters to the states general, Dec. [14/] 24, Add. Ms. 31510, 199–200. Hewitson, ed., *Bellingham Diary*, Dec. 15, 16, 17, 1688. On the Irish fright, the precursor of the French Revolution's "Grande Peur," see also Beddard, *Kingdom*, esp. 45, 82–85; Evans, "Revolution," *YAJ*, 278., and notes 91 and 92 below.

91. Peter Shackerley to "Great Sir!" [Blathwayt], Chester Castle, Dec. 13, 1688, Add. Ms. 38695, 103, and same to Lt. Gen. [Sir John] Werden, Dec. 15, 1688, *ibid.*, 104, and see 19. Shackerley's problems were compounded by the presence in the town of Col. Henry Gage's Catholic recruits, Hosford, *Nottingham*, 105. Cruickshanks, *By Force or Default?*, 35–37, paints Shackerley as a loyalist and the Irish fright as a panic manufactured to oust his ilk.

92. See also George Hilton Jones, "The Irish Fright of 1688: Real Violence and Imagined Massacre," *BIHR* 40 (1982): 148–53; Miller, "Militia and Army," *HJ* 4: 675–78; Mackintosh, *The Revolution*, 531–32.

93. *The English Currant* #2, Dec. 14, 1688; *The Universal Intelligence*, Dec. 11, 1688; Davis, *Second, Queen's*, 2: 77; Feversham to Preston, Windsor, Dec. 17, 1688, HMC, *Graham Ms.*, 421; the lords to Dartmouth, Dec. 11, 1688, HMC,

Dartmouth Ms., 1: 229, and see 230; Van Citters to the states general, Dec. 11/21, 1688, Add. Ms. 31510, 197; Mackintosh, *The Revolution,* 534; Clarke, ed., *James Second,* 2: 259–61; Feiling, *Tory Party,* 239.

94. Beddard, *Kingdom,* esp. 41, 57, 74, 80, 81; Beddard, "Loyalist Opposition," *BIHR* 40: 106; Beddard, "The Guildhall Declaration of 11 December 1688 and The Counter-Revolution of the Loyalists," *HJ* 11 (1968), 404–405, 411–12. Webb, *Governors-General,* #49, p. 263–75. See below, chapter six, for Vaughan's remarkable support of Churchill when he was accused of planning another putsch. Personal and cultural details, but nothing of politics, are given by Major Francis Jones, "The Vaughans of Golden Grove," *Transactions of the Honorable Society of Cymrodorion,* Session 1963, Pt. I, esp. 129–36. See also, Davies, *Gentlemen and Tarpaulins,* 197.

95. Webb, *Governors-General,* #198, pp. 378–403; Beddard, *Kingdom,* 38, 39, 71–72, 107, 109, 150–51, 160, 162.

96. Webb, *Governors-General,* #198, pp. 378–403; H. Horwitz, "Parliament and the Glorious Revolution," *BIHR* 47 (1974): 37; Beddard, "Anti-Popery and the London Mob, 1688," *HT* 38 (July 1988), 37, and "Guildhall Declaration" *HJ* 11: 413, 416–19.

97. Sachse, "Mob," *JBS* 4, 26–31, 37–38.

98. On Selwyn, see Webb, *Governors-General,* #58. *London Courant* #2, Dec. 12–15; Beddard, *Kingdom,* 44, 46, 96; *The Universal Intelligence* #2, Dec. 15, 1688; Philip Frowde to Dartmouth, London, Dec. 11, 1688, HMC, *Dartmouth Ms.,* I: 230; Clarke, ed., *James Second,* 2: 256–57; HMC, *Le Fleming Ms.,* 230.

99. Van Citters to the states general, Reading, Dec. [11/]21, Westminster, Dec. [14/24], 1688, Add. Ms. 31510, 197–98. *Two Illustrious Generals,* 26; *The Universal Intelligence* #2, Dec. 15, 1688.

100. *The English Currant* #2, Dec. 14, 1688; *The London Mercury,* Dec. 15, 1688; Davis, *Second, Queen's,* 2: 64; Padget, *New "Examen,"* 186–87. A warrant for Penn's arrest was issued Feb. 27, 1688/9, to which he demurred because he was preparing "to depart for America." On Penn's symbolic importance (and political isolation) see Bill Speck, "Religion's Role in the Glorious Revolution," *HT* 38 (July 1988): 32. See also Browning, ed., *Reresby,* Dec. 10, 1688, p. 539. Baltimore's commission, dated Oct. 10, 1688, is in S.P. 44/165, 108.

101. *The Universal Intelligence* #1, Dec. 11, 1688; W.O. 4/1, 117–18; Hamilton, *First Guards,* 1: 311; Beddard, *Kingdom,* 105, 116.

102. Van Citters to the states general, Dec. [14/]24, 1688, Add. Ms. 31510, 200; Egerton Ms. 2621, 84.

103. Beddard, *Kingdom,* 56–60; Powys, ed., *Anthony a'Wood,* 273–74. For the view that the populace that first welcomed James and then William was not fickle but, like so many eminent persons, were deceived by the prince's Declaration, see Tim Harris, "London Crowds," in Cruickshanks, *By Force or Default?,* 56. For Turner's (and probably, Churchill's) position, see Horwitz, "Parliament," *BIHR* 47: 37. In retrospect, it is hard to dispute Ailesbury: "a man must have been of a very weak discernment not to have comprehended that the prince came over for three crowns, not to redress grievances" (Buckley, ed., *Memoirs,* 223).

104. Berwick, *Memoirs*, 35; Philip Musgrave to Dartmouth, Dec. 11, 1688, HMC, *Dartmouth Ms.*, 1: 231, and see 234, 236; *The Universal Intelligence #3*, Dec. 18, 1688; Thompson, ed., *Hatton Correspondence*, 2: 123; HMC, *Le Fleming Ms.*, 230; Clarke, ed., *James Second*, 2: 261n., 262, 264–65, 273. Since the crisis of the Oxford parliament in 1681, three companies of the Coldstream had been quartered in the royal mews to offset the politically unreliable First Guards: Major P. R. Adair "The Coldstream Guards, c. 1680," *JSAHR* 40: 111–13; Mackinnon, *Coldstream Guards*, 163–66, Appendix #61, 70; Dalrymple, ed., *Memoirs*, 3: 275; Hamilton, *First Guards*, 1: 318–19; Davis, *Second, Queen's*, 2: 78; "Depart" in Mackintosh, *The Revolution*, 708–709 and continuation, 552–53, 548.

105. *Two Illustrious Generals*, 26; *The Universal Intelligence #3*, Dec. 18, and #5, Dec. 26, 1688; *The London Courant #1*, Dec. 18, #4, Dec. 22, *The London Mercury #5*, Dec. 27, 1688. The quotation is from *The English Currant #3*, Dec. 19, 1688. The quarters are listed at the head of *The London Gazette #2411*, Dec. 17–20, 1688. Hamilton, *First Guards*, 1: 317–20; Geiter and Speck, eds., *Reresby*, 545, Jan. 22, 1688/9: "And yet the Citty was soe pleased with their deliverers that they did not perceive their deformity, nor the oppression they laid under, which was much greater than what they felt from the English army." So too whig historians. Burnet's remark to Herbert about the army's second thoughts is quoted by Beddard, *Kingdom*, 62.

106. Report of the deputies for foreign affairs to the states, Oct. 8, 1688, Add. Ms. 31511, 11. See also the princes's declarations of 10 and 24 October 1688, Beddard, *Kingdom*, 124–50.

107. Routh, ed., *Burnet's History*, 3: 359; HMC, *Le Fleming Ms.*, 230; *The Orange Gazette #5*, Jan. 17, 1688/9.

108. Recit di Depart Du Roi, Mackintosh, *The Revolution*, 710, 712, and see *The Continuation*, 435, 439, 547, 564–65; Turner, *James II*, 452, 454; Miller, *James II*, 208–9. Harleian Ms. 6585, f. 280b; Clarke, ed., *James Second*, 2: 223, 255n, 259–60, 268, 272, 273, 275–77; Ailesbury, *Memoirs*, 1: 224. Routh, ed., *Burnet's History*, 341, 345n., implies that this scare tactic was Halifax's, as does "a Court Lady," possibly that infamous Jacobite intriguer, Eleanor Wall, Lady Oglethorpe, Cleveland's chamberwoman and Churchill's correspondent, especially in the interest of her son, James Edward, the Guards officer and founder of Georgia. Geiter and Speck, eds., *Reresby*, Feb. 2, 1688/9, 549–50, 552–53, 563.

Book III: Army and Revolution

epigraph: *Lives of the Two Illustrious Generals*, 30, The author of the *Lives* heard this prophecy related by the grand pensionary, Hensuis, when Marlborough was being constituted captain general of the allies.

Chapter Five: The Coup in the Colonies: 1689–1690

1. *The London Courant*, #4, Dec. 19, 1688; HMC, *Dartmouth Ms.*, 1: 249; *The English Currant*, #8, Jan. 2–4, 1688/9; John Childs, *The British Army of William*

III (Manchester, 1987), 17. Of the thirty-three officers in Cornbury's dragoons on Jan. 1, 1689, only twelve remained with the corps twelve months later, Atkinson, *Royal Dragoons*, 56–57.

2. "We are under a Conquest," wrote Bishop Compton to Archbishop Sancroft, but it was a Protestant one. Brown, "Compton," *HMPEC* 25:34–35. So too Bishop Burnet wrote three years later. The fact of conquest was a truth unwelcome to whigs (then and since). Burnet's observation was burned by the public hangman as contrary to William's second declaration, which disavowed "that wicked design of conquering the Nation." That "wicked attempt at conquest" would leave the nation at the discretion of the conqueror (as the American colonies were already held to be), Beddard, ed., *Kingdom*, 149. For Sancroft's observation see Robert Beddard, "The Unexpected Whig Revolution of 1688," in Beddard, ed., *Revolutions of 1688"* (Oxford, 1991), 44. See also M. P. Thompson, "The Idea of Conquest in Controversies over the 1688 Revolution," *JHI* 38 (1977), 33–46. That conquest conferred legitimacy on kings was a doctrine acceptable to Anglicans: Gerald M. Straka, *Anglican Reaction to the Revolution of 1688* (Madison, 1962), Ch. 5. Quotation from Geiter and Speck, eds., *Reresby*, 547.

3. *Ibid.*, 553; William's declaration of Oct. 10, 1688, Beddard, ed., *Kingdom*, 148.

4. *The English Currant*, #3, Dec. 14–19, 1688, and see #5, 7, 9. Sir John Fenwick, the Jacobite conspirator, succinctly described William's security system: the few English troops at home were dispersed in country quarters and rotated regularly, while "the main army [was] always abroad, where the only service they could do [King James] was desert to the French, who would not receive them because they would not trust them," HMC, *Buccleuch Ms.*, 2: Part 1, 396. [Hare,] *Marlborough*, 17. The whig denunciation is in [Wharton to William,] Dec. 25, 1689, Dalrymple, ed., *Memoirs*, vol. 3, p. 95–108, Appendix to Pt. II, Bk. IV; *ibid.*, (2d ed., London, 1773), 2: 85. Macaulay, *History*, 3: 1215; *London Gazette*, #2411, 2412, Dec. 17, 24, 1688; Feiling, *Tory Party*, 249.

5. Beddard, "Unexpected Revolution," in Beddard, ed. *Revolutions of 1688*, 64–65, 72–75, 86–87.

6. Foxcroft, *Halifax*, 2: 202–203: William's remark "shewd 1. that Ld. Churchill was very assuming, wch hee did not like; 2. It shewed a jealousy still of the Princess and that side of the house." William's "jealousy of being thought to be governed" did not immediately take effect but, "like some slow poison, worked at a great distance of time." All this was the more troubling to everyone involved, as William's provocation was Churchill's persuasion of a reluctant Anne to give way to William in the succession. See also, Halifax's memoranda in Add. Ms. 51511, 28, 40, 43; Churchill, *Marlborough*, 1: 276.

7. "Proceedings on the Crown," esp. Jan. 29, 30, Feb., 6, 1688/9, Add. Ms. 61538, 2–10. Culpepper and Lovelace were prominent among those who voted to declare the throne vacant. Grafton, Clarendon, Nottingham, Rochester, Craven, Ormonde, and Dartmouth dissented. James's old retainers observed that a regency was better for the king "than setting his Crowne upon another Head wch except by Force is never to be reverst," Beddard, ed., "Loyalist Op-

position," *BIHR* 40 (1967), 107; Mark Goldie, "The Political Thought of the Anglican Revolution," Beddard, ed., *Revolutions of 1688*, 109–10. For Turner, see Feiling, *Tory Party*, 250–51, 253. The Diary of Henry Hyde, earl of Clarendon, Jan. 27, Feb. 5, 1688/9, Singer ed., *Clarendon Correspondence*, 2: 214, 260; Halifax's memorandum, Dec. 30, 1688, Add. Ms. 51511, 28; Geiter and Speck, eds., *Reresby*, 551.

8. *Conduct of the Duchess of Marlborough*, 16–17; *Two Illustrious Generals*, 27; Atkinson, *Marlborough*, 59–60. Note that the deciding vote to declare the throne vacant was cast by that ancient enemy of James Stuart, the earl of Carlisle, former governor-general of Jamaica, standing on his crutches: Clarendon Diary, Feb. 6, 1688/9, Singer, ed., *Clarendon Correspondence*, 2: 261, and see 255; Webb, *Governors-General*, 95–97. Feiling, *Tory Party*, 249. Churchill abstained from the vote to declare William and Mary king and queen, *ibid.*, 254. See also Beddard, "Unexpected Revolution," Beddard, ed., *Revolutions of 1688*, 89–92, who stresses Sarah's role in arranging spiritual advice for Anne, and see Horwitz, "Parliament," *BIHR* 47: 43, 45–47. The motion to make William king was offered to the lords by the marquis of Winchester (afterwards duke of Bolton), Francis Nicholson's patron and colonel of the Leeward Islands legion. Winchester's son made the motion in the commons. See n. 15, below. See also Gregg, *Anne*, 69–71. Churchill conveyed to the lords Princess Anne's plea that the lords "concur with the Commons," in offering the crown to William and Mary, and Anne's statement that "for the good of the Nation and safety of the Protestant religion she was heartily willing to acquise therein."

9. S.P. 44/165, 265; Coxe, *Marlborough*, 1: 43; Atkinson, *Marlborough*, 102; Wolsey, *Marlborough*, 2: 64; Dalton, ed., *Army Lists*, 3: 1; [Hare,] *Marlborough*, 17; Clarendon Diary, Jan. 13, 1688 [/89], Singer, ed., *Clarendon Correspondence*, 2: 245. W.O. 5/5, 103–104; Lediard, *Marlborough*, 1: 87; John Childs, *The Nine Years' War and the British Army, 1688–1697: The Operations in the Low Countries* (Manchester, 1991), 100.

10. Webb, *Governors-General*, #27; Charnock, *Biographia Navalis*, 1: 59–61; Latham and Matthews, eds., *Pepys*, June 14, 1665, 6: 127; Clarendon, *History*, 1, par. 101, 105. A fourth earl, whose mark on his time was to become a general of royalist artillery (*ibid.*, 7: 113, p. 396, n.6), briefly succeeded but died without heirs in June 1679. The title being extinguished, Churchill was free to choose it. It is likely that James Ley, earl of Marlborough, was the source of the Blenheim Ms. on "the Empire of the Great Mogul." It was governed "by keeping a Standing Army in every Province" and by the Mogul himself being "allways at the head of a Powefull Army," Add. Ms. 61358, 90–111, esp. 76. On his faith, see James Earl of Marlborough, *Old James*, near the coast of Holland, April 24, 1665, quoted in Granville Penn, *Memorials of the Professional Life & Times of Sir William Penn Knt.* (London, 1833), 2: 430–32 & n.; Webb, *Governors-General*, #7; Davies, *Gentlemen and Tarpaulins*, 111.

11. *The London Mercury or Moderate Intelligencer*, #6, Dec. 27 to 31, 1688; *The Universal Intelligence*, #7, Dec. 29 to Jan. 1 1688 [/9]; Sir Charles Littleton to Lord Hatton, Apr. 9, July 16, 30, 1689, Add. Ms. 29578, 204, 215, 216b; Thompson, ed., *Hatton Correspondence*, 2: 129–30, and see 131.

12. *The Orange Gazette*, #2, Dec. 31 to Jan. 3, 1688/9; Littleton to Blathwayt, Mar. 14, 15, 1688/9, Add. Ms. 38695, 146–48, Thompson, ed., *Hatton Correspondence*, 2: 129–30; Littleton to Hatton, Apr. 9, July 30, [16]89, Add. Ms. 29578, 204, 216; W.O. 5/5, 108; Childs, *Army of William III*, 17; Charles D. Ellestad, "The Mutinies of 1689," *JSAHR* 53 (1975): 9ff. Littleton did not give up the Sheerness government until July 12/22, 1690, when Queen Mary wrote to ask the king how to dispose of it, Dalrymple, ed., *Memoirs*, vol. 3, p. 162, App. to Pt. II, Bk. IV.

13. Dalton, ed., *Army Lists*, 3: 102, 128; S.P. 44/165, 182, 429, dates the commission Jan. 15, 1689/90. Webb, *Governors-General*, #58.

14. Shackerly to Blathwayt, Jan. 7, 14, 23, 26, 29, 1688 [/9], Add. Ms. 3695, 124, 128, 134, 136, 138; Blathwayt to Shackerly, Jan. 10, 1688/9, W.O. 4/1, 120; Crawford to Geo. Clarke, Feb. 13, 1689, Egerton Ms. 2618, 158; Halifax memoranda, Add. Ms. 51511, 28, 62. Lediard, *Marlborough*, 1: 86–87; Wolsey, *Marlborough*, 2: 119, 120, 125; Coxe, *Marlborough*, 1: 42; Ashley, *Marlborough*, 27–28.

15. Churchill, *Marlborough*, 1: 276–77. This was the case even for the dispatch of the fourteen regiments with Kirke to Ireland, W.O. 4/1, 129–30, where the orders were signed "Churchill" and then "Schomberg." His commission as captain-general was dated in June 1689, S.P. 44/165, 316. Webb, "Blathwayt," *WMQ* 26 (1969): 373–81. On Schomberg, see John Childs, "For God and for Honor," *HT* 38 (July 1986), 46–52. Note the dispatch of the Irish to the emperor, W.O. 4/1, 127. Webb, Officers and Governors . . . , Ph.D. Dissertation, University of Wisconsin, Madison (1965), Appendix I, p. 26–28; Webb, *Governors-General*, 153; W. L. Grant and James Munro, eds., *Acts of the Privy Council, Colonial*, 3: Ap. I, II, V and 5: Ap. 1; C.O. 5/1300; *CSPD 1689–1690*, 248: Shrewsbury to Bolton, Sept. 10, 1689: "As to Captain Nicholson, his Majesty is as yet undecided how he shall dispose of his government of New York but however he succeeds in this I doubt not but he will feel the benefit of your recommendation." Lieutenant Colonel Holt was breveted to command before he left for the West Indies, but Bolton's other lieutenant colonel was not promoted as he was not going to serve out of the kingdom. See #8, above.

16. Van Citters to the states general, Nov. 23, 1688, Add. Ms. 31510, 174; *CSPC 1689–1692*, #109; Dalton, ed., *Army Lists*, 2: 75, 115, 228–29. Marlborough stripped his own troop of the Life Guards to officer the Flanders expedition, another example of the Life Guards' function as an officer training corps. Compare *ibid.*, 2: 117 with 3: 20. On Belasyse at York, see Childs, *Dictionary*; Browning, ed., *Reresby*, 530. For Colchester s.v. "Savage, Richard, 4th Earl Rivers," Childs, *Dictionary*.

17. Webb, *Governors-General*, #56; Hewitt, ed., *Bellingham Diary*, 37; C.O. 5/1, 11–25; Foxcroft, *Halifax*, 2: 233–38; Murison, Blathwayt's Empire, 135–36.

18. [Sir Robert Southwell or Blathwayt, to Nottingham or Marlborough,] Mar. 23, 1688/9, Blathwayt Papers BL 418, Huntington Library, printed in Michael G. Hall, Lawrence H. Leder, and Michael G. Kammen, eds., *The Glorious Revolution in America, Documents in the Colonial Crisis of 1689*, (New York, 1964, 1972), 67–69. On the circumstances of this document, see Webb, "Blathwayt,"

WMQ 26: 377–79. The memorandum is endorsed with the date and two phrases: "Copy to the Earle of Nottingham. Touching a Conjunction with the Dutch in the West Indies." The addressee is alerted to "Our Interest in the West Indies," both in the islands and on the continent, and, if the author is protected from the whigs, is promised political information as well. "This business which yor Lopp has now in Charge, namely how to regulate a Conjunction of Our Forces with Holland," was as much Marlborough's business, as the English military chief, as it was Nottingham's, as secretary of state. The ideas in the memorandum were, by 1689, more clearly identified with Blathwayt than with his old chief at the colonial office, Southwell. They had not changed when Blathwayt put them to Marlborough in 1701. For a photocopy of the endorsement, and for helpful correspondence, I am indebted to Mary L. Robertson, Curator of Manuscripts at the Huntington. The exception to Dutch exclusion was the allied recapture of St. Eustasius from the French, William Thomas Morgan, "The British West Indies During King William's War (1689–97)," *JMH*, 2 (1930): 387. Webb, "Blathwayt," *WMQ* 26: 373–74; Simon Groenveld, " 'J'equippe une flotte tres considerable': The Dutch Side of the Glorious Revolution," Beddard, ed., *Revolutions of 1688*, 242.

19. "Marleborough" for the Hudson's Bay Co. to the King, referred to the privy council committee, Apr. 25, 1689, C.O. 135/1, ff. 68–70, pp. 122–26.

20. These estimates reflect points made to the author by Professor J. R. Jones. See Feiling, *Tory Party*, 255; John Childs, *The Nine Years War and the British Army, 1689–1697* (Manchester, 1991), 25–27; Childs, *British Army of William III*, 252–53; John Brewer, *The Sinews of Power, War, Money, and the English State 1683–1783* (New York, 1989), Table 2.1; D. W. Jones, *War and Economy* (Oxford, 1988), 7–11.

21. Rich, *Hudson's Bay Company*, 256; Morgan, "British West Indies," *JMH*, 2: 387; Blathwayt to Marlborough, May. 28, 1701, Add. Ms. 9722, 127–28; Webb, "Blathwayt," WMQ, 26: 411. Fears that the Dutch would take "Canada" from the French were voiced also in New England, Thomas Hutchinson, *The History of the Colony and Province of Massachusetts Bay*, Lawrence Shaw Mayo, ed. (Cambridge, Mass., 1936), 1: 337.

22. Memorandum of March 23, 1688/9, Huntington BL 418, and Hall, Leder, and Kammen, eds., *Revolution Documents*, 67.

23. *Ibid.*, 68, 69.

24. The king's proclamation, Sept. 28, 1688, *London Gazette*, #2386, Sept. 27 to Oct. 1, 1688.

25. Andros's proclamation, Whitmore, ed., *Andros Tracts*, 75n–76n; Randolph to the privy council committee, "Common Gaole, Boston," May, 29, 1689, *ibid.*, 3: 232; *NYCD*, 3: 578–83; Webb, "Trials of Andros," in Martin, ed., *Nation-Making*, 42–45. There is some indication that Bostonians had heard of William's invasion as early as mid-December 1688: Jo. George to Sec. Admiralty, June 12, 1689, C.O. 5/905, 122.

26. The declaration of April 18, 1689, Whitmore, ed., *Andros Tracts*, 1: 11–19, and see 55; Viola Florence Barnes, *The Dominion of New England* (New Haven, 1923; New York, 1960), 241–42; An Account of the Forces Raised in New England, *CSPC, 1689–1692*, #912; Webb, "Trials," *Nation-Making*, 44, n. 32. Richard S. Dunn, *Puritans and Yankees*, (Princeton, N. J., 1962), 251–52; C.O. 135/1, 69b; Randolph to the Committee, Oct. 8, 1688, May 29, 1689, *NYCD*, 3: 579, 581 and *CSPC 1689–1692*, #152.

27. The provincial commanders' complaints are in C. M. Andrews, ed., *Narratives of the Insurrections 1675–1690* (New York, 1915, 1967), 247–48. Their realization that war strengthens the executive was expressed by "AB" in Whitmore, ed., *Andros Tracts*, 1: 193–94. The loyalist counterstrike by "CD" is in *ibid.*, 255–56, 261, 263, and 2: 207–209. A judicious summary is Hutchinson's, *History*, 1: 314–15.

28. Richard R. Johnson, *Adjustment to Empire: The New England Colonies 1675–1715* (New Brunswick, N. J. 1981), 88; Whitmore, ed., *Andros Tracts*, 1: 171–73; Cotton Mather, *Decennium Luctuosum* (1699), in C. H. Lincoln, ed., *Narratives of the Indian Wars 1675–1699* (New York, 1913, 1941), 186–95. The Maine forces are listed in *CSPC 1689–92*, #912. See also #902 for the regular companies. On Lt. Jordan's discipline, see #207–208; Whitmore, ed., *Andros Tracts*, 2: 155, 173.

29. Sr Edmund Andros's Account, Rec'd 27 May 1690, *NYCD*, 3: 722–26; Whitmore, ed., *Andros Tracts*, 1: 150–52, 156, 171; 3: 18–27, esp. 21–22; *CSPC 1689–1692*, #901–902; Andrews, ed., *Narratives*, 229–36.

30. *CSPC 1689–1692*, #207, 208, in which Lt. John Jordan describes the antisocial frontiersmen and the consequent coup at Pemaquid, Ap. 27, 1689. Whitmore, ed., *Andros Tracts*, 1: 150–56; Hall et al., eds., *Documents*, 57–58.

31. Andrews, ed., *Narratives*, 197, 231.

32. "A Particular Account of the Late Revolution at Boston in the Colony and Province of Massachusetts," Andrews, ed., *Narratives*, 196; Nicholson &c. to Andros, March 2, 1688/9, *NYHSC* 1 (1868): 242–43; Randolph to the Committee, May 29, 1689, *CSPC 1689–1692*, #152: *NYCD* 3: 582; Randolph to [Edwyn Stede,] "Gaol in Boston, May 16th '89," Robert Noxon Toppan, ed., *Edward Randolph*, (Boston, 1899), 4: 264–65; Andrews, ed., *Narratives*, 323.

33. John Nelson [to St. Castine, Mar. 16, 1689,], in Ian Steele, "Origins of Boston's Revolutionary Declaration," *NEQ*, 62: 76–77; [Increase Mather,] "A Vindication of New England," Whitmore, ed., *Andros Tracts*, 2: 50–52. "The soldiers Charges Against Sr. E. Andros," *ibid.*, 1: 150–51; Hall et al., eds., *Documents*, 58; Barnes, *Dominion*, 241; Johnson, *Adjustment*, 87.

34. Samuel Mather's Account, Whitmore, ed., *Andros Tracts*, 3: 145n.; Nathaniel Byfield's Account, Samuel Prince's Account, Andrews, ed., *Narratives*, 170–75, 180–81, 187–90; The Petition of John Riggs, *CSPC 1689–92*, #282 and see #261 I; John Riggs's Narrative, C.O. 5/905, 85–87; Callieres to Seignelay, Jan. 1688 [/90], *NYCD* 9: 404–405: "the Recent Revolution in England will change the face of American affairs. . . . Chevalier Andros, now Governor-General of New England and New York . . . is Protestant, so that there is no reason to hope that he will remain faithful to the King of England, and we expect that he will not only urge the Iroquois to continue the war against us but that he will even furnish them with Englishmen to lead them. . . . " Callieres also anticipated that the Treaty of Neutrality was effectively abrogated if only because the

Dutch of New York would "submit to the orders of the Prince of Orange, and even force their Governor, did he not consent, to acknowledge him," *ibid.*, 408.

35. Whitmore, ed., *Andros Tracts*, 2: 50, 52. N.B. that the mutiny in Maine had two or three stages: the provincial desertions that followed Andros's departure, the deposition of his officers, and the dispersion of the red-coated soldiers. Some episodes followed news of the Maine deserters' revolt in Boston. Others were obedient to the orders of the coup's council of safety: *CSPC 1689–92*, #152, 407; Andrews, ed., *Narratives*, 204–205, 233; *NYCD* 3: 582–84. Following the coup in Boston, Pemaquid was deserted by the provincials, Maj. Brockholes was carried prisoner to Boston, and the regulars under James Weems were overwhelmed. At Newcastle, Lt. Jordan was sent prisoner to Boston and the post was deserted, On the Kennebeck, Major Thomas Savage and the provincial officers rose against Lt. Col. MacGregorie. Then those who had not already done so, deserted the forts: Whitmore, ed., *Andros Tracts*, 3:31–32, but see 35–36.

36. *Ibid.*, 2: 194; "AB" in Hall et al., eds., *Documents*, 47–50; Barnes, *Dominion*, 238 n. 17. There is no reason to doubt that, as he said, John Winslow brought "William of Orange's Declarations" to Boston from Nevis, on April 4, 1689. These would have been the declarations of Oct. 10, Nov. 20, and [Hugh Specke's] spurious "third Declaration of the Prince of Orange," dated Nov. 28, 1688. These are quite distinct from the Nottingham declaration of Nov. 22/26 and the Guildhall declaration of Dec. 11, the items that Steele conjectures Winslow brought to Boston. Steele, "Origins," *NEQ* 63: 77. William's declarations are printed in Beddard, ed., *Kingdom*, 124–50. The prince's declarations, which were usually combined with his letters to the armed forces, especially that to the English army of October 28, 1688, quite sufficed to authorize the military coup at Boston. They were the more likely to have done so because they preceded the Nottingham and Guildhall statements by two months. See *A Compleat Collection of Papers, in twelve parts* (London, 1689), I #7, 15; II #1, 6, 9. On the militia revolt, see "AB" in Hall, et al., eds., *Documents*, 49–50 and Whitmore, ed., *Andros Tracts*, 2: 194.

37. Andros's letter of Apr. 16, 1688, in Hutchinson, *History*, 1: 316–17; Webb, *Governors-General*, 198.

38. *CSPC 1689–92*, #407; David S. Lovejoy, *The Glorious Revolution in America* (New York, 1972), 238, but see 242; George Chalmers, *An Introduction to the History of the Revolt of the American Colonies* (Boston, 1845), 1: 207. Some confirmation of Mather's theory is offered by [Burnet's?] publication of Mather's "Narrative of the Miseries of New England," in the *Compleat Collection*, V #10. On the Mather mission, see Andrews, ed., *Narratives*, 271–75, and Mather himself, *ibid.*, 276–97, esp. 277.

39. William of Orange's order of Jan. 12, 1688/9, C.O. 5/905, 42 "to Sr Edm Andros, for Officers Civill and Military, except Papists, to keep their Imployments" is marginally noted: "upon the Application of Sr. Wm. Phipps and Mr Mather this letter was stopped. . . . " The other relevant documents are printed in Robert Earle Moody and Richard Clive Simmons, eds., *The Glorious Revolution in Massachusetts, Selected Documents, 1689–1692* (Boston, 1982), 428–38.

The communications issues are canvassed in Ian K. Steele, *The English Atlantic 1675–1740* (New York, 1986), Ch. 6, esp. 104. See also, Webb, *Governors-General*, 35; Johnson, *Adjustment*, 87; Lovejoy, *Glorious Revolution*, 281–288. On Jan. 1688/9 planning, see also "CD" in Andrews, *Narratives*, 257; Whitmore, ed., *Andros Tracts*, 1: 71–72; 2: 210; 3: 194, 226; *CSPC 1689–92*, #152, 285, 407; Barnes, *Dominion*, 237–38. On the new regime's imperial intentions, see *NYCD* 3: 578, and for the restoration of Compton's American religious jurisdiction, see *ibid.*, 688 and *CSPC 1689–92*, #992, 1164 VII.

40. Barnes, *Dominion*, 241–42; Whitmore, ed., *Andros Tracts*, 1: 11–12; 3: 145–46; Andrews, ed., *Narratives*, 182, 186–87, 199–202; *CSPC 1689–92*, #96, #261 II.

41. Note that the puritan elite recognized that the provincial army, and the organizers of the eight Boston companies who made the crucial arrests, "consists of such as were no freemen in the Old Government" (Moody and Simmons, eds., *Documents*, 359) and who did not approve of the resumption of the charter and the restoration of puritan rule. *CSPC 1689–92*, #885; and see Richard R. Johnson, *John Nelson* (New York, 1991), 55.

42. Randolph to the privy council committee, May 29, July 23, 1689, *CSPC 1689–92*, #152, 285; *NYCD* 3: 510, 581, 740, 901; Johnson, *Nelson*, 46–47, 51–52; Johnson, *Adjustment*, 85, 89–90; Andrews, ed., *Narratives*, 173, 198n.; 200–201, 207, 209, 263; "AB" in Whitmore, ed., *Andros Tracts*, 2: 196; Hall, et al., eds., *Documents*, 50.

43. "Mr Riggs his Narrative of the Proceedings at Boston in New England in Seizing the Government there," C.O. 5/905, p. 85; *CSPC 1689–92*, #261; Nathaniel Byfield, *An Account of the Late Revolution in New England* (London, 1689) rpr. Whitmore, ed., *Andros Tracts*, 1: 3–4, 2: 195; Andrews, ed., *Narratives*, 170–173, 199–200, 213–214; Cotton Mather, "Life of Phips," *Magnalia Christi Americana* (Hartford, 1853), 52; Barnes, *Dominion*, 239; Johnson, *Adjustment*, 90–91; Dunn, *Puritans and Yankees*, 254–55; *CSPC 1689–92*, #196 I, II; #261 III. The allegation of Lt. Condon's Catholicism is [Increase Mather's] in Whitmore, ed., *Andros Tracts*, 2: 36, although it appears to be contradicted by Condon himself in his log. Compare the Appendix, "Inglorious Revolution: The Channel Fleet in 1688."

44. Rose Paybook, ADM 33/123; Jo. George to Sec. Admiralty, Rose at Boston N Engld June the 12th 1689, C.O. 5/905, 122. That the allegations were Small's, and that he was widely believed in Boston, appear in the *Rose* Log for June 16, 1689, ADM 51/3955, 134v–135. See also *CSPC 1689–92*, #196, 774; Whitmore, ed., *Andros Tracts*, 2: 194–95; Hall et al., eds., *Documents*, 50–51.

45. Riggs's Narrative, C.O. 5/905, 85; Rose Log, ADM 51/3955, 134; Andrews, ed., *Narratives*, 171–72, 200, 207, 259; Addresses of Boston's Anglicans to the king, Whitmore, ed., *Andros Tracts*, 2: 10–14; and see 44, 45n–55, 211–212, but see 198–99; *CSPC 1689–92*, #510, 742, 1217; 1239; Johnson, *Adjustment*, 77, 84, 99–100; Hall et al., eds., *Documents*, 51.

46. Mather, *Magnalia Christi Americana*, 2: 588–89. The governor's party included the remainder of the Anglican elite, headed by the colonel of the City Regiment, who was a founder of King's Chapel, Charles Lidget. Andrews, ed.,

Narratives, 171, 173, 174, 187–88, 217; *CSPC 1689–92,* #96; Barnes, *Dominion,* 242, n.27. On Lt. Treffrey, see *CSPC 1689–92,* #283, and see #261 I. The governor-general blamed the dissident councilors and the charter magistracy for recruiting the two thousand men who "appeared under arms at Boston under the command of those who were officers in the sayd former popular government," Andrews, ed., *Narratives,* 232, and see 172, 175–82, 200.

47. The declaration was printed by a practiced whig pamphleteer, Benjamin Harris. See Webb, *1676,* 186, and, for Harris's latest prints, see Steele, "Origins," *NEQ* 62: 79n. Harris reprinted in Boston the "Declaration of the Nobility, Gentry and Commonality at the Rendezvous at Nottingham, November 22, 1688" and "The Declaration of the Lords Spiritual and Temporal . . . Assembled at Guildhall 11th Decemb. 1688," Evans #465. The Boston Declaration of April 18, 1689, Whitmore, ed., *Andros Tracts,* 1: 11–19; *CSPC 1689–92,* #261 I; the Nottingham declaration, Ducket, ed., *Penal Laws,* 113–15; *A Second Collection of Papers Relating to the Present Juncture of Affairs in England* (London, 1689).

48. Despite Ian K. Steele's assertion ("Origins," *NEQ* 62: 79–80, and Steele, *English Atlantic,* 105–106), the Nottingham and Boston declarations have almost nothing in common, save for the phrase about "patterns." The differences reflect the distinction between the coup in process at Nottingham (the Nottingham Declaration referred to a prospective parliament only) and the triumph of William a month afterward (the Boston declaration referred to what "Orders from his Highness with the *English Parliament,* shall direct"). Still, Steele's larger point, that the Boston elite trod in English footsteps, is clearly correct. See [Increase Mather,] "Vindication," Whitmore, ed., *Andros Tracts,* 2: 50–51 and Byfield in Andrews, ed., *Narratives,* 181. See Chapter Four, n. 65.

49. Hutchinson, *History,* 1: 317.

50. Summons to Sir Edmund Andros to Surrender the Fort, At the Town House in Boston, April 18, 1689, C.O. 5/905, 97; Riggs's Narrative, *ibid.,* 85, and see p. 143; *CSPC 1689–92,* #261 III, and see #510, 33; Andrews, ed., *Narratives,* 182, 188, 201–203, 232; Johnson, *Nelson,* 52.

51. Whitmore, ed., *Andros Tracts,* 1: 6; 2: 8–9; *Rose* Log, April 18, 1689, ADM 51/3955, Pt. 7 (350v).

52. Riggs's Narrative, C.O. 5/905, 86; *CSPC 1689–92,* #261; Andrews, ed., *Narratives,* 189, 205–206. For the alternative account, that Randolph conveyed Andros's advice to Treffrey at the Fort and he to Pippon at the Castle, see *ibid.,* 202, 206; Whitmore, ed., *Andros Tracts,* 2: 197–98; Hall, et al., eds., *Documents,* 51. See also Johnson, *Nelson,* 54–55.

53. Prince in Andrews, ed., *Narratives,* 188; George to [Pepys,] June 12, 1689, C.O. 5/905, 123; *CSPC 1689–92,* #196.

54. *Rose* Log, Sat. 20 Ap. 1689, ADM 51/3955, Pt. 7, 134; Riggs's Narrative, C.O. 5/905, 87. Prince (Andrews, ed., *Narratives,* 188) has the Castle surrender first and then its guns, with those of the fort batteries, forced the *Rose* to capitulate.

55. Andrews, ed., *Narratives,* 189, 190, 198, 103, 204; George to [Pepys], June 12, 1689, *ibid.,* 216–17, and C.O. 5/905, 122–23; John Gorham Palfrey, *History* *of New England During the Stuart Dynasty* (Boston, 1870), 3: 582. On the peculiar religious character of the Massachusetts rising, see Barnes, *Dominion,* 251–53.

56. *CSPC 1689–92,* #510; Hutchinson, *History,* 1: 325–27; Whitmore, ed., *Andros Tracts,* 2: 199; Hall et al., eds., *Documents,* 52: "the Sword yet continued in every man's hands, and for divers weeks the colony continued without pretence to *Civil Government.*"

57. Hutchinson, *History,* 1: 328; William Pencak, *War, Politics & Revolution in Provincial Massachusetts* (Boston, 1981), 18.

58. Webb, "Trials," Martin, ed., *Nation-Making,* 43–53; *NYHSC* 1: 264, 266.

59. "A Short Account of the loss of Pemaquid Fort, New England," *CSPC 1689–92,* #316, and see #286 I, 291; "The Journal of Dr Benjamin Bullivant" *MHSP* 1878, 106; *CSPC 1689–92,* #885; Barnes, *Dominion,* 260.

60. Webb, "Nicholson," *WMQ,* 23: 521–23; *NYCD* 3: 423–24, 428–30, 465, 467, 477, 503–505, 506–13, 568–69, 579–80, 583–84, 590–97; C.O. 138/5, 78–80; C.O. 135/1, 69b, and above, Chapter Four.

61. *NYCD* 3: 655; Hall et al., eds., *Documents,* 98.

62. Randolph to Blathwayt, Oct. 2, 1688, CWWB, 1, #5; *CSPC 1689–1692,* #617, and see #350, 362, 459, 690, 1127; "Address of the Militia of New York to William and Mary," June 1689; Captain Leisler to same, Aug. 20, 1689, *NYCD* 3: 583–84, 615–16, and see 630, 655–66, 671–72, 676, 732.

63. Churchill to James II, Nov. 23, 1688, Churchill, *Marlborough,* 1: 263–64; Webb, "Nicholson," *WMQ,* 23: 522–26; Nicholson &c. to Committee, May 15, 1689, *NYCD* 3: 574–76 and see 577, 583–85, 590; *CSPC 1689–1692,* #902; *NYHSC* 1: 267. Andrews, ed., *Narratives,* 376: "all professed Papists to assist in making Arbitrary Placats, and forcing obedience to them from a Protestant free People."

64. *NYHSC* 1: 241, 253, 258–59; *NYCD* 3: 591, 614, 660; John Romeyn Brodhead, *History of the State of New York* (New York, 1871), 2: 527–28; David William Voorhees, In Behalf of the true Protestants religion: the Glorious Revolution in New York, Ph.D. Dissertation, New York University, 1988; Webb, "Nicholson," *WMQ,* 23: 523–24; Nicholson to Lt. Col. Allyn, Dec. 4, 1688, J. Hammond Trumbull, ed., *The Public Records of the Colony of Connecticut* (Hartford, 1859), 3: 454–55; *CSPC 1689–92,* #671; Hall et al., eds., *Documents,* 102.

65. Robert Livingston to Randolph, Mar. 22, 1688/9, Toppan, ed., *Randolph,* 4: 262; *NYHSC* 1: 246; *NYCD* 3: 584, 591; *CSPC 1689–92,* #1429.

66. Representation of Ens. Jost Stol, Nov. 16, 1689, *NYCD* 3: 632. Leisler, Sergeant William Churchill (or Churcher) & Stoll had now established a subaltern system for bypassing or coercing the commissioned officers of the city regiment. They used it whenever they felt their hold on power slipping, *ibid.,* 638. Webb, "Nicholson," *WMQ,* 23: 523–24.

67. *NYCD* 3: 584, 591, 598, 603, 637, 568. Some of the noncoms asked Col. Bayard to lead the coup, the alternative being assassination. Bayard refused, but, apparently, four captains (Leisler needed no threats) did not. Note the similarities between New York's mutiny and that at Portsmouth.

68. Nicholson &c. to the privy council committee, May 15, 1689, C.O. 5/905, 82; *NYHSC* 1: 245, 259–60, 273. Contrast W.O. 4/1, 117; Stephanus Van Courtland to Andros, July 9, 1689, *NYCD* 3: 591–2 and see 603; *CSPC 1689–1692*, Addenda, #2736–2739. On the export of the Protestant putsch southwards from Boston, see Barnes, *Dominion*, 248–50.

69. *NYCD* 3: 592, 668; declaration of Suffolk Freeholders, May 3, [1689], *ibid.*, 577; *CSPC 1689–1692*, #104; C.O. 5/1081, 3, 3A, on the Queen's County coup. See also, Hall et al., eds., *Documents*, 56, 103–104; *NYHSC* 1: 252–53; Voorhees, Revolution in New York, 127.

70. Nicholson, flypse, Cortland, and Bayard to privy council committee, May 15, 1689, C.O. 5/905, 82; Captain Leisler to King William, Aug. 20, 1689, *NYCD* 3: 614, and see 668. *CSPC 1689–92*, #1746.

71. *NYCD* 3: 592, 593. There *was* a French plan to blockade the province by sea and invade it by land, which eventuated in the destruction of Schenectady. Details are in *ibid.*, 9: esp. 422–26, 428–30, 440–47, 452. Nicholson &c. to Committee, May 15, 1689, C.O. 5/905, 81–84, ptd. *NYCD* 3: 574–76, 592; *CSPC 1689–1692*, #121, 190–92, 1740.

72. That key coupster, Albert Bosch, sergeant of Cuyler's company, heard the exchange from outside Nicholson's window. *NYHSC* 1: 254–55, 267, 279; Voorhees, Revolution in New York, 133; Trumbull, ed., *Records of Connecticut*, 3: 460–63; Whitmore, ed., *Andros Tracts*, 3: 33, 37. Militia address, *NYCD* 3: 583–84. There was the usual class and political division between cavalry and infantry in the New York provincial army. The troopers (who had to provide their own mount, horse furniture, sword, and pistols) refused to support the coup after the first hysteria evaporated. Leisler arrested eight troopers for refusing to agree that some visiting Harvard students were French papist counterrevolutionaries, *ibid.*, 615–16. *NYHSC* 1: 254–55, 268, 269–70, 277, 288. The Leislerian account is in O'Callaghan, ed., *DNHY* 2: 3–4 and see 388–90. *NYCD* 3: 614–16, 654–57; Andrews, ed., *Narratives*, 375–401.

73. *NYCD* 3: 614–16, 654–57; Andrews, ed., *Narratives*, 375–401.

74. [Colonel of the City Regiment, Nicholas Bayard,] "A Modest and Impartial Narrative," Andrews, ed., *Narratives*, 325, and *NYCD* 3: 669; *CSPC 1689–92*, #121, 160, 458; *NYCD* 3: 504, 577, 584, 634, 637; *NYHSC* 1: 288, 292–93, 295.

75. In civilian life, Sergeant Churchill, or "Churcher," was a mason and Jost Stoll, Leisler's second, a barkeep. *CSPC 1689–92*, #458; *NYCD* 3: 669; *DHNY* 2: 3–4; Hall et al., eds., *Documents*, 111.

76. *NYCD* 3: 585, 717; *CSPC 1689–92*, #175, 187–89.

77. "A Declaration of the Inhabitants Soujers," May 31, 1689, *DHNY* 2: 10, 27, 28–30, 55; *NYCD* 3: 583–84, 589–90, 594–95, 598–602, 603, 606, 615–17, 621, 633, 641–42, 646, 654, 671, 673, 675, 682, 684, 709, 716, 717; C. O. 5/1081, 21, 57, cited in Lovejoy, *Glorious Revolution*, 256, 284; Hall et al., eds., *Documents*, 109–10; *NYHSC* 1: 268, 270, 28, 288–90; Bartholomew de Roux (of Minvell's company), Sept. 26, 1689, *CSPC 1689–1692*, 1458, and the Huguenot fort laborer Daniel de Clarke, Sept. 26, 1689, *ibid.*, #459, and see 171–73, 175, 211, 216, 221, 241, 242, 274, 288–89, 302, 319–20, 322, 359, 360–62, 365, 450, 567, 632, 899, 955, 1084, 1246.

78. Andrews, ed., *Narratives,* 366–67, 387–88, 389.

79. *CSPC 1689–1692,* #1246.

80. *NYCD* 3: 629–32, 656–57, 671.

81. "Complaint from Heaven with a Huy and Crye and Petition out of Virginia and Maryland," C.O. 1/36, 213–18, ptd. *AMD* 5: 134–52; analyzed in Webb, *1676,* 70–79. On Coode's testimony, see *ibid.,* 79–83. Andrews, *Colonial Period,* 2: 343–45, 347–48, 378–79; Russell R. Menard, "From Servant to Freeholder . . . ," *WMQ* 30(1973): 37–74; David W. Jordan, "John Coode, Perennial Rebel," *MHM* 70(1975): 2–4, 7–8; *EJC* 1: 419.

82. On the 1681 crisis, see above, chapter three; Webb, *Governors-General,* 299–13, 393–425, 447–51, 461–62.

83. Jordan, "Coode," *MHM* 70: 8, 10–11, 13; Andrews, *Colonial Period,* 2: 349, 350–51; and see note 84.

84. *CSPC 1681–85,* #184, 256, 260, 275, 351; *AMD* 5: 300–301, 329–32; 7: 124, 137–38; 15: 326, 388–90, 391; Michael Kammen, "Causes of the Maryland Revolution of 1689," *MHM* 55(1960): 296, 323; Lovejoy, *Glorious Revolution,* 86, 90. The remark was afterward made about John Wilkes.

85. *AMD* 5: 134–52, 312–54; *CSPC 1681–1685,* p. 92, #180, 184, 185, 195, 275, 313, 319, 391, 397, 448. The generational issue was raised by Bernard Bailyn in his influential essay, "Politics and Social Structure in Virginia," James Morton Smith, ed., *Seventeenth-Century America* (Chapel Hill, 1959), 90–115, and has been developed for Maryland by the dextrous prosopography of Louis Green Carr and David William Jordan, *Maryland's Revolution of Government 1689–1692* (Ithaca, 1974), 18, 31–34, 37–43, 53–55.

86. Andrews, *Colonial Period,* 2: 352n., 356–63; *AMD* 15: 250; *CSPC 1689–92,* #25, 290, 394, 422; Lovejoy, *Glorious Revolution,* 92–97; Chapter Four, p. 163, above.

87. Bernard C. Steiner, "The Protestant Revolution in Maryland," *AHAR 1897,* 283–88, wisely remarks that "the close relation of the colonists to the mother country, and of colonial politics to the course of affairs in England, can not be urged too strongly."

88. *AMD* 8: 63; "Proceedings and Acts of the General Assembly . . . St. Mary's," Nov. 14–Dec. 8, 1688, *AMD* 13: 147–64; Andrews, *Colonial Period,* 2: 329, 368–71; Beverley McAnear, ed., "Mariland's Grevances Wiy The Have Taken Op Arms," *JSH* 8 (1942): 402, 403.

89. *Ibid.,* 404.

90. Councilors to Proprietor, Mattapany, Jan. 19, 1688, *AMD* 8:65.

91. *Ibid.,* 56–57, 62–65, 67; *CSPC 1689–92,* #1195, 1204, 1206; Steiner, "Protestant Revolution," *AHAR 1897,* 290; Andrews, *Colonial Period,* 2: 371–72; Carr and Jordan, *Maryland's Revolution,* 46–47.

92. *AMD* 8: 70–76, 77–78, 82–85, 88, 101–107; *CSPC 1689–92,* #290, 1206; McAnear, ed., "Mariland's Grevences," *JSH* 8: 405; *AHAR 1897,* 291–98; Kammen, "Causes," *MHM* 55: 317–18, 321–29.

93. Kammen (*ibid.,* 319) also observes that the proprietor had conceded militia commissions to the lesser, Protestant, gentry simply because they were not lucrative. Fairfax Harrison, "Parson Waugh's Tumult," *VMHB* 30 (1922): 32–

37; Carr and Jordan, *Maryland's Revolution*, 46–48. For Brent, see also *VHMB* 1 (1893): 123–24; 12 (1904/5): 441; 15 (1906/7): 94.

94. *AMD* 8: 70–87; *CSPC 1689–92*, #56; McAnear, ed., "Mariland's Grevances," *JSH* 8: 405.

95. C.O. 5/1358, 3–4; *EJC* 1: 106–107; *AMD* 8: 112–14; *CSPC 1689–92*, #389–90, 394, 1427; McAnear, ed., "Mariland's Grevances," *JSH* 8: 404; Andrews, *Colonial Period*, 2: 372n; Carr and Jordan, *Maryland's Revolution*, 51–52; Love-joy, *Glorious Revolution*, 261.

96. Spencer to Blathwayt, June 10, 1689, CWWB, 18 #3; *AMD* 8: 112.

97. *CSPC 1689–92*, #194, 1267 (which links 1676, 1681, and 1689); *AMD* 8: 107–16, 118–19, 156–57.

98. *AMD* 8: 101–107; Andrews, ed., *Narratives*, 305–14; *CSPC 1689–92*, #290.

99. *AMD* 8: 107–108, 116, 151, 155–57, 161, 225–28.

100. On the leaders of the coup, see the biographical appendices in Carr and Jordan, *Maryland's Revolution*.

101. *AMD* 8: 108–11, 117, 120, 154, 159, 245–47; 13: 231–32, 239–41, 241–47; *CSPC 1689–92*, #315.

102. McAnear, ed., "Mariland's Grevances," *JSH* 8: 408; Steiner, "Protestant Revolution," *AHAR 1897*, 307–12, 318–19. Coode-Leisler, *DHNY* 2: 225–26; 248–50; 266–68. Carr and Jordan, *Maryland's Revolution*, 64–74, 80–81, report a 56 percent change in military commissions, contrasted with but 23 percent in civil appointments.

103. *AMD* 8: 99, 123–24, 167–68, 199, 207, 233–36; Carr and Jordan, *Maryland's Revolution*, 102, 263–80.

104. *CSPC 1689–92*, #976, 1029, 1287–89, 1714, 1765–68. Note that, while Jowles and Chesseldyne were named to Copley's council, Coode, having made a very bad impression on Blathwayt, was not: Blathwayt to Copley, Feb. 28, 1692/3, CWWB, 18 #4.

105. *AMD* 8: 235–36, 263–80; *CSPC 1689–92*, #923, 924, 976, 1023, 1026, 1028–30, 1297, 1317. Childs, *Army of William III*, 35–36; Browning, *Danby*, 1: 445–46, 486, 477–78; *CSPD 1689–90*, #137; *CSPD 1690–91*, 12, 68; Geiter and Speck, eds., *Reresby*, 571; *CJ* 10: 191, 265–68; *CTB* 9: 1431, 1836; Webb, "Nicholson," *WMQ* 23: 527–28, 533–34.

106. *Ibid.*, 527–28; *CSPC 1689–92*, #924, 1023. See n. 8, 15, above.

107. Webb, "Nicholson," *WMQ* 23: 533.

108. Webb, *Governors-General*, 404–22; *EJC* 1: 104; "Some Questions Proposed to Us, their Majesties Council of Virginia," 7 July, 1692, C.O. 5/1306, #114 (2). Spencer to Blathwayt, June 22, 1688, CWWB, 15 #5. It was only when the political order was in flux in the metropolis that proconsuls needed to be particularly concerned about ever-present protests. It was thus that Mather secured a hearing against Andros and Ludwell against Effingham. Both protests were dismissed when the crisis passed. See C.O. 5/1305, 17, I, for an example. Circular letter to the governors-general, Oct. 16, 1688, C.O. 138/6, 135–38; Randolph to Blathwayt, Oct. 2, 1688, CWWB, 1 #5.

109. *CSPC 1689–92*, #91, 92; CWWB, 16 #5; C.O. 5/1305, #7.

110. *Ibid.; EJC,* 1: 104; Harrison, "Parson Waugh's Tumult," *VMHB* 30: 31–37; Carr and Jordan, *Maryland's Revolution,* 48–49.

111. Spencer to the privy council committee, Apr. 29, 1689, C.O. 5/1305, 2; *CSPC 1689–92,* #93; same to Blathwayt, June 10, 1689, CWWB, 18 #5; Nicholson to same, June 10, 1691, *ibid.,* 15 #2; same to privy council committee, Aug. 20, 1690, C.O. 5/1306, 43.

112. Steele, "Governors or Generals," *WMQ* 46: 309, makes the point that the Virginia elite did not declare martial law. It is not clear that they had authority to do so in the absence of the governor-general. As the councilors seized the popular leaders by force and without warrant and imprisoned them without trial, it is also not clear what need the councilors had of martial law. Indeed, King James defended and Prince William conquered the British Isles without recourse to martial law, so that the issue seems moot. Both defender and invader recurred to the hallowed principle (often applied in America) that *inter armes, leges silens:* that armed conflict suspends the civil law and introduces the law of force and necessity without any need of proclamations. For the situation, in law and practice, in Virginia, see Webb, *Governors-General,* 344–45, esp. n. 28; 353–54. Spencer to Blathwayt, Apr. 27, 1689, bears the laconic endorsement "Rec'd 26 Aug 1689/For Ammunition," CWWB, 16 #5.

113. Smyth Kelli to Blathwayt, Port Royal, Jamaica, May 27, 1689, Rec'd July 28, 1689, *ibid.,* 22 #9. In both Ireland and Jamaica (as in Virginia), the "Cromwellian" conquerors were far more radical than the stay-at-home partisans of the Protectorate. The determination of the restored monarchy to suppress them was proportionally greater. The exaggeration was characteristic of provincial politics, the politics of experiment and extremism. On this, see Webb, *Governors-General,* 39–49, 151–210, and, for Virginia, Webb, *1676,* 27, 35.

114. William Henry, Prince of Orange, to Sr. Fr. Watson, 11 Jan. 1688/9, C.O. 138/6, 146–51.

115. Dep. Auditor Wilson to Blathwayt, May 10; Attorney General Simon Musgrave to same, Aug. 30, 1690, CWWB, 26 #1; on the *Almiranta,* see the naval appendix below.

116. Instructions to Albemarle, Aug. 15, 1687, C.O. 138/5, 334–35. Albemarle was a shameless, or stupid, witness against himself. See esp. his letters to the committee, Dec. 19, 1687, Feb. 11, 1687/8, March 6, 15, 1687/8, May 11, Aug. 8, 1688, C.O. 138/6, 80, 83, 86–91, 109–15, 139–43, and the special instructions in *ibid.,* 261–93, and see note 117, below.

117. Albemarle's support for Father Churchill appears in C.O. 138/6, 120. The assembly's fears for the Church of England are recorded in Add. Ms. 12429, 160. The privy council rejoinder is in *ibid.,* 160–161b. Father Churchill's electoral activities are complained of in *ibid.,* 182b–183. The king and council to President Sir Francis Watson and council, Nov. 30, Dec. 1, 1688, C.O. 138/6, 144–46; Hender Molesworth to Blathwayt, Mar. 7, 1687/8, CWWB, 25 #6; Albemarle to same, Feb. 11, 1687/8, *ibid.,* 21 #1; Samuel Barry to the king, n.d., Add. Ms. 12429, 159b; Musgrave to the privy council committee, May 12, 1688, C.O. 138/6, 210–14.

118. Musgrave to Blathwayt, Aug. 30, 1690; Watson to Blathwayt, June 6, 1689, CWWB, 27 #4; circular letter to the governors-general, Oct. 16, 1688, C.O. 138/6, 135–36.

119. On the Watson case, see Steele, "Governors or Generals," *WMQ*, 44: 306–307; Kelli to Blathwayt, May 27, 1689, CWWB, 22 #9; Musgrave to committee, May 12, 1688, C.O. 138/6, 210–12 on "mechanics, barbers, & tapmen" in office; Molesworth to Shrewsbury, April 17, *ibid.*, 166–69. Molesworth, Beckford &c. had sponsored laws which conferred ever-increasing authority on the field officers of the provincial regiments. See Add. Ms. 12429, 151b. That the island was governed by the provincial army appears in president & council to committee, n.d., C.O. 138/6, 332–34. The role of the Royal African Co. factors is outlined in *ibid.*, 287–300.

120. Watson to Blathwayt, June 6, 1689, CWWB, 27 #4; Watson to committee, June 6, 1689, C.O. 138/6, 222–26.

121. Atty. Gen. Musgrave asked Blathwayt (Aug. 30, 1690, CWWB, 27 #1) whether he should prosecute Watson for his conduct during the coup. See also Kelli to Blathwayt, June 5, 1689, *ibid.*, 22 #10; *CSPC 1689–92*, #980; Prince of Orange to Watson, Jan. 11, 1688/9, C.O. 138/6, 146–51 and see 156–57; Watson to privy council committee, Mar. 15, 1688[/9], *ibid.*, 215–21. Watson had also refused to restore Lynch's anti-pirate policies or to remove Albemarle's appointees, as he wrote to Blathwayt, Nov. 16, 1688 (filed in spring, 1689), *ibid.*, 174–77.

122. *CSPC 1689–92*, #89, 109, 116–20, 127, 198, 234, [229], 264, 270, 271, 273, 274, 292, 410, 413, 429, 533, 557, 588, 640, 876, 980, 1187, 1207, 1212; William III to president & council of Jamaica, Feb. 22, 1689/9, C.O. 138/6, 156–57; Shrewsbury to privy council committee, June 13, 1689, *ibid.*, 177. Molesworth's commissions (full martial law powers as captain general and vice admiral were included after being debated by the privy council committee), *ibid.*, 182–202. See his deathbed petition, *ibid.*, 164–73. Inchiquin's commissions were ordered Sept. 18, 1689, *ibid.*, 229 and issued Dec. 5, *ibid.*, 230–69. Inchiquin to the privy council committee, July 6, 1692, reported his arrival and shrewdly summarized provincial politics, *ibid.*, 336–40, Coad, *Providence*, 29, 38, 46.

123. Vincent T. Harlow, *Christopher Codrington* (Oxford, 1928), 16; W.O. 4/1, 148–53; Webb, Officers and Governors, Appendix I; Morgan, "British West Indies," *J.M.H*, 2: 383.

124. Lediard, *Marlborough*, 1: 89–92. Compare C.O. 135/1, 69, Blathwayt's memo. of Nov. 16, 1687, Huntington Library; *NYCD*, 3: 509; *CSPC 1685–88*, 48, and p. 187–97 above. See also Chandler, *Marlborough*, 29–30. As the wording of the declaration made clear, as a soldierly authoritarian, King William was especially concerned to reinforce the respect paid to the governors, whether of general's or colonel's rank, Humphrey Bland, *A Treatise of Military Discipline* (6th ed., London, 1746), 199–201.

125. C.O. 135/1, f. 70b–72; Churchill, *Marlborough*, 1: 415; HMC, *Le Fleming Ms.*, 284, 293, 297. Hudson's Bay Co. Papers, University of London Ms. 147, 11, records the memorial to William, "as the exorbitant encroachments of the

French almost everywhere necessitated the War." On the Oct. return of "a pink from Hudson's Bay, richly laden with furs," see HMC, *Finch Ms.*, 2: 499.
126. *CSPC 1689–92*, #120, 123, 124, 164, 265, 395, 397, 1207, 1212, 1384; S. P. 44/165, 369, 379, 394.
127. Webb, "Blathwayt," *WMQ* 25: 374–75; above, 154–55; Webb, *Governors-General*, #204.
128. Hill to Blathwayt, Aug. 25, 1692, CWWB, 39 #4; Morgan, "British West Indies," J.M.H., 2: 386–87. Thomas Spencer, "A True and Faithful Relation of the Proceedings of the forces . . . under Christopher Codrington, 1689–1690," *Harleian Misc.*, II (London, 1809), 564–75. And see Chapter Six, note 45, below. A contemporary pamphlet voiced the suspicion that William III used West Indian assignments to rid himself of certain alienated English officers ("The Dear Bargain," cited by Morgan, "British West Indies," 391 n.) just as Cromwell had done in Jamaica, Webb, *Governors-General*, 159.

Chapter Six: A Decade of Dissent: 1689–1698

1. C.O. 135/1, ff. 70–75, p. 126–54; W.O. 4/1, 134, 135; S.P. 44/165, 266–69. Marlborough's power to promote immediately put him at odds with Ormonde, colonel of the second troop of the Life Guards: Arthur, *Household Cavalry*, 236n. Chandler, *Marlborough*, 30–31; Taylor, *Marlborough*, 2: 453; Childs, *Army of William III*, Ch. 1 and p. 14. Childs contends that Marlborough acted here, as always, simply as a mercenary leader of professional soldiers, without political goals or patriotic sentiments. Certainly, this was the view of Marlborough's enemies. On additions to Marlborough's original force, see Knight, *Buffs*, 1: 283, 297; Luttrell, *Brief Relation*, 1: 503; HMC, *Kenyon Ms.*, 218; Hamilton, *First Guards*, 1: 329–30; Childs, *Nine Years' War*, 100–101.
2. HMC, *Le Fleming Ms.*, 242; Walton, *British Army*, 391–95; Dalton, ed., *Army Lists*, 2: 134. Marlborough's notorious bread contracts seem to date from his first divisional command. He "made a bargain with a Jew for 4d a loaf, and sold it to the Soldiers for 6d," so Halifax wrote of Marlborough in May 1690, Add. Ms. 51511, 28. See also Jones, *War and Economy*, 36; Childs, *British Army of William III*, 250–51. Marlborough to the King, June 17, 1690, *CSPD, 1690–91*, 34, Dalrymple, ed., *Memoirs*, 3, p. 263, App. to Bk. VII, finds the earl "extremely fretted" at Guise's accusation that Marlborough had deposited £30,000 in Holland. He did send home 6,500 guineas with Portland and 4,700 with Schulemberg, but his pay as commander of the English division was only £2,190 p.a.
3. Charles D. Ellestad, "The Mutinies of 1689," *JSAHR* 53 (1975): 9, 11–17; W.O. 4/1, 125–26; *CSPD 1689–90*, 17.
4. *CJ*, 10: 49, 69; Anchitell Grey, *Debates in the House of Commons* (London, 1769), 9: 164–69; W.O. 4/1, 125–36.
5. Ferguson, *Scots Brigade*, 1: 567; Chandler, *Marlborough*, 31; Geiter and Speck, eds., *Reresby*, 563–64, 565–67.
6. Ferguson, *Scots Brigade*, 1: 569; William Crammond, Pocket Diary, 1688–

1691, Add. Ms. 29878, 35; Churchill, *Marlborough*, 1: 278, 286; Dalton, ed., *Army Lists*, 2: 244–45; S.P. 44/165, 376; S.P. 8/5, 48, 62, 124; Knight, *Buffs*, 1: 290. William III's compliments to Marlborough on Waldeck's reports are dated July 6/16, 1689, Blenheim Ms. A.1.11; Add. Ms. 61101, f. 7.

7. The basic account of Walcourt is Crammond's Diary, Add. Ms. 29878, 33. [Hare,] *Marlborough*, 18–19, has a variant on the early part of the action, in which Marlborough's detachment of cavalry provokes the French attack, after which Marlborough's troopers are called up to cover Hodges's retreat. HMC, *Finch Ms.*, 2: 231–32. As usual, the French took out their frustration on civilians, burning two villages. Chandler, *Marlborough*, 31; Childs, *Nine Years' War*, 116–17; [Richard Cannon, comp.,) *Historical Record of the Third Regiment* . . . (London, 1839), 131; Sir F. Maurice, *The 16th Foot* (London, 1931), 2–3, 5; Mackinnon, *Coldstream Guards*, 202–203; Waldeck's despatch of Aug. 25, 1689 (o.s.) in *London Gazette*, #2482, Aug. 22–26.

8. *Ibid.*, #2483, Aug. 27–29, 1689; and see, Arthur, *Household Cavalry*, 1: 237, who places the initiative for the attack with Marlborough, but he is scarcely mentioned by Childs, *Nine Years' War*, 122–23. The conclusion is Crammond's, Add. Ms. 29878, 33.

9. *Historie De Jean Churchill Duc De Marlborough* (Paris, 1808), 1: 56–57; Lediard, *Marlborough*, 1: 93; Churchill, *Marlborough*, 1: 281; Chandler, *Marlborough*, 33; William III to Marlborough, Sept. 3/13, 1689, Blenheim Ms. A. 1. 11; Add. Ms. 61101, f. 11; Coxe, *Marlborough*, 1: 48–49. [Richard Cannon, comp.], *Royal Fusiliers*; Dalton, ed., *Army Lists*, 3: 20. Note that George Churchill was his brother's cornet and major in the Life Guards, *ibid.*, 177.

10. Taylor, *Marlborough*, 2: 456–57; Coxe, *Marlborough*, 1: 46. Dalrymple, *Memoirs*, vol. 1, p. 414–17, Part II. Bk. VII, and p. 455–57, Bk. IV, describes the division between the sisters, due in part to Anne's sense of her sovereign sacrifice, due even more to her affinity to the tories, and due most of all to the machinations of Sarah. William then took the part of his wife and "the piques of women became the quarrels of parties, and of the public" (*ibid.*, 456), as the parliamentary grant struggle manifested. On the Denmark finances and the grant, see Gregg, *Anne*, 76–79.

11. On sales and cabinets, see Halifax's memos of August 1690, Add. Ms. 51511, 28. Feiling, *Tory Party*, 246–54. [Wharton to William,] Dec. 25, 1689, Dalrymple, ed., *Memoirs*, vol. 3, p. 107, App. to Pt. II, Bk. IV; *ibid.*, (2d ed., London, 1773), 2: 94: "the design was plain to give the princess a great revenue, and make her independent upon your Majesty, that she might be the head of a party against you." The most balanced account is still Lediard's, *Marlborough*, 1: 104–10. General Wolsey's reflections (*Marlborough*, 2: 112–28) on the relations of the Churchills to William, Mary, and Anne are interesting but speculative. See *Conduct of the Duchess of Marlborough*, 26. Sarah's fuller analysis is in Blenheim Palace Ms. F.1.16, Add. Ms. 61101, f. 42. On all such questions see, Frances Harris, *A Passion for Government The Life of Sarah Duchess of Marlborough* (Oxford, 1991), here 55–57.

12. Beddard, "Unexpected Revolution," Beddard, ed., *Revolutions of 1688*, 77; Atkinson, *Royal Dragoons*, 58 (silently following DeAinslie, *Royal Dragoons*, 29), attributes Cornbury's dismissal to his father's opposition to William. Note too that Grafton lost the First Guards' command as the king cut down the Churchill connection. HMC, *Downshire Ms.*, 1: pt. 1, 318–19, 327; Wolsey, *Marlborough*, 2: 126–27, 131; S. P. 44/165, 47/153, 369. HMC, *Le Fleming Ms.*, 297.

13. Dalton, ed., *Army Lists*, 3: 162; Newsletter, June 3, 1690, HMC, *Downshire Ms.*, 1: pt. 1, 347; Atkinson, *Marlborough*, 110–11. Monmouth's madness was neatly captured by Sec. Vernon's memorandum, James, ed., *Vernon Correspondence*, 2: 345–49.

14. Hamilton, *First Guards*, 1: 341–44; HMC, *Finch Ms.*, 2: 278, 313, 347–48, gives six as the number of English warships lost, notes the risk to the army in Ireland and to the convoys from America, and so the customs that support the war. See *ibid.*, 360, where "the Chief" is said to have but five thousand foot and a thousand horse. Wolsey, *Marlborough*, 2: 141; Dalrymple, *Memoirs*, vol. 1, p. 474–75, 481–86, Pt. II, Bk. V, vol. 3, p. 160, App. to same; Mahan, *Sea Power*, 160–65; Ogg, *James II and William III*, 352–55; Ehrman, *Navy*, 350–51, gives quite a different account of four Dutch battleships lost and only one English but the result was the same: "the French found themselves in command of the Channel." Mackinnon, *Coldstream Guards*, 206–207; Routh, ed., *Burnet's History*, 4: 93–97; William III to Marlborough, July 9/19, 1690, Blenheim Ms. A.1.11, Add. Ms. 61101, f. 15. The English under Brigadier Churchill did not reach Waldeck until after Fleurus had been lost. On July 15, 1690, Danby begged William to come home with the troops, or at least to "send somebody more able than our present generall to conduct our military affairs," Browning, *Danby*, II, 181.

15. In general, among contemporary accounts, see George Story, *Impartial History of the Affairs of Ireland* (London, 1693), and, among modern accounts, J. G. Simms, *War and Politics in Ireland 1649–1730* (London, 1986). Note that James II's reign in Ireland coincided with the interregnum in America. England attended to its colonies in order of imperial importance. It could never cope simultaneously with widespread disturbance in Ireland and America. As in the *causus belli* of the war with France, so in his decision to go to Ireland, William responded to the priorities of English imperialism. On the latter, see Ogg, *James II and William III*, 254. On the American Jacobites, see Coode to Leisler, Apr. 4, Leisler to Coode, June 27, 1690, *DHNY* 2: 225–27, 266–69.

16. Among the survivors of the siege was Richard Kane, journalist of the Royal Irish, Marlborough's drillmaster, and governor-general, Dalton, ed., *Army Lists*, 3: 83; Kane, *Campaigns*, 13, 15, 17. W.O. 4/1, 142, 143. Charnock, *Biographia Navalis*, 2: 167; Stephen Martin Leake, ed., *The Life of Sir John Leake*, ed., Geoffrey Callendar, (Naval Records Society, 1920) 1: 26–31, records Leake's relief of Londonderry after 111 days. Kirke, looking on from the *Swallow*, gave Leake a company in his regiment. *London Gazette*, #2480, Aug. 15–19; #2481, Aug. 19–22; #2484, Aug. 29–Sept. 1, 1689. Hunter's presence appears to be indicated in Blenheim Ms. CCXXI, Add. Ms. 61321, 29. Ogg, *James II and William III*, 250–51; Chandler, *Marlborough*, 34.

17. On the horrors of Dundalk camp. see Simms, *War and Politics*, 91–104; *London Gazette*, #2482, Aug. 22–26, 1689; Kane, *Campaigns*, 14, 15, 16, 17, 20,

21; Parker, *Memoirs*, 16–18, E. A. H. Webb, *History of the Suffolk (12th) Regiment 1685–1913* (London, 1914), 13.

18. Story, *Impartial History*, 35–39, has the dreadful details. Dalton, ed., *Army Lists*, 3: 107n; [Richard Cannon,] *Historical Record of The Eighth, Or, The King's Regiment of Foot . . .* (London, 1844), 17–18; Geoffrey Powell, *The Green Howards (The 19th Regiment of Foot)* (London, 1968), 21; Webb, *Governors-General*, #152.

19. Blathwayt to the lords justices, Aug. 8, n.s., 1695, Add. Ms. 9722, 89–90; Webb, "Blathwayt," *WMQ*, 26: 396.

20. *CSPC 1689–92*, #2600; Andrews, *Colonial Period*, 3: 317–26; Gary B. Nash, *Quakers and Politics 1681–1726* (Princeton, 1968), 201–205; James S. Leamon, War, Finance and Faction in Colonial New York, the Administration of Governor Benjamin Fletcher, Ph.D. Dissertation, Brown University, 1961.

21. Leamon, "Governor Fletcher's Recall," *WMQ* 20 (1963): 527–42; Webb, "Blathwayt," *WMQ* 26: 402; Lawrence H. Leder, *Robert Livingston* (Chapel Hill, 1961), 101–102, 114–16, 122–24.

22. Dalton, ed., *Army Lists*, 1: 125; 3: 78, 116; Walton, *British Army*, 80; Bayard's Narrative, *NYCD*, 577–84; *NYHSC*, I: 299–334.

23. Council of N.Y. to Blathwayt, Jan. 11, 1691/2, CWWB, 8 #1; *CSPC 1693–1696*, #1911, 1919, 2054, but see 1976.

24. Fletcher to Blathwayt, Yorke-America, August 15, 18, 22, '93, CWWB, 8 #3.

25. Fletcher [to Blathwayt,] Jan. 22, 1693/4, Aug. 20, 1696, CWWB 8, #5; and see #8, #9, #10; *CSPC 1689–92*, #1212.

26. Dalton, ed., *Army Lists*, 3: 107; Charnock, *Biographia Navalis*, 2:143–44. Fairburne was the nephew of the Tangier governor-general and a volunteer with Marlborough at Cork. See the Appendix: "Inglorious Revolution: The Channel Fleet in 1688."

27. Dalton, ed., *Army Lists*, 2: 83, 109, 123. Kane was present as a lieutenant in Skeffington's (Londonderry) Regiment and was promoted into Meath's (Royal Irish) in Nov. 1692. Kane, *Campaigns*, 22ff; Walton, *British Army*, 80; Lt. Col. G. Le M. Gretton, *The Campaigns and History of the Royal Irish Regiment From 1684 to 1902* (Edinburgh and London, 1911), 5–6.

28. HMC, *Finch Ms.*, 2: 326; Parker, *Memoirs*, 21. Cornbury had lost his post in the Denmark household for refusing to accompany Prince George to Ireland (Singer, ed., *Clarendon Correspondence*, 2: 314–15), presumably because the service would involve an attack on King James. On Prince George's ambitions, see Gregg, *Anne*, 80. William's staff also included Prince George of Hesse-Darmstadt, afterwards captor and governor-general of Gibraltar. Routh, ed., *Burnet's History*, 4: 90–91; Kane, *Campaigns*, 21; Hewitson, ed., *Bellingham Diary*, 130 (30 June 1690); Simms, *War and Politics*, 106; *London Gazette*, #2572, July 3–7, 1690; Story, *Impartial History*, 75–76.

29. Simms, *War and Politics*, 130–31, says William's right wing numbered "about 15,000." Webb, *Governors-General*, #58, 167; E. A. H. Webb, *12th*, 16–21, Pl. #4; R. H. Raymond Smithies, *Historical Record of the 40th (2d Somerset) Regiment . . . 1717–1893* (Devonport, 1894), 496; Dalton, ed., *Army Lists*, 3: 53,

54, 73, 112n; H. M. Walker, *A History of the Northumberland Fusiliers 1674–1902* (London, 1919), 30–31.

30. Simms, *War and Politics*, 109–13, quotes Brewer to Th. Wharton, July, 1690, Carte Ms., 79. See also Southwell to Nottingham, July 1, 2, 1690, HMC, *Finch Ms.*, 2: 326, 329. HMC, *Tenth Report, Appendix V*, 123–36 is an Irish account of James II's occupation of Ireland and of this "skirmish" at the Boyne.

31. Story, *Impartial History*, 77–82; Hewitson, ed., *Bellingham Diary*, 131–32; Dalton, ed., *Army Lists*, 5: 295.

32. On Hamilton, afterwards earl of Orkney and marshal of England, see Dalton, ed., *Army Lists*, 3: 155; Webb, *Governors-General*, Appendix #203.

33. Story, *Impartial History*, 82–85; Sir Henry Everett, *The History of the Somerset Light Infantry . . . [13th] 1685–1914* (London, 1934), map. f. p. 25. HMC, *Fingal Ms.*, 136. Fifteen hundred or two thousand of King James's men fell, the most noted of whom was lord Dongan, brother of the governor-general of New York, Thomas Dongan, who succeeded to the title, was reconciled with King William, recovered something of the family estates in Ireland, and led another generation of British soldiers to fight in Portugal.

34. Crammond, Diary, May 8–July 20 [o.s.], 1690, Add. Ms. 29878, 29; HMC, *Finch Ms.*, 2: 328–31, 361–63, 365, 372–74, 384, 433; HMC, *Le Fleming Ms.*, 284, 297 (Aug. 12, Oct. 18, 1690); Lediard, *Marlborough*, 1: 95; Nottingham to the king, July 15, 1690, Dalrymple, ed., *Memoirs*, vol. 3, 124–26, App. to Pt. II, Bk. 5; *ibid.* (2d. ed., London, 1773) 2: 107–10. *The London Gazette*, #2571, June 20–July 3, 1690, which reported the approaches to the Boyne, also reported the first news of the naval battle. Israel, ed., *Anglo-Dutch Moment*, map, 127; Ian B. Cowan, "The Revolution of 1688–1689 in Scotland, *ibid.*, 177.

35. On Marlborough's restraint, see *Two Illustrious Generals*, 28, and Coxe's opinion in Add. Ms. 9199, 135. Taylor, *Marlborough*, 2: 460; Lediard, *Marlborough*, 1: 98; Mary to William, 7/17 8, 1690, 26/5 8/9, 1690, Dalrymple, *Memoirs*, vol. 1, p. 503–504, Pt. II., Bk. V, vol. 3, p. 134, 135, App. Bk. VI; same to same, Sept. 1/Aug. 22, 1690, *ibid.*, 193–94; *ibid.*, (2d ed., London, 1773), 2: esp. 197; William III to Marlborough, Camp at Limerick, Aug. 14/24, Blenheim Ms. A.1.11, Add. Ms. 61161, f. 17. Queen Mary (by Nottingham), Aug. 25 [1690], orders to reduce Cork and Kinsale, Blenheim Ms. H.8, Add. Ms. 61136, (170). Marlborough also sought an admiral's flag for his brother. Danby's response was to say that "if Churchill have a flag, he will be called the flag by favour as his brother is called the general of favour." Danby cut Marlborough's convoy and criticized his arrangements (Danby to William, Aug. 29, 1690, Browning, *Danby*, 2: 188–89) while begging the king for the provost marshal's place in the Leeward Islands for a client. Naturally, Danby was "mightily dissatisfied with the business of Kinsale," Mary to William, Sept. 5/ Aug. 26, 1690, Dalrymple, ed., *Memoirs*, App. Bk. VI, 197.

36. Blathwayt to Clarke, 8 mo., 21/31, 1690, quoted in Wolsey, *Marlborough*, 2: 155–56 and see 157n. Everett, *Somerset*, 24–25. [Cannon,] *3d*, does not include the regiment in the Cork expedition. Cowper, *King's Own*, 63, 65; John Mackensie Semple, "Marlborough's Siege of Kinsale," *JSAHR* 18 (1939), 183; [Cannon,] *8th*, 18; Dalton, ed., *Army Lists*, 3: 338. Fletcher's corps came weak

out of Ireland and suffered so much from desertion in Portsmouth that Marlborough sought to replace it with eight companies of the First Guards, HMC, *Finch Ms.*, 2: 433, and see 438, 460.

37. William to Marlborough, Limerick, Aug. 14/24, 1690, Add. Ms. 61336, printed in Churchill, *Marlborough*, 1: 287–88; Mare R to Marlborough, Whitehall, Aug. 25, 1690, Add. Ms. 61336, 170; Lediard, *Marlborough*, 1: 101–102; HMC, *Finch Ms.*, 2: 414, 430–31, 441, 449, 459; Berwick, *Memoirs*, 77–78; Dalrymple, ed., *Memoirs*, 3: 197.

38. Marlborough to Nottingham, "Portchmouth," Aug. 30, Sept. 1, 5, 15, 17, 1690, HMC, *Finch Ms.*, 2: 438, 440, 446, 458, 460. Crammond Diary, Aug. 20–31, 1690, Add. Ms. 29878, 29.

39. On the French evacuation, see HMC, *Finch Ms.*, 437. Three episodes unnoticed by Marlborough's biographers suggest some of the tensions between the commander of this English national expedition and the Dutch king. Marlborough appears to have ignored William's order of Sept. 11 to return to London. Certainly he did not obey that of Sept. 14: to give up his command to Count Solms as soon as Cork was essayed, *ibid.*, 452, 457. The French were further informed by a Jacobite that Marlborough had made a special trip up "from Portsmouth the see the King, makeing this compliment Sir, I think myself extreamly happy to see your Majesty safely returned and [to] have the honor to kiss your hand before I goe upon this expedition, to which King William answer'd very coldly, my Lord I had rather you should have stay'd at Portsmouth, you have cost me three tides, and you are come up without leave," *ibid.*, 464. Parker, *Memoirs*, 28; Atkinson, *Marlborough*, 115; HMC, *Le Fleming Ms.*, 290, 291. On Carmarthen's (Danby's) intent to "ruin" Marlborough on this occasion, see Halifax's memo of Oct. 24, 1692, Add. Ms. 51511, 61. Fitzroy, *Grafton*, 69–70, 73, 75, 77–79.

40. HMC, *Finch Ms.*, 2: 465; Atkinson, *Marlborough*, 114, 116; HMC, *Le Fleming Ms.*, 293, 294. Lediard, *Marlborough*, 1: 97, puts the capture of the Cat Fort on September 27. Cramond Diary, Add Ms. 29878, 28–27; Taylor, *Marlborough*, 2: 462; Story, *Impartial History*, 141; HMC, *Fingal Ms.*, 145–46.

41. [Hare,] *Marlborough*, 23–24; Lediard, *Marlborough*, 1: 97; Churchill, *Marlborough*, 1: 287, and 289–290, where he follows Taylor, *Marlborough*, 2: 463. Dalrymple, *Memoirs*, I: p. 504, Pt. II. Bk. V; Rev. David C. A. Agnew, *Protestant Exiles from France* (London, 1871), 2: 183.

42. Lediard, *Marlborough*, 1: 98; Cramond Diary, Add. Ms. 29878, 28b–34, quoted in Chandler, *Marlborough*, 40; Taylor, *Marlborough*, 2: 464; Fitzroy, *Grafton*, 79–80; Story, *Impartial History*, 142.

43. [Hare,] *Marlborough*, 25–27; Lediard, *Marlborough*, 1:98–99; Everett, *Somerset* [13th], 27. Jacobites said that the surrender was owing to a shortage of ammunition and the guile of Protestant clergy, HMC, *Finch Ms.*, 2: 471. William's felicitations to Marlborough, Oct. 4/14, 1690, Blenheim Ms. A.1.11, Add. Ms. 61101, f.8. Simms, *War and Politics*, 117–27; s.v. "Macelligott, Roger," Childs, *Dictionary*.

44. Lediard, *Marlborough*, 1: 99; Nottingham to Marlborough, Aug. 29, 1690, quoted French despatches, intercepted by a Dutch privateer, as saying that "tho' there be 3,000 men in Kinsale, with great quantities of ammunition, and the Governor very zealous for the late King James, yet there is not very much to be hoped from them, and that there needs no more to take the town than to appear before it," HMC, *Finch Ms.*, 2: 437, and see 476. Routh, ed., *Burnet's History*, 4: 108. Details of Fort Charles, built from 1667 to 1670, are in *JSAHR* 16 (1937), 174. The same *Gazette* (#2602, Oct. 16–20, 1690) that recorded the investment of Kinsale featured a long account from Barbados of the recapture of St. Kitts by Colonel Christopher Codrington's forces. The governor-general of the Leeward Islands was seconded by Col. Henry Holt of Boltons (2d), the 15th Regiment's clone, and by Sir Timothy Thornhill, in command of the provincial troops raised by Col. James Kendall, the defier of James II, now governor-general of Barbados. The Irish renegades whom they captured in the French garrison of St. Kitts were sent to slave in Virginia.

45. Story, *Impartial History*, 144. Taylor, *Marlborough*, 2: 466. Semple (*JSAHR* 18: 183) writes that the assault force of 1,100 were British. Cramond's Diary, Add. Ms. 29878, 24–23, makes this an altogether smaller affair than do the modern authors, numbering the attackers 1,000 to 1,200 and the garrison only about 400. [Hare,] *Marlborough*, 28, has the defenders numbering only 450 men. Webb, *Governors-General*, #75, 76.

46. Story, *Impartial History*, 144–45; Lediard, *Marlborough*, 100, 101; Atkinson, *Marlborough*, 18; Wolsey, *Marlborough*, 2: 212–13; HMC, *Le Fleming Ms.*, 296, 299, 301; Chandler, *Marlborough*, 42 is corrected from Cramond's Diary, Add. Ms. 29878, 24–22. Mordaunt's brother was with his troops and was killed at Kinsale, HMC, *Finch Ms.*, 2: 474. For the Kinsale governor, s.v. "Scott, Sir Edward," Childs, *Dictionary*.

47. [Hare,] *Marlborough*, 28–30.

48. Marquis D'Albyville to James II, [Oct. 27/] Nov. 6, 1690, Taylor, *Marlborough*, 2: 471. If Marlborough left Kinsale in such haste that he did not see the breach filled (*ibid.*, 474), it was contrary to his later practice. This was, of course, his first siege in command. Dalrymple, ed., *Memoirs*, vol. 1, p. 505, Pt. II. Bk. V.; [Cannon,] *Royal Fusiliers*, 10; Wolsey, *Marlborough*, 2: 216, 218; Everett, *Somerset* [13th], 27; Lediard, *Marlborough*, 101–102; Churchill, *Marlborough*, 1: 293–94; Coxe, *Marlborough*, 1: 51; Fortescue, *British Army*, 1: 352. The earliest version of the king's estimate is quoted from *Two Illustrious Generals*, 29.

49. HMC, *Le Fleming Ms.*, 301, Newsletter, Nov. 1, 1690: Marlborough to succeed Schomberg as master general of the ordnance and to be created duke of Albemarle, a title resonant of military king-making and vacant because of the death of the second duke in his government of Jamaica. See also *ibid.*, 302; Atkinson, *Marlborough*, 120; Wolsey, *Marlborough*, 2: 242, places these events in the following winter.

50. Atkinson, *Marlborough*, 120–26; Life of James the Second in Macpherson, ed., *Original Papers*, 1: 236–38; Clarke, ed., *James Second*, 2: 444, 446–50; Bradley, ed., *Ailesbury Memoirs*, 2: 391–92; Thompson, ed., *Hatton Correspondence*, 2: 170; Burnet's Rough Draft, Harleian Ms. 6584, 66, 68–69; Routh, ed., *Burnet's History*, 4: 152–53. Wolsey, *Marlborough*, 2: 226–33. Dalrymple, ed., *Memoirs*, vol. 1, pp. 519–21, Pt. II, Bk. VI, is a full statement of the nationalist case against William, put forward by the Churchills, Cornbury, and Princess Anne. See also *ibid.*, vol. 3, p. 213, App. to Bk. VI; and *ibid.*, 265, 267, 269, App. to Bk. VII. Defoe, *Marlborough*, 11.

51. HMC, *Le Fleming Ms.*, 310; Albert Lee, *History of the Tenth Foot* (Aldershot, 1911), 1: 41, 43; Webb, *Governors-General*, Chapter 2, esp. 61, 68–69; Atkinson, *Marlborough*, 127; Wolsey, *Marlborough*, 2: 274–75; Chandler, *Marlborough*, 43; Davis, *Second, Queen's*, 2: 154–55.

52. Dalton, ed., *Army Lists*, 3: 171; Atkinson, ed., *Marlborough*, 128; Lee, *Tenth Foot*, 45; *Two Illustrious Generals*, 30. S.v. officers' and regimental names in Webb, *Governors-General*, Appendix. There is some question whether this John Webb is the officer promoted in the Guards on his return from Virginia or is John Richmond Webb, formerly of the Queen's Dragoons, wounded fighting for King James in 1688, and afterwards distinguished in combat at Wynendale and in politics for his hostility to Marlborough (for which he was commissioned governor of the Isle of Wight from the date of Marlborough's fall in 1711 until his reinstatement in 1715).

53. Lee, *Tenth Foot*, 45–46; Maurice, *16th*, 3–5, 13–14; Chandler, *Art of War*, Ch. 5–7.

54. Lediard, *Marlborough*, 1: 103; Coxe, *Marlborough*, 1: 56; S. H. F. Johnson, *The History of the Cameronians . . .* (Aldershot, 1957), 1: 47; Arthur, *Household Cavalry*, 257–59, App. A; Edward D'Auvergne, *Relation of the Most Remarkable Transactions in the Campaign of 1691* (London, 1692); HMC, *14th Report*, Pt. 3, 123; Ranke, *England*, 5: 23–24. Childs, *Nine Years' War*, 172–75, discusses this action from the French side.

55. *Two Illustrious Generals*, 30, variously improved by Lediard, *Marlborough*, 1: 103; Coxe, *Marlborough*, 1: 56; Wolsey, *Marlborough*, 2: 237; Churchill, *Marlborough*, 1: 308.

56. Lediard, *Marlborough*, 1: 104; HMC, *Portland Ms.*, 3: 477; *CSPD 1690–1691*, 547; Arthur, *Household Cavalry*, 1: 258n.

57. Prince George and Princess Anne to King William, Aug. 2, 1691, Dalrymple, ed., *Memoirs*, vol. 3, pp. 272–73, App. to Pt. II, Bk. VII, and see *ibid.*, 555–57, 559; *ibid.*, (2d ed., London, 1773), 2, App. to Pt II, 229–30; Coxe, *Marlborough*, 1: 59, 68; Gregg, *Anne*, 82, 83–84; *CSPD 1690–1691*, 468; Princess Anne to James II, Dec. 1, 1691, Life of James the Second, in Macpherson, ed., *Original Papers*, 1: 241–42; Clarke, ed., *James Second*, 2: 475–78; Ranke, *England*, 5: 42–44.

58. *Ibid.*, 7: 177; Wolsey, *Marlborough*, 2: 243, 245; 263; Routh, ed., *Burnet's History*, 4: 151–53; "A Memorial, November 1692—After the Affair of La Hogue," Nairne Papers, in MacPherson, *Original Papers*, 1: 440; Gregg, *Anne*, 84–88; Baxter, *William III*, 299–300; Coxe, *Marlborough*, 1: 61, 67; Defoe, *Marlborough*, 11; HMC, *7th Report*, App., *Denbigh Ms.*, 220; Dalrymple, *Memoirs*, vol. 1, p. 554, pt. II, Bk. VII: "The officers of the army, who are accustomed to complain of the want of preferment, because their complaints carry an implication of their merits, now imputed every disappointment to foreign influence; and being apt, from their manners, to take the lead in all conversation, and, from their want of occupation, to mingle in all companies, they spread their own discontents every where among others."

59. Lediard, *Marlborough*, 1: 105–106; Ranke, *History*, 5: 42; HMC, *Portland Ms.*, 3: 489.

60. Defoe, *Marlborough*, 11, implicates Solms in Marlborough's disgrace. Lord Basil Hamilton to the duke of Hamilton, Jan. 21, 1692, Dalrymple, ed., *Memoirs* (2d ed., London, 1773) 2: App. to Pt. 2, 230. *Conduct of the Duchess*, 28, 58; Lediard, *Marlborough*, 1: 107, 110; Coxe, *Marlborough*, 1: 59–60; Gregg, *Anne*, 84–85; HMC, *7th Report*, App., *Denbigh* Ms., 220.

61. James Blair to Nicholson, London, Feb. 27., 1692, Nicholson Papers, Williamsburg; Defoe, *Marlborough*, 11; Thompson, ed., *Hatton Correspondence*, 170, 176, 180, 195, 249; Beer, ed., *Evelyn Diary*, Jan. 20, Feb. 28, 1692, 5: 86, 90.

62. Anon. [to Portland,] HMC, *Finch Ms.*, 4: 114–15, warned of an imminent invasion to be supported by Marlborough who, "by the Princess' intercession to the late king and the Lord Godolphin to the Queen, and his own promises to ingage a great part of armey, has gott his pardon with assurances from King James that he shall have his favour if he succeed." The prince and princess, Beaufort, and Danby were all said to have assured James that the nobility and gentry would receive him "upon terms." The ranks of officers who "are already ingaged in this designe" were given in four senior cavalry formations and the Inniskilling Horse; both Foot Guards corps and nine infantry regiments (all save the Inniskilling foot, raised before 1688); and the Tower Hamlets regiment of the London trained bands. See also *ibid.*, 122–25, 137; Baxter, *William III*, 298–99; Childs, *Army of William III*, 64–65. Hales's regimental agent was Adam de Cardonnel, Blathwayt's deputy secretary at war, afterwards Marlborough's military secretary. So the regimental accounts are in the Blenheim Ms., Add. Ms. 61331, 61411, 61412. Cardonnel's commission is also in the Blenheim Papers, Add. Ms. 61336, 168–69. Regimental opinion was that Colonel Hales was removed simply because Nottingham coveted the fees to be paid by his replacement. That officer, Col. Geoffrey Lloyd, however, was so much a Williamite that he corresponded with Cardonnel in Dutch (*ibid.*, 54). The career of another of Marlborough's followers is encapsulated in the memorial of Lt. Col. Rodney to the duke, Add. Ms. 61294, 72. Rodney had brought a troop home from Tangier to join Churchill's dragoon regiment. Then he had served in the Irish garrison but was purged as a Protestant. Joining the Guards in London, he participated in lord Churchill's coup. So he won back his troop in the Royal Dragoons, "till your Grace was put in the Tower," and Rodney was cashiered as Marlborough's client. At the peace, Marlborough rescued Rodney, using his connection with Admiral Russell to get Rodney a commission as lieutenant colonel of Holt's marines when they returned from the West Indies.

63. HMC, *Finch Ms.*, 4: 127, 136, 137–38, 142, 230, 342, 347–48, 474–75, 500–501, but Russell's staff was not suspect, *ibid.*, 131. *Conduct of the Duchess*, 43; Littleton to Hatton, May 5, [1692,] Thompson, ed., *Hatton Correspondence*, 2: 176; Lediard, *Marlborough*, 1: 111–12; Coxe, *Marlborough*, 1: 62–65, 69–70; Wolsey, *Marlborough*, 2: 257, 271, 280–81; [Sprat,] Bishop of Rochester, "A Relation of the Late Wicked Contrivance," *Harleian Misc.*, 10: 1–27, esp. 15,

25. Ehrman, *Navy*, 391; Dalrymple, *Memoirs*, vol. 1, pp. 563, 565, Pt. II. Bk. VII, wrote of Marlborough that, "there was no medium between putting it out of his power to do mischief, and trusting the fate of the kingdom to his hands." See also Sir John Fenwick's confession, *ibid.*, 3: 275–80; *ibid.* (2d ed., London, 1773), 2, App. to Pt. II., 235.

64. Defoe, *Marlborough*, 11; [the Jamaican official to Dykveldt,], Jan. 26/Feb. 5, 1693, HMC. *Denbigh Ms.*, 220; Thompson, ed., *Hatton Correspondence*, 2: 180; HMC, *Finch Ms.*, 4: 260; Campbell, *Lives of the Admirals*, 31; Lediard, *Marlborough*, 1: 112–13; Coxe, *Marlborough*, 1: 70; Taylor, *Marlborough*, 2: 484–85; A. S. Tuberville, *The House of Lords in the Reign of William III*, 70–72; Dalrymple, *Memoirs*, vol. 1, p. 564, Pt.II, Bk. VIII; Luttrell, *Brief Relation*, 2: 617, 619.

65. Wolsey, *Marlborough*, 2: 288–89; Atkinson, *Marlborough*, 140–41; Taylor, *Marlborough*, 2: 485; HMC, *Denbigh Ms.*, 213, 220; Godfrey Davies, "The Reduction of the Army After the Peace of Ryswick, 1697," *JSAHR* 28 (1950): 15–16n, 26n, 27; Ashley, *Marlborough*, 30–31. As Ogg (*James II and William III*, 379) points out, the generals of infantry and of cavalry, four of six lieutenants general (all save Marlborough and Ormonde), and three of five major generals in the "English" army were not English. Childs, *Nine Years' War*, 203, admits Solms's "incompetence, a lack of professionalism, and shortage of imagination and initiative," but says that Solms's alleged hatred of the British "bulldogs" was "dirt" thrown at Solms by "political generals," i.e., Marlborough. Marlborough advocated a reformed Treason Act and, recalling lord Delamere's plea, demanded that trials of peers for treason be held before the entire body of the lords: Thompson, ed., *Hatton Correspondence*, 2: 211; see also p. 327 n. 78, above.

66. Mahan, *Sea Power*, 173; Charnock, *Biographia Navalis*, 1: 408–409; Ehrman, *Navy*, 498–510; HMC, *Downshire Ms.*, 1: 429, 436; Thompson, ed., *Hatton Correspondence*, 2: 201; HMC, *Portland Ms.*, 3: 529–34. "The customs duties under William III brought in practically as much as the excise duties, and more than two-thirds as much as the land tax," Morgan, "British West Indies," *JMH* 2: 381. The situation was a bit more complicated than that. Customs revenue was close to excise income from 1695 until it exceeded it in 1699, Brewer, *Sinews*, figure 4.2.

67. Capt. Robert Wroth [to Rupert Browne,] July 23, 1693, HMC, *Downshire Ms.*, 1, pt. 1, 423–24, and see 424–25; HMC, *House of Lords Ms.*, n.s. 1: #765, esp. Capt. Martin's Narrative and Sir George Rooke's Account, pp. 200–205, 215–27; HMC, *Portland Ms.*, 3: 529–34; Fortescue, *British Army*, 1: 372–78; Hamilton, *First Guards*, 1: 371–78; Mackinnon, *Coldstream Guards*, 230–35, 272; Childs, *Nine Years' War*, 233–40.

68. Hamilton, *First Guards*, 1: 280; Thompson, ed., *Hatton Correspondence*, 2: 194–95; "Remarks upon the *London Gazette* relating to the Streights-Fleet and the Battle of Landen in Flanders," (Pamphlet, London, 1693, Bodleian Library, Oxford); HMC, *Downshire Ms.*, 1: 427.

69. Charles Hatton to Christopher, Lord Hatton, Aug. 24, 1693, Thompson, ed., *Hatton Correspondence*, 2: 195–96, 197; Wolsey, *Marlborough*, 2: 290, 300–301; Luttrell, *Brief Relation*, 3:172, s.v. 8/29/93.

70. Childs, *Army of William III*, ch. 3, is a full account, but his labeling of some senior officers, and so the expedition, as "whiggish" (221) seems open to question. See also, *ibid.*, 228–30; Clarke, ed., *James Second*, 2: 521–23; Macpherson, ed., *Original Papers*, 1: 487; Wolsey, *Marlborough*, 2: 312–13; Ehrman, *Navy*, 514–15; *London Gazette* #2983, June 11–14, 1694.

71. Childs, *Army of William III*, 222, 224–26, follows Jacobite sources to suggest that Marlborough was motivated by jealousy of Tollemache (Talmarsh). This case is marred by such inconsistencies as variously dating Louis XIV's letter to Vauban in a span from April 4, 1694 (267) to May 1 1694 (225). In any case, Childs admits that Marlborough's communication was dated May 3, 1694, that is, that he betrayed the Brest expedition after Louis XIV had already ordered defenses against it prepared. But Marlborough's behavior was despicable, unless all the evidence in the case was forged. The issue is complicated because none of the original Jacobite reports from England survive. Rather, decipherments, purported translations, draft projects, and other writings by the St. Germain secretariat embody the information about alleged Jacobite conspiracies in England, Marlborough's and the army officers' supposed plots among them. The balance of scholarly opinion is that Marlborough et al. did communicate with St. Germain, but only as a precaution and without either prejudicing allied operations or offering particular proposals for the restoration of James II. See Macaulay, *England*, 5: 2442–50; Paget, *New Examen*, 15–31; E. M. Lloyd, "Marlborough and the Brest Expedition, 1694," *EHR*, 9 (1894): 130–32; Parnell, "Macpherson," *ibid.*, 12: 254–84; Davies, "Macpherson," *ibid.*, 35: 367–76; Churchill, *Marlborough*, 1: 368. That Marlborough and Godolphin acted here to protect Anne as well as themselves is argued by Gregg, *Anne*, 83.

72. Shrewsbury to the king, June 22July 2, 1694; reply, July 15, William Coxe, ed., *Private And Original Correspondence of Charles Talbot, Duke of Shrewsbury with King William* (London, 1821), 44–47; Coxe, *Marlborough*, 1: 72–73; a variant appears in Churchill, *Marlborough*, 1: 392; and hints appear even in Defoe, *Marlborough*, 16. See also, Wolsey, *Marlborough*, 2: 321.

73. Lediard, *Marlborough*, 1: 113–15; Gregg, *Anne*, 100–102, 112; *Conduct of the Duchess*, 77; Luttrell, *Brief Relation*, Jan. 15, 1694/5 3: 426. It was on this occasion that Sarah introduced her cousin and ward Jack Hill to the court as a page to Prince George. Her account of the Hill family is in Blenheim Ms. G I 9.

74. *Conduct of the Duchess*, 79; Gregg, *Anne*, 103; Shrewsbury to Russell, Jan. 29, 1694/5, Coxe, ed., *Shrewsbury Correspondence*, 220; Coxe, *Marlborough*, 1: 75.

75. Blenheim Ms. E.17, quoted by Gregg, *Anne*, 103, and see 105; *Conduct of the Duchess*, 79–81; Churchill, *Marlborough*, 1: 397. On the siege, July 1–Sept. 5, 1695, n.s., see generally: Chandler, *Art of War*, ch. 15; *An Exact Journal of the Seige of Namur* . . . (London, 1695); Edward D'Auvergne, *The History of the Campaign in Flanders for the Year 1695* . . . (London, 1696); and Childs, *Nine Years' War*, ch. 8.

76. D'Auvergne, *Campaign of 1695*, 161–67, 171; Chandler, *Marlborough*, 28; Coxe, ed., *Shrewsbury Correspondence*, 103–104.

77. Peter Laslett, "John Locke, the Great Recoinage, and the Origins of the Board of Trade," *WMQ*, 14 (1957), 320–402; Ogg, *James II and William III*, ch.

14, esp. 405, 422; *ibid.*, 433; *CTB*, xi, 37; Davies, "Reduction of the Army," *JSAHR*, 28: 15; the king to Shrewsbury, July 20/30, 1696, Coxe, ed., *Shrewsbury Correspondence*, 129; *CSPD 1696–1697*, 286–87; Childs, *Nine Years' War*, 305–306, 320–21.

78. See also, Ogg, *James II and William III*, 412–13, 435; Morgan, "British West Indies," *JMH* 2: 405–406; D. W. Jones, *War and Economy in the Age of William III and Marlborough* (London, 1988), 20–26, 47–48, Table 5.1; Brewer, *Sinews*, 119–22.

79. Routh, ed., *Burnet's History*, 4: 361–70; Paul Grimblot, ed., *Letters of William III, and Louis XIV* . . . (London, 1848), 1: 228, 236, 239, 248–49, 254; Davenport, *Treaties*, 2: 350–65; Coxe, ed., *Shrewsbay Correspondence*, 375, 377.

80. Routh, ed., *Burnet's History*, 4: 374–75; Childs, *Army of William III*, ch. 8; Schwoerer, *No Standing Armies!*, 156–59.

81. *CJ*, Oct. 28, 1696; *CSPD 1697*, 454, gives an average size of 90,172, plus officers, and see 484 for the ministry's proposed reduction to 30,000. Brewer, *Sinews*, 31, 42, Table 2.1; Mackinnon, *Coldstream Guards*, 2: 277; Schowerer, *No Standing Armies!*, 157.

82. *Cal. S. P. Dom.*, *1697*, 511–12 on 35,000 proposed to 10,000 allowed by the commons; Fortescue, *British Army*, 1: 383–84, 386–87; Davies, "Reduction," *JSAHR*, 28: 15, 61n; Shaw, ed., *CTB 1697*, 24, 30 Je. 1697, payment for the Dutch Guards of Princess Anne's escort.

83. *Ibid. 1695–1702*, ccx–ccxi, cccxxxiii, ccclvii–ix, for the army debt, 1692–98, and payments to Dec. 18, 1699; Davies, "Reduction," *JSAHR*, 2: 15–17; Macaulay, *England*, 6: 2742–43; *CSPD 1697*, 505–507; James, ed., *Vernon Correspondence*, 1: 460–61, 2: 85; "A Short History of Standing Armies," *State Tracts*, 2: 667; Schowerer, *No Standing Armies!*, 168–69, gives a figure of 33,615 in 1698; Childs, *Army of William III*, 89, 196–97; *CJ* 12: 356–58. Dec. 13, 16, 1698.

84. *CJ*, Jan. 18, 1697/8, Apr. 27, 1699, Jan. 3, 1698; Davies, "Reduction," *JSAHR*, 28: 18, 19.

85. *Ibid.*, 20, 30, 31; Grimblot, *Letters of William III and Louis XIV*, 1: 149, 150–51, and see 343 for the suggestion that the nonpayment of arrears preserved the tax-base requisite for English opposition to France. On the enormous, unprecedented, and transforming cost of the army under William III, see Childs, *Army of William III*, 153; C. M. Clode, *The Military Forces of the Crown* (London, 1869), 1: 369; Brewer, *Sinews*, 37–42; Tables 2.1, 2.2; Routh, ed., *Burnet's History*, 4: 406; Schowerer, *No Standing Armies*, 179n; *CSPD 1698*, 128–29. The obvious identity of marines with empire made them attractive to the same tory sentiment that approved of large naval expenditures, James, ed. *Vernon Correspondence*, 2: 390, 394–95, 396–97, 405. Schowerer, *No Standing Armies!*, 181, speaks of "the isolationists of the seventeenth century, interested in the fleet, colonies, and overseas dominion" but hostile to a continental war to contain France. This was a xenophobic imperialism, but hardly "isolationist." Childs, *Army of William III*, takes much the same view, and associates the "blue water" strategy with the country party. Fortescue, *British Army*, 1: 390n., lists fifty-seven regiments on foot in the British kingdoms, with a ratio of one officer to every ten men. Dalton, ed., *Army Lists*, 4: passim, records promotions, etc. in forty-four regiments in Britain during 1698 and changes in forty-two regiments in Britain and the West Indies in 1699. Obviously, the army was not disbanded, but active duty forces on the English establishment were reduced to something like 25,000 of all ranks by 1699. This was a dramatic reduction from the 87,500 of 1697, but not even close to the 10,000 demanded by parliament and said to be the case by Childs, *Army of William III*, 185. But see *ibid.*, 203, for a total of 24,600, and see also Davies, "Reduction," *JSAHR*, 28: 23–24. On the Jan. 1698/9 vote of £350,000 for the army and the specifics of reduction, see Thompson, ed., *Hatton Correspondence*, 2: 238–39.

86. Davies, "Reduction," *JSAHR*, 28: 23–24. The king had kept more than 30,000 troops under arms, 14,834 in England, 15,488 in Ireland, 1,258 in America, and 600 invalids. Childs, *Army of William III*, 200–202. James, ed., *Vernon Correspondence*, 2: 230–31, 235–36; Luttrell, *Brief Relation*, 4: 462–63; *CSPD 1698*, 128–29, 427–28; *CJ*, 12: 359–60, Dec. 17, 1698, resolves reduction to 7000 officers and men; Schowerer, *No Standing Armies!*, 169; Fortescue, *British Army*, 1: 388; Wolsey, *Marlborough*, 2: 342–45; Fifth, *Commentary*, 145–47.

87. Somers to Shrewsbury, Dec. 29, 1698, Coxe, ed., *Shrewsbury Correspondence*, 572–77; Churchill, *Marlborough*, I: 439; Macaulay, *England*, 6: 2869, 2882.

88. William III to Hensius, Mar. 29/Apr. 8, 1698, Grimblot, ed., *Letters of William III and Louis XIV*, 1: 348–49, and see 339–40; James, ed., *Vernon Correspondence*, 2: 235, 236–37, 241–42, 243–44, 245, 246–48, 250–59, 269–70, 415; HMC, *Downshire Ms.*, 1: pt. 2, 767.

89. Webb, *Governors-General*, #75, 76. On Sept. 20, Vernon reported the Codrington succession to the Leeward Islands' commanders and commented that "perhaps they had better take one that has his fortunes made, than one that should make them there," James, ed., *Vernon Correspondence*, 2: 178. The Codringtons were perhaps the richest family in the English Antillies. See Vincent T. Harlow, *Christopher Codrington* (Oxford, 1928).

90. HMC, *House of Lords Ms.*, n.s., 3: 313–14; D. W. Prowse, *A History of Newfoundland from the English, Colonial, and Foreign Records* (London, 1896), 214–24; Harold A. Innes, *The Cod Fisheries* (New Haven, 1940); John Reeves, *History Of The Government Of The Island Of Newfoundland* (London, 1793), 22–24; Webb, *Governors-General*, 351.

91. *Ibid.*, #178; HMC, *Downshire Ms.*, 1: pt. 2, 700–701; James, ed., *Vernon Correspondence*, 2: 85–87; Dickinson, "Richards Brothers," *JSAHR*, 46: 78, 84. Other officers in Gibson's regiment at Newfoundland were Roger Handasyde, the major's son, and Robert Lilburne, both of whom were left in the St. John's garrison when the fleet sailed for England. James Stanhope, afterwards earl Stanhope, had transferred from Gibson's (26th) Regiment to the 1st Guards for the Namur campaign. Dalton, ed., *Army Lists*, 3: 381, 4: 46, 151. On Gibson's difficulties in the Portsmouth administration, see Childs, *Army of William III*,

96–97, and note 40, above. Blathwayt to Admiralty Sec., Mar. 15, 1696/7, HMC, *House of Lords Ms.*, n.s., pt. 3, #1378 (c. 1, p. 318); #1378 (c. 2, p. 327), HMC, *Buccleuch Ms.*, 2: pt. 2, 453; James, ed., *Vernon Correspondence*, 1: 192.

92. English captains often deserted their convoys to hunt prizes. C.f. the Barbados disaster, *ibid.*, I: 247, 254; Daniell, *Cap of Honour*, 23–24; Stock, comp., *Proceedings*, 2: 233n, et seq.; HMC, *House of Lords Ms.*, n.s., 3, pt. 2, #1378 (h), 337–40. On the extensive refortification of St. John's, see MFQ 772, 10691.

93. Michael Richards in particular denied that the boats and sails of the fleet were given over to fishing (HMC, *House of Lords Ms.*, n.s. 3, pt. 2, 345), but the vast bulk of the testimony supports the text. Charnock, *Biographia Navalis*, 2: 342–44, exonerates Norris, blaming the army officers instead, but notes that (Gibson's) fortifications did protect the fleet from the outward bound French squadron. Norris's instructions (HMC, *House of Lords Ms.*, n.s. 3: pt. 2, #1738 (c)) are for an assault on Newfoundland and the fisheries, not, as Charnock, and others following him, say, Hudson Bay. See also *ibid.*, (cl), 324, 334; (h3), 349; *CSPD 1697*, 286–87; Prowse, *Newfoundland*, 224. The regiment's terrible losses at Newfoundland, including Alexander Gibson, opened commissions in the 26th for two subsequent staff stalwarts of Marlborough, George Watkins and Luke Spicer, as well as for Gibson's own son, Dalton, ed., *Army Lists*, 4: 210.

94. HMC, *House of Lords Ms.*, n.s., 3: pt. 2, xxxiii, 315; James, ed., *Vernon Correspondence*, 2: 85–87, 89. The Churchill connection's success in publishing the naval failure at St. John's appears in such military chronicles as Kane, *Campaigns*, 95.

95. The address of the lords, April 17, 1699, Stock, comp., *Proceedings*, 2: 299–304n; Gibson to the council of trade and plantations, Mar. 10, 1698, *CSPC 1697–1698*, 130; HMC, *House of Lords Ms.*, n.s., 3 pt. 2, 317. Note also that Sir Edward Seymour and the Devon adventurers took this opportunity to collect and enact all of the regulations favoring the fishing admirals and discouraging planters (and governors), Stock, comp., *Proceedings*, 2: 295–96; Reeves, *Newfoundland*, 11–12, 31; Prowse, *Newfoundland*, 225–27. Webb, *Governors-General*, 495–97; Glanvill J. Davies, "Military Leadership at Newfoundland Before 1729," *JSAHR*, 59 (1981): 194–200. For Marlborough's continuing patronage of these Newfoundland veterans, who had "Endured very great hardships by ye intemperance of yt Climate," see the memorial of Capt. [George] Watkins (a.d.c. to Charles Churchill) to Marlborough, Add. Ms. 61297, 82. It is a mark of the widening gap between the Marlborough moderates and the Hyde right wing of the princess's party that, when the Norris case was reheard in 1701, it had become a tory cause and none of the moderates supported the minority lords' protest, Mar. 8, 1701, Stock, comp., *Proceedings*, 2: 377.

96. *London Gazette* #3402, June 16–20, 1698; James, ed., *Vernon Correspondence*, 2: 104, 106, 111. Marlborough took a seat in the cabinet, Sunday, June 19, and was then sworn as a privy councilor, hours before Portland returned to London. Lediard, *Marlborough*, 1: 117–20, quotes *Two Illustrious Generals*, 33, as does Churchill, *Marlborough*, 1: 432, Coxe, *Marlborough*, 1: 86–89, and Wolsey, *Marlborough*, 2: 338.

97. See also, Ashley, *Marlborough*, 31–32; Chandler, *Marlborough*, 48–49. Burnet was named preceptor to the duke and his history (Routh, ed., *Burnet's History*, 4: 385–386n, 451–53) is even more unctuous than usual on this subject. As the head of the Gloucester household, Marlborough became extremely protective of the tutor/bishop when he was attacked in the commons, although it was a partisan case, the first of many, in which he could no longer control his tory brother, George: James, ed., *Vernon Correspondence*, 2: 386–89. See also Lediard, *Marlborough*, 1: 123–24; Atkinson, *Marlborough*, 150; Wolsey, *Marlborough*, 2: 337–40. Marlborough's increased influence and imperial range appeared anew on June 7, when Vernon reported the parliamentary "accommodation" between the old and the new East India companies: "I believe my Lord Godolphin and Lord Marlborough have mediated it." The key issue was the valuation of the old company's "forts and castles" in India. James, ed., *Vernon Correspondence*, 2: 68n, 75–76, 95–96. Marlborough himself was a parliamentary investigator into East India affairs, he was a substantial investor in old East India Company stock, and he initially approved the merger, Add. Ms. 61358, 180–217, 222, 228; Add. Ms. 61363, 17. On the regency, see *ibid.*, 126, 130. With Marlborough's reentry into government came "a little fit of the gout," *ibid.*, 140; *London Gazette* #3410, July 16, 1698.

98. *Conduct of the Duchess*, 84; Churchill, *Marlborough*, 1: 432. Although Carmarthen was dismissed, the government of Hull finally passed not to Churchill but to the duke of Newcastle together with the lieutenancy of the East Riding of Yorkshire. On Godfrey, see James, ed., *Vernon Correspondence*, 2: 81; on Hull, *ibid.*, 299, 333, and, on George Churchill's admiralty appointment, at Marlborough's "instance," *ibid.*, 361.; James, ed., *Vernon Corres.*, 2: 124, 177–78, 182–83 (where Sir Isaac Newton was said to be named Gloucester's mathematics tutor). See n. 73, above.

99. Sunderland's promise of Dec. 31, 1699 is in Blenheim Papers A. 1. 11, Add. Ms. 61126, 9. Coxe, *Marlborough*, 1: 90–91, 95–98; James, ed., *Vernon Correspondence*, 2: 356. Sunderland's return to the ministry at this moment was therefore also a favorable omen for the Churchill connection: *ibid.*, 364n, 392, 398–99, 435. The Marlboroughs had just married their eldest daughter, Henrietta, to Godolphin's heir, and the princess had also given £5,000 toward her dowry, Churchill, *Marlborough*, 1: 436–38.

100. Grimblot, ed., *Letters of William III, and Louis XIV*, 1: 348; Marlborough [to Shrewsbury,] May 11, [1700,] HMC, *Buccleuch Ms.*, 2: pt. 2, 647.

Appendix: Inglorious Revolution: The Channel Fleet in 1688

Epigraph printed in Mark. K. Brown, ed., *The Works of George Savile Marquis of Halifax* (Oxford, 1989), 1: 295, n.3.

1. Routh, ed., *Burnet's History*, 3: par. 762; Edward P. Powley, *The English Navy in the Revolution of 1688* (Cambridge, 1928), 4.
2. The political significance of the Mordaunt mission is asserted by J. K. Laughton, "Mordaunt, Charles, third Earl of Peterborough, *DNB*. Laughton's

assertion finds no support in the log of the flagship, ADM 52/35 *Foresight*, Part 2; in Florence E. Dyer, *The Life of Admiral Sir John Narborough* (London, 1931); or in Peter Earle, *The Wreck of the Almiranta Sir William Phips and the Search for the Hispaniola Treasure* (London, 1979). Perhaps it would be unreasonable to expect more than circumstantial evidence in such a case. On Myngs and the Jamaica station, see Webb, *Governors-General*, 184, 216. For Narborough on the Tangier station (where the *Foresight* had been his favorite ship), see Routh, *Tangier*, 1: 143–44. Myngs passed the Tangier command to Herbert. Narborough died on the eve of the return voyage, much to the disappointment of the officers of the Channel Fleet, HMC, *Dartmouth Ms.*, 2: 54.

3. See also, Charnock, *Biographia Navalis*, III, 316; Powey, *English Navy*, 9–10; Albemarle to Dartmouth, Nov. 27, 1687; Mar. 8, 1687/8, HMC, *Dartmouth Ms.*, 2: 135–36. Ducket, ed., *Penal Laws*, 286. The *Assistance*, Narborough's other command at Tangier, brought out Albemarle to Jamaica, before being ordered to help protect the treasure from Mordaunt. The Jamaica council accepted Albemarle's hint that they should withhold their consent that he should go in command: Ward, *Albemarle*, 297; *CSPC 1685–1688*, #1640, p. 507. Some of the wreckers sailed from the Bahama Banks rendezvous to Boston. There, much to their resentment, Governor-General Andros claimed the king's share of the treasure, one-half of the 10,274 ounces of plate and coin. Andros asked the privy council for permission to invest the king's share in fortifying Boston. The crews doubtless peddled other things than Spanish silver in the markets of Massachusetts. Edward Randolph to Sir Nicholas Butler, Mar. 29, 1688, CWWB, 1 #5; Andros to the privy council committee, Ap. 4, 1688, C.O. 905/62, 12. Some £250,000 may have been distributed in English America from the wreck.

4. Davies, *Gentlemen and Tarpaulins*, 111, 191, 198, 203–13; Davies, "The Navy, Parliament and Political Crises in the Reign of Charles II," *HJ* 36 (1986): 282–83. Like Grafton, Herbert had to exhibit a sudden display of conscience before King James to justify his defiance: Luttrell, *Brief Relation*, 1: 397; Dalrymple, ed., *Memoirs, 3:* App. to Pt. I, 271; Powey, *English Navy*, 11; Routh, ed., *Burnet's History*, 3: par. 762; Muilenberg, "Embassy," *Nebraska Studies*, 20: 141.

5. Pepys to Dartmouth, Oct. 26, 1688, HMC, *Dartmouth Ms.*, 1: 171; Childs, *Army and Revolution*, 142–44, 148–59; Davies, *Gentlemen and Tarpaulins*, 214. Dalrymple, *Memoirs* (2d ed., London, 1773), 2: 228–31; *EHD* 8: 120–23.

6. Pepys Ms. 2859, p. 37; Davies, *Gentlemen and Tarpaulins*, 213–14; Fitzroy, *Grafton*, 9–11.

7. On Tangier, military professionalism, and on the Tangier regimental connections, see Webb, *Governors-General*, index, s.v. "Tangier" and "Tangier Regiments." See also note 23, below.

8. On Berry, see note 17, below. Only Arthur Hastings of the *Woolwich* and Stephen Ackerman of the *Dreadnought* were leading naval conspirators without also holding army commissions. See the lists of naval conspirators in Van Citters's despatches, Add. Ms. 31510, John Knox Laughton, ed., *Memoirs Relating to the Lord Torrington*, Camden Society, n.s. XLVI (London, 1889), and in this text. Several of these dual commanders are listed by Dalton, *Army Lists*, II, xxi, and s.v. Dalton's index. See also Webb, *Governors-General*, "Index of Persons," and Webb, *1676*, s.v. these officers. Note that such noted commanders in America as John Graydon of the *Quaker Ketch* (HMC, *Dartmouth Ms.*, 138), also served in the Channel Fleet (as captain of the *Sandadoe*), "and very fortunate it proves to her Captaine, by giveing him an opportunity for attoneing for his errors abroad (said to be great both in numbers and weight) . . . ," Pepys to Dartmouth, Oct. 11, 1688, *ibid.*, 156–57, Pepys to Dartmouth, Oct. 14, 17, *ibid.*, 160, 166. These "errors" perhaps related to his Newfoundland command: "he has made a very extra-ordinary Admirall in his last station."

9. Josiah Burchett, Esq., Secretary of the Admiralty, *Complete History Of the most Remarkable Transactions At Sea . . .* (London, 1719), 410; Davies, *Gentlemen and Tarpaulins*, 107, 205, 212.

10. *Ibid.*, 205; Van Citters to the states general, 28 Sept. 1688, Add. Ms. 31510, 145. On Berry's obstructionism, see Luttrell, *Brief Relation*, July 31, 1688, and Berry to Dartmouth, Oct. 14, 1688, HMC, *Dartmouth Ms.*, 1: 159.

11. Fitzroy, *Grafton*, 9–12, 54; Powey, *English Navy*, 16–19, but, on Strickland's conversion, see Geiter and Speck, eds. *Reresby*, 503–504, 582.

12. Routh, ed., *Burnet's History*, 3: par. 755; Laughton, ed., *Torrington Memoirs*, 18–19; s.v. "Byng, George," *DNB*, III, 567–70; Davies, *Gentlemen and Tarpaulins*, 200–203.

13. See also, Burchett, *Complete History*, 407–11.

14. *Ibid.*, 410; Davies, *Gentlemen and Tarpaulins*, 197, 199, 207; Davies, "Parliament," *HJ* 36: 284; Davies, "James II and the Admirals," 88: Rawlinson Ms. D, 148, f.1–2, Bodleian.

15. HMC, *Dartmouth Ms.*, 1: 138, 142, 276; III, 55. Press warrants were not issued until 25 September. One hundred seventy of the *Resolution*'s 370-man complement were soldiers. The morale of Dartmouth's fleet will not have been improved by the arrival of 318 more soldiers from three disaffected regiments. Laughton, ed., *Torrington Memoirs*, 20, 23; J. R. Tanner, "Naval Preparations of James II in 1688," *EHR* 8 (1893), 275; Powey, *English Navy*, 24–25. For Dartmouth's challenge to Herbert, Sept. 4, 1688, see Egerton Ms., 2621, 9–10.

16. Laughton, ed., *Torrington Memoirs*, 22–23, 28; Powey, *English Navy*, 37–38, 46–47, 49; the king to Dartmouth, Oct. 5, 26, 1688; S. Pepys to same, Oct. 7, 17, HMC, *Dartmouth Ms.*, 1: 144–46, 170; 3: 55. Some confusion, both at the time and since, has attended the fact that, while the Prince of Orange had assembled fifty-nine warships, only thirty-two were ships of the line ("battleships"). If all the capital ships King James had ordered out had actually joined Dartmouth's fleet, it would have had thirty-eight ships of the line. See Admiral Sir Herbert Richmond, *The Navy as an Instrument of Policy, 1558–1724* (Cambridge, 1953), 196.

17. Charnock, *Biographia Navalis*, 1: 143–56; Webb, *Governors-General*, esp. 350–59; Webb, *1676*, 128–31, 219, 237, 238, 314–15; Davies, *Gentlemen and Tarpaulins*, 194, 212.

18. HMC, *Dartmouth Ms.*, 1: 259, 261; George Churchill to navy commissioners, Oct. 24, 1688, ADM 106/383, 208.

19. HMC, *Dartmouth Ms.*, 1: 170.

20. Clarke, ed., *James the Second*, 2: 207. For Grafton's plan to board Hastings's ship so as to be present in the fleet during the crisis, see HMC, *Dartmouth Ms.*, 1: 3: 56. Powey, *English Navy*, 67–68; Davies, *Gentlemen and Tarpaulins*, 224; Davies, "James II . . . and the Admirals," Cruickshank, ed., *By Force or Default*, 98–99.

21. Laughton, ed., *Torrington Memoirs*, 2–18; Brian Turnstall, ed., *The Byng Papers* (Naval Records Society, 1930), xvii–xxx; Dalton, ed., *Army Lists*, II, xxii, 27, 135, 208; *DNB*, III, 567.

22. The meeting may have been chaired by Ormonde. c.f. HMC, *Ormonde Ms.*, n.s. VIII, 4, 6, 8, 13–14. Laughton, ed., *Torrington Memoirs*, 26–28; Dalton, ed., *Army Lists*, I, 257; II, 27.

23. To all Commanders of Ships and Seamen, Sept. 28, 1688, Egerton Ms., 2621, 12–13; *An Impartial Account of Some Remarkable Passages in the Life of Arthur Earl of Torrington* (London, 1691), 12–13; #63 in the Collection of Tracts 1603–1675, BL 100 * (65). For Herbert's distinction of Churchill, see Playfair, *Scourge of Christendom*, 138–39. Davies, *Gentlemen and Tarpaulins*, 185, 187, 195, 205, 212. Peter Le Fevre, "Charles Kirke," *Mariner's Mirror*, 68 (1982), 327–28; Le Fevre, "Tangier, the Navy and Its Connection with the Glorious Revolution," *ibid.*, 73 (1987), 187–89; Le Fevre, "Matthew Aylmer," *ibid.*, 206–208.

24. Laughton, ed., *Torrington Memoirs*, 26–27; Powey, *English Navy*, 67–69. The king himself had written Dartmouth on 11 Oct. 1688, while the fleet was still at the buoy of the Nore, advising a cruise to the coast of Holland, HMC, *Dartmouth Ms.*, 1: 158. The king changed his mind on Oct. 27, *ibid.*, 175, and Dartmouth thought the season too advanced to risk the shoals of Holland, *ibid.*, 3: 60–61. For the assertion that Herbert had "undertaken to find ways to prevail with most of [Dartmouth's] fleet to revolt to the Prince of Orange" and that the prince's second sailing awaited assurances of success, s.v. Oct. 26, 1688, *ibid.*, 174. Journal of Captain Grenville Collins, *ibid.*, 56. Grafton himself may have come down from London again to further the conspiracy, *ibid.*, and see Fitzroy, *Grafton*, 59–60. Burchett, *Transactions at Sea*, I, 414. Clyve Jones, "The Protestant Wind of 1688: Myth and Reality," *ESR* 3 (1973): 214.

25. [Burnet] claimed that accounts of storm damage to the Dutch fleet were exaggerated "to lull a great man a-sleep," "Expedition," *Harleian Misc.*, 1: 449; HMC, *Dartmouth Ms.*, 1: 190, 191, 194; 3: 56–57, 61; 5: 177, 213; Laughton, ed., *Torrington Memoir*, 29; Powey, *English Navy*, 79–81; Add. Ms. 29578, 194, 196. The unusual overcrowding of Columbine's flyboat also caused an overestimate of the numbers of troops carried aboard the Dutch fleet.

26. HMC, *Dartmouth Ms.*, 3: 56; ADM 106/383, 208. Constable may have been the officer of this name who was an associate of Albemarle, Churchill's major in the Horse Guards (Dalton, ed., *Army Lists*, 2: 16, 60, 111, 116), and shareholder with Mordaunt in the Hispaniola treasure syndicate, but Davies (*Gentlemen and Tarpaulins*, 210), points out that Constable was a Catholic and a client of Dartmouth's. Van Citters to the states general, 12 Nov. (n.s.) 1688, Add Ms. 31510, 224–25.

27. HMC, *Dartmouth Ms.*, 3: 57, 61–62, 1: 184–86; Littleton to Hatton, Sheerness, Nov. 6, 1688, Add. Ms. 29578, 194; Davies, *Gentlemen and Tarpaulins*, 211, 213; Richmond, *Sea Power*, 197; Laughton, ed., *Torrington Memoirs*, 29; Powey, *English Navy*, 82–86; Jones, "Protestant Wind," *ESR*, 3: 218–19. Four observations may be made on William's course. The western landing sites must have offered dramatic advantages because the Yorkshire coast was half the distance and William had embarked from ports far to the east in order to use an east wind to sail north. He did sail halfway to Yorkshire before Zeulstein arrived with intelligence that James expected a northern landing and that the English fleet would not interfere. After this, the wind veered enough to give the invasion fleet a broad reach on the starboard tack during daylight hours through the Narrows of the Pas de Calais toward the objective, the port of Dartmouth. The final wind shift put the fleet into Torbay instead.

28. HMC, *Dartmouth Ms.*, 3: 57, 62, 66; Add. Ms. 29578, 199. The king considered the *Centurion*'s grounding the result of criminal mismanagement and ordered the master court-martialed, *ibid.*, 5: 193–94, 208. On her crew's desertion, see *ibid.*, 200, and, on the *Newcastle*, *ibid.*, 202.

29. Russell to Herbert, Exeter, 13 8br 1688, Egerton Ms., 2621, 47; Dartmouth-Berkeley correspondence, HMC, *Dartmouth Ms.*, 1:, 205, 210–11, and see 181, 260, 261. William commissioned Berkeley admiral and colonel of marines. Dalton, ed., *Army Lists*, II, 1; Powey, *English Navy*, 68; Laughton, ed., *Torrington Memoirs*, 29, 32; Fitzroy, *Grafton*, 63–64. Note that the same suspect source (Clarke, ed., *James the Second*, 2: 208) alleges both plots, but it gains some credibility because Davies, "James II . . . and the Admirals," Cruickshanks, ed., *By Force or Default*, 98–99, takes it quite seriously.

30. HMC, *Dartmouth Ms.*, 1: 212, 271–72; 3: 57, 66–69; 5: 191–92, 195–96, 203, 205–206.

31. *Ibid.*, 1: 220.

32. *Ibid.*, 214–216, 220, 272, 273–74, 275–276, Laughton, ed., *Torrington Memoirs*, 30; Powey, *English Navy*, 124–25; Berwick, *Memoirs*, 32.

33. *Ibid.*, 35–36; Harleian Ms. 6845, 282.

34. Laughton, ed., *Torrington Memoirs*, 30–32; Dalton, ed., *Army Lists*, II, 208.

35. HMC, *Dartmouth Ms.*, 1: 219, 223, 224, 272, 273; 3: 58, 69; Dalrymple, ed., *Memoirs*, App. to Pt. I, 314; Laughton, ed., *Torrington Memoirs*, 32, 33; Clarke, ed. *James the Second*, 208; Fitzroy, *Grafton*, 60; Add. Ms. 51511, 10.

36. Laughton, ed., *Torrington Memoirs*, 33; HMC, *Dartmouth Ms.*, 1: 224–26, 230, 244, 277, 278; 3: 58.

37. The surrender letter is not in HMC, *Dartmouth Ms.*, but is printed by Powey, *English Navy*, 143–44, from F. Devon, *Vindication of the first Lord Dartmouth* (London, 1856), Appendix X. *Ibid.*, XI is the prince's reply, dated at Windsor, Dec. 16, 1688. HMC, *Dartmouth Ms.*, 1: 231–32, 235, 236. 283–85; 3: 58–59, 69; Laughton, ed., *Torrington Memoirs*, 35–36; Powey, *English Navy*, 152. Constable of the *St. Albans*, Shovell of the *Dover*, Aylmer of the *Swallow*, Ashby of the *Defiance*, and Hastings of the *Woolwich*, had acted early in lord Churchill's coup. With the remaining captains of Berry's squadron, Stafford Fairburne, and George Rooke among them, they rose to be the admirals whose fortunes were linked with John Churchill's. In Sir John Berry's new squadron, George Byng held his first post rank as captain of the *Constant Warwick*, beginning a career in command that concluded with the destruction of the Spanish fleet off Cape Passaro. Berry became commissioner of the navy to William III. He was poisoned on board ship in February 1691, supposedly by King James's loyalists because of Sir John's central part in the coup d'état. Compare the text with the lists in Powey, *English Navy*, 57–59 and 152, and see Charnock, *Biographia Navalis*, I, 143–56.

38. HMC, *Dartmouth Ms.*, 1: 235, 242, 249, 251, 285–92. Mackintosh, *The Revolution*, 474, 581; Singer, ed., *Clarendon Correspondence*, 2: 337–39.

Index

A NOTE ABOUT THE AUTHOR

Stephen Saunders Webb was born in Syracuse, New York, in 1937. He received a B.A. from Williams College and an M.S. and a Ph.D. from the University of Wisconsin. He has taught at St. Lawrence University, The College of William & Mary, and Syracuse University, where he is Professor of History in the Maxwell School. He has been a Fellow of The Institute of Early American History and Culture; The Charles Warren Center, Harvard; The National Endowment for the Humanities; and the John Simon Guggenheim Memorial Foundation. He is the author of *The Governors-General: The English Army and the Definition of the Empire, 1569–1681* (1979) and *1676: The End of American Independence* (1984).

A NOTE ON THE TYPE

This book was set in Janson, a typeface long thought to have been made by the Dutchman Anton Janson, who was a practicing typefounder in Leipzig during the years 1668–1687. However, it has been conclusively demonstrated that these types are actually the work of Nicholas Kis (1650–1702), a Hungarian, who most probably learned his trade from the master Dutch typefounder Dirk Voskens. The type is an excellent example of the influential and sturdy Dutch types that prevailed in England up to the time William Caslon (1692–1766) developed his own incomparable designs from them.

Composed by ComCom, an R. R. Donnelley & Sons Company,
Allentown, Pennsylvania
Printed and bound by R. R. Donnelley & Sons Company,
Harrisonburg, Virginia
Designed by Robert C. Olsson